Much of Jefferson Davis' life and career has been obscured in controversy and misinterpretation. This full, carefully annotated edition will make it possible for scholars to reassess the man who served as President of the Confederacy and who in the aftermath of war became the symbolic leader of the South.

For almost a decade a dedicated team of scholars has been collecting and documenting Davis' papers and correspondence for this multi-volume work. The first volume includes not only Davis' private and public correspondence but also the important letters and documents addressed to and concerning him. Two autobiographical accounts, a detailed genealogy of the Davis family, and a complete bibliography are also included.

The volume covers Davis' early years in Mississippi and Kentucky, his career at West Point, his first military assignments, and his tragic marriage to Sarah Knox Taylor. Together, the letters and documents unfold a human story of the first thirty-two years of a long life that later became filled with turbulence and controversy.

Jefferson Davis at an Early Age

THE PAPERS OF
Jefferson Davis

VOLUME 1
1808–1840

EDITED BY
Haskell M. Monroe, Jr.
AND
James T. McIntosh

LOUISIANA STATE UNIVERSITY PRESS
BATON ROUGE
1971

ISBN 0-8071-0943-6
Library of Congress Catalog Card Number 76-152704

Manufactured in the United States of America
Printed by The TJM Corporation, Baton Rouge, Louisiana
Designed by Jules B. McKee

INTRODUCTION

by Bruce Catton

JEFFERSON DAVIS occupies a place unlike any other in the list of well-remembered Americans.

He is the great loser—the leader of the Lost Cause, the man who headed a split-off republic that did not live. For a long time he was blamed by both sides alike—by Southerners for the Confederacy's failure to survive; by Northerners for trying so hard to make it survive. On one hand it was argued that with a wiser, more capable man to lead, the Southern Confederacy might have risen above its built-in limitations; on the other hand, it was held that if he had been less rigid and obstinate the reunion of the sections might have been brought about with less bloodshed. Everything, it seemed, was his fault.

As the years passed after Appomattox these judgments changed. Southerners began to see Davis in a new light—as a helpless scapegoat, as a martyr to the Lost Cause. When he was captured by Union soldiers on his flight across Georgia he was locked up in a casemate at Fort Monroe, and for a time it seemed likely that the Federal authorities would try him for treason and, if they got the verdict they wanted, would hang him as a traitor. (At one stage the government even seemed disposed to fix on Davis part of the responsibility for Abraham Lincoln's assassination, although this charge presently collapsed under the weight of its own absurdity.)

It should be pointed out that many Northerners doubted the wisdom of proceeding against Davis as a traitor. Chief Justice Salmon P. Chase remarked: "His capture was a mistake. His trial will be a greater one. We cannot convict him of treason. Secession is settled. Let it stay settled." Davis himself welcomed the idea of a trial. For one thing, it would end the harrowing uncertainty under which he lived; his health was bad, he was given rigorous treatment, and it was often charged that the government hoped he would die in prison. For another, Davis believed that if he were put on trial he would be able to show that the act of secession was legally justifiable. (Apparently this same feeling haunted the Chief Justice of the United States.) Davis was finally indicted for treason but he was never brought to trial, and at last—two years after his capture—Davis was released from prison. He remained on bail for some time, and now and then the authorities asserted that he would presently be tried, but it never happened and at last the charges against him quietly expired.

Through all of this the things men said and thought about Davis began to change. A few prominent ex-Confederates like Vice President Alexander Stephens and Generals Joseph E. Johnston and P. G. T. Beauregard continued to criticize him, alleging that he had been one of the great handicaps the Confederate cause had had to bear, but they aroused a diminishing response. Increasingly, Southerners came to see him as one who had suffered much and accomplished much for the common cause; and in the course of time Davis became the most revered man in the South, a popular hero whose rare appearances were greeted by cheering crowds, with aging veterans of the war raising the Rebel yell in his honor. As leading ex-Confederates died, one by one, in the course of time, Davis came to seem the very embodiment of the adored, romantic nation that had not lived. Ranks were closed; by the end of his life Davis was the Confederate hero incarnate.

The change in attitude, naturally enough, came much more slowly in the North, where very different emotions were involved. I remember that my own family nourished a thin legend that we had some sort of blood relationship with Davis—my mother's family came from southern Indiana, down near the Ohio River, and there was a Davis in it somewhere. Nobody ever bothered to trace the exact relationship, however, and this bothered my mother; and she told me that one day, sometime in the early years of the twentieth century, she asked her father why he didn't look into the matter, because it seemed to her that if we were actually related to Jefferson Davis we ought to know about it. Her father looked at her indignantly. "What!" he cried. "That *Rebel*?" And that ended it.

That sort of attitude was probably typical, half or three-quarters of a century ago. But the years passed, "Rebel" ceased to be such a terrible word, and Northerners began to take another look at the Confederate president. As time went on they found him well worth looking at. He had a quality, somehow, and as the hot passions of the

1860's finally died out it became possible for men to look at him objectively.

Davis had several qualities not too common among leaders in public life. He had unquestioned integrity, for one; integrity, unending courage, a flawless dedication to duty, and a constitutional inability to collapse under pressure. It seems likely that he never really despaired of the Confederate cause until the moment the Yankee cavalry made him a prisoner. If he guided some of his generals with a tight rein, some of them indeed needed it; if, fighting for state rights, he asserted the overreaching authority of the Richmond government in a way that brought dismay to men like Georgia's Governor Brown, it can only be said that he had a war to win and that it would infallibly have been lost quite rapidly without a high degree of centralized control. If he lacked the flexibility to suffer fools gladly, it must be admitted that a good many arrant fools got in his way at one time or another.

He was, in short, an extremely able man. To be sure, under his presidency the Confederacy at last came to total defeat; but who could have done any better with it? From the beginning, it was overmatched. Taking the long view that is possible now that more than a century has passed, we are compelled to ask—not why the Confederacy finally died, but how it remained alive so long? Davis had an impossible assignment, and he did about as well with it as anyone could have done. As a mental exercise, try running down the list of Southern leaders who, in 1861, might conceivably have been elected president instead of Davis. Most of them, obviously, would not have done nearly as well as Davis did, and it is hard to think of anyone of whom one can confidently say that he would have done better. The great trouble with the Confederacy was that its president was required to solve a number of problems that were inherently insoluble.

Agreed, then, that Jefferson Davis was a man who is bound to be remembered? Beyond question; and since he will be remembered, he might as well be understood. We need to get better acquainted with him, and that is precisely the reason why this extensive collection of his writings is presented. As a man progresses from youth to manhood, and on through manhood to death, he leaves tracks on paper, and if he had sufficient stature it is important to collect those traces of his progress and put them between covers. Davis had stature; here are the tracks.

It seems that in some ways Davis was a late bloomer. A careful examination of his comings and goings during his first thirty years or more reveals few indications that he is on his way to greatness. His West Point record was, to be blunt about it, more or less undistinguished. As a young officer in the old army he was simply one of many young officers; he did his job, endured the monotony of frontier posts without complaint, and at last resigned from the army to become a Mississippi planter. You will have to look very hard at this part of the record to see a future president of the Southern Confederacy.

You will get one or two surprises, however.

One of the adjectives that is usually applied to President Davis is the word "austere." He had that quality, certainly, but apparently he came by it late in life. It certainly is not in evidence in his West Point record. During his first year at the military academy, Davis skipped out and with friends went down to Benny Havens' famous saloon, which was off-limits to cadets on pain of dismissal. He was caught, court-martialled, and sentenced to be dismissed, but in view of his past good conduct a remission of the sentence was ordered and Davis stayed on. A year later he was again at Benny Havens' when the authorities descended on the place; Davis got away, but in his flight he fell off a cliff and was hospitalized for a long time. He was also detected, with a number of others, making and consuming eggnog in barracks, for which he was confined to quarters. In June of 1828 the record shows that with 137 demerits Davis ranked 163rd in conduct out of 208 cadets.

Without visible signs of austerity, Davis made his way through West Point. He seems to have disliked Yankees from the beginning. Not long after his arrival he writes to his older brother Joseph saying that the Yankees in the cadet corps "are not such as I formed an acquaintance with on my arrival. . . . nor are they such associates as I would at present select." He added, caustically: "you cannot know how pittiful they generally are."

It must be admitted that Davis was somewhat standoffish—a trait noted later in life by some of his political opponents. After graduation, while he was a young lieutenant on a frontier post, Davis was court-martialled on charges that he had behaved toward his commanding officer with disrespect. He beat this rap without trouble, but one remark made at the trial is memorable. One of the court, who knew him well, asked the complaining witness: "Might not the usual manner of the accused be considered disrespectful or even contemptuous by one not well acquainted with him?"

These things, to be sure, amount to very little. The ardent spirit that led him to forbidden drinking parties was overlaid, as he grew mature, with the most rigid self-control; and if his impatience with anybody else's restraint, and his proud manner that seemed contemptuous to one who did not know him well, cropped out now and then during his presidency, and made trouble for him—well, great men have their foibles, and Davis had the defects of his qualities. It may well be that at Richmond he made enemies out of men who would have been his supporters if he had been more flexible; yet his very inflexibility, in the impossible job that was given him, was one of his strengths.

In any case, he has to be taken as he was, and there is no better way to see him as he really was than to examine the record as it appears in these papers. The very fact that the immense effort to collect, edit, and arrange these papers was so much worth doing testifies to the position he has finally come to occupy in the nation's story. He followed an impossible dream and lost, served it to the best of his substantial ability, and finally went down in defeat; but he was a memorable American, central actor in one of the republic's greatest stories, an indomitable character who could be broken but who could not be bent. In these volumes the record speaks about him. It tells a story that deserves attention.

GENERAL VIEW OF THE WORK

by Frank E. Vandiver

JEFFERSON DAVIS' long and important career in American affairs during the nineteenth century serves as the justification for this series—a series which will attempt to present his writings and recorded actions as completely and accurately as possible. Because the editors have thought in broad terms, *The Papers of Jefferson Davis* will also attempt to provide sufficient background material to enable the reader to make his own appraisal of the man and his age.

Since Davis was a man whose business was chiefly transacted by correspondence, this edition will seek to present not only the public and private letters written by him, but also those important letters and documents addressed to him. Obviously the plan is to present a complete or definitive edition of Davis' papers, but since such exhaustiveness is impossible to achieve, certain caveats are in order. In later volumes, many items, routine official correspondence, for example, will simply be calendared. In the first two or three volumes, a different rule will prevail. Here, where bulk is no particular problem—many of the early Davis papers being either lost or destroyed—a more comprehensive approach will be used. Many letters and documents which under the usual limitations might be classified as routine are included. The board of advisory editors felt justified in adopting a different method in the first volumes since so much of Davis' early career remains clouded in mystery, controversy, or misinterpretation.

Even with the limitations, the edition will inevitably reach large proportions. Present estimates look toward twenty to twenty-five volumes, with one or two supplemental volumes at the end. Letters and documents are presented in chronological order, and each volume will have a chronology of Davis' life for the period covered in that volume, plus a list of sources cited in the footnotes. In addition to the index in each volume, a complete bibliography and index will appear in the last volume of the set. Genealogical charts will appear in every third or fourth volume, beginning with the first; subsequent charts will present the additional genealogy of the Davis family and will offer corrections and additions to the previous charts.

Needless to say, such an undertaking requires the interest, enthusiasm, and support of many. Since the inception of the Davis project almost a decade ago, myriad people and organizations have cooperated to make the scheme a reality. First among the organizations is the Jefferson Davis Association, a nonprofit corporation chartered under the laws of Texas in 1963. Among the early incorporators were Cooper K. Ragan, William P. Hobby, Jr., and the late Palmer Bradley. Mr. Ragan volunteered his aid as an attorney, and has served faithfully as secretary-treasurer of the association. Once organized, the association asked a group of distinguished historians to serve on an editorial advisory board for the *Papers*; one of these consultants Bell I. Wiley, persuaded the Southern Company of Atlanta through its president, Harllee Branch, Jr., to make a grant of several thousand dollars which served as the initial financial base of the project. In 1965 the association secured the vital support of the William Stamps Farish Fund of Houston—and that fund has sustained the work of the editorial staff consistently for the past six years.

Through the unstinting help of the late Allan Nevins, essential cooperation came from the National Civil War Centennial Commission, which awarded the project the commission's gold medallion and urged all libraries and scholars to assist in collecting Davis materials. The National Historical Publications Commission, with the active support of its director, Oliver W. Holmes, approved *The Papers of Jefferson Davis* as worthy of support, made grants which permitted the employment of Karl L. Trever, a peerless archivist, and worked with the National Archives to make available microfilm copies of its extensive Davis holdings. Without the faith and generosity of all these people and organizations, the Jefferson Davis Association could not have survived and the *Papers* would not have appeared.

From the vantage point of an adviser, privileged to look in from the outside, I have watched the editorial staff grow in competence and, perhaps more importantly, maintain their enthusiasm. My gratitude to Haskell Monroe, James McIntosh, Miss Lynda Lasswell, Miss Kathleen Davis, Mrs. Mary Castañeda, Mrs. Mary Dix, and Mrs. Gene Riddle can be shown only in affection.

ACKNOWLEDGMENTS

PUBLICATION OF this volume would have been impossible without the cooperation and generous assistance of many individuals and institutions. We here gratefully acknowledge all support, both moral and material, accorded us during the existence of the project.

Vital financial support and continuing assistance have been provided by a number of organizations, particularly: the William Stamps Farish Fund; the Southern Company, through its subsidiaries, the Alabama Power Company, Georgia Power Company, Gulf Power Company of Florida, and the Mississippi Power Company; the National Historical Publications Commission; the William P. Hobby Foundation; and the Miami-Yulee Chapter of the United Daughters of the Confederacy.

We extend our thanks also to many other organizations and individuals who have supported the project generously since its inauguration: Adam G. Adams, Ralph L. Ardis, Jr., Ed Arnold, Maddrey W. Bass, James T. Beachum, V. L. Bedsole, Mrs. C. L. Blackburn, Rosanna A. Blake, William A. Bond, the late Palmer Bradley, H. S. Brannen, Edward Clark, H. M. Clement, Everett K. Cooper, Jr., Leonard G. Corby, Roy H. Cullen, Edward W. Dvorak, Robert D. Farish, Father Anton J. Frank, Kathleen H. Gilleland, John A. Glass, Joseph S. Guernsey, Herbert L. Harper, Emma Cortez Harris, Louise W. Hicks, Anne T. Hill, William P. Hobby, Jr., Samuel R. Hoene, Thomas B. Jeffries, Jr., William A. Kirkland, J. H. Knox, Mrs. M. B. Koonce, Mary L. Lasswell, McDaniel Lewis, Walter E. Long, C. T. Martoccia, W. H. Mason, C. E. Maxwell, Mrs. J. F. Mitchell, R. G. Murray, Steven J. Nobles, Mary Moody Northen, L. B. Pope, Cooper K. Ragan, J. Newton Rayzor, R. C. Reed, Robert H. Roser, Alvin Seippel, Lieutenant Colonel Alvin L. Small, AUS

(Ret.), Mrs. J. A. Steele, Henry S. Stroupe, Frank E. Vandiver, Worth Wicker, Frederick E. Williams, Jr., T. T. Wentworth, Jr., Harrison Weymouth, Jr., Benjamin N. Woodson, Pattie R. Wyche.

Also, the State of Alabama; the Chicago Civil War Round Table; Children of the Confederacy (Florida); the Civil War Centennial Commission and the several commissions of Alabama, Cumberland Gap (Tennessee), Florida, Louisiana, Mississippi, North Carolina, Richmond, South Carolina, Tennessee, and Virginia; C. S. Hammond & Company; Jay I. Kislak Foundation; Orlando Federal Savings & Loan Association; Peoples National Bank of Miami Shores; Tennessee Sons of Confederate Veterans; the following chapters of the United Daughters of the Confederacy: Brierfield, Richmond, Pat Cleburne, Davis-Reagan, Varina Davis, Florida Division, James B. Gordon, John B. Hood, and Robert E. Lee; the Wortham Foundation.

For direct sponsorship and use of physical facilities, we are grateful to the administration and board of governors of Rice University. To the United States Congress, we extend our appreciation for financial grants made to us through the National Historical Publications Commission.

Karl Trever, former Special Assistant to the Archivist of the United States for Presidential Libraries, has performed excellent and invaluable service as a member of the editorial staff, working in Washington, D.C. We are obligated to the following members of the staff of the National Archives, without whose work in the finding, cataloging, and filming of Davis material this volume would have been disastrously incomplete: Sarah D. Jackson and Elmer O. Parker, who assisted the editorial staff with special research problems; Mary Alliene Johnson, who did the greater part of the microfilming; Albert U. Blair; Elaine Everly; Maizie Johnson; Richard Maxwell; Dorothy B. Pickering; and Vera C. Rockwell.

The director of the National Historical Publications Commission, Oliver W. Holmes, has been of great assistance, and we thank him particularly for helping us gain the services of H. B. Fant and Richard E. Beringer. Mr. Fant made it possible for us to obtain Davis items easily through his comprehensive inventories of holdings of the Library of Congress, and has aided the editors with detailed searching in various collections. Professor Beringer, a fellow of the Commission, was chosen to work on the project for the 1969–70 academic year; we were fortunate in having such an able, painstaking, and patient historian on the staff. His experience was invaluable to us, and his unstinting labor contributed immeasurably to the preparation of Volume 1.

Collection of documents and research materials necessitated calling on private collectors and private and public depositories in all states; we wish to thank the many who responded, and especially the following individuals who have given more than generously of their time, attention, and knowledge: Anna B. Allan, University of North Carolina Library, Chapel Hill; Virgil L. Bedsole, Louisiana State University Library, Baton Rouge; James R. Bentley, The Filson Club, Louisville, Kentucky; Francis L. Berkeley, Jr., University of Virginia Library, Charlottesville; W. A. Blackledge, "Beauvoir," Biloxi, Mississippi; John W. Bonner, Jr., University of Georgia Library, Athens; the late Peter A. Brannon, Alabama Department of Archives and History, Montgomery; Eleanor S. Brockenbrough, Museum of the Confederacy, Richmond, Virginia; the late Mary Givens Bryan, Georgia Department of Archives and History, Atlanta; Amelia K. Buckley, Keeneland Race Course Library, Keeneland, Kentucky; Jacqueline Bull, University of Kentucky, Lexington; Henry Cadwalader, Historical Society of Pennsylvania, Philadelphia; Charlotte Capers, Mississippi Department of Archives and History, Jackson; Marie T. Capps, United States Military Academy Library, West Point, New York; Alexander P. Clark, Princeton University Library, Princeton, New Jersey; G. Glenn Clift, Kentucky Historical Society, Frankfort; C. F. W. Coker, North Carolina Department of Archives and History, Raleigh; Howson W. Cole, Virginia Historical Society, Richmond; Margaret Cook, College of William and Mary, Williamsburg, Virginia; J. Isaac Copeland, University of North Carolina Library, Chapel Hill; H. Bartholomew Cox, National Historical Publications Commission, Washington, D.C.; Mary R. Davis, Emory University Library, Atlanta; William S. Dix, Princeton University Library, Princeton, New Jersey; Katherine M. Epps, National Historical Publications Commission, Washington, D.C.; David E. Estes, Emory University Library, Atlanta; Anne Freudenberg, University of Virginia Library, Charlottesville; Mary I. Fry, Henry E. Huntington Library and Art Gallery, San Marino, California; George R. Gilkey, University of Wisconsin, La Crosse; J. Harcourt Givens, Historical Society of Pennsylvania, Philadelphia; Virginia R. Gray, Duke University Library, Durham, North Carolina; Lida L. Greene, Iowa Department of History and Archives, Des Moines; Connie Griffith, Tulane University Library, New Orleans; Josephine L.

Harper, State Historical Society of Wisconsin, Madison; Laura S. Harrell, Mississippi Department of Archives and History, Jackson; Carroll Hart, Georgia Department of Archives and History, Atlanta; Lilla M. Hawes, Georgia Historical Society, Savannah; W. Edwin Hemphill, editor, *Papers of John C. Calhoun*, University of South Carolina, Columbia; James J. Heslin, New-York Historical Society, New York City; Robert W. Hill, New York Public Library, New York City; Elbert Hilliard, Mississippi Department of Archives and History, Jackson; William S. Hoole, University of Alabama Library, Tuscaloosa; Milo B. Howard, Jr., Alabama Department of Archives and History, Montgomery; E. L. Inabinet and Clara Mae Jacobs, South Caroliniana Library, University of South Carolina, Columbia; H. G. Jones, North Carolina Department of Archives and History, Raleigh; Virginia K. Jones, Alabama Department of Archives and History, Montgomery; Milton Kenin, Historical Society of Pennsylvania, Philadelphia; Fay Kidd, National Historical Publications Commission, Washington, D.C.; John D. Kilbourne, Maryland Historical Society, Baltimore; Adele D. Leonard, New York State Library, Albany; Louis H. Manarin, Virginia State Library, Richmond; Helen S. Mangold, Henry E. Huntington Library and Art Gallery, San Marino, California; Elsa B. Meier, Louisiana State University Library, Baton Rouge; John Miller, New York Public Library, New York City; Richard W. Norton, R. W. Norton Art Gallery, Shreveport, Louisiana; the late Joseph O'Donnell, United States Military Academy Library, West Point; Harriet C. Owsley, Tennessee State Library and Archives, Nashville; James W. Patton, University of North Carolina Library, Chapel Hill; Kermit J. Pike, Western Reserve Historical Society, Cleveland; Mary B. Prior, South Carolina Historical Society, Charleston; James Rabun, Emory University Library, Atlanta; William M. E. Rachal, co-editor, *Papers of James Madison*, University of Chicago; Peggy Richards, Louisiana State Historical Museum, New Orleans; Stephen T. Riley, Massachusetts Historical Society, Boston; Peter Rippe, Museum of the Confederacy, Richmond, Virginia; Mattie Russell, Duke University Library, Durham, North Carolina; Marcelle Schertz, Louisiana State University Library, Baton Rouge; Fred Shelley, National Historical Publications Commission, Washington, D.C.; John Y. Simon, editor, *Papers of Ulysses S. Grant*, Southern Illinois University, Carbondale; Harmon Smith, Georgia Department of Archives and History, Atlanta; Sam B. Smith, Tennessee State Library and Archives, Nashville; Lewis M. Stark,

New York Public Library, New York City; Susan B. Tate, University of Georgia Library, Athens; Mary Lewis Ulmer, Clayton Library, Houston; William J. Van Schreeven, Virginia State Library, Richmond; the late Sarah A. Verner, University of Alabama Library, Tuscaloosa; Carolyn A. Wallace, University of North Carolina Library, Chapel Hill; Alene Lowe White, Western Reserve Historical Society, Cleveland; Sandra and James Wilson, "Beauvoir," Biloxi, Mississippi; James Wooldridge, Mississippi Department of Archives and History, Jackson.

Many others have also contributed Davis documents and extensive research materials, or have been otherwise exceedingly helpful in the preparation of this volume; we are greatly indebted to them: S. M. Arnold, John McDonnell Barb, M.D., Mrs. George S. Bennett, the late Palmer Bradley, Richard T. Colquitt, E. Merton Coulter, John Dale, Jr., Curtis Carroll Davis, Philip F. Detweiler, Dorman David, Amanda Geisenberger, Richard Harwell, Thomas R. Hay, Joseph Johnson, J. Ambler Johnston, Barbara and E. B. Long, the late Albert B. Moore, Mrs. James Polk Morris, Jr., the late Allan Nevins, Ralph Newman, the late Rembert Patrick, the Reverend DeWolf Perry, the Reverend Francis P. Prucha, S.J., Cooper K. Ragan, Frank G. Rankin, Ottilie B. Redus, Mary Louise Dement Rugg, Elsie O. and Philip D. Sang, Ann Louise Stone, and Hudson Strode.

Descendants and relatives of the Davis family have strongly and consistently encouraged and aided the editors, and many have done special research for us. They have allowed us to use their private manuscript collections and have sent us genealogical and biographical information on members of the Davis family. We especially wish to acknowledge the assistance of Jefferson Hayes-Davis, Davis' grandson, who graciously allowed us to use a number of hitherto unpublished Davis letters which will appear in this and future volumes. Similar gratitude is due to Lucinda Ballard Dietz, Robert D. Farish, Libbie Rice Farish, Floyd R. Farrar, Maude W. Farrar, Alfred F. Ganier, Benjamin H. Goldberger, the late Anna F. Goldsborough, Francis F. Goldsborough, Margaret Y. Graves, Anne Purnell and Fred C. Jackson, Nancy White Johnson, the late Elizabeth O'Kelley Kerrigan, Douglas McL. More, Beulah S. Watts, John Tobin White, Betty White Wills, Mrs. Ralph Wood, and Beverly M. Young.

Our colleagues on the faculty and staff of Rice University have unfailingly aided us in all aspects of preparation for publication. Chancellor Carey Croneis, Professors Katherine F. Drew, S. W. Higginbotham, Harold M. Hyman, and the late Professor Andrew F. Muir provided constant support and expert historical guidance. The late Hardin Craig, Jr., former librarian, and present librarian Richard O'Keeffe, and their staff—especially Marvine Brand, James W. Dyson, Georgia A. Frazer, Monika Orr, Richard H. Perrine, Guylene Willcox, Mary Jo Wonders, and Gilberta Zingler—have always been efficient and most helpful. Many other members of the Rice community, more than we can enumerate here, have been of assistance to the project, but we certainly wish to thank Jackie Church, Ron Guercio, Marian Jordan, Susie Vandiver, and Georgia I. Van Wie.

The Jefferson Davis Association has benefitted over a long period of time from the services of part-time employees, graduate students, and undergraduates, including Antoinette Boecker, Major John H. Bradley, Patricia K. Brito, Cynthia Fraser, Major William R. Griffiths, Major John A. Hixson, Lee Hyman, Patricia Long, Geoffrey J. and Gregory Norris, David A. Pace, Lynn D. Roberts, Steven Shannon, Dr. Richard J. Sommers, Major Thomas R. Stone, and Larry W. Turner.

A special debt is, of course, due our colleagues at the Louisiana State University Press—to Charles East, Leslie Phillabaum, Jules B. McKee, Albert Crochet, and especially to Martha Lacy Hall, our editor, whose unfailing patience, encouragement, and good humor made an exacting task easier, indeed, even pleasant.

Throughout the preparation of this volume, the editors have been inspired by the excellence achieved by Julian P. Boyd in his supervision of *The Papers of Thomas Jefferson.*

Extensive as the foregoing acknowledgments may be, we are certain that still others who have assisted the project have been overlooked. Thus, we conclude with general—and very sincere—thanks to all who facilitated our task.

EDITORIAL STAFF

Haskell M. Monroe, Jr., Editor
James T. McIntosh, Editor

Richard E. Beringer, Fellow of the
National Historical Publications Commission

Lynda Lasswell, Assistant Editor
Gene Jones Riddle, Editorial Associate
Mary S. Castañeda, Editorial Assistant
Kathleen Davis, Editorial Assistant
Mary S. Dix, Editorial Assistant
Karl L. Trever, Editorial Assistant

JEFFERSON DAVIS ASSOCIATION

Board of Directors

THE PAPERS OF JEFFERSON DAVIS

Board of Advisory Editors

EDITORIAL METHOD

ALTHOUGH THE preparation of the first volume of the writings and recorded actions of Jefferson Davis entailed a number of difficult decisions, the decision to print from photoduplicates was a relatively easy one. Indeed, given the limitations imposed by time and money, no other decision was possible. In addition to the apparent editorial advantages, the use of photocopies made possible the accumulation of a complete collection of Davis documents. Interested scholars will no longer be forced to travel from repository to repository, for by agreement with Rice University, the entire file of documents and notes will be deposited, upon completion of the project, in the Fondren Library, Rice University, Houston, Texas.

Closely related to the decision to use photofacsimiles was the decision to gather for the purposes of comparison every known version of a Davis document, be it draft, copy, or original. Although locating letterbook and retained copies has been—particularly in the case of the materials in the National Archives—a relatively easy task, the acquisition of recipients' copies has often been not only difficult, but at times impossible. Many of them, those not tucked away in forgotten trunks, are in the hands of autograph dealers whose catalogs frequently tantalize the impecunious editor by listing desirable Davis items at a price far above his power to pay. No doubt the dealers' market justifies the price as well as a certain element of secretiveness, but sometimes—as when trying to discover the new owner of a Davis letter—such practices seem designed to frustrate the historical editor. The task of acquiring copies of the letters sent to Davis has been further complicated by the fact that many of the letters, particularly those belonging to the early period of his life, were either seized or destroyed by Union forces during the war. And of those that escaped destruction, many have been so scattered that they too appear irretrievably lost. Still the search for fugitive Davis letters continues and, although difficult, is sometimes rewarded by an important find. No doubt a supplementary volume will be required for those letters discovered after the publication of the volumes in which they chronologically belong.

Letters mentioned as having been sent that have not been found are so noted. Missing letters of great or potentially great importance will be accorded special treatment: when the necessary information on dating and content permits, they will be treated as items and entered in their proper chronological places.

Although the editorial decisions made in regard to the collecting, cataloging, and filing of documents—a manageable file being an editorial *sine qua non*—were of fundamental importance, those made concerning the method of printing were of equal, if not greater, significance. Central to and controlling the method of presentation was the decision of the editors to transcribe each document as accurately as possible. Fully aware that every transcription no matter how accurate loses something of the original, the editors have evolved a methodology which, tempered by the need for clarity, is both flexible enough to accommodate the various documents of the first volume and hopefully elastic enough to embrace the problems of future volumes.

A flexible methodology was particularly desirable for the first volume since the editorial decision to print all known documents signed by and addressed to Davis as well as selected contemporary notices meant that a great variety of materials had to be treated. Indeed, subsequent volumes will merely calendar much that has been printed here. Because the available sources are so often incomplete and inaccurate, the editors felt justified in printing any item that would explain or clarify events in Davis' early life.

Many of the documents relating to the early life of Davis—particularly those that simply record his actions—do not lend themselves to literal presentation. In such cases it was decided to present the documents in either an extracted or abstracted form. This is notably so in the case of official returns which, while affording important information about Davis, also include much irrelevant matter that has been deleted. While principally employed with military documents, the abstract and extract have also been used in a number of documents wherein Davis is mentioned but is neither sender nor recipient.

Finally—before discussing the specific methods used in presenting the documents themselves—it should be mentioned that the editors have attempted to treat each item as an entity in itself, supplying with each all the information needed for its clear understanding. Cross-referencing has consequently been extensively employed, and while sometimes intrusive it was felt that it would be less so than the needless repetition of information supplied elsewhere.

Since a number of items may be printed on a single page, the editors decided that some device beyond pagination was necessary for efficient CROSS-REFERENCING. Thus arabic numerals have been assigned to each item to designate volume and item numbers. Printed in the margin opposite the title, the first arabic number denotes the volume, and the second indicates the item number; e.g., the Samuel Davis to Jefferson Davis letter of June 25, 1823, becomes "1:5."

The HEADING of an individual letter is titled "To . . . " or "From . . . , " Davis' name being understood. In letters to or from others, both the sender's and the recipient's names are printed in full, as in the following example: "Sarah Knox Taylor Davis to Margaret Mackall Smith Taylor." Documents such as speeches, courts martial, certificates, and others of a similar nature are given their official titles, or, if there be none, the editors have supplied them.

When it is necessary to explain background or where logic dictates that certain information is necessary for the understanding of a particular manuscript, an EDITORIAL NOTE is positioned between the heading and the place and date line.

The salutation and PLACE AND DATE LINE are treated as the first line of text, with the following exceptions: where the place and date line is too lengthy; where the salutation and place and date line both carry numbered footnotes. In all cases, the place and date lines appear as written, save for abstracts where the form has been modernized. Regardless of where the date appears in the manuscript—after the signature or in the margin of a letterbook—for the sake of uniformity it is always printed in the upper right hand corner of the document. When the place and date are derived from internal evidence, the editors have placed them within square brackets in modern form. If the date or place has been supplied from a postmark or an endorsement, the editors will indicate the source in an explanatory footnote.

Some documents such as the post returns are not fully dated, the day of the month being omitted. Since they are monthly returns, they have been arbitrarily assigned the last day of their respective months, the day appearing in square brackets. Other documents, the pay registers for example, although fully dated, have no place of origin. In these cases the place, when known, has been supplied, again in square brackets.

All SALUTATIONS appear as written; however, the inside address is not considered a part of the salutation and is not printed.

Standard PARAGRAPH INDENTION is used. It is commonplace in nineteenth-century manuscripts for the writer to end a paragraph in midline and return to the left margin without indention. Whenever this occurs, extraneous punctuation, if any, is eliminated and the modern form of paragraphing is employed.

In SPELLING, GRAMMAR, and CAPITALIZATION, the rule of literal presentation is followed. If a word is misspelled it will appear so without the annoying [*sic*] or intrusive [corrected spelling]. When a misspelling occurs, the reader may assume that it is simply a literal presentation and not a typographical error. Misspelled proper names will also be left as they appear, but will be corrected in the explanatory footnotes. The letter writer, whose intentions are sometimes difficult to determine, will be given the benefit of the doubt when "i" and "e," "a" and "o," or "u" and "o" look alike. Words capitalized for no apparent reason are left as written, but if the writer's intention is unclear, he is again given the benefit of the doubt and the correct form is followed.

Normally, PUNCTUATION is left as it appears; however, in the place and date line, archaic forms have been dropped and modern usage employed. Wherever double punctuation has been used, the more correct—according to modern practices—of the two forms has been retained. When the dash is used as terminal punctuation, it has been, if followed by a capital letter, changed to a period and, when followed by a lower case letter, retained. For the most part, when quotation marks have been used as an apostrophe or when the colon has been utilized as a comma or period, it has been silently corrected. In those letters where punctuation has been omitted and the omission makes the reading unclear, a "pause" has been employed—that is, an extended space—to indicate the absence of punctuation in the original document. If, however, the addition of the pause makes two or more readings possible, the document has been allowed to stand as it is and a clarifying note has been added.

All SUPERSCRIPT is lowered.

When word or phrase REPETITION occurs or when a page ends with a word, and the same word is repeated at the beginning of the next page, the repetitions are silently deleted. If, however, the repetition seems to have a psychological significance, it is retained.

If easily understood, ABBREVIATIONS and CONTRACTIONS are retained as written, but if in the opinion of the editors they are not immediately recognizable, they are expanded within square brackets. The ampersand and the form "&c" are retained as well as monetary signs and the various units of weight and measurement.

All AUTHOR DEVIATION FROM LINEAL PRESENTATION—insertions, corrections, strikeouts, marginalia—is placed within angle brackets: "I arrived here <Dec. 26th> with a severe cough"; "I hope you will come down <—in the course of the—> <and Mary must come with> you"; "The fall was <—illegible—> arrested." Strikeouts, preceded and followed by short dashes, are placed in angle brackets, as in two of the examples above. If the type of deviation is other than a strikeout, an explanatory note is subjoined.

EDITORIAL INSERTIONS and CORRECTIONS are enclosed in square brackets.

The COMPLIMENTARY CLOSE and SIGNATURE are treated as the last line of the text.

All substantive ENDORSEMENTS are printed after the signature line of the document on which they appear. The physical description of the endorsement is given in square brackets at the left margin. If there is more than one endorsement, an arabic number has been used with the descriptive symbol, for example: [AES 1], [AE 2]. Although clerical information is technically an endorsement, much of it concerns such matters as filing and has been eliminated. However, relevant clerical data or that conceivably relevant, such as the date of receipt, have been included and are printed in the descriptive footnote.

If an ENCLOSURE is an integral part of the letter transmitting it or if it has the same place and date line, it is printed with its cover letter. In such cases, the abbreviation "[Encl]" is positioned in the left margin below the signature line of the cover letter, and the enclosed letter or document follows. If, on the other hand, the letter has a different place and date line, it is printed apart from its cover letter in its proper chronological order with the necessary cross-references.

The DESCRIPTIVE NOTE follows immediately upon the document itself and includes the following: the character of the document, that is, whether it is an ALS, ADS, a copy, or a printed form; the location, i.e., the repository holding the document or, if privately owned, the owner as of the given year; the collection, if any, to which the document belongs; and, in the case of abstracts and extracts, the number of filmed exposures needed to acquire a complete copy. When more than one version of a document is recorded, the first listed is always the version printed. The descriptive note also chronicles the condition of the manuscript—whether torn or otherwise incomplete, the person to whom the letter is addressed, the postmark if used in establishing the date or place, the presence of a seal, the signature if not printed with the document itself, as well as relevant clerical endorsements. Notice is always given when the letter includes enclosures or is itself an enclosure. Finally, the descriptive note provides not only a listing of where the document has previously appeared in print but, in addition, any unusual provenance.

The EXPLANATORY FOOTNOTES are numbered consecutively after each document and identify persons, places, and things, whenever possible. The first time a person appears, a brief biographical sketch is given; thereafter whenever he is mentioned, a cross-reference to the sketch will follow, for example: "Lewis Cass (sketch, 1:349, *n.* 5)" or if the person noted is a member of the Davis family, a reference to the genealogical chart is included, e.g., "Amanda Davis Bradford (sketch, 1:363, *n.* 29; 1:Appendix IV, Entry 21)." Nicknames, pseudonyms, initials, misspelled proper names and titles used as names are identified and, if necessary, expanded or corrected. Places and such things as legislative bills, political movements, and military orders are identified. In addition, the explanatory footnote is used for presenting conflicting evidence and interpretations as well as the reminiscences of Davis and others.

SYMBOLS AND ABBREVIATIONS

AD	Autographed Document
ADS	Autographed Document Signed
ADf	Autographed Draft
ADfS	Autographed Draft Signed
AE	Autographed Endorsement
AES	Autographed Endorsement Signed
AL	Autographed Letter
ALbCS	Autographed Letterbook Copy Signed
ALS	Autographed Letter Signed
AN	Autographed Note
ANS	Autographed Note Signed
D	Document (unaddressed items, such as proclamations, speeches, oaths, deeds, commissions, warrants, etc., not in the author's handwriting and not signed by him)
DAB	*Dictionary of American Biography*
Df	Draft
DfS	Draft Signed
DS	Document Signed
E	Endorsement
Encl	Enclosure
ES	Endorsement Signed
L	Letter
LbC	Letterbook Copy
LbCS	Letterbook Copy Signed
LS	Letter Signed
MS	Manuscript (a general category used when other descriptions are inapplicable)
NA	National Archives
NS	Note Signed
OED	*A New English Dictionary on Historical Principles*
RG	Record Group

CONTENTS

CONTENTS

CONTENTS

CONTENTS

CONTENTS

CONTENTS

CONTENTS

CONTENTS

CONTENTS

CONTENTS

CONTENTS

CONTENTS

CONTENTS

CONTENTS

CONTENTS

CONTENTS

CONTENTS

1838

CONTENTS

ILLUSTRATIONS

ILLUSTRATIONS

AUTOBIOGRAPHY OF JEFFERSON DAVIS 1:1

Editorial Note: The following autobiography has been extracted from its proper chronological order and printed here in preference to printing it in an appendix because it could not, except in an arbitrary way, be exactly dated. More importantly, the editors believe that it might constitute an effective introduction to both set and volume in that it affords, as the *Papers* frequently do not, a historical sequence of events, a framework into which the various Davis documents might be placed for better understanding. Finally, it has been included at this point since it presents certain problems, such as the question of Davis' birthdate, that do not appear elsewhere and that must be explained at the beginning of the volume if the contradictions implicit in the documents themselves are to be reconciled and understood.

Footnoting in this document will be held to a minimum and will be confined, save for the above-mentioned exception, to explaining errors of print or fact.

Beauvoir, Miss., November, 1889

I was born, June 3, 1808,[1] in Christian County, Ky., in that part of it which, by a subsequent division, is now in Todd County. At this place has since arisen the village of Fairview, and on the exact spot where I was born has been constructed the Baptist church of the place. My father, Samuel Davis, was a native of Georgia, and served in the War of the Revolution, first in the "mounted gun-men," and afterward as captain of infantry at the siege of Savannah. During my infancy my father removed to Wilkinson County, Miss. After passing through the County Academy, I entered Transvaal College,[2] Kentucky, at the age of sixteen,[3] and was advanced as far as the senior class when I was appointed to the United States Military Academy at West Point; which I entered in September, 1824. I graduated in 1828, and then, in accordance with the custom of cadets, entered active service with the rank of lieutenant, serving as an officer of infantry on the Northwest frontier until 1833, when, a regiment of dragoons having been created, I was transferred to it. After a successful campaign against the Indians I resigned from the army, in 1835, being anxious to fulfil a long-existing engagement with a daughter of Colonel Zachary Taylor, whom I married, not "after a romantic elopement," as has so often been stated, but at the house of her aunt and in the presence of many of her relatives, at a place near Louisville, Ky. Then I became a cotton planter in Warren County, Miss. It was my misfortune, early in my married life, to lose my wife; and for many years thereafter I lived in great seclusion on the plantation in the swamps of the Mississippi. In 1843 I for the first time took part in the political life of the country. Next year I was chosen one of the Presidential electors at large of the State; and in the succeeding year was elected to Congress, taking my seat in the House of Representatives in December, 1845. The proposition to terminate the joint occupancy of Oregon, and the reformation of the tariff, were the two questions arousing most public attention at that time, and I took an active part in their discussion, especially in that of the first.

During this period hostilities with Mexico commenced, and in the legislation which the contest rendered necessary my military education enabled me to take a somewhat prominent part.

In June, 1846, a regiment of Mississippi volunteers was organized at Vicksburg, of which I was elected colonel. On receiving notice of the election, I proceeded to overtake the regiment, which was already on its way to Mexico, and joined it at New Orleans. Reporting to General Taylor, then commanding at Camargo, my regiment, although the last to arrive—having been detained for some time on duty at the mouth of the Rio Grande—was selected to move with the advance upon the city of Monterey.[4] The want of transportation prevented General Taylor from taking the whole body of volunteers who had reported there for duty. The Mississippi regiment was armed entirely with percussion rifles. And here it may be interesting to state that General Scott, in Washington, endeavored to persuade me not to take more rifles than enough for four companies, and objected particularly to percussion arms, as not having been sufficiently tested for the use of troops in the field. Knowing that the Mississippians would have no confidence in the old flint-lock muskets, I insisted on their being armed with the kind of rifle then recently made at New Haven, Conn.—the Whitney rifle. From having been first used by the

Mississippians, these rifles have always been known as the Mississippi rifles.

In the attack on Monterey[4] General Taylor divided his force, sending one part of it by a circuitous road to attack the city from the west; while he decided to lead in person the attack on the east. The Mississippi regiment advanced to the relief of a force which had attacked Fort Lenaria,[5] but had been repulsed before the Mississippians arrived. They carried the redoubt, and the fort which was in the rear of it surrendered. The next day our force on the west side carried successfully the height on which stood the bishop's palace, which commanded the city.

On the third day the Mississippians advanced from the fort which they held, through lanes and gardens, skirmishing and driving the enemy before them until they reached a two-story house at the corner of the Grand Plaza. Here they were joined by a regiment of Texans, and from the windows of this house they opened fire on the artillery and such other troops as were in view. But, to get a better position for firing on the principal building of the Grand Plaza, it was necessary to cross the street, which was swept by canister and grape, rattling on the pavement like hail; and as the street was very narrow it was determined to construct a flying barricade. Some long timbers were found, and, with pack-saddles and boxes, which served the purpose, a barricade was constructed.

Here occurred an incident to which I have since frequently referred with pride. In breaking open a quartermaster's storehouse to get supplies for this barricade, the men found bundles of the much-prized Mexican blankets, and also of very serviceable shoes and pack-saddles. The pack-saddles were freely taken as good material for the proposed barricade; and one of my men, as his shoes were broken and stones had hurt his feet, asked my permission to take a pair from one of the boxes. This, of course, was freely accorded; but not one of the very valuable and much-prized Mexican blankets was taken.

About the time that the flying barricade was completed arrangements were made by the Texans and Mississippians to occupy houses on both sides of the street for the purpose of more effective fire into the Grand Plaza. It having been deemed necessary to increase our force, the Mississippi sergeant-major was sent back for some companies of the First Mississippi which had remained behind. He returned with the statement that the enemy was behind us, that all our troops had been withdrawn, and that orders had been three times sent to me to return. Governor Henderson, of Texas, had accompanied the Texan troops, and on submitting to him the question what we should do under the message, he realized—as was very plain—that it was safer to remain where we were than—our supports having been withdrawn—to return across streets where we were liable to be fired on by artillery, and across open grounds where cavalry might be expected to attack us. But, he added, he supposed the orders came from the general-in-chief, and we were bound to obey them. So we made dispositions to retire quietly; but, in passing the first square, we found that our movement had been anticipated, and that a battery of artillery was posted to command the street. The arrangement made by me for crossing it was that I should go first; if only one gun was fired at me, then another man should follow; and so on, another and another, until a volley should be fired, and then all of them should rush rapidly across before the guns could be reloaded. In this manner the men got across with little loss. We then made our way to the suburb, where we found that an officer of infantry, with two companies and a section of artillery, had been posted to wait for us, and in case of emergency, to aid our retreat.

Early next morning General Ampudia, commanding the Mexican force, sent in a flag and asked for a conference with a view to capitulation. General Taylor acceded to the proposition, and appointed General Worth, Governor Henderson, and myself, commissioners to arrange the terms of capitulation. General Taylor received the city of Monterey,[4] with supplies, much needed by his army, and shelter for the wounded. The enemy gained only the privilege of retiring peacefully, a privilege which, if it had not been accorded, they had the power to take by any one of the three roads open to them. The point beyond which they should withdraw was fixed by the terms of capitulation, and the time during which hostilities were to be suspended was determined on by the length of time necessary to refer to and receive answers from the two governments. A few days before the expiration of the time so fixed, the Government of the United States disapproved of the capitulation, and ordered the truce to be immediately terminated. By this decision we lost whatever credit had been given to us for generous terms in the capitulation, and hostilities were to be resumed without any preparations having been made to enable General Taylor, even with the small force he had, to advance farther into the enemy's country. General

Taylor's letter to Mr. Marcy, Secretary of War, was a very good response to an unjust criticism; and in the *Washington Union* of that time I also published a very full explanaton of the acts of the commissioners, and of the military questions involved in the matter of capitulation in preference to continuing the siege and attack.

General Taylor, assuming that it was intended for him to advance into the interior of Mexico, then commenced to prepare himself for such a campaign. To this end he made requisitions for the needful transportation, as well as munitions, including, among other supplies, large india-rubber bags in which to carry provisions for days, and which, being emptied before we reached the desert of sixty miles, would, by being filled with water, enable his troops and horses to cross those desert plains. These and other details had been entered into under the expectation that the censure of the treaty of Monterey[4] meant a march into the interior of Mexico. Another thing required was a new battery of field-pieces to take the place of the old Ringgold battery, which by long service had become honey-combed. When all these arrangements were nearly completed it was decided to send General Scott, with discretionary powers, which enabled him to take nearly all the tried troops General Taylor had, including even the engineer then employed in the construction of a fort, and the battery of new guns to replace the old ones, which were deemed no longer safe, but which, under the intrepid Captain Bragg, afterward did good service in the battle of Buena Vista.

General Taylor, with the main body of his army, went to Victoria, and there made arrangements to send them all to report to General Scott, at Vera Cruz, except the small force he considered himself entitled to as an escort on his route back to Monrerey[4] through an unfriendly people. That escort consisted of a battery of light artillery,[6] a squadron of dragoons, and the regiment of Mississippi riflemen. With these he proceeded through Monterey[4] and Saltillo to Agua Nueva, where he was joined by the division of General Wool, who had made the campaign of Chihuahua.

General Santa Anna, commanding the army of Mexico, was informed of the action which had been taken in stripping General Taylor of his forces, and was also informed that he had at Saltillo only a handful of volunteers, which could be easily dispersed on the approach of an army. Thus assured, and with the prospect of recovering all the country down to the Rio Grande, Santa Anna advanced upon Agua Nueva.

General Taylor retired to the Angostura Pass, in front of the Hacienda of Buena Vista, and there made his dispositions to receive the anticipated attack. As sage as he was brave, his dispositions were made as well as the small force at his command made it possible. After two days of bloody fighting General Santa Anna retired before this little force, the greater part of which had never before been under fire.

The encounter with the enemy was very bloody. The Mississippians lost many of their best men, for each of whom, however, they slew several of the enemy. For, trained marksmen, they never touched the trigger without having an object through both sights; and they seldom fired without drawing blood. The infantry against whom the advance was made was driven back, but the cavalry then moved to get in the rear of the Mississippians, and this involved the necessity of falling back to where the plain was narrow, so as to have a ravine on each flank.

In this position the second demonstration of the enemy's cavalry was received. They were repulsed, and it was quiet in front of the Mississippians until an aide came and called from the other side of the ravine, which he could not pass, that General Taylor wanted support to come as soon as possible for the protection of the artillery on the right flank. The order was promptly obeyed at double quick, although the distance must have been nearly a mile. They found the enemy moving in three lines upon the batteries of Captain Braxton Bragg and the section of artillery commanded by George H. Thomas. The Mississippians came up in line, their right flank opposite the first line of the advancing enemy, and at a very short range opened fire. All being sharpshooters, those toward the left of the line obliqued to the right, and at close quarters and against three long lines very few shots could have missed. At the same time the guns of Bragg and Thomas were firing grape. The effect was decisive; the infantry and artillery of the enemy immediately retired.

At the close of the day Santa Anna bugled the retreat, as was supposed, to go into quarters; but when the next sun rose there was no enemy in our front.

The news of this victory was received in the United States with a degree of enthusiasm proportionate to the small means with which it was achieved; and generosity was excited by the feeling that General Taylor had been treated with injustice. Thenceforward the march of "old Rough and Ready" to the White House was a foregone conclusion.

In this battle, while advancing to meet the enemy, then pressing some of our discomfited volunteers on the left of the field of battle, I received a painful wound, which was rendered more severe in consequence of remaining in the saddle all day, although wounded early in the morning. A ball had passed through the foot, leaving in the wound broken bones and foreign matter, which the delay had made it impossible then to extract. In consequence I had to return home on crutches.

In the meantime a Senator of Mississippi had died, and the Governor had appointed me his successor. Before my return home President Polk had also appointed me Brigadier-General of Volunteers; an appointment which I declined on the ground that volunteers are militia, and that the Constitution reserved to the State the appointment of all militia officers. This was in 1847. In January, 1848, the Mississippi Legislature unanimously elected me United States Senator for the rest of the unexpired term; and in 1850 I was re-elected for the full term as my own successor. In the United States Senate I was Chairman of the Military Committee; and I also took an active part in the debates on the Compromise measures of 1850, frequently opposing Senator Douglas, of Illinois, in his theory of squatter sovereignty, and advocating, as a means of pacification, the extension of the Missouri Compromise line to the Pacific. When the question was presented to Mississippi as to whether the State should acquiesce in the Compromise legislation of 1850, or whether it should join the other Southern States in a Convention to decide as to the best course to pursue in view of the threatened usurpations of the Federal Government, I advocated a Convention of the Southern States, with a view to such co-operation as might effectually check the exercise of constructive powers, the parent of despotism, by the Federal Government.

The canvass for Governor commenced that year. The candidate of the Democratic party was by his opponents represented to hold extreme opinions—in other words, to be a disunionist. For, although he was a man of high character and had served the country well in peace and war, this supposition was so artfully cultivated that, though the Democratic party was estimated to be about eight thousand in majority, when the election occurred in September the Democratic candidates for a Convention were defeated by a majority of over seven thousand, and the Democratic candidate for Governor withdrew.

The election for Governor was to occur in November, and I was called on to take the place vacated by the candidate who had withdrawn from the canvass. It was a forlorn hope, especially as my health had been impaired by labors in the summer canvass, and there was not time before the approaching election to make such a canvass as would be needed to reform the ranks of the Democracy. However, as a duty to the party I accepted the position, and made as active a campaign as time permitted, with the result that the majority against the party was reduced to less than one thousand. From this time I remained engaged in quiet farm-labors until the nomination of Franklin Pierce, when I went out to advocate his election, having formed a very high opinion of him as a statesman and a patriot, from observations of him in 1837 and 1838, when he was in the United States Senate.

On his election as President, I became a member of his cabinet, filling the office of Secretary of War during his entire term.

During these four years I proposed the introduction of camels for service on the Western plains, a suggestion which was adopted. I also introduced an improved system of infantry tactics; effected the substitution of iron for wood in gun-carriages; secured rifled muskets and rifles and the use of Minié balls; and advocated the increase of the defences of the sea-coast, by heavy guns and the use of large-grain powder.

While in the Senate I had advocated, as a military necessity and as a means of preserving the Pacific Territory to the Union, the construction of a military railway across the continent; and, as Secretary of War, I was put in charge of the surveys of the various routes proposed. Perhaps for a similar reason—my previous action in the Senate—I was also put in charge of the extension of the United States Capitol.

The administration of Mr. Pierce presents the single instance of an executive whose cabinet witnessed no change of persons during the whole term. At its close, having been re-elected to the United States Senate, I re-entered that body.

During the discussion of the Compromise measures of 1850 the refusal to extend the Missouri Compromise line to the Pacific was early put on the ground that there was no constitutional authority to legislate slavery into or out of any territory, which was in fact and seeming intent a repudiation of the Missouri Compromise; and it was so treated in the Kansas-Nebraska bill.

Subsequently, Mr. Douglas, the advocate of what was called squatter-sovereignty, insisted upon the rights of the first immigrants into the territory to decide upon the question whether migrating citizens might take their slaves with them; which meant, if it meant anything, that Congress could authorize a few settlers to do what it was admitted Congress itself could not do. But out of this bill arose a dissension which finally divided the Democratic party, and caused its defeat in the Presidential election of 1860.

And from this empty, baseless theory, grew the Iliad of our direst woes.

When Congress met, in the fall of 1860, I was appointed one of a Senate Committee of Thirteen to examine and report on some practicable adjustment of the controversies which then threatened the dissolution of the Union. I at first asked to be excused from the Committee, but at the solicitation of friends agreed to serve, avowing my willingness to make any sacrifice to avert the impending struggle. The Committee consisted of men belonging to the three political divisions of the Senate: the State-rights men of the South; the Radicals of the North; and the Northern Democrats; with one member who did not acknowledge himself as belonging to any one of the three divisions—Mr. Crittenden, an old-time Whig, and the original mover of the Compromise Resolutions. When the Committee met it was agreed that, unless some measure which would receive the support of the majority of each of the three divisions could be devised, it was useless to make any report; and, after many days of anxious discussion and a multiplicity of propositions, though the Southern State-rights men and the Northern Democrats and the Whig, Mr. Crittenden, could frequently agree, they could never get a majority of the Northern Radicals to unite with them in any substantive proposition. Finally, the Committee reported their failure to find anything on which the three divisions could unite. Mr. Douglas, who was a member of the Committee, defiantly challenged the Northern Radicals to tell what they wanted. As they had refused everything, he claimed that they ought to be willing to tell what they proposed to do.

When officially informed that Mississippi had passed the ordinance of secession, I took formal leave of the Senate, announcing for the last time the opinions I had so often expressed as to State sovereignty, and, as a consequence of it, the right of a State to withdraw its delegated powers. Before I reached home I had been appointed by the Convention of Mississippi commander-in-chief of its army, with the rank of Major-General, and I at once proceeded with the task of organization. I went to my home in Warren County in order to prepare for what I believed was to be a long and severe struggle. Soon a messenger came from the Provisional Confederate Congress at Montgomery, bringing the unwelcome notice that I had been elected Provisional President of the Confederate States. But, reluctant as I was to accept the honor, and carefully as I had tried to prevent the possibility of it, in the circumstances of the country I could not refuse it; and I was inaugurated at Montgomery, February 18, 1861, with Alexander H. Stephens, of Georgia, as Vice-President.

From this time to the fall of the Confederate Government my life was part of the history of the Confederacy and of the war between the States. It is impossible, therefore, to follow it in detail.

In the selection of a cabinet I was relieved from a difficulty which surrounds that duty by the President of the United States; for there were no "sections" and no "party" distinctions. All aspirations, ambitions, and interest had been merged in a great desire for Confederate independence.

In my inaugural address I asserted that necessity, not choice, had led to the secession of the Southern States; that, as an agricultural people, their policy was peace and free commerce with all the world; that the constituent parts, not the system of government, had been changed.

The removal of the troops from Fortress Moultrie to Fort Sumter, the guns of which threatened the harbor of Charleston, and the attempt to throw reinforcements into that fort—thus doubly breaking a pledge that matters should be kept *in statu quo*—constituted the occasion as well as the justification of the opening of fire upon Fort Sumter. Speedily following this event came the call for a large army by Mr. Lincoln, and the secession of other Southern States as the consequence of this unmistakable purpose of coercion.

Virginia, which had led in the effort, by a Peace Conference, to avert national ruin, when she saw the Constitution disregarded and the purpose to compel free States by military force to submit to arbitrary power, passed an Ordinance of Secession, and joined the Confederate States.

Shortly after this, as authorized by the Provisional Congress, I removed the Confederate capital from Montgomery to Richmond.

Among the many indications of good-will shown when on my way to and after my arrival at Richmond was the purchase of a very fine residence in Richmond, by leading citizens. It was offered as a present; but, following a rule that had governed my action in all such cases, I declined to accept it. I continued to live in Richmond until the Confederate forces were compelled to withdraw from the defences of the capital.

That event was not quite unexpected, but it occurred before the conditions were fulfilled under which General Lee contemplated retreat. After General Lee was forced to surrender, and General Johnson[7] consented to do so, I started, with a very few of the men who volunteered to accompany me, for the trans-Mississippi; but, hearing on the road that marauders were pursuing my family, whom I had not seen since they left Richmond, but knew to be *en route* to the Florida coast, I changed my direction, and, after a long and hard ride, found them encamped and threatened by a robbing party. To give them the needed protection I travelled with them for several days, until in the neighborhood of Irvinville, Ga., when I supposed I could safely leave them. But, hearing, about nightfall, that a party of marauders were to attack the camp that night, and supposing them to be pillaging deserters from both armies, and that the Confederates would listen to me, I awaited their coming, lay down in my travelling clothes, and fell asleep. Late in the night my colored coachman aroused me with the intelligence that the camp was attacked; and I stepped out of the tent where my wife and children were sleeping, and saw at once that the assailants were troops deploying around the encampment. I so informed my wife, who urged me to escape. After some hesitation I consented, and a servant-woman started with me carrying a bucket as if going to the spring for water. One of the surrounding troops ordered me to halt, and demanded my surrender. I advanced toward the trooper, throwing off a shawl which my wife had put over my shoulders. The trooper aimed his carbine, when my wife, who witnessed the act, rushed forward and threw her arms around me, thus defeating my intention, which was, if the trooper missed his aim, to try to unhorse him and escape with his horse. Then, with every species of petty pillage and offensive exhibition, I was taken from point to point until incarcerated in Fortress Monroe. There I was imprisoned for two years before being allowed the privilege of the writ of habeas corpus.*

At length, when the writ was to be issued, the condition was imposed by the Federal Executive that there should be bondsmen influential in the "Republican" party of the North, Mr. Greeley being specially named. Entirely as a matter of justice and legal right, not from motives of personal regard, Mr. Greeley, Mr. Gerrit Smith, and other eminent Northern citizens went on my bond.

In May, 1867, after being released from Fortress Monroe, I went to Canada, where my older children were, with their grandmother; my wife, as soon as permitted, having shared my imprisonment, and brought our infant daughter with her. From time to time I obeyed summonses to go before the Federal Court at Richmond, until, finally, the case was heard by Chief Justice Chase and District Judge Underwood, who were divided in opinion, which sent the case to the Supreme Court of the United States, and the proceedings were quashed, leaving me without the opportunity to vindicate myself before the highest Federal Court.

After about a year's residence in Canada I went to England with my family under an arrangement that I was to have sixty days' notice whenever the United States Court required my presence. After being abroad in England and on the Continent about a year, I received an offer of an appointment as President of a Life Insurance Company. Thereupon I returned to this country, and went to Memphis and took charge of the company. Subsequently I came to the Gulf Coast of Mississippi, as a quiet place where I could prepare my work on "The Rise and Fall of the Confederate Government." A friend from her infancy, Mrs. Dorsey shared her home with me, and subsequently sold to me her property of Beauvoir, an estate of five or six hundred acres, about midway between Mobile and New Orleans. Before I had fully paid for this estate Mrs. Dorsey died, leaving me her sole legatee. From the spring of 1876 to the autumn of 1879

* For a fuller account of my arrest see statements of United States Senator Reagan; W. R. Johnston,[8] President Tulane University; F. R. Lubbock, Treasurer of Texas; B. N. Harrison, Esq., of New York City, all eye-witnesses. Also "The Rise and Fall of the Confederate Government," page 700, vol. ii.; and for my life at Fortress Monroe, "The Prison Life of Jefferson Davis," by Dr. L. J. J. Craven;[9] New York: Carleton, 1866.

I devoted myself to the production of the historical work just mentioned. It is an octavo book, in two volumes of about seven hundred pages each. I have also from time to time contributed essays to the *North American Review* and BELFORD'S MAGAZINE, and have just completed the manuscript of "A Short History of the Confederate States of America," which is expected to appear early in 1890.

Since settling at Beauvoir, I have persistently refused to take any active part in politics, not merely because of my disfranchisement, but from a belief that such labors could not be made to conduce to the public good, owing to the sectional hostilities manifested against me since the war. For the same reason I have also refused to be a candidate for public office, although it is well known that I could at any time have been re-elected a Senator of the United States.

I have been twice married, the second time being in 1844,[10] to a daughter of William B. Howell, of Natchez, a son of Governor Howell, of New Jersey. She has borne me six children—four sons and two daughters. My sons are all dead; my daughters survive. The elder is Mrs. Hayes, of Colorado Springs, Col., and the mother of four children. My youngest daughter lives with us at Beauvoir, Miss. Born in the last year of the war, she became familiarly known as "the daughter of the Confederacy."

JEFFERSON DAVIS.

MS not found. Text from Davis, "Autobiography of Jefferson Davis," *Belford's Magazine*, IV (1889–90), 255–66. Also printed: J. W. Jones, *Memorial Volume*, 27–42, variant version. According to Jones (p. 27), the publishers stated that the above autobiography " 'was dictated by Mr. Davis as he lay sick in bed one morning at Beauvoir a few weeks before his death, and was taken down in shorthand by a Northern guest, whose manuscript was revised by the old statesman before it was mailed to the Belford Company, who had solicited it for a biographical cyclopaedia they had undertaken.' "

1 Although 1808 has been accepted as the correct year of Davis' birth and although in both autobiographies (1:1, 2) he lists it as such, it may well have been, as he himself at one time believed, not 1808 but 1807. In a letter to W. H. Sparke that reflects his uncertainty, Davis wrote, "There has been some controversy about the year of my birth among the older members of my family, and I am not a competent witness in the case, having once supposed the year to have been 1807, I was subsequently corrected by being informed it was 1808, and have rested upon that point because it was just as good, and no better than another" (February 19, 1858 [Museum of the Confederacy, Richmond, Virginia]).

Just exactly when Davis determined to accept 1808 as the year of his birth is unknown. While the matter is not, perhaps, of great importance, it has caused not only some confusion but also has made suspect the dates that

Davis ascribes to the early events of his life.

[2] Transylvania University, Lexington, Kentucky.

[3] An excellent example of the type of statement that has, because of the uncertainty as to the year of Davis' birth, given rise to a number of errors. If Davis was born in 1807, he would of course have entered Transylvania in 1823. If, on the other hand, he was born in 1808, he obviously entered in 1824. Equally obvious, in this case at least, Davis was remembering 1807 as the year of his birth, for he could not have intended to write as he does that he entered both Transylvania and West Point in the same year, that is, 1824.

[4] Monterrey.

[5] El Tortín de Tenería.

[6] Two batteries of light artillery (J. H. Smith, *War with Mexico*, I, 368).

[7] Joseph E. Johnston.

[8] William Preston Johnston.

[9] John J. Craven.

[10] Davis married Varina Howell on February 26, 1845, not 1844 (Marriage bond, Book F, 69 [County Clerk's Office, Adams County Courthouse, Natchez, Mississippi]).

EXTRACT

Jefferson Davis, Ex-President of the Confederate States of America: A Memoir 1:2

Editorial Note: As in the case of the preceding item, annotation in the following document will be confined to explaining errors of print or fact, as well as those problems that do not elsewhere appear. The printed version of this autobiography is divided into chapters and, in addition, has a number of insertions. Both chapter divisions and insertions have been removed in order to present the autobiography as an uninterrupted account.

[Beauvoir, Mississippi, November 1889]

Three brothers came to America from Wales in the early part of the eighteenth century. They settled at Philadelphia.

The youngest of the brothers, Evan Davis, removed to Georgia, then a colony of Great Britain. He was the grandfather of Jefferson Davis.[1] He married a widow, whose family name was Emory. By her he had one son, Samuel Davis, the father of Jefferson Davis.

When Samuel Davis was about sixteen years of age his widowed mother sent him with supplies to his two half-brothers, Daniel and Isaac Williams, then serving in the army of the Revolution. Samuel, after finding his brothers were in active service, decided to join them, and thus remained in the military service of Georgia and South Carolina until the close of the war. After several years of service he gained sufficient experience and confidence to raise a company of infantry in Georgia. He went with them to join the revolutionary patriots, then besieged at Savannah.

At the close of the war he returned to his home. In the meantime his mother had died, and the movable property had been scattered. The place was a wreck. It was a home no more; so he settled near Augusta. His early education had qualified him for the position of county clerk, and the people, who had known him from boyhood, gave him that office.

There was only one political party in those days—the Whigs. The Tories had been beaten or driven away. During his service in South

Carolina he had met my mother, and after the war they were married. Her maiden name was Jane Cook. She was of Scotch-Irish descent, and was noted for her beauty and sprightliness of mind. She had a graceful poetic mind, which, with much of her personal beauty, she retained to extreme old age. My father, also, was unusually handsome, and the accomplished horseman his early life among the "mounted men" of Georgia naturally made him. He was a man of wonderful physical activity.

The last time I saw my father he was sixty-four years of age. He was about to mount a tall and restless horse, so that it was difficult for him to put his foot in the stirrup. Suddenly he vaulted from the ground into the saddle without any assistance. He was usually of a grave and stoical character, and of such sound judgment that his opinions were a law to his children, and quoted by them long after he had gone to his final rest, and when they were growing old.

My parents lived near Augusta, Ga., where they had a farm, on which they resided until after the birth of several children, when they moved to what was then known as the Green River country, in the southwestern part of Kentucky. There my father engaged in tobacco-planting and raising blooded horses, of which he had some of the finest in the country.

I was born on the 3d of June, 1808,[2] in what was then Christian County. The spot is now in Todd County, and upon the exact site of my birthplace has since been built the Baptist church of Fairview.

During my infancy my father removed to Bayou Têche, in Louisiana; but, as his children suffered from acclimatization, he sought a higher and healthier district. He found a place that suited him about a mile east of Woodville, in Wilkinson County, Miss. He removed his family there, and there my memories begin.

My father's family consisted of ten children, of whom I was the youngest. There were five sons and five daughters, and all of them arrived at maturity excepting one daughter.[3] My elder brother, Joseph, remained in Kentucky when the rest of the family removed, and studied law at Hopkinsville in the office of Judge Wallace. He subsequently came to Mississippi, where he practised his profession for many years, and then became a cotton-planter, in Warren County, Miss. He was successful both as a planter and a lawyer, and, at the beginning of the war between the States, possessed a very large fortune.

Three of my brothers bore arms in the War of 1812, and the fourth was prevented from being in the army by an event so characteristic of the times, yet so unusual elsewhere, that it may be deemed worthy of note. When it was reported that the British were advancing to the attack of New Orleans, the men of Wilkinson County, who were then at home, commenced volunteering so rapidly that it was deemed necessary to put a check upon it, so as to retain a sufficient number at home for police purposes. For this purpose a county court, consisting of a justice and quorum, ordered a draft for a certain number of men to stay at home.[4] This draft stopped my brother, who was about to start for New Orleans—making him the exception of my father's adult sons who were not engaged in the defence of the country during the War of 1812.

The part of the county in which my father resided was at that time sparsely settled. Wilkinson County is the southwestern county of the State. Its western boundary is the Mississippi River. The land near the river, although very hilly, was quite rich. Toward the east it fell off into easy ridges, the soil became thin, and the eastern boundary was a "pine country." My father's residence was at the boundary line between the two kinds of soil. The population of the county, in the western portion of it, was generally composed of Kentuckians, Virginians, Tennesseeans, and the like; while the eastern part of it was chiefly settled by South Carolinians and Georgians, who were generally said to be unable to live without "lightwood"—which is fat pine. The schools were kept in log-cabins, and it was many years before we had a "County Academy."

Mississippi was a part of the territory ceded by Georgia to the United States. Its early history was marked by conflicts with the Spanish authorities, who had held possession, and who had a fort and garrison in Natchez.

During the administration of President Adams a military force was sent down to take possession of the country. It was commanded by General Wilkinson, for whom the county in which we lived was named. He built a fort overlooking the Mississippi, and named it, in honor of the President, Fort Adams. There is still a village and river-landing by that name.

My first tuition was in the usual log-cabin school-house; though in the summer, when I was seven years old,[5] I was sent on horseback through what was then called "The Wilderness"—by the country of the Choctaw and Chicasaw nations—to Kentucky, and was placed in a Catholic institution then known as St. Thomas, in Washington County, near the town of Springfield.

In that day (1815)[6] there were no steam-boats, nor were there stage-coaches traversing the country. The river trade was conducted on flat- and keel-boats. The last-named only could be taken up the river. Commerce between the Western States and the Lower Mississippi was confined to water-routes. The usual mode of travel was on horseback or afoot. Many persons who had gone down the river in flat-boats walked back through the wilderness to Kentucky, Ohio, and elsewhere. We passed many of these, daily, on the road.

There were, at that time, places known as Stands, where the sick and weary ofttimes remained for relief, and many of these weary ones never went away. These Stands were log-cabins, three of them occupied by white men who had intermarried with the Indians. The first, in the Choctaw nation, was named Folsom; then came the Leflores, known as the first and second French camps. The fourth was that of a half-breed Chicasaw, at the crossing of the Tennessee River. When the traveller could not reach the house at which he had intended to stop, he found it entirely safe to sleep, wrapped in blankets, in the open air. It was the boast of the Choctaws that they had never shed the blood of a white man, and, as a proof of their friendship, they furnished a considerable contingent to the war against the Creek Indians, who were allies of the British.

The party with which I was sent to Kentucky consisted of Major Hinds (who had command of the famous battalion of Mississippi dragoons at the battle of New Orleans), his wife, his sister-in-law, a niece, a maid-servant, and his son Howell, who was near my own age, and, like myself, mounted on a pony. A servant had a sumpter mule with some supplies, besides bed and blankets for camping out. The journey to Kentucky occupied several weeks.

When we reached Nashville we went to the Hermitage. Major Hinds wished to visit his friend and companion-in-arms, General Jackson. The whole party was so kindly received that we remained there for several weeks. During that period I had the opportunity a boy has to observe a great man—a stand-point of no small advantage—and I have always remembered with warm affection the kind and tender wife who then presided over his house.

General Jackson's house at that time was a roomy log-house. In front of it was a grove of fine forest trees, and behind it were his cotton and grain fields. I have never forgotten the unaffected and well-bred courtesy which caused him to be remarked by court-trained diplomats, when President of the United States, by reason of his very impressive bearing and manner.

Notwithstanding the many reports that have been made of his profanity, I remember that he always said grace at his table, and I never heard him utter an oath. In the same connection, although he encouraged his adopted son, A. Jackson, Jr., Howell Hinds, and myself in all contests of activity, pony-riding included, he would not allow us to wrestle; for, he said, to allow hands to be put on one another might lead to a fight. He was always very gentle and considerate.

Mrs. Jackson's education, like that of many excellent women of her day, was deficient; but in all the hospitable and womanly functions of wife and hostess she certainly was excelled by none. A child is a keen observer of the characteristics of those under whom he is placed, and I found Mrs. Jackson amiable, unselfish, and affectionate to her family and guests, and just and mild toward her servants. The undeserved slanders that had been launched against her for political purposes had served to render her husband more devoted to her, and her untimely death was unquestionably the heaviest grief of his life.

Our stay with General Jackson was enlivened by the visits of his neighbors, and we left the Hermitage with great regret and pursued our journey. In me he inspired reverence and affection that has remained with me through my whole life.

The Kentucky Catholic School, called St. Thomas' College, when I was there, was connected with a church. The priests were Dominicans. They held a large property; productive fields, slaves, flour-mills, flocks, and herds. As an association they were rich. Individually, they were vowed to poverty and self-abnegation. They were diligent in the care, both spiritual and material, of their parishioners' wants.

When I entered the school, a large majority of the boys belonged to the Roman Catholic Church. After a short time I was the only Protestant boy remaining, and also the smallest boy in the school. From whatever reason, the priests were particularly kind to me—Father Wallace,[7] afterward Bishop of Nashville, treated me with the fondness of a near relative.

As the charge has been frequently made that it is the practice of the priests in all their schools to endeavor to proselyte the boys confided to them, I may mention an incident which is, in my case at least, a refutation. At that period of my life I knew, as a theologian, little of the true creed of Christianity, and under the influences which surrounded me I thought it would be well that I should become a Catholic, and went to the venerable head of the establishment, Father Wilson, whom I found in his room partaking of his frugal meal, and stated to him my wish. He received me kindly, handed me a biscuit and a bit of cheese, and told me that for the present I had better take some Catholic food.

I was so small at this time that one of the good old priests had a little bed put in his room for me. There was an organized revolt among the boys one day, and this priest was their especial objective point. They persuaded me to promise to blow out the light which always burned in the room; so, after everything was quiet I blew it out; then the insurgents poured in cabbages, squashes, biscuits, potatoes, and all kinds of missiles. As soon as a light could be lit, search was made for the culprits, but they were all sound asleep and I was the only wakeful one. The priests interrogated me severely, but I declared that I did not know much and would not tell that. The one who had especial care of me then took me to a little room in the highest story of the monastery and strapped me down to a kind of cot, which was arranged to facilitate the punishment of the boys; but the old man loved me dearly and hesitated before striking me a blow, the first I should have received since I had been with the monks. He pleaded with me, "If you will tell me what you know, no matter how little, I will let you off." "Well," said I, "I know one thing, I know who blew out the light." The priest eagerly promised to let me off for that piece of information and I then said, "I blew it out." Of course I was let off, but with a long talk which moved me to tears and prevented me from co-operating with the boys again in their schemes of mischief.

I had been sent so young to school, and far from home, without my mother's knowledge or consent, that she became very impatient for my return. Neither then, nor in the many years of my life, have I ceased to cherish a tender memory of the loving care of that mother, in whom there was so much for me to admire and nothing to remember save good.

Charles B. Green, a young Mississippian, who was studying law in Kentucky, had acted as my guardian when I was at school there, and he returned with me to Mississippi. We left Bardstown to go home by steamer from Louisville; for, then, steam-boats had been put on the river.

At that time, as well as I can remember, there were three steam-boats on the Mississippi—the Volcano, the Vesuvius, and the AEtna. We embarked on the AEtna. A steam-boat was then a matter of such great curiosity that many persons got on board to ride a few miles down the river, where they were to be landed, to return in carriages. The captain of the AEtna, Robinson De Hart, had been a sailor in his earlier days, and he always used a speaking-trumpet and spy-glass when landing the boat to take wood. Our voyage was slow and uneventful, and we reached home in safety.

I had been absent two years, and my brother Isaac accompanied me home, stopped at the village near my father's house, and told me to go on and conceal my identity to see if they would know me. I found my dear old mother sitting near the door, and, walking up with an assumed air to hide a throbbing heart, I asked her if there had been any stray horses round there. She said she had seen a stray boy, and clasped me in her arms.

After we had become somewhat calmer, I inquired for my father, and was told he was out in the field. I, impatient of the delay, went there to meet him. He was a man of deep feeling, though he sought to repress the expression of it whenever practicable; but I came to him unexpectedly. Greatly moved he took me in his arms with more emotion than I had ever seen him exhibit, and kissed me repeatedly. I remember wondering why my father should have kissed so big a boy.

My father was a silent, undemonstrative man of action. He talked little, and never in general company, but what he said had great weight with the community in which he lived. His admonitions to his children were rather suggestive than dictatorial. I remember a case in point, which happened after my return from Kentucky, while I was at the County Academy.

A task had been assigned me in excess of my power to memorize. I stated the case to the teacher, but he persisted in imposing the lesson. The next day it had not been mastered, and when punishment was threatened I took my books and went to my father. He said, "Of course, it is for you to elect whether you will work with head or hands; my son could not be an idler. I want more cotton-pickers and will give you work."

The next day, furnished with a bag, I went into the fields and worked all day and the day after. The heat of the sun and the physical labor, in conjunction with the implied equality with the other cotton-pickers, convinced me that school was the lesser evil. This change of opinion I stated to my father when coming from the field, after my day's cotton had been weighed. He received the confidence with perfect seriousness, mentioned the disadvantages under which a man, gently bred, suffers when choosing a laborer's vocation, and advised me, if I was of the same opinion the next day, to return to school; which I did, and quietly took my accustomed place. He had probably arranged with the teacher to receive me without noticing my revolt.

The dominies of that period were not usually university men. Indeed their attainments and the demands of their patrons rarely exceeded the teaching of "the three R's," and the very general opinion held by that class was that the oil of birch was the proper lubricator for any want of intelligence. I well remember two boys, with whom I went to school, one of them dull, the other idle, but both of them full, broad-shouldered boys, able to bear the infliction, which they rarely failed to receive, of one or more floggings a day. The poor boy who could not learn took it very philosophically, but the other insisted that whipping a boy was very apt to make him a lying hypocrite.

The method of instruction in these old log school-houses was very simple. It consisted solely of a long copy-book—the qualifications required of the teacher being that he should be able to write at the head of each page the pot-hooks, letters, and sentences which were to be copied by the pupil on each line of the paper.

As the pupil advanced, he was required to have a book for his sums. He worked out the examples in the arithmetic, and, after a sufficient amount of attention, he was required to copy this into a book, which, when it was completed, was the evidence that he understood arithmetic. After some time a bright boy could repeat all the rules; but if you asked him to explain why, when he added up a column of figures, he set down the right and carried the left-hand figure, he could give the rule, but no reason for it. And I am not sure that, as a general thing, the teacher could have explained it to him.

The log-cabin schools were not public schools in the sense in which that term is used to-day—for the teacher was supported by the fees charged every pupil.

I was next sent to school in Adams County, Miss., to what was called, and is still known as, Jefferson College. I was then about ten years of age.[8] The principal was a man of great learning, qualified to teach pupils more advanced than those he received. There was an adjacent department (over which a Scotchman presided) to teach the smaller children, and his methods were those of the earlier times—to prescribe the lesson and whip any boy who did not know it.

The path along which I travelled to the school-house passed by the residence of an old dominie who had a great contempt for Latin. Why, he never told me, nor could he have told me, as he knew nothing about it; but whenever he saw me walking along the path, he would shout out, grinningly, "How are you getting along with you hic, haec, hoc?" I had been there but a short time when the County Academy of Wilkinson was organized, and I returned home and went daily from my father's house to the school-house until I was sufficiently advanced to be sent to the college known as the Transylvania University of Kentucky.

At the head of the County Academy was a scholarly man named John A. Shaw, from Boston. He took on himself, also, the duty of preaching every Sunday; but as there was no church, he held his meetings in the court-house. The boys of the Academy were required to attend, and very soon they became his only audience; when, like a conscientious, sensitive man, he notified the trustees that he would preach no more. He explained to them that with him it was a profession; that he agreed to preach for a stipulated salary; but, unless he thought he was doing good, which the absence of the people showed to be doubtful, he was neither willing to preach nor to receive the salary. He continued solely under the pay received as principal of the Academy.

He was a quiet, just man, and I am sure he taught me more in the time I was with him than I ever learned from any one else. He married in our county, and after the death of his wife returned to Massachusetts; but, whether he acquired new tastes during his residence in the South, or from whatever reason, he returned after some years to New Orleans, where he was Superintendent of the Public Schools when I last heard from him. I was very much gratified to learn that he remembered me favorably, and mentioned it to one of his pupils who had been named for me. He was the first of a new class of teachers in our neighborhood, and was followed by classical scholars who raised the standard of ability to teach and of the pupils to learn.

The era of the dominies whose sole method of tutition was to whip the boy when he was ignorant has passed.

From the Academy presided over by Mr. Shaw I went to Lexington, Ky., to enter the Transylvania University. Having usually been classed with boys beyond my age, I was quite disappointed to find that the freshmen of the college I wanted to enter were much younger than myself, and I felt my pride offended by being put with smaller boys. My chief deficiency was in mathematics, which had been very little taught in the Academy. The professor of mathematics, Mr. Jenkins, kindly agreed to give me private lessons, and I studied under him for the balance of the session and through the vacation, so as to enable me to pass examination as a sophomore. He was a classical scholar as well as a mathematician, but he had very poor material to work upon, as it was mainly languages and metaphysics that were considered desirable to know at that time. His health failed while I was taking lessons from him, leaving me in the meantime to study as much as I could or would; he availed himself of the vacation for going away.

After I had been for some time studying by myself, a senior from Louisiana, who had taken some interest in me, inquired how I was getting along. I told him how far I had gone. He was very much surprised, undertook to examine me, and found that I did not recollect the letters that were put on the figures in the book, which he told me were necessary. I began at the beginning to memorize the letters. When the professor returned, and I explained to him the difficulty encountered, he laughed and told me that if the senior knew his letters that was all he ever did know, and he would rather I should learn the problem without the letters than with them; by which I was greatly relieved.

Our professor of languages was a graduate of Trinity College, Dublin—a fine linguist, with the pronunciation of Latin and Greek taught in that College, which I then believed, and yet believe, to be the purest and best of our time.

The professor of these last-named branches, and vice-president of the University, was a Scotchman, Rev. Mr. Bishop, afterward president of a college in Ohio (Kenyon, I believe it was), a man of large attainments and very varied knowledge. His lectures in history are remembered as well for their wide information as for their keen appreciation of the characteristics of mankind. His hero of all the world was William Wallace.

In his lectures on the history of the Bible his faith was that of a child, not doubting nor questioning, and believing literally as it was written.

About this I remember a funny incident. He was arguing for a literal construction of the Testament, and said that valuable doctrines were lost in the habit of calling those teachings of our Lord "Eastern allegories." "Now, my hearers, I will, if you please, read one of the passages with the words, 'Eastern allegories' where your learned friends think they occur. 'And all the Eastern allegories besought him, saying, Send us into the swine that we may enter into them, and he forthwith gave them leave. And the Eastern allegories went out, and entered into the swine; and the herd ran violently down a steep place into the sea.' "

Mr. Bishop was going on gravely reading when a titter aroused him. He looked up astonished, and said, "Sobriety becometh the house of God."

A vulgar boy, in the junior class, committed some outrage during the recitation, which Dr. Bishop chose to punish as became the character of the offender. His inability to draw a straight line on the blackboard caused him to keep a very large ruler, broad and flat, with which he used to guide the chalk. Calling the boy to him, he laid him across his knee and commenced paddling him with the big ruler. The culprit mumbled that it was against the law to whip a collegiate. "Yes," said the old gentleman, momentarily stopping his exercise, "but every rule has its exceptions, Toney." Then he whacked him again, and there would not have been a dissenting voice if the question had been put as to the justice of the chastisement.

Among my college mates in Transylvania was a tall country boy, true-hearted and honest, with many virtues but without grace or tact. The sight of him always seemed to suggest to Mr. Bishop the question of the Catechism, "Who made ye, Dauvid?" to which Atchison always answered, "Gaud," and Mr. Bishop invariably responded, "Quite right, Dauvid; quite right." I left him in the college when I went to West Point, and afterward, when I met him in the United States Senate, in which he was one of the Senators from Missouri, my first greeting was, "Who made ye, Dauvid?" I loved him when we were boys, and he grew with growing years in all the graces of manhood. David R. Atchison, now no more, but kindly remembered even by those who disagreed with him politically, was a man of unswerving courage and stainless honor.

The University of Transylvania was fortunate in so far that its alumni were favorites in public life. My dear and true friend, George W. Jones, of Iowa, was of our class, and with me, also, in the Senate of the United States; S. W. Downs, of Louisiana, was a graduate of Transylvania, and so was Edward A. Hannegan, both of whom were subsequently United States Senators. When I was serving my first term as United States Senator, I was one of six graduates of Transylvania who held seats in that chamber.

In my time, the college proper (over which the very brilliant Horace Holly[9] presided), consisted of a medical department, with such distinguished professors as Drake, Dudley, Blythe, Cook,[10] Richardson, Caldwell, and others. The law department was well, although not so numerously attended as the medical and theological; its professor was that real genius, Jesse Bledsoe, who was professor of common law. Some sectarian troubles finally undermined the popularity of the President of the Transylvania University, and the institution has probably never recovered the high reputation it had in 1820, and the years immediately following.

There I completed my studies in Greek and Latin, and learned a little of algebra, geometry, trigonometry, surveying, profane and sacred history, and natural philosophy.

I passed my examination for admission to the senior class,[11] and as it was so long ago I may say that I had taken an honor, when I received intelligence of the death of my father. He died on July 4, 1824, at the age of sixty-eight.

My oldest brother, who then occupied to me much the relation of a parent, notified me that he had received the news of my appointment as a cadet in the United States Military Academy; and, fearing the consequences of being graduated at the early age of seventeen, he insisted that I should proceed at once to West Point. Of course I disliked to go down from the head class of one institution to the lowest in another; but I yielded and went to West Point, to find that I was too late; that all the candidates had been admitted in June or the first of September; that the classes were engaged in their studies; and that the rule was absolute as to the time of admission. But Captain (afterward General) Hitchcock, then on duty in the Academy, had known my family when he was on recruiting duty in Natchez, and asked a special examination for me. Chance favored me. There was just then a Mr. Washington, who had been permitted, on account of his health, to leave the Academy for a year or two. He had gone to France, and, because of his name, had received the advantage of the Polytechnique. He had returned to find that his class had been graduated, and asked to be examined on the full course. The staff were in session examining Mr. Washington. This chance caused me also to be examined, and to be admitted out of rule.

As soon as permission was given to appear before the staff, Captain Hitchcock came and told me that I would be examined, particularly in arithmetic. He asked, "I suppose you have learned arithmetic?" To which I had to answer in the negative. But I added that I had learned some algebra and some geometry, and also some application of algebra. He was quite alarmed, and went off and got me an arithmetic, telling me to study as much as I could of fractions and proportion. I had hardly commenced when an order came to bring me before the staff. The professor of mathematics asked me one or two questions in regard to vulgar fractions and the difference between vulgar and decimal fractions, which I knew enough algebra to answer, and then asked how, the three terms of a direct proportion being given, I would put the fourth. I answered that the proportion was that the fourth should bear to the third the relation that the second did to the first. "Certainly, certainly," he said, probably thinking that I knew a great deal more than I did. Then they requested me to read and to write; and as I did so legibly, the French professor was authorized to determine what section of French I was to be put in, and to examine me upon languages. To his gratification he learned that I read Greek, and launched into a discussion of some questions as to the construction of Greek, with which he was so delighted that he kept on till the superintendent stopped him, and that broke up my examination.

Since that time I have never believed that an examination formed a very conclusive rule of decision upon the qualification of a person subjected to its test.

I had consented to go to the Academy for one year, and then to the University of Virginia, which was just beginning to attract attention in quarters remote from it.

But at the end of the year, for various reasons, I preferred to remain, and thus continued for four years, the time allotted to the course.

When graduated, as is the custom at West Point, we were made brevet second lieutenants, and I was assigned to the infantry, and, with others of the same class, ordered to report to the School of Practice at Jefferson Barracks, near St. Louis, Mo.

When I entered the United States Military Academy at West Point that truly great and good man, Albert Sidney Johnston, had preceded me from Transylvania, Ky.; an incident which formed a link between us, and inaugurated a friendship which grew as years rolled by, strengthened by after associations in the army, and which remains to me yet, a memory of one of the greatest and best characters I have ever known. His particular friend was Leonidas Polk, and when Johnston was adjutant of the corps Polk was the sergeant-major. They were my seniors in the Academy, but we belonged to the same "set," a name well understood by those who have been ground in the Academy mill.

Polk joined the Church from convictions produced, as I understood, from reading "Gregory's Letters"—a noted religious work of that day—aided by the preaching of our eloquent and pious chaplain, who had subsequently a wide reputation as Bishop McIlvaine.

A word as to chaplain McIlvaine. In appearance and manner he seemed to belong to the pulpit, and he had a peculiar power of voice rarely found elsewhere than on the stage. From its highest tones it would sink to a whisper, and yet be audible throughout the whole chapel. His sermons, according to the usage of his Church—the Episcopalian—were written beforehand; but, occasionally, he would burst forth in a grand tide of oratory, clearly unpremeditated, and more irresistible than it probably would have been had it been carefully written. For example: He was once preaching, and, just behind him, was visible the mountain pass through which the Hudson flows, when a gathering storm was seen approaching West Point. That coming storm he wove into his sermon, so that the crash of one fitted into a great outburst of the other. They seemed to belong to one another—the sermon and the storm.

Among the cadets then and subsequently distinguished was Alexander D. Bache, the head of the first or graduating class, when I entered the Academy. He was a grandson of Benjamin Franklin,[12] and, to the extraordinary genius of his grandfather, was added an elementary education in physical science. He had a power of demonstration beyond that of any man I ever heard; so much so that, by way of illustration, I have often stated that I believe he could explain the highest astronomical problems to any one of good understanding, if he would acknowledge at the beginning his entire ignorance and admit when he did not understand any point in the progress of the demonstration. He graduated at the head of his class in 1828. He resigned after a few years' service in the Engineer Corps of the army, became President of Girard College, and went abroad to study the European system of instruction.

After his return from Europe we met, and he told me that the thing which surprised him most was the system of the West Point Academy, where any boy, regardless of his endowments or previous preparation, was required to learn the same things in the allotted time; and implied that, what astonished him most was that he should have gone through the Academy without even realizing that. In defence of the institution I reminded him that it was not intended for popular education, but to prepare as many as were required from year to year for appointments in the army; that, therefore, it might well be that one might have a genius for something not specially required of a soldier, and be unable to learn a thing that was needful. The consequence would be that he would have to carry his talents into some calling for which he was especially endowed.

To take this extraordinary genius for illustration, though he readily mastered every branch of the curriculum of the Military Academy, and would doubtless have been useful as an engineer in the army, his career as a civilian proved that another field was more peculiarly his, and that he could there render greater service to his country. In the year 1842, on the decease of Mr. Hasler,[13] Professor Bache was appointed Superintendent of the Coast Survey, and introduced methods and established rules in regard to triangulation and deep-sea soundings which have given to the American coast and sea border the best charts, I think, in existence, and which will remain for Bache an enduring monument. A great-grandson of Benjamin Franklin and grandson of Alexander Dallas, Secretary of State under Mr. Jefferson's administration, he seemed to have inherited the common-sense and the power to apply science to the utilities of life of the one, and the grace and knowledge of men possessed by the other.

In the succeeding class, the cadet who held the first place was William H. C. Bartlett, of Missouri. He is a man of such solid merit and exemption from pretensions that I am sure he will pardon me for stating in regard to him what may be a useful incentive to others under like embarrassments. The C in his name stands for Chambers, the Colonel of the First Infantry, who was interested in the boy and secured for him an appointment as cadet, when Chambers was gratefully added to his Christian name as a token of his obligation. His own preparation had been so small that, in addition to learning his lessons at night, he told me that he had to use a dictionary to find out the meaning of the words in the text, and an English grammar to teach him how to construct his sentences in demonstrations. Yet, despite these drawbacks, he led his class from first to last.

After graduation he was assigned to the Corps of Engineers, and afterward was employed as Assistant Professor of Engineering in the Academy. After serving in the construction of several military works, he became Professor of Natural and Experimental Philosophy in the Military Academy, where he was growing old with insufficient compensation, and which post he resigned to accept the better pay of actuary in the Mutual Life Insurance Company.

In his conduct there was a total want of self-assertion, and a modesty which rendered him prone to believe that others possessed the same capacity as himself. For example, he offered me the last book he wrote on natural philosophy. With thanks I told him "it had more mathematics, no doubt, than I could master." "No," he answered, "you might say there are no mathematics in it." And to him there seemed to be very little, because in a page he would have a little equation, easily decipherable to him, but involving a world of trouble to one of less knowledge and mathematical genius.[14]

MS not found. Text from Varina Howell Davis, *Jefferson Davis, Ex-President of the Confederate States of America: A Memoir* (2 vols., New York: Belford, 1890), I, 3–27, 32–41. According to Mrs. Davis, her husband "during the last year of his life . . . yielded to the repeated requests, both of his personal friends and publishers, to write an autobiography. Shortly before his last journey to Briarfield he dictated to a friend, as an introductory chapter, this account of his ancestry and early boyhood. He was too weak to sit up long at a time, and lay in bed while his friend and I sat by and listened" (*Memoir*, I, 2–3).

[1] Hudson Strode states that Davis knew very little about his ancestors and that he was indifferent to genealogy in general, which he considered both undemocratic and un-American (*American Patriot*, 441). This assertion is, in part at least, effectively borne out, for here Davis mistakenly says that his paternal grandfather had been born in Wales. That he at one time knew differently is attested by his father's letter to him of June 25, 1823 (1:5), in which Samuel Davis writes that Philadelphia was "the most beautiful City I ever Saw the place where my father drew his first breath." Davis' error has been not only perpetuated but enlarged upon by a number of genealogists who, having accepted an erroneous premise, have been led far afield in their efforts to discover the American beginnings of the Davis family. Perhaps the most suc-

cessful of the various attempts made to trace the Davis genealogy is that undertaken by Kirk Bentley Barb. Unlike other investigators he most logically began his search of the records in Philadelphia. Briefly stated, his contention is "that . . . Evan Davis . . . was the original Welsh immigrant ancestor of Jefferson Davis in America, that he was Jefferson Davis' great-grandfather, and that Jefferson Davis belonged to the fourth generation of his family in this country and not to the third as he himself thought" (1:Appendix III, 493). Whether Barb's thesis regarding the origin of the Davis family is correct does not concern us here, since our study is limited to Jefferson Davis and his immediate family; although his contention seems more firmly based on fact than most, it remains for the professional genealogists to either accept or reject his hypothesis. For other theories regarding the origin of the Davis family, see the following: H. A. Davis, *The Davis Family*; N. D. Smith, "Reminiscences," *Confederate Veteran*, XXXVIII, 178–82; Whitsitt, *Genealogy*. Yet another investigation—a copy of which the editors have been unable to locate—by Creed T. Davis maintains that the Davises were descended from one Evan Davis, an early settler in Lancaster County, Virginia (Strode, *American Patriot*, 440–41).

[2] See 1:1, *n.* 1 for a discussion of the problem concerning Davis' date of birth.

[3] Davis here has reference to his youngest sister, Mary Ellen Davis Davis (sketch, 1:528, *n.* 5; 1:Appendix IV, Entry 23), who died at an early age after "a short and severe illness," on March 2, 1824, at Woodville, Mississippi (Woodville *Republican*, March 2, 1824), and not, as heretofore believed, his sister Matilda, who died March 16, 1834 (1:419).

[4] See also Davis to McGehee, September 16, 1888, D. Rowland, *Papers*, X, 79, for further, although similar, information about the men of Wilkinson County and the War of 1812.

[5] Here Davis is calculating his age from 1808, as witness the records of the College of St. Thomas (1:3, *n.* 2), which state that he arrived on July 10, 1816. Evidently the journey to Kentucky began before June 3, when he was still seven.

[6] If we are to accept the records of St. Thomas (1:3, *n.* 2), the year was 1816, and not 1815, as Davis here states.

[7] Apparently Davis has confused the name of either Richard Pius Miles—later bishop of Nashville—or William Thomas Willett with that of Wallace, for according to V. F. O'Daniel, there was no Father Wallace at St. Thomas at the time of Davis' enrollment (*A Light of the Church*, 192).

[8] Davis is here calculating his age from the year 1808.

[9] Horace Holley (sketch, 1:24, *n.* 7).

[10] Neither Robert Peter in *The History of the Medical Department of Transylvania University* nor the university catalogues list a "Cook" as having been a professor in the medical school for the years 1821–24. Peter does, however, list a certain John Esten Cooke as having been appointed professor of the theory and practice of medicine in 1827. Although Cooke does not appear to have been at Transylvania during the period of Davis' residence, it is to him that Davis is no doubt referring. The two perhaps met during the great cholera epidemic of 1833, when both doctor and soldier were in Lexington (see 1:357 and 1:361, *n.* 4 for evidence of Davis' presence in Lexington), where each in his own way was attempting to alleviate the suffering (Peter, *Medical Department of Transylvania*, 60, 166).

[11] It is of interest to note that Davis, contrary to contemporary style, speaks of his final junior examinations as senior admission examinations. Compare this manner of speaking with his statement (p. lxxvi) that he passed examination as a sophomore. In both cases he is speaking of being admitted to the next or higher class, that is, the junior and senior classes respectively. See 1:6,

n. 2 for discussion of Davis' period of residence at Transylvania.

[12] Bache was, as Davis himself says on page lxxxi, the great-grandson of Franklin and not, as here mentioned, his grandson (*DAB*).

[13] Ferdinand R. Hassler died on November 20, 1843 (*DAB*).

[14] "Here ended the dictation that had my husband's life been spared, he intended to continue, giving a full and familiar history of his public and private life. While on his sick-bed he told me, 'I have not told what I wish to say of my classmates Sidney Johnston and [Leonidas] Polk. I have much more to say of them. I shall tell a great deal of West Point, and I seem to remember more every day'" (V. Davis, *Memoir*, I, 41–42).

DAVIS CHRONOLOGY, 1808–1840

Editorial Note: The italicized entries are taken from the memoirs of Davis or his wife, and are unsupported by other primary sources.

1807/1808	
June 3	*Born in Christian County (now Todd) on a site that has since become a part of Fairview, Kentucky*
1809/1810	*Family moves to the Bayou Têche country of Louisiana and shortly thereafter to Wilkinson County, Mississippi*
1816	*Travels with Major Thomas Hinds and party to Kentucky; stops to visit for several weeks with Andrew Jackson at "The Hermitage"*
July 10	Enrolls at St. Thomas College, near Springfield, Kentucky; in attendance for two years
1818–1823	*Returns to Mississippi; enters Jefferson College in Adams County; later transfers to the Wilkinson County Academy and lives at home in Woodville*
1823	
Spring	*Goes to Lexington, Kentucky, and prepares for examinations at Transylvania University*
Fall	Enters the junior class at Transylvania University
1824	
March 11	Appointed a cadet at the United States Military Academy

June 18	Delivers first formal speech at the Junior Exhibition of Transylvania University
July 4	Father, Samuel Emory Davis, dies
July 7	Accepts appointment to West Point
September	*Arrives at West Point after admission deadline but is permitted to take the entrance examination*; admitted and attends until graduation in July 1828
1825	
July 14–20	On furlough
August 1	Arrested for being off limits July 31 in violation of Academy regulations
August 3	Testifies at his court martial
August 4	Presents his defense; found guilty of two charges, but court recommends remission of sentence of dismissal
1826	
June 23	Appointed fourth sergeant of the first company for the annual summer encampment
August 7–20	On furlough
August 30	Appointed sergeant of the color guard; serves through February 1827
December 25	Arrested and confined to quarters at the beginning of the "Eggnog Riot"
1827	
January 19	Testifies on the eleventh day of the court of inquiry investigating the "Eggnog Riot"
February 7	Testifies for the defense in the trial of Walter B. Guion on the eleventh day of the "Eggnog" court martial
February 8	Returns to duty upon release from arrest
1828	
July 1	Is graduated from West Point and appointed brevet second lieutenant of infantry

July 14	Granted leave until October 30
August 26	Writes from Lexington, Kentucky, requesting furlough extension to December 31; request granted on September 8
1829	
January 11	Reports to Jefferson Barracks
March 24	Ordered to report to the headquarters of the First Infantry at Fort Crawford
May	Present at Fort Winnebago, not assigned to a company; stationed at Fort Winnebago until June 1831
May–June	Serves as acting assistant commissary of subsistence
August 29	Ordered attached to Company C
September 1	In command of Company B until October 31
October	In pursuit of deserters
December 22	Absent on leave
1830	
January	Present for duty at Fort Winnebago
April	Relieves the acting assistant quartermaster at Fort Winnebago
May 1	Relieves the acting assistant commissary of subsistence
July 25	Ordered in pursuit of deserters
1831	
March 15	Appointed a second lieutenant of the First Infantry
April 16	Joins and assumes command of Company B
June 24	Leaves Fort Winnebago
June 26	Arrives at Fort Crawford

June 27	Leaves Fort Crawford; relinquishes command of Company B
June 28	Arrives at Fort Armstrong
June 30	Officially concludes duties as acting assistant commissary of subsistence and acting assistant quartermaster
July 2	Leaves Fort Armstrong
July 5	Returns to Fort Crawford; stationed there until March 1833
July	On special duty superintending a saw mill on the Yellow River in Iowa
September	On leave
October 11	Ordered to Dubuques Mines to prevent hostilities between the miners and the Indians; remains there until March 1832
November 1	Serves the detachment at Dubuques Mines as acting assistant commissary of subsistence until March 26, 1832
1832	
March 26	Leaves Fort Crawford on furlough
March 31	Checks his pay account with the paymaster at St. Louis
April 14	Writes headquarters of the Western Department from Woodville, Mississippi, requesting a furlough extension
August 18	Reports for duty at Fort Crawford
September 4	Arrives with Black Hawk and other Indian prisoners at Galena, Illinois
September 10	Arrives with prisoners at Jefferson Barracks
October 3	Writes from Memphis, Tennessee, requesting permission to complete furlough
November	Continues furlough through December

CHRONOLOGY

1833	
Winter	Present for duty at Fort Crawford in January; *dispatched a second time to Dubuques Mines to prevent hostilities between the Indians and the miners*
March 4	Appointed second lieutenant of Dragoons
June	On recruiting duty in Lexington, Kentucky
July 11	Joins the Dragoons at Jefferson Barracks
August 29/30	Appointed adjutant of Dragoons
October 2–21	Serves as acting staff officer to brigade
November 20	Leaves Jefferson Barracks with the Dragoons for Fort Gibson
December 14	Arrives at Camp Jackson, near Fort Gibson
1834	
February 4	Resignation as adjutant of Dragoons accepted; transfers to Company F
May 10	Appointed first lieutenant of Dragoons
June 17–30	In command of Company F
June 18	Leaves Fort Gibson with the Dragoons on an expedition to the villages of the Kiowa and Wichita tribes in what is now southwestern Oklahoma
August 16	Returns with the expedition to Fort Gibson
September 1	Appointed acting assistant commissary of subsistence for a special encampment, later named Camp Jones
September 3	Leaves Fort Gibson for Camp Jones
November 10/11	Returns sometime after November 10/11 to Fort Gibson; concludes his duty as acting assistant commissary of subsistence at Camp Jones; commands Company E until December 24
December 24	In arrest after altercation with superior officer

	climaxes period of disagreement between the two
1835	
February 12–17	Testifies at his court martial
February 19	Presents his defense; acquitted of charges
March 2	Requests forty-day leave of absence; writes letter of resignation to be submitted if he does not return from leave Testifies in Lucius B. Northrop court martial
March 9	Again testifies in Northrop court martial
March 10	Request for furlough granted
March 26	Signs oath of allegiance at Port Gibson, Mississippi
April 20	Fails to return from furlough; letter of resignation dated
May 12	Letter of resignation forwarded to headquarters
June 17	Marries Sarah Knox Taylor near Louisville, Kentucky; leaves with bride for Mississippi
June 30	Resignation becomes effective
September 15	Sarah Knox Taylor Davis dies at "Locust Grove" plantation near Bayou Sara, Louisiana; Davis seriously ill at the same time
Winter	*Travels to Havana, Cuba, to recover health;* returns via New York and Washington
1836	
	Lives at plantation of his brother while clearing and planting "Brierfield" property
1837	
November	Travels to New York, Philadelphia, Baltimore, and Washington
December 26	Arrives at Washington

CHRONOLOGY

1838	
January 1	Attends White House reception
April 5	Leaves Washington for Philadelphia; plans to proceed via Pittsburgh to Mississippi
July	Back in Mississippi
1839–1840	
	Cultivates "Brierfield," his plantation twenty miles below Vicksburg, Mississippi

THE PAPERS OF JEFFERSON DAVIS

Volume 1

1808–1840

ABSTRACT

Register and Account Book, St. Thomas College[1] 1:3

[Near Springfield, Kentucky,] July 10, 1816[2]

Lists the arrival[3] of Jefferson Davis and the receipt of $65.[4]

D (Archives, the Dominican Province of Saint Joseph, Washington, D.C.). Document faded and almost indecipherable. Printed: O'Daniel, *A Light of the Church*, 184; Pitt, "Two Early Catholic Colleges," *Filson Club History Quarterly*, XXXVIII, 136. A number of years ago, when the parlors of the second St. Rose's Convent were being redecorated, a fragment of a St. Thomas register and account book was found behind the lathing. The above entry was a part of such and had evidently been thrust there in order to stop a rat-hole—an act of vandalism that led to the preservation of one of the two extant St. Thomas documents (O'Daniel, *A Light of the Church*, 182).

1 The College of St. Thomas Aquin near Springfield, Kentucky, the first Catholic college west of the Allegheny Mountains, was founded in either 1808 or 1809. "It is impossible to assign an exact date to the opening of the secular College of St. Thomas. . . . The new church of St. Rose was dedicated on Christmas Day, 1809. Prior to that date, either late in 1808 or early in 1809, the secular school was opened, although the building was not completed" (Pitt, "Two Early Catholic Colleges," *Filson Club History Quarterly*, XXXVIII, 133–34).

2 Although Davis recalled that he entered the College of St. Thomas in 1815 (1:2, lxx), the college register is undoubtedly correct in stating that he arrived on July 10, 1816. That Davis erred regarding the date is not too surprising when one remembers not only the uncertainty concerning the year of his birth (1:1, *n.* 1), but also the fact that he dictated both the *Belford's* and the *Memoir* accounts from a sick bed in the last year of his life when his memory might well have been less than its best (J. W. Jones, *Memorial Volume*, 27).

3 The trip overland from Mississippi to Kentucky was made via the Natchez Trace in the company of Major Thomas Hinds. Although Davis does not, in his account of the journey, mention the trace by name, he nonetheless effectively identifies it by giving the various stands or waystations at which the party stopped (1:2, lxx; E. Rowland, "Marking the Natchez Trace," Mississippi Historical *Publications*, XI, 353). To Davis perhaps the most memorable event of the trip was the stopover of several weeks at General Andrew Jackson's home, "The Hermitage," where Hinds, who had served under his old friend Jackson at the Battle of New Orleans, was eager to spend some time. In a letter written October 25, 1885, to Andrew Jackson, Jr., Davis recalled, "In the 'Longago' Genl Hinds with his son Howell, and myself, made a visit to The Hermitage and a boy of about our own age, say between seven and nine was our companion while there and his name was Andrew Jackson. I am now so old that I may well doubt whether my former playmate be still living, but if so, and you are he please accept the cordial salutation which belongs to my remembrance of those early days" (Andrew

Jackson Papers, Library of Congress).

[4] Apparently a part payment of Davis' board and tuition. On Easter Sunday, 1815, the tuition and board at St. Thomas were raised from $75 to $125. Opposition to the increase from the students and the patrons of the school caused the charge to be lowered to $100 (O'Daniel, *A Light of the Church*, 183–84). Whether Davis entered under the $125 or $100 rule is unknown, since the exact date of the compromise solution is uncertain. Although the above register gives no indication of who actually paid the $65, it was probably Davis' guardian, Charles B. Green (1:2, lxxii).

ABSTRACT

1:4 Register and Account Book, St. Thomas College[1]

[Near Springfield, Kentucky,] May 3, 1817

Lists the receipt of $50 from Jefferson Davis "(teste[2] Hill)," and remarks "Maise[3] fifty dollars and four and half cents. Booked."

D (Archives, the Dominican Province of Saint Joseph, Washington, D.C.). Document faded and almost indecipherable. Printed: O'Daniel, *A Light of the Church*, 184. See 1:3 for provenance.

[1] See 1:3, *n.* 1 for St. Thomas.

[2] Archaic term used before the name of a person when he is cited as a witness or as an authority for a particular transaction (*OED*).

[3] Archaic term, a variant of *mease*, which in turn is a variant of *mese*, or the more modern *mess* (*OED*). Although O'Daniel says (*A Light of the Church*, 184) that the word means allowance, a more accurate interpretation would seem to be board.

1:5 From Samuel Emory Davis

MY DEAR SON JEFFERSON Philadelphia June 25 1823

I have a few minutes past taken your letter[1] out of the post office which has afforded me inexpressible <satisfaction>[2] it being the only information which I have received since I left the Mississippi Country Tho I have wrote often and from various places, my Journey has been unpleasant and expensive[3] I have been delayed of necessity about Seven Weeks only arrived here last Thursday noon in bad health and [con]tinue much the Same I have left James[4] & my horses at a little Village Called Harford in Maryland[5] seventy two miles from here from there I came in Mail Stages to Wilmington where I took passage in a Steam boat to this place which is the most beautiful City I ever Saw the place where my father drew his first

St. Rose Priory and St. Thomas College

Joseph E. Davis

breath[6] & the place if I had applied some thirty year ago I might now have been immensely rich but I fear all is lost here by the lapse of time yet I shall continue to search every thing to the extent before I leave here which will likely be late in Aug. or early in Septr. as <such>[7] you can write me again before I leave here. I am much pleased to find that you are at College[8] perhaps on my return Voyge I may come thro Kentucky if so I shall call and see you but if otherways I know where you are and shall frequently write to you while my hand can hold a pen let me be where I may which is very uncertain   I had frequently applyed at this post office got Nothing before your letter and got that broke open which had been done by a man of my name   whenever I leave here or before I shall write you that you may not send any thing to be broken open after I am gone   if any discovery should be made favorable to my interest I shall be sure to let you know in due time & should I never return or See you any more <—your father pra—>[9] I have notify'd you where I have left your boy James he is in the care of a David Malsby in the Village aforenamed   I have also Written the same to David Bradford.[10] Remember the short lessons of instruction offered you before our parting   use every possible means to acquire usefull knowledge as knowledge is power the want of which has brought mischiefs and misery on your father in old age. That you may be happy & shine in society when your father is beyond the reach of harm is the most ardent desire of <—my—> his heart. Adieu my Son Jefferson   your father   SAML. DAVIS[11]

ALS (Personal Papers, Samuel E. Davis, Accession No. 26130, Virginia State Library, Richmond); L, typed copy (C. Seymour Bullock Papers, Southern Historical Collection, University of North Carolina Library, Chapel Hill). Although torn and faded, the manuscript is nonetheless legible. Addressed: "Mr. Jefferson Davis Lexington K." Printed: Whitsitt, *Genealogy*, 12–14; Strode, *American Patriot*, 25–26; Strode, *Private Letters*, 6–7. Douglas S. Freeman states that this most interesting letter—interesting in that it affords proof that it was not Davis' grandfather, as some biographers and Davis himself maintained, but rather his great-grandfather who emigrated from Wales (1:2, *n.* 1)—was presented early in 1909 to the Virginia State Library by Mr. S. S. P. Patterson of Richmond. Beyond the fact that Patterson acquired the letter from one Byron A. Nevins of Albany, New York, nothing further is known of its provenance (Freeman to Whitsitt, February 25, 1909, Whitsitt, *Genealogy*, 12).

1 Davis' letter to his father has not been found.

2 In the margin.

3 Davis' father (see *n.* 11 below) made the journey in an unsuccessful attempt to recover a lost inheritance (see Barb, "Genealogy of Davis," 20–

23 [typescript in Mississippi Department of Archives and History]).

[4] James Pemberton, a trusted slave who, according to W. L. Fleming ("Davis and the Negro Problem," *Sewanee Review*, XVI, 408), was given to Davis by his mother as a body servant when he entered the army. Although this letter speaks of Pemberton as Davis' property, the apparent contradiction need not be one, since Fleming may be speaking of the legal deeding of Pemberton to Davis; the letter, on the other hand, may refer to an informal family understanding. See also 1:9, *n.* 7 for the contradictory evidence of William Stamps, who, in a letter to Davis, July 3, 1874, says that Pemberton was sold to Joseph E. Davis just prior to the death of Samuel Emory in 1824. Whatever the legal circumstances may have been, there is no doubt that Pemberton accompanied Davis in his army career from September 1829 until Davis' resignation in 1835 (see 1:152–481, *passim*). He took charge of Davis' funds and arms and frequently accompanied him on dangerous expeditions—most notably the 1834 expedition of the Dragoons from Fort Gibson, in what is now Oklahoma, to the lands of the Kiowa and Wichita Indians, then collectively referred to as the Comanches and Pawnee Picts (1:420, *n.* 6). In 1831—the exact date is unconfirmed—when Davis lay seriously ill with pneumonia, Pemberton nursed him back to health (V. Davis, *Memoir*, I, 81). Again, during the illness that followed the death of Davis' first wife, Sarah Knox Taylor, in 1835, it was Pemberton who cared for his master (*ibid.*, 165). In 1836 when Davis returned from his recuperative trip to Cuba and the eastern part of the United States, he made Pemberton manager of his plantation (*ibid.*, 176). Together the two built the first house at "Brierfield"—described by Mrs. Davis as a "cat and clayed" house (*ibid.*, 202–203)—and together they cleared and prepared the fields for cultivation. In 1845, when Davis went to Congress as a member of the House of Representatives, Pemberton remained behind to manage the plantation. In the following year, when given the choice of going with Davis to the Mexican War or remaining behind, Pemberton decided to remain, believing he could best serve Davis by running "Brierfield" (*ibid.*, 284–85). When Davis returned from the war on a brief furlough, he made his will. James, having been asked if he wished to be free in the event of Davis' death, replied that he would continue serving Mrs. Davis during her lifetime, but that after her death, he would like to have his freedom (*ibid.*, 311). The personal relationship apparently existing between master and slave is best described by Mrs. Davis in her *Memoir*, I, 176–77, wherein she says, "They were devoted friends, and always observed the utmost ceremony and politeness in their intercourse, and at parting a cigar was always presented by Mr. Davis to him. James never sat down without being asked, and his master always invited him to be seated, and sometimes fetched him a chair. James was a dignified, quiet man, of fine manly appearance, very silent, but what he said was always to the point. His death, which occurred from pneumonia in 1850, during our absence, was a sore grief to us, and his place was never filled."

[5] Originally called Harford Town for Henry Harford, son of the last Lord Baltimore, Harford—now known as the village of Bush—was the first seat of Harford County (Writers of the W.P.A., *Maryland*, 325).

[6] Samuel's father Evan Davis (1:Appendix IV, Entry 11) was born in Pennsylvania about 1729; he was the first generation of his line born in the New World, his parents having emigrated from Wales. Evan's father Evan had made provision for his son to be apprenticed to a blacksmith, but on reaching his majority the younger Evan with his brother Joseph moved

south about 1750. It is generally agreed that Evan went first to South Carolina, where he married Mrs. Mary Emory Williams about 1755, then to Georgia, where his son Samuel was born *ca.* 1756. Evan died about 1758 (1:Appendix III, 502).

[7] Interlined.

[8] Transylvania Seminary, established in 1783 by the General Assembly of Virginia for the District of Kentucky, opened a school in Lexington in 1789. Three years later, a group of prominent men in Lexington formed the Transylvania Land Company, which bought land in Lexington to give to the seminary in 1793. After a quarrel over leadership of the school, the Baptist and Presbyterian factions compromised, and Transylvania University was opened in 1799. Plagued by religious controversy and financial instability, Transylvania graduated only twenty-two students in its first nineteen years. Finally, in 1817, the board of trustees elected Horace Holley, a Unitarian minister from Boston, president; under his administration, Transylvania achieved a position of eminence unmatched west of the Alleghenies. Holley attracted faculty members with national reputations, and saw to the enlargement of facilities and curriculum improvements, especially in the medical and law schools. But Holley's liberal religious views were anathema to local Presbyterians, Baptists, and Methodists, and in 1827 he left Transylvania. After his resignation, the school entered a period of decline caused in part by rapid changes in administration; in 1829 a fire destroyed the main campus buildings. After a brief recovery under Methodist control in the early 1840's, Transylvania continued to decline, and during the Civil War was used as a grammar school. From 1865 to 1878 the institution prospered as Kentucky University; in 1908 the name was changed to Transylvania College, and is now Transylvania University (Miller, "Transylvania University," *Filson Club History Quarterly*, XXXIV, 305–12; Townsend, "Transylvania University," in Kerr [ed.], *History of Kentucky*, II, 1049–60; Collins, *History of Kentucky*, II, 183–86; Sonne, *Liberal Kentucky, passim*).

[9] Although the phrase is partially obscured by the strikeout, it appears to read "your father pra[ys]."

[10] Probably David Bradford (1:Appendix IV, Entry 71), Samuel's son-in-law, who was an attorney. His father, also named David, was reportedly one of the leaders of the 1794 Whiskey Rebellion in Pennsylvania. He escaped government prosecution by moving to Louisiana, where he eventually acquired several thousand acres of land (H. A. Davis, *The Davis Family*, 92–94). Although the younger David later acquired a portion of his father's property in West Feliciana Parish (Notarial Record B, October 10, 1822, p. 545 [West Feliciana Parish Courthouse, St. Francisville, Louisiana]; see also 1:363 and 1:419), he seems to have devoted more time to law and politics than to planting. For example, he was superintendent of the mint at New Orleans from 1837 to 1839 (*American Almanac* [1839], 100, [1840], 157). A notice placed on December 8, 1843, in the Richmond (Louisiana) *Compiler* announced his intent to practice law "in the District Court in this and the other Parishes of the Ninth Judicial District of this State, and in the Parish and Probate Courts of this Parish." It was in Richmond that Bradford incurred the hostility of John T. Mason that led to Bradford's assassination in 1844. Davis reported on the event in a letter of March 15, 1844, to Varina Howell, his wife-to-be, saying "I have just returned from the performance of a most painful and melancholy duty. My Brother-in-law David Bradford was assassinated day before yesterday. I went out to his late residence yesterday and returned to-day bringing with me my Sister and her Children" (Hudson Strode, Tuscaloosa, Alabama, 1969;

see also 1:Appendix IV, *n.* 98). Probably the most accurate account of the "fatal rencounter"—that is, the shooting of Bradford by John T. Mason on a Richmond street—may be found in the *Compiler* of March 15, 1844. Accounts of the incident in this issue of the *Compiler*, in the Vicksburg *Weekly Whig* (March 25, April 8, 1844), and in the Vicksburg *Sentinel* (March 18, 1844) report that Mason, armed with a shotgun, confronted Bradford in what was more or less a duel. The *Weekly Whig* and the *Sentinel* record that a disagreement had existed between Bradford and Mason. Both issues of the *Weekly Whig* note that Bradford had publicly challenged Mason to settle the dispute. Mason was brought to trial for murder in May 1844, and a hesitant jury found him not guilty, "or in other words, the jury pronounced the act excusable homicide" (Richmond *Compiler*, May 24, 1844).

11 Samuel Emory Davis (1:Appendix IV, Entry 13), Davis' father, was born *ca.* 1756, the son of Evan and Mary Emory Williams Davis, then residing in Georgia (1:2, lxviii). Within at most a few years after Samuel's birth, Evan died, leaving Mary to provide for three children: Daniel and Isaac Williams, sons by her first marriage, and Samuel (1:Appendix IV, *nn.* 8, 10). When the Revolutionary War began, these half brothers, of whom Samuel was apparently very fond, volunteered to serve with South Carolina troops; Samuel likewise enlisted early in the conflict (1:2, lxvii). While Davis notes only that his father was "in the military service of Georgia and South Carolina until the close of the war" (1:2, lxvii), H. A. Davis records that Samuel served first as a private soldier with a South Carolina company of "mounted gunmen" under Colonel Elijah Clark. Sometime in 1779 Samuel organized and led a company of troops, probably mounted infantry (H. A. Davis, *The Davis Family*, 38; Knight, *The Real Davis*, 7). One account (H. A. Davis, *The Davis Family*, 38) states that he participated in the battle at Kettle Creek, Georgia (February 14, 1779), and led his own company in the siege of Augusta (April–June 1781). Davis concurs (1:2, lxvii) that his father led troops in the siege of Savannah (September–October 1779).

At the close of the war, Samuel returned home to find that his mother had died and her property fallen into disrepair. Soon after his return to Georgia, Samuel was chosen clerk of the courts and married Jane Cook (daughter of William Cook) whom Samuel had met in South Carolina during the war (1:2, lxviii). Samuel was compensated for his service in the war by a grant of land in Georgia. Whether he ever lived on the land is not certain, but Samuel and Jane Davis did reside in Georgia, where their first five children were born, until *ca.* 1797 (1:Appendix IV, *n.* 19). A patent for 1,000 acres was also granted to Samuel Davis by South Carolina. Although Davis believed his family went directly from Georgia to Kentucky (1:2, lxviii), H. A. Davis contends that after leaving Georgia they lived in Barren and Logan counties in South Carolina before moving on to Kentucky, Louisiana, and finally to what became Wilkinson County, Mississippi (H. A. Davis, *The Davis Family*, 38, 40, 80–83). The Davis property there was first known as "Poplar Grove" and later as "Rosemont" (*ibid.*, 38; see also 1:395, *n.* 1). There is evidence that a Samuel Davis bought some land in Wilkinson County from Nancy Viles in 1810, having made arrangements for the purchase in 1808 (Land Record, Book A, 179 [Chancery Clerk's Office, Wilkinson County Courthouse, Woodville, Mississippi]). In 1823 Samuel made a futile journey to Philadelphia in hopes of recovering an inheritance from his father's family (see the reference in *n.* 3 above). While visiting his son Joseph in Warren County, Mississippi, in the summer of 1824, Samuel became ill and died (H. A. Davis, *The Davis Family*, 39–40; see also 1:9, *nn.* 4 and 7).

ABSTRACT

A Catalogue of the Officers and Students of Transylvania University[1] 1:6

Lexington, Kentucky, January 1824

Lists Jefferson Davis of Wilkinson County, Mississippi, as a junior,[2] rooming at the J. Ficklin[3] residence.

D, printed catalogue (Frances Carrick Thomas Library, Transylvania University, Lexington, Kentucky).

1 See 1:5, *n.* 8 for Transylvania.

2 After studying privately through the spring and summer (1:2, lxxvi), Davis entered the junior class of Transylvania University in the fall of 1823 (Autobiographical Sketch [Huntington Miscellaneous Collection, 2161, Henry E. Huntington Library and Art Gallery, San Marino, California]; 1:1, liii).

At first reading, the *Memoir* account (1:2, lxxvi) seems to contradict the above and to support the more commonly held view that Davis attended Transylvania from 1821 to 1824. The editors, however, believe that a closer reading will reveal that Davis said, or rather intended to say, that he went to Transylvania where he was disappointed to find that the authorities, because of his deficiency in mathematics, wished him to enter the freshman class. Unhappy with such an arrangement and wishing to be placed with boys more nearly his own age or even "beyond [his] age," Davis and the authorities agreed that he would be permitted to take private instruction in math "the balance of the session and through the vacation" so that in the fall he might be classified as a sophomore and take the qualifying examinations for admission to the junior class.

The most misleading of Davis' statements is the one in which he says that he studied under a private tutor "so as to enable [him] to pass examination as a sophomore." To interpret this to mean that Davis took an examination to enter the sophomore class would be to say that he entered the same class which he objected to in the first place. Here Davis is speaking of the final sophomore examinations as junior admission examinations. See also 1:2, *n.* 11 for discussion of a similar statement.

3 J. Ficklin's home in Lexington, where Davis boarded during the spring term of 1824, was at the southwest corner of High and Limestone streets. Joseph Ficklin "served as the city's fifth postmaster from 1822 to 1843" (Coleman, "Samuel Woodson Price," *Filson Club History Quarterly*, XXIII, 7–8) and as editor of the Kentucky *Gazette* (Wagers, *Education of a Gentleman*, 7). He was, according to Mrs. Davis, a friend of the Davis family, and as such welcomed Jefferson as one of his own. Mrs. Davis further relates that in 1852 she and Davis were in Lexington and that while there the Ficklins entertained them. During the course of the evening, Mrs. Ficklin, in speaking of Davis, said, "Jeff is the same dear boy he was when he was sixteen" (*Memoir*, I, 29–31).

ABSTRACT

1:7
Notice of an Exhibition by the Members of the Junior Class of Transylvania University[1]

Lexington, Kentucky, June 14, 1824

Jefferson Davis of Mississippi is reported as being scheduled to deliver "An Address on Friendship" as part of a junior class "Exhibition," to be presented to "The friends of learning" in the chapel on Friday, June 18, 1824, at 10:00 A.M.[2]

Text from Lexington *Kentucky Reporter*, June 14, 1824. Printed: Wagers, *Education of a Gentleman*, 34.

[1] See 1:5, *n.* 8 for Transylvania.

[2] The legislature of Kentucky, which founded Transylvania University, provided that "there shall be annually a public examination . . . beginning on the first Wednesday before commencement, in the studies of the preceding year" (Kentucky House *Journal*, 1824, p. 235). In accordance with the dictum of the legislature and sometime prior to the publication of this notice, Davis passed his examinations, taking an honor in the process (see 1:2, lxxviii, for Davis' recollection of the event). Having won an honor, he was given the privilege of addressing the annual junior exhibition. His efforts were evidently successful, for, in reporting on the exhibition, the *Monitor* mentions that "Davis on Friendship made friends of the hearers" (clipping from the [Lexington, Kentucky] *Monitor*, June 22, 1824, in Mrs. Horace Holley's scrapbook [Frances Carrick Thomas Library, Transylvania University, Lexington, Kentucky], cited in Wagers, *Education of a Gentleman*, 35).

1:8
To John C. Calhoun

Lexington, July 7th 1824 Transylvania Univer[1]

SIR,[2]

The commission of Cadet granted the undersigned March 11th, and remitted to Natchez, on accountt of my absence was forwarded here.[3] I accept it.

am not able to go on before sept. for reasons I will explain to the superintendent[4] on my arrival.[5] Yours &C JEFFERSON DAVIS

ALS, facsimile (New York *Daily Graphic*, September 7, 1877). Indexed, not found (NA, RG 107 Records of the Office of the Secretary of War, Letters Received, D–51[18], 1824). Addressed: "J. C. Calhoun." Printed: Cutting, *Political Soldier*, 17; McElroy, *The Unreal and the Real*, I, 12; D. Rowland, *Papers*, I, 1; Strode, *American Patriot*, 28; Wagers, *Education of a Gentleman*, 35.

[1] See 1:5, *n.* 8 for Transylvania.

[2] At the time of this letter, John C. Calhoun (1782–1850) was the secretary of war under President James Monroe. Serving variously as vice president, senator from South Carolina, and secretary of state, he was renowned both as politician and as political philosopher (*DAB*). To Davis he was a revered figure and political guide; in later years Davis wrote that in his early manhood he "enjoyed the personal acquaintance of Mr. Calhoun, and perhaps received especial consideration from the fact that, as Secretary of War, he had appointed me a cadet in the United States Military Academy" (Davis, "Calhoun," *North American Review*, CXLV, 258).

[3] Davis' commission, which has not been located, was, as he says, remitted to Natchez, the distributing office for the state of Mississippi. The postmaster, who was required by law "to open all mails," evidently forwarded it to him at Lexington (*American State Papers*, Class VII, Post Office Department, 113).

[4] Sylvanus Thayer (sketch, 1:74, *n.* 6) was superintendent at West Point.

[5] No documentary evidence has been found concerning Davis' delay in leaving for West Point before September. The death of his father on July 4, 1824 (see 1:9), may have been the reason for his late departure. However, the delay may have been occasioned by a certain reluctance to leave a friendly and familiar place, for, as Davis says, he "disliked" going from the head class of one institution to the lowest of another (1:2, lxxviii). The West Point appointment was Joseph E. Davis' idea, and Davis agreed to it reluctantly and only after having received his brother's assurance that if, after a trial term of one year, he found that he did not like it, he would be permitted to go to the University of Virginia (1:2, lxxix).

To Susannah Gartley Davis 1:9

DEAR SISTER,[1] Lexington, August 2d '24

It is gratifying to hear from a friend,[2] especially one from whom I had not[3] so long as yourself, but the intelligence contained in yours,[4] was more than <sufficient to mar>[5] the satisfaction of hearing from any one. You must imagine, I cannot describe the shock my feelings sustained, at that sad intelligence. In my Father[6] I lost a parent ever dear to me, but rendered more so (if possible), by the disasters that attended his dclining years.[7]

When I saw him last,[8] he told we would probably never see each other again, but I still hoped to meet him once more But Heaven has refused my wish. This is the second time, I have <been>[5] doomed to receive the heart rending intelligence of the *Death* of a *friend.*[9] God only knows, whether or not it will be the last. If all the dear friends of my childhood are to be torn from earth, I care not how soon I may follow. I leave in a short time for West-Point,[10] State of New York, where <—I—> it will always give me pleasure to hear from you. Kiss the Children[11] for Uncle Jeff. Present me affectionately to

Brother Isaac,[12] tell him I would be happy to hear from him. And to yourself the sincere regard of Your Brother, JEFFERSON

ALS (Jefferson Davis Papers, Frances Carrick Thomas Library, Transylvania University, Lexington, Kentucky). Addressed: "Mrs. Susannah Davis, Warrenton, Warren Cty. Mississippi." Printed: V. Davis, *Memoir*, I, 32–33; Dodd, *Jefferson Davis*, 23; W. L. Fleming, "Early Life," Mississippi Valley Historical *Proceedings, 1915–16*, IX, 175; D. Rowland, *Papers*, I, 2; Strode, *American Patriot*, 28–29; Strode, *Private Letters*, 7; Whitsitt, *Genealogy*, 15–16; Winston, *High Stakes*, 9–10.

[1] Susannah Gartley (also spelled Garthy, Guerthy, and Guertly) Davis (1:Appendix IV, Entry 55), wife of Davis' brother Isaac.

[2] The letter advising Davis of the death of his father has not been found.

[3] The word "heard" is obviously omitted.

[4] Davis here has reference to the death of his father, Samuel E. Davis, on July 4, 1824 (see 1:2, lxxviii).

[5] Interlined.

[6] Samuel E. Davis (sketch, 1:5, *n.* 11; 1:Appendix IV, Entry 13).

[7] Although it is not certain, it may be assumed that he was referring here to his father's financial difficulties—difficulties that ultimately resulted in the loss of his property at Woodville, Mississippi. The specific and complicated circumstances of Samuel's financial troubles and of his death are related in a letter written to Davis by William Stamps, second husband of Davis' sister Lucinda, on July 3, 1874:

"My recollection of the transaction which took place between Your Father and Your Brother Joe [Joseph Emory Davis] is that in May, 1822 your Brother Joe bought of your Father his plantation near Woodville in this County for which he was to give him the sum of Five Thousand Dollars, out of which sum he was to pay John Brown something over Two thousand Dollars, which your Father owed Brown for the place: I do not think Your Brother Joe at the time paid your Father More than five hundred Dollars of the purchase money at the time, and at the same time Your Father gave your Brother Joe a Bill of sale for all his Negroes for which he never paid one dime the negroes were Bob & his wife Farah, Charles, Jim Pemberton, Sampson and Charity, which negroes at the time would have sold in the open Market for about Three thousand Dollars: It may be unpleasent to you (as it was with Many others) to know the sale of the land and Negroes to your Brother Joe was in Consequence of your Fathers liabilities as Security for Robert Davis [Davis' brother-in-law] for a Considerable amount in fact so Much so that with the Judgement of Jno. Brown would utterly have ruined him. As to your Father or yourself being dependent on your Brother the idea is absur[d] [a]nd all who knew your Father would so assert

"Your Brother Joe never assumed any ownership over the negroes until after the death of your Father and the manner in which they came into his possession was thus—Your Father had the Negroes in the Crop with your Brother Samuel in 1823 or '24 I cannot state which year (but I think it was in 1824, when some Misunderstanding takeing place between your Father & your Brother Samuel, he took his Negroes to Vicksburg bought a Boat and Shipped them with himself to the place of your Brother Joe plantation, then managed by Your Brother Isaac, your Father took the Fever on the River and died within five or six days after landing; Nothing was ever done after by any one of the Family all Conceding that whatever he had belonged [to]

Jefferson Davis his son who was off at school" (Jefferson Davis Papers, Frances Carrick Thomas Library, Transylvania University, Lexington, Kentucky).

The land transaction between Joseph E. Davis and his father, filed June 15, 1822, was for property valued at $5,000 on the headwaters of Thompson's Creek and Buffalo—the same tract of approximately 256 acres conveyed to Samuel Davis by John Brown (Land Record, Book C, 274 [Chancery Clerk's Office, Wilkinson County Courthouse, Woodville, Mississippi]). Brown sold his land to Samuel Davis in April 1820 for over $2,000 (Land Record, Book C, 200–203 [*ibid.*]).

[8] See 1:2, lxviii for Davis' recollection of when he last saw his father.

[9] The "friend" to whom Davis here refers was his youngest sister, Mary Ellen (sketch, 1:528, *n.* 5; 1:Appendix IV, Entry 22).

[10] Davis accepted his West Point appointment in July (1:8), and arrived there in September (1:14, *n.* 2).

[11] Virtually nothing is known of the elder son (1:Appendix IV, Entry 56) of Isaac and Susannah Davis—not even his name. Most authorities agree that he was born in either 1823 or 1824 and that he was killed during a violent storm from which the "Hurricane" plantation derived its name (V. Davis, *Memoir*, I, 48). Whether the storm was a cyclone in 1827 (Strode, *American Patriot*, 94) or a hurricane in the early 1830's (H. A. Davis, *The Davis Family*, 84; "List of Hurricanes," *De Bow's Review*, XXIII, 513–17) has not been ascertained. In 1824 Susannah and Isaac Davis had only one known child.

[12] Isaac Williams Davis (1:Appendix IV, Entry 19), Davis' brother, was born in October 1792 in Wilkes County, Georgia (H. A. Davis, *The Davis Family*, 83). During the War of 1812, Isaac served as a private in a troop of volunteer dragoons, and about 1822 married Susannah Gartley. Apparently after his brother Joseph bought a plantation on Davis Bend about 1818 (Davis *v.* Bowmar, 441 [Mississippi Department of Archives and History, Jackson]), Isaac managed the property while Joseph continued practicing law. In a violent storm that ravaged the region (see *n.* 11 above), Isaac's leg was broken and one of his sons was killed (Strode, *American Patriot*, 94). Soon after, Isaac moved near Canton, Mississippi, where he became a planter (*ibid.*, 50; Trist Wood Papers, Box 12, Folder 8 [Southern Historical Collection, University of North Carolina Library, Chapel Hill]). H. A. Davis states that he died before 1860 (*The Davis Family*, 84).

ABSTRACT

Monthly Return 1:10

West Point, New York, September 30, 1824

Lists Jefferson Davis as having been admitted to the Military Academy.

DS (U.S. Military Academy Archives), 2. Signed: "H. H. Gird, Lieut. Actg. Adjt. S. Thayer Lt Col Comdg." Documents such as this pertaining to Davis' career at the Academy present an unusual and difficult problem. Many of them were lost in a fire that destroyed the Old Academy Building in 1838 (Smith to DeRussy, February 22, 1838 [U.S. Military Academy Archives]) and were subsequently copied by a group of officers who were sent to Washington for the purpose of rebuilding the Academy records. Consequently it is difficult, if not impossible, to determine whether a document is an original, a contemporary duplicate, or a later copy of either an original or duplicate. The confusion is compounded by the fact that a number of the items which were supposedly destroyed in the fire and later recopied bear apparently authentic signatures which would seem to indicate that they are not copies, but originals. The difficulty has been resolved by giving to each document the designation, *e.g.*, D, DS, DS copy, LbC, or LbCS, that its physical appearance seems to warrant.

ABSTRACT

1:11

Monthly Conduct Report

U.S. Military Academy, September 30, 1824

Lists Cadet J. Davis and 83 other cadets out of a total of 259 as "distinguished for Correct Conduct" during September.[1]

DS (NA, RG 94 Records of the Adjutant General's Office, Records Relating to the U.S. Military Academy, Monthly Conduct Reports, Entry 231), 2. Signed: "S. Thayer Lt Col Supnd. Mil Acady."

[1] See 1:116, which confirms the fact that Davis had no offenses during September.

ABSTRACT

1:12

Monthly Conduct Report

U.S. Military Academy, October 31, 1824

Lists Cadet J. Davis as having committed one offense during October.[1]

DS (NA, RG 94 Records of the Adjutant General's Office, Records Relating to the U.S. Military Academy, Monthly Conduct Reports, Entry 231), 2. Signed: "S. Thayer Lt Col Supnd Mil Acady."

[1] Compare Davis' record of delinquencies (1:116) which, unlike the above, lists him as having committed three offenses during October.

ABSTRACT

Monthly Return 1:13

West Point, New York, October 31, 1824

Lists Cadet Davis as being present and sick.[1]

DS (U.S. Military Academy Archives), 2. Signed: "H. H. Gird, Lieut. Actg. Adjt. S. Thayer Lt Col Comdg."

[1] That the Davis here mentioned is Jefferson and not some other is confirmed by the muster roll of the same date (see 1:14), which lists Jefferson Davis as present and sick.

ABSTRACT

Muster Roll of the Corps of Cadets 1:14

West Point, October 31, 1824

Lists Jefferson Davis, United States Military Academy, Corps of Cadets commanded by Major William J. Worth,[1] as admitted September 1, 1824,[2] and present at the post. Remarks: "Sick."

DS (U.S. Military Academy Archives), 8. Signed: "W J Worth M[a]j[or] Com[mandin]g Corps Muster[in]g & Insp[ectin]g Offr."

[1] William J. Worth (1794–1849) was born in Hudson, New York, had a common school education, then moved to Albany and engaged in commerce until the War of 1812. He served as Winfield Scott's aide, and was brevetted captain and major. He was lamed for life from a wound received at Lundy's Lane, but continued to serve in the army until his death. From 1820 to 1828 he was commandant of cadets at West Point and was promoted to colonel of the Eighth Infantry in 1838, serving in the Seminole Wars. Worth was conspicuous for his gallantry in the Mexican War, under the commands of Zachary Taylor and Scott. He was in command of the Department of Texas and a brevet major general when he died of cholera (*DAB*).

[2] In spite of the fact that the records list Davis as having entered the Academy on September 1, it is more likely that he entered late in September (W. L. Fleming, "Davis at West Point," Mississippi Historical *Publications*, X, 248). If such be the case, the September 1 entry date can be explained as an effort on the part of the authorities to make the event conform, on paper at least, to the Academy regulations which provided that "no cadet shall be examined for admission after that time [June 30], unless he shall have been prevented from joining, by sickness, or some other unavoidable cause; in which case, he may be examined on the 1st of September following, and if then found qualified, may be admitted accordingly" (*Regulations of the Military Academy* [1823], 19). No documentary proof, other than that afforded by Davis' autobiographical account (1:2, lxxviii) and by his letter to Calhoun (1:8), has been found. If Davis left Lexington on or about September 1, as the Calhoun letter seems to say, he obviously did not enter the Academy until after that date.

ABSTRACT

1:15
Monthly Conduct Report

U.S. Military Academy, November 30, 1824

Lists Cadet F. J. Davis[1] as having committed two offenses during November.[2]

DS (NA, RG 94 Records of the Adjutant General's Office, Records Relating to the U.S. Military Academy, Monthly Conduct Reports, Entry 231), 2. Signed: "S. Thayer Lt Col Supnd Mil Acady."

[1] Davis' initials are here reversed. According to Strode, the "F" in Davis' name stood for Finis (*American Patriot*, 3).

[2] See 1:116 for a list of Davis' delinquencies.

ABSTRACT

1:16
Consolidated Conduct Report

U.S. Military Academy, December 31, 1824

Lists Cadet F. J. Davis[1] as having committed three offenses during the months of July through December.[2]

DS (NA, RG 94 Records of the Adjutant General's Office, Records Relating to the U.S. Military Academy, Monthly Conduct Reports, Entry 231), 2. Signed: "S. Thayer Lt Col Supnd Mil Acady." Endorsed: "No report for June 1824."

[1] Davis' initials are here reversed and refer to Jefferson Finis (Strode, *American Patriot*, 3).

[2] Although the total of three delinquencies agrees with 1:12 and 1:15, it does not agree with Davis' record of delinquencies (1:116).

ABSTRACT

1:17
Muster Roll of the Corps of Cadets

West Point, December 31, 1824

Lists Jefferson Davis, United States Military Academy, Corps of Cadets commanded by Major William J. Worth,[1] as present at the post.

DS (U.S. Military Academy Archives), 18. Signed: "W. J Worth M[a]j[or] Com[mandin]g Corps Mustering & Insp[ect]ing Offr."

[1] William J. Worth (sketch, 1:14, *n.* 1).

12 JANUARY 1825

ABSTRACT

Semiannual Muster Roll of the Corps of Cadets 1:18

West Point, December 31, 1824

Lists Jefferson Davis of Mississippi, United States Military Academy, Corps of Cadets commanded by Major William J. Worth,[1] as being age seventeen years, six months,[2] and as present at the post, having been admitted to the fourth class[3] September 1, 1824.[4]

DS (NA, RG 94 Records of the Adjutant General's Office, Records Relating to the U.S. Military Academy, Semiannual Muster Rolls of Cadets, Entry 227), 11; DS (U.S. Military Academy Archives). Signed: "W. J Worth Maj Com[mandin]g Corps, Mustering & Insp[ectin]g Officer Countersigned S. Thayer Lt Col Supnd Mil Acady."

[1] William J. Worth (sketch, 1:14, *n.* 1).

[2] Davis' age is here figured from 1807 (see 1:1, *n.* 1).

[3] The fourth class at West Point was the freshman class; according to the regulations of the Academy, "The cadets shall be formed in four distinct annual classes, corresponding with the four years of study; that is to say, all cadets employed on the first year's course, shall constitute the fourth, or lowest class; those on the second year's course, shall constitute the third class; those on the third year's course, shall constitute the second class; and those on the fourth year's course, shall constitute the first class" (*Regulations of the Military Academy* [1823], 13–14).

[4] See 1:14, *n.* 2 for a discussion of the date Davis entered West Point.

To Joseph Emory Davis 1:19

DEAR BROTHER,[1] West Point, Jany. 12, 25

Yours of the 13th[2] was gratefully received last night, was supprised that you had not received a letter from me[2] for the time specified, on opening a letter[2] from Sister L, Stamps[3] & finding the same complaint, when I recollected having <written>[4] to both her and yourself at the sametime concluded, (what you least expected to be the cause of not having heard from me,) that something had happened to the mail.

As for your fear that I might be confined in the guard-house[5] I trust ever to have enough prudence to keep from being confined.

You mentioned Brother Isaac[6] had some intention of moving to Kentucky. I hope this only a romantic notion of his, which will die away as soon as it arose. Kentucky being the last <place>[4] I would go to for the purpose of making a subsistence.[7]

The long silence of both Brothers Isaac, & Saml[8] has not a little supprised me. I opened a communication and finished it,[2] so let it rest.

Say to Florida[9] I received her letter and answered,[2] addressing at St Francisville the place whence she wrote me.[10] If you bring her on with you[11] I have no doubt but the trip will be improving and interesting to her, it would besides give me great pleasure to see her.

I have to make a request of you which having made so often before, I feel a delicacy in making again, indeed I had not expected it would be necessary again, but it is that you would if convenient in your next remit me some Cash, I expect my pay generally to satisfy cvery demand, hope entirely, which however depends entirely upon the company I keep. *The Yankee part of the corps find their pay entirely sufficient some even more, but these are* <*not*>[4] *such as I formed an acquaintance with on* my arrival, it having originated in the introductory letters I brought on with me; *nor are they such associates as I would* <—illegible—> *at present select,*[12] enough of this as you have never been connected with them, you cannot know *how pittiful they generally* are.[13]

Am happy to hear of the restoration of your health, I hope after your visit to the North you will entirely <feel>[4] free from the effects of the ill health you have lately experienced.

Let me hear from you. Your Brother, JEFFERSON

ALS (Special Collections, Murphy Library, Wisconsin State University—La Crosse). Purloined from the Davis plantation on June 19, 1863, by one "Beauford" and forwarded by him to "Dr Sir," this most interesting letter eventually found its way to the Wisconsin State University at La Crosse. Although the complete provenance is unknown, it is possible to trace some of the steps by which the letter came to rest in Wisconsin. On June 19, 1863, Beauford wrote from the U.S.S. *Carondelet* near Vicksburg: "Enclosed you will find a letter written by Jefferson Davis, a long time ago. even at that early age evincing his Contempt for the *Yankees* we lay within a couple of Miles of his plantation, his Brother Joseph's plantation is within a mile of where we lay. I have just been taking a stroll over both places where I picked up the letter" (Special Collections, Murphy Library, Wisconsin State University—La Crosse). Just how the letter passed from "Dr Sir" into the hands of Ellis B. Usher is unknown, but that it did so is indisputable. The following quotation from an article by Albert H. Sanford ("Ellis B. Usher Donor Of Historical Volumes to Teachers College," La Crosse *Tribune and Leader-Press*, April 26, 1931) is self-explanatory: " 'Besides his books, pamphlets and many newspaper clippings included in the gift, he and Mrs. Usher contributed numerous relics of considerable historical value. Prominent among these is a collection of autographs that was originally made about 100 years ago. . . . Most interesting is a letter by Jefferson Davis when he was a cadet at West Point in 1821 [1825].' " George R. Gilkey, chairman of the department of history, Wisconsin State University, La Crosse, in a letter to the editor, January 26, 1967, suggested the possibility that Usher obtained the

Davis letter from his uncle, Cyrus Woodman, a collector of autographs and a person of consequence in the early history of Wisconsin (Usher, "Cyrus Woodman," *Wisconsin Magazine of History*, II, 393–412).

[1] Joseph Emory Davis (1784–1870), Davis' eldest brother (1:Appendix IV, Entry 15), was born in Georgia and moved with the family to Kentucky, then to Mississippi. He read law in Kentucky and Mississippi and was admitted to the bar in 1812. An officer in the Mississippi Dragoons during the War of 1812, Joseph served in Thomas Hinds's command at the Battle of New Orleans (Shields, *Natchez: Its Early History*, 188). He practiced in Pinckneyville and Greenville before moving to Natchez, where he formed a partnership with Thomas B. Reed in 1820. He was one of the trustees of Trinity Church, Natchez, at its incorporation in 1822 (*ibid.*, 248). After retiring from practice in 1827, he concentrated on the management and development of "Hurricane," his plantation on the Mississippi River south of Vicksburg, and became quite wealthy. Joseph Davis was married on October 5, 1827, to Eliza Van Benthuysen of New Orleans, who helped him rear his three daughters by a previous marriage. A lifelong Jeffersonian Democrat, Joseph took an active role in local politics; he was a delegate to the state constitutional convention in 1817, chairman of the Shipping Committee of Vicksburg and the Vicksburg Cotton Convention in 1842, and a nominee to the state Democratic convention in 1843. During the Civil War, he was forced to abandon his plantation, but returned to Vicksburg after the war and died there (Lynch, *Bench and Bar of Mississippi*, 73–78). He was Davis' confidant and guardian and, because of the vast difference in their ages, seems to have been more a father than a brother. Davis said of him in 1884: "He was my beau ideal when I was a boy and my love for him is to me yet a sentiment than which I have none more sacred . . ." (Davis to Mitchell, February 7 [Lise Mitchell Papers, Howard-Tilton Memorial Library, Tulane University, New Orleans]). It is believed that Davis may have obtained his 1824 appointment to the Military Academy through Joseph's influence (Knight, *The Real Davis*, 17; Schaff, *Davis: Life and Personality*, 10; DeLeon, "The Real Jefferson Davis," Southern Historical *Papers*, XXXVI, 81). Joseph also managed their father Samuel's estate; to compensate Davis for his part of the inheritance, Joseph gave him "Brierfield" plantation in 1835, and loaned him money to begin life as a planter (Winston, *High Stakes*, 20–21; Eckenrode, *President of the South*, 32; Davis *v.* Bowmar, 62 [Mississippi Department of Archives and History, Jackson]).

[2] The mentioned letters have not been found.

[3] Lucinda Farrar Davis Davis Stamps (1:Appendix IV, Entry 20), one of Davis' five sisters, was born June 5, 1797, in Christian County, Kentucky (H. A. Davis, *The Davis Family*, 84). About 1816 she married Hugh Davis, who, within a year of their marriage, drowned while crossing the Homochitto River. A son, Hugh Robert, was born in 1818 (see 1:Appendix IV, *nn.* 80, 81). On March 5, 1820, Lucinda married William Stamps (Marriage Records [Wilkinson County Courthouse, Woodville, Mississippi]); they had four children—Jane Davis, Anna Aurelia, William, Jr., and Isaac Davis Stamps. For a time they lived on their 1,500-acre plantation near Woodville before moving to Fort Adams (Woodville [Mississippi] *Republican*, November 24, 1834; Lloyd, *Steamboat Directory*, 95–101). Later still they moved to "Rosemont," which had been Jane Cook Davis' home near Woodville, where Lucinda died on December 14, 1873 (More, Genealogical Data [Jefferson Davis Association, Rice Univer-

sity, Houston]; H. A. Davis, *The Davis Family*, 84).

[4] Interlined.

[5] Although no record exists proving that Davis was actually confined to a guardhouse, he was arrested a number of times during his West Point career. See 1:34 for evidence of his first arrest.

[6] Isaac W. Davis (sketch, 1:9, *n.* 12; 1:Appendix IV, Entry 19), was at this time managing Joseph E. Davis' plantation, "Hurricane." Evidently Isaac had become somewhat dissatisfied with his position and was thinking of moving to Kentucky to improve it.

[7] Davis lived in Lexington in 1823–24 while attending Transylvania University (1:6, *n.* 2).

[8] Samuel Davis (1:Appendix IV, Entry 17), Davis' brother and third son of Samuel Emory and Jane Cook Davis, was born *ca.* 1788–89 in Wilkes County, Georgia, and moved with his parents to Kentucky, Louisiana, and finally Mississippi (H. A. Davis, *The Davis Family*, 81). When the War of 1812 began, Samuel volunteered as a private soldier and served in the army for several years (Strode, *American Patriot*, 9; H. A. Davis, *The Davis Family*, 81). He returned from the war to help his father on the family farm near Woodville, Mississippi. About 1818 Samuel married Lucy Throckmorton; they had six children, the eldest and only one to leave descendants settling in Boise, Idaho (*ibid.*, 81; Strode, *American Patriot*, 30; De Leon, *Belles, Beaux and Brains*, 77). Samuel Davis died about 1835 (H. A. Davis, *The Davis Family*, 81).

[9] Relatively little is known of Davis' niece, Florida A. Davis McCaleb Laughlin (1:Appendix IV, Entry 28), eldest daughter of Joseph E. Davis and his first wife (1:Appendix IV, *n.* 25). If Florida was fifty-seven years old on July 2, 1875, as she stated in a legal deposition (Davis *v.* Bowmar, 378 [Mississippi Department of Archives and History, Jackson]), she would have been about twelve at the time of her marriage to David McCaleb in 1830 (Woodville [Mississippi] *Republican*, November 13, 1830). The couple made their home at "Diamond Place," a plantation of about 1,200 acres given to Florida by her father (Strode, *American Patriot*, 117). Florida was widowed in the late 1840's. On July 17, 1848, she signed a marriage bond with Edmund C. Laughlin (O'Neill, "Warren County Marriages," *Journal of Mississippi History*, XXX, 214). She had no children, but Florida and her second husband adopted some of his nephews (H. A. Davis, *The Davis Family*, 80).

[10] Evidently Florida was visiting one of her aunts, Anna Davis Smith or Amanda Davis Bradford, both of whom lived with their families in West Feliciana Parish, Louisiana.

[11] The trip to which Davis refers was one which Joseph E. Davis, in company with Mr. and Mrs. William B. Howell (Davis' future father- and mother-in-law), made to West Point in the summer of 1825. See V. Davis, *Memoir*, I, 49–51, for a discussion of the trip and of the impression made upon the Howells by Davis. Apparently Florida Davis had intended going with her father and friends to West Point.

[12] The most intimate of Davis' acquaintances at the Academy were Leonidas Polk and Albert Sidney Johnston. In later years Davis wrote, "They were my seniors in the Academy, but we belonged to the same 'set,' a name well understood by those who have been ground in the Academy mill" (1:2, lxxx).

[13] Here Davis, in asking his brother for money, violates paragraph 127 of the regulations which provided that "No cadet shall apply for, or receive money from his parents, or from any person whomsoever . . . any violation of which will be considered a positive disobedience of orders, and punished accordingly" (*Regulations of the Military Academy* [1823], 28). Although

the regulation had been a dead letter prior to the superintendency of Lieutenant Colonel Sylvanus Thayer, he, in his efforts to improve the discipline of the Academy, attempted to enforce it—much to the disgust of the cadets. Leonidas Polk, a contemporary of Davis at the Academy, mentioned the difficulty of living within the pay that each cadet received when he wrote to his father that "exactly like nineteen twentieths of the corps, I am indebted to the aforesaid tailor, merchant, etc., the major part of my next month's pay . . . and things are so arranged that there seems to be no remedy. Not even the rigid economy of the Yankees can withstand it" (W. M. Polk, *Leonidas Polk*, I, 81). Cadets "received $16 per month pay and two rations, equivalent in all to $28 per month" (W. L. Fleming, "Davis at West Point," Mississippi Historical *Publications*, X, 264–65). The underlining in this paragraph appears to have been added at a later date by someone other than Davis.

ABSTRACT

Monthly Conduct Report 1:20

U.S. Military Academy, January 31, 1825

Lists Cadet J. Davis as having committed one offense during January.[1]

DS (NA, RG 94 Records of the Adjutant General's Office, Records Relating to the U.S. Military Academy, Monthly Conduct Reports, Entry 231), 2. Signed: "S. Thayer Lt Col Supnd Mil Acady." Endorsed: "No reports for the months of Augt. & Decr. 1824, but these are included in Consolidated report No. 50."

[1] Compare the Record of Delinquencies (1:116), which lists Davis as having committed no offenses during January.

ABSTRACT

Merit Roll 1:21

U.S. Military Academy, January [31,] 1825

Ranks Cadet J. Davis at the general examination given in January 1825 as fifty-fourth out of ninety-one members of the fourth class[1] in mathematics, and nineteenth out of ninety-one members of the fourth class in French.

D (NA, RG 94 Records of the Adjutant General's Office, Records Relating to the U.S. Military Academy, Merit Rolls, Entry 230), 7.

[1] See 1:18, *n.* 3 for an explanation of the West Point class system.

ABSTRACT

1:22 Roll of Cadets

West Point, New York, February 1, 1825

Lists Cadet Jefferson Davis of Mississippi, fourth class,[1] as admitted to the Academy September 1, 1824,[2] at the age of seventeen years, two months.[3] His parent is recorded as Mrs. Jane Davis,[4] of Woodville,[5] Wilkinson County, Mississippi.

DS (NA, RG 94 Records of the Adjutant General's Office, Records Relating to the U.S. Military Academy, Rolls of Cadets, filed with Entry 227), 9. Signed: "H. H. Gird, Lieut. actg. adjt. S. Thayer Lt Col Supnd Mil Acady." Endorsed: "The 2nd Roll as reqd. by the Mily. Academy Order of 12 March 1824"; in a different hand, "Copied."

[1] See 1:18, *n.* 3 for a discussion of the West Point class system.

[2] See 1:14, *n.* 2 for an explanation of the date of Davis' admission to West Point.

[3] Davis' age is figured from the year 1807. See 1:1, *n.* 1 for a discussion of the problem of Davis' age.

[4] Jane Cook Davis (1:Appendix IV, Entry 14), Davis' mother, was born *ca.* 1760–61 in North Carolina. She married Samuel Emory Davis after the Revolutionary War, having met him in South Carolina during the war (1:2, lxviii; H. A. Davis, *The Davis Family*, 38–40). Of Scotch-Irish descent (1:2, lxviii), she was, according to Schaff (*Davis: Life and Personality*, 4), the daughter of a famous Baptist minister. After her husband's death in 1824, Jane Davis continued to live at "Rosemont," near Woodville, until her death in October 1845. Varina Davis describes her as a lovely older lady: "On our visit to Woodville I was introduced to Mr. Davis' mother, who, though she . . . had attained her eighty-fifth year [eighty-fourth, see 1:Appendix IV, *n.* 13], was still fair to look upon. Her eyes were bright, her hair was a soft brown, and her complexion clear and white as a child's. His [Davis'] dutiful attentions to her, and the tender love he evinced for his sisters and family, impressed me greatly" (*Memoir*, I, 200).

[5] Woodville, county seat of Wilkinson County since the early 1800's, is thirty-five miles south of Natchez and fifteen miles from the Mississippi River. A thriving community, Woodville contained about 800 inhabitants by 1835. The *Republican*, oldest newspaper in Mississippi, was first published there in 1812, and in 1831 Woodville became a terminus of the state's first railroad (see 1:328, *n.* 7). A number of prominent individuals lived in or near Woodville, which was the site of several academies and churches (*Encyclopedia of Mississippi History*, II, 991–92; Writers of the W.P.A., *Mississippi*, 344–46; [Ingraham], *South-West*, II, 178–80).

ABSTRACT

Monthly Conduct Report 1:23

U.S. Military Academy, February 28, 1825

Lists Cadet J. Davis as having committed one offense during February.[1]

DS (NA, RG 94 Records of the Adjutant General's Office, Records Relating to the U.S. Military Academy, Monthly Conduct Reports, Entry 231), 2. Signed: "S. Thayer Lt Col Supndt. Mil. Acady."

[1] Both this conduct report and Davis' record of delinquencies (1:116) agree.

EXTRACT

Notice of a Celebration 1:24

Lexington, Kentucky March 7, 1825

Tuesday[1] being the birth day of our illustrious WASHINGTON, the day was celebrated by the Military and the Citizens agreeable to the arrangements announced in our last. At 11 o'clock the Episcopal Church was crowded. The Rev. J. Tomlinson[2] addressed the throne of grace when appropriate Orations were delivered by Gustavus Adolphus Henry,[3] on the part of the Union Philosophical Society[4] and by Robert J. Breckinridge[5] Esq. on behalf of the Whig Society.[4] After the Orations were concluded, the U. P. Society dined at Mr. Giron's[6] attended by President Holley,[7] Judge Bledsoe,[8] Dr. Caldwell,[9] Dr. Richardson,[10] Professor Roche[11] and R. H. Chinn[12] Esq. as invited guests.

Patrick Henry[13] Presided assisted by W. B. Redd[14] as Vice President. The following toasts were drunk with the applause of the company. . . . By W. B. Redd To the health and prosperity of Jefferson Davis, late a Student of Transylvania University,[15] now a Cadet at West Point—May he become the pride of our country, the idol of our army.

Text from Lexington *Kentucky Reporter*, March 7, 1825, p. 1.

[1] According to the perpetual calendar, February 22 fell on a Tuesday, thirteen days prior to this notice.

[2] Joseph S. Tomlinson (1802–53) was born in Kentucky of a poor fam-

ily. He entered Transylvania as an orphan, was in Davis' class, and graduated with honors. Licensed to preach in the Methodist church before graduation, Tomlinson was appointed to the faculty of Augusta College, Bracken County, Kentucky, in 1825, and in time became the second president of the Methodist school. He was admitted to the circuit in 1825, graduated regularly to deacon and elder, and finally obtained the D.D. degree. When the Methodist church schism occurred in 1844, Augusta was closed, and Tomlinson accepted a professorship at Ohio University at Athens. He was elected president of the university a year later, but declined the appointment because of ill health. After the death of one of his sons, he evidently became a victim of a "melancholy form of mental derangement" which worsened with time and ended in suicide (*Catalogue of Transylvania University* [1824]; Redford, *History of Methodism in Kentucky*, III, 295–99; Cannon, "Education, Publication, Benevolent Work, and Missions," *History of American Methodism*, I, 554–55).

[3] Gustavus A. Henry (1804–80), born in Kentucky, was graduated first in the class of 1825 at Transylvania. A lawyer, he first practiced in Hopkinsville, and served in the Kentucky legislature. Sometime after his marriage in 1833, he moved to Clarksville, Tennessee. He was in the Tennessee legislature, a Whig presidential elector in 1840, an unsuccessful candidate for the United States Congress in 1843, 1844, and 1852, and in 1853 lost to Andrew Johnson in the gubernatorial race. He was elected a senator to the 1862 Confederate Congress, and served until the end of the war. Afterwards, he resumed his law practice at Clarksville, and in 1874 was chairman of the Tennessee Democratic convention (*National Cyclopaedia*, XIII, 131; *Appleton's*; Henry, *History of the Henry Family*, 118–25; Moore and Foster, *Tennessee*, IV, 823–24).

[4] One of the two rival literary debating societies at Transylvania. According to Wagers, "These societies occupied a unique position in the life of the campus providing much of the social, as well as a cultural and intellectual stimulus. The dinners which they sponsored were occasions for discussing every conceivable topic, with the added zest of numerous toasts in wines of rare vintage" (*Education of a Gentleman*, 31).

[5] Robert Jefferson Breckinridge (1800–71), uncle of John C. Breckinridge, was born near Lexington, educated at Jefferson College and Yale, and was graduated from Union College in 1819. He then studied law at Lexington and began his practice in 1824. Elected to the state legislature, 1825–28, he turned to the Presbyterian church for a new career after the deaths of two of his children, being licensed to preach in 1832. He served at the Second Presbyterian Church in Baltimore in 1832, succeeding his brother. From 1845 to 1847 he was president of Jefferson College in Pennsylvania, then became superintendent of public instruction in Kentucky until 1851. The Danville Theological Seminary offered him a professorship in 1851, a position he accepted and retained until his resignation in 1869. He resided in Danville until his death (*DAB*).

[6] Mathurin Giron emigrated from France to Kentucky at approximately the turn of the century, and by 1811 had established a confectionery shop with Henry Terrass in Lexington, on Mill near Short Street. Later Peter J. Robert was co-owner, then Giron became sole proprietor. He bought an interest in the house on Mill Street in 1818, and purchased another on the southwest side of Short so that the buildings joined in the rear, forming a right angle. From 1821 to 1824, the Lexington Juvenile Library was located in Giron's Short Street building. An 1829 deed book refers to a brick house on

Short Street used by Giron as a ballroom and supper room. The confectionery was sold in 1844, and the Girons may then have moved to Maysville, where Felicity, "wife of M. Giron," died in 1848 (Doty, *Confectionery of Monsieur Giron*, 12–21; Leavy, "Memoir of Lexington," Kentucky Historical *Register*, XLI, 132, 325; Clift [ed.], "Kentucky Marriages and Obituaries," *ibid.*, XL, 394; Wagers, *Education of a Gentleman*, 38).

[7] Horace Holley (1781–1827), Unitarian minister and educator, was born in Connecticut, attended Williams College, and was graduated from Yale in 1803. After briefly studying law, he returned to Yale to study theology. He was a pastor in Fairfield and Boston until appointed third president and professor of mental philosophy at Transylvania in 1818. Under Holley's leadership, the college was reorganized, the curriculum improved, and the law and medical schools revived. Conflicts with local Presbyterians over control of the school led to his resignation in 1827 and he moved to New Orleans, where he hoped to found a new college. He had barely begun his work there when he suddenly died on a summer sea voyage (*DAB*; Wagers, *Education of a Gentleman*, 3–10). See 1:2, lxxviii for Davis' comment on Holley.

[8] Jesse Bledsoe, born in Virginia in 1776, was educated at Transylvania and was an outstanding classical scholar. He was a prominent lawyer and member of the Kentucky legislature, and in 1808 was appointed Kentucky secretary of state. A United States senator, 1813–15, he was a circuit judge and professor of common and statute law at Transylvania from 1822. He later became a minister and moved to Mississippi in 1833, then to Texas in 1835. He died in Nacogdoches in 1836 (*Biographical Encyclopaedia of Kentucky*, 52; *Catalogue of Transylvania University* [1823]). See 1:2, lxxviii for Davis' estimate of Bledsoe as a professor of law.

[9] Charles Caldwell (1772–1853) was born in North Carolina, obtained his M.D. (1796) at the University of Pennsylvania, where he later taught science. In 1819 he accepted an invitation to found the medical department at Transylvania and was "Professor of the Institutes and Teacher of Materia Medica." Acting as agent for Transylvania, he toured Europe (1821), purchasing books for the university library. In 1837 he became first professor at what was then the Louisville Medical Institute (now University of Louisville), a post he held until his retirement in 1849 (*DAB*; *Catalogue of Transylvania University* [1821]). See 1:2, lxxviii for mention of Caldwell by Davis.

[10] William H. Richardson, M.D., was a member of the medical faculty at Transylvania from 1817 until his death in 1845. Richardson received his training at the University of Pennsylvania medical school, and by 1815 was acting trustee at Transylvania. Professor of obstetrics and the diseases of women and children, he also served as dean of the faculty, 1821–22. In 1824 he was made a director of the Transylvania Botanic Garden Association; he died in Fayette County, Kentucky (Peter, *Transylvania University*, 15–16, 33–35, 110; Leavy, "Memoir of Lexington," Kentucky Historical *Register*, XLI, 120, 126; Jillson, "Bibliography of Lexington," *ibid.*, XLIV, 262; Clift [ed.], "Kentucky Marriages and Obituaries," *ibid.*, XL, 277). See 1:2, lxxviii for mention of Richardson by Davis.

[11] John Roche, a graduate of Trinity College, Dublin, was appointed to the faculty of Transylvania by Horace Holley as a tutor in Latin and Greek. By 1828 Roche was a professor in the ancient languages. He died at Transylvania, aged fifty-five, in 1849 (Sonne, *Liberal Kentucky*, 172; Ham, "Broadsides and Newspapers in the John M. McCalla Papers," Kentucky Historical *Register*, LIX, 62; Barrickman, "Marriages and Deaths," *ibid.*, L, 144). See 1:2, lxxvi for Davis' estimate of Roche.

[12] Richard H. Chinn, a lawyer, emigrated to Lexington from Carlisle, Pennsylvania, in the late 1780's. He was a private in Captain N. S. G. Hart's Lexington Light Infantry Company in the War of 1812, and was captured at the Battle of Raisin River. Chinn served on the Transylvania board, was a state representative from Fayette County in 1831, and a state senator, 1833–37. He later moved to New Orleans, where he also practiced law. He died in Tensas Parish in 1847 (Leavy, "Memoir of Lexington," Kentucky Historical *Register*, XLI, 339; Ham, "Broadsides and Newspapers in the John M. McCalla Papers," *ibid.*, LIX, 62; Clift [ed.], "Kentucky Marriages and Obituaries," *ibid.*, XL, 377; Peter, *Transylvania University*, 148, 154; Peter, *History of Fayette County*, 65–66, 420; Collins, *History of Kentucky*, II, 170; Clift, *Remember the Raisin!*, 192; Clift to McIntosh, February 2, 1970 [Jefferson Davis Association, Rice University, Houston]).

[13] Patrick Henry (1801–64), elder brother of Gustavus Adolphus Henry, was elected brigadier general of Tennessee militia in 1837 but moved to Mississippi in 1839. A lawyer, he served in the Mississippi legislature as a Whig representative from Madison County (1848, 1850), and lived in Brandon, Mississippi, from 1858 until his death (Henry, *History of the Henry Family*, 108–17; D. Rowland, *Official and Statistical Register, 1908*, p. 88).

[14] Waller B. Redd (1806–43) was in Davis' class at Transylvania and, according to one source, was Davis' closest friend at school (Wagers, *Education of a Gentleman*, 12). Redd's father was a carriage manufacturer in Lexington, and a "much esteemed citizen." Waller later served as state senator from Fayette County. He married Rebecca, daughter of a Revolutionary War veteran, Colonel William Allen, in 1831, and their six sons were all soldiers in the Confederate Army (*Catalogue of Transylvania University* [1824]; Conkwright [comp.], Redd family notes, October 1933 [Redd family file, The Filson Club, Louisville, Kentucky]; *Reminiscences of Richard Menefee Redd*, 28).

[15] Transylvania University, which Davis attended in 1823–24 (see 1:5, *n.* 8).

ABSTRACT

1:25

Monthly Conduct Report

U.S. Military Academy, March 31, 1825

Lists Cadet J. Davis as having committed five offenses during March.[1]

DS (NA, RG 94 Records of the Adjutant General's Office, Records Relating to the U.S. Military Academy, Monthly Conduct Reports, Entry 231), 2. Signed: "S. Thayer Lt Col Supnd Mil Acady."

[1] See Davis' record of delinquencies (1:116) for the types of offenses he committed during March.

ABSTRACT

Monthly Conduct Report 1:26

U.S. Military Academy, April 30, 1825

Lists Cadet Davis,[1] along with fifteen other cadets, as having "committed the greatest number of Offences" during April. Davis is charged with eleven infractions.[2]

DS (NA, RG 94 Records of the Adjutant General's Office, Records Relating to the U.S. Military Academy, Monthly Conduct Reports, Entry 231), 2. Signed: "S. Thayer Lt. Col Supnd Mil Acad."

[1] That the Davis here listed is Jefferson is made apparent by the muster rolls which list only one Davis as being enrolled at the Academy at the time.

[2] See 1:116 for a list of Davis' April delinquencies.

ABSTRACT

Monthly Conduct Report 1:27

U.S. Military Academy, May 31, 1825

Lists Cadet Davis as having committed one offense during May.[1]

DS (NA, RG 94 Records of the Adjutant General's Office, Records Relating to the U.S. Military Academy, Monthly Conduct Reports, Entry 231), 2. Signed: "S. Thayer Lt Col Supnd Mil Acady."

[1] The Record of Delinquencies (1:116) agrees in charging Davis with one offense during May.

ABSTRACT

Consolidated Monthly Conduct Report 1:28

U.S. Military Academy, June 26, 1825

Lists Cadet Davis as having committed twenty-five offenses during the period from July 1, 1824, to June 26, 1825.[1]

DS (NA, RG 94 Records of the Adjutant General's Office, Records Relating to the U.S. Military Academy, Monthly Conduct Reports, Entry 231), 2. Signed: "S. Thayer Lt Col Supnd Mil Acady."

[1] Compare Davis' record of delinquencies (1:116) which charges him with twenty-eight offenses for the same period of time.

ABSTRACT

1:29
Merit Roll

[U.S. Military Academy,] June [30,] 1825

Ranks Cadet Davis forty-third out of seventy-one members of the fourth class[1] in mathematics, and eighteenth out of seventy-one members of the fourth class in French.[2]

D (NA, RG 94 Records of the Adjutant General's Office, Records Relating to the U.S. Military Academy, Merit Rolls, Entry 230), 5.

[1] See 1:18, *n.* 3 for a discussion of the West Point class system.

[2] An example of the tests taken by the cadets at the Military Academy in June 1825 is printed in the *American State Papers*, Class V, Military Affairs, III, 150–51.

ABSTRACT

1:30
Yearly Merit Roll

U.S. Military Academy, June [30,] 1825

Ranks Cadet Davis thirty-second out of seventy-one members of the fourth class,[1] with 103 merits in mathematics and 83 merits in French, for a total of 186.[2]

DS (NA, RG 94 Records of the Adjutant General's Office, Records Relating to the U.S. Military Academy, Merit Rolls, Entry 230), 5. Signed: "S. Thayer Lt Col Supnd Mil Acady."

[1] See 1:18, *n.* 3 for an explanation of the West Point class system.

[2] According to paragraph 1367 of army regulations, "The relative importance of the studies in each particular class (excepting the 1st,) in forming the general merit-roll of that class, shall be specifically determined by the academic board . . . ." For the first class the board determined as follows: "*Conduct* 3; *Engineering and the science of war* 3; *Mathematics* 3; *Natural Philosophy* 3; *Practical Military Instruction* 2; *Chemistry and Mineralogy* 2; *Geography, History, and Ethics* 2; *French* 1; *Drawing* 1." The board further determined that "in forming the general merit-rolls of the 2d, 3d, and 4th classes, the subjects of each course shall have weight as follows: 2d class–*Philosophy* 3; *Chemistry* 1; *Drawing* 1. 3d. class–*Mathematics* 3; *French* 1; *Drawing* ½. 4th class–*Mathematics* 2; *French Language* 1" (*General Regulations of the Army* [1825], 378).

ABSTRACT

Semiannual Muster Roll of the Corps of Cadets 1:31

West Point, New York, June 30, 1825

Lists Jefferson Davis of Mississippi, fourth class,[1] United States Military Academy, Corps of Cadets commanded by Major William J. Worth,[2] as being age eighteen years,[3] and as present at the post.

DS (NA, RG 94 Records of the Adjutant General's Office, Records Relating to the U.S. Military Academy, Semiannual Muster Rolls of Cadets, Entry 227), 8; DS (U.S. Military Academy Archives). Signed: "Chs. F. Smith Adjt. of Corps W. J Worth Maj Com[mandin]g & Must[erin]g Off. Countersigned S. Thayer Lt Col Comdg Supnd Mil Acady."

1 See 1:18, *n.* 3 for a discussion of the West Point class system.

2 William J. Worth (sketch, 1:14, *n.* 1).

3 Davis' age is figured from the year 1807. See 1:1, *n.* 1 for a discussion of the problem of Davis' year of birth.

ABSTRACT

Roll of Cadets[1] 1:32

West Point, New York, July 1, 1825

Lists Cadet Jefferson Davis, of Woodville,[2] Wilkinson County, Mississippi, third class,[3] as admitted to the Academy September 1, 1824,[4] at the age of seventeen years, two months, and as presently eighteen years of age.[5] His parent is recorded as Mrs. Jane Davis[6] of Woodville, Wilkinson County, Mississippi.

DS (NA, RG 94 Records of the Adjutant General's Office, Records Relating to the U.S. Military Academy, Rolls of Cadets, filed with Entry 227), 9. Signed: "S. Thayer Lt Col Supnd Mil Acady."

1 Save for the fact that Davis' age and class are adjusted as he grows older, the subsequent rolls of cadets afford substantially the same information and have therefore been omitted.

2 See 1:22, *n.* 5 for Woodville.

3 See 1:18, *n.* 3 for an explanation of the West Point class system.

4 See 1:14, *n.* 2 for a discussion of the date Davis entered West Point.

5 Davis' age is figured from 1807. See 1:1, *n.* 1 for a discussion of the problem concerning the birth date of Davis.

6 Jane Cook Davis (sketch, 1:22, *n.* 4; 1:Appendix IV, Entry 14).

ABSTRACT

1:33 **Orders No. 87**

West Point, July 14, 1825

Cadet Jefferson Davis has "leave of absence" [1] until July 20 when he "will report himself at this post for duty." By order of Major Worth[2] H. H. GIRD[3]

Lieutenant and Adjutant.

LbC, transcription from letterbook copy in the War Department (U.S. Military Academy Archives), 1.

[1] In all probability Davis' leave was granted so that he might be with his brother, Joseph E. Davis, and the William B. Howells, who visited Davis at West Point in the summer of 1825. See V. Davis, *Memoir*, I, 49–51 and 1:19 for Davis' notice of the proposed journey.

[2] William J. Worth (sketch, 1:14, *n.* 1).

[3] Henry H. Gird was born in New York and died at New Orleans. He was a cadet at the Military Academy, 1818 to 1822, when he was graduated and promoted to brevet second lieutenant. He served at West Point as assistant instructor of infantry tactics, 1822 to 1824, and as adjutant, 1824 to 1827. After resigning from the army in 1829, he became professor of mathematics and natural philosophy at the College of Louisiana and ultimately was made president of the same institution. He was employed in the United States Branch Mint when he died in 1845, at the age of forty-four (Cullum, *Biographical Register*, I, 286).

1:34 **Orders No. 95**

Editorial Note: On Sunday, July 31, Davis and four other cadets were discovered by Captain E. A. Hitchcock at Benny Havens', "a public house or place where spirituous liquors [were] sold" (1:36), located some two miles from West Point. Arrested the next day, as the following order indicates, they were tried by a general court martial which, sitting at the time of their arrest, had been reconvened on July 30 "for the trial of such prisoners as [might] be brought before it" (Orders No. 62, July 22, 1825 [NA, RG 153, Court Martial Records, H–61, 1825]).

U. S. Military Academy, West Point, 1st. August 1825

Cadets J. Davis, Meade,[1] Allison,[2] Hays,[3] & Swift,[4] charged with violating several of the prohibitions contained in the 1408th.[5] and 1415[6] paragraphs of the general army Regulations, are hereby arrested. By order of Mayor Worth[7] H. H. GIRD[8]

Lt. and Adjt.

LbC, transcription from letterbook copy in the War Department (U.S. Military Academy Archives).

[1] Theophilus Mead, son of Richard K. Mead of Brunswick County, Virginia, entered the Academy on either September 1, 1821 (Semiannual Muster Roll of Cadets, June 30, 1825 [NA, RG 94, Records Relating to the U.S. Military Academy, Entry 227]), or September 14, 1821 (Roll of Cadets, July 1, 1825 [NA, RG 94, Records Relating to the U.S. Military Academy, Rolls of Cadets, filed with Entry 227]). Mead, like Davis, appears to have entered later than September 1, but unlike Davis, in Mead's case the records indicate some possible irregularity. He was "dismissed" by a general court martial September 3, 1825 (Monthly Conduct Report, November 30, 1825 [NA, RG 94, Records Relating to the U.S. Military Academy, Entry 231]).

[2] James Allison, son of Mrs. Matilda Allison of Carthage, Smith County, Tennessee, entered the Academy on July 1, 1822 (Roll of Cadets, July 1, 1825 [NA, RG 94, Records Relating to the U.S. Military Academy, Rolls of Cadets, filed with Entry 227]), and was "discharged" August 4, to take effect December 27, 1825 (Monthly Conduct Report, September 30, 1825 [NA, RG 94, Records Relating to the U.S. Military Academy, Entry 231]).

[3] Samuel J. Hays, son of Jane Donelson Hays (James, *Andrew Jackson*, 371) of Jackson, Madison County, Tennessee, and ward and nephew of Andrew Jackson, entered the Academy on July 1, 1823 (Roll of Cadets, July 1, 1825 [NA, RG 94, Records Relating to the U.S. Military Academy, Rolls of Cadets, filed with Entry 227]), and, after having been absent without leave (Muster Roll of the Corps of Cadets, April 30, 1826 [U.S. Military Academy Archives]), "Resigned to take effect the 30th. of June 1826" (Semiannual Muster Roll of Cadets, June 30, 1826 [NA, RG 94, Records Relating to the U.S. Military Academy, Entry 227]).

[4] James F. Swift of Wilmington, North Carolina, son of General Joseph G. Swift of Brooklyn, New York, entered the Academy on July 1, 1821 (Roll of Cadets, July 1, 1825 [NA, RG 94, Records Relating to the U.S. Military Academy, Rolls of Cadets, filed with Entry 227]), and was dismissed from the service by sentence of a general court martial September 3, 1825 (Monthly Conduct Report, November 30, 1825 [NA, RG 94, Records Relating to the U.S. Military Academy, Entry 231]). General Swift, first graduate of the Military Academy, was, as commandant of the Corps of Engineers, the ex officio superintendent of the Military Academy (1812–17) and at the time of his son's dismissal held the politically important post of surveyor of the United States revenue for the port of New York (Cullum, *Biographical Register*, I, 51–56).

[5] Paragraph 1408 provided: "No cadet shall drink, nor shall bring or cause to be brought, into either barracks or camp, nor shall have in his room or otherwise in his possession, wine, porter, or any other spirituous or intoxicating liquor; nor shall go to any inn, public house, or place where any of those liquors are sold, without permission from the superintendent, on pain of being dismissed the service of the United States" (*General Army Regulations* [1825], 384).

[6] Paragraph 1415 stated that "No cadet shall go beyond the walls of West Point, or such other limits as may be prescribed" (*General Army Regulations* [1825], 385).

[7] William J. Worth (sketch, 1:14, *n.* 1).

[8] Henry H. Gird (sketch, 1:33, *n.* 3).

EXTRACT

1:35 # Proceedings of a General Court Martial—Third Day Trial of Theophilus Mead

Editorial Note: Theophilus Mead, the first of the five cadets to be tried for having violated the rules of the Academy by going to Benny Havens', was brought before the court martial on the third day of its session. The first two days were concerned with the trial of Peter Radcliff—a cadet, unconnected with the incident at Havens', who had overstayed his leave and who, when he did return to the Point, compounded his fault by returning visibly and noisily drunk. Toward the close of the third day's session, Davis, who had been called as a witness for the defense, testified as to whether or not Cadet Mead drank any ardent spirits during the "frolic" [1] at Benny Havens'.

West Point, New York August 2d. 1825

The Court met pursuant to adjournment.

Present.

Brevet Maj. Worth,[2] President.

Members.

Capt. Legate[3] Capt. Hitchcock[5]
Lieut. Lowd[4] Lieut. Kinsley[6]
Lieut. C. G. Smith,[7] Supernumerary member.
Lieut. H. H. Gird,[8] Special Judge advocate

Absent.

Lieut. Webster[9]—Member.
Lieut. Ross,[10] Supernumerary member. . . .

Cadet Jefferson Davis, of the U. S. Mil. Acad. a witness for the defence, being duly sworn, answers as follows:

Ques. by Pris. Did you see me drink ardent spirits[11] on the 31st of July, 1825, at Mr. Havens',[12] or at any other place?

Ans. No. I did not.

Ques. by Pris. Have you any reason to believe that I made use of ardent spirits on the day specified?

Ans. I have reason to believe that he did not drink any.

Ques. by J. Adv. Had the prisoner no opportunity of drinking spirituous liquor without being observed by you, on the 31st July, 1825?

Ans. He could have done it.

Ques. by Prest. of Ct. Were you in company with the prisoner on Sunday last? If so–state the time when–and where?

Ans. I was in company with him part of that day. I cannot answer further without criminating myself.

Ques. by Prest. of Ct. What opportunities had you of judging whether the prisoner did or did not use intoxicating liquor?

Ans. I saw him frequently. Besides I know it is contrary to his habits.

Ques. by a Mem. Have you been frequently in company with the accused, and do you know whether he has refused, <–liquors–> to drink liquor?

Ans. I have been intimately acquainted with him ever since I have been a Cadet. I have never known him to drink spirits, but whenever I have seen it presented to him he has refused it.

DS (NA, RG 153 Records of the Office of the Judge Advocate General [Army], Court Martial Records, H–61, 1825), 90.

[1] The word "frolic" is used advisedly, for Mrs. Davis, in describing a similar occasion, said that Davis and a fellow cadet "went down to Bennie Havens's on a little frolic" (*Memoir*, I, 52).

[2] William J. Worth (sketch, 1:14, *n.* 1).

[3] Thomas C. Legate, captain in the Artillery Corps, was born in Massachusetts and entered the army in 1812. He became a captain in 1820, was brevetted major in 1830, and resigned in 1836 (Heitman, *Historical Register*, I, 626). See Davis to Jones, August 8, 1882 (D. Rowland, *Papers*, IX, 185), for Davis' reference to Legate as a close friend. See also 1:291 for their association at Dubuques Mines.

[4] Allen Lowd was born in Massachusetts and appointed second lieutenant of the Corps of Artillery on May 1, 1814. Ultimately he was brevetted major (May 9, 1846) for gallant conduct in the defense of Fort Brown, Texas. He died in 1854 (Heitman, *Historical Register*, I, 644).

[5] Ethan Allen Hitchcock (1798–1870) was born in and appointed to the Military Academy from Vermont. Son of Samuel Hitchcock, a United States circuit judge, and grandson of the Revolutionary patriot Ethan Allen, he entered the Military Academy at the age of sixteen and was graduated in 1817. From 1824 to 1827 he acted as assistant instructor of infantry tactics at the Academy and later (1829–33) as the commandant of cadets. He rose by the usual stages to the rank of lieutenant colonel (1842) and was brevetted brigadier general during the Mexican War for gallant and meritorious conduct in the Battle of Molino del Rey. Hitchcock resigned in 1855 and wrote several monographs on literature and philosophy. In the Civil War, he was appointed major general of volunteers and served as commissioner for exchange of prisoners of war and finally as commissary general of prisoners of war (*DAB*; Cullum, *Biographical Register*, I, 167–79). Davis' and Hitchcock's careers crossed a number of times and the results were not always pleasant. In addition to the episode at Benny Havens', Hitchcock discovered Davis and others in another rather serious infraction of the rules. In December of

1826 and prior to the beginning of the "Eggnog Riot," Davis and a number of his friends were discovered by Hitchcock surreptitiously preparing and drinking eggnog (see 1:68, *n.* 3 for a further discussion of Davis' involvement). Whether or not any lasting animosity developed as a consequence of these two rather unpleasant encounters is unknown, but the fact that Davis and Hitchcock did quarrel at a later date is a matter of record. In contrast, see 1:2, lxxviii for Davis' statement that Captain Hitchcock had met his family when on recruiting duty at Natchez—a statement made probable by the fact that Hitchcock was earlier stationed (1821–23) in the area of Davis' home (Cullum, *Biographical Register*, I, 168)—and that when Davis arrived at West Point too late to be legally admitted, it was due to Hitchcock's influence that he was permitted to take his admission examination.

[6] Zebina J. D. Kinsley was born and died in New York. Appointed in 1814 to the Military Academy, he was graduated in 1819 and served in various posts in New England until 1820 when he was made assistant instructor of infantry tactics at the Academy. In 1835 he resigned from the army and from 1838 until his death in 1849 was the principal of a "Classical and Mathematical School" located near West Point (Cullum, *Biographical Register*, I, 211). Called "Old Detestation" by the cadets for his zeal in enforcing the Academy regulations (T. J. Fleming, *West Point*, 54), Kinsley seems to have incurred the particular dislike of Davis. According to Mrs. Davis, "One of the professors [Kinsley], at sight, had taken a great dislike to Cadet Davis. . . . The professor tried to entrap the boy into errors in recitation, and he, in turn, endeavored to find an opportunity to 'get even' with the man in authority. One day the professor was giving a lecture on presence of mind being one of the cardinal qualities needful for a soldier. He looked directly at his young enemy and said he doubted not that there were many who, in an emergency, would be confused and unstrung, not from cowardice, but from the mediocre nature of their minds. . . . A few days afterward, while the building was full of cadets, the class were being taught the process of making fire-balls, and one took fire. [T. J. Fleming, *ibid.*, 54, says that Davis lit the fuse of the grenade himself.] The room was a magazine of explosives. Cadet Davis saw it first, and calmly asked of the doughty instructor, 'What shall I do, sir? This fire-ball is ignited.' The professor said, 'Run for your lives,' and ran for his. Cadet Davis threw it out of the window and saved the building and a large number of lives thereby" (*Memoir*, I, 52–53).

[7] Charles G. Smith was born in Connecticut and died in 1827 at the age of twenty-nine at Fort Moultrie, South Carolina. A cadet at the Military Academy from 1818 to 1822, he was graduated and promoted in the army to second lieutenant on July 1, 1822. After having served in garrison at Fort Moultrie and Fortress Monroe, Virginia, he was appointed assistant instructor of infantry tactics at West Point in 1825 (Cullum, *Biographical Register*, I, 278–79).

[8] Henry H. Gird (sketch, 1:33, *n.* 3).

[9] Horace Webster (1794–1871), cadet at the Military Academy from 1815 to 1818, was born in Vermont and died at Geneva, New York. Shortly after taking part in the above court martial proceedings, he resigned his position as principal assistant professor of mathematics at West Point, and after serving as professor of mathematics and natural philosophy at Geneva College, New York, became the principal of the Free Academy, later the College of the City of New York (Cullum, *Biographical Register*, I, 187).

[10] Edward C. Ross, a cadet at the Military Academy from 1817 to 1821, was born in Pennsylvania. After graduation, he served until 1833 both as the

assistant professor and as the principal assistant professor of mathematics at the Academy. Resigning from the army in 1839, he was appointed professor of mathematics at Kenyon College in 1840, and later professor of mathematics and natural philosophy at the Free Academy in New York City, where he died in 1851, aged fifty (Cullum, *Biographical Register*, I, 268–69).

11 Although we cannot know for sure, Davis may be using an old cadet trick by which they tried to escape incriminating one another. When they drank together, they drank with their faces turned away from one another so that if called upon to testify whether such a one drank or not, they could say that "they had not 'seen' Cadet So-and-So drinking" (T. J. Fleming, *West Point*, 57).

12 Benny Havens, a veteran of the War of 1812, began his career as a tavern keeper sometime between 1822 and 1824, and remained, in spite of official displeasure, a West Point tradition until his death in 1877. His home and tavern were located on the shore of the Hudson River some two miles from the Point—a distance that made his place all the more attractive to the cadets since it was less likely to be checked by officers than other, closer establishments (T. J. Fleming, *West Point*, 55; Latrobe, *Reminiscences of West Point*, 27; Church, *Reminiscences*, 19). Although cadets were forbidden to visit Benny Havens', they frequently did and in addition memorialized Benny and his establishment in a seemingly endless song of doggerel verse:

"To our comrades who have fallen,
one cup before we go,
They poured their lifeblood freely
out *pro bono* publico;
No marble points the stranger to
where they rest below,
They lie neglected far away from
Benny Havens Oh!"

(W. L. Fleming, "Davis at West Point," Mississippi Historical *Publications*, X, 263).

EXTRACT

Proceedings of a General Court Martial—Fourth Day Trial of Theophilus Mead and Jefferson Davis 1:36

Editorial Note: On the fourth day of the court martial, the cases of Radcliff and Mead were continued. Davis was recalled in the Mead case in order to testify to his understanding of what was meant by the term "ardent spirits." Later in the course of the day's proceedings the cases of Hays, Allison, and Davis were begun. Davis' testimony has been extracted.

West Point, New York August 3d. 1825

The Court met persuant to adjournment.

Present.

Brevet Maj. Worth,[1] President.

Members.

Capt. Legate,[2]	Capt. Hitchcock[4]
Lieut. Lowd,[3]	Lieut. Kinsley[5]

Lieut. C. G. Smith,[6] Supernumerary member.
Lieut. H. H. Gird,[7] Special Judge advocate.

Absent.

Lieut. Webster,[8] member.
Lieut. Ross,[9] Supernumerary member. . . .

Cadet J. Davis (before examined) called by the Court for some explanation of his former testimony, answers as follows:

Ques. by the Court. You have stated in your former testimony that the prisoner[10] did not use in your presence ardent spirits or intoxicating liquor; now state what kind of liquor or beverage was drank by the prisoner during the time you were with him on Sunday?

Ans. I believe the prisoner drank cider and I believe the prisoner drank <—wine—> porter,[11] which, of course I did not understand to be spirituous liquors. . . .

Cadet Jefferson Davis, of the U. S. M. Acad. a prisoner for trial, being asked if he had any objection to any of the members of the Court, replied in the negative.

Capt. Hitchcock, being in his place, then objected to himself as in the case of Cadet Mead, and the Court decided to excuse Capt. Hitchcock from sitting in this case.[12]

The vacancy thus occasioned was supplied by the Supernumerary member Lt. Smith, to whom the prisoner declined making any objection, and the Court was duly sworn.

The prisoner objected to being tried on <the>[13] charges preferred against him, because the new Regulations were to him in the nature of an *ex post facto* law,[14] having never been published to his corps.

The Court in secret session decided that the charges were in due form.

The prisoner was then arraigned on the following charges, prefered by order of his Comdg offr. Maj. Worth, viz:

Charge 1st. Violating the 1415th paragraph of the General army Regulations.

Specification. In this—that the said Cadet Davis, did, on Sunday, the 31st of July, 1825, <—at some place in the vicinity of West Point,—> go beyond the limits prescribed to Cadets at West-Point, without permission.

Charge 2d. Violating the 1408th paragraph of the General army Regulations.

Specification 1st. In this—that the said Cadet Davis, on Sunday the

Benny Havens' Tavern

Drawing of a warrior by Jefferson Davis

31st of July, 1825, at some place in the vicinity of West Point, did drink spirituous and intoxicating liquor.

Specification 2d. In this—that the said Cadet Davis, on Sunday the 31st of July, 1825, did go to a public house or place where spirituous liquors are sold, kept by one Benjamin Havens,[15] at or near Buttermilk Falls,[16] and distant about two miles from the Post of West-Point.

The prisoner pleaded—to the 1st Charge and its Specification—Guilty; to the 1st Spec. 2d Ch. not Guilty; to the 2d Spec. 2d Ch. Guilty; to the 2d Charge—Guilty of violating so much of the 1408th paragraph of the General army Regulations as prohibits going to a public house or place where liquors are sold, and not Guilty of the remainder.

Capt. Hitchcock, asst. Insr. of Tactics, U. S. Mil. Acad. a witness for the prosecution, being duly sworn, says: I saw the prisoner at the time specified about two miles from West-Point. He was in company with several Cadets (at a house kept I believe by Mr. Havens) all of whom except one appeared to be under the influence of spirituous liquor. I did not see Mr. Davis make use of any liquor, and judged that he had used it more perhaps from the circumstances in which I saw him than from either his conduct or appearance generally. On his perceiving me he exhibited extreme embarrassment bordering upon weakness. It might have proceeded from being found in the circumstances I stated—but <a part of it>[13] I attributed to the use of spirituous liquor. I did not observe him particularly; my attention was more drawn to the conduct of another one who was near him.

Ques. by Pris. Did said Cadet Davis appear to the witness to have used spirituous and intoxicating liquor?

Ans. There were some appearances of it. I have not a doubt of it.

Maj. Worth, Insr. of Tactics, a witness for the defence, being duly sworn, <—says:—> answers as follows:

Ques. by Pris. What has been my <—general—> conduct and general deportment since a Cadet?

Ans. The prisoner's conduct and general deportment to the best of my knowledge and belief has been marked by correct and strict attention to his duty, and he has not prior to the present accusation—committed any offence which called for animadversion. His deportment as a Gentleman has been unexceptionable.

Capt. Hitchcock, on the part of the defence, answers as follows:

Ques. by Pris. What has been my conduct and general deportment since a Cadet?

Ans. I am under the impression the prisoner's conduct and general deportment has been correct. I have observed nothing to the contrary prior to the matter which is now a subject of charge.

At the prisoner's request he was allowed until to-morrow morning at 9 o'clock to prepare his defence.

DS (NA, RG 153 Records of the Office of the Judge Advocate General [Army], Court Martial Records, H–61, 1825), 90.

1 William J. Worth (sketch, 1:14, *n.* 1).

2 Thomas C. Legate (sketch, 1:35, *n.* 3).

3 Allen Lowd (sketch, 1:35, *n.* 4).

4 Ethan Allen Hitchcock (sketch, 1:35, *n.* 5).

5 Zebina J. D. Kinsley (sketch, 1:35, *n.* 6).

6 Charles G. Smith (sketch, 1:35, *n.* 7).

7 Henry H. Gird (sketch, 1:33, *n.* 3).

8 Horace Webster (sketch, 1:35, *n.* 9).

9 Edward C. Ross (sketch, 1:35, *n.* 10).

10 The prisoner was Theophilus Mead (sketch, 1:34, *n.* 1).

11 Porter: short for porter's ale or beer. So called because it was originally made for or drunk chiefly by porters or other lower-class laborers (*OED*).

12 Captain Hitchcock objected to himself in Davis' case as he did in the cases of the other four cadets "on account of his having made the report on which the charges against the prisoner are founded, and because he (Capt. Hitchcock) will be the principal witness against the prisoner" (NA, RG 153, Court Martial Records, H–61, 1825, 20).

13 Interlined.

14 See 1:37, Davis' defense, for a more complete presentation of his contention that the new regulations were ex post facto. The old regulation under which Davis maintained he should be judged reads as follows: "Any cadet who shall play at cards, or any game of chance, or who shall, without permission, procure or use wine or spirituous liquors, or shall go to any inn or public house, shall be dismissed the service" (Paragraph 98, *Regulations of the Military Academy* [1823], 23). Compare with the newer regulation, 1:34, *n.* 5.

15 Benny Havens (sketch, 1:35, *n.* 12).

16 A cadet who entered the Academy in 1818 described the falls: "Buttermilk Falls was the limit of many a Saturday's walk from West Point. . . . The road to Buttermilk Falls was a rough one, turning aside somewhat in one place, to avoid what had been a small battery intended to command an approach to the main fortifications at the Point. Beyond the battery the road descended, and there was level ground on the left. . . . Continuing down the road . . . we reached the few houses that then formed the village of 'Buttermilk Falls.' The only house that I can now recall was a low, one-storied frame building, painted red, with white door and window trimmings, that overhung the river on the east, and, on the south, the ravine of the mountain stream, which, when there was water enough, fell in foam down the white-faced, sloping rock into the Hudson, producing the appearance that gave to the spot its name" (Latrobe, *Reminiscences of West Point*, 27).

4 AUGUST 1825

EXTRACT

Proceedings of a General Court Martial—Fifth Day Trial of Jefferson Davis 1:37

Editorial Note: On the fifth day of the court martial, the cases of Radcliff, Allison, Mead, and Davis were concluded with each presenting his defense.

West Point, New York August 4th, 1825

The Court met pursuant to adjournment.

Present.
Major Worth,[1] President.

Members.

Capt. Legate[2] Capt. Hitchcock[4]
Lieut Lowd[3] Lieut. Kinsley[5]
Lieut. C. G. Smith,[6] Supernumerary member.
Lieut. H. H. Gird,[7] Special Judge Advocate

Absent.
Lieut. Webster,[8] Member,
Lieut. Ross,[9] Supy. member. . . .

The Court then resumed the case of Cadet Davis who made the following Defence:

Mr. President & Gentlemen of the Court.

It is with feelings of the greatest embarassment that I address you, tried by laws which with respect to my knowledge have but just sprung into existence, since the deeds for which I am arraigned were done.

I conciede that (in the spirit of the term) these laws can be considered only as "expost facto" since i<'—n—>solated as we are from the rest of the world, orders can date their existence only from the time when published in the corps. The efficasey of these regulations then cannot be said to have commenced prior to our arrest, as we had no opportunity to know what they were, or had any order to obey them if perchance we had known them, as I before stated said laws must be held as "*ex post facto*" *laws*.[10]

Having plead guilty to the charge of leaving the post circumstances may perhaps in some degree justify the deed. it will be recollected that on the 31st. ultimo the rain was excessive, my tent was flooded[11] so that I could not remain in it with any satisfaction, the disperse bugle blew I met by chance with some of my friends who like myself were at a loss to know what to do, and all in want of comfortable shelter, thus urged by circumstances without premeditation wandered too far.

Haveing been further charged with using spirituous and intoxicating liquor, and mark what testimony to establish it, that I was seen in company with Cadets and the witness judged more from surrounding circumstances than my conduct that I had used spirituous liquor, was emberassed—perhaps the effect of Drinking, why this conclusion, the fact of being caught was certainly enough to have confused any Cadet, and it appears to me that this conclusion would have been far more immediate. I cannot believe that the Court would if previously acquainted with the circumstances have shown so little respect to my feelings as to have charged me (on such weak evidence) with conduct so contrary to principles of a soldier & a man of honor.

Having without due meditation plead guilty to the charge of visiting a public house and place where liquors are sold would wish here if in order to qualify so much as relates to calling B. Havens[12] a public house as I believe this cannot be established, admit liquors are sold at the place above mentioned, I think it a matter of the smallest importance as the construction which I would suppose was intended to be laid on this paragraph, was if a Cadet visited such a place and *bought* spirituous liquors, it could not have been for merely visiting such a place since the stores which we are allowed to visit do contain spirituous liquors and these liquors are sold. As no evidence has been produced to prove that we did procure or use spirituous liquor it matters not whether the storekeeper was obligated not to sell it or not under such obligation.

I do trust that the Court will bear in mind the maxim that it is better a hundred guilty should escape than one rightuous person be condemned, and on testimony so circumstantial shall confidentially look forward to an honorable acquital.

(signed) Jefferson Davis.

The Court was then cleared, and proceeded to <–set–> conclude the cases of Cadets Mead[13] & Davis. . . .

In the Case of Cadet Davis:

The Court after mature deliberation on the testimony adduced, find the prisoner Cadet Jefferson Davis, Guilty of both the 1st &

2d Charges preferred against him and their specifications. The Court sentence him to be dismissed from the service of the United States, but in consideration of his <—past—> <former>[14] good conduct <—respe—> <respectfully>[14] recommend the remission of said sentence.[15]

The Court adjourned to meet again to-morrow morning at half past nine o'clock.

DS (NA, RG 153 Records of the Office of the Judge Advocate General [Army], Court Martial Records, H–61, 1825), 90; D, typed copy, Davis' defense (Walter Lynwood Fleming Collection, New York Public Library). Signed: "H. H. Gird Lieut. & adjt. Spec[ial] Judge Advocate W. J Worth Major U S army President the Court." Transmitted: Macomb to Jones, October 11, 1825 (NA, RG 153 Records of the Office of the Judge Advocate General [Army], Court Martial Records, H–61, 1825).

[1] William J. Worth (sketch, 1:14, *n.* 1).

[2] Thomas C. Legate (sketch, 1:35, *n.* 3).

[3] Allen Lowd (sketch, 1:35, *n.* 4).

[4] Ethan Allen Hitchcock (sketch, 1:35, *n.* 5).

[5] Zebina J. D. Kinsley (sketch, 1:35, *n.* 6).

[6] Charles G. Smith (sketch, 1:35, *n.* 7).

[7] Henry H. Gird (sketch, 1:33, *n.* 3).

[8] Horace Webster (sketch, 1:35, *n.* 9).

[9] Edward C. Ross (sketch, 1:35, *n.* 10).

[10] See 1:34, *n.* 5 and 1:36, *n.* 14 for the regulations being discussed.

[11] Of the previous year's encampment, Church wrote: "My recollections of my first encampment appear to me quite vivid, and yet I call to mind nothing disagreeable, except the confinement and strict discipline. . . . We were encamped on the same spot now made so comfortable. Not a single shade tree near—not even sentry boxes for shelter in times of storm—no board floors, simply oil cloths to keep us from the dampness of the ground, a single ditch around the tent to drain the water" (*Reminiscences*, 16).

[12] Benny Havens (sketch, 1:35, *n.* 12).

[13] Theophilus Mead (sketch, 1:34, *n.* 1).

[14] Interlined.

[15] Contemporary notice of the results of this court martial is found in the journal of Samuel Peter Heintzelman, who, while a cadet, wrote, "The proceedings of the Court-Martials in the cases of several of the cadets came out this evening. Cadet R . . . ff [Radcliff] was tried for conduct unbecoming an Officer and Gentleman and dismissed the service, four more were tried for leaving the Post, going to a public house and drinking spirituous liquors and sentenced to be dismissed the service. Cadets H—s [Hays] and D . . s [Davis] were remitted on account of their former good conduct. Cadet Sw . . s [Swift's] is left for farther consideration and Cadet M—s [Mead's] is approved" (typescript in Virginia State Library, Richmond, 44–45).

EXTRACT

1:38

Alexander Macomb to Sir

SIR,[1] Engineer Department August 27. 1825

The proceedings of the General Court-Martial[2] of which Major Worth[3] is President, and before which was tried Cadets Peter A Radcliff,[4] Theophilus Mead,[5] Saml J Hays,[6] Jefferson Davis, James Allison[7] and James F Swift,[8] have been handed to me by Major Vandeventer,[9] with your decision thereon, except in the case of Swift, which was not acted upon for the want of the necessary information with regard to his standing &c &c.... I have the honor to be With perfect respect Sir, Your most ob st AL. MACOMB[10]

M[ajor] G[eneral] Ch[ief] Eng[ineer].

LS (NA, RG 94 Records of the Adjutant General's Office, Records Relating to the U.S. Military Academy, Letters Relating to the Military Academy, Entry 210), 4; LbC (NA, RG 77 Records of the Office of the Chief of Engineers, Miscellaneous Letters Sent, II, 393–94).

1 "Sir" was Secretary of War James Barbour (NA, RG 77, Miscellaneous Letters Sent, II, 393–94).

2 See 1:35–37 for the proceedings of the general court martial.

3 William J. Worth (sketch, 1:14, *n.* 1).

4 Peter A. Radcliff (1:35, Editorial Note).

5 Theophilus Mead (sketch, 1:34, *n.* 1).

6 Samuel J. Hays (sketch, 1:34, *n.* 3).

7 James Allison (sketch, 1:34, *n.* 2).

8 James F. Swift (sketch, 1:34, *n.* 4).

9 Christopher Van De Venter (also Van Deventer) was born in New York in 1789. From 1808 to 1809 he was a cadet at the Military Academy and after graduation served as a second lieutenant in a number of Atlantic posts. A veteran of the War of 1812, he was assistant adjutant general, 1815–16, and General Joseph E. Swift's aide in 1816. He resigned from the army, and in 1817 was appointed chief clerk in the War Department, where he became a friend of John C. Calhoun. Van De Venter rented "Oakley," Calhoun's Georgetown residence in July 1826, but left Washington after he was fired from his clerkship in February 1827. He moved to Buffalo and entered business, then returned to Washington, where he died in 1838 (Cullum, *Biographical Register*, I, 91; Whitehill, *Dumbarton Oaks*, 41–45).

10 Alexander Macomb (1782–1841) was born at Detroit. A veteran of the War of 1812, he rose in the ranks until he became the commanding general of the United States Army in 1828, a position which he continued to fill until his death in 1841. Macomb was one of the first student officers to complete the course of instruction at West Point and later was one of those, along with Peter B. Porter, the secretary of war, responsible for the abolition of the whiskey ration in 1830. Writer as well as soldier, he authored *A Treatise On Martial Law and Courts-Martial* (Charleston, 1809), and later in his life, *The Practice of Courts Martial* (New York, 1840). He died in Washington (*DAB*).

EXTRACT

Military Academy Orders No. 19 1:39

Engineer Department Washington August 29th 1825

At the general Court Martial,[1] of which Major W. J. Worth,[2] of the 1st regiment of artillery is President, first convened at West Point, in the State of New York, by virtue of Orders No 41 issued by the Adjutant General[3] of the Army on the 19th of May 1825, and reconvened by virtue of Orders No. 62 [4] issued by the same officer on the 22d of July last, which Court commenced its session under the second convention on the 30th of July and continued it by adjournment to the 8th of August last, was tried . . . . Cadet Jefferson Davis on the following charges and specifications, viz;

Charge 1st. Violating the 1415th paragraph[5] of the general army regulations.

Specification. In this, that the said Cadet Davis did on Sunday the 31st July 1825 go beyond the limits prescribed to Cadets, at West Point, without permission.

Charge 2d. Violating the 1408th paragraph[6] of the general army regulations.

Specification. In this, that the said Cadet Davis on Sunday the 31st July 1825, at some place in the vicinity of West Point, did drink spirituous and intoxicating liquor

Specification 2d. In this, that the said Cadet Davis on Sunday the 31st July 1825 did go to a public house or place where sperituous liquors are sold, kept by one Benjamin Havens,[7] at or near Buttermilk Falls,[8] and distant about two miles from the post of West Point.

The prisoner pleaded to the 1st Charge and its specification guilty; to the 1st spec. 2d Ch. not guilty; to the 2d Spec 2d Ch. guilty; to the 2d Charge guilty of violating so much of the 1408th paragraph of the general army regulations as prohibits going to a public house or place where liquors are sold, and not guilty of the remainder.

The Court after mature deliberation on the testimony adduced find the prisoner Cadet Jefferson Davis guilty of both the 1st and 2d charges preferred against him, and their specifications. The Court Sentence him to be dismissed from the Service of the United States; but in consideration of his former good conduct respectfully recommend the remission of said sentence.[9] . . .

The foregoing proceedings are approved. Cadets Radcliff[10] and

Mead[11] are dismissed accordingly. Cadets Hays[12] and Davis, in consideration of the recommendation of the general Court Martial, are pardoned; and will return to their duty. The case of Cadet Swift[13] is suspended for further consideration. By order of the Secretary of War.[14] AL. MACOMB[15]

Majr Genl Inspector of the Mily. Acdy.

DS (NA, RG 153 Records of the Office of the Judge Advocate General [Army], Court Martial Records, H–61, 1825), 10; LbC (NA, RG 94 Records of the Adjutant General's Office, Records Relating to the U.S. Military Academy, Academy Orders, 1814–67, I, 84–87); LbC, transcription from letterbook copy in the War Department (U.S. Military Academy Archives).

1 See 1:35–37 for the proceedings of the general court martial.

2 William J. Worth (sketch, 1:14, *n.* 1).

3 The adjutant general was Roger Jones (sketch, 1:123, *n.* 6).

4 See Editorial Note, 1:34 for mention of Orders No. 62.

5 See 1:34, *n.* 6 for paragraph 1415 of army regulations.

6 See 1:34, *n.* 5 for paragraph 1408 of army regulations.

7 Benny Havens (sketch, 1:35, *n.* 12).

8 See 1:36, *n.* 16 for a description of Buttermilk Falls.

9 See 1:37 for the disposition of Davis' case.

10 Peter Radcliff (1:35, Editorial Note).

11 Theophilus Mead (sketch, 1:34, *n.* 1).

12 Samuel J. Hays (sketch, 1:34, *n.* 3).

13 James F. Swift (sketch, 1:34, *n.* 4).

14 The secretary of war was James Barbour.

15 Alexander Macomb (sketch, 1:38, *n.* 10).

ABSTRACT

1:40

Monthly Return

West Point, New York, August 31, 1825

Lists Cadet J. Davis "Present. In Arrest." [1]

DS (U.S. Military Academy Archives), 2. Signed: "H. H. Gird, Lieut. & Adjt. S. Thayer Lt Col Supnd Mil Acady Comdg."

1 See 1:34 for evidence of Davis' arrest on August 1, 1825.

ABSTRACT

1:41

Muster Roll of the Corps of Cadets

West Point, New York, August 31, 1825

Lists Jefferson Davis, United States Military Academy, Corps of

31 OCTOBER 1825

Cadets commanded by Major William J. Worth,[1] as present at the post. Remarks: "In arrest." [2]

DS (U.S. Military Academy Archives), 11. Signed: "A. S. Johnston Adjt. of Corps W. J Worth Maj Com[mandin]g & Mustering & Insp[ectin]g Offr."

[1] William J. Worth (sketch, 1:14, *n.* 1).

[2] See 1:34 for evidence of Davis' arrest.

ABSTRACT

Monthly Conduct Report 1:42

U.S. Military Academy, September 30, 1825

Lists Cadet J. Davis as having committed four offenses during September,[1] and being punished for "violation of 1408 & 1415 par Army Regs" [2] on July 31. Remarks: "Sentenced by genl. ct. martl. to be dismissed the service. Sentence remitted on recommendation of the court." [3]

DS (NA, RG 94 Records of the Adjutant General's Office, Records Relating to the U.S. Military Academy, Monthly Conduct Reports, Entry 231), 2. Signed: "S. Thayer Lt Col Comdg."

[1] Compare Davis' record of delinquencies (1:116) for the month of September 1825, which conforms to the above and lists him as having committed four offenses during the month.

[2] See 1:34, *nn.* 5, 6 for the provisions of paragraphs 1408 and 1415.

[3] See 1:37, p. 41 for Davis' sentence and its remission.

ABSTRACT

Monthly Conduct Report 1:43

U.S. Military Academy, October 31, 1825

Lists Cadet J. Davis as having committed two offenses during October.[1]

DS (NA, RG 94 Records of the Adjutant General's Office, Records Relating to the U.S. Military Academy, Monthly Conduct Reports, Entry 231), 2. Signed: "S. Thayer Lt Col Supndt."

[1] See 1:116 for confirmation of the fact that Davis committed two offenses during October.

ABSTRACT

1:44
Muster Roll of the Corps of Cadets

West Point, New York, October 31, 1825

Lists Jefferson Davis, United States Military Academy, Corps of Cadets commanded by Major William J. Worth,[1] as present at the post.

DS (U.S. Military Academy Archives), 10. Signed: "John B. Grayson Acting Adjt of the Corps W. J Worth Maj Comd Corps."

[1] William J. Worth (sketch, 1:14, *n.* 1).

ABSTRACT

1:45
Monthly Conduct Report

U.S. Military Academy, November 30, 1825

Lists Cadet J. Davis as having committed one offense during November.[1]

DS (NA, RG 94 Records of the Adjutant General's Office, Records Relating to the U.S. Military Academy, Monthly Conduct Reports, Entry 231), 2. Signed: "S. Thayer Lt Col Suprd Mil Acady."

[1] The Record of Delinquencies (1:116) lists Davis as having committed six offenses during November.

ABSTRACT

1:46
Monthly Conduct Report

U.S. Military Academy, December 31, 1825

Lists Cadet J. Davis as having committed one offense during December.[1]

DS (NA, RG 94 Records of the Adjutant General's Office, Records Relating to the U.S. Military Academy, Monthly Conduct Reports, Entry 231), 2. Signed: "S. Thayer Lt Col Supnd Mil Acady."

[1] The Record of Delinquencies (1:116) lists Davis as having committed three offenses during December and not, as stated above, one.

ABSTRACT

Semiannual Muster Roll of the Corps of Cadets 1:47

West Point, New York, December 31, 1825

Lists Jefferson Davis of Mississippi, third class,[1] United States Military Academy, Corps of Cadets commanded by Major William J. Worth,[2] as being eighteen years, six months,[3] and as present at the post.

DS (NA, RG 94 Records of the Adjutant General's Office, Records Relating to the U.S. Military Academy, Semiannual Muster Rolls of Cadets, Entry 227), 10; DS (U.S. Military Academy Archives). Signed: "A. S. Johnston Adj Corps E A Hitchcock Capt Com[mandin]g Corps App[rove]d S. Thayer Lt Col Supnd Mil Acady."

[1] See 1:18, *n.* 3 for a discussion of the class system at West Point.

[2] William J. Worth (sketch, 1:14, *n.* 1).

[3] Davis' age is figured from 1807. See 1:1, *n.* 1 for a discussion of the problem of Davis' birth year.

ABSTRACT

Monthly Conduct Report 1:48

U.S. Military Academy, January 31, 1826

Lists Cadet J. Davis and 72 other cadets out of a total of 237 as "distinguished for Correct Conduct" during January.[1]

DS (NA, RG 94 Records of the Adjutant General's Office, Records Relating to the U.S. Military Academy, Monthly Conduct Reports, Entry 231), 2. Signed: "S. Thayer Lt Col Comdg."

[1] See 1:116 for confirmation of the fact that Davis had no offenses during January 1826.

ABSTRACT

Merit Roll 1:49

U.S. Military Academy, January [31,] 1826

Ranks Cadet Jefferson Davis at the general examination given in January 1826 as thirty-fourth out of fifty-three members of the third class[1] in mathematics, sixteenth out of fifty-three members of the third class in French, and twenty-third out of fifty-four members of the third class in drawing.

D (NA, RG 94 Records of the Adjutant General's Office, Records Relating to the U.S. Military Academy, Merit Rolls, Entry 230), 6; D, copy, transcription from letterbook copy in the War Department (U.S. Military Academy Archives).

[1] See 1:18, *n.* 3 for an explanation of the West Point class system.

ABSTRACT

1:50 ## Monthly Return

West Point, New York, January 31, 1826

Lists Cadet Davis[1] as being present and sick.

DS (U.S. Military Academy Archives), 2. Signed: "H. H. Gird, Lieut. & adjt. S. Thayer Lt Col Comdg."

[1] The Davis here mentioned is probably Jefferson but may be John P. Davis, who entered the Academy on July 1, 1825. Although it is impossible to know positively, the fact that John P. Davis is usually referred to by his full name or as J. P. Davis is perhaps suggestive that, in this case at least, it is Jefferson and not John who is listed as being ill (Semiannual Muster Roll, December 31, 1825 [NA, RG 94, Records Relating to the U.S. Military Academy, Entry 227]).

ABSTRACT

1:51 ## Monthly Conduct Report

U.S. Military Academy, February 28, 1826

Lists Cadet J. Davis and 68 other cadets out of a total of 236 as "distinguished for Correct Conduct" during February.[1]

DS (NA, RG 94 Records of the Adjutant General's Office, Records Relating to the U.S. Military Academy, Monthly Conduct Reports, Entry 231), 2. Signed: "S. Thayer Lt Col Supnd Mil Acady."

[1] Compare Davis' record of delinquencies (1:116) for further evidence of the fact that Davis had no offenses during February.

ABSTRACT

Monthly Conduct Report 1:52

U.S. Military Academy, March 31, 1826

Lists Cadet J. Davis as having committed five offenses during March.[1]

DS (NA, RG 94 Records of the Adjutant General's Office, Records Relating to the U.S. Military Academy, Monthly Conduct Reports, Entry 231), 2. Signed: "S. Thayer Lt Col Supnd Mil Acady." Endorsed: "Recd 26 Apr 1826."

[1] See 1:116 for further evidence of Davis' five offenses during March.

ABSTRACT

Monthly Conduct Report 1:53

U.S. Military Academy, April 30, 1826

Lists Cadet J. Davis as having committed four offenses during April.[1]

DS (NA, RG 94 Records of the Adjutant General's Office, Records Relating to the U.S. Military Academy, Monthly Conduct Reports, Entry 231), 2. Signed: "S. Thayer Lt. Col Supnd Mil Acady."

[1] See 1:116 for further evidence of the fact that Davis committed four offenses during April.

ABSTRACT

Monthly Return 1:54

West Point, New York, May 31, 1826

Lists Cadet Davis[1] as being present and sick.

DS (U.S. Military Academy Archives), 2. Signed: "H. H. Gird, Lieut. & Adjt. S. Thayer Lt Col Comdg."

[1] It is not possible to know whether the Davis here listed is Jefferson or John P. See 1:50, *n.* 1 for discussion of a similar problem.

ABSTRACT

1:55 **Battalion Order No. 43**

West Point, June 23, 1826

Cadet Davis is appointed "4th. Sergt." of the first company[1] for the forthcoming encampment.[2] By command of Major Worth.[3]

J. M. Berrien[4]
Adjutant of the Corps.

LbC, transcription from letterbook copy in the War Department (U.S. Military Academy Archives), 2.

[1] According to paragraph 135 of the regulations, "The cadets will be arranged . . . for encampment into four companies. These companies shall form one battalion, to be commanded by the instructor of infantry tacticks" (*Regulations of the Military Academy* [1823], 29).

[2] Prior to the Thayer administration, cadets were permitted to go on vacation from mid-July to the end of August. But beginning in 1818, general vacations were abolished and the corps went into the first of its annual summer encampments (T. J. Fleming, *West Point*, 37–40). Paragraph 46 of the Academy regulations provided that "There will be an encampment of the cadets annually to commence on the 1st day of July, and end on the 31st day of August next ensuing; during which, the instruction shall be exclusively military" (*Regulations of the Military Academy* [1823], 13).

[3] William J. Worth (sketch, 1:14, *n.* 1).

[4] John M. Berrien, born in New Jersey, and appointed to the Academy from Pennsylvania, was graduated in 1826 and served as an assistant teacher of drawing and assistant instructor of tactics, 1826–28. He was a first lieutenant, Fifth Infantry, on topographical duty when he resigned in 1836. He became a civil engineer and died at Detroit in 1876, aged seventy-three (Cullum, *Biographical Register*, I, 378).

ABSTRACT

1:56 **Merit Roll**

U.S. Military Academy, June [30,] 1826

Ranks Cadet Davis at the general examination given in June 1826 as thirty-third out of forty-nine members of the third class[1] in mathematics, sixteenth out of forty-nine members of the third class in French, and fifteenth out of forty-nine members of the third class in drawing.

DS (NA, RG 94 Records of the Adjutant General's Office, Records Relating to the U.S. Military Academy, Merit Rolls, Entry 230), 5; D, copy, transcription from letterbook copy in the War Department (U.S. Military Academy Archives). Signed: "S. Thayer Lt. Col Supnd Mil Acady."

[1] See 1:18, *n.* 3 for a discussion of the West Point class system.

ABSTRACT

Yearly Merit Roll 1:57

U.S. Military Academy, June [30,] 1826

Ranks Cadet J. Davis twenty-ninth out of forty-nine members of the third class,[1] with 154 merits in mathematics, 78 merits in French, and 52 merits in drawing, for a total of 284.[2]

DS (NA, RG 94 Records of the Adjutant General's Office, Records Relating to the U.S. Military Academy, Merit Rolls, Entry 230), 5; D, copy, transcription from letterbook copy in the War Department (U.S. Military Academy Archives). Signed: "S. Thayer Lt Col Supnd Mil Acady."

[1] See 1:18, *n.* 3 for a discussion of the West Point class system.

[2] See 1:30, *n.* 2 for the West Point grading system.

ABSTRACT

Muster Roll of the Corps of Cadets 1:58

West Point, New York, June 30, 1826

Lists Jefferson Davis, United States Military Academy, Corps of Cadets commanded by Major William J. Worth,[1] as present at the post. Remarks: "Sick 4th. Sergt.[2] 1st. Company Corps of Cadets."

DS (U.S. Military Academy Archives), 7. Signed: "Jno M Berrien Adjt Corps of Cadets W. J Worth Maj Com[mandin]g &c."

[1] William J. Worth (sketch, 1:14, *n.* 1).

[2] See 1:55 for evidence of Davis' appointment as fourth sergeant of the first company.

ABSTRACT

Semiannual Muster Roll of the Corps of Cadets 1:59

West Point, New York, June 30, 1826

Lists Jefferson Davis of Mississippi, third class,[1] United States Military Academy, Corps of Cadets commanded by Major William J. Worth,[2] as being age nineteen years,[3] and as present at the post. Remarks: "4th. Sergt.[4] 1st. Comp[an]y Corps of Cadets–Sick."

DS (NA, RG 94 Records of the Adjutant General's Office, Records Relating to the U.S. Military Academy, Semiannual Muster Rolls of Cadets, Entry 227), 9; DS (U.S. Military Academy Archives). Signed: "Jno M Berrien Adj Corps W. J Worth Maj Com[mandin]g Corps."

[1] See 1:18, *n.* 3 for a discussion of the West Point class system.

[2] William J. Worth (sketch, 1:14, *n.* 1).

[3] Davis' age is figured from 1807. See 1:1, *n.* 1 for a discussion of the problem of Davis' year of birth.

[4] See 1:55 for evidence of Davis' appointment as fourth sergeant of the first company.

ABSTRACT

1:60 Battalion Order No. 47

Camp Jackson,[1] West Point, July 10, 1826

Cadet J. F. Davis and twenty-one other cadets "are detailed for a weeks tour of laboratory duty. The party will be commanded and reported to Lieut Kinsley."[2] By command of Major Worth.[3]

JNO. M. BERRIEN[4]
Adjutant of the Corps.

LbC, transcription from letterbook copy in the War Department (U.S. Military Academy Archives), 1.

[1] Camp Jackson was the name given to the summer camp. See 1:55, *n.* 1 for a discussion of the annual summer encampment.

[2] Zebina J. D. Kinsley (sketch, 1:35, *n.* 6).

[3] William J. Worth (sketch, 1:14, *n.* 1).

[4] John M. Berrien (sketch, 1:55, *n.* 4).

ABSTRACT

1:61 Orders No. 114

West Point, August 7, 1826

Cadet Jefferson Davis has leave of absence until August 20. By order of Major W. J. Worth.[1]

Z. J. D. KINSLEY[2]
Lieutenant and Acting Adjutant.

LbC, transcription from letterbook copy in the War Department (U.S. Military Academy Archives), 1.

[1] William J. Worth (sketch, 1:14, *n.* 1).
[2] Zebina J. D. Kinsley (sketch, 1:35, *n.* 6).

ABSTRACT

Battalion Order No. 70 1:62

West Point, August 30, 1826

Cadet Davis is appointed sergeant of the color guard[1] in a reorganization of the corps.

LbC, transcription from letterbook copy in the War Department (U.S. Military Academy Archives), 1.

[1] See 1:55 for Davis' previous appointment as fourth sergeant of the first company.

ABSTRACT

Monthly Return 1:63

West Point, New York, August 31, 1826

Lists Cadet J. Davis as being present and sick.[1]

DS (U.S. Military Academy Archives), 2. Signed: "H. H. Gird, Lieut. & adjt. S. Thayer Lt Col Supnd Mil Acady Commdg."

[1] Davis is listed present and sick on all subsequent monthly returns through November 1826 (1:Appendix V, 531). It was evidently to this four-month period that Mrs. Davis was referring when she wrote, "While at West Point Mr. Davis came near escaping all the anguish and turmoil of his life by a fall. He and Emile Laserre [La Sére], a fellow-cadet, went down to Bennie Havens's on a little frolic—of course without leave. There was a rumor of one of the instructors coming, and the two young men rushed off by a short cut to get back to barracks, and Cadet Davis fell over the bank, and as he afterward found, he had been precipitated sixty feet to the river bank. Fortunately he caught at a stunted tree, which broke the force of his fall, though it tore his hands dreadfully. . . . He lay ill many months afterward, and was expected to die for some weeks" (*Memoir*, I, 52). In a letter to his wife dated October 11, 1865, Davis wrote: "When a Cadet I lay for more than four months in Hospital and rarely saw any one even when it was thought I was about to die, then some of my friends were allowed to stay with me at night" (Strode, *Private Letters*, 187).

ABSTRACT

1:64
Muster Roll of the Corps of Cadets

West Point, New York, August 31, 1826

Lists Jefferson Davis, United States Military Academy, Corps of Cadets commanded by Major William J. Worth,[1] as present at the post. Remarks: "Sergt of the colour guard[2]–Sick in Hospital."

DS (U.S. Military Academy Archives), 8. Signed: "Thos. S. Trask Adjt. of the Corps W. J Worth Maj Com[mandin]g & Mustering & Insp[ectin]g officer."

[1] William J. Worth (sketch, 1:14, *n.* 1).

[2] See 1:63, *n.* 1 for a discussion of Davis' illness. See also 1:Appendix V, 531 for a calendar of monthly reports that list Davis as being ill from August through November.

ABSTRACT

1:65
Monthly Conduct Report

U.S. Military Academy, September 30, 1826

Lists Cadet J. Davis and 80 other cadets out of a total of 254 as "distinguished for correct conduct" during September.[1]

DS (NA, RG 94 Records of the Adjutant General's Office, Records Relating to the U.S. Military Academy, Monthly Conduct Reports, Entry 231), 2. Signed: "S. Thayer Lt Col Supnd Mil Acady."

[1] See 1:116 for confirmation of the fact that Davis committed no offenses during September.

ABSTRACT

1:66
Monthly Conduct Report

U.S. Military Academy, October 31, 1826

Lists Cadet J. Davis and 79 other cadets out of a total of 247 as "distinguished for correct conduct" during October.[1]

DS (NA, RG 94 Records of the Adjutant General's Office, Records Relating to the U.S. Military Academy, Monthly Conduct Reports, Entry 231), 2. Signed: "S. Thayer Lt Col Supndt Mil Acady."

[1] See 1:116 for confirmation of the fact that Davis committed no offenses during October.

ABSTRACT

Monthly Conduct Report 1:67

U.S. Military Academy, November 30, 1826

Lists Cadet J. Davis as having committed one offense during November.[1]

DS (NA, RG 94 Records of the Adjutant General's Office, Records Relating to the U.S. Military Academy, Monthly Conduct Reports, Entry 231), 2. Signed: "S. Thayer Lt Col Supndt Mil Acady." Endorsed: "Recd. Decr. 16. 1826."

[1] See 1:116 for confirmation of this offense.

ABSTRACT

Battalion Order No. 98 1:68

West Point, December 26, 1826

Cadet Sergeant[1] J. Davis and twenty-two other cadets "are hereby *arrested*[2] & confined to qrs under the usual restrictions, charged with being concerned in the riotous proceedings which took place <—yester—> on the morning of the 25th."[3] By command of Major W. J. Worth.[4]

THOMAS S. TRASK[5]
Adjutant of the Corps.

LbC, transcription from letterbook copy in the War Department (U.S. Military Academy Archives), 1.

[1] See 1:62 for evidence of Davis' having been appointed sergeant of the color guard.

[2] The underlining here appears to be in pencil and may have been added at a later date.

[3] On the morning of December 25, 1826, the cadets at the Military Academy defied the authorities and held, as had been their wont in years past, a number of Christmas drinking parties. See the testimony of Cadet Lieutenant Nathaniel J. Eaton, a witness for the defense, in the trial of Cadet William P. N. Fitzgerald on February 17, 1827, who, in reply to a question, stated that it had been the custom for the cadets to drink spirituous liquors in each other's rooms before reveille on Christmas morning and that he had never before known the officers to interfere (NA, RG 153, Court Martial Records, BB–96, 1827, p. 65).

The officers of the Academy, who, at the direction of Superintendent Thayer had been endeavoring to suppress all drinking, even that sanctioned by custom (T. J. Fleming, *West Point*, 57), had been alerted. When they interfered, the cadets, their anger aroused, rioted and drove the tactical officers who attempted to restrain them either to the safety of their rooms or from the barracks altogether. Davis, unlike most of the other twenty-two cadets, was arrested not for having taken part in the riot but for being absent from his room and for having attended, in defiance of regulations, a Christmas drinking party. After his arrest he went, as ordered, to his room in the South Barrack where he apparently fell asleep, thus missing the riot and the consequent court martial.

[4] William J. Worth (sketch, 1:14, *n.* 1).

[5] Thomas S. Trask was born in Vermont and was appointed to the Military Academy in 1822. After graduation he served at Jefferson Barracks, Missouri, where at the early age of twenty-four he died (Cullum, *Biographical Register*, I, 398).

1:69

Military Academy Order No. 49

Engineer Department, Washington, December 30th, 1826

It having been reported to this Department, that on or about the night of the 24th and morning of the 25th instant, certain irregularities and disorders[1] were committed at the post of West-Point, in the state of New-York, a Court of Inquiry—to consist of Brevet Major W. J. Worth,[2] of the 1st Artillery, President, and 2d Lieut. Henry H. Gird,[3] of the 4th Artillery, Recorder, with two other members to be detailed by the Superintendent[4] of the Military Academy at West-Point, will assemble at said post of West-Point as soon as practicable, and investigate the origin and circumstances of the said irregularities and disorders, and report the facts connected therewith to the said Superintendent; who will—should he, upon his examination of the facts reported by the Court of Inquiry,[5] be of opinion that there are just grounds for the institution of a Court Martial, in relation to the matters presented by the Court of Inquiry, detail accordingly, without delay, a General Court Martial,[6] to consist of Captain Thomas C. Legate,[7] of the 2d Artillery, President, 2d Lieutenant Henry H. Gird, of the 4th Artillery, Judge Advocate, with five members and two supernumerary members, (that being the greatest number that can be assembled without manifest injury to the service), to be detailed by the said Superintendent and the said Superintendent will prefer charges against all delinquents to be tried by the said Court Martial, with such other persons as may be brought before it. The whole of the proceedings both of the Court of Inquiry and of the General Court Martial will be transmitted to this Department, through the Superintendent, to be laid before the Secretary of War.[8] By order of the Secretary of War, Signed ALEX. MACOMB,[9]

Maj. Gen. Inspr. Mil. Acad.

D, copy (NA, RG 153 Records of the Office of the Judge Advocate General [Army], Court Martial Records, BB-96, 1827).

[1] See 1:68, *n.* 3 for a discussion of the irregularities occurring at West Point on December 24–25.

[2] William J. Worth (sketch, 1:14, *n.* 1).

[3] Henry H. Gird (sketch, 1:33, *n.* 3).

[4] The superintendent of the Military Academy was Sylvanus Thayer (sketch, 1:74, *n.* 6).

[5] See 1:75–81 for the court of inquiry proceedings.

[6] See 1:83, 86, 90 for the court martial.

[7] Thomas C. Legate (sketch, 1:35, *n.* 3).

[8] James Barbour was the secretary of war.

[9] Alexander Macomb (sketch, 1:38, *n.* 10).

ABSTRACT

Monthly Conduct Report **1:70**

U.S. Military Academy, December 31, 1826

Lists Cadet J. Davis as having committed three offenses during December,[1] and being punished since December 26 for "being concerned in the riot[ou]s proceedgs. of the 25.[2] . . . In Arrest & Confinement." [3]

DS (NA, RG 94 Records of the Adjutant General's Office, Records Relating to the U.S. Military Academy, Monthly Conduct Reports, Entry 231), 2. Signed: "S. Thayer Lt Col Supndt. Mil Acady."

[1] The Record of Delinquencies (1:116) also lists Davis as having committed three offenses during December.

[2] See 1:68, *n.* 3 for a discussion of the riotous proceedings of December 24–25.

[3] See 1:68 for evidence of Davis' arrest.

ABSTRACT

Monthly Return **1:71**

West Point, New York, December 31, 1826

Lists Cadet Davis "Present. In Arrest." [1]

DS (U.S. Military Academy Archives), 2. Signed: "H. H. Gird, Lieut. & Adjt. S. Thayer Lt Col Comdg."

[1] Davis was arrested December 26, 1826 (1:68).

ABSTRACT

1:72 Muster Roll of the Corps of Cadets

West Point, New York, December 31, 1826

Lists Jefferson F. Davis, United States Military Academy, Corps of Cadets commanded by Major William J. Worth,[1] as present at the post. Remarks: "Sergt. Colour Guard[2] In arrest & conft." [3]

DS (U.S. Military Academy Archives), 8. Signed: "Thos. S. Trask Adjt. of the Corps W. J. Worth Maj Com[mand]ing Corps & Mustering Offr."

[1] William J. Worth (sketch, 1:14, *n.* 1).

[2] See 1:62 for evidence of Davis' having been made the sergeant of the color guard.

[3] See 1:68 for the order first arresting Davis.

ABSTRACT

1:73 Semiannual Muster Roll of the Corps of Cadets

West Point, New York, December 31, 1826

Lists Jefferson F. Davis of Mississippi, second class,[1] United States Military Academy, Corps of Cadets commanded by Major William J. Worth,[2] as being age nineteen years, six months,[3] and as present at the post. Remarks: "Sergt of the Colour Guard.[4] In arrest & Conft." [5]

DS (U.S. Military Academy Archives), 9; D, copy (NA, RG 94 Records of the Adjutant General's Office, Records Relating to the U.S. Military Academy, Semiannual Muster Rolls of Cadets, Entry 227). Signed: "Thos. S. Trask Adjt. of the Corps W. J Worth Maj Com[mandin]g Corps & Mustering offr."

[1] See 1:18, *n.* 3 for a discussion of the West Point class system.

[2] William J. Worth (sketch, 1:14, *n.* 1).

[3] Davis' age is figured from the year 1807. See 1:1, *n.* 1 for a discussion of the problem of Davis' age.

[4] See 1:62 for evidence of Davis' having been made sergeant of the color guard.

[5] Davis was arrested on December 26 (1:68).

1:74 Orders No. 3

U. S. Mil. Academy West-Point, 7th Jan. 1827

In accordance with Military Academy Orders, No. 49, (1826)[1]

7 JANUARY 1827

Capt. E. A. Hitchcock[2] of the 1st Infantry, and Lieut. Wm. Bryant,[3] of the 3d Artillery, are detailed as members of the Court of Inquiry, of which Brevet Major W. J. Worth,[4] of the 1st Artillery, is President; which Court will convene to-morrow morning at nine o'clock, in the office of the Adjutant of Cadets.[5] By order of Lieut. Col. Thayer,[6] Signed

H. H. GIRD,[7]
Lieut. & Adjt.

D, copy (NA, RG 153 Records of the Office of the Judge Advocate General [Army], Court Martial Records, BB-96, 1827).

1 See 1:69 for Order No. 49.

2 Ethan A. Hitchcock (sketch, 1:35, *n.* 5).

3 William Bryant, born in Virginia, had been a cadet, 1822–26, and was a second lieutenant and assistant professor of chemistry, mineralogy, and geology in 1827. He later served as assistant professor of engineering and in various garrisons until his resignation from the army in 1835. He was an Episcopal clergyman and principal of Botetourt Academy, Virginia, at the time of his death at age forty-two in 1846 (Cullum, *Biographical Register*, I, 365–66).

4 William J. Worth (sketch, 1:14, *n.* 1).

5 Thomas S. Trask (sketch, 1:68, *n.* 5) was the adjutant of the cadets.

6 Sylvanus Thayer (1785–1872) was born in Braintree, Massachusetts, attended Dartmouth College, and was graduated from West Point in 1808. After distinguished service in the Corps of Engineers in the War of 1812, he was brevetted major in 1815. He spent two years in Europe on professional duty, studying military schools, armies, and fortifications, and was appointed superintendent of the Academy in 1817, a post he held until 1833. Known as a firm disciplinarian, Thayer was respected by cadets and instructors for his fairness without regard for political patronage. In his sixteen-year tenure as superintendent, Thayer earned, as a consequence of his many reforms, the title of "Father of the Military Academy." He had classes divided into small sections on the model of the École Polytechnique, where cadets were instructed according to ability and rate of progress. The number of textbooks was increased and the curriculum expanded to include more science and engineering, in order to train men not only for the army, but also for civilian positions. Faculty members were carefully selected and encouraged to try new techniques in instruction. Summer camps were instituted in lieu of long summer vacations, and the cadets were allowed their own officers. A demerit system was introduced in September 1825, whereby the number of demerits received would influence class standing; the demerit list was to be published annually for the information of parents and guardians (Post Orders No. 122, September 25, 1825 [U.S. Military Academy Archives]; T. J. Fleming, *West Point*, 57; see 1:118, *n.* 1 for a discussion of the new demerit system and 1:116 for Davis' record of delinquencies). Thayer did not receive the same support for his authority from President Andrew Jackson as he had previously enjoyed, and, after a long series of difficulties with officials in Washington, he tendered his resignation in January 1833. In March of the same year, he was brevetted colonel and he left West Point in July. He remained in the Corps of Engineers, and

among other assignments, directed the construction of the Boston harbor defenses. Brevetted brigadier general for long and faithful service, he retired in 1863 and died in his home town at the age of eighty-seven (*DAB*; T. J. Fleming, *West Point*, 3–87; Cullum, *Biographical Register*, I, 81–87; Weigley, *United States Army*, 145–47).

[7] Henry H. Gird (sketch, 1:33, *n.* 3).

EXTRACT

1:75 Proceedings of a Court of Inquiry—First Day Case of Seventy Cadets

West-Point, 8th January, 1827

The Court met pursuant to the foregoing orders.

Present

Brevet Maj. W. J. Worth,[1] (1st Art.) President
Capt. E. A. Hitchcock,[2] (1st Inf.) } Members
2d Lieut. Wm. Bryant,[3] (3d Art.) } Members
2d Lieut. Henry H. Gird,[4] (4th Art.) Recorder

The Court was duly sworn.

Capt. E. A. Hitchcock, being duly sworn, gave testimony as follows: viz:

The Court. State to the Court, such circumstances as are within your knowledge, having reference to, or connection with, the riotous and disorderly proceedings[5] which occurred in the North Barrack[6] under your command, on the evening of the 24th and morning of the 25th December, 1826.

Witness. About 4 o'clock on the morning of the 25th December last, I heard some walking through the halls of the barrack–and soon after walked through the halls myself to ascertain if there was any disorder in the barrack. I perceived nothing worthy of <–notice–> particular notice and returned to my room; but hearing the walking of the Cadets (as I presumed) to continue–with some increase of noise–I again walked through the halls of the Barrack . . . . I observed a collection of Cadets at No. 5.[7] I entered this room and found in it–Cadet Bibb,[8] Aisquith,[9] Bomford,[10] J. L. Thompson,[11] Roberts,[12] Sullivan,[13] Carr,[14] Guion,[15] C. J. Wright[16] and Temple,[17] who were not occupants of the room. The occupants of the room were Cadets Sevier,[18] T. M. Lewis,[19] Cobb[20] & Farrelly[21] the first three of whom were present. As to the presence of the latter, I am not positive, I think he was present and left the room soon after I entered. While I was in the room, Cadet J. Davis entered, saying "Put away that liquor, boys." I immediately arrested him and ordered him to his quarters; and gave a general order to those who were not occupants of the room to retire to their quarters. As soon as they had left the room—a noise of hallooing commenced in the barrack—which I had no doubt proceeded from some of them. After I had returned to my own room acts of violence were commenced in the barrack, such as throwing sticks of wood against my own door, and my windows very soon after were assailed with stones and every glass broken but three. It was about this time that some person commenced beating the drum. I at first thought it was the commencement of reveillee, but discovering the contrary by the irregularity of the beat, descended to the guard-room[22] from which the noise proceeded and found Cadet Bibb standing immediately over the drum—the head of which was broken in. I ordered Cadet Bibb to his quarters in arrest. While descending to the guard room—there were a considerable number of Cadets in the halls and upon the stairs—and many sticks of wood were thrown which as I supposed were aimed at me. One slightly touched my arm. The Cadets however had dispersed—with the exception of Cadet Bibb before-mentioned. From this time forward—until after the regular beat of reveillee—there was an uninterrupted noise in and about the Barrack—such as throwing billets of fire-wood and stones and the discharge of firearms. Many of the windows (glass and sashes) were broken, as also the banisters of the stairway. . . . At this time—many clubs were thrown in the hall—from which I was obliged to seek protection in my own room.

For perhaps half an hour during the morning—I was with Lieut. Thornton[23] (who was associated with me in the <—command—> <service>[24] of the Barrack) at his room, after having ordered the Officer of the Day[25] to report to the Commandant of Cadets that great disorder prevailed in the Barrack and that it was impossible for me to quell it. After I returned to my room I was informed that several Cadets had been near my room calling me out with threats. Major Worth (Commandant of the Cadets) in a short time came into my quarters—about which time the riot or disorder ceased. . . .

The Court adjourned to meet again to-morrow morning at nine o'clock.

DS (NA, RG 153 Records of the Office of the Judge Advocate General [Army], Court Martial Records, BB–96, 1827), 153.

[1] William J. Worth (sketch, 1:14, *n.* 1).

[2] Ethan A. Hitchcock (sketch, 1:35, *n.* 5).

[3] William Bryant (sketch, 1:74, *n.* 3).

[4] Henry H. Gird (sketch, 1:33, *n.* 3).

[5] See 1:68, *n.* 3 for additional information on the riotous proceedings of December 24–25.

[6] One of two barracks, the other being the South Barrack, built for the accommodation of the cadets. Completed in 1817, it was four stories high and "less than 100 feet distant from the northeastern corner" of the South Barrack (Boynton, *West Point*, 255).

[7] Room No. 5 was on the second floor of the North Barrack (Court of Inquiry, March 3, 1827 [NA, RG 153, Court Martial Records, BB–96, 1827, Part II], 320).

[8] Lucien I. Bibb, an 1827 graduate of West Point, was from Frankfort, Kentucky, and after graduation served at Fortress Monroe, as an instructor at West Point, and on ordnance duty in Virginia, where he died in 1831, aged twenty-four (Cullum, *Biographical Register*, I, 389; Roll of Cadets, February 1, 1827 [NA, RG 94, Records Relating to the U.S. Military Academy, Rolls of Cadets, Entry 227]).

[9] William E. Aisquith was admitted to the Academy from Leesburgh, Virginia, in 1823. He was graduated in 1827, and served at two garrisons before his dismissal in 1832. Five years later, he was reappointed to the First Artillery, participated in the Florida War of 1837–38, and the Canadian border disturbances, and served at various posts until 1845 when he was cashiered. After the Mexican War, during which he was a volunteer orderly sergeant and soldier in the First Artillery, he was recommended for reappointment but was not confirmed by the Senate. From 1848 until his death in Washington in 1856, he was a marine sergeant and clerk (Cullum, *Biographical Register*, I, 391–92; Roll of Cadets, February 1, 1827 [NA, RG 94, Records Relating to the U.S. Military Academy, Rolls of Cadets, Entry 227]).

[10] George C. Bomford, son of future Chief of Ordnance George Bomford of Washington, D.C., was admitted to the Academy in 1824 at the age of sixteen. By sentence of a court martial, he was dismissed effective May 31, 1827 (Entrance Register of Cadets [U.S. Military Academy Archives]).

[11] James L. Thompson, from Dandridge, Tennessee, was graduated in 1828. He was to serve at Jefferson Barracks, many frontier forts, and in the military occupation of Texas before his resignation in 1846. He became a farmer in Michigan and died by drowning in 1851, at the age of forty-six (Cullum, *Biographical Register*, I, 415; Entrance Register of Cadets [U.S. Military Academy Archives]).

[12] Samuel Roberts, from Alabama, was a member of the 1824–28 West Point class, but failed to be graduated as he was dismissed by the sentence of a court martial in May 1827 (Entrance Register of Cadets [U.S. Military Academy Archives]).

[13] George R. Sullivan (later George R. J. Bowdoin), admitted to the Academy from Boston, was graduated in 1829 and served in the army only three years. He was an attorney in New York, 1832–70, and died in London, England, aged sixty, in 1870 (Cullum, *Biographical Register*, I, 443; Entrance Register of Cadets [U.S. Military Academy Archives]).

[14] Dabney O. Carr, a member of the 1829 class, was from Charlottesville, Virginia, but was not graduated. He resigned effective May 31, 1827 (Entrance Register of Cadets [U.S. Military Academy Archives]).

[15] Walter B. Guion, son or ward of John Isaac Guion, a prominent Missis-

sippi politician, was dismissed from the Academy by sentence of a court martial in May 1827. He became a captain of topographical engineers in 1838 and resigned four years later (Heitman, *Historical Register*, I, 483; Entrance Register of Cadets [U.S. Military Academy Archives]). See Davis' testimony (1:80) to the effect that he and Guion were roommates.

[16] Crafts J. Wright was born in 1808 in New York (Wright to Davis, February 18, 1878, D. Rowland, *Papers*, VIII, 111) and attended the Academy, 1823–28, where he was reportedly Davis' roommate (St. Louis *Globe-Democrat*, December 7, 1889, Sec. 1, p. 3). Having resigned his commission soon after graduation in 1828, he was a counselor-at-law and newspaper editor, then served as a colonel of volunteers in the Union Army, 1861–62. He was superintendent of the United States Marine Hospital in Chicago, 1875–83. A lifelong friend and correspondent of Davis, he died in Chicago in 1883 (Cullum, *Biographical Register*, I, 418).

[17] Robert E. Temple, born in Vermont, was graduated in 1828 and served as an assistant professor at West Point until 1830. He was Winfield Scott's aide, 1832–33, and participated in the Seminole War. After his resignation in 1839, he became an attorney in New York and was state adjutant general, 1846–47. He was reappointed as colonel, Tenth Infantry, in 1847 and served in the Mexican War. He died in 1854 at Albany, New York, aged forty-five (Cullum, *Biographical Register*, I, 407).

[18] Robert Sevier was graduated from West Point in 1828, having been appointed from Tennessee. He served at southern and frontier posts and participated in the Black Hawk War before resigning in 1837. He became a farmer and merchant and was a Missouri circuit court clerk, 1845–65. He died in Missouri in 1879, aged seventy-two (Cullum, *Biographical Register*, I, 411).

[19] Thomas M. Lewis entered the Academy from Morganfield, Kentucky, in 1824. He failed to be graduated because of his dismissal in May 1827 by sentence of a general court martial (Entrance Register of Cadets [U.S. Military Academy Archives]).

[20] Samuel K. Cobb, born in South Carolina and appointed from Alabama in 1824, was graduated in 1828 and served at Jefferson Barracks, on the Red River in Louisiana, and at Fort Towson before his death in New Orleans in 1834. He was twenty-eight (Cullum, *Biographical Register*, I, 416–17).

[21] David M. Farrelly was admitted to West Point from Meadville, Pennsylvania, in 1824 and was dismissed by sentence of a general court martial in May 1827 (Entrance Register of Cadets [U.S. Military Academy Archives]).

[22] The guard room was on the lower story of the North Barrack just east of the only entrance then in use, the north entrance being fastened up (Church, *Reminiscences*, 19–20).

[23] William A. Thornton, assistant instructor of infantry tactics at West Point, 1826–29, was an 1825 graduate of the Academy. He was born in New York and served in the army over forty years. He served during the nullification crisis and the Florida War and transferred to the Ordnance Corps from Fourth Artillery in 1838. Until his death in New York in 1866 at the age of sixty-three, Thornton was stationed mostly in the Northeast on various ordnance boards. He was brevetted brigadier general in 1865 (Cullum, *Biographical Register*, I, 346–47).

[24] Interlined.

[25] Nathaniel J. Eaton was the officer of the day (Court of Inquiry, February 22, 1827 [NA, RG 153, Court Martial Records, BB–96, 1827, Part II], 140).

EXTRACT

1:76 ## Proceedings of a Court of Inquiry—Second Day Case of Seventy Cadets

West Point, 9th January, 1827

The Court met pursuant to adjournment.

Present
Maj. Worth,[1] President,
Capt. Hitchcock,[2] } Members
Lieut. Bryant,[3] }
Lieut. Gird,[4] Recorder....

Cadet Edgar M. Lacey,[5] being duly sworn, and examined by the Court, answers as follows:

Ques. Where are you quartered? and were you in the North Barrack, during the riot on the morning of the 25th?

Ans. I am quartered in the South Barrack[6]–No. 21;[7] and was not in the North Barrack during any part of the riot

The Court–State to the Court such circumstances as may come under your observation connected with the disorderly and riotous proceedings which took place in the Barracks, particularly the North, on the night of the 24th, or morning of the 25th December, 1826, and such facts pertinent to this inquiry as you may have heard?

Witness. I saw Cadet J. W. Collins[8] [a few] minutes past seven–between reveillee and breakfast–with a club in his hand. Before reveillee–perhaps six o'clock–Cadet Stocker[9] came to my room. He asked me why I did not come over to the north barrack observing that they had plenty of fun aboard, and I think he said that they were breaking windows. From six to half past six o'clock–there was a noise in the room adjoining mine.[10] This noise appeared to proceed principally from Cadet J. F. Davis. I am familiar with his voice. From the language he used I supposed him to be intoxicated. I think that the cause of the riot was the orders[11] given that the Superintendents[12] should sit up all night on duty.

Ques. Are you aware, or do you believe, that any orders were given, or measures taken, other than those of a preventive character, and such as are not uncommon to check disorderly conduct and enforce the rules and regulations of the Institution?

Ans. I believe that no orders were issued but such as would tend to prevent riotous conduct and disorder. I think, however that it was unusual to order the Superintendents to sit up all night.

Ques. Do you suppose from Cadet Stocker's manner and language that he was engaged in the proceedings of which he spoke, and wished you to join in them?

Ans. I do.

Ques—In what light do the Cadets view the riotous proceedings of the 25th—so far as you are acquainted?

Ans. In a disgraceful light. I have heard many express their opinion on it. I have had very little conversation with those who are supposed to be concerned in it, but my impression is—that the generality of the Corps consider it as a disgrace<—ful—> to the Corps. . . .

The Court adjourned—to meet again at nine o'clock, to-morrow morning.

DS (NA, RG 153 Records of the Office of the Judge Advocate General [Army], Court Martial Records, BB-96, 1827), 153.

[1] William J. Worth (sketch, 1:14, *n.* 1).

[2] Ethan A. Hitchcock (sketch, 1:35, *n.* 5).

[3] William Bryant (sketch, 1:74, *n.* 3).

[4] Henry H. Gird (sketch, 1:33, *n.* 3).

[5] Edgar M. Lacey, born in New York, was graduated in the class of 1827 and served in the Fifth Infantry at Jefferson Barracks and Forts Howard, Winnebago, and Crawford. He died at the age of thirty-two at Prairie du Chien, Michigan Territory, in 1839 (Cullum, *Biographical Register*, I, 400).

[6] Completed in 1815, the South Barrack was constructed of stuccoed stone and consisted of a central building with two wings at each end. The building was demolished in 1849 (Boynton, *West Point*, 254–55).

[7] No. 21 was next door to Davis' room. See *n.* 10 below.

[8] James W. Collins was admitted from Baltimore in 1823, but failed to be graduated having been dismissed by sentence of a general court martial in May 1827 (Roll of Cadets, February 1, 1827 [NA, RG 94, Records Relating to the U.S. Military Academy, Rolls of Cadets, Entry 227]; Muster Roll of the Corps of Cadets, August 31, 1827 [U.S. Military Academy Archives]).

[9] John C. Stocker, from Philadelphia, failed to be graduated with his class in 1827 having been dismissed by sentence of a general court martial in May of that year (Roll of Cadets, July 1, 1827 [NA, RG 94, Records Relating to the U.S. Military Academy, Rolls of Cadets, Entry 227]; Semiannual Muster Roll of the Corps of Cadets, December 31, 1826 [*ibid.*]).

[10] See 1:80 for Davis' statement that he roomed in No. 19.

[11] Charles W. Whipple, superintendent of the first division (second floor) of the North Barrack, testified: "I received orders on the night of the 24th December last, from Major Worth, through the adjutant of the Corps, that I should be accountable for the good order of my division during the night"

(Court of Inquiry, January 10, 1827 [NA, RG 153, Court Martial Records, BB–96, 1827, Part II], 320).

12 Each division (floor) reserved for the accommodation of the cadets of both the North and South barracks had a superintendent. They were "selected from those cadets who act as captains and lieutenants in the corps. They [were] charged with a general supervision of their division. It [was], accordingly, their duty to notice, and report all irregularities and infringements of regulations, and such other offenses, which, though not specified, are nevertheless contrary to good order and discipline. . . . It [was their] duty, in the event of noise, scuffling, or any improper conduct whatever, to repair instantly to the spot, order the parties to their rooms, and forthwith to make report of the circumstances to the commandant of the barrack, or, in his absence, to the officer of the week . . ." (*Regulations of the Military Academy* [1823], 36).

EXTRACT

1:77

Proceedings of a Court of Inquiry—Fourth Day
Case of Seventy Cadets

West Point, 11th January, 1827

The Court met pursuant to adjournment.

Present.
Maj. Worth,[1] President.
Capt. Hitchcock,[2] Lieut. Bryant,[3] } Members.
Lieut. Gird,[4] Recorder. . . .

Cadet Robert Sevier,[5] being duly sworn and examined, testifies as follows:

I am Quarter Master's Sergeant in the Corps of Cadets. I room in No. 5,[6] North Barrack.[7] My room-mate, Cadet T. M. Lewis[8] had been using spirituous liquor, I should judge from his conduct on the morning of the 25th December last. He left his room I think before reveillee, he was out during the riot. Cadet Fitzgerald[9] came into my room that morning, he had a cutlass or sword, he was somewhat disorderly.

Ques. Was there any liquor in your room during that morning?

Ans. There was.

Ques. By whom introduced?

Ans. I did not see any one bring it in, but I heard Cadets Farrelly[10] and T. M. Lewis say something from which I infer that they brought it in. The liquor was contained in two jugs—each of which might contain about half a gallon.

Witness says further—Cadet Cobb[11] seemed somewhat disorderly. I should suppose he had drank some liquor in the room that morning. I think I heard Cadet Farrelly say he went after the liquor, which I understood came from Havens'.[12] Cadet J. L. Thompson[13] came to my room before the riot commenced; he went away when ordered by Capt. Hitchcock. Cadet J. F. Davis came to my room before the riot commenced. Capt. Hitchcock was in the room at the time. Cadet Davis said as he came in, "Put away the grog, Capt. Hitchcock is coming," or something to that effect. Cadet Davis, I think had been there previously. Cadet Guion[14] was in my room also before the commencement of the riot; also Cadet Temple,[15] and, I believe, Cadet Drayton.[16] The greater part of the liquor was made into egg-nog. I believe Cadet J. F. Davis invited me to drink. I think I saw Cadet Temple with some eggs. Cadet Aisquith[17] was also in the room. He came before the riot commenced. Cadet Farrelly left the room sometime between tattoo and reveillee, on the night of the 24th December last. He was gone long enough to go a mile or two. He made a remark when he came back, that he had obtained liquor somewhere and that he had deposited it somewhere: he said something about the Quartermaster or Quartermaster's office. The noise in the barrack commenced soon after Capt. Hitchcock came to my room.

The Court. State to the Court the occurrences at your room from the time Capt. Hitchcock entered.

Witness. When Capt. Hitchcock came to the room there were several persons there: he ordered them to their quarters, and I believe they went out. He asked me if there was any liquor in the room: I did not directly answer. After looking sometime for liquor, he requested that the trunks might be opened. Cadet Farrelly was absent. I did not see Capt. Hitchcock touch any trunk or any article in any trunk. I dont recollect whether any trunk was opened except my own: I opened that myself.

Ques. Standing by your trunk, would you have known, if Capt. Hitchcock had touched it?

Ans. I should have known it.

Ques. Would you not have known it if he had touched any other trunk?

Ans. I believe I should have known.

Ques. Did Capt. Hitchcock open the trunk of Cadet Farrelly? or request it to be opened, after it was stated that Cadet Farrelly was absent?

Ans. He did not open it to the best of my recollection. I could not say that Capt. Hitchcock did request Cadet Farrelly's trunk to be opened after it was stated that he was absent.

Ques. Do you believe that any representation of the transactions which took place in your room while Capt. Hitchcock was present, was made to any Cadet or Cadets, calculated to occasion the disorderly proceedings which afterwards ensued?

Ans. I do not think there was time for any such representation before the riot commenced.

Ques. Do you believe that after the riot commenced, any representation of those transactions was made, calculated to heighten or continue it?

Ans. I do not know. I was not placed so as to hear.

Witness says further. Cadet Fitzgerald came into my room before we were up, sometime before reveillee: he was then sober: he aroused the room-mates and did not remain long. He returned afterwards—before reveillee—he had then a small cutlass: he drew it out and brandished it: his conduct was rather disorderly. I should suppose he was excited. I could not say whether he was intoxicated.

Cadet Hamilton[18] was in my room after the riot; and Cadet Mercer[19] also—before the riot. I think Cadet Roberts was there sometime in the morning. The liquor was brought in sometime in the night. I think I have heard Cadet Farrelly say since that I was not awake when it was brought. It was dark in the back-room[20] when Cadet J. F. Davis invited me to drink. I did not see him drink.

Ques. Do you know or have you any reason to believe that any person did invite any other to come to your room, on the morning of the 25th, for the purpose of drinking, or for any other purpose?

Ans. I do not know of any invitation being given. I believe it was made known to Cadet Guion's room[21] and to Cadet Temple's that there would be a party in my room and that there would be liquor in my room sometime <—in—> about Christmas. The latter I believe was as much concerned as others.

Witness says further. Some days before the 25th Cadet Temple being in my room, I believe, made a proposition that we should have some liquor brought into the barracks. Cadets Tilghman,[22] J. F. Davis & Temple were to procure such articles as were necessary for a drinking party. They were to be obtained in the most convenient manner. The party which took place in my room Christmas morning was the one agreed upon. No precautions were taken but such as are usual. I have heard Cadet Roberts[23] remark that he had thrown a tub—referring to the time of the riot. I have heard Cadet Guion state probably that he was instrumental or something of that kind in commencing the riot. I think he said if it had not been for him there would have been nothing of it.

Ques. Do you think a correct representation of what occurred in your room, relative to the trunks, would have had a tendency to increase or continue the riot?

Ans. I should suppose if such a representation had been made it would have had an effect to increase it.

Ques. Upon which part of the Corps do you think it would have had such an effect—on the more reasonable or the excited?

Ans. It would have had an effect on any one I presume though on those who were excited probably more than others.

Ques. Do you suppose that the circumstances warranted Capt. Hitchcock in believing that there was liquor in your room?

Ans. Yes. He might have inferred it from the appearance of the room and from the remark of Cadet Davis. He asked if there had been any there that morning? I answered that remained to be determined or something to that effect. I did not see the liquor, brought in.

Ques. Are you aware that the introduction into the barracks or use of liquor, is prohibited, under severe penalties? [24]

Ans. Yes.

Ques. So far as you have had an opportunity of forming an opinion, in what light are the riotous proceedings of the 25th December last, viewed by a majority of the Cadets?

Ans. I should think it was not approved at present.

Ques. Have you heard any person express any approbation of those proceedings?

Ans. I have heard Cadet Lewis say that he was glad they had taken place or something to the amount. . . .

The Court adjourned to meet again at nine o'clock to-morrow morning.

DS (NA, RG 153 Records of the Office of the Judge Advocate General [Army], Court Martial Records, BB-96, 1827), 153.

[1] William J. Worth (sketch, 1:14, *n.* 1).

[2] Ethan A. Hitchcock (sketch, 1:35, *n.* 5).

[3] William Bryant (sketch, 1:74, *n.* 3).

[4] Henry H. Gird (sketch, 1:33, *n.* 3).

[5] Robert Sevier (sketch, 1:75, *n.* 18).

[6] See 1:75, *n.* 7 for location of room No. 5.

[7] See 1:75, *n.* 6 for description of the North Barrack.

[8] Thomas M. Lewis (sketch, 1:75, *n.* 19).

[9] William P. N. Fitzgerald, admitted to the Academy in 1824 from Ogdensburgh, New York, was not graduated. He was dismissed in May 1827 by sentence of a general court martial (Entrance Register of Cadets [U.S. Military Academy Archives]).

[10] David M. Farrelly (sketch, 1:75, *n.* 21).

[11] Samuel K. Cobb (sketch, 1:75, *n.* 20).

[12] Benny Havens (see 1:35, *n.* 12).

[13] James L. Thompson (sketch, 1:75, *n.* 11).

[14] Walter B. Guion (sketch, 1:75, *n.* 15).

[15] Robert E. Temple (sketch, 1:75, *n.* 17).

[16] Thomas F. Drayton was born in South Carolina in 1808 (Drayton to Davis, June 14, 1889, D. Rowland, *Papers*, X, 123) and died there in 1891, the last surviving member of the 1828 West Point class (*Register of Graduates* [1964], 535). He entered West Point in 1823, and remained Davis' friend until Davis' death. At the time of his resignation from the army in 1836, Drayton was a second lieutenant of the Sixth Infantry. He was a planter, railroad engineer, and member of the South Carolina senate before his appointment as brigadier general in the Confederate Army, 1861–65 (Cullum, *Biographical Register*, I, 417; Warner, *Generals in Gray*, 75–76).

[17] William E. Aisquith (sketch, 1:75, *n.* 9).

[18] James W. Hamilton first entered the Academy in 1819 with an appointment from Missouri, but failed to be graduated (*American State Papers*, Class V, Military Affairs, IV, 318). He evidently reentered on December 8, 1824, and was discharged effective January 29, 1827, by the academic board of the Academy (Semiannual Muster Roll of the Corps of Cadets, February 28, 1827 [NA, RG 94, Records Relating to the U.S. Military Academy, Entry 227]). The roll of cadets, February 1–July 1, 1826, states that he was the son of Major Thomas Hamilton of Fort Snelling and that he was at the time of his admission residing at St. Louis (NA, RG 94, Records Relating to the U.S. Military Academy, Rolls of Cadets, filed with Entry 227). He enlisted as a first lieutenant in the Battalion of Mounted Rangers in 1832 and served as regimental adjutant until August 1835, when he was cashiered. Hamilton was a first lieutenant in the Second Dragoons at the time of his death in 1837 (Heitman, *Historical Register*, I, 493).

[19] Hugh W. Mercer was born in Virginia in 1808 and was graduated from West Point in 1828. Appointed to the Artillery Corps, he served in southern garrisons and was Winfield Scott's aide, 1832–34, before resigning in 1835. An officer in the Georgia militia, 1835–45, and cashier in a Savannah bank, 1841–61, he entered the Confederate Army when Georgia seceded, and was quickly promoted to brigadier general. After September 1864 he saw no active service, having been commander at Savannah the greater part of the war. When the war ended he returned to banking, then moved to Baltimore. He died in Germany in 1877 (Cullum, *Biographical Register*, I, 406–407; Warner, *Generals in Gray*, 216–17).

[20] Some of the rooms of the North Barrack "were divided in two, by a thin board partition, one part a sleeping room and the other a parlour or study" (Church, *Reminiscences*, 20).

[21] Guion and Davis roomed in No. 19 South Barrack; see 1:80.

[22] Richard C. Tilghman was graduated second in the 1828 West Point

class. A native of Maryland, Tilghman served in the First Artillery at southern garrisons and on staff duty until his resignation in 1836. He became a United States civil engineer, 1837–46, then a farmer in Maryland. He declined an appointment as quartermaster of the state militia in 1867 and died in 1879, aged seventy-two, in Centreville, Maryland (Cullum, *Biographical Register*, I, 406).

[23] Samuel Roberts (sketch, 1:75, *n.* 12).

[24] See 1:34, *n.* 5 for the regulation prohibiting drinking.

EXTRACT

Proceedings of a Court of Inquiry—Fifth Day 1:78
Case of Seventy Cadets

West-Point, 12th January, 1827

The Court met pursuant to adjournment.

Present.
Maj. Worth,[1] President.
Capt. Hitchcock,[2] } Members.
Lieut. Bryant,[3] }
Lieut. Gird,[4] Recorder....

Cadet Thomas Drayton,[5] being duly sworn and examined, testifies as follows:

I am Sergeant-Major in the Corps of Cadets and quarter in No. 2, South Barrack.[6] I saw—after breakfast—on the 25th December last Cadet J. F. Davis in a state of intoxication and also Cadet Whitehurst,[7] the latter in the Mess-Hall. I have heard Cadets Guion,[8] J. L. Thompson[9] and J. F. Davis, in conversation on the events of the morning of the 25th in which it was said that they had better not talk about it as they might be called upon to give evidence, or to that effect. On the evening of the 24th it was designed to have a party. I knew there was to be a collection in No. 5.[10] I had no invitation there, until the morning of the 25th. Cadet Guion then called for me to go there. I knew previously that there was going to be a party there. On Saturday—the day before—I heard them talking about it and knew they had an intention to have a party the next morning. I believe Cadets Guion & Farrelly[11] provided the materials for this party. These gentlemen were engaged so to do, at the time I have mentioned. I have heard Cadet Guion say since that he went to Havens's[12] for the liquor, and that Cadet Farrelly went with him....

The Court adjourned to meet again to-morrow morning at nine o'clock.

DS (NA, RG 153 Records of the Office of the Judge Advocate General [Army], Court Martial Records, BB-96, 1827), 153.

1 William J. Worth (sketch, 1:14, *n.* 1).
2 Ethan A. Hitchcock (sketch, 1:35, *n.* 5).
3 William Bryant (sketch, 1:74, *n.* 3).
4 Henry H. Gird (sketch, 1:33, *n.* 3).
5 Thomas F. Drayton (sketch, 1:77, *n.* 16).
6 See 1:76, *n.* 6 for a description of the South Barrack.
7 Daniel W. Whitehurst, of Georgetown, South Carolina, was admitted in 1826 and ordered discharged by the general court martial in January 1827 (Entrance Register of Cadets [U.S. Military Academy Archives]).
8 Walter B. Guion (sketch, 1:75, *n.* 15).
9 James L. Thompson (sketch, 1:75, *n.* 11).
10 No. 5 was on the second floor of the North Barrack. See 1:75, *n.* 7.
11 David M. Farrelly (sketch, 1:75, *n.* 21).
12 Benny Havens (see 1:35, *n.* 12).

EXTRACT

1:79 Proceedings of a Court of Inquiry—Seventh Day Case of Seventy Cadets

West-Point, 15th January, 1827

The Court met pursuant to adjournment.

Present.
Maj. Worth,[1] President.
Capt. Hitchcock,[2] }
Lieut. Bryant,[3] } Members.
Lieut. Gird,[4] Recorder....

Cadet Dabney O. Carr,[5] being duly sworn and examined, testifies as follows:

I quartered in No. 41, South Barrack,[6] on the 25th December last. On that morning, I got up between 3 and 4 o'clock, I presume. Cadet Burnley[7] came over to my room before I was up and invited the occupants of my room over to his room. Previously a day or two before he <had>[8] invited us <to come>[8] over and drink egg-nogg, on Christmas morning. I went over. I met Capt. Hitchcock. He ordered me to my quarters. I returned to my quarters. Afterwards I went back again. I went on the 1st Division (2d Story)[9] into Cadet Mercer's[10] room. Several gentlemen were there—among them Cadets Lewis[11] and Mercer. I left there and went into Cadet Farrelly's[12] room.[13] I went into the back-room,[14] where there was a table at which they were making egg-nog. Once or twice the operations were suspended—as some one was coming. Some one asked me to see if Capt. Hitchcock was coming. When I returned they were talking about making another bucket of egg-nog. Capt. Hitchcock then came in. Cadet Davis came in afterwards, and said, "Put away the grog, Captain Hitchcock is coming," or words to that effect. Capt. Hitchcock recognized all who were in the room. He ordered me to my room. I came over to the South Barrack,[15] when I first heard a noise, and then went back and into the hall of the 2d Story. I only recognized one person though there were many there. Some one cried, "Stand out of the way, Guion[16] is going to shoot Captain Hitchcock." Guion turn to <—him—> the person, and shook his finger at him and said—"Dont mention my name again to-night." Capt. Hitchcock came out of his room with a lamp in his hand, and they all ran down stairs.

Afterwards I went over with Cadet Temple[17] to his room. We stayed there about half an hour—during which they were breaking windows in the North Barrack. We went over again. I then saw Cadet Guion looking for something, which he said was a pistol loaded with ball. With a candle I looked and found a pistol and gave it to Cadet Guion. I went into Cadet Farrelly's room. Cadet Gard[18] came in. He appeared to be in a great passion. "Fellows," he said, "the bombardiers[19] are coming. Let us go to the door." Then he swore and stamped. This was the first I heard of that report. . . .

The Court adjourned to meet to-morrow, at 9. a.m.

DS (NA, RG 153 Records of the Office of the Judge Advocate General [Army], Court Martial Records, BB-96, 1827), 153.

1 William J. Worth (sketch, 1:14, *n.* 1).

2 Ethan A. Hitchcock (sketch, 1:35, *n.* 5).

3 William Bryant (sketch, 1:74, *n.* 3).

4 Henry H. Gird (sketch, 1:33, *n.* 3).

5 Dabney O. Carr (sketch, 1:75, *n.* 14).

6 See 1:76, *n.* 6 for a description of the South Barrack.

7 William R. Burnley, from Russellville, Alabama, entered West Point at the age of sixteen in 1825. He was discharged May 1827 by sentence of a general court martial (Entrance Register of Cadets [U.S. Military Academy Archives]).

8 Interlined.

9 See 1:76, *n.* 12 for a discussion of the various divisions of the barracks.

10 Hugh W. Mercer (sketch, 1:77, *n.* 19).

[11] Thomas M. Lewis (sketch, 1:75, *n.* 19).
[12] David M. Farrelly (sketch, 1:75, *n.* 21).
[13] Farrelly's room was No. 5 North Barrack. See 1:75 for the occupants of room No. 5.
[14] See 1:77, *n.* 20 for an explanation of "back room."
[15] See 1:76, *n.* 6 for a description of the South Barrack.
[16] Walter B. Guion (sketch, 1:75, *n.* 15).
[17] Robert E. Temple (sketch, 1:75, *n.* 17).
[18] Benjamin F. Gard was a cadet from Ohio who entered the Academy in 1824 at age twenty. Arrested in March 1828 for having violated paragraph 1408 of the army regulations (see 1:34, *n.* 5), he resigned prior to the graduation of his class in July (Monthly Conduct Report, March 31, 1828 [NA, RG 94, Records Relating to the U.S. Military Academy, Entry 231]; Entrance Register of Cadets [U.S. Military Academy Archives]).
[19] "Bombardiers" was the name given by the cadets to a detachment of regular artillery troops stationed at West Point (T. J. Fleming, *West Point*, 58; Church, *Reminiscences*, 32).

EXTRACT

1:80
Proceedings of a Court of Inquiry—Eleventh Day Case of Seventy Cadets

West-Point, 19th January, 1827

The Court met pursuant to adjournment.

Present.
Major Worth,[1] President.
Capt. Hitchcock,[2] } Members.
Lieut. Bryant,[3] }
Lieut. Gird,[4] Recorder.

Cadet Samuel K. Cobb,[5] being duly sworn and examined, testifies as follows:

I quartered in No. 5, North Barrack,[6] on the 25th December last. Cadets Aisquith,[7] Carr,[8] Bibb,[9] Mercer,[10] Guion,[11] Thompson,[12] J. F. Davis, Temple[13] and J. B. Magruder,[14] were in my room that morning before reveillee. There was spirituous liquor in my room then. I was informed afterwards that the liquor was put in Cadet Farrelly's[15] trunk, when Capt. Hitchcock came to the room, at that time. After Capt. Hitchcock came in–he ordered the visitors to their rooms. He then asked me who was orderly. I told him Cadet Sevier.[16] He then had some conversation with Cadet Sevier, which I did not hear, except that I heard Cadet Sevier reply that something was to be determined in future. What he alluded to I did not understand. I heard Capt. Hitchcock say, after he had looked round some time, "I must have these trunks opened." Cadet Sevier, I think it was, then threw open a couple of trunks with his foot. Cadet T. M. Lewis[17] said–pointing to a trunk–that was Cadet Farrelly's trunk, and he was absent and it could not be opened. Cadet J. F. Davis came into the room soon after Capt. Hitchcock, (and while the <latter>[18] was there,) <–and–> saying "Boys, put away that grog. Capt. Hitchcock is coming." Capt. Hitchcock inspected the room, before he looked at the trunks.

Cadet Jefferson F. Davis, being duly sworn and examined, testifies as follows:

I quartered in No. 19, South Barrack,[19] on the 25th December last. I have heard Cadet J. L. Thompson say that some one had struck him on the head <with a club>[18] that morning, while he was standing–in the dark–on the back-stairs; which person he supposed to be an officer as he had on a Citizen's dress. Cadet Guion came to my room, (he is a room-mate of mine,) and told me that the bombardiers[20] were coming, and got a pistol; this was about one o'clock on that morning, I suppose. It was sometime after I returned to my room. I was asleep when he came for it. . . .

The Court adjourned to meet again to-morrow morning at ten o'clock.

DS (NA, RG 153 Records of the Office of the Judge Advocate General [Army], Court Martial Records, BB-96, 1827), 153.

[1] William J. Worth (sketch, 1:14, *n.* 1).
[2] Ethan A. Hitchcock (sketch, 1:35, *n.* 5).
[3] William Bryant (sketch, 1:74, *n.* 3).
[4] Henry H. Gird (sketch, 1:33, *n.* 3).
[5] Samuel K. Cobb (sketch, 1:75, *n.* 20).
[6] No. 5 was on the second floor of the North Barrack. See 1:75, *nn.* 6, 7.
[7] William E. Aisquith (sketch, 1:75, *n.* 9).
[8] Dabney O. Carr (sketch, 1:75, *n.* 14).
[9] Lucien I. Bibb (sketch, 1:75, *n.* 8).
[10] Hugh W. Mercer (sketch, 1:77, *n.* 19).
[11] Walter B. Guion (sketch, 1:75, *n.* 15).
[12] James L. Thompson (sketch, 1:75, *n.* 11).
[13] Robert E. Temple (sketch, 1:75, *n.* 17).
[14] John B. Magruder, born in Virginia in 1807, was a cadet at the Academy, 1826–30, and was appointed to the Seventh Infantry. He was transferred to the First Artillery in 1831, and served in the Florida and Mexican wars, being brevetted lieutenant colonel in 1847 for gallant and meritorious conduct at Chapultepec. Magruder resigned from the army in 1861 and was appointed brigadier, then major general in the Confederate Army the same year. After the Civil War he joined the

Mexican imperial forces as a major general. He retired to Houston, Texas, after the downfall of Maximilian and died there in 1871 (Cullum, *Biographical Register*, I, 455–56; Warner, *Generals in Gray*, 207–208; *DAB*).

[15] David M. Farrelly (sketch, 1:75, *n.* 21).

[16] Robert Sevier (sketch, 1:75, *n.* 18). See 1:77 for Sevier's testimony.

[17] Thomas M. Lewis (sketch, 1:75, *n.* 19).

[18] Interlined.

[19] Davis roomed with Guion in No. 19 in the South Barrack.

[20] See 1:79, *n.* 19 for the bombardiers.

EXTRACT

1:81

Proceedings of a Court of Inquiry—Twelfth Day
Case of Seventy Cadets

West Point, 20th January, 1827

The Court met pursuant to adjournment.

Present
Major Worth,[1] President.
Capt. Hitchcock,[2] } Members.
Lieut. Bryant,[3] }
Lieut. Gird,[4] Recorder. . . .

The Court of Inquiry report, as required, for the information of the Superintendent,[5] the fact—that the mutinous, riotous and disorderly proceedings which took place in and about the North-Barrack, on the morning of the 25th December last, originated in the immoderate use of liquor,[6] brought to the barracks several days previous by certain Cadets. . . .

The Court adjourned *sine die.*

W. J. Worth
Maj. & Prest. Ct. of Inquiry
H. H. Gird,
Lieut. & Adjt. Recorder of Ct. of Inquiry.

DS (NA, RG 153 Records of the Office of the Judge Advocate General [Army], Court Martial Records, BB-96, 1827), 153.

[1] William J. Worth (sketch, 1:14, *n.* 1).

[2] Ethan A. Hitchcock (sketch, 1:35, *n.* 5).

[3] William Bryant (sketch, 1:74, *n.* 3).

[4] Henry H. Gird (sketch, 1:33, *n.* 3).

[5] Sylvanus Thayer (sketch, 1:74, *n.* 6).

[6] In 1883 Davis wrote to his nephew's wife Mary Stamps to inquire what her father, Benjamin Grubb Humphreys,

had said of him and the Christmas riot. Humphreys, who attended the Academy at the same time as did Davis, and who, unlike Davis, had been dismissed for his part in the riot, was believed by Davis to be the author of an injurious story about him and the West Point riot. Davis wrote: "I recollect you once told me that your Father had said, to illustrate the difference between his luck & mine that I had got drunk so as not to participate in the Xmas riot & that he not getting drunk had on that occasion, performed acts for which he was dismissed. Now though the fact was not as he supposed but that I was arrested and confined to my quarters before the riot commenced as I believe I then explained to you more fully the story did not seem of sufficient importance to induce me to write to your father about it. The whole affair formed the basis for an exhaustive inquiry & the record will show what each cadet did & to what each Cadet testified under oath. The result was that nothing was found on which to frame charges against me, though if anyone had testified that I was drunk I should certainly have been brought before a court to answer to the charge. Very recently a story was put in circulation vastly different from that mentioned by you & in some of its particulars highly injurious to me. When I asked for the authority it was said to be the late Genl Humphreys, therefore it is that I wish to learn from you what he really did say & if he erroneously or from hearsay said anything to give colour to the story in circulation I shall have to resort to the old record for my vindication" (May 30, 1883 [Mrs. I. D. Stamps Farrar, New Orleans, 1968]).

In after years Humphreys, recalling his experiences at the Academy and his part in the Christmas riot, wrote: "I reached West Point in June 1825 and had no difficulty at the examination. . . . I was greatly pleased with the military life the camp, the drill and other duties and exercises. I pursued my studies with diligence and success, conforming to all rules and obeying all orders, until I became involved in a Christmas spree ending in a riot. A court of inquiry placed me under arrest in March and confined me to my quarters under charges of 'riotous, and disorderly conduct'. A court martial justly sentenced me and thirty-eight [nineteen] others, including Walter Guion, to be expelled from service of the U. States. I have ever regretted my error and regard it as one of the greatest personal misfortunes of my life. . . . One of the specifications against me was being drunk. As my father had ever regarded drunkenness with horror, I took special pains to prove my innocence. On this specification I was found *not guilty* by the Court" ("Autobiography," ed. Rainwater, *Mississippi Valley Historical Review*, XXI, 237–38).

Orders No. 9 1:82

U. S. Military Academy, West-Point, 25th January, 1827

In accordance with Military Academy Order No. 49,[1] of the last year, the following Officers are detailed as members of the General Court Martial to be held at this post, and of which Captain Thomas C. Legate[2] has been appointed President; viz:

1st Lieut. S. S. Smith,[3] (3d Art.)
1st Lieut. E. C. Ross,[4] (4th Art.)
2d Lieut. Jas. Grier,[5] (5th In.) } Members.
2d Lieut. T. B. Wheelock,[6] (2d Art.)
2d Lieut. R. P. Parrot,[7] (3d Art.)
Brevet 2d Lieut. W. H. C. Bartlett,[8] (Engrs.) } Supernumerary
2d Lieut. T. J. Cram,[9] (4th Art.) } Members.

The Court thus composed will convene in the Treasurer's office, to-morrow morning, at eleven o'clock. By order of Lieut. Col. Thayer,[10] Signed H. H. GIRD,[11]
Lieut. & Adjt.

D, copy (NA, RG 153 Records of the Office of the Judge Advocate General [Army], Court Martial Records, BB-96, 1827).

1 See 1:69 for Order No. 49.

2 Thomas C. Legate (sketch, 1:35, *n.* 3).

3 Samuel S. Smith, born in and appointed to the Academy from Delaware, was graduated in 1818. He served as assistant and principal assistant of mathematics, 1818–23, and was a teacher of natural and experimental philosophy from September 1823 until the time of his death in Delaware in 1828 (Cullum, *Biographical Register*, I, 186–87).

4 Edward C. Ross (sketch, 1:35, *n.* 10).

5 James Grier was a cadet, 1817–21, from New York. He served in the Second Artillery at various garrisons until his transfer to the Fifth Infantry and appointment to the Academy as assistant instructor of infantry tactics in 1825. He died in 1828 at age thirty at Jefferson Barracks, Missouri, while on recruiting service (Cullum, *Biographical Register*, I, 270).

6 Thompson B. Wheelock of Massachusetts attended West Point, 1818–22. He served in various garrisons, in the Fourth, Third, and Second artilleries until his resignation in 1829. He was president of Woodward College, Cincinnati, Ohio, 1830–33, and was reappointed to the army with the rank of first lieutenant of Dragoons in 1833. Having served in several garrisons and in the Seminole War, he died in Florida, aged thirty-five, in 1836 (Cullum, *Biographical Register*, I, 282).

7 Robert P. Parrott (1804–77), born in New Hampshire, attended the Academy, 1820–24, and after graduation served on the faculty there for five years. At the time of this court martial, he was assistant professor of mathematics. He resigned in 1836, a captain of ordnance, and became superintendent of the West Point Foundry Association, Cold Spring, New York, 1836–37 (Blake, *History of Putnam County, N. Y.*, 239–40; *DAB*), also called the West Point Iron and Cannon Foundry (Cullum, *Biographical Register*, I, 326; *Appleton's*; *National Cyclopaedia*, V, 366). Parrott experimented in the manufacture of ordnance, and in 1861 patented an improved expanded projectile for rifled ordnance and a design for strengthening cast-iron cannon. "Parrott projectiles" and "Parrott guns" were used extensively in the Civil War by the Union Army. Parrott had also served as first judge of the Court of Common Pleas, Putnam County, New York. He retired from the foundry in 1877 and died in Cold Spring (*DAB*).

8 William H. C. Bartlett was born in Pennsylvania, appointed to the Acad-

emy from Missouri in 1822, and was graduated at the head of his class in 1826. For Davis' reminiscence of Bartlett, see 1:2, lxxxi. He served in the Corps of Engineers, and was a member of the West Point faculty almost continuously from 1827 to 1871, when he retired as professor of natural and experimental philosophy. Author of several scientific monographs, he was associated after his retirement with a New York insurance company and died in 1893 (Cullum, *Biographical Register*, I, 364–65; Heitman, *Historical Register*, I, 196).

[9] Thomas J. Cram, born in New Hampshire, entered West Point in 1822. He served in the Second and Fourth artilleries and on the Academy faculty from his graduation in 1826 until his resignation in 1836; in January 1827 he was assistant professor of mathematics. After a brief period as a railroad engineer, he was reappointed to the Corps of Topographical Engineers with the rank of captain in 1838, and transferred to the Corps of Engineers as lieutenant colonel in 1863. Brevetted brigadier general and major general for faithful and meritorious service in 1866, he retired from active service in 1869 and died in Philadelphia in 1883 at the age of eighty (Cullum, *Biographical Register*, I, 366).

[10] Sylvanus Thayer (sketch, 1:74, *n.* 6).

[11] Henry H. Gird (sketch, 1:33, *n.* 3).

EXTRACT

Proceedings of a General Court Martial—First Day Trial of William E. Aisquith 1:83

Editorial Note: Of the seventy cadets implicated in the riotous proceedings of December 24–25, nineteen were eventually tried. All Davis' testimony and mention of Davis have been either extracted or abstracted from the proceedings, which ended March 15.

West Point, U. S. Military Academy, 26th January, 1827

Present.

Captain Thomas C. Legate,[1] (2d Art.)	President.
1st Lieut. S. S. Smith,[2] (3d Art.)	Members.
1st Lieut. E. C. Ross,[3] (4th Art.)	
2d Lieut. Jas. Grier,[4] (5th In.)	
2d Lieut. T. B. Wheelock,[5] (2d Art.)	
2d Lieut. R. P. Parrot,[6] (3d Art.)	
Brevet 2d Lieut. W. H. C. Bartlett,[7] (Engrs.)	Supernumerary members.
2d Lieut. T. J. Cram,[8] (4th Art.)	
2d Lieut. H. H. Gird,[9] Judge Advocate....	

Capt. Ethan A. Hitchcock,[10] Assistant Instructor of Tactics in the

U. S. Mil. Academy, a witness for the prosecution, being duly sworn says:

I saw Cadet Aisquith[11] on the morning of the 25th December last, about 5 o'clock, before reveillee. He was in room No. 5,[12] in the North-Barrack,[13] at this post. There were several Cadets in the room who were not occupants of the room. I gave them all orders to retire to their quarters. I think I gave a special order to Cadet Aisquith to retire to his quarters. I am well convinced of this: there is a bare possibility of mistake only. Most of the visitors in the room, were in the back-room around a table. The lights—2 candles—had recently been extinguished, when I entered the room. While I was in the room, a Cadet[14] entered saying "Put away that liquor," or words to that effect. After the visitors had retired, I inquired of the orderly of the room,[15] if there was liquor in the room. He declined giving a <positive>[16] answer. I saw no liquor in the room. I had no doubt the purpose of the assemblage was that of amusement, and from the remark of the Cadet entering the room, and the orderly's not answering my question, I had no doubt there had been liquor in the room. The time I saw the prisoner was about an hour or an hour and a quarter before the proper time for reveillee. It was before the riot or noise commenced in the Barrack.

DS (NA, RG 153 Records of the Office of the Judge Advocate General [Army], Court Martial Records, BB-96, 1827, Part I), 222.

1 Thomas C. Legate (sketch, 1:35, *n.* 3).
2 Samuel S. Smith (sketch, 1:82, *n.* 3).
3 Edward C. Ross (sketch, 1:35, *n.* 10).
4 James Grier (sketch, 1:82, *n.* 5).
5 Thompson B. Wheelock (sketch, 1:82, *n.* 6).
6 Robert P. Parrott (sketch, 1:82, *n.* 7).
7 William H. C. Bartlett (sketch, 1:82, *n.* 8).
8 Thomas J. Cram (sketch, 1:82, *n.* 9).
9 Henry H. Gird (sketch, 1:33, *n.* 3).
10 Ethan A. Hitchcock (sketch, 1:35, *n.* 5).
11 William E. Aisquith (sketch, 1:75, *n.* 9).
12 See 1:75, *n.* 7.
13 See 1:75, *n.* 6 for a description of the North Barrack.
14 The cadet was Davis. See 1:77, 79, 80.
15 The orderly was Robert Sevier (sketch, 1:75, *n.* 18). See also 1:80.
16 Interlined.

ABSTRACT

Monthly Conduct Report 1:84

[U.S. Military Academy,] January 31, 1827

Lists Cadet J. Davis and 60 other cadets out of a total of 221 as "distinguished for Correct conduct" during January.[1]

DS (NA, RG 94 Records of the Adjutant General's Office, Records Relating to the U.S. Military Academy, Monthly Conduct Reports, Entry 231), 2. Signed: "S. Thayer Lt Col Comdg."

[1] The Record of Delinquencies (1:116) states that Davis had no offenses during January.

ABSTRACT

Merit Roll 1:85

U.S. Military Academy, January [31,][1] 1827

Ranks Cadet J. Davis at the general examination given in January 1827 as twenty-ninth out of forty-three members of the second class[2] in natural philosophy, twenty-third out of forty-three members of the second class in chemistry, and thirty-ninth out of forty-three members of the second class in drawing.

DS (NA, RG 94 Records of the Adjutant General's Office, Records Relating to the U.S. Military Academy, Merit Rolls, Entry 230), 6; D, copy, transcription from letterbook copy in the War Department (U.S. Military Academy Archives). Signed: "Military Academy West Point 20th. Jany 1827 S. Thayer Lt Col Supndt. Mil. Acady."

[1] The inconsistency of dating in this document, *i.e.*, between the date line and that appearing in the signature line of the descriptive footnote, can be explained, but not reconciled. The various merit rolls have been arbitrarily assigned to the last day of their respective months because the greater number of them bear no date at all.

[2] See 1:18, *n.* 3 for an explanation of the West Point class system.

EXTRACT

1:86 Proceedings of a General Court Martial—Eleventh Day Trial of Walter B. Guion

West Point, U. S. Military Academy, 7th February, 1827
Present–as before. . . .

Cadet Jefferson F. Davis, a witness for the defence, being duly sworn, answers as follows:

Ques. Pris. Do you not recollect that the prisoner[1] came into your room on the morning of the 25th December–and got a pistol, and did he not state at that time that it was to oppose the Artillery Company[2] who were reported to have been turned out?

Ans. He did.

DS (NA, RG 153 Records of the Office of the Judge Advocate General [Army], Court Martial Records, BB–96, 1827, Part I), 222. Signed: "H. H. Gird, Lieut. & Adjt. Judge Advocate W. J. Worth Major U S A Prest. the Court."

[1] The prisoner was Guion, Davis' roommate (sketch, 1:75, *n.* 15).

[2] The cadets called the regulars belonging to the Artillery Company the bombardiers (see 1:79, *n.* 19).

1:87 Orders No. 14

U. S. M. Academy West Point. 8th Feby 1827

Cadet J. F. Davis is hereby released from <—his—> arrest.[1] he will accordingly return to his duty. By order of Lt Col Thayer[2]

H. H. GIRD[3]
Lt & adj't

LbC, transcription from letterbook copy in the War Department (U.S. Military Academy Archives).

[1] Davis was under arrest from December 26, 1826 (1:68), to February 8, 1827. Mrs. Davis writes, although the records do not completely substantiate her statement, that "Cadet ——— [Guion], his room-mate, was discovered and dismissed with several others. Davis was implicated unjustly. Because his room-mate had been mistaken for him he would not explain, and consequently was under arrest for a long period, and his already numerous demerits received a considerable addition" (*Memoir*, I, 54).

[2] Sylvanus Thayer (sketch, 1:74, *n.* 6).

[3] Henry H. Gird (sketch, 1:33, *n.* 3).

ABSTRACT

Monthly Conduct Report 1:88

[U.S. Military Academy,] February 28, 1827

Lists Cadet J. Davis and 51 other cadets out of a total of 218 as "distinguished for correct conduct" during February.[1]

DS (NA, RG 94 Records of the Adjutant General's Office, Records Relating to the U.S. Military Academy, Monthly Conduct Reports, Entry 231), 2. Signed: "S. Thayer Lt Col Comdg." Endorsed: "Recd. 20. March 1827."

[1] The Record of Delinquencies (1:116) substantiates the above.

ABSTRACT

Muster Roll of the Corps of Cadets 1:89

West Point, New York, February 28, 1827

Lists Jefferson F. Davis, United States Military Academy, Corps of Cadets commanded by Major William J. Worth,[1] as present at the post. Remarks: "Sergt. of the Colour G[uar]d." [2]

DS (U.S. Military Academy Archives), 7. Signed: "Thos. S. Trask Adjt. of the Corps W. J. Worth Majr. Com[mandin]g Corps Mustering & Insp[ectin]g Offr."

[1] William J. Worth (sketch, 1:14, *n.* 1).

[2] See 1:62 for evidence of Davis' having been appointed sergeant of the color guard.

EXTRACT

Proceedings of a General Court Martial—Thirtieth Day Trial of James M. Berrien 1:90

West Point, U. S. Military Academy, 1st March, 1828 [1]

Present—all—except Lieut. Cram,[2] Supernumerary member, absent sick. . . .

Cadet Samuel A. Roberts,[3] a witness for the defence, being duly sworn, answers as follows:

Ques. Pris.[4] Were you not in No. 5,[5] North-Barrack,[6] at the time

Capt. Hitchcock[7] entered and was not Cadet Guion[8] there at the same time: this on the night of the 24th or morning of the 25th December, 1826?

Ans. I believe he did not order him. I saw him halt Cadet Guion and take his name

Ques. Pris. If Capt. Hitchcock had ordered Cadet Guion to his room would you not have heard him?

Ans. I presume I would.

Ques. J. Adv[9]–How <–wher–> near were you to Capt. Hitchcock at the time he ordered Cadet Guion to halt?

Ans. Five feet.

Ques. J. Adv. At what time precisely did Capt. Hitchcock take Cadet Guion's name? Was it before or after he turned to Cadet Thompson?[10]

Ans. I cannot say.

Ques. Court. Who were the individuals in the room?

[To this question a member objected. The Court was cleared, and decided not to sustain the objection. The Court was then opened.][11]

Ans. There was Cadets Guion, Thompson, Sullivan,[12] Bomford,[13] J. F. Davis, and I think Cadets Bibb[14] and Temple[15] were there.

Ques. Court–Name as many of the individuals who received an order to go to their rooms as you recollect?

Ans. Cadets Sullivan and Davis did I am certain, and whether Cadet Bibb did or not I am not certain.

Ques. J. Adv. Did Capt. Hitchcock in giving his orders to those gentlemen as far as you heard speak in a low voice or not?

Ans. He spoke in an audible voice.

Ques. J. Adv. The question is–did he speak in a low voice.

Ans. He spoke to them so that I heard him.

Ques. J. Adv. When he gave those orders which you heard were you as near to him as the gentlemen he ordered.

Ans. I was not.

Ques. J. Adv. How much farther were you?

Ans. When he spoke to Cadet Davis I was in the back-room.[16] Cadet Davis was at the fire-place in the front-room. Capt. Hitchcock walked up to Cadet Davis. The others were in the back-room. I was myself there and so was Capt. Hitchcock. I believe Capt. Hitchcock was standing in the door of the back-room and as they came to the door he ordered them to go to their quarters. I was standing about five feet from the door. . . .

The prisoner requests the Court to refer to and consider the evidence of Capt. Hitchcock, as given in the case of Cadet Guion, so far as relates to the matter in issue: which the Court grants.

No further evidence was offered on the part of the defence; and the Judge Advocate requested further proceeding to be postponed until to-morrow morning, which the Court granted.

DS (NA, RG 153 Records of the Office of the Judge Advocate General [Army], Court Martial Records, BB–96, 1827, Part II), 364. Signed: "H. H. Gird, Lieut. & adjt. Judge Advocate. W. J Worth Major U S army Prest. the Court."

1 Obviously a clerical error, since the year should be 1827.

2 Thomas J. Cram (sketch, 1:82, *n.* 9).

3 Samuel A. Roberts (sketch, 1:75, *n.* 12).

4 The prisoner was John M. Berrien (sketch, 1:55, *n.* 4).

5 See 1:75, *n.* 7 for further information on the location of room No. 5.

6 See 1:75, *n.* 6 for a description of the North Barrack.

7 Ethan A. Hitchcock (sketch, 1:35, *n.* 5).

8 Walter B. Guion (sketch, 1:75, *n.* 15).

9 Henry H. Gird (sketch, 1:33, *n.* 3) was the judge advocate (1:83).

10 James L. Thompson (sketch, 1:75, *n.* 11).

11 Brackets in the original text.

12 George R. Sullivan (sketch, 1:75, *n.* 13).

13 George C. Bomford (sketch, 1:75, *n.* 10).

14 Lucien I. Bibb (sketch, 1:75, *n.* 8).

15 Robert E. Temple (sketch, 1:75, *n.* 17).

16 See 1:77, *n.* 20 for an explanation of the "back-room."

ABSTRACT

Monthly Conduct Report 1:91

[U.S. Military Academy,] March 31, 1827

Lists Cadet J. Davis as having committed one offense during March.[1]

DS (NA, RG 94 Records of the Adjutant General's Office, Records Relating to the U.S. Military Academy, Monthly Conduct Reports, Entry 231), 2. Signed: "S. Thayer Lt Col Comdg."

1 The Record of Delinquencies (1:116) does not list Davis with any offenses during March.

EXTRACT

1:92 ## Order No. 55

U. S. M. Academy West Point 24 April 1827

Cadet Rousseau[1] is transferd to the 2nd & Cadet J. Davis to the 3rd Section[2] of Chemistry. By order W. H. C. BARTLETT[3]
Lt & Act Adjt

LbC, transcription from letterbook copy in the War Department (U.S. Military Academy Archives), 1.

[1] Gustave S. Rousseau (1806–79) was born in Louisiana, where his father had been the commanding general of Spain's Mississippi River warships, 1792–1803. Rousseau was in the 1828 West Point graduating class and served at Jefferson Barracks, 1828–29 and 1830–31, but was not there when Davis arrived in January 1829, contrary to Mrs. Davis' statement (*Memoir*, I, 55; Post Return, January 1829 [NA, RG 94, Post Returns, Jefferson Barracks]). See also Northrop to Davis, April 17, 1879, for a comment on Rousseau at Jefferson Barracks (D. Rowland, *Papers*, VIII, 379). Rousseau resigned from the army in 1833 and was a bank cashier, sheriff, and brigadier general of Louisiana militia before the Mexican War, in which he served briefly. After the war he continued as chief of the militia until 1855 and managed his plantation at Bayou Goula. He was counselor-at-law in Plaquemine from 1858 until his death (Clement, *Plantation Life*, 150–55; Cullum, *Biographical Register*, I, 415). Davis evidently followed Rousseau's career, for he noted his death in a letter to Northrop (April 25, 1879, D. Rowland, *Papers*, VIII, 384).

[2] Thayer introduced the system "of dividing classes into sections with constant transfer from one to another, according to preparation and ability of the students . . ." (W. L. Fleming, "Davis at West Point," Mississippi Historical *Publications*, X, 252). The first section of a class, which included the better students, was taught by the head of the department, while the others were taught by various assistants (T. J. Fleming, *West Point*, 31).

[3] William H. C. Bartlett (sketch, 1:82, *n.* 8).

ABSTRACT

1:93 ## Monthly Return

West Point, New York, April 30, 1827

Lists Cadet J. F. Davis as being present and sick.

DS (U.S. Military Academy Archives), 2. Signed: "Wm H C Bartlett Lieut & act adjt S. Thayer Lt. Col Comdg." Endorsed: "Recd. May 10th."

ABSTRACT

Muster Roll of the Corps of Cadets 1:94

West Point, New York, April 30, 1827

Lists Jefferson F. Davis, United States Military Academy, Corps of Cadets commanded by Major William J. Worth,[1] as present at the post. Remarks: "Sick."

DS (U.S. Military Academy Archives), 7. Signed: "N. J. Eaton Actg. Adjt of the Corps. W. J Worth Maj Com[mandin]g Corps Mustering & Insp[ectin]g offr."

[1] William J. Worth (sketch, 1:14, *n.* 1).

ABSTRACT

Yearly Conduct Report 1:95

[U.S. Military Academy,] June 30, 1827

Ranks Cadet Jefferson Davis, second class,[1] 101st out of 202 cadets with seventy demerits for the year.[2]

D (NA, RG 94 Records of the Adjutant General's Office, Records Relating to the U.S. Military Academy, filed with Merit Rolls, Entry 230), 1.

[1] See 1:18, *n.* 3 for an explanation of the West Point class system.

[2] See 1:116 for a detailed list of Davis' delinquencies.

ABSTRACT

Merit Roll 1:96

[U.S. Military Academy,] June [30,][1] 1827

Ranks Cadet J. Davis at the general examination given in June 1827 as thirtieth out of thirty-seven members of the second class[2] in natural and experimental philosophy, twenty-second out of thirty-seven members of the second class in chemistry, and thirty-third out of thirty-seven members of the second class in drawing, landscape and topography.

D (NA, RG 94 Records of the Adjutant General's Office, Records Relating to the U.S. Military Academy, Merit Rolls, Entry 230), 5; D, copy, transcription from letterbook copy in the War Department (U.S. Military Academy Archives). Endorsed: "Handed in by Col. Thayer June 29th."

[1] See 1:85, *n.* 1 for an explanation of the inconsistent dates of this item.

[2] The West Point class system is discussed in 1:18, *n.* 3.

ABSTRACT

1:97

Yearly Merit Roll

[U.S. Military Academy,] June [30,][1] 1827

Ranks Cadet Jefferson Davis twenty-ninth out of thirty-seven members of the second class,[2] with 130 merits in philosophy, 55 merits in chemistry, and 41 merits in drawing, for a total of 226.[3]

D (NA, RG 94 Records of the Adjutant General's Office, Records Relating to the U.S. Military Academy, Merit Rolls, Entry 230), 5; D, copy, transcription from letterbook copy in the War Department (U.S. Military Academy Archives). Endorsed: "Handed in by Col. Thayer June 29th."

[1] See 1:85, *n.* 1 for an explanation of the inconsistency in dating.

[2] The West Point class system is discussed in 1:18, *n.* 3.

[3] See 1:30, *n.* 2 for an explanation of the West Point system of grading.

ABSTRACT

1:98

Muster Roll of the Corps of Cadets

West Point, New York, June 30, 1827

Lists Jefferson F. Davis, United States Military Academy, Corps of Cadets commanded by Major William J. Worth,[1] as present at the post.

DS (U.S. Military Academy Archives), 7. Signed: "E Sterett Adjt. of Corps."

[1] William J. Worth (sketch, 1:14, *n.* 1).

ABSTRACT

1:99

Semiannual Muster Roll of the Corps of Cadets

West Point, New York, June 30, 1827

Lists Jefferson F. Davis of Mississippi, second class,[1] United States

Military Academy, Corps of Cadets commanded by Major William J. Worth,[2] as being age twenty years,[3] and as present at the post.

DS (NA, RG 94 Records of the Adjutant General's Office, Records Relating to the U.S. Military Academy, Semi-annual Muster Rolls of Cadets, Entry 227), 6; DS (U.S. Military Academy Archives). Signed: "W. J Worth Major Commanding."

[1] See 1:18, *n.* 3 for a discussion of the West Point class system.

[2] William J. Worth (sketch, 1:14, *n.* 1).

[3] Davis' age is figured from the year 1807. See 1:1, *n.* 1 for a discussion of the year of Davis' birth.

ABSTRACT

Battalion Order No. 50 1:100

Camp Wood,[1] [West Point,] July 5, 1827

Cadet Davis, and thirty-three other members of the first class, "will recite in Tactics daily from 2 to 4 P. M." By order of Major Worth.[2]

GEORGE E. CHASE[3]
Adjutant Corps of Cadets.

LbC, transcription from letterbook copy in the War Department (U.S. Military Academy Archives), 1.

[1] See 1:55, *nn.* 1, 2 for discussion of the summer encampment at West Point.

[2] William J. Worth (sketch, 1:14, *n.* 1).

[3] George E. Chase, cadet from Massachusetts, entered West Point in 1824 and was graduated in 1828. At the time of his resignation from the army in 1833, he was a second lieutenant of the Third Artillery. He became a United States civil engineer in 1839, and died at age thirty-nine in 1844 in Florida (Cullum, *Biographical Register*, I, 409).

ABSTRACT

Battalion Order No. 67 1:101

Camp Wood,[1] West Point, August 5, 1827

Cadet Davis, along with thirty-one other members of the first class,[2] is assigned to receive "daily instruction in fencing from M. Simon Sword—Mr." [3]

LbC, transcription from letterbook copy in the War Department (U.S. Military Academy Archives), 1.

[1] See 1:55, *nn.* 1, 2 for discussion of the summer encampment at West Point.

[2] See 1:18, *n.* 3 for a discussion of the West Point class system.

[3] Louis S. Simon was swordmaster at the Military Academy from 1826 until his resignation in 1831. Prior to his appointment to fill the vacancy caused by the death of swordmaster P. Truinque, Simon had been employed for several years at a seminary in New York City (Heitman, *Historical Register*, I, 887; NA, RG 94, Records Relating to the U.S. Military Academy, Correspondence Relating to the Military Academy, 1826, No. 178).

EXTRACT

1:102

Order: Laboratory Duty

Camp Wood[1] West-Point Aug. 15th 1827

Cadets Gard,[2] (squad marcher) Brockway,[3] C. J. Wright,[4] Davis, Drayton,[5] Van Wyck,[6] Penrose[7] & Gardinier[8] are detailed for Laboratory duty. The second laboratory section[9] is relieved from that duty. Hereafter the Second fencing section will attend at ½ past 9 A.M. & the 4th Section from 5 to 6 A. M. . . . By Command of Major Worth[10]

GEORGE E. CHASE[11]
Adjutant Cadets.

LbC, transcription from letterbook copy in the War Department (U.S. Military Academy Archives), 1.

[1] See 1:55, *nn.* 1, 2 for a discussion of the summer encampment at West Point.

[2] Benjamin F. Gard (sketch, 1:79, *n.* 18).

[3] Thomas C. Brockway was born in Connecticut and appointed to the Academy in 1824. After graduation he served from 1829 until 1831 in Indian territory, both at Fort Gibson and on the military road. At the time of his death at Fort Gibson in 1831 at the age of twenty-six, he was a second lieutenant in the Seventh Infantry (Cullum, *Biographical Register*, I, 418).

[4] Crafts J. Wright (sketch, 1:75, *n.* 16).

[5] Thomas F. Drayton (sketch, 1:77, *n.* 16).

[6] Philip R. Van Wyck was born in New Jersey and appointed to West Point in 1824. He was graduated in 1828 but was not commissioned because of deafness. He was appointed and served as a United States civil engineer from 1828 until his death by drowning in the Tennessee River in 1832, at the age of twenty-five (Cullum, *Biographical Register*, I, 419; Heitman, *Historical Register*, I, 985).

[7] James W. Penrose was appointed to the Academy from Missouri in 1824 and was graduated and commissioned in 1828. He served in the Black Hawk and Seminole wars and was brevetted major for gallantry in the Mexican War in 1847. He died in garrison in New York at the age of forty-one in 1849 (Cullum, *Biographical Register*, I, 419; Heitman, *Historical Register*, I, 783).

[8] John R. B. Gardenier was born in New York and attended the Academy, 1823–28, where he was an intimate friend of Davis (W. L. Fleming, "Davis at West Point," Mississippi Historical

Publications, X, 266). A veteran of the Black Hawk, Seminole, and Mexican wars, he was a captain of the First Infantry and on sick leave at the time of his death in Arkansas in 1850, at the age of forty-two (Cullum, *Biographical Register*, I, 418).

9 See 1:92, *n.* 2 for a discussion of the West Point system of dividing classes into sections.

10 William J. Worth (1:14, *n.* 1).

11 George E. Chase (1:100, *n.* 3).

EXTRACT

Battalion Order No. 80 1:103

West-Point Septr 6th 1827

The following Cadets, vis: Morrison,[1] Adams,[2] Lane,[3] Mather,[4] Ba[ker],[5] Thompson,[6] Torrence,[7] Gard,[8] Davis, C. J. Wright,[9] Van Wyck,[10] Drayton,[11] Brockwa[y],[12] Foster,[13] Gardenier[14] & Penrose,[15] of the first Class[16] will attend daily at the L[ab]oratory from 4 to ½ past 5 P. M. to receive instruction in Pyrotechny[17] from [Lt.] Kinsley.[18] Cadet Drayton will take command of the squad, and he wi[ll] be held responsible that the above-named Cadets march to & from the L[ab]. They will not be excused from evening parade. . . .

By order of Lieut. Thornton[19] GEORGE E. CHASE[20]
Adjt of the Corps.

LbC, transcription from letterbook copy in the War Department (U.S. Military Academy Archives), 1. Manuscript worn.

1 William L. E. Morrison, born in Missouri, was a cadet at the Academy from 1824 until graduation in 1828. He resigned from the army, still a brevet second lieutenant of the Second Infantry, in 1830. A civil engineer, he died in Illinois, aged twenty-five, in 1835 (Cullum, *Biographical Register*, I, 416; Heitman, *Historical Register*, I, 729).

2 Thomas B. Adams, cadet at West Point, 1824–28, was born in Massachusetts and died in Florida in 1837 at age twenty-eight. He served in the Seminole War and attained the rank of first lieutenant of Second Artillery (Cullum, *Biographical Register*, I, 410).

3 John F. Lane was born in Kentucky, attended the Academy, 1824–28, and was an instructor there after graduation. He was colonel of the Creek Volunteers in the Seminole War and died in Florida at the age of twenty-six in 1836 (Cullum, *Biographical Register*, I, 409–10).

4 William W. Mather (1804–59) was born in Connecticut, a descendant of Richard Mather, the Puritan clergyman. After graduation from West Point in 1828, he was science instructor there for six years. He resigned from the army as a first lieutenant in 1836, and had a distinguished career as professor, engineer, and author in the natural sciences until his sudden death in Ohio (*DAB*; Cullum, *Biographical Register*, I, 412–13).

5 William H. Baker, born in Michigan, was graduated from West Point in 1828 and resigned from the army in 1831, a second lieutenant of the Fourth

Infantry. In 1835 he died in Michigan, aged twenty-six (Cullum, *Biographical Register*, I, 414).

[6] James L. Thompson (sketch, 1:75, *n.* 11).

[7] Samuel Torrence, born in Pennsylvania, was a cadet, 1823–28, and served as second lieutenant of the Fourth Infantry on the frontier and in the Black Hawk War. He died in Illinois at the age of twenty-six in 1832 (Cullum, *Biographical Register*, I, 417).

[8] Benjamin F. Gard (sketch, 1:79, *n.* 18).

[9] Crafts J. Wright (sketch, 1:75, *n.* 16).

[10] Philip R. Van Wyck (sketch, 1:102, *n.* 6).

[11] Thomas F. Drayton (sketch, 1:77, *n.* 16).

[12] Thomas C. Brockway (sketch, 1:102, *n.* 3).

[13] Amos Foster was born in New Hampshire, graduated in 1828 from the Academy, and was a twenty-seven-year-old second lieutenant of the Fifth Infantry in Michigan when he was killed by a soldier in 1832 (Cullum, *Biographical Register*, I, 417).

[14] John R. B. Gardenier (sketch, 1:102, *n.* 8).

[15] James W. Penrose (sketch, 1:102, *n.* 7).

[16] See 1:18, *n.* 3 for a discussion of the West Point class system.

[17] The fireball incident mentioned in connection with the Zebina J. D. Kinsley biographical sketch (1:35, *n.* 6) may well have occurred during this particular class.

[18] Zebina J. D. Kinsley (sketch, 1:35, *n.* 6).

[19] William A. Thornton (sketch, 1:75, *n.* 23).

[20] George E. Chase (sketch, 1:100, *n.* 3).

ABSTRACT

1:104

Monthly Return

West Point, New York, September 30, 1827

Lists Cadet Davis as being present and sick.

DS (U.S. Military Academy Archives), 2. Signed: "F. L. Griffith Adjt S. Thayer Lt Col Comdg." Endorsed: "Recd 6 Augt."

ABSTRACT

1:105

Monthly Conduct Report

U.S. Military Academy, November 30, 1827

Lists Cadet J. Davis as having committed one offense during November.[1]

DS (NA, RG 94 Records of the Adjutant General's Office, Records Relating to the U.S. Military Academy, Monthly Conduct Reports, Entry 231), 2. Signed: "S. Thayer Lt. Col Supndt. Mil. Academy."

[1] Davis' record of delinquencies (1:116) also shows that he had one offense during November.

ABSTRACT

Monthly Conduct Report 1:106

U.S. Military Academy, December 31, 1827

Lists Cadet J. Davis as having committed two offenses during December.[1]

DS (NA, RG 94 Records of the Adjutant General's Office, Records Relating to the U.S. Military Academy, Monthly Conduct Reports, Entry 231), 2. Signed: "S. Thayer Lt Col Supnd Mil Acady."

[1] Contrary to the above, Davis' record of delinquencies (1:116) lists him as having committed three offenses during December.

ABSTRACT

Semiannual Muster Roll of the Corps of Cadets 1:107

West Point, New York, December 31, 1827

Lists Jefferson F. Davis of Mississippi, first class,[1] United States Military Academy, Corps of Cadets commanded by Major William J. Worth,[2] as being age twenty years six months,[3] and as present at the post.

DS (U.S. Military Academy Archives), 8. Signed: "George E. Chase Adjt Corps of Cadets."

[1] See 1:18, *n.* 3 for a discussion of the West Point class system.

[2] William J. Worth (sketch, 1:14, *n.* 1).

[3] Davis' age is figured from 1807. See 1:1, *n.* 1 for a discussion of the year of Davis' birth.

ABSTRACT

Battalion Order No. 4 1:108

West Point, January 21, 1828

Cadet J. F. Davis and fifteen other cadets are organized into a "Hose Company" [1] under the supervision of Lieutenant Winder.[2] "In case of fire, Cadets Magruder[3] and Davis will repair to the *fire-plug*. They will see a hose properly attached to the same, and regulate the supply of water."

WM A. THORNTON,[4]
Lieut. Commanding Corps.

LbC, transcription from letterbook copy in the War Department (U.S. Military Academy Archives), 1.

1 Of a similar type duty, Albert E. Church wrote: "We had a small hand fire-engine, which was seldom required, and well drilled fire organizations. It was my lot to be captain of the fire company during my graduating year [1828]" (*Reminiscences*, 22).

2 John H. Winder (1800–65) was the son of Brigadier General William H. Winder, who served in the War of 1812. John Winder was born in Maryland and attended West Point, 1814–20. He resigned from the army in 1823, and was reappointed in 1827 as a second lieutenant in the First Artillery. From November 1827 to September 1828, he was assistant instructor of infantry tactics. Davis recalled in later years, "Of Gen. Winder as an instructor of tactics when we were cadets, I had no particular knowledge; my acquaintance with him in the old army was mainly from the reports, and my estimate of him thus formed was that he was a gallant man, and a good officer" (Davis to Wright, February 12, 1876, D. Rowland, *Papers*, VII, 495). After service in various garrisons, Winder was in the Seminole and Mexican wars, and was brevetted lieutenant colonel in 1847 for gallant conduct. Having resigned his commission in April 1861, he was appointed a brigadier general in the Confederate Army and provost marshal of Richmond, and was later commissary general of prisoners east of the Mississippi. Winder died in South Carolina (*DAB*; Cullum, *Biographical Register*, I, 252–53; Warner, *Generals in Gray*, 340–41).

3 John B. Magruder (sketch, 1:80, *n.* 14).

4 William A. Thornton (sketch, 1:75, *n.* 23).

ABSTRACT

1:109 **Monthly Conduct Report**

U.S. Military Academy, January 31, 1828

Lists Cadet J. Davis as having committed two offenses during January.[1]

DS (NA, RG 94 Records of the Adjutant General's Office, Records Relating to the U.S. Military Academy, Monthly Conduct Reports, Entry 231), 2. Signed: "S. Thayer Lt. Col Supnd Mil Acady."

1 See 1:116, which, confirming the above, lists Davis as having committed two offenses during January.

ABSTRACT

Merit Roll 1:110

U.S. Military Academy, January 31, 1828

Ranks Cadet J. Davis at the general examination given in January 1828 as twenty-fifth out of thirty-four members of the first class[1] in engineering, thirteenth out of thirty-four members of the first class in rhetoric and moral philosophy, twenty-second out of thirty-four members of the first class in chemistry and mineralogy, and twenty-sixth out of thirty-four members of the first class in artillery.

D (NA, RG 94 Records of the Adjutant General's Office, Records Relating to the U.S. Military Academy, Merit Rolls, Entry 230), 6; D, copy, transcription from letterbook copy in the War Department (U.S. Military Academy Archives).

[1] See 1:18, *n.* 3 for an explanation of the West Point class system.

ABSTRACT

Monthly Conduct Report 1:111

U.S. Military Academy, February 29, 1828

Lists Cadet J. Davis as having committed two offenses during February.[1]

DS (NA, RG 94 Records of the Adjutant General's Office, Records Relating to the U.S. Military Academy, Monthly Conduct Reports, Entry 231), 2. Signed: "S. Thayer Lt Col Supnd Mil Acady."

[1] The Record of Delinquencies (1:116) confirms that Davis committed two offenses during February.

ABSTRACT

Monthly Conduct Report 1:112

U.S. Military Academy, March 31, 1828

Lists Cadet J. Davis as having committed two offenses during March.[1]

DS (NA, RG 94 Records of the Adjutant General's Office, Records Relating to the U.S. Military Academy, Monthly Conduct Reports, Entry 231),

2. Signed: "S. Thayer Lt Col Supnd Mil Acady." Endorsed: "Recd from the War Department Septr 23rd 1828."

[1] The Record of Delinquencies (1:116) lists Davis with only one offense during March.

ABSTRACT

1:113 ## Monthly Conduct Report

U.S. Military Academy, April 30, 1828

Lists Cadet J. Davis as having committed four offenses during April.[1]

DS (NA, RG 94 Records of the Adjutant General's Office, Records Relating to the U.S. Military Academy, Monthly Conduct Reports, Entry 231), 2. Signed: "S. Thayer Lt. Col Supnd Mil Acady."

[1] The Record of Delinquencies (1:116) confirms that Davis committed four offenses during April.

ABSTRACT

1:114 ## Order No. 67

U.S. Military Academy, May 4, 1828

Cadet J. F. Davis and eight other cadets "will attend Laboratory duties at 4 O'Clock P. M. until further orders. . . ." By order of Lieutenant Colonel Thayer[1]

F. L. GRIFFITH,[2]
Adjutant.

LbC, transcription from letterbook copy in the War Department (U.S. Military Academy Archives), 1.

[1] Sylvanus Thayer (sketch, 1:74, *n.* 6).

[2] Frederick L. Griffith, a cadet at the Academy from Virginia, 1814–17, was graduated as a third lieutenant in the Corps of Artillery. (The grade third lieutenant was evidently abolished March 2, 1821, by "An Act to reduce and fix the military peace establishment of the United States" whereby the Ordnance Department was merged with the artillery and each regiment of artillery was reorganized [*Statutes at Large of the United States*, III (1846), 615]). After service in the Seminole campaign, 1817–18, he was assigned to various garrisons and was first lieutenant of Second Artillery and adjutant at West Point, May 1827 to September 1831. He died at age thirty-five in 1832 in Alexandria, D.C. (Cullum, *Biographical Register*, I, 161).

ABSTRACT

Order No. 70 1:115

U.S. Military Academy, May 6, 1828

Cadet J. Davis and seven other cadets are to "attend the Fencing-Master,[1] every other day from 6 to 7 A. M. . . ." By order of Lieutenant Colonel Thayer[2]

F. L. GRIFFITH,[3]
Adjutant.

LbC, transcription from letterbook copy in the War Department (U.S. Military Academy Archives), 1.

[1] Louis S. Simon (sketch, 1:101, *n.* 3) was the fencing master.

[2] Sylvanus Thayer (sketch, 1:74, *n.* 6).

[3] Frederick L. Griffith (sketch, 1:114, *n.* 2).

EXTRACT

Record of Delinquencies of the Corps of Cadets[1] 1:116

[West Point, New York,] June 5, 1828

Davis. J

Absent from G[uar]d Mounting	16	Oct 1824
Dis[obedience] of ord[ers]	17	
Absent from g[uar]d mounting	17	
Visiting in Study Hours[2]	3	Nov
Dis[obedience] of ord[ers]	18	
Violation of 93. Par. Reg.[2]	28.	"
" " " " "	13	Feb 1825
" " " " "	5	March
Fender insecurely placed[3]	19	
Door not Closed	28.	
Visiting in Study Hours[2]	31.	
Ab[sent] from qrs.	"	
" " "	6.	April
" " Class parade[4]	6.	
Late at " "	6.	
Absent from qrs.	12	April
Bad police	13.	
Ab[sent] from qrs.	14.	
" " marching to French[4]	18.	

Cot down after reveille.[5]		23.	
Ab[sent] from qrs. from 7 'till 11. P.M.		23.	
Ab[sent] from Reveille		23.	
Ab[sent] from qrs. from 8 untill 9 P.M.		23.	
Long hair at Inspection.[6]		24.	
Dis[obedience] of B[attalion] O[rder] No 40.		17.	May.
Ab[sent] from drill		8	June
Bed not strapped 30′ after rev[eille][5]		17.	
Room not policed		24.	
Not Marching from Mess Hall[7]		5	July
Orderly paper not posted[8]		17	
Ab[sent] from 12 O Clock Drill		29	
" " Eve[ning] Parade		31	
In rear rank at Ev[ening] Parade		4	Augt.
Candlestick out of Place		10	Sepr.
Carrying his musket improperly on Drill		12	
Dis[obedience] of Post order No 117		26	
Bed not strapped 30′ after rev[eille][5]		29	
Candlesticks out of order		3	Oct
Name not Posted as orderly[8]		Excused "	
Bad Police. (Foul clothes not in Clothes Bag)		2	Novr
Ab[sent] from Art[iller]y drill		9	
Dis[obedience] of Special order and not to be found for drill		9	
Ab[sent] from Inf[antr]y drill		11	
Making unnecessary noise in S[tudy] H[ours]		27	
Ab[sent] from Church[9]		27	
" " Qrs. in S[tudy] H[ours]	4	23	Decr.
Visiting in S[tudy] H[ours][2]	3	31.	
" " " "	3	31.	
Ab[sent] from Reveille	5	9	March
" " Parade	5	11	
" " Reveille	5	20	
" " "	5	28	
Leaving the Academy during the first hour of recitation[10]	6	28	

Neglect of Fender[3]	3	4	April
Bed not strapped 30′ after Reveille[5]	7	11	
Ab[sent] from qrs. between 7 & 8 PM	3.	11	
" " Parade	5	24	
Improper conduct firing his musket from the window of his room	2	2	May
In bed after reveille	7	14	
Late at reveille		7	June
Bed not strapped[5]		23	
Neglect of duty as Compy Police Officer		21	*July*
Neglect of Police	1	25	Nov
Us[in]g Sp[iri]t[ou]s Liquors[11]	8	25	Decr
Disord[erl]y conduct in B[arrac]ks[11]	4	"	"
Ab[sent] from Qrs after taps[11]	8	24	"
Ab[sent] from church[9]		8	April 1827
Dis[o]b[edienc]e of special order in not going to Church when ordered		"	"
Allowing noise on his post		13	"
Ab[sent] from Philosophy		14	"
In Bed after Rev[eille]		27	"
Absent from Qrs (12 & 1) A.M.		29	"
Inattention on drill		7	June
Ab[sent] from Qrs. (8 & 9) P.M.		12	
" " Drill		28	July
In bed 30 min after Rev[eille]		12	[illegible]
Leaving the mess hall without permission		6	1827 Aug
Ab[sent] from B[arrac]ks (8.9) P.M		2	Sept
In rear rank at parade		5	"
Ab[sent] from Laboratory		6	"
" " parade		20	"
Out of uniform in mess sq[ua]d		"	"
Going to mess-Hall without Marching[7]		18	"
Spitting on the floor		4	Oct
Inattention on p[ara]d[e]		21	Nov
Bed not strapped 30′ after Rev[eille]		2	Decb’

In mess hall after the Batt[alion]s [Rise?] [12]	25	
Bed not made 30′ after Rev[eille]	31	"
		1828
Vis[itin]g (10 & 11) A.M.	5	Jany
Cooking in Qrs. (7 & 8) P. M[13]	18	"
Abs[ent] from Church[9]	19	Feby
Not n[oting?] ch[angin]g[?] off[icer] G[uar]d	"	"
In bed 30′ after Reve[ille]	15	March
Visiting 11 & 12	2	Apl
Going to Engineering before the proper time	12	"
Visiting 3 & 4	16	"
Ab[sent] from Reve[ille]	27	"
" " "	11	May
" " "	13	May
In bed 30′ after Reve[ille]	13	"
Abs[ent] from Qrs. after Taps[2]	5	June

LbC, transcription from letterbook copy in the War Department (U.S. Military Academy Archives), 3.

[1] "The Superintendent will cause a registry to be kept of all the delinquencies and punishments which may take place at the Academy . . ." (*Regulations of the Military Academy* [1823], 29).

[2] Paragraph 93 of the *Regulations of the Military Academy* [1823], 22, provided that "No cadet is to visit another's room, or be absent from his own, in study hours, or between tattoo and reveillé, without permission from the proper authority."

[3] Of a similar offense, Albert E. Church wrote, "To prevent danger from fires, each [cadet] room was furnished with a large sheet-iron fender, which it was the duty of the person leaving the room, without an occupant, to place before the fire. This was the prolific source of reports of 'fender not up' to the orderly . . ." (*Reminiscences*, 22).

[4] Paragraphs 140 and 141 of the regulations provided that "When the weather will permit, the classes and sections will be formed on the battalion parade ground. In bad weather they will be formed in the lower hall of the north barrack . . . Every cadet, while on the class parade, or while marching to and from the academy, is required to observe perfect silence and regularity" (*Regulations of the Military Academy* [1823], 30).

[5] Although Church wrote that the cadets spread their mattresses on the floor and that they had no bedsteads of any kind (*Reminiscences*, 21), it would appear from Davis' violation that cots were in use at this time.

[6] Although cadets were permitted at this time to wear their hair in whatever style they wished, the typical short haircut not being required until after 1825 (Church, *Reminiscences*, 63), Davis evidently went too far.

[7] The regulations provided that "At the signal for breakfast, dinner, and supper, the squads are to be formed in front of the south barrack by their respective carvers, acting as squad

marchers, after which, they will be marched to the commons under the command of the superintendent of the lower mess hall, assisted by the superintendent of the upper hall" (*Regulations of the Military Academy* [1823], 32).

[8] Paragraph 178 of the regulations provided that "The cadets in rotation act as orderlies to their respective rooms. They are detailed weekly, and enter upon their duties every Sunday morning. . . . He will, on entering upon his duties as orderly, post his name in some conspicuous place in his room; and he is not to be relieved until his room shall have been inspected, and found in good order" (*Regulations of the Military Academy* [1823], 35).

[9] "On Sundays, except during the hours of divine service, at which all academick officers and cadets must strictly attend, every cadet will attend to reading or study at his own room" (*Regulations of the Military Academy* [1823], 23).

[10] The regulations provided that "No cadet will be allowed to go out of his academy till after one hour from its commencement, nor then, except on a necessary occasion. Cadets who get permission to go out, will return as quickly as possible. Any cadet who remains out longer than ten minutes, will be deemed guilty of disobedience of orders" (*Regulations of the Military Academy* [1823], 31).

[11] Offenses charged against Davis during the course of the eggnog riot of December 24–25, 1826.

[12] According to Major John A. Hixson, a 1960 graduate of West Point, the command "battalions rise" is given today, as it was then, to signal the end of a meal. Evidently Davis stayed longer than was allowed.

[13] "All cooking in quarters, or giving entertainments, within or out of quarters, is strictly prohibited" (*Regulations of the Military Academy* [1823], 22).

Order No. 88 1:117

U. S. Military Academy 6th June 1828

Cadet J. F. Davis, for absenting himself from Quarters last night 'till 12 o'clock, is hereby placed in arrest.[1] He will confine himself <—illegible—> to his room. By order of Lt Col. Thayer,[2] (Signed)

F. L. GRIFFITH[3]
Adjutant.

LbC, transcription from letterbook copy in the War Department (U.S. Military Academy Archives).

[1] The last entry on the Record of Delinquencies, confirming the above, lists Davis as "Abs[ent] from Qrs. after Taps" on June 5 (1:116).

[2] Sylvanus Thayer (sketch, 1:74, *n.* 6).

[3] Frederick L. Griffith (sketch, 1:114, *n.* 2).

ABSTRACT

1:118 Yearly Conduct Report

[U.S. Military Academy,] June [30,] 1828

Lists Cadet Jefferson Davis as having committed thirty "offences" during the past academic year (two of the second class, five of the third class, three of the fourth class, six of the fifth class, seven of the sixth class, and seven of the seventh class), for a total of 137 "Proportional Demerit[s]." On this basis Davis is ranked 163rd in conduct out of 208 cadets.[1]

D (NA, RG 94 Records of the Adjutant General's Office, Records Relating to the U.S. Military Academy, Monthly Conduct Reports, Entry 231), 5.

[1] On September 25, 1825, a new demerit system was instituted at West Point whereby it was determined that "Rolls will . . . be published annually exhibiting the number of offences of each degree of criminality charged to each cadet on the record of delinquencies & his relative merit according to the following rules. 1st The offences will be classified as follows 1st class—Mutinous Conduct 2d Positive disobedience of a special Order Breach of arrest Neglect of duty On post Forcing a sentinels post Refusing attendance on duty when specially named Irreverence at church Ungentlemanly Conduct. use of spirituous liquors Profanity & other immoralities Absence from quarters after Tattoo Gross disrespect to a Superior Officer 3 Disrespectful conduct to any superior Absence from quarters at night before Tattoo Visiting in study hours, absence from Barracks Neglect of fires. Insubordinate conduct 4 Disorderly Conduct in Barracks, at Parades with arms Academies & Mess. Leaving Academy & not returning 5 Absence from church, Academies & drills 6 Absence from Parades, Inspections, Roll-calls & Marching off guard. Neglect of duty as Orderly. Disorderly at Parades without arms & Marching to meals & acadamies Absence from quarters in study hours during the day 7 In bed after reveille & before Tattoo. Late at Inspections. Absence from the academy more than 10 Minutes Bad police of rooms 2d The degree of criminality of each offence will be distinguished by Numbers as follows For the first class of offences No 10 Second 8 Third 5 Fourth 4 Fifth 3 Sixth 2 Seventh 1 . . . . For each year (after the first) that a Cadet may be a member of the Institution, his offences shall be made to count more, by adding to the number expressing his demerit one sixth for his second, one third for his third, and one half for his fourth year" (Post Orders No. 122, September 25, 1825 [U.S. Military Academy Archives]). According to the above, Davis accumulated during his senior year a total of 92 demerits which, when multiplied by one and one-half, becomes 138. The additional point is apparently an arithmetical error. Beginning with the June 7 entry, the Record of Delinquencies (1:116) lists Davis with twenty-nine offenses, not thirty as the above indicates.

ABSTRACT

Yearly Merit Roll 1:119

U.S. Military Academy, June [30,] 1828

Ranks Cadet Jefferson Davis twenty-third out of thirty-three members of the first class, with 154 merits in mathematics, 78 in French, 130 in natural philosophy, 41 in drawing, 174 in engineering, 116 in chemistry and mineralogy, 146 in rhetoric and moral philosophy, 132 in tactics, 62 in artillery, and 219 in conduct, for a total of 1,252 in general merit;[1] upon the basis of these scores he is recommended for promotion into the infantry.[2]

D (NA, RG 94 Records of the Adjutant General's Office, Records Relating to the U.S. Military Academy, Merit Rolls, Entry 230), 5; D, copy, transcription from letterbook copy in the War Department (U.S. Military Academy Archives).

[1] See 1:30, *n.* 2 for a discussion of the West Point grading system.

[2] See 1:122, *n.* 5 for a discussion of Davis' appointment to the infantry.

ABSTRACT

Semiannual Muster Roll of the Corps of Cadets 1:120

West Point, New York, June 30, 1828

Lists Jefferson F. Davis of Mississippi, first class,[1] United States Military Academy, Corps of Cadets commanded by Major William J. Worth,[2] as being age twenty-one years,[3] and as absent from the post. Remarks: "Furloughed till August 28th. 1828."[4]

DS (NA, RG 94 Records of the Adjutant General's Office, Records Relating to the U.S. Military Academy, Semiannual Muster Rolls of Cadets, Entry 227), 7; DS (U.S. Military Academy Archives). Signed: "W. J Worth Maj Com[mandin]g Mustering & Insp[ectin]g offr."

[1] See 1:18, *n.* 3 for a discussion of the West Point class system.

[2] William J. Worth (sketch, 1:14, *n.* 1).

[3] Davis' age is figured from 1807. See 1:1, *n.* 1 for a discussion of the year of Davis' birth.

[4] Davis' furlough until August 28 was evidently granted by the West Point authorities. The War Department extended the furlough for two months (1:122). See 1:124 for Davis' request for an additional extension and 1:126 for approval of his request.

ABSTRACT

1:121 Entrance Register of Cadets

[West Point, New York,] July 1, 1828

Lists Jefferson Davis of Mississippi as having entered the Academy September 1, 1824,[1] and as having been promoted to brevet second lieutenant of infantry July 1, 1828.[2]

D (U.S. Military Academy Archives).

[1] See 1:14, *n.* 2 for a discussion of the date Davis entered West Point.

[2] Davis' appointment as brevet second lieutenant is discussed in 1:122, *n.* 5.

EXTRACT

1:122 Order: Promotions and Appointments[1]

Department of War July 14th, 1828

The following promotions and appointments in the Army have been made by the President of the United States,[2] since issuing the order of May 28th, 1828.[3] . . . *Appointments* . . . Second Lieutenants by Brevet, from the Military Academy. . . . *For the Infantry*. . . . 23. Cadet Jefferson Davis[4] . . . The above named Cadets having passed their final examination at the Military Academy and been recommended by the Academic Staff for appointments in the several Corps of the Army set opposite their respective names; are accordingly attached to those Corps by brevet, as supernumerary Second Lieutenants,[5] to rank from the 1st. July 1828. They will be allowed, unless otherwise directed by special order, to avail themselves of the usual indulgence of leave of absence, until the 30th October,[6] on which day they will severally report themselves at such places, and for such duty, as shall be assigned to them respectively, by the General in Chief,[7] who will in the mean time, make the same known to the Army in General Orders.[8] By Command of the President P. B. PORTER[9]

Secretary of War.

LbC (NA, RG 94 Records of the Adjutant General's Office, War Department Orders and Circulars, Orders, V, 58–60), 3. Endorsed: "True Entry. R. Jones."

[1] Davis was appointed brevet second lieutenant in the First Infantry by a War Department order of December 31, 1828 (1:132). He was recommended for appointment to the rank of brevet

second lieutenant December 22, 1828, (1:131), and confirmed by the Senate January 22, 1829 (1:136).

[2] John Quincy Adams.

[3] The adjutant general's order of May 28 may be found in NA, RG 94, War Department Orders and Circulars, Orders, I, 1–4.

[4] Davis graduated twenty-third in a class of thirty-two and according to the custom of the time was appointed upon the recommendation of the academic staff to the infantry (1:119). The artillery was generally considered to be the more desirable service and was reserved, if desired, for those cadets who had the right of choice because of their distinguished academic records (W. P. Johnston, *Life of Gen. Albert Sidney Johnston*, 13).

[5] Davis' appointment by brevet to the infantry, as supernumerary second lieutenant, was, as Davis himself wrote in after years (see 1:2, lxxix), the rank customarily given to the graduates of the Military Academy. A brevet rather than a regular commission was granted to the graduates of the Academy because the laws providing for the establishment of the army declared that each company shall have a certain number of officers and no more. The number of young graduates each year made it apparent that all of them could not be placed, and the President of the United States was authorized to attach them as brevet second lieutenants to any regiment where they were needed, with the understanding that they were to receive their regular commission in the lowest grade as soon as a vacancy occurred. They were called supernumerary lieutenants because they were over and above the number of officers allowed by law to every company and not because they were more than could be usefully employed (F. Robinson, *Organization of the Army*, I, 88).

[6] See 1:124 for Davis' request for a furlough extension. See also 1:126 for the granting of the requested extension.

[7] Alexander Macomb was general-in-chief (sketch, 1:38, *n.* 10).

[8] See 1:123 for the mentioned orders.

[9] Peter B. Porter (1773–1844), born in Massachusetts, had a distinguished career in the War of 1812 as a major general of New York Volunteers, and in the state and national legislatures before he was appointed secretary of war in June 1828; he served until March 1829. He was a close friend of Henry Clay and a Whig presidential elector in 1840. He died at Niagara Falls (*DAB*).

ABSTRACT

Order No. 37 1:123

Adjutant General's Office, Washington, July 15, 1828

The brevet second lieutenants of infantry mentioned in the July 14 order[1] of the secretary of war[2] are ordered to report to the Infantry School of Practice at Jefferson Barracks[3] by October 30.[4] By order of Major General Macomb.[5]

R. JONES,[6]
Adjutant General.

LbCS (NA, RG 94 Records of the Adjutant General's Office, War Department Orders and Circulars, Orders, V, 60), 1.

[1] See 1:122 for an extract of the July 14 order.

[2] Peter B. Porter (sketch, 1:122, *n.* 9) was secretary of war.

[3] On July 10, 1826, four companies of the First Infantry commanded by Major Stephen Watts Kearny established a camp on the west bank of the Mississippi River below St. Louis. In honor of the President, the camp was named "Cantonment Adams," but on October 23, 1826, Roger Jones, the adjutant general, ordered that the new post be named "The Jefferson Barracks" and further ordered that it should become an "Infantry School of Practice." According to the custom of the day, all newly commissioned lieutenants were sent, depending upon whether attached to the artillery or to the infantry, to Fortress Monroe, Virginia, or Jefferson Barracks, Missouri, for a course of instruction in what we today would call basic training (Webb, "Jefferson Barracks," *New Mexico Historical Review*, XXI, 190; Davis to Reeves, December 16, 1847 [Cullum file of graduates, U.S. Military Academy Archives]).

[4] Davis was granted a furlough until October 30. See 1:122.

[5] Alexander Macomb (sketch, 1:38, *n.* 10).

[6] Roger Jones (1789–1852), born in Virginia, entered the Marine Corps in 1809, transferred to the Third Artillery in 1812 as a captain, and fought in the War of 1812, notably at Chippewa, Fort Erie, and Lundy's Lane. He was major and assistant adjutant general, 1813–15, and assumed the post of adjutant general of the army in 1825 as colonel. He was brevetted major general in 1848 for meritorious conduct in the performance of his duties during the Mexican War, and died in Washington, D.C., having been adjutant general for twenty-seven years (*Appleton's*; Heitman, *Historical Register*, I, 582).

1:124

To Winfield Scott

Lexington[1] August 26th 1828

SIR[2]

I was unavoidably detained in the north until the commencement of the sickly season[3] rendered it imprudent for me to return home (Mississippi)

After an absence of nearly six years[4] I feel desirous of remaining some time with my relations, and as the furlough I received on leaving the Point expires in Oct. next[5] before which month it would be unsafe for me to visit Missi. I would respectfully ask from you an extension of my furlough until the 31st of December next[6] Yours respctfly

J. F. DAVIS
Brvt 2d Lieut Inft.

[PS] (<–illegible–>)

ALS (S. M. Arnold, St. Louis, 1969). Indexed, not found (NA, RG 94 Records of the Adjutant General's Office, Letters Received, D–82, 1828). Addressed: "To Majr Genl W. Scott Comdg. Western Dept."

[1] Lexington, Kentucky, was the site of Transylvania University which Davis attended, 1823–24. The letter af-

fords proof that Davis did not go directly home after graduation, but that he visited in the North and in Kentucky before going to Mississippi.

[2] Winfield Scott was born near Petersburg, Virginia, in 1786 and died at West Point in 1866. His long and often controversial military career began with brief service in a Virginia cavalry troop in 1807. After practicing law for a short time, he obtained a commission as captain of artillery in 1808. On the eve of the War of 1812, he was promoted to lieutenant colonel and was brevetted major general after the Battle of Lundy's Lane. Scott served on various army boards after the war and wrote several treatises on temperance and military policies; in 1834–35 he personally revised and enlarged *Infantry-Tactics* (3 vols., New York, 1835), which remained a standard until the Civil War. Scott was ordered to the West during the Black Hawk War, but did not participate as his command was struck by cholera (see 1:Appendix II, 486, *n.* 15). President Jackson commissioned Scott to observe the nullification crisis in South Carolina in 1832, and to prosecute the Creek and Seminole War in 1835, but relieved him from command because of delays. In 1838 Scott was charged by President Van Buren with the task of pacification of the Canadian frontier and with conducting hostile Cherokees from South Carolina and Tennessee to Mississippi. Scott became general-in-chief in 1841 and undertook a successful naval and land campaign against General Antonio López de Santa Anna to Mexico City in 1847, ending the Mexican War. Unsuccessful Whig presidential candidate in 1852, he became lieutenant general in 1855, the first since Washington to hold that rank. When Davis became secretary of war, animosity between him and Scott caused the latter to move his headquarters to New York City. In late 1860 he attempted unsuccessfully to secure the reinforcement of military installations in the South, and in early 1861, just before the outbreak of the war, he returned headquarters to Washington to supervise preparations for defense of the capital. Later that year, Scott retired from active service because of age and physical disability (*DAB*; see also Elliott, *Winfield Scott*).

[3] That season of the year when disease was most prevalent, usually the summer and fall, when yellow fever often killed whole communities. "Usually the first cases were diagnosed in July, their number would mount in August, hold steady in September, and then gradually decline through October, with occasional ones turning up in November" (Duffy [ed.], *History of Medicine*, II, 125).

[4] In stating that he had been absent from Mississippi for nearly six years, Davis furnishes further proof that he attended Transylvania University for a period of little over a year and a half, and not three years as has heretofore been maintained (see 1:6, *n.* 2).

[5] See 1:122 for the furlough granted until October 30.

[6] See 1:126 for the order granting Davis a furlough extension.

ABSTRACT

Register of Payments to Officers 1:125

[Washington, D.C.,] August 31, 1828

Lists payment by Paymaster T. J. Leslie[1] to Second Lieutenant

Jefferson Davis, First Infantry,[2] $127. Amount includes pay and allowance for Davis and one servant,[3] for July and August.

D (NA, RG 99 Records of the Office of the Paymaster General, Register of Payments to Officers, IV, 27), 1.

[1] Thomas J. Leslie, born in England and appointed from Pennsylvania, was graduated from West Point in the Corps of Engineers in 1815. He served as paymaster at the Academy, 1815–21 and 1822–38, and treasurer of the Academy, 1816–41. Brevetted lieutenant colonel, colonel, and brigadier general in 1865 for fifty years' "faithful and meritorious performance of duty in the Pay Department," he was retired in 1869, and died five years later at age seventy-seven in New York City (Cullum, *Biographical Register*, I, 141–42).

[2] Although this document lists Davis' unit as First Infantry, he wrote in later years that he was first assigned to the Sixth Infantry, at the school of practice, Jefferson Barracks (Davis to Reeves, December 16, 1847 [Cullum file of graduates, U.S. Military Academy Archives]).

[3] The name of the servant is unknown, unless it was "David," who is listed on Davis' May 1829 pay voucher (1:144). Each second lieutenant was entitled to keep one servant and was allowed "pay, rations, and clothing of a private soldier, or money in lieu thereof. The ration to be calculated at twenty cents, and the clothing at the contract price of Infantry clothing" (*General Army Regulations* [1825], 287–88).

1:126

Special Order No. 99

Adjutant Genl's. Office Washington 8 Sept. 1828

The furlough[1] granted to Brevet Second Lieut. J F. Davis of the Infantry, is hereby extended to the 31st. of December Next,[2] when he will report in person, to the Commanding officer at Jefferson Barracks,[3] agreeably to order No 37.[4]

By Order of Major Genl. Macomb.[5]

S. Cooper[6]
Aide de Camp
ac[ting] as[sistant] a[djutant] Genl

LbC (NA, RG 94 Records of the Adjutant General's Office, War Department Orders and Circulars, Special Orders, II, 46–47).

[1] See 1:122 for the furlough that Davis received upon graduation.

[2] See 1:124 for Davis' request for a furlough extension.

[3] The commanding officer at Jefferson Barracks was officially Henry Atkinson (sketch, 1:301, *n.* 7), although Davis actually reported to Bennet Riley (see 1:138, *n.* 2). For Jefferson Barracks, see 1:123, *n.* 3.

[4] See 1:123 for Order No. 37.

[5] Alexander Macomb (sketch, 1:38, *n.* 10).

[6] Samuel Cooper (1798–1876), an 1815 graduate of the Military Academy, served most of his army career on staff duty in Washington, where he became adjutant general of the army with the rank of colonel in 1852.

Although born in New Jersey, his marriage to a granddaughter of George Mason, his purchase of a Virginia estate, and his friendship with Davis made him Southern in his feelings. With the outbreak of the Civil War, he resigned his commission and offered his services to the Confederacy, where his administrative abilities were invaluable. He was senior officer of the Confederate Army throughout the war, and was adjutant general and inspector general. Captured at the end of the war, he retired after his parole and release to his estate near Alexandria, Virginia (*DAB*).

ABSTRACT

Register of Payments to Officers 1:127

[Washington, D.C.,] September 30, 1828

Lists payment by Paymaster T. J. Leslie[1] to Second Lieutenant Jefferson Davis, First Infantry, $62.50. Amount includes pay and allowance for Davis and one servant,[2] for September. Remarks: "Transfd. a/c for Octob. to be pd by P m Tallmadge." [3]

D (NA, RG 99 Records of the Office of the Paymaster General, Register of Payments to Officers, IV, 27), 1.

1 Thomas J. Leslie (sketch, 1:125, *n.* 1).

2 See 1:125, *n.* 3.

3 Charles B. Tallmadge, born in New York, was first appointed as an assistant district paymaster in 1814 and was major and paymaster from June 1818. He was serving in New York City in 1828, and died four years later (Heitman, *Historical Register*, I, 944; *American State Papers*, Class V, Military Affairs, III, 670).

ABSTRACT

Monthly Return 1:128

West Point, New York, September 30, 1828

Lists receipt of Special Order 99, dated September 8,[1] "Granting a furlough to Bt. 2d Lt J F Davis of Infy till 31 Decr 1828." [2]

DS (U.S. Military Academy Archives), 2. Signed: "F. L. Griffith Adj. S. Thayer Lt. Col Comdg." Endorsed: "Recd 6 Augt."

1 See 1:126.

2 The extension was granted at Davis' request (1:124).

ABSTRACT

1:129 **Register of Payments to Officers**

[Washington, D.C.,] October 31, 1828

Lists payment by Paymaster C. B. Tallmadge[1] to Second Lieutenant Jefferson Davis, First Infantry, $63.50. Amount includes pay and allowance for Davis and one servant,[2] for October.

D (NA, RG 99 Records of the Office of the Paymaster General, Register of Payments to Officers, IV, 27), 1.

[1] Charles B. Tallmadge (sketch, 1:127, *n.* 3).
[2] See 1:125, *n.* 3.

ABSTRACT

1:130 **Post Return**

Jefferson Barracks,[1] October [31,][2] 1828

Lists Jefferson Davis and ten other brevet second lieutenants of infantry as absent without leave.[3] Remarks: "Absent–Furloughs expired 30th Octr. 1828."[4]

Printed form, filled in and signed (NA, RG 94 Records of the Adjutant General's Office, Post Returns, Jefferson Barracks), 2. Signed: "J. D. Searight Lieut. & Act. Post Adjt. A R Woolley Lt Col U S Infty." Endorsed: "(*Recd. Novr. 28th. 1828.*)"

[1] See 1:123, *n.* 3.
[2] Since the post returns bear no date beyond the month of the year, they have been assigned, for the purpose of chronological placement, to the last day of their respective months.
[3] Evidently notice of the furlough extension which Davis was granted (see 1:126) was not received at Jefferson Barracks, for he is listed on the October–December post returns as being absent without leave (Post Returns, November, December, 1828 [NA, RG 94, Jefferson Barracks]).
[4] See 1:122 for the furlough granted until October 30.

ABSTRACT

1:131 **Promotions and Appointments List**[1]

Adjutant General's Office, Washington
December 22, 1828

Cadet Jefferson Davis is recommended for appointment as brevet second lieutenant of infantry,[2] to be ranked from July 1, 1828.

LbC (NA, RG 107 Records of the Office of the Secretary of War, Letters to the President, II, 213–16), 2. Transmitted: Porter to the President, December 22, 1828 (NA, RG 107 Records of the Office of the Secretary of War, Letters to the President, II, 212). Printed: *Senate Executive Journal*, III, 631–33.

[1] This list of recommended promotions and appointments was transmitted to the Senate by letter of President John Quincy Adams, January 7, 1829, and appears under the proceedings of January 15, 1829. The appointments of Davis and the other officers included in the President's letter were referred to the Committee on Military Affairs on January 15 and were reported back to the Senate and confirmed on January 22, 1829. See *Senate Executive Journal*, III, 631–33, 635, and Senate Resolution, January 22, 1829 (1:136).

[2] Davis was appointed to the infantry by the War Department order of July 14, 1828 (1:122), and further appointed to the First Infantry by a War Department order, December 31, 1828 (1:132).

ABSTRACT

Order: Promotions and Appointments 1:132

Department of War, December 31, 1828

Cadet Jefferson Davis is appointed brevet second lieutenant, First Infantry,[1] effective July 1, 1828. "Cadets acting as Supernumerary Officers of the Army, in virtue of their Brevets,[2] shall hereafter be promoted to Vacancies of the lowest grade in the Regiment or Corps to which they are assigned. . . ." By command of the President.[3]

P. B. PORTER[4]
Secretary of War.

LbC (NA, RG 94 Records of the Adjutant General's Office, War Department Orders and Circulars, Orders, V, 119–22), 3.

[1] Davis was appointed to the infantry by orders of the War Department dated July 14, 1828 (1:122). He was recommended for nomination as brevet second lieutenant in the promotion list of December 22, 1828 (1:131), and confirmed January 22, 1829 (1:136).

[2] See 1:122, *n.* 5 for a discussion of brevet commissions and supernumerary officers.

[3] John Quincy Adams.

[4] Peter B. Porter (sketch, 1:122, *n.* 9).

ABSTRACT

Order No. 66 1:133

Adjutant General's Office, Washington
December 31, 1828

Brevet second lieutenants whose appointments are announced by

the War Department order of December 31, 1828,[1] "will report by letter[2] to their respective Colonels" [3] for assignment to companies. By order of Major General Macomb.[4] R. JONES[5]
Adjt. Gen

LbCS (NA, RG 94 Records of the Adjutant General's Office, War Department Orders and Circulars, Orders, V, 122–23), 1.

1 See 1:132.

2 Davis' letter has not been found.

3 Davis was appointed to the First Infantry (1:132), and probably reported to Colonel John McNeil (sketch, 1:151, *n.* 3), commander of the regiment which was headquartered at Fort Crawford (Gordon, *Compilation of Registers of the Army*, 363, 375).

4 Alexander Macomb (sketch, 1:38, *n.* 10).

5 Roger Jones (sketch, 1:123, *n.* 6).

ABSTRACT

1:134

Register of Payments to Officers

[Washington, D.C.,] December 31, 1828

Lists payment by Paymaster T. Biddle[1] to Second Lieutenant Jefferson Davis, First Infantry, $126. Amount includes pay and allowance for Davis and one servant,[2] for November and December.

D (NA, RG 99 Records of the Office of the Paymaster General, Register of Payments to Officers, IV, 27), 1.

1 Thomas Biddle, Jr., born in Philadelphia in 1790, was a veteran of the War of 1812; he commanded the artillery in the defense of Fort Erie, fought at Lundy's Lane, and was brevetted major in 1814. Major and paymaster in 1821 to rank from 1820, he was, in 1828, the paymaster at St. Louis (*American State Papers*, Class V, Military Affairs, III, 670). Biddle quarrelled with Missouri Representative Spencer Pettis on the United States Bank issue in 1830, and a duel followed in 1831. Because of Biddle's defective eyesight, the dueling distance was shortened to five feet, and both men were mortally wounded at the first shots (Heitman, *Historical Register*, I, 217; *Appleton's*; *National Cyclopaedia*, VII, 533; Hempstead, "I at Home: Part IX," ed. Jensen, Missouri Historical *Bulletin*, XXII, 443).

2 See 1:125, *n.* 3.

1:135

To the War Department

Jefferson Barracks[1] Mo. Jany. 21st 1829

SIR[2]

I received yesterday my letter of appointment[3] as Brevet 2d. Lieut.

of Infantry containing instructions to communicate through you my acceptance or non-acceptance of the same and in obedience thereto I now inform you of my acceptance of said appointment the duties of which I have been performing since early in the present <month,>[4] in pursuance of orders[5] from the General in Chief[6]—I am a native Kentucky—Very Respctly J. F. DAVIS

Brvt. Lt. Inft.

ALS (NA, RG 94 Records of the Adjutant General's Office, Letters Received, D–17, 1829). Addressed: "For the War department from Jefferson F. Davis graduate of 1828." Endorsed: "[Received] Feb. 11. 1829."

[1] Jefferson Barracks, see 1:123, *n.* 3.

[2] "Sir" was probably Secretary of War Peter B. Porter (sketch, 1:122, *n.* 9).

[3] Davis' letter of appointment has not been found.

[4] Interlined. Davis was present for duty January 11 (1:138).

[5] See 1:126.

[6] Alexander Macomb (sketch, 1:38, *n.* 10).

ABSTRACT

Senate Resolution 1:136

In the Senate of the United States, January 22, 1829

The Senate confirms the appointment of, among others, "Jefferson Davis to be Br. 2d. Lt. of Infy. 1 July 1828.[1]. . . Attest . . ."

WALTER LOWRIE[2]

LbC (NA, RG 94 Records of the Adjutant General's Office, Records of the Appointment, Commission, and Personnel Branch, Register of Confirmations of Officers, United States Army, Senate Resolutions of Consent to Promotions and Appointments, I, 49–52), 3. Printed: *Senate Executive Journal*, III, 635, variant version.

[1] Davis was appointed to the infantry by a War Department order of July 14, 1828 (1:122), and further appointed to the First Infantry by a War Department order of December 31, 1828 (1:132). He was recommended for nomination as brevet second lieutenant in the promotions and appointments list of December 22, 1828 (1:131).

[2] Walter Lowrie was born in Scotland in 1774 or 1784 and had been a schoolteacher, justice of the peace, and state senator before he was elected Democratic senator from Pennsylvania in 1819. After one term he was elected secretary of the Senate, in which capacity he served from 1825 to 1836. Lowrie founded the congressional prayer meeting and temperance society and was secretary of the West Foreign Missionary Society. From 1836 until the time of his death in New York City in 1868, he was the secretary of the Board of Foreign Missions of the Presbyterian Church (*DAB*; *Appleton's*; Nevin [ed.], *Encyclopaedia of the Presbyterian Church*, 454–55).

ABSTRACT

1:137

Register of Payments to Officers

[Washington, D.C.,] January 31, 1829

Lists payment by Paymaster T. Biddle[1] to Second Lieutenant Jefferson Davis, First Infantry, $63.50. Amount includes pay and allowance for Davis and one servant,[2] for January.

D (NA, RG 99 Records of the Office of the Paymaster General, Register of Payments to Officers, IV, 27), 1.

[1] Thomas Biddle (sketch, 1:134, *n.* 1).
[2] See 1:125, *n.* 3.

ABSTRACT

1:138

Post Return

Jefferson Barracks,[1] January [31,] 1829

Lists Brevet Second Lieutenant Jefferson Davis, First Infantry, present at the post.[2] Remarks: "11 Jany. 1829 For Duty." [3]

Printed form, filled in and signed (NA, RG 94 Records of the Adjutant General's Office, Post Returns, Jefferson Barracks), 2. Signed: "Geo. W. Waters L[ieutenant] & Act. Post Adjt.
B Riley Capt." Endorsed: "Entd. (Rcd. 23. Feby 1829)."

[1] See 1:123, *n.* 3.

[2] According to McElroy, Davis later recalled his arrival at the Barracks: " 'Being . . . something of a martinet, I arrayed myself in full uniform and made my way to the regimental headquarters. The Colonel and Lieutenant-Colonel being absent [Colonel Henry Atkinson was absent on special duty and Lieutenant Colonel Abram R. Woolley was in arrest (Post Return, January 1829 [NA, RG 94, Jefferson Barracks]).]—or perhaps one or both of these positions being vacant—the command of the regiment had devolved upon [Brevet] Major (afterward Colonel and brevet Major-General) Bennet Riley. The Major was not in, and I was directed to the Commissary to find him. Repairing to the place indicated, I found Major Riley, alone, seated at a table with a pack of cards before him, intently occupied in a game of solitaire. In response to my formal salute, he nodded, invited me to take a seat, and continued his game. Looking up after a few minutes, he inquired: 'Young man, do you play solitaire? Finest game in the world! You may cheat as much as you please and have nobody to detect it.' " (*The Unreal and the Real*, I, 20–21). The same story is related in "History of Jefferson Barracks" (typescript in Missouri Historical Society, St. Louis), 14–15.

[3] See 1:135 for Davis' letter in which he says that he has been at Jefferson Barracks since early January.

From Roger Jones 1:139

SIR, Adjt. Gener. Office Washington 9. Febry. 1829

Your communication of the 16. Ulto.[1] to the Secretary of War[2] respecting your letter of appointment has just been received & in answer to your inquiry, I have to inform you that your appointment as brevet 2. Lieut of Infantry,[3] with the appointments of the rest of the Class of graduates of 1828, were sent to Lieut Colonel Thayer[4] at West Point, for distribution. I am, Sir Respectfully Your Obt Servt.

(sigd.) R. JONES[5]
Adj. Genl.

LbC (NA, RG 94 Records of the Adjutant General's Office, Letters Sent, VIII, 230). Addressed: "Bvt. 2 Lieut Jefferson Davis 1st. Infantry Jefferson Barracks Missouri."

[1] Davis' letter of January 16 has not been found.

[2] Peter B. Porter was secretary of war (sketch, 1:122, *n.* 9).

[3] Davis' appointment is missing.

[4] Sylvanus Thayer (sketch, 1:74, *n.* 6).

[5] Roger Jones (sketch, 1:123, *n.* 6).

ABSTRACT

Register of Payments to Officers 1:140

[Washington, D.C.,] February 28, 1829

Lists payment by Paymaster T. Biddle[1] to Second Lieutenant Jefferson Davis, First Infantry, $60.50. Amount includes pay and allowance for Davis and one servant,[2] for February.

D (NA, RG 99 Records of the Office of the Paymaster General, Register of Payments to Officers, IV, 27), 1.

[1] Thomas Biddle (sketch, 1:134, *n.* 1).

[2] See 1:125, *n.* 3.

ABSTRACT

Register of Payments to Officers 1:141

[Washington, D.C.,] March 31, 1829

Lists payment by Paymaster T. Biddle[1] to Second Lieutenant Jefferson Davis, First Infantry, $63.50. Amount includes pay and allowance for Davis and one servant,[2] for March.

D (NA, RG 99 Records of the Office of the Paymaster General, Register of Payments to Officers, IV, 27), 1.

[1] Thomas Biddle (sketch, 1:134, *n.* 1).
[2] See 1:125, *n.* 3.

ABSTRACT

1:142

Post Return

Jefferson Barracks,[1] March [31,] 1829

Lists Brevet Second Lieutenant Jefferson Davis, First Infantry, and other officers, as dropped. Remarks: "Ordered to their Regiments[2] 24 March. Dep. Hd. Qrs."

Printed form, filled in and signed (NA, RG 94 Records of the Adjutant General's Office, Post Returns, Jefferson Barracks), 2. Signed: "Alb. S. Johnston Lieut & Adjt 6th Regt & Post B Riley Capt." Endorsed: "Received 27 April."

[1] See 1:123, *n.* 3.
[2] The headquarters of the First Infantry was at Fort Crawford, Prairie du Chien, Michigan Territory (Gordon, *Compilation of Registers of the Army*, 387, 401). Although the extant records of Fort Crawford do not confirm that Davis was sent there from Jefferson Barracks, it is not unusual for post returns to omit officers not garrisoned at the post. Transient officers were not usually noted, although they may have been there awaiting assignment.

ABSTRACT

1:143

Register of Payments to Officers

[Washington, D.C.,] April 30, 1829

Lists payment by Paymaster T. Biddle[1] to Second Lieutenant Jefferson Davis, First Infantry, $62.50. Amount includes pay and allowance for Davis and one servant,[2] for April.

D (NA, RG 99 Records of the Office of the Paymaster General, Register of Payments to Officers, IV, 27), 1.

[1] Thomas Biddle (sketch, 1:134, *n.* 1).
[2] See 1:125, *n.* 3.

ABSTRACT

Pay Voucher 1:144

Fort Winnebago,[1] May 31, 1829

Brevet Second Lieutenant J. F. Davis, First Infantry, acknowledges that he has received $63.50 from Paymaster David Gwynne.[2] Amount includes pay, and allowance for one servant, for May 1829. The servant is described as David,[3] yellow, five feet six inches in height, with black hair and eyes.

Printed form, filled in and signed (NA, RG 217 Records of the United States General Accounting Office, Paymasters' Accounts, Gwynne 13,350, Voucher 70), 3. Signed: "J. F. Davis Brvt. 2nd Lt. 1st Infty."

1 Fort Winnebago was established in October 1828 at the portage of the Fox and Wisconsin rivers in response to the growing threat of war with Indian tribes aroused by the incursions of lead miners into that part of Michigan Territory. Its strategic location made Fort Winnebago a vital link in the line of forts from Green Bay to the Mississippi River, especially during the Black Hawk War. With time, the importance of the posts in this northwest region lessened, and, with the approach of war with Mexico in 1845, Fort Winnebago was evacuated. In 1853, as secretary of war, Davis ordered the sale of the property comprising his first post (Turner, "Fort Winnebago," Wisconsin Historical *Collections*, XIV, 66, 95; Prucha, *Broadax and Bayonet*, 24).

2 David Gwynne, born in Maryland, joined the army in 1812 as a first lieutenant of the Nineteenth Infantry. Later he became a regimental paymaster, 1812–13. Major and paymaster in 1816, he resigned from the army in 1830 and died in 1849 (Heitman, *Historical Register*, I, 485).

3 The "David" here mentioned as Davis' servant is of interest since it has been thought that James Pemberton was with Davis during his entire army career. See 1:5, *n.* 4.

ABSTRACT

Register of Payments to Officers 1:145

[Washington, D.C.,] May 31, 1829

Lists payment by Paymaster D. Gwynne[1] to Second Lieutenant Jefferson Davis, First Infantry, $63.50. Amount includes pay and allowance for Davis and one servant,[2] for May.

D (NA, RG 99 Records of the Office of the Paymaster General, Register of Payments to Officers, IV, 27), 1.

1 David Gwynne (sketch, 1:144, *n.* 2).
2 David was the servant's name (1:144).

ABSTRACT

1:146

Post Return

Fort Winnebago,[1] May [31,] 1829

Lists Brevet Second Lieutenant J. F. Davis, First Infantry, present at the post. Remarks: "Ordered to this post and not attached to any company." [2]

Printed form, filled in and signed (NA, RG 94 Records of the Adjutant General's Office, Post Returns, Fort Winnebago, 1828–45), 2. Signed: "D. E Twiggs Major 1 In[fantry]." Endorsed: "Recd. 2 July. 1829."

[1] See 1:144, *n.* 1.

[2] Although the exact date of Davis' arrival at Fort Winnebago is unknown, it may be that he left Fort Crawford with Company B, which left Prairie du Chien, May 2 (Post Return, May 1829 [NA, RG 94, Fort Crawford, 1817–34]) and arrived at Fort Winnebago, May 9 (Post Return, May 1829 [NA, RG 94, Fort Winnebago, 1828–45]). See 1:133, *n.* 3 for Davis' assignment to Fort Crawford.

ABSTRACT

1:147

Post Return

Fort Winnebago,[1] June [30,] 1829

Lists Brevet Second Lieutenant J. F. Davis, First Infantry, present at the post. Remarks: "On Extra duty.[2] Not attached to any company."

Printed form, filled in and signed (NA, RG 94 Records of the Adjutant General's Office, Post Returns, Fort Winnebago, 1828–45), 2. Signed: "D E Twiggs Major 1st Infty." Endorsed: "Recd. 3d. Augt."

[1] See 1:144, *n.* 1.

[2] The "extra duty" here mentioned was duty Davis performed as acting assistant commissary of subsistence (1:185).

ABSTRACT

1:148

Register of Fresh Beef Contracts

[Washington, D.C.,] July 28, 1829

Records that Lieutenant J. F. Davis, acting for Lieutenant Thomas P. Gwynn,[1] contracted with William Clark to supply Fort Winnebago[2] with fresh beef at 5.75 cents per pound for the period September 1829 through August 1830.

D (NA, RG 192 Records of the Office of the Commissary General of Subsistence, Register of Fresh Beef Contracts, 1820–56), 1.

1 Thomas P. Gwynn, born in Virginia, was a cadet at the Military Academy (1813–18) but was not graduated with his class. He was a first lieutenant in the First Infantry from 1824 until his promotion in 1833. He served in the Mexican War and died a major, Fifth Infantry, in 1861 (*Register of Graduates* [1964], 205; Heitman, *Historical Register*, I, 485). Gwynn was the acting assistant commissary of subsistence and acting assistant quartermaster at Fort Winnebago, and was absent from the post on staff duty during part of July and August 1829 (Post Returns, July, August 1829 [NA, RG 94, Fort Winnebago, 1828–45]). During that time Davis appears to have taken his place.

2 See 1:144, *n*. 1.

ABSTRACT

Post Return 1:149

Fort Winnebago,[1] Michigan Territory,[2] July [31,] 1829

Lists Brevet Second Lieutenant J. F. Davis, First Infantry, present at the post. Remarks: "On Extra duty.[3] order of Maj. Twiggs[4] 21 June 1829. Not attached to any Company."

Printed form, filled in and signed (NA, RG 94 Records of the Adjutant General's Office, Post Returns, Fort Winnebago, 1828–45), 2. Signed: "D E Twiggs Major 1s Infy." Endorsed: "Recd. 1st. Septr."

1 Fort Winnebago—see 1:144, *n*. 1.

2 Michigan Territory was formed in 1805 from the northern part of the territory of Indiana, and was first governed under the terms of the Northwest Ordinance. In 1819 the new territory was authorized to elect a delegate to Congress and in 1836 was admitted to the Union (*Statutes at Large of the United States*, II [1845], 309–10, III [1861], 482–83, V [1846], 49–50).

3 The pay voucher (1:185) lists Davis as the acting assistant commissary of subsistence for only May and June of 1829. The nature of this "extra duty" is unknown. It may be that the "extra duty" was supervision of the construction at Fort Winnebago (1:451).

4 David E. Twiggs (1790–1862), son of a Revolutionary War general, was born and died in Georgia. He attended Franklin College, Athens, and studied law in Augusta before his first military service as a captain, then brevet major, in the War of 1812. A major in the First Infantry from 1825, he was assigned to direct construction of Fort Winnebago in August 1828 and remained there until summer of 1831, when he was promoted to lieutenant colonel of the Fourth Infantry. He distinguished himself in the Mexican War under the commands of both Zachary Taylor and Winfield Scott, was brevetted major general, and awarded a gold sword for gallantry by Congress in 1847. Dismissed from the army in

March 1861 because of his surrender of the Department of Texas, he was made a Confederate major general but was too old for active service (*DAB*; Heitman, *Historical Register*, I, 976; Warner, *Generals in Gray*, 312; Turner, "Fort Winnebago," Wisconsin Historical *Collections*, XIV, 69–76; Beers, "Western Military Frontier," 79; F. Robinson, *Organization of the Army*, II, 117–28).

ABSTRACT

1:150

Post Return

Fort Winnebago,[1] Michigan Territory,[2] August [31,] 1829

Lists Brevet Second Lieutenant J. F. Davis, Company C, First Infantry, present at the post. Remarks: "Attached to Company by order of Maj. Twiggs[3] 29 Aug. 1829."

Printed form, filled in and signed (NA, RG 94 Records of the Adjutant General's Office, Post Returns, Fort Winnebago, 1828–45), 2. Signed: "T J Beall Major U S Army." Endorsed: "Recd. 9th Octr."

[1] See 1:144, *n.* 1.
[2] See 1:149, *n.* 2.
[3] David E. Twiggs (sketch, 1:149, *n.* 4).

ABSTRACT

1:151

Company Muster Roll

Fort Winnebago,[1] August 31, 1829

Lists Brevet Second Lieutenant Jefferson F. Davis of Captain Thomas J. Beall's[2] Company C, First Regiment of Infantry commanded by Colonel J. McNeil,[3] as present, "Attached to Comp. by order of Maj. Twiggs[4] 29 Aug 1829." Report covers July and August, 1829.

Printed form, filled in and signed (NA, RG 94 Records of the Adjutant General's Office, Muster Rolls of Regular Army Organizations, First Infantry, Company C), 2. Signed: "T J Beall, B[reve]t Major 1st. Infty." Endorsed: "Adjt Genls. Office 9th. Octr. 1829. Corrected in this Office Recd. Octr. 9th. 1829. Entered."

[1] See 1:144, *n.* 1.

[2] Thomas J. Beall, born in the District of Columbia, was appointed to West Point from Maryland and was graduated in 1811. A veteran of the War of 1812, he was brevetted major in 1828, transferred to the First Infantry in January 1829, and served at Fort Winnebago, 1829–30, and in 1831. He died, aged forty, in garrison at Fort Armstrong, Illinois, in 1832 (Cullum, *Biographical Register*, I, 96–97).

[3] John McNeil (1784–1850), born in New Hampshire, was brevetted lieutenant colonel and colonel for gallantry in the War of 1812 at the battles of

Chippewa and Niagara. He joined the First Infantry as lieutenant colonel in 1818 and became its colonel in 1826. Brevetted brigadier general in 1824, he was a United States commissioner at treaty negotiations at Fort Crawford in August 1829 and resigned in 1830 to become surveyor of the port of Boston. He died in Washington, D.C. (*Appleton's*; Heitman, *Historical Register*, I, 679; Washburne, "Col. Henry Gratiot," Wisconsin Historical *Collections*, X, 250–51).

[4] David E. Twiggs (sketch, 1:149, *n.* 4).

ABSTRACT

Pay Voucher

1:152

Fort Winnebago,[1] September 30, 1829

Brevet Second Lieutenant Jefferson F. Davis, First Infantry, acknowledges that he has received $262 from Paymaster Major David Gwynne.[2] Amount includes pay, and allowance for one servant,[3] for June through September 1829, and additional pay for commanding Company B in September.[4] The servant is described as "Jas. Pemberton dark," five feet ten inches in height.

Printed form, filled in and signed (NA, RG 217 Records of the United States General Accounting Office, Paymasters' Accounts, Gwynne 13,715, Voucher 63), 3. Signed: "J. F. Davis Lt. 1st. Infty."

[1] See 1:144, *n.* 1.

[2] David Gwynne (sketch, 1:144, *n.* 2).

[3] James Pemberton (sketch, 1:5, *n.* 4).

[4] Davis commanded Company B from September 1 through October 31, 1829 (1:185).

ABSTRACT

Register of Payments to Officers

1:153

[Washington, D.C.,] September 30, 1829

Lists payment by Paymaster D. Gwynne[1] to Second Lieutenant Jefferson Davis, First Infantry, $262. Amount includes pay and allowance for Davis and one servant,[2] for June through September, and for temporary duty "Com[mandin]g 'B' Co. from 1 Sept."[3]

D (NA, RG 99 Records of the Office of the Paymaster General, Register of Payments to Officers, IV, 27), 1.

[1] David Gwynne (sketch, 1:144, *n.* 2).

[2] James Pemberton (sketch, 1:5, *n.* 4).

[3] For Davis' period of command, see also 1:152, 185.

ABSTRACT

1:154 Post Return

Fort Winnebago,[1] Michigan Territory[2]
September [30,] 1829

Lists Brevet Second Lieutenant J. F. Davis, Company C, First Infantry, present at the post. Remarks: "On Extra Duty[3] Order of Major Twiggs[4] 21 June 1829."

Printed form, filled in and signed (NA, RG 94 Records of the Adjutant General's Office, Post Returns, Fort Winnebago, 1828–45), 2. Signed: "T J Beall B[reve]t Major 1st Infty." Endorsed: "Recd. 2 Novr."

[1] See 1:144, *n.* 1.

[2] See 1:149, *n.* 2.

[3] Davis was commanding Company B (1:153).

[4] David E. Twiggs (sketch, 1:149, *n.* 4).

1:155 To George Bomford

Fort Winebago[1] M[ichigan] T[erritory,][2]

SIR[3] Oct. 1st 1829

Enclosed I transmit you the quarterly Ordinance return of light Company "B" 1st Infty.

The Musket & Belt mentioned in the return were lost by the men to whom they had been issued. Very Respctfly. I have the honorer to be yr. obt. Servt.

J. F. DAVIS
Lt Comdg. Co. "B"[4]

ALS (NA, RG 156 Records of the Office of the Chief of Ordnance, Letters Received, D–80, 1829). Addressed: "To Lt. Col. Geo. Bomford Ordinance officer." Endorsed: "Recd. Nov. 2d. An[swere]d Dec 21." Enclosure missing.

[1] See 1:144, *n.* 1.

[2] See 1:149, *n.* 2.

[3] George Bomford (1782–1848), eighth graduate of the Military Academy, class of 1805, was in the Corps of Engineers and Ordnance Department, served in the War of 1812, and invented bomb cannon (howitzers) under the name "Columbiads." He continued with ordnance duties in the First Artillery from 1821, when ordnance and artillery were merged (*Statutes at Large of the United States*, III [1846], 615). With the organization of the Ordnance Corps in 1832, he was promoted to colonel and chief of ordnance. In 1842 he became inspector of arsenals, ordnance, arms, and munitions of war, the post he held at the time of his death at Boston (Cullum, *Biographical Register*, I, 58–59; *Who Was Who*).

[4] Davis was commanding the company from September 1 (1:153).

8 OCTOBER 1829

Certificate of Enlistment 1:156

Fort Winnebago[1] 8th October 1829

<-STATE-> *Territory* OF *Michigan*[2]

I, *John M. Oliver* born in *Albany* in the state of *New York* aged *thirty one* years, and by occupation a *Soldier* DO hereby acknowledge to have voluntarily enlisted this *eighth* day of *October* 1829 as a SOLDIER in the ARMY of the UNITED STATES of AMERICA, for the period of FIVE YEARS, unless sooner discharged by proper authority: Do also agree to accept such bounty, pay, rations, and clothing, as is or may be established by law. And I, *John M Oliver* *do solemnly swear*, that I will bear true faith and allegiance to the UNITED STATES of AMERICA, and that I will serve them *honestly and faithfully* against all their enemies or opposers whomsoever; and that I will observe and obey the orders of the President of the United States,[3] and the orders of the Officers appointed over me, according to the Rules and Articles of War.

Sworn and subscribed to, at *Fort Winnebago*
this *8th.* day of *October* 1829
BEFORE *T J Beall*[4]
Major Commdg

John M. *his* X *mark* *Oliver*

I CERTIFY, ON HONOR, That I have carefully examined the above named Recruit, agreeably to the General Regulations of the Army, and that in my opinion he is free from all bodily defects and mental infirmity, which would, in any way, disqualify him from performing the duties of a Soldier. *L. Abbott*[5] *Examining Surgeon. U. S. A*

I CERTIFY, ON HONOR, That I have minutely inspected the Recruit, *John M Oliver* previous to his enlistment, who was entirely sober when enlisted; and that in accepting him as duly qualified to perform the duties of an able bodied Soldier, I have strictly observed the Regulations which govern the Recruiting Service. This Recruit has *Gray* eyes, *Dark* hair, *Dark* complexion, is *five* feet *seven* inches high. *J. F. Davis* *Recruiting Officer.*

RECEIVED of *J. F. Davis Lieut.* of the United States' Army, this *eighth* day of *October* 1829 *Six* Dollars, in part of my bounty for enlisting in the Army of the United States, for five years.

(Signed Duplicates.)

$6.00 *John M.* *his* X *mark* *Oliver*

WITNESS, *T J Beall*

Printed form, filled in and signed (NA, RG 217 Records of the United States General Accounting Office, Second Auditor's Office, Second Auditor's Accounts, Account 13,710); printed form, filled in and signed (NA, RG 94 Records of the Adjutant General's Office, Enlistment Records). Endorsed in Davis' hand: "John M. Oliver enlisted at Fort Winebago M[ichigan] T[erritory] this eighth day of Octbr. Anno Domini 1829. By J. F. Davis Lt 1st Infty."

[1] See 1:144, *n.* 1.

[2] See 1:149, *n.* 2.

[3] The President was Andrew Jackson (sketch, 1:239, *n.* 2).

[4] Thomas J. Beall (sketch, 1:151, *n.* 2).

[5] Lucius Abbott, an assistant surgeon, 1828–34, was born in Connecticut. He was first stationed at Fort Winnebago, 1828–33, and at the time of his resignation was stationed at Detroit (Heitman, *Historical Register*, I, 150; Gordon, *Compilation of Registers of the Army*, 393, 487, 536). Abbott was on leave from Fort Winnebago, July 1830–May 1831, and returned June 20, 1831, with a detachment of recruits. He resigned after some difficulties with his medical examining board (NA, RG 94, Personal Papers, Medical Officers and Physicians).

1:157 Statement of Bounty Account Current

October 8th. 1829

Dr. United States In Acct. Current

With Lieut J. F. Davis 1st. Infy for Bounty, Premium, for October 1829

date		Amount	
		Dolls	Cts
October 8th. 1829	To Amount of Bounty as pr. Acct	6	00
		6	00

I Certify that the above account Current Exhibits a true statement of monies paid away by me the eigtht of October 1829, and that there is a Ballance due from the United States to me—of eight Dollars.[1]

J. F. Davis
Lt. 1st. Infty.

DS (NA, RG 217 Records of the United States General Accounting Office, Second Auditor's Office, Second Auditor's Accounts, Account 13,710).

[1] Authorization for the $8 payment was given in January 1830 (1:165–67); $2 was the premium, in addition to $6 bounty (1:158).

Recruiting Account 1:158

at Fort Winnebago[1] October [31,] 1829
Recruiting Account of Lt J. F. Davis 1st. Infy for October 1829.[2]

No	Names in Alphabetical Order	Age	Size		Enlistment		Bounty			Premium	Bounty & Premium	Remarks
			Feet	Inches	date of	Period of	Allowed	$ Paid	$ due			
1st.	Oliver. John. M	31	5	7	8 October 1829	5 Years	12	6	6	2	8	
							"	6	"	2	8[3]	

J. F. Davis
Lt. 1st. Infty.

DS (NA, RG 217 Records of the United States General Accounting Office, Second Auditor's Office, Second Auditor's Accounts, Account 13,710). Endorsed: "at Fort Winnebago En-l[istment]s Has the above man been mustered present?"; in a different hand, "*A Re-enlistment* Mustered on On Furlough the 31st. Octr 1829. In Compy B. 1st. Infy."

[1] See 1:144, *n.* 1.

[2] See 1:156 for the enlistment certificate.

[3] Authorization for the $8 payment was given in January 1830 (1:165–67).

ABSTRACT

1:159 **Post Return**

Fort Winnebago,[1] Michigan Territory[2]
October [31,] 1829

Lists Brevet Second Lieutenant J. F. Davis, Company C,[3] First Infantry, as absent on detached service.[4] Remarks: "In pursuit of Deserters Order of Major Beall[5] 20th. Octr 1829."

Printed form, filled in and signed (NA, RG 94 Records of the Adjutant General's Office, Post Returns, Fort Winnebago, 1828–45), 2. Signed: "T J Beall B[reve]t Major 1st Infty." Endorsed: "Ent[ere]d. Recd. 9 Jany. 1830."

[1] See 1:144, *n.* 1.
[2] See 1:149, *n.* 2.
[3] For evidence that Davis was attached to Company C, see 1:150.
[4] Evidence that Davis was not at the fort is further strengthened by a statement of General David Hunter who recalled that he first saw Davis in October 1829 in Chicago "in search of deserters" (Hunter to Wentworth, May 18, 1881, cited in Wentworth, *Early Chicago: Fort Dearborn*, 28).
[5] Thomas J. Beall (sketch, 1:151, *n.* 2).

ABSTRACT

1:160 **Company Muster Roll**

Fort Winnebago,[1] Michigan Territory[2]
October 31, 1829

Lists Brevet Second Lieutenant J. F. Davis of Captain Thomas J. Beall's[3] Company C, First Regiment of Infantry commanded by Colonel John McNeil,[4] "Absent on detached service, in pursuit of deserters.[5] order of Major Beall, October 20. 1829." Report covers September and October 1829.

Printed form, filled in and signed (NA, RG 94 Records of the Adjutant General's Office, Muster Rolls of Regular Army Organizations, First Infantry, Company C), 2. Signed: "T J Beall B[reve]t Major U S A." Endorsed: "*Proves*. Recd. Janry. 9th. *1830*. Entered."

[1] See 1:144, *n.* 1.
[2] See 1:149, *n.* 2.
[3] Thomas J. Beall (sketch, 1:151, *n.* 2).
[4] John McNeil (sketch, 1:151, *n.* 3).
[5] See 1:159, *n.* 4.

From the Office of the Quartermaster General[1] 1:161

SIR, November 26th. 1829

Your Clothing Return and vouchers for the 3d. quarter of the present year,[2] has been received and examined at this Office, and sent to the Treasury for settlement.[3] I am, Sir &c.

LbC (NA, RG 92 Records of the Office of the Quartermaster General, Letters Sent Relating to Clothing, II, 408). Addressed: "Lt J. F Davis 1st. Regiment Infantry Fort Winnebago."

[1] The quartermaster general was Thomas S. Jesup (sketch, 1:174, *n.* 4).

[2] The clothing return and vouchers have not been found.

[3] The return was sent to the second auditor's office (Office of the Quartermaster General to the second auditor, November 26, 1829 [NA, RG 92, Letters Sent Relating to Clothing, II, 407]).

ABSTRACT

Post Return 1:162

Fort Winnebago,[1] Michigan Territory[2]
November [30,] 1829

Lists Brevet Second Lieutenant J. F. Davis, Company C, First Infantry, present at the post. Remarks: "For Duty."

Printed form, filled in and signed (NA, RG 94 Records of the Adjutant General's Office, Post Returns, Fort Winnebago, 1828–45), 2. Signed: "T J Beall Major U S A." Endorsed: "Receivd. 18 March."

[1] See 1:144, *n.* 1.

[2] See 1:149, *n.* 2.

ABSTRACT

Post Return 1:163

Fort Winnebago,[1] Michigan Territory[2]
December [31,] 1829

Lists Brevet Second Lieutenant J. F. Davis, Company C, First Infantry, as absent with leave.[3] Remarks: "By order of Maj Beall[4] 22nd. Decr. 1829."

Printed form, filled in and signed (NA, RG 94 Records of the Adjutant General's Office, Post Returns, Fort Winnebago, 1828–45), 2. Signed: "G A

Spencer Capt 1st Infty." Endorsed: "Ent[ere]d Recd. 18 March 1830."

[1] See 1:144, *n.* 1.

[2] See 1:149, *n.* 2.

[3] Davis' leave was, in all probability, the occasion of a visit that he made to George Wallace Jones. In after years Jones, a lifelong friend of Davis, wrote, " 'The next I knew of "Jeff," as we used to call him, was in 1829. . . . It was late in the year, and late, one night, when a lieutenant and a sergeant rode up to my log-cabin at Sinsinawa Mound, about fifty miles from Fort Crawford, and inquired for Mr. Jones. I told him that I answered to that name. The lieutenant then asked me if they could remain there all night. I told him that they were welcome to share my buffalo robes and blankets, and that their horses could be coralled with mine on the prairie.

" 'The officer then asked me if I had ever been at the Transylvania University. I answered that I had been there from 1821 to 1825.

" ' "Do you remember a college boy named Jeff Davis?" '

" ' "Of course I do." '

" ' "I am Jeff." '

" 'That was enough for me. I pulled him off his horse and into my cabin, and it was hours before either of us could think of sleeping.

" 'Lieutenant Davis remained at my cabin for some days, and after the unconstrained manner of early frontier life we had a delightful time' " (V. Davis, *Memoir*, I, 58–59).

[4] Thomas J. Beall (sketch, 1:151, *n.* 2).

ABSTRACT

1:164

Semiannual Company Muster Roll

Fort Winnebago,[1] Michigan Territory[2]
December 31, 1829

Lists Brevet Second Lieutenant J. F. Davis of Captain Thomas J. Beall's[3] Company C, First Regiment of Infantry commanded by Colonel McNeil,[4] as "Attached to compy 'C.[5] by order of Maj. Twiggs,[6] 29. Aug. 1829. Absent with leave, 22 December, 1829." [7] Report covers July through December 1829.

Printed form, filled in and signed (NA, RG 94 Records of the Adjutant General's Office, Muster Rolls of Regular Army Organizations, First Infantry, Company C), 2. Signed: "E. G. Mitchell 2nd Lt 1st Infty G C Spencer Capt 1st Infty." Endorsed: "Proves Recd. March 18, 1830. Entered."

[1] See 1:144, *n.* 1.

[2] See 1:149, *n.* 2.

[3] Thomas J. Beall (sketch, 1:151, *n.* 2).

[4] John McNeil (sketch, 1:151, *n.* 3).

[5] Davis commanded B Company September 1–October 31 (1:152, 185).

[6] David E. Twiggs (sketch, 1:149, *n.* 4).

[7] For a conjecture on Davis' leave activities, see 1:163, *n.* 3.

ABSTRACT

Bounty Payment 1:165

[Washington, D.C.,] January 22, 1830

James Eakin[1] approves the claim of Lieutenant J. F. Davis, First Infantry, for $8 due him "For bounty paid, and premium on, one man[2] inlisted at Fort Winnebago[3] in october 1829."

DS (NA, RG 217 Records of the United States General Accounting Office, Second Auditor's Office, Second Auditor's Accounts, Account 13,710), 2. Signed: "James Eakin chf clk." Endorsed in Eakin's hand, "rep[lied] 22 Jany. 1830"; in a different hand, "Treasury Department 2d. Comptrollers Office Jany 23d 1830 Lt Jn Davis a/c."

[1] James Eakin, from New Jersey, was the chief clerk in the second auditor's office from at least 1830 until 1844 (*American Almanac* [1831–45], *passim*; Trever to McIntosh, May 8, 1970 [Jefferson Davis Association, Rice University, Houston]). Among other duties, the second auditor received and settled all accounts relating to the recruiting service (*American Almanac* [1832], 130).

[2] John M. Oliver; see 1:156 and 1:158.

[3] See 1:144, *n.* 1.

ABSTRACT

Appropriation Certificate No. 8265 1:166

Treasury Department, Second Auditor's Office
January 22, 1830

W. B. Lewis,[1] second auditor, certifies that the United States owes Lieutenant J. F. Davis, First Infantry, $8 "for recruiting disbursements made in october 1829,[2] at Fort Winnebago[3]. . . ."

Printed form, filled in and signed (NA, RG 217 Records of the United States General Accounting Office, Second Auditor's Office, Second Auditor's Accounts, Account 13,710), 1. Addressed: "To <—Richard Cutes—>, <*Isaac Hill,*> Esq. Second Comptroller of the Treasury." Signed: "W. B. Lewis." Endorsed: "I ADMIT and certify the above, this *23d* day of *January 1830. Isaac Hill,* Second Comptroller."

[1] William B. Lewis (1784–1866), born in Virginia, moved to Tennessee at an early age. His marriage to the daughter of a prominent planter near Nashville led to important contacts, including a lifelong friendship with Andrew Jackson. Lewis served as Jackson's quartermaster in the Natchez and Creek campaigns, 1812–13, and worked in the presidential campaigns of 1824 and 1828. With the accession of Jackson to the presidency in 1829, Lewis became second auditor of the Treasury Department, a resident of the White House, and a member of the "Kitchen Cabinet." He retired to his

home near Nashville in 1845 and lived in relative seclusion until his death (*DAB*). The second auditor's office handled accounts of the army relative to pay, subsistence, clothing, contingent disbursements, medicine and medical claims, recruiting, ordnance, and disbursements in the Indian Department (*American Almanac* [1832], 130).

[2] See 1:156–58 for Davis' recruiting documents.

[3] See 1:144, *n.* 1.

1:167

From William B. Lewis

SIR, 25 January 1830

The Treasurer U S.[1] will transmit you $8.00 the amount of your account for recruiting disbursements[2] made in October last at Fort Winnebago[3]—on the receipt of which be pleased to forward an acknowledgment to this Office.

Should you have any further accounts of a like nature with the foregoing, you will be pleased to refer, on the Statement, to the Rolls where your recruits are to be found mustered present. W. B. L.[4]

LbC (NA, RG 217 Records of the United States General Accounting Office, Second Auditor's Office, Letters Sent, XIV, 410). Addressed: "Lieut. J. F. Davis, 1 Inf. Fort Winnebago, via Green Bay."

[1] The secretary of the treasury was Samuel D. Ingham.

[2] See 1:156–58 for Davis' October recruiting documents.

[3] See 1:144, *n.* 1.

[4] William B. Lewis (sketch, 1:166, *n.* 1).

1:168

From the Office of the Quartermaster General[1]

SIR, January 30th. 1830

Your Clothing Return[2] for part of the 4th. quarter of last year, has been received and examined at this office, and sent to the Treasury for settlement[3] I am, Sir &c.

LbC (NA, RG 92 Records of the Office of the Quartermaster General, Letters Sent Relating to Clothing, III, 18). Addressed: "Lt J. F Davis 1st Infantry Fort Winnebago M[ichigan] T[erritory]."

[1] Thomas S. Jesup (sketch, 1:174, *n.* 4) was quartermaster general.

[2] Davis' clothing return has not been found.

[3] Sent to the second auditor (January 30, 1830 [NA, RG 92, Letters Sent Relating to Clothing, III, 18]).

ABSTRACT

Post Return 1:169

Fort Winnebago,[1] Michigan Territory[2]
January [31,] 1830

Lists Brevet Second Lieutenant J. F. Davis, Company C, First Infantry, present at the post. Remarks: "For Duty."

Printed form, filled in and signed (NA, RG 94 Records of the Adjutant General's Office, Post Returns, Fort Winnebago, 1828–45), 2. Signed: "T J Beall Br[evet] Major U S A." Endorsed: "Entd. Recd. 17th April."

[1] See 1:144, *n*. 1.
[2] See 1:149, *n*. 2.

ABSTRACT

Post Return 1:170

Fort Winnebago,[1] Michigan Territory[2]
February [28,] 1830

Lists Brevet Second Lieutenant J. F. Davis, Company C, First Infantry, present at the post. Remarks: "On Extra Duty."

Printed form, filled in and signed (NA, RG 94 Records of the Adjutant General's Office, Post Returns, Fort Winnebago, 1828–45), 2. Signed: "T J Beall B[reve]t Major U S A." Endorsed: "Ent[ered] Recd. 7th. April."

[1] See 1:144, *n*. 1.
[2] See 1:149, *n*. 2.

ABSTRACT

Company Muster Roll 1:171

Fort Winnebago,[1] Michigan Territory[2]
February 28, 1830

Lists Brevet Second Lieutenant J. F. Davis of Captain Thomas J. Beall's[3] Company C, First Regiment of Infantry commanded by Colonel John McNeil,[4] as present on extra duty. Report covers January and February 1830.

Printed form, filled in and signed (NA, RG 94 Records of the Adjutant General's Office, Muster Rolls of Regular Army Organizations, First Infantry, Company C), 2. Signed: "T J Beall Br[evet] Major 1st Infty." Endorsed: "Proves. Recd. April 5th 1830. Entered."

[1] See 1:144, *n.* 1.

[2] See 1:149, *n.* 2.

[3] Thomas J. Beall (sketch, 1:151, *n.* 2).

[4] John McNeil (sketch, 1:151, *n.* 3).

1:172

From William B. Lewis

SIR, 25 March 1830

The Treasurer U S.[1] will transmit you $24.00 the amount of your account for recruiting disbursements made at Fort Winnebago[2] in November last[3]—on the receipt of which be pleased to forward an acknowledgment to this Office.

Referring to my letter of the 25 Jany.[4] last, I am &c. W. B. L.[5]

LbC (NA, RG 217 Records of the United States General Accounting Office, Second Auditor's Office, Letters Sent, XV, 11). Addressed: "Lieut. Jeffn. F. Davis, 1 Inf. Ft. Winnebago, via Greenbay."

[1] Samuel D. Ingham was secretary of the treasury.

[2] See 1:144, *n.* 1.

[3] The recruiting documents for November have not been found.

[4] The January 25 letter is 1:167.

[5] William B. Lewis (sketch, 1:166, *n.* 1).

1:173

To George Bomford

Fort Winebago[1] March 31st 1830

SIR[2]

In the absence of the commanding officer (Maj Twiggs)[3] I send you a return of Ardinance and Ordinance stores containing the expenditures made since 30th June 1829 which appears from records left by Maj. Twiggs in my possession to be the date of the last return sent to your office.

The musket powder expended was used in obtaining stone necessary in the construction of Barracks. Very respectfuly I have the honor to be Your obt. servant JEFN. DAVIS

Lt. 1st. Infty.

ALS (NA, RG 156 Records of the Office of the Chief of Ordnance, Letters Received, D–4, 1830). Addressed: "For Col. G. Bomford Ordinance officer." Endorsed: "Recd. May 31st. an[swere]d. June 5"; in a different hand, "Tell him to send Abstract of Expenditure." Enclosure missing.

[1] See 1:144, *n.* 1.

[2] George Bomford (sketch, 1:155, *n.* 3).

[3] David E. Twiggs (sketch, 1:149, *n.* 4) had been on furlough since October 1829, and returned to the fort in June 1830 (Post Returns, October 1829–June 1830 [NA, RG 94, Fort Winnebago, 1828–45]).

ABSTRACT

Thomas P. Gwynn to Thomas S. Jesup 1:174

Fort Winnebago,[1] [Michigan Territory][2]
April 10, 1830

Gwynn[3] transmits a number of reports to the quartermaster general,[4] apologizes for the way in which post reports were made out, and states that he has "been relieved from the duties of A[cting] A[ssistant] Q. m. for the present by Lt. Davis . . . ."[5]

LS (NA, RG 92 Records of the Office of the Quartermaster General, Consolidated Correspondence File, Fort Winnebago, G–97, 1830), 3. Addressed: "Gen. T. S. Jessup Q M Gen U. S. A. Washington City D. C." Signed: "T P Gwynn Lt act[ing] ass[istant] Q M." Endorsed: "Recd June 8th. 1830." Enclosures missing.

[1] See 1:144, *n.* 1.

[2] See 1:149, *n.* 2.

[3] Thomas P. Gwynn (sketch, 1:148, *n.* 1) left on furlough April 28 (Post Return, April 1830 [NA, RG 94, Fort Winnebago, 1828–45]).

[4] Thomas S. Jesup (1788–1860), a Virginian, was quartermaster general for forty-two years (1818–60), having been first commissioned a second lieutenant in 1808. Jesup served as General William Hull's brigade major and adjutant general in the War of 1812 and was brevetted lieutenant colonel and colonel in 1814 for his conduct in the battles of Chippewa and Lundy's Lane. Even though the army was greatly reduced after the war, he was retained as an infantry major and was major general by 1828. In the Seminole War (1836–38) Jesup commanded the army in Florida. He is credited with a massive and efficient reorganization of the Quartermaster Department, and was honored by having two army posts named for him. He died in Washington and was succeeded by Lieutenant Colonel Joseph E. Johnston (*DAB*; Heitman, *Historical Register*, I, 573; Risch, *Quartermaster Support of the Army*, *passim*).

[5] Davis also relieved Gwynn in the office of assistant commissary of subsistence (1:175).

1:175
Order No. 42

Fort Winnebago[1] April 30th. 1830

Brevet 2nd. Lieut Jefferson Davis will releive Lieut Gwynn[2] Asst. Comy. Subs[3] for this Post from the duties appurtaining to that appointment By Order of Maj Beall[4] J F. DAVIS
Lt ac[ting] Adjt.

DS (Beauvoir, Jefferson Davis Shrine, Biloxi, Mississippi).

[1] See 1:144, *n.* 1.

[2] Thomas P. Gwynn (sketch, 1:148, *n.* 1).

[3] Davis also relieved Gwynn as assistant quartermaster (1:174).

[4] Thomas J. Beall (sketch, 1:151, *n.* 2).

ABSTRACT

1:176
Report of Persons and Articles Employed and Hired

Fort Winnebago,[1] April [30,] 1830

Lieutenant J. F. Davis, acting assistant quartermaster, certifies that he paid $161.33 during the month of April for the hire of Peter Pauquette,[2] François Roy,[3] and Elijah Wentworth, and their wagons, carts, and oxen, to haul stone for new barracks, and to pay P. G. Hambaugh,[4] a clerk in the Quartermaster Department.

DS (NA, RG 92 Records of the Office of the Quartermaster General, Reports of Persons and Articles Hired), 2. Signed: "J. F. Davis actg. A[ssistant] Q. M."

[1] See 1:144, *n.* 1.

[2] Peter Pauquette (also Pierre, Paquette, Poquett, and Poquette) was an interpreter, trader, and agent of the American Fur Company at Portage. He may have been born in St. Louis in 1796 (Turner, "History of Fort Winnebago," Wisconsin Historical *Collections*, XIV, 80), although two sources state that his birthdate was 1800 and his parentage French and Winnebago (Clark, "Early Times at Fort Winnebago," *ibid.*, VIII, 316; Merrell, "Pioneer Life in Wisconsin," *ibid.*, VII, 374). Pauquette acted often as a Winnebago interpreter and served as a government scout in the Black Hawk War. In September 1836, Henry Dodge, governor of the Territory of Wisconsin, was directed by the War Department to treat with the Winnebagoes at Portage for the sale of their lands east of the Mississippi. Pauquette attended the council as interpreter until he was killed by a Winnebago chief October 17, 1836. Pauquette's farm, Bellefontaine, was located on the Green Bay military road twelve miles northeast of Fort Winnebago, and the town of Poynette, Wisconsin, was first named Pauquette after him (*Dictionary of Wisconsin Biography*, 279; Clark, "Early Times at Fort Winnebago," Wisconsin Historical *Collec-*

tions, VIII, 316–20; De La Ronde, "Personal Narrative," *ibid.*, VII, 355–58; Merrell, "Pioneer Life in Wisconsin," *ibid.*, VII, 373–76, 382–91; [Thwaites], "The Wisconsin Winnebagoes: An Interview with Moses Paquette," *ibid.*, XII, 399–404; Turner, "History of Fort Winnebago," *ibid.*, XIV, 80–81; H. E. Cole, "The Old Military Road," *Wisconsin Magazine of History*, IX, 60; Kellogg, "The Agency House at Fort Winnebago," *ibid.*, XIV, 444; Starin, "Diary of a Journey to Wisconsin in 1840," *ibid.*, VI, 212).

[3] François Roy (variously spelled Francais, Francois, Francis, Franc, and Roi, Le Roy, Laroy, le Roy) resided from 1810 to 1828 at the Fox-Wisconsin portage on the east side of the Fox River, the site of Fort Winnebago. One source states he was at the portage from 1812 to 1818 ([Thwaites], "Narrative of Andrew J. Vieau, Sr.," Wisconsin Historical *Collections*, XI, 223*n.*), and, according to De La Ronde, he was still there as late as May 29, 1828 ("Personal Narrative," *ibid.*, VII, 346). François Roy was the son of Joseph Roy, who settled in Green Bay before 1785, and the husband of Thérèse Lecuyer. After the death of his father-in-law, he took over the latter's business at Portage, hauling boats and cargo, and trading with the Winnebago Indians. When Fort Winnebago was established in 1828, the government purchased his home and trading facilities (NA, RG 92, Letters Sent, XIII, 474–75; Turner, "History of Fort Winnebago," Wisconsin Historical *Collections*, XIV, 69–72), and Roy left the locality, although it is not known where he moved. A July 1830 letter places him in Portage ([Thwaites (ed.)], "Documents Relating to the Catholic Church in Green Bay," *ibid.*, XIV, 165–66), and there is evidence he lived there at least between April and July 1830, since he appears on reports of persons and articles employed and hired for April, May, June, and July 1830 (NA, RG 92). He probably moved to Green Bay no later than 1830 or 1831, for he subscribed money for the Catholic church there prior to the publication of a subscription listing in the summer of 1831 ([Thwaites (ed.)], "Documents Relating to the Catholic Church in Green Bay," Wisconsin Historical *Collections*, XIV, 175). Another source maintains he was living on the Wisconsin River from 1828 to 1831, when he moved to Green Lake ([Thwaites (ed.)], "The Fur-Trade in Wisconsin, 1815–1817," *ibid.*, XIX, 396*n.*). There was a Francis le Roy keeping a tavern and boardinghouse at the portage in 1839, and there is also a mention of a Roy twelve miles from Fort Winnebago in 1838 ([Thwaites], "Narrative of Alexis Clermont," *ibid.*, XV, 455; Kemper, "A Trip through Wisconsin in 1838," *Wisconsin Magazine of History*, VIII, 436–37). Francis Roy is listed as an employee or debtor of the Helena, Wisconsin, shot tower from 1831 to 1833 (Libby, "Chronicle of the Helena Shot-tower," Wisconsin Historical *Collections*, XIII, 340*n.*). These references could be to the same person or to relatives; in any case, clear identification is complicated by uncertain orthography (see, for example, Grignon, "Seventy-two Years' Recollections," *ibid.*, III, 289–90; Lockwood, "Early Times and Events in Wisconsin," *ibid.*, II, 109; Titus, "Historic Spots in Wisconsin," *Wisconsin Magazine of History*, III, 186).

[4] P. G. Hambaugh was under contract as a clerk as early as November 1829, but by 1845 he had established a trading post in Florida (NA, RG 92, Reports of Persons and Articles Hired; NA, RG 92, Letters Sent, XIV, 343; *House Reports*, 29th Cong., 1st Sess., No. 278).

1:177 To Thomas S. Jesup

Fort Winnebago[1] May 5th. 1830

SIR,[2]

I have the honor of informing you that the duties of Quarter Master have divolved on me[3] for the present as will appear from authority herewith inclosed.

The imperfect knowledge <I>[4] have of the distances of the different Military Posts in the united States has induced me to call on you for a Scale of distances.[5]

You will oblige me by forwarding it immediately on the receipt of this. Verry respectfully Your Mo. Obt. Sert. JEFN. DAVIS
actg. A[ssistant] Q. M.

LS (Jefferson Davis Association, Rice University, Houston). Indexed, not found (NA, RG 92 Records of the Office of the Quartermaster General, Letters Received, D–83, 1830). Addressed: "Genl. T. S. Jessup Q M Gen U. S. A. Washington City." Enclosure missing.

[1] See 1:144, *n.* 1.

[2] Thomas S. Jesup (sketch, 1:174, *n.* 4).

[3] Davis assumed the assistant quartermaster duties in April (1:174).

[4] Interlined.

[5] The scale of distances was sent to Davis June 8 (1:180).

ABSTRACT

1:178 Report of Persons and Articles Employed and Hired

Fort Winnebago,[1] May [31,] 1830

Lieutenant J. F. Davis, acting assistant quartermaster, certifies that he paid $310.50 during the month of May for the hire of carts, wagons, and oxen to haul stone and lime for new barracks and to pay a clerk[2] in the Quartermaster Department.

DS (NA, RG 92 Records of the Office of the Quartermaster General, Reports of Persons and Articles Hired), 2. Signed: "J F. Davis ac[ting] A[ssistant] Q. M." Transmitted: Davis to Jesup, June 4, 1830 (NA, RG 92 Records of the Office of the Quartermaster General, Letters Received, D–108, 1830). Acknowledged: The Office of the Quartermaster General to Davis, July 19, 1830 (1:188).

[1] See 1:144, *n.* 1.

[2] P. G. Hambaugh (1:176, *n.* 4).

To George Gibson 1:179

Fort Winnebago[1] June 4th. 1830

SIR[2]

I have the honor of inclosing to you a monthly return of Sub. Stores received & issued at this Post during the month of May 1830

148 pounds of Candles are taken up on the return as received of Lt. Denny,[3] but no invoice of the Same. As Soon as an invoice can be procured it Shall be forwarded. I am Sir Verry respectfully Your Mo. Obt. Sert.

J. F. DAVIS
ac[ting] A[ssistant] C[ommissary] S[ubsistence]

LS (NA, RG 192 Records of the Office of the Commissary General of Subsistence, Letters Received, D–959, 1830). Addressed: "Gen. Geo. Gibson Com[missary] Gen. U. S. A. Washington City D. C." Endorsed: "[Received] June 26th." Enclosure missing. Acknowledged: Gibson to Davis, July 2, 1830 (NA, RG 192 Records of the Office of the Commissary General of Subsistence, Letters Sent, VII, 495).

1 See 1:144, *n.* 1.

2 George Gibson, born in Pennsylvania in 1783, was first commissioned in 1808 as a captain in the Fifth Infantry, and served in the War of 1812. Promoted to colonel in 1816, he was quartermaster general supporting Andrew Jackson in the Seminole War, then commissary general of subsistence from 1818. He was brevetted brigadier general in 1826, and major general in 1848 for meritorious conduct in performing his duties in the Mexican War. Gibson died in 1861 at Washington, D.C. (Heitman, *Historical Register*, I, 453; *Appleton's*; Risch, *Quartermaster Support of the Army*, 179–83, 247–48).

3 St. Clair Denny, born in Pennsylvania, was graduated from West Point in 1822 and appointed to the Fifth Infantry. Denny had served in various garrisons, and was a first lieutenant and assistant quartermaster at Fort Howard, Wisconsin, October 1830–January 1834. He resigned in 1839 but was reappointed as major and paymaster in 1841, serving in the 1841–42 Florida war and at several other posts until his death in 1858 at Pittsburgh, at the age of fifty-eight (Cullum, *Biographical Register*, I, 287).

From the Office of the Quartermaster General[1] 1:180

SIR. June 8th. 1830

In compliance with the request contained in your letter of the 5th. instant,[2] I transmit herewith, a copy of the table of Post Offices and distances, by which you will be governed, in your payments of Transportation. You will turn it over to your successor, on being relieved from duty in the Quarter Master's Department.

LbC (NA, RG 92 Records of the Office of the Quartermaster General, Letters Sent, XIV, 326). Addressed: "Lt. Jefferson Davis, A[cting] A[ssistant] Qr. Mr. Fort Winnebago." Enclosure missing.

[1] Thomas S. Jesup was quartermaster general (sketch, 1:174, *n.* 4).

[2] See 1:177 for Davis' May 5 request.

[3] Davis was acting assistant quartermaster until he left Fort Winnebago in June 1831 (1:267, 279).

ABSTRACT

1:181

The Office of the Quartermaster General[1] to Thomas P. Gwynn

[Washington, D.C.,] June 15, 1830

Lieutenant T. P. Gwynn[2] is informed that his accounts have been sent to the third auditor[3] of the Treasury for settlement. Remarks on the vouchers note the reason for heavy wear on tents used by detached parties and point out Gwynn's failure to deduct Sundays from the extra duty days for which "Lt. E. F. Davis"[4] was paid $126.40 for the period June 21, 1829, to January 1, 1830.

LbC (NA, RG 92 Records of the Office of the Quartermaster General, Letters Sent, XIV, 342–43), 1. Addressed: "Lieut. T. P. Gwynn, 1st. Infantry."

[1] Thomas S. Jesup was quartermaster general (sketch, 1:174, *n.* 4).

[2] Thomas P. Gwynn (sketch, 1:148, *n.* 1).

[3] Peter Hagner (sketch, 1:199, *n.* 5) was third auditor.

[4] Although Davis is mistakenly referred to as "E. F.," there is little doubt that Jefferson is the Davis intended.

1:182

To Thomas S. Jesup

Act. Asst Qr. Mrs. Office
Fort Winnebago[1] June 19th. 1830

SIR[2]

Your letter dated March 25th. 1830,[3] covering a Statement of remarks on Lt. T. P. Gwynn's[4] accounts and property return for the 4th quarter of 1829 has been received at this Office. Also a letter[3] from the 3d Auditor[5] accompanied by a Sheet of remarks on Lt. Gwynn's acts. for the 3d. & 4th. Quarter of 1829 has been received.

The letter from the Treasury Department calls for the duplicates of Sundry vouchers belonging to the 3d. quarter of 1829, to be corrected and forwarded as early as possible. Lt. Gwynn left this post in May last[6] for Washington City, and carried with him all the Vouchers for disbursments of money at this Office during the time he acted as Quarter Master.[7] It is therefore out of my power to furnish the Vouchers called for.

Letter from Treasury Department Says, "*Muster Rolls* are wanting, Say, from October '28 to May '29, inclusive". Remarks from Qr. Mr. Genls. Office and 3rd. Auditor require Muster rolls from 1st. July to 31st. December 1829. On examining the extra duty rolls filed in this office I find that they have been made out regularley every month from the 1st. of October 1828 to the present time. I also find letters from the Qr. M. Genl. filed in this office, acknowledging the receipt of Muster rolls for May October and December 1829 and also Jany. & Feby. 1830. If it is absolutely necessary to forward other Muster rolls please apprize me of it: inform at the Same time the months they are required for, and it Shall be attended to. I am Sir Verry respecty. Your mo. obt. Sert. JF. DAVIS

ac[ting] A[ssistant] Q. Master

LS (NA, RG 92 Records of the Office of the Quartermaster General, Letters Received, D–107, 1830). Addressed: "Genl. T. S. Jessup Qr. Mr. Genl. U. S. A. Washington City D. C." Endorsed: "Recd July 19th. 1830."

1 See 1:144, *n.* 1.

2 Thomas S. Jesup (sketch, 1:174, *n.* 4).

3 The letters and statements have not been found.

4 Thomas P. Gwynn (sketch, 1:148, *n.* 1).

5 The third auditor of the Treasury Department was Peter Hagner (sketch, 1:199, *n.* 5).

6 Gwynn left Fort Winnebago April 28 (Post Return, April 1830 [NA, RG 94, Fort Winnebago, 1828–45]).

7 Davis relieved Gwynn as assistant quartermaster and commissary in April (1:174, 175).

ABSTRACT

Report of Persons and Articles Employed and Hired 1:183

Fort Winnebago,[1] June [30,] 1830

Lieutenant J. F. Davis, acting assistant quartermaster, certifies that he paid $231 during the month of June for the hire of carts, wagons, and oxen to haul lumber for new barracks and to pay a clerk[2] in the Quartermaster Department.

DS (NA, RG 92 Records of the Office of the Quartermaster General, Reports of Persons and Articles Hired), 2. Signed: "J. F. Davis ac[ting] A[ssistant] Q M."

[1] See 1:144, *n.* 1.
[2] P. G. Hambaugh; see 1:176, *n.* 4.

ABSTRACT

1:184
Register of Fresh Beef Contracts

[Washington, D.C.,] July 1, 1830

Records that Lieutenant J. F. Davis contracted with Wallace Rowan[1] to supply Fort Winnebago[2] with fresh beef at 4.99 cents per pound for the period September 1830 through August 1831.

D (NA, RG 192 Records of the Office of the Commissary General of Subsistence, Register of Fresh Beef Contracts, 1820–56), 1.

[1] Wallace Rowan (also spelled Willis, Wallis and Rowin, Rowen) was from Indiana. For a time he mined unsuccessfully in Kentucky and in the lead country near Platteville, Wisconsin, then became a trader in the Fort Winnebago area. About 1830 he built a one-room residence and trading post on Lake Mendota along the Green Bay military road, but abandoned it when the Black Hawk War erupted. After the war he sold the cabin and by 1835 had a claim at Squaw Point on the eastern bank of Lake Monona. In 1838 he moved to Poynette where he operated an inn, the only building in town. From Poynette he migrated to Baraboo and, with Abraham Wood, opened a sawmill in 1840. He died at Baraboo ("The Question Box," *Wisconsin Magazine of History*, III, 239–40; Starin, "Diary of a Journey to Wisconsin," *ibid.*, VI, 212; H. E. Cole, "The Old Military Road," *ibid.*, IX, 50; Draper, "Michel St. Cyr," Wisconsin Historical *Collections*, VI, 397–99; J. D. Butler, "Taychoperah," *ibid.*, X, 76–77).

[2] See 1:144, *n.* 1.

ABSTRACT

1:185
Pay Voucher

Fort Winnebago,[1] July 4, 1830

Lieutenant J. F. Davis, First Infantry, acknowledges that he has received $603.30 from Paymaster William Piatt.[2] Amount includes pay, and allowance for one servant,[3] for October 1829 through June 1830, and additional pay for commanding Company B in October 1829 and acting as assistant commissary of subsistence in May and June 1829. The servant is described as "James a Slave."

Printed form, filled in and signed (NA, RG 217 Records of the United States General Accounting Office, Paymasters' Accounts, Piatt 14,473, Voucher 20), 3. Signed: "J. F. Davis Lt. 1st. Infty."

[1] See 1:144, *n.* 1.

[2] William Piatt, major and paymaster from New Jersey, was a veteran of the War of 1812. Having received a wound at the Battle of New Orleans, he was brevetted lieutenant colonel for gallant conduct. He was discharged in 1815 but recommissioned in May 1830. At the time of his death in 1834, he was listed in the army register as a colonel in the Pay Department (Gordon, *Compilation of Registers of the Army*, 536; Heitman, *Historical Register*, I, 790).

[3] James Pemberton (sketch, 1:5, *n.* 4).

ABSTRACT

Register of Payments to Officers 1:186

[Washington, D.C.,] July 4, 1830

Lists payment by Paymaster W. Piatt[1] to Second Lieutenant Jefferson Davis, First Infantry, $603.30. Amount includes pay and allowance for Davis and one servant,[2] for October 1829 through June 1830. Remarks: "Com[mandin]g 'B' Co. Octob. A[cting] C[ommissary] S[ubsistence] &c May & June."[3]

D (NA, RG 99 Records of the Office of the Paymaster General, Register of Payments to Officers, IV, 27), 1.

[1] William Piatt (sketch, 1:185, *n.* 2).

[2] James Pemberton (sketch, 1:5, *n.* 4).

[3] Davis' claim for pay as acting assistant commissary of subsistence referred to May and June 1829. See pay voucher, July 4, 1830 (1:185).

To George Gibson 1:187

Fort Winnebago[1] July 6th. 1830

SIR[2]

Inclosed I have the honor of forwarding a return of provisions received and issued at this <Post>[3] during the month of June 1830. I also forward my a/current for the months of May and June 1830.

I have not received of Lt. St Clair Denny[4] an invoice of Some Candles which were taken up on my last returns, but as Soon as it comes to hand it Shall be forwarded.

I also inclose a Contract[5] entered in to with W. Rowin[6] for Sup-

plying this Post with fresh beef the ensuing year. I am Sir Verry respecty. Your Mo. Obt. Sert.
J. F. DAVIS
ac[ting] A[ssistant] C[ommissary] S[ubsistence]

LS (NA, RG 192 Records of the Office of the Commissary General of Subsistence, Letters Received, D-971, 1830). Addressed: "Genl. Geo. Gibson Com[missary] Gen U. S. A. Washington City." Endorsed: "Recd. 6 Augt." Enclosures missing. Acknowledged: Gibson to Davis, August 6, 1830 (NA, RG 192 Records of the Office of the Commissary General of Subsistence, Letters Sent, VIII, 27).

1 See 1:144, *n.* 1.

2 George Gibson (sketch, 1:179, *n.* 2).

3 Interlined.

4 St. Clair Denny (sketch, 1:179, *n.* 3).

5 The beef contract was registered July 1 (1:184).

6 Wallace Rowan (sketch, 1:184, *n.* 1).

1:188

From the Office of the Quartermaster General[1]

SIR: July 19th. 1830

I have received your letter of the 14th. ultimo,[2] enclosing a Muster Roll of Soldiers on extra duty,[3] and a Report of Persons and articles hired for the month of May;[4] and also that of the 19th Ultimo,[5] in relation to the defects pointed out in the accounts of Lieut. Gwynn,[6] your predecessor.[7] In reply to the latter, I have to remark, that the Muster Rolls received at this Office from Lieut. Gwynn and of which you find my acknowledgements, are retained upon the files of my Office, whilst those required of him, were necessary to accompany his accounts to the Treasury Department. The regulations (No. 1.086)[8] distinctly enjoin, that duplicate Muster Rolls shall be executed, one of which to be transmitted direct to me, and the other to be filed in support of the pay rolls. This latter requirement, escaped the attention of Lt. Gwynn, as he informs me verbally, and recourse has been had to the rolls transmitted to me, which should remain in my Office for administrative purposes, but which, under the circumstances of his case, have been handed over to the Treasury Department. I have gone thus into detail on the subject, to prevent you from falling into a like error with your predecessor.

LbC (NA, RG 92 Records of the Office of the Quartermaster General, Letters Sent, XIV, 379). Addressed: "Lieut. Jefferson Davis, Acting Asst. Quarter Master, Fort Winnebago via Green Bay, Michigan."

1 Thomas S. Jesup (sketch, 1:174, *n.*

4) was quartermaster general.

[2] Davis' letter of June 14 is missing.

[3] The May muster roll of soldiers on extra duty has not been found.

[4] Davis' report for May is 1:178.

[5] Davis' letter of June 19 appears as 1:182.

[6] Thomas P. Gwynn (sketch, 1:148, *n.* 1).

[7] Gwynn turned over his duties as acting assistant quartermaster (see 1:174) and as acting assistant commissary of subsistence (see 1:175) to Davis upon Gwynn's leaving Fort Winnebago for the East.

[8] Article 69, paragraph 1086, is printed on page 235 of *General Army Regulations* for 1825.

ABSTRACT

Report of Persons and Articles Employed and Hired 1:189

Fort Winnebago,[1] Michigan Territory[2]
July [31,] 1830

Lieutenant J. F. Davis, acting assistant quartermaster, certifies that he paid $113 during the month of July for the hire of carts, a wagon, and oxen to haul bricks and lime for new barracks and to pay a clerk[3] in the Quartermaster Department.

DS (NA, RG 92 Records of the Office of the Quartermaster General, Reports of Persons and Articles Hired), 2. Signed: "J. F. Davis ac[ting] A[ssistant] Q. M."

[1] See 1:144, *n.* 1.

[2] See 1:149, *n.* 2.

[3] P. G. Hambaugh; see 1:176, *n.* 4.

ABSTRACT

Post Return 1:190

Fort Winnebago,[1] Michigan Territory[2]
July [31,] 1830

Lists Brevet Second Lieutenant J. F. Davis, Company C, First Infantry, as absent on special duty. Remarks: "On detached service, in pursuit of Deserters.[3] Order of Maj. Twiggs[4] 25. July (*1830*)."

Printed form, filled in and signed (NA, RG 94 Records of the Adjutant General's Office, Post Returns, Fort Winnebago, 1828–45), 2. Signed: "D. E. Twiggs Major 1st Ifty." Endorsed: "Entd. Recd. 31. Augst."

[1] See 1:144, *n.* 1.

[2] See 1:149, *n.* 2.

[3] In a letter to James D. Butler dated February 22, 1885, Davis reminisced about an expedition or expeditions which he made to the Four Lakes

region while on detached service. Although Davis writes that the expedition was made in the summer of 1829, the official records do not list him as being on detached service at that time. An extract of the letter follows: "When on detached service I think I encamped one night about the site of Madison. . . . Fort Winnebago had been occupied but a short time before my arrival there and I think nothing was known to the Garrison about the Four Lakes before I saw them. Indeed Sir, it may astonish you to learn, in view of the densely populated condition of that country, that I, and the file of soldiers who accompanied me, were the first white men who ever passed over the country between the Portage of the Wisconsin & Fox rivers and the then, Village of Chicago" (File 1885, State Historical Society of Wisconsin, Madison).

[4] David E. Twiggs (sketch, 1:149, *n.* 4).

1:191 To George Gibson

Fort Winnebago[1] August 2nd. 1830

SIR[2]

I have the honor of inclosing to you a return of Provisions received and issued at this Post during the month of July 1830.

I also inclose <–you–> the Invoice promised you in a former letter[3] to accompany the return of May 1830[4] I am Verry respecty. Your Mo. Obt. Sert.

J. F. DAVIS

ac[ting] A[ssistant] C[ommissary] S[ubsistence]

LS (NA, RG 192 Records of the Office of the Commissary General of Subsistence, Letters Received, D–984, 1830). Addressed: "Genl. Geo. Gibson Com[missary] Genl. U. S. A. Washington City." Endorsed: "Recd. 7 Sep." Enclosures missing.

[1] See 1:144, *n.* 1.

[2] George Gibson (sketch, 1:179, *n.* 2).

[3] The invoice for candles is mentioned in 1:179 and 1:187.

[4] The return for May was transmitted in 1:179.

1:192 From Joshua B. Brant

Asst. Quarter Master's Office
Saint Louis August 3rd. 1830

SIR,

Your letters of the 30th. of June and 8th July ultimo,[1] the former advising me of your draft in favour of J. E. Heron[2] Esqr. for $151. and the latter informing me of the Course you had thought proper to pursue in obtaining funds from this office, have been received, and in reply to both I have to state that, in consequence of the advance having been made by the Sutler, the draft has been paid, otherwise it would have been returned for the approval of the Commanding Officer[3] as instructed by the Q Mr. Genl,[4] to whom I have transmitted a Copy of your Communication of the 8th. ult. and now apprise you that no draft of yours will hereafter be paid by me at this Office, unless authenticated in the manner heretofore directed.[5] Respectfuly I have the honour to be Sir Your ob. Sevt J. B. BRANT[6]

A[ssistant] Q. M. U. S. A

LS (NA, RG 108 Records of the Headquarters of the Army, Letters Received, 1830). Addressed: "Lieut. Jef. Davis Act[ing] Asst Qr Master USA Fort Winnebago M[ichigan] T[erritory]." Endorsed: "Recd Oct 25th. 1830." Enclosed: Jesup to Macomb, October 29, 1830 (1:215).

1 Davis' letters of June 30 and July 8 have not been found.

2 James E. Heron, born in Pennsylvania, was assistant commissary of purchases, 1813–21, and sutler at Mackinaw, Forts Dearborn, Howard, Leavenworth, and Jesup until 1843. He died in 1845 (Heitman, *Historical Register*, I, 525; Ellis, "Fifty-Four Years' Recollections," Wisconsin Historical *Collections*, VII, 241*n*.; [Thwaites (ed.)], "Fur-Trade in Wisconsin, 1812–25," *ibid*., XX, 278*n*.).

3 Davis' commanding officer was David E. Twiggs (sketch, 1:149, *n*. 4).

4 Thomas S. Jesup (sketch, 1:174, *n*. 4) was the quartermaster general.

5 See also 1:205, 211, 215 for Brant's quarrel with Davis.

6 Joshua B. Brant, from Connecticut, entered the army a private in 1813 and was brevetted first lieutenant for gallantry at Fort Erie in 1814. He was regularly promoted to captain and assistant deputy quartermaster general in 1819, to major and quartermaster in 1832, and to lieutenant colonel and deputy quartermaster general from 1838 until his resignation in 1839 (Heitman, *Historical Register*, I, 241).

Order No. 93

1:193

Fort Winnebago[1] August 12, 1830

A board of survey, will convene forthwith to inspect Qr Masters stores, reported unfit for use, The board will consist of Maj Beall[2] & Capt Spencer[3] members—asst Surgeon Abbott[4] will perform the duties of Secretary of the board By order of Maj. Twiggs[5]

(Signed) J. F. DAVIS

Lt & a[cting] Adj

[ES 1] Fort Winnebago Augt. 13th 1830

Pursuant to the above order the board have examined Six boats belonging to the Qr Masters[6] Department and find them unfit for ser-

vice & irreparable on account of age,[7] L. ABBOTT
Ass[istant] Surg U. S. A Secretary
T J BEALL
Bt Major U S. A.
G C SPENCER
Capt 1st Infty

[E 2] Lt. Davis is not entitled to a credit for the articles condemned by the board of survey until they are disposed of under the provisions of 1.001 & 1.002 general regulations.[8] Q M. GEN. OFFICE

D, copy (NA, RG 217 Records of the United States General Accounting Office, Third Auditor's Office, Third Auditor's Accounts, Account 10,523). Enclosed: Davis to Jesup, October 25, 1830 (1:214).

1 See 1:144, *n.* 1.

2 Thomas J. Beall (sketch, 1:151, *n.* 2).

3 George C. Spencer, a Virginian appointed from Indiana, was commissioned a second lieutenant of the First Infantry February 13, 1818, became captain in 1822, and resigned from the army in December 1831 (Heitman, *Historical Register*, I, 910).

4 Lucius Abbott (sketch, 1:156, *n.* 5).

5 David E. Twiggs (sketch, 1:149, *n.* 4).

6 Thomas S. Jesup was the quartermaster general (sketch, 1:174, *n.* 4).

7 See 1:223 for remarks on this survey report.

8 Article 69, paragraph 1001, provides for a board of survey to examine damaged and unfit quartermaster stores, and to report whether or not the damage was caused by neglect. Paragraph 1002 states that stores damaged from causes other than neglect of the quartermaster were to be sold at public auction (*General Army Regulations* [1825], 218–19).

1:194 From the Office of the Quartermaster General[1]

SIR, August 14th. 1830

If you should find it more convenient to receive the funds and supplies required at Fort Winnebago[2] from St. Louis, than from Detroit, a duplicate of each monthly estimate and Summary Statement made to this office should be sent to the Assistant Quarter Master[3] there to enable him to provide in time for the payment of your drafts.

If you should receive funds &c from Detroit, duplicates of your estimates and Summary Statements must be sent to the Assistant Quarter Master.[4]

LbC (NA, RG 92 Records of the Office of the Quartermaster General, Letters Sent, XIV, 432). Addressed: "Acting Asst. Qr. Master, at Fort Winnebago, Michigan Territory. (Lieut. Jefferson Davis.)"

[1] The quartermaster general was Thomas S. Jesup (sketch, 1:174, *n.* 4).

[2] See 1:144, *n.* 1.

[3] The assistant quartermaster at St. Louis was Joshua B. Brant (sketch, 1:192, *n.* 6). See 1:192 for Brant's reprimand of Davis.

[4] The assistant quartermaster at Detroit was Henry Whiting (sketch, 1:208, *n.* 2).

Order No. 95

1:195

Fort Winebago[1] M[ichigan] T[erritory][2]
August 15th 1830

A board of survey[3] will convene at 11 Oclock A. M. to inspect public oxen & a Horse reported unfit for use.

The board will consist of Maj. Beall,[4] Capt Spencer[5] & Lt Burbank[6] members. The junior member will perform the duties of Secretary. By Order of Major Twiggs[7] (Signed) J. F. DAVIS
Lt. &. Act. Adjt.

[ES] The board met pursuant to the above order & examined one horse & five oxen belonging to the Qr. Master's Department; which they find unfit for public use, in consequence of old age stiff joints, & long service.[8]

T J BEALL
Bt Major U S A
G C SPENCER
Capt 1st. Infty
S. BURBANK
Lt. & Secretary

D, copy (NA, RG 217 Records of the United States General Accounting Office, Third Auditor's Office, Third Auditor's Accounts, Account 10,523). Enclosed: Davis to Jesup, October 25, 1830 (1:214).

[1] See 1:144, *n.* 1.

[2] See 1:149, *n.* 2.

[3] See 1:193, *n.* 8 for the regulations concerning boards of survey.

[4] Thomas J. Beall (sketch, 1:151, *n.* 2).

[5] George C. Spencer (sketch, 1:193, *n.* 3).

[6] Sidney Burbank, son of Sullivan Burbank, a veteran of the War of 1812, was born in Massachusetts and was appointed to the First Infantry from West Point in 1829. He served at several frontier posts, in the Black Hawk War, the 1840–41 Seminole War, and the Civil War, being brevetted brigadier general (Union Army) at Gettysburg. After forty years' service, he retired in 1870 and died at Newport, Kentucky, in 1882 at the age of seventy-five (Cullum, *Biographical Register*, I, 432–33).

[7] David E. Twiggs (sketch, 1:149, *n.* 4).

[8] See 1:223 for remarks on this survey report.

1:196

To Thomas S. Jesup

Fort Winnebago[1] Augt. 15th. 1830

SIR[2]

I have the honor of enclosing to you my property returns and accounts current for the 2nd. Quarter of 1830. They Should have been forwarded Sooner but have been detained in consequence of my absence on duty.[3]

I have made Seperate returns of those articles belonging to the New Barracks, and also a Separate A/Current for disbursments on account of New Barracks.

By instructions contained in a letter[4] from the Qr. Mr. Genl. to Lt Gwynn[5] I have discontinued returning the Tents on the property return. I receipted to Lt Gwynn for fourteen Tents, Nine of which number were on hand and five represented to be in the hands of an Officer at that time Stationed up the Ouisconsin river, procuring timber; That officer on his return to this Post informs me that he has two Tents in his hands belonging to the Q. M. department. The Number therefore on hand at this time is eleven I am Respecty. Your Mo. Obt. Sert.

J. F. DAVIS
ac[ting] A[ssistant] Q. M.

LS (NA, RG 92 Records of the Office of the Quartermaster General, Consolidated Correspondence File, Fort Winnebago, D–145, 1830). Addressed: "Genl. T S Jessup Q M Genl. U. S. A." Endorsed: "Recd. Septr. 7th." Enclosures missing.

[1] See 1:144, *n.* 1.

[2] Thomas S. Jesup (sketch, 1:174, *n.* 4).

[3] On July 25 Davis was ordered on detached service to pursue deserters (1:190).

[4] See 1:181 for Jesup's letter to Gwynn.

[5] Thomas P. Gwynn (sketch, 1:148, *n.* 1).

1:197

From Thomas S. Jesup[1]

SIR: August 17th. 1830

Annexed you will receive a copy of a communication, addressed to me from the War Department, rescinding so much of the Regulation of the 11th. of June 1828,[2] as grants a per diem allowance to Officers employed with working parties[3] under the direction of the Quarter Master's Department. Your payments on that account, will cease from the date of that communication.

[Encl]

SIR, War Department August 16th. 1830

The regulation of the 11th. June 1828,[2] allowing extra compensation of eighty cents per day to officers not of the Staff, employed with working parties under the direction of the Quarter Master's Department is rescinded, and you will give orders accordingly. Very Respectfully, (signed) P. G. RANDOLPH[4]

Acting Secretary of War

LbC (NA, RG 92 Records of the Office of the Quartermaster General, Letters Sent, XIV, 435). Addressed: "(Circular) . . . Lieut. J Davis. . . ."

1 Thomas S. Jesup (sketch, 1:174, *n.* 4).

2 The regulation of June 11, 1828, is found in NA, RG 92, Orders Received from the War Department, I (1818–31), 260–61. The new rule of August 16, 1830, made Davis uncertain about the validity of his and other officers' claims to compensation for duty performed before the new rule became effective (1:224). Davis was told to submit his claim (1:240), which he did (1:264); and it was accepted (1:276).

3 Other than the Twiggs to Jesup letter printed as 1:451, the above item is one of few contemporary documents proving that Davis supervised, as he states in his letter to Jones, January 5, 1872, the construction parties at Fort Winnebago (1:264, *n.* 11).

4 Dr. Philip G. Randolph, chief clerk in the War Department, was interim secretary after the resignation of John H. Eaton in the summer of 1831. Randolph was Eaton's brother-in-law, and was involved in the dispute between Eaton and Samuel D. Ingham over Eaton's second wife, Peggy O'Neale Timberlake, which finally led to dissolution of the cabinet and Randolph's dismissal in 1831 (*American Almanac* [1831], 132; *Biographical Directory of the American Congress*, 16; Wiltse, *Calhoun: Nullifier*, 108; Pollack, *Peggy Eaton*, 160–65).

From the Office of the Quartermaster General[1] 1:198

SIR. Augt. 19th. 1830

To enable me to comply with a recent order of the War Dept,[2] I wish you to furnish me with a special report of the progress made in the erecting of Barracks & other public buildings[3] at Fort Winnebago.[4]

The report should designate each building with the number & size of the rooms, whether completely finished or not—and if not when it is probable it will be completed. The improvements of the grounds—whether the appropriation will be sufficient to finish the entire work in a manner to ensure suitable accommodation and comfort to the garrison.

If a further appropriation be necessary the estimate should be furnished in time to be included in my annual estimate.[5] I am Sir &c.

LbC (NA, RG 92 Records of the Office of the Quartermaster General, Letters Sent, XIV, 441). Addressed: "The Actg. Asst. q m. at Ft. Winnebago. M[ichigan] Ter."; in a different hand, "(Lieut Jefferson Davis)."

[1] The quartermaster general was Thomas S. Jesup (sketch, 1:174, *n.* 4).

[2] A directive of August 7, 1830, signed by Philip G. Randolph, acting secretary of war, was sent to all heads of bureaus asking an estimate of appropriations required before October 20, a statement of money drawn and remitted through the third quarter, and a report on construction of roads and public works (NA, RG 92, Letters Received from the Secretary of War, Book 10, S289 [1830]).

[3] Davis' reply is 1:212, dated October 15.

[4] See 1:144, *n.* 1.

[5] Jesup's annual report was dated November 30, and made no mention of the Fort Winnebago expenses (*American State Papers*, Class V, Military Affairs, IV, 609–11). See also 1:240, *n.* 6 describing congressional appropriations for the construction of barracks.

1:199

From Peter Hagner

SIR, Aug. 25th. 1830.

The Com. Genl of Sub[1] has referred to this office your acct. as actg. ass[istant] Com[missar]y of Sub[sisten]ce at Fort Winnebago,[2] for the qr ending 30th. June 1830,[3] which has been examined and reported to the 2d. Comptroller[4] of the Treasury for his decision thereon, & is returned resulting in a balance remaining due the U. States of Three hundred & fifty seven dollars & fifty three cents, Differing from your statement, seven cents—which is explained in a statement here annexed for your government. Respectfully Your ob. Servt

PETER HAGNER[5]
Aud.

LbC (NA, RG 217 Records of the United States General Accounting Office, Third Auditor's Office, Miscellaneous Letters Sent, LIV, 268). Addressed: "Lt. J. Davis, a[cting] a[ssistant] C[ommissary] S[ubsistence] Fort. Winnebago." Enclosure missing.

[1] The commissary general of subsistence was George Gibson (sketch, 1:179, *n.* 2).

[2] See 1:144, *n.* 1.

[3] Davis' account has not been found.

[4] The second comptroller in 1830 was James B. Thornton (sketch, 1:244, *n.* 1).

[5] Peter Hagner (1772–1850) was born in Philadelphia of German parentage and attended the University of Pennsylvania, but was not graduated. He became an accountant in the War Department, then located in Philadelphia, in 1793, and was the first to hold the post of third auditor of the Treasury when the office was created in 1817. Called "watchdog of the Treasury," he was twice commended by votes of Congress for his services before his resignation in 1849. He died in Washington, D.C. (*DAB*; *National Cyclopaedia*, XXII, 372; *Appleton's*). Hagner's duties as third auditor in-

cluded auditing all Quartermaster Department accounts as well as those for army subsistence, fortifications, internal improvements, pensions, war claims, and the Military Academy (*American Almanac* [1832], 130).

ABSTRACT

Report of Persons and Articles Employed and Hired 1:200

Fort Winnebago,[1] Michigan Territory[2]
August [31,] 1830

Lieutenant J. F. Davis, acting assistant quartermaster, certifies that he paid $53 during the month of August for the hire of oxen and a cart to haul stone and lime for new barracks and to pay a clerk[3] in the Quartermaster Department.

DS (NA, RG 92 Records of the Office of the Quartermaster General, Reports of Persons and Articles Hired), 2. Signed: "J. F. Davis Lt. & ac[ting] A[ssistant] Q. Master." Transmitted: Davis to Jesup, September 10, 1830 (NA, RG 92 Records of the Office of the Quartermaster General, Letters Received, D-178, 1830).

[1] See 1:144, *n.* 1.
[2] See 1:149, *n.* 2.
[3] The clerk was P. G. Hambaugh (see 1:176, *n.* 4).

ABSTRACT

Post Return 1:201

Fort Winnebago,[1] Michigan Territory[2]
August [31,] 1830

Lists Brevet Second Lieutenant J. F. Davis, Company C, First Infantry, present at the post. Remarks: "On Extra Duty."

Printed form, filled in and signed (NA, RG 94 Records of the Adjutant General's Office, Post Returns, Fort Winnebago, 1828–45), 2. Signed: "D. E Twiggs Major 1 Ifty." Endorsed: "Entd. Recd. 18th. Octr."

[1] See 1:144, *n.* 1.
[2] See 1:149, *n.* 2.

To George Gibson 1:202

Fort Winnebago[1] September 6th. 1830

SIR[2]

Herewith I have the honor of inclosing my return of provisions received and issued at this Post during the month of August 1830. I am respctfly. Your Mo. Obt. Sert. J. F. DAVIS

Lt. &. ac[ting] A[ssistant] C[ommissary] S[ubsistence]

LS (NA, RG 192 Records of the Office of the Commissary General of Subsistence, Letters Received, D-994, 1830). Addressed: "Genl. Geo. Gibson Com[missary] Genl. U. S. A. Washington." Endorsed: "Recd. 18 Octr." Enclosure missing. Acknowledged: Gibson to Davis, November 8, 1830 (NA, RG 192 Records of the Office of the Commissary General of Subsistence, Letters Sent, VIII, 107).

[1] See 1:144, *n.* 1.

[2] George Gibson (sketch, 1:179, *n.* 2).

1:203 From George Gibson

SIR, 7 Septr. 1830

Your return for July[1] has been examined in this office and found correct, with the exception of converting 3678 rations of extra Whiskey into bulk, you make it 118 gallons 2 gills, should be 114 gallons 30 gills. The correction Can be made in your next return after you receive this. GEO. GIBSON[2]

c[ommissary] G[eneral] s[ubsistence]

LbC (NA, RG 192 Records of the Office of the Commissary General of Subsistence, Letters Sent, VIII, 52). Addressed: "Lt. J. F. Davis A[cting] A[ssistant] C[ommissary] S[ubsistence] Fort Winnebago."

[1] Davis' July return was transmitted in 1:191.

[2] George Gibson (sketch, 1:179, *n.* 2).

1:204 From the Office of the Quartermaster General

SIR, September 8th. 1830

Your money and property accounts, for the Department proper and new Barracks at Fort Winnebago,[1] for the second quarter of the present year,[2] after the usual examination at this Office, are transmitted[3] to the 3d. Auditor[4] of the Treasury for settlement.

Remarks have been made on some of your vouchers, a statement of which you will receive herewith.

The Abstract which you denominated C should have been B.

[Encl] Statement of remarks on the accounts of Lieut. J. F. Davis, acting assistant Quarter Master at Fort Winnebago, for the second Quarter of 1830.

On account of New Barracks.

Abstract B. Voucher 1 Francis Roy[5]–Hauling lumber $262– "Mark to receipt not witnessed."

Quarter Master's Department.

Abstract C. Voucher 3. Geo. W. Hoffman–articles for firing a salute on 4th. of July 1830–$3.25–"Referable to 2nd. Auditor." [6]

QUARTER MASTER GENERAL'S[7] OFFICE

LbC (NA, RG 92 Records of the Office of the Quartermaster General, Letters Sent, XIV, 487). Addressed: "Lieut. Jefferson Davis, Acting Asst. Quarter Master, Fort Winnebago."

[1] See 1:144, *n.* 1.

[2] Davis' money and property accounts for the second quarter of 1830 have not been found, but were transmitted to the quartermaster general in August (1:196).

[3] Jesup transmitted the accounts to Hagner on September 8, 1830 (NA, RG 92, Letters Sent, XIV, 486–87).

[4] The third auditor was Peter Hagner (sketch, 1:199, *n.* 5).

[5] François Roy (sketch, 1:176, *n.* 3).

[6] William B. Lewis was the second auditor (sketch, 1:166, *n.* 1).

[7] Thomas S. Jesup (sketch, 1:174, *n.* 4).

To Joshua B. Brant 1:205

Fort Winnebago[1] Sept. 19th. 1830

SIR[2]

Not wishing to retain your letter[3] (herewith inclosed) in my Office, I return it with assurances that I Shall avoid making any call on you, which it may be optionary with you to grant or refuse. Very respectfully Your Mo. Obt. Sert.

J. F. DAVIS

Lt. & ac[ting] A[ssistant] Q. Master

P. S. having received no answer to my communication accompanying a requisition for Stationary,[4] necessity has compelled me to make a requisition on Lt St Clair Denny[5] a. a. Q. M. at Green Bay

J. F. DAVIS

Lt. & ac. A. Q. M.

LS (NA, RG 108 Records of the Headquarters of the Army, Letters Received, 1830). Addressed: "Capt. J. B. Brant Asst. Q. Master U. S. A. St Louis Missouri." Endorsed: "Prairie du Chien M[ichigan] T[erritor]y [received] Sept 25"; in a different hand, "Recd Oct. 25th. 1830." Enclosure:

Brant to Davis, August 3, 1830 (1:192). Enclosed: Brant to Jesup, October 13, 1830 (1:211); Jesup to Macomb, October 29, 1830 (1:215).

[1] See 1:144, *n*. 1.
[2] Joshua B. Brant (sketch, 1:192, *n*. 6).
[3] Brant's letter of August 3 to Davis is 1:192.
[4] Davis' request for stationery has not been found, and according to Brant, was never received (1:211).
[5] St. Clair Denny (sketch, 1:179, *n*. 3).

ABSTRACT

1:206

Report of Persons and Articles Employed and Hired

Fort Winnebago,[1] Michigan Territory[2]
September [30,] 1830

Lieutenant J. F. Davis, acting assistant quartermaster, certifies that he paid $30 during the month of September for the hire of a clerk[3] in the quartermaster's office.

DS (NA, RG 92 Records of the Office of the Quartermaster General, Reports of Persons and Articles Hired), 2. Signed: "J. F. Davis L[ieutenant] ac[ting] A[ssistant] Q Master." Endorsed: "Recd. Decr. 6. 1830."

[1] See 1:144, *n*. 1.
[2] See 1:149, *n*. 2.
[3] The clerk was P. G. Hambaugh (see 1:176, *n*. 4).

1:207

To George Gibson

Fort Winnebago[1] Oct. 1st. 1830

SIR[2]

I have the honor of inclosing to you a return of Provisions received and issued during the month of September 1830, and also an Account current of monies received and expended in the Commissarys Dept. at this Post during the third Quarter of 1830. Verry respectfully Your Mo. Obt. Sert. J. F. DAVIS

Lt. ac[ting] A[ssistant] C[ommissary] S[ubsistence]

LS (NA, RG 192 Records of the Office of the Commissary General of Subsistence, Letters Received, D-1002, 1830). Addressed: "Genl. Geo. Gibson Com[missary] Genl. U. S. A." Endorsed: "Recd. 22 Nov." Enclosures missing.

[1] See 1:144, *n*. 1.
[2] George Gibson (sketch, 1:179, *n*. 2).

ABSTRACT

The Office of the Quartermaster General[1] to Henry Whiting 1:208

[Washington, D.C.,] October 8, 1830

Major Whiting,[2] the assistant quartermaster at Detroit, is notified that both he and Captain Brant[3] at St. Louis may be called upon to pay drafts for quartermaster expenses[4] at Fort Winnebago.[5]

LbC (NA, RG 92 Records of the Office of the Quartermaster General, Letters Sent, XV, 67), 1. Addressed: "Major H. Whiting, Assistant Quarter Master, Detroit."

[1] The quartermaster general was Thomas S. Jesup (sketch, 1:174, *n.* 4).

[2] Henry Whiting, assistant quartermaster at Detroit, enlisted as a cornet in a regiment of light dragoons in 1808 and served through the War of 1812, being retained as a first lieutenant in the Fifth Infantry at the close of the war. Whiting was brevetted major in 1824 and promoted to major in 1835. He was colonel and assistant quartermaster general and had been brevetted brigadier general for gallantry in the Mexican War at the time of his death in 1851 (Heitman, *Historical Register*, I, 1030).

[3] Joshua B. Brant (sketch, 1:192, *n.* 6).

[4] See also 1:194.

[5] See 1:144, *n.* 1 for Fort Winnebago.

ABSTRACT

Pay Voucher 1:209

Fort Winnebago,[1] October 8, 1830

Lieutenant J. F. Davis, First Infantry, acknowledges that he has received $213.10 from Paymaster Colonel W. Piatt.[2] Amount includes pay, and allowance for one servant,[3] for July through September 1830, and additional pay for duty as acting assistant commissary of subsistence[4] during the same period. The servant is described as "James a Slave."

Printed form, filled in and signed (NA, RG 217 Records of the United States General Accounting Office, Paymasters' Accounts, Piatt 14,905, Voucher 19), 3. Signed: "J. F. Davis Lt 1st. Infty ac[ting] A[ssistant] C[ommissary] S[ubsistence]."

[1] See 1:144, *n.* 1.

[2] William Piatt (sketch, 1:185, *n.* 2).

[3] James Pemberton (sketch, 1:5, *n.* 4).

[4] See 1:175 for evidence of Davis' appointment as acting assistant commissary of subsistence.

ABSTRACT

1:210 Register of Payments to Officers

[Washington, D.C.,] October 8, 1830

Lists payment by Paymaster W. Piatt[1] to Second Lieutenant Jefferson Davis, First Infantry, $213.10. Amount includes pay and allowance for Davis and one servant,[2] for July through September. Remarks: "$20. A[cting] A[ssistant] C[ommissary] S[ubsistence].[3] [illegible]."

D (NA, RG 99 Records of the Office of the Paymaster General, Register of Payments to Officers, IV, 27), 1.

[1] William Piatt (sketch, 1:185, *n.* 2).

[2] James Pemberton (sketch, 1:5, *n.* 4).

[3] See 1:175 for Davis' appointment as acting assistant commissary of subsistence.

1:211 Joshua B. Brant to Thomas S. Jesup

Asst Quarter Master's Office
Saint Louis Oct. 13. 1830

GENERAL[1]

Viewing the conduct of Lieut Jef. Davis in returning to me the communication herewith,[2] as insubordinate and highly disrespectful, I have considered it proper to Submit the Same for your consideration; requesting at the Same time, that you will be pleased to give me your instructions as to the course most advisable to be pursued in relation to this case.[3]

The requisitions for Stationary mentioned in the postcript in his letter have not been received at this Office; the Calls from out posts, whether for funds or Supplies, have, I can Confidently affirm, been always promptly & punctually attended to. With high respect I have the honour to be, Sir, Your mo. ob. Servt. J. B. BRANT[4]
A[ssistant] Q. M

LS (NA, RG 108 Records of the Headquarters of the Army, Letters Received, 1830). Addressed: "Major Genl Thos. S. Jesup Q M. Genl. U. S. A Washington City." Endorsed: "Recd Oct 25th. 1830." Enclosures: Brant to Davis, August 3, 1830 (1:192); Davis to Brant, September 19, 1830 (1:205). Enclosed: Jesup to Macomb, October 29, 1830 (1:215).

[1] Thomas S. Jesup (sketch, 1:174, *n.* 4).

[2] See 1:205 for Davis' return of a previous letter from Brant.

[3] See 1:215 for Jesup's recommendation.

[4] Joshua B. Brant (sketch, 1:192, *n.* 6).

15 OCTOBER 1830

To Thomas S. Jesup 1:212

Fort Winebago[1] M[ichigan] T[erritory][2]

SIR[3] Oct 15th. 1830

Enclose I send you a trachee[4] of this Fort with an explanatory sheet containing an estimate of funds required to complete the work[5] and to that I now add the amount of outstanding debts (say) 1300 Dollars. Very Respctfly–I have the honor–to be Yr. mo. obt. Servt.

J. F. DAVIS

L[ieutenant] ac[ting] A[ssistant] Q. M.

[Encl 1: see pages 158–59] Plan of Fort Winnebago. 1830

[Encl 2] Explanation to draught of Fort Winebago M[ichigan] T[erritory]

The exterior tracé is a square of 80 yds represented by A B C D. The block houses at the angles A & B are of similar construction and equal size being two story buildings made of hewed pine logs[6] 8 inches thick the lower story 22 ft. square and 8 ft. 4 inches high the upper story's sides are parallel to those of the lower one and project 2 ft. height 7 ft. 8 inches each story furnished on every side with musketry port holes the lower story floored with two inch <–illegible–> pine plank is entered by a door at (a') the upper story floored with inch plank is entered by a trap door in the middle of it accessible by a moveable stair way–covered by a bevelled roof of pine shingles. The remaining buildings of the garrison are composed of a basement story (constructed of sand stone) 9 ft. high 5 ft below and four ft. above the ground next in ascending order a story framed in the usual manner sheeted & weather boarded the space between the studs filled in with block and clay then lathed to receive plaister the partition walls are lathed on both sides and not filled in, the garret is divided into rooms the gable ends filled as the outer walls below, the partition walls lathed as those of the first story. The partition walls of the cellar are some of wood some of stone which will be noticed. The double line with branches at the extremities represents a door without branches a window. E F G H is the Commissary and Qr. Master's store is 72 feet in length and 21 in breadth a porch (supported by turned columns) in front 11 ft deep.

The basement story is divided into two rooms the one 50 the other 20 ft long line of division on plan (g h) each room is entered

[Encl 1]

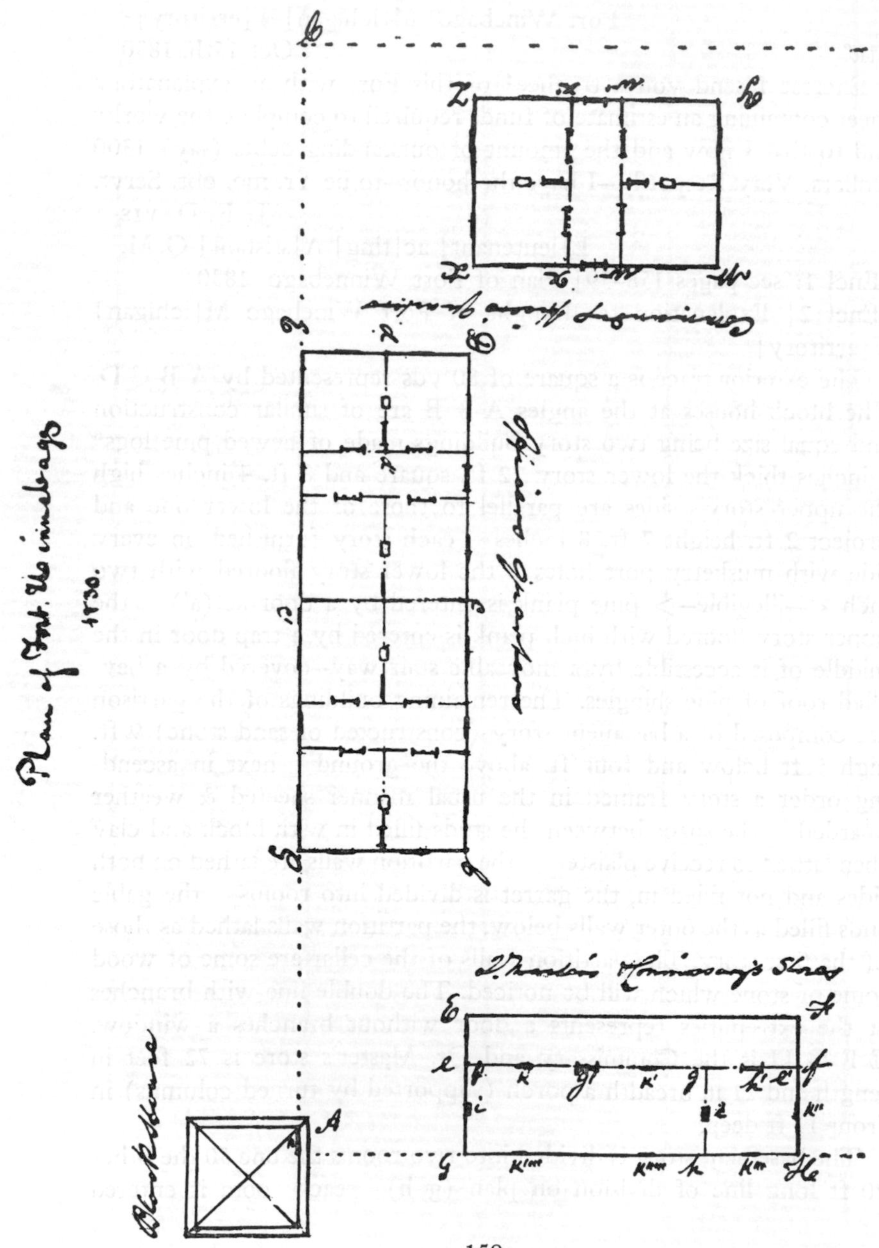

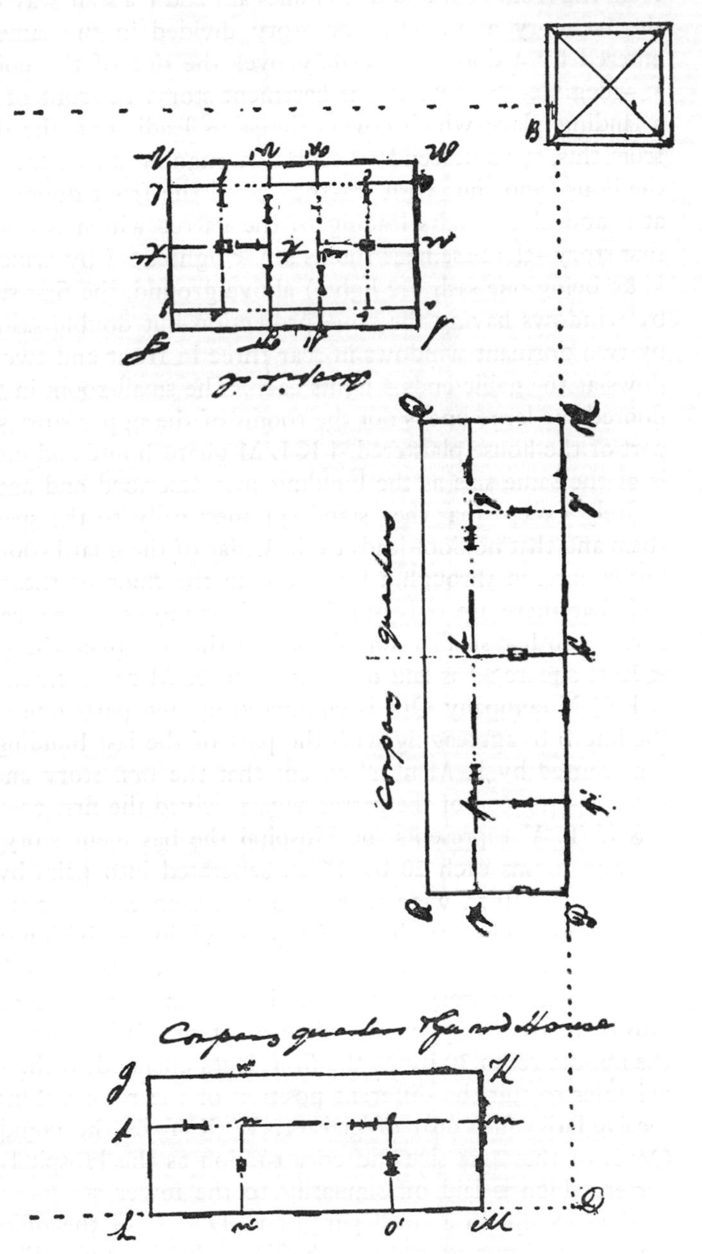
Block House
Company quarters
Company quarters & Guard House

from the front at g' and h' chimnies at i and i' a stair way leading into the 1st story at f'. The first story divided in the same manner is entered by a door immediately over the one of the corresponding <–illegible–> story in the basement story. In front of the door is a landing place which covers the steps leading to the door below, from this, steps descend on each side running down the side wall of the house and thus with <–the–> all the front doors of the Fort, at f' and e' are stairs leading to the garret which is divided as the first story—the basement rooms are <lighted>[7] by windows at k & k' &c being one sash (12 lights) above ground, the first story lighted by windows having the same projection but double sash the garret by two dormant windows in rear three in front and two small windows at the gable ends 6 lights each. The small room in the cellar is floored the large one is not the rooms of the upper stories floored no part of the house plaistered. J K L M guard house and company Qrs is of the same size as the building just described and agrees with it entirely except that they stand symmetrically to the space between them and that no door leads to the cellar of the guard room (l h n n') but is entered through a trap door in the floor of the guard room and that there are only small grated windows to this cellar. In the garret another small room similar to the one over the guard room <20 ft square>[7] is laid off at the end K M represented o o' m M. R P Q N company Qrs. is composed of two parts one each side of the line b b' agreeaging with the part of the last building described represented by K M n' n" except that the first story and the small room at each end of the garret have received the first coat of plaister

S U T. V represents the Hospital the basement story composed of four rooms each 20 by 16 ft. seperated into pairs by a passage S' T' U' V' 10 ft. wide with a door at each end   at the back end a stair way leading to the 1st Story which in its division corresponds with the basement story   a stair in the same relative position as that of the basement story leads hence into to the garret which is divided into three rooms by the lines b c & e f the end rooms 10 by 26 ft. the middle room 30 by 26 the fire places changed to the sides of the chimnies to suit the different position of the rooms. This house has received the first coat of plaister. W X Y Z[8] the comdg. officer's Qrs is of the same size and construction as the Hospital except the garret which is laid off similarily to the lower story—this house is finished except in a small part of it. D E C G the officers Qrs. is composed of two parts one each side of the line c c' similar and equal to Comdg. off's Qrs—except the passage is only 8 ft wide and has in the first story no back door this house has received only the "scratch coat." The buildings would have been completed but for the want of hair[9] which I have in vain endeavoured to procure since the failure of the person who had I was informed agreed to furnish became known to me. The Old buildings have been removed to make Stables wash houses a bakehouse and some of them were given the Indian Agent[10] &C a Carpenter's shop has been erected 30 by 20 ft 8 feet high and a Blacksmith's shop 20 by 18 ft. 8 ft high both frame houses—sinks in such quantities as required.

The Comissary store is built so as to be readily converted into compy. Qrs—should they be wanting for that purpose. Those parts <of the grounds>[7] that most wanted improvement have been attended to during the summer and all necessary labour may be drawn (I think) from <men>[7] who labour for punishment to complete the proposed improvements of the parade which is all that is required.

To complete <the>[7] work (I think) 17.00.00 Dollars will be required the Magazine is the only building now to be erected picketing and plaistering are the principal.

The distance we send for timber is great. I will endeavour to procure hair from the Indians this fall.

The pickets cannot be got here before next spring until which time the work will be almost entirely suspended the plaistering if we had hair could be finished in a month The completion of the work depending on these contingencies I cannot say when it will take place.

<note>[11]

In the first building described the petition walls of the cellar are all wood 2nd n n' stone 3rd b b' stone 4th all wood 5th all stone 6th c c' stone.

ALS (NA, RG 92 Records of the Office of the Quartermaster General, Consolidated Correspondence File, Fort Winnebago, D-216, 1830). Addressed: "To Maj. Genl. T. Jessup *Q. M. Genl.*" Endorsed: "Recd Decr. 9th. 1830." Enclosure 1: AD (NA, RG 92 Records of the Office of the Quartermaster General, Cartographic Records, Map 101). Enclosure 2: AD (NA, RG 92 Records of the Office of the Quartermaster General, Consolidated Correspondence File, Fort Winnebago, D-216, 1830).

[1] See 1:144, *n.* 1.

[2] See 1:149, *n.* 2.

[3] Thomas S. Jesup (sketch, 1:174, *n.* 4).

[4] Davis undoubtedly intended to use the French word tracé.

[5] Davis is replying to Jesup's letter of August 19 (1:198).

[6] Pine logs for construction of the

fort were procured some ten miles up the Wisconsin River from the portage and were floated downstream (Ellis, "Upper Wisconsin Country," Wisconsin Historical *Collections*, III, 437; Clark, "Early Times at Fort Winnebago," *ibid.*, VIII, 310). See also 1:264, *n.* 11.

[7] Interlined.

[8] It was evidently in the commanding officer's quarters (building WXYZ on the plan) that Mrs. John Kinzie, wife of the Indian agent, found an impressive piece of furniture built under Davis' supervision. Called a "Davis," it was an elaborate wardrobe, combining "clothes-press, store-room, and china-closet." For a detailed description, see Kinzie, *Wau-Bun*, 91–92. Major David E. Twiggs, commanding the garrison, was later to praise Davis' skill as a construction superintendent (1:451).

[9] Davis later requested hair from the assistant quartermaster at Detroit (see 1:264).

[10] The Indian agent was probably John Harris Kinzie, who left Detroit September 6 for Fort Winnebago, via Green Bay (Kinzie, *Wau-Bun*, xx *et passim*). The Kinzies' daughter later described the friendship between her parents and Davis, and recalled that the young officer had once given up his quarters to Mrs. Kinzie (Gordon to Davis, September 1, 1864 [Museum of the Confederacy, Richmond]). See also *n.* 8 above.

[11] In the margin.

1:213

From Philip G. Randolph

SIR, War Department, *October 20, 1830*

You are hereby informed, that the President[1] of the United States has promoted you to the rank of *Second Lieutenant* in the *First* Regiment of the United States *Infantry* to take effect from the *first* day of *July 1828. vice 2d Lt. J. W. Kingsbury,*[2] *promoted:* should the Senate, at their next session, advise and consent thereto, you will be commissioned accordingly. *You will report by letter*[3] *to the Commanding Officer*[4] *of your Regiment. (Signed)* *P. G. Randolph,*[5]
Actg. Secretary of War.

Printed letter, filled in and signed (NA, RG 94 Records of the Adjutant General's Office, Records of the Appointment, Commission, and Personnel Branch, Letters of Army Promotions, I, 36). Addressed: "For, 2d Lieut. Jefferson Davis, 1st Infantry, Fort Winnebago."

[1] Andrew Jackson (sketch, 1:239, *n.* 2).

[2] James W. Kingsbury, born in Connecticut, attended West Point, 1819–23, but was not graduated. He was commissioned second lieutenant in the First Infantry in 1823, was captain by 1837, and then became a military storekeeper. He resigned from the army in 1843 and died ten years later (Heitman, *Historical Register*, I, 601).

[3] Davis' letter has not been found.

[4] The commander of the First Infantry was Willoughby Morgan (sketch, 1:237, *n.* 4).

[5] Philip G. Randolph (sketch, 1:197, *n.* 4).

To Thomas S. Jesup

1:214

Fort Winnebago[1] October 25th. 1830

SIR[2]

I have the honor of forwarding my a/cs current and property returns for the third quarter of 1830.[3]

In Voucher No. 6. Abstract B. Barracks, Twenty Dollars have paid to McLane[4] a deserter. That amt. was paid him previous to his desertion and for which he has receipted Since his apprehension.

Voucher No. 8 Abstract B. Barracks Eleven 55/100 Dollars have been deducted from that Voucher and charged in Abstract B. Qr. Mrs. Department, it being the amount paid to E[xtra] Duty men for procuring Hay during the quarter. This should have been embraced in a Seperate Voucher, but was not noticed untill after the payment.

Sixteen oxen have been purchased in the quarter per order of Maj. Twiggs,[5] who has directed me to explain to you the necessity of the purchase, which was twofold. Viz: building materials and fuel even to be hauled from a considerable distance, and the oxen on hand were worn down by hard use during the Summer.

By reference to certificate No. 2 it will be Seen that five oxen and one horse have been condemned,[6] and not having met with an opportunity to Sell them without Sacrifice I have determined to Keep them untill Spring which may be done without expense to the government, and when they may be Sold probibly to advantage

Six Mackinaw[7] Boats have also been condemned[8] two I do not believe they will Sell for any thing for they are completely rotten. The remaining four will be disposed of as soon as an opportunity offers. I have the honor to be Respectfully Your Mo. Obt. Sert.

J. F. DAVIS

L[ieutenant] ac[ting] A[ssistant] Q. Master

LS (NA, RG 217 Records of the United States General Accounting Office, Third Auditor's Office, Third Auditor's Accounts, Account 10,523). Addressed: "Genl. T. S. Jessup Q M Genl. u S. a. Washington City." Endorsed: "Referred to the 3d Auditor with the accounts. Q. M. Gen. Office Decr. 21. 1830." In a different hand, "Recd Decr. 6th. 1830." Enclosures: Order No. 93, August 12, 1830, and survey report (1:193); Order No. 95, August 15, 1830, and survey report (1:195); other enclosures missing. Acknowledged: From the Office of the Quartermaster General to Davis, December 21, 1830 (1:223).

1 See 1:144, *n*. 1.

2 Thomas S. Jesup (sketch, 1:174, *n*. 4).

3 Except for the survey reports,

Davis' accounts current and property returns for the third quarter of 1830 have not been found.

[4] Alexander McLean, a private in K Company, was recruited in Boston by First Lieutenant Henry Bainbridge in 1829 for five years. When he enlisted he gave his occupation as laborer and his age as thirty-one. McLean deserted from Fort Winnebago July 27, 1830, and was apprehended August 11. He was discharged in April 1833 at Fort Armstrong on account of disability (NA, RG 94, Register of Enlistments, XXXVIII).

[5] David E. Twiggs (sketch, 1:149, *n.* 4).

[6] See 1:195.

[7] The mackinac, or mackinaw—the words were used interchangeably—was a flat-bottomed boat, sometimes with oars and sails, used on the upper Great Lakes at this time. The word "mackinac" came into English from the Canadian French adaptation of an Ojibway term (*Dictionary of American English*). The mackinac evidently varied greatly in length, from ten to fifty feet, and was five to seven feet broad (Brunson, "Early Times in Old Northwest," Wisconsin Historical *Proceedings, 1904*, p. 168). A picture is in Nichols, *Atkinson*, facing page 195. One traveller described the mackinac boat carrying her party in 1830 as a craft thirty feet long and having posts in the center supporting a canvas roof and curtains (Kinzie, *Wau-Bun*, 42).

[8] See 1:193 for the board of survey report.

1:215

Thomas S. Jesup to Alexander Macomb

GENERAL,[1] qr. Mr. Gen's Office Octr. 29th. 1830

I respectfully submit for your consideration a letter of Cap't. J. B. Brant,[2] enclosing one from Lieutenant Jefferson Davis, Acting as quarter Master at Fort Winnebago—also an official letter of Cap't. Brant to Lieu't. Davis which the latter returned to Cap't. Brant.[3] The conduct of Lieu't. Davis is so repugnant to every sound principle of service, that I hope it will not be allowed to pass without the animadversion it deserves. I have the honor to be Sir, Your Obt Sevt.

TH. S. JESUP[4]
q. m. Genl.

LS (NA, RG 108 Records of the Headquarters of the Army, Letters Received, 1830); LbC (NA, RG 92 Records of the Office of the Quartermaster General, Letters Sent, XV, 97). Addressed: "Maj. Genl. Alexr Macomb. Commg the Army, Washington City." Enclosures: Brant to Jesup, October 13, 1830 (1:211); Davis to Brant, September 19, 1830 (1:205); and Brant to Davis, August 3, 1830 (1:192).

[1] Alexander Macomb (sketch, 1:38, *n.* 10).

[2] Joshua B. Brant (sketch, 1:192, *n.* 6).

[3] Davis' and Brant's letters are 1:192, 205. Brant's letter to Jesup concerning the complaint is 1:211.

[4] Thomas S. Jesup (sketch, 1:174, *n.* 4).

Jefferson Barracks

Fort Winnebago

ABSTRACT

Report of Persons and Articles Employed and Hired 1:216

Fort Winnebago,[1] Michigan Territory[2]
October [31,] 1830

Lieutenant J. F. Davis, acting assistant quartermaster, certifies that he paid $30 during the month of October for the hire of a clerk[3] in the quartermaster's office.

DS (NA, RG 92 Records of the Office of the Quartermaster General, Reports of Persons and Articles Hired), 2. Signed: "J. F. Davis L[ieutenant] ac[ting] A[ssistant] Q. Master." Transmitted: Davis to Jesup, November 4, 1830 (NA, RG 92 Records of the Office of the Quartermaster General, Letters Received, D-213, 1830). Acknowledged: The Office of the Quartermaster General to Davis, December 8, 1830 (NA, RG 92 Records of the Office of the Quartermaster General, Letters Sent, XV, 165).

[1] See 1:144, *n.* 1.
[2] See 1:149, *n.* 2.
[3] P. G. Hambaugh (see 1:176, *n.* 4).

To George Gibson 1:217

Fort Winnebago[1] November 3rd. 1830

SIR[2]

I have the honor of forwarding a return of provisions received and issued at this Post during the month of October 1830.

I have neglected to deduct from the amount of Beans on hand, twenty one Bushels one Gallon, which were condemned in May last, as per Certificate herewith, untill the present return.

I have also corrected an error commited in the return of July as noticed in your letter of the 7th. September last.[3] I am Verry respectfully Your mo. Obt. Sert. J. F. DAVIS

L[ieutenant] ac[ting] A[ssistant] C[ommissary] Subsistence

LS (NA, RG 192 Records of the Office of the Commissary General of Subsistence, Letters Received, D-1011, 1830). Addressed: "Genl. Geo. Gibson Com[missary] Genl. U. S. a. Washington City." Endorsed: "Recd. 6 Decr." Enclosure missing.

[1] See 1:144, *n.* 1.
[2] George Gibson (sketch, 1:179, *n.* 2).
[3] See 1:203 for Gibson's letter of September 7.

1:218 From George Gibson

Sir, 25 November 1830

In making out the monthly return enclosed, you will perceive you have brought forward, from august return[1] the quantity of provisions in the upper line in place of the lower, which makes a difference of the whole month of August issues in your provision account.

The abstracts are retained in this office and will be placed with your September return, when received corrected.

Geo. Gibson[2]
C[ommissary] G[eneral] S[ubsistence]

LbC (NA, RG 192 Records of the Office of the Commissary General of Subsistence, Letters Sent, VIII, 123). Addressed: "Lt. J. F. Davis A[cting] A[ssistant] C[ommissary] S[ubsistence] Fort Winnebago." Enclosure missing.

[1] Davis' August return was acknowledged on November 8 (see 1:202, descriptive footnote).

[2] George Gibson (sketch, 1:179, *n.* 2).

ABSTRACT

1:219 Report of Persons and Articles Employed and Hired

Fort Winnebago,[1] Michigan Territory[2]
November [30,] 1830

Lieutenant J. F. Davis, acting assistant quartermaster, certifies that he paid $30 during the month of November for the hire of a clerk[3] in the quartermaster's office.

DS (NA, RG 92 Records of the Office of the Quartermaster General, Reports of Persons and Articles Hired), 2. Signed: "J. F. Davis L[ieutenant] ac[ting] A[ssistant] Q. M." Acknowledged: The Office of the Quartermaster General to Davis, January 11, 1831 (NA, RG 92 Records of the Office of the Quartermaster General, Letters Sent, XV, 233).

[1] See 1:144, *n.* 1.

[2] See 1:149, *n.* 2.

[3] The hired clerk was P. G. Hambaugh (see 1:176, *n.* 4).

To George Gibson 1:220

Fort Winnebago[1] Decr. 3rd. 1830

SIR.[2]

Inclosed I have the honor of forwarding a return of provisions received and issued at this Post during the month of November 1830. I am verry respecty. Your mo. Obt. Sert. J. F. DAVIS

L[ieutenant] ac[ting] A[ssistant] C[ommissary] S[ubsistence]

LS (NA, RG 192 Records of the Office of the Commissary General of Subsistence, Letters Received, D-1019, 1830). Addressed: "Genl. Geo. Gibson Com[missary] Genl U. S. A." Endorsed: "[Received] Jany 10th. 1831." Enclosure missing.

[1] See 1:144, *n.* 1.

[2] George Gibson (sketch, 1:179, *n.* 2).

From William B. Lewis 1:221

SIR, 14 December 1830

I return you the inlistment which accompanied your recruiting account for October last,[1] that the oath prescribed by law[2] may be administered to the recruit,[3] and that your Signature may be affixed to his descriptive Certificate.

I avail myself of the occasion to repeat my request, that the necessary remarks may be made in the proper column of your recruiting account, as to muster, agreeably to the form herewith sent.

W. B. L.[4]

LbC (NA, RG 217 Records of the United States General Accounting Office, Second Auditor's Office, Letters Sent, XV, 316). Addressed: "Lieut. J. F. Davis, 1 Inf. Fort Winnebago—via Greenbay." Enclosure missing.

[1] The recruiting documents are printed as 1:156–58.

[2] The oath can be found in the tenth article of war (*General Army Regulations* [1825], 410).

[3] John M. Oliver—see 1:156.

[4] William B. Lewis (sketch, 1:166, *n.* 1).

ABSTRACT

1:222
Promotions and Appointments List[1]

Adjutant General's Office, Washington
December 14, 1830

Brevet Second Lieutenant Jefferson Davis is recommended for promotion to second lieutenant, First Regiment of Infantry, to be ranked from July 1, 1828.

MS not found. Text from *Journal of the Executive Proceedings of the Senate of the United States of America* (90 vols., Washington: Duff Green, Government Printing Office, 1828–1948), IV, 131–33. Signed: "R. Jones, Ad't. Gen'l." Endorsed: "Respectfully submitted to the Secretary of War. Al. Macomb, Major-Gen'l, Comm'g the Army." Transmitted: Eaton to the President, December 14, 1830 (*Senate Executive Journal*, IV, 131).

1 This list was further transmitted to the Senate by letter of President Jackson, December 17, 1830, and appears under the proceedings of that day. The nominations of Davis and the other officers included in the adjutant general's roster were referred to the Committee on Military Affairs December 17 and were reported back to the Senate and confirmed February 28, 1831. See *Senate Executive Journal*, IV, 130–33, 134, 166, and Senate Resolution, February 28, 1831 (1:234).

1:223
From the Office of the Quartermaster General

SIR, December 21st. 1830

Your money and property accounts, for the Third quarter of the present year,[1] for the Quarter Master's Department proper and New Barracks at Fort Winnebago,[2] after the usual examination at this office, are transmitted to the proper offices of the Treasury[3] for settlement.

You will receive herewith a statement of remarks. Stationary used in the discharge of your duty as Acting Assistant Quarter Master should be entered in Abstract J, instead of abstract L, supported by the proper certificate as a voucher.

Expenditures on account of Contingencies, or such as are chargeable in Abstract C, should not be noticed in account current of the Quarter Master's Department, but a separate account should be rendered—and the two accounts should not have any connection with one another.

[Encl] Statement of remarks on the accounts of Lieutenant J. F. Davis, acting assistant quarter Master at Fort Winnebago, for the Third quarter of 1830.

Abstract C. Voucher 2. Charles Young[4]–apprehending a deserter $10.00. "Date of apprehension and delivery wanting."

4. S. D. Scott–apprehending deserters $30.00 "See remark on Voucher 2."

Proceedings of Board of Survey Nos. 1&2. "Lieutenant Davis is not entitled to a credit for the articles condemned by the board of Survey,[5] until they are disposed of under the provisions of 1.001 and 1.002 General Regulations." [6]

Barracks Fort Winnebago.

Abstract B. Voucher 3. Josiah Barbour–Transporting Sundries $15.00 "Mark to receipt not witnessed."

QUARTER MASTER GENERAL'S[7] OFFICE

LbC (NA, RG 92 Records of the Office of the Quartermaster General, Letters Sent, XV, 194–95). Addressed: "Lieut. Jefferson Davis, Acting Asst. Quarter Master, Fort Winnebago, M[ichigan] T[erritory]."

[1] Except for 1:193, 195, Davis' money and property accounts for the third quarter have not been located. These accounts were transmitted to Jesup in 1:214.

[2] See 1:144, *n.* 1.

[3] Jesup transmitted Davis' accounts by letters of the same date to the second and third auditors (NA, RG 92, Letters Sent, XV, 194).

[4] Charles Young, sergeant in Company C, enlisted April 1829 for five years, and was promoted to sergeant October 1, 1830. He was recruited by First Lieutenant Elias Phillips in Albany, New York (Semiannual Muster Roll, December 31, 1830 [NA, RG 94, First Infantry, Company C]).

[5] The boards of survey referred to were convened by Order No. 93, August 12, 1830 (1:193), and Order No. 95, August 15, 1830 (1:195); both were forwarded in Davis to Jesup, October 25, 1830 (1:214).

[6] For paragraphs 1001–1002, see 1:193, *n.* 8.

[7] The quartermaster general was Thomas S. Jesup (sketch, 1:174, *n.* 4).

To Thomas S. Jesup 1:224

Qr. Masters office

Fort Winebago[1] M[ichigan] T[erritory,][2] Dec 30th 1830

SIR[3]

Several accounts have been lately presented by officers of the post for extra services rendered previous to august 16th 1830.[4] Feeling some doubt whether the orders of that date stopped payments for services previously rendered or only for those of a subsequent date I deferred settling the claims and refer to you for instruction.

Previous to the 1st of April 1830 I performed certain duties for this Dept.[5] for which I was borne on extra duty—on that day I relieved the A[cting] A[ssistant] Qr. Master[6] of the post and in addition to the new duties which thus devolved upon me continued to perform those for which I had been borne on extra duty.

On the 1st. of May 1830 I relieved the Asst. Com. Sub.[7] and continued to perform the duties required of me in Q. M. Dept. as heretofore.

I have been paid for extra services in the Commissary's Dept.[8] by the pay-master and wish to know if I am entitled to any compensation for the services performed in Q. M. Dept. from the 1st of April 1830 to this date Very Respctfly I have the honor to be yr. mo. obt. servt.

J. F. Davis
L[ieutenant] ac. A. Q. M.

ALS (NA, RG 92 Records of the Office of the Quartermaster General, Consolidated Correspondence File, Fort Winnebago, D–53, 1831). Addressed: "For Genl. T. S. Jessup Qr. M. genl. U. S. A. Washington D. C." Endorsed: "Recd. March 5. 1831."

[1] See 1:144, *n.* 1.

[2] See 1:149, *n.* 2.

[3] Thomas S. Jesup (sketch, 1:174, *n.* 4).

[4] See 1:197 for the order of August 16, 1830. The quartermaster general's office requested Davis to submit the claims in question (1:240), which he did (1:264), and they were accepted (1:276).

[5] Davis' extra duty probably began on June 21, 1829 (see 1:147, 149, 181).

[6] See 1:174 for Gwynn's statement that he was relieved by Davis as acting assistant quartermaster.

[7] The order by which Davis relieved Gwynn as the acting assistant commissary of subsistence is printed as 1:175.

[8] See 1:209, 210.

1:225

From Peter Hagner

Sir, Dec. 30. 1830

Your a/c for disbursements during the 2d. & 3d. qrs of 1830,[1] have been audited & reported to the 2d. Comptroller[2] for his decision thereon, by whom they have been returned to this office, exhibiting a balance due *from* you on a/c qm. Dpt of $1120.75 & a balance due *to* you on a/c of "Barracks at Ft. Winnebago" of $182.09 (the latter sum will be transferred to your credit on a/c qm. Dpt.) differing in the aggregate from your statements $1174.86 which the enclosed sheet of remarks will explain. Respectfully Your obt. St

PETER HAGNER[3]
Aud.

[PS] Vo[ucher] 1. B. 2 qr '30 Barracks
Vo[ucher] 3 B 3 qr '30 Barracks. are enclosed.

LbC (NA, RG 217 Records of the United States General Accounting Office, Third Auditor's Office, Miscellaneous Letters Sent, LV, 292). Addressed: "Lt. J. F. Davis, a[cting] a[ssistant] qm Fort Winnebago." Enclosures missing.

[1] Davis' accounts have not been found, but his second quarter return was transmitted to the third auditor September 8 (NA, RG 92, Letters Sent, XIV, 486–87); his third quarter return was sent to the quartermaster general October 25 (1:214).

[2] The second comptroller was James B. Thornton (sketch, 1:244, *n.* 1).

[3] Peter Hagner (sketch, 1:199, *n.* 5).

ABSTRACT

Report of Persons and Articles Employed and Hired 1:226

Fort Winnebago,[1] Michigan Territory[2]
December [31,] 1830

Lieutenant J. F. Davis, acting assistant quartermaster, certifies that he paid $30 during the month of December for the hire of a clerk[3] in the Quartermaster Department.

DS (NA, RG 92 Records of the Office of the Quartermaster General, Reports of Persons and Articles Hired), 2. Signed: "J. F. Davis L[ieutenant] ac[ting] A[ssistant] Q. M."

[1] See 1:144, *n.* 1.

[2] See 1:149, *n.* 2.

[3] The clerk was P. G. Hambaugh (see 1:176, *n.* 4).

To George Gibson 1:227

Fort Winnebago[1] January 1st. 1831

SIR[2]

Herewith I have the honor of inclosing to you a return of provisions received and issued at this Post during the month of December 1830, and also an Account Current exhibiting a Statement of all monies received and disbursed in the Subsistence Department during the 4th. Quarter of 1830.

By reference to the A/Current it will appear that all the funds left in the hands of the A[ssistant] Commissary of this Post have been expended, and the Department will fall in debt by the end of the first Quarter of 1831, about $300.

It will be a great convenience to the A. Com. to receive funds by the last of march next, if arangements can be made to that effect. I am verry respectfully Sir Your Mo. Obt. Sert. J. F. DAVIS

L[ieutenant] ac[ting] a[ssistant] C[ommissary] S[ubsistence]

LS (NA, RG 192 Records of the Office of the Commissary General of Subsistence, Letters Received, D–1032, 1831). Addressed: "For General Geo. Gibson Com[missary] General U. S. A. Washington City *D. C.*" Endorsed: "[Received] March 5th. 1831." Enclosures missing.

[1] See 1:144, *n.* 1.

[2] George Gibson (sketch, 1:179, *n.* 2).

1:228 From Peter Hagner

SIR, Jan. 11th. 1831

The Com. Genl of Sub[1] has transmitted to this office, your a/c & vouchers for the Qr ending the 30th. Sept last;[2] & the Same have been by me audited and reported to the Second Comptroller[3] of the Treasury for his decision thereon, by whom they have been returned to this office, with the following result.

A balance is found to be due from you to the U. S of Eighty eight dollars & forty eight cents, differing from your Statement 7 cents,[4] which is the difference arising on Settlement of your a/c the 17 August last, a Statement of which was forwarded to you on that day, but not noticed in your present a/c. Respectfully Your obt St

PETER HAGNER[5]

Aud.

LbC (NA, RG 217 Records of the United States General Accounting Office, Third Auditor's Office, Miscellaneous Letters Sent, LV, 328). Addressed: "Lt. J. F. Davis Act[ing] Ass[istant] Com[missary] of Sub. Fort. Winnebago."

[1] The commissary general of subsistence was George Gibson (sketch, 1:179, *n.* 2).

[2] See 1:207 for Davis' letter transmitting his third quarter accounts current.

[3] In 1831 the second comptroller was

James Thornton (sketch, 1:244, *n.* 1).
[4] See 1:199 for Hagner's letter advising Davis of the seven-cent difference between their accounts.
[5] Peter Hagner (sketch, 1:199, *n.* 5).

ABSTRACT

Report of Persons and Articles Employed and Hired 1:229

Fort Winnebago,[1] Michigan Territory[2]
January [31,] 1831

Lieutenant J. F. Davis, acting assistant quartermaster, certifies that he paid $30 during the month of January for the hire of a clerk[3] in the Quartermaster Department.

DS (NA, RG 92 Records of the Office of the Quartermaster General, Reports of Persons and Articles Hired), 2. Signed: "J. F. Davis L[ieutenant] a[cting] a[ssistant] Q. M." Acknowledged: The Office of the Quartermaster General to Davis, April 6, 1831 (NA, RG 92 Records of the Office of the Quartermaster General, Letters Sent, XV, 379).

[1] See 1:144, *n.* 1.
[2] See 1:149, *n.* 2.
[3] P. G. Hambaugh was the clerk hired (see 1:176, *n.* 4).

To George Gibson 1:230

Fort Winnebago[1] February 2nd. 1831

SIR[2]

I have the honor of inclosing to you a return of provisions received and issued at this Post during the month of January 1831. I am respectfully Your Mo. Obt. Sert. J. F. DAVIS
L[ieutenant] a[cting] a[ssistant] C[ommissary] S[ubsistence]

LS (NA, RG 192 Records of the Office of the Commissary General of Subsistence, Letters Received, D–1041, 1831). Addressed: "Genl. Geo. Gibson Com[missary] Genl. u. S. a. Washington City. D. C." Endorsed: "Recd. 5th. April." Enclosure missing.

[1] See 1:144, *n.* 1.
[2] George Gibson (sketch, 1:179, *n.* 2).

1:231

To Thomas S. Jesup

Fort Winnebago[1] M[ichigan] T[erritory][2]
February 3rd. 1831

SIR[3]

Having from personal observation, acquired Some Knowledge of the different routes, leading from this place, and thinking that you have not probably been possessed of Such information, I herewith transmit, (in Compliance with Art. 975 Genl. Regs.)[4] the following remarks for which, were their imperfections less, I would offer the novelty of the Subject as an apology.

The usual channel of communication between this place and Fort Howard,[5] Green Bay, is by the Fox River,[6] distance nominally 180 miles, probably it is greater. This river rises in a lake[6] three miles South East of Fort Winnebago and has a general direction of about half a degree north of east, Current Slow, banks low and generally marshy, course winding, channel usually deep enough for boats of 30 tons burthen, but the changes of direction are too Sudden to admit of an advantagious navigation by those above the class called Mackenac,[7] about 10 tons burthen. About 25 miles from its Source this river receives a tributary, up to which there is always water enough for Mackenaw boats but above which it is Sometimes necessary to lighten them of half their lading. The obstructions to the navigation of the Fox River by the last mentioned discription of boats are, three lakes[8] where detentions on account of wind are frequent, one rapid where it is necessary to make half loads, and two where all the lading must be discharged and carried around by land.[9] In descending this latter operation may usually be avoided at one of rapids. By land the distance from this to Fort Howard is about 110 miles, a plain trace.[10] Obstructions, one deep marsh about 200 yards wide, another about one mile wide, three boggy bayoux and many deep ravines, the Fox River must be crossed three times twice by ferry and once by a difficult ford at one of the rapids. The first half of the route uninhabited, the Second half very thinley inhabited— This route might be placed on better ground (free from the two first and third obstructions) without Sensibly increasing the distance.[11]

The usual route from this to Fort Crawford[12] (Prairie du Chien) is by the Ouisconsin River, distance nominally 180 miles. The Ouisconsin rises West of North and has a general direction from this place to its confluence with the Mississippi, South of West, is a broad

Strait Stream Studded with Islands, its channel frequently interrupted with Sand bars,[13] which in a low Stage of Water occludes its navigation to boats above the Size of the Mackenac, and renders it to these tedious and difficult. Above this place (I have been informed) the river is equally navigable for one hundred miles or further with the exception of one rapid Sixty miles hince. By land the distance to Fort Crawford is about 120 miles, a plain trace used by Waggons except about eight miles. Obstacles, the Fox River crossed at the garrison ferry, a creek about four miles hence,[14] Seldom Swimming, about 40 feet wide, on the opposite Side of which is a deep marsh about 250 yards wide, three miles thence another about 75 yards wide, twelve miles thence another less difficult about 20 yards wide, thence no difficulty until the road inclines to the Ouisconsin, within eight miles of which the ground is broken and is that part of the road not used by Waggons, the river is passed by a ferry and thence the road is good to Fort Crawford about nine miles distant. The first Sixty miles of this road is uninhabited, the latter thinly Settled. A road might be obtained with <—out—> little labour which would reduce the first 50 miles to about 40 and occupy better ground than the present one. The character of the Ouisconsin's borders being broken the bearing of this road is too much South, a more direct route would be found on the right bank, but then it would be necessary to cross two rivers which when the ice is forming or dissolving (a period in this climate too considerable to be neglected) would cause detentions.

To Fort Dearborn[15] (Chicago) is 180 miles, for the first 30 miles the route the Same as to Fort Crawford, then only an obscure trace in Some places difficult to follow until within a few miles of Chicago. After the road Separates from that leading to Fort Crawford, the obstacles are three deep marshes 150—100—& 50 yards Wide in wet Seasons wider, three rivers Vizt. The Chicago passed by a ferry at Fort Dearborn the Fox*[16] River 137 and the Rock River 75 miles hence, both usually Swimming. Rock River the one of that name which empties into the Mississippi at Rock Island, rises near lake Winnebago of the Fox River about 70 miles hence, communicates with a chain of lakes[17] (near where the chicago trace crosses it) four in number and extending in a westwardly direction about 50 miles. usually a Mackinaw boat could pass from the Rock River to the

* The Second of that name distinguished by a dash over it from the one near this Post.

head of these lakes about 30 miles South of this place, though in dry Seasons the communication between the 2nd. and 3rd. of the "Four Lakes" is broken. Near this the Rock River receives another tributary from the East, below which it is probibly navigable at all times by "Keal boats" of 30 tons burthen. Its current is Swift its channel deep and Single, occasionally interrupted by Shoals. I speak only of the upper part of this river from observation but I have been informed that the general character is the Same to its mouth. The route to chicago is uninhabited. The distance might be diminished 25 or 30 miles, and those obstacles noticed in discribing the route to Fort Crawford avoided. The direction is South East and the road Should not cross the Fox River.

To Galena[18] Illinois is about 120 miles. The route for the first 60 miles the Same as to Fort Crawford, after which a waggon road much used and for a natural one unusually good. The first half of the rout has been noticed, the latter is thickly Settled and without obstructions. By changing the position of the road ten or fifteen miles might be gained without any loss in the quality of the ground, which would reduce the distance to Galena to 95 or 100 miles. "Gratiots Grove" [19] is a Post Office on the route to Galena and 15 miles this Side of that place.

The Country around Galena is well Supplied with waggons and Stores may be transported by the waggon load at $1.00 per hundred pounds.

All of the routes noticed lie in a country richly clothed with grass.

Whilst the troops of this garrison belong to the western Department and their Regitl. Head Qrs. is at Prairie du Chien, the route to Galena as a general Channel of Communication possesses many advantages which will readily Suggest themselves.

Having never taken any notes nor intended when traveling on these routs to give a description of them, I am only able to give a partial (and perhaps a very inacurate) one. I have the honor to be respectfully Your Mo. Obt. Sert.

J. F. Davis

L[ieutenant] a[cting] a[ssistant] Q.M.

LS (NA, RG 92 Records of the Office of the Quartermaster General, Consolidated Correspondence File, Fort Winnebago, D–67, 1831). Addressed: "Genl. T. S. Jesup Qr Mr Genl. U. S. A." Endorsed: "Recd April 5. 1831."

[1] See 1:144, *n.* 1.

[2] See 1:149, *n.* 2.

[3] Thomas S. Jesup (sketch, 1:174, *n.* 4).

[4] Article 69, paragraph 975, made it the duty of the quartermaster general to be familiar with the frontier, its resources, means of transportation, routes of communication between posts and armies, and depot sites (*General Army Regulations* [1825], 213).

[5] Fort Howard was established in 1816 as American settlers moved into the Northwest after the War of 1812. Green Bay had been the site of a French post, La Baye, 1745–61, and the British Fort Edward Augustus, 1761–1815. The garrison was withdrawn in 1841, regarrisoned after the Mexican War, and abandoned in 1852 (Prucha, *Guide to Military Posts*, 79; Davidson, *In Unnamed Wisconsin*, 201–202).

[6] The Fox River is about 175 miles long and flows to Portage (Fort Winnebago) to a point about one and one-half miles from the Wisconsin River, to which it is now connected by a canal. It originates now in Swan Lake, although at least two nineteenth-century maps show its source farther to the east (Ford, *History of Illinois*, ed. Quaife, I, facing p. 155; [Thwaites], "Narrative of Morgan L. Martin," Wisconsin Historical *Collections*, XI, facing p. 400). For a contemporary drawing showing Swan Lake with the marsh and forest vegetation, see Catlin, *North American Indians*, II, facing page 206.

[7] For mackinac, see 1:214, *n.* 7.

[8] The three lakes mentioned in the navigation of the Fox to Fort Howard are probably Lakes Puckaway, Butte des Morts, and Winnebago, the three largest of the five lakes between Portage and Green Bay. Lakes Buffalo and Little Butte des Morts sometimes do not appear on nineteenth-century maps; the former may have been considered only a wide stretch of the river, and the latter a part of Lake Winnebago (see Ford, *History of Illinois*, ed. Quaife, I, facing p. 155).

[9] At the lower, or northern, end of Lake Winnebago there were rapids where, as Davis wrote, half loads were necessary (Lockwood, "Early Times and Events in Wisconsin," Wisconsin Historical *Collections*, II, 109). There were two required portages between Lake Winnebago and Green Bay: at Grand Chute (near Appleton), seven to eight miles from the rapids; at Kakalin (now Kaukauna) where there was a one-mile portage at the Stockbridge Indian settlement, about twenty miles from Fort Howard at Green Bay (Davidson, *In Unnamed Wisconsin*, 123, 129–30; Kemper, "Journal of an Episcopalian Missionary's Tour," Wisconsin Historical *Collections*, XIV, 413*n.*; Stambaugh, "Report on Wisconsin Territory," *ibid.*, XV, 415–18; Tanner, "Wisconsin in 1818," *ibid.*, VIII, 292). For a detailed description of the route, see Arndt, "Pioneers and Durham Boats," Wisconsin Historical *Proceedings, 1912*, pp. 189–215.

[10] By land to Fort Howard, the route led for the first seventy miles through fields and marshes of wild rice, past Green Lake, and through a swamp to Butte des Morts, just south of Lake Winnebago (Kinzie, *Wau-Bun*, 78, 86; Whittlesey, "Recollections of a Tour," Wisconsin Historical *Collections*, I, 73–75).

[11] A military road from Green Bay to Prairie du Chien had been planned to pass through Portage; it was surveyed in 1831–32, and the order for construction given in 1835 (Cole, "The Old Military Road," *Wisconsin Magazine of History*, IX, 47–50). For a contemporary map of the region, see [Thwaites], "Narrative of Morgan L. Martin," Wisconsin Historical *Collections*, XI, facing page 400.

[12] Fort Crawford was established in June 1816, as a result of the same westward movement which led to the construction of Fort Howard (see *n.* 5 above). The post was temporarily abandoned, 1826–27, and in 1830 was moved to new barracks on higher ground south of the first site. Fort Crawford was twice abandoned and reoccupied before it was closed in

1856 (Prucha, *Guide to Military Posts*, 68).

[13] Navigation of the Wisconsin is difficult, as Davis says, because of shifting sandbars, but is possible for small craft for about 200 miles of its 430-mile length (*Webster's Geographical Dictionary*).

[14] On a modern map, Duck Creek is the first stream shown on the route to Fort Crawford south of Fort Winnebago, and is approximately five miles distant. Yet on an 1829 map, there is an unidentified stream about four miles from the garrison, and Duck Creek appears to be some eight miles away ([Thwaites], "Narrative of Morgan L. Martin," Wisconsin Historical *Collections*, XI, facing p. 400).

[15] Fort Dearborn was first built in 1803 on the present site of Chicago, destroyed in 1812, and reoccupied by 1816. It was vacant from 1823 to 1828 and for other short periods before its abandonment in 1836 (Prucha, *Guide to Military Posts*, 71).

[16] The Fox River mentioned in connection with Fort Dearborn is a 220-mile-long river flowing south from southeast Wisconsin to the Illinois River at Ottawa.

[17] The Four Lakes form a chain of lakes in Dane County, southern Wisconsin, near present-day Madison. The fourth, farthest to the north, is Lake Mendota, the third, to the southeast, is Lake Monona, the second is Lake Waubesa, and the first is Lake Kegonsa (see J. D. Butler, "Taychoperah," Wisconsin Historical *Collections*, X, 64–69, for a description). The lakes are not presently connected by the Yohara River, which runs toward the Rock River from Lake Kegonsa. However, maps of the period and the presence of a town called Indian Ford near the point where the junction could have been indicate there probably was a water connection in Davis' time (Ford, *History of Illinois*, ed. Quaife, I, facing p. 155; [Thwaites], "Narrative of Morgan L. Martin," Wisconsin Historical *Collections*, XI, facing p. 400; Libby, "Chronicle of the Helena Shot-Tower," *ibid.*, XIII, 373).

[18] Galena was the largest lead mining settlement on the Fever River, six miles from its junction with the Mississippi in Jo Daviess County, Illinois ([Thwaites], "Notes on Early Lead Mining," Wisconsin Historical *Collections*, XIII, 291–92).

[19] Gratiot's Grove, northeast of Galena in Michigan Territory, was founded about 1826 by Henry and Jean Pierre Bugnion Gratiot, who established a lead smelting center there. The spot was selected for its abundance of timber, necessary for the furnaces (Washburne, "Col. Henry Gratiot," Wisconsin Historical *Collections*, X, 245–49).

1:232

The Office of the Quartermaster General[1] to Henry Whiting

SIR,[2] February 25th. 1831

I have received your letter dated the 31st. of January, covering a Summary Statement for that month. I anticipate no difficulty in relation to the drafts of Lieutenant Davis, as an appropriation[3] will probably be made at the present Session to cover them; but you will pay no other drafts of that officer on account of the Barracks until further orders. Any remittance made to him must be on account of the Quarter Master's Department.

You are authorized to draw on me for a sum not exceeding four thousand dollars, in drafts of such amount as you may find the most readily negociable.

LbC (NA, RG 92 Records of the Office of the Quartermaster General, Letters Sent, XV, 303–304). Addressed: "Major H. Whiting."

[1] The quartermaster general was Thomas S. Jesup (sketch, 1:174, *n.* 4).

[2] Henry Whiting (sketch, 1:208, *n.* 2).

[3] For the barracks appropriation, see 1:240, *n.* 6.

From George Gibson 1:233

SIR, 26 February 1831

After the delivery and inspection at Green Bay[1] of the subsistence contracted for with Messrs. Gidings & Co. intended to supply that post and Fort Winnebago,[2] the Asst. Commissary of Subs., Lieut. A. S. Hooe,[3] will turn over to be transported by the quarter Master's department the following provisions.

The prices annexed are what they cost at Green Bay, to which you will add in sales to officers &c the cost of transportation.

180	barrels	of	Pork	at	$10.25
375	"	"	Flour	"	4.62
165	bushels	"	Beans	"	1.00
2640	pounds	"	Soap	"	.06½
1200	"	"	Candles	"	.13
60	bushels	"	Salt	"	1.00
700	gallons	"	Vinegar	"	.18

Lieut. Hooe will send you no Whiskey—as to this article, instructions will shortly be sent to you.[4] G. G.[5]

LbC (NA, RG 192 Records of the Office of the Commissary General of Subsistence, Letters Sent, VIII, 224). Addressed: "Lt. J. F. Davis A[cting] A[ssistant] C[ommissary] S[ubsistence] Fort Winnebago."

[1] Green Bay was the site of Fort Howard (see 1:231, *n.* 5).

[2] See 1:144, *n.* 1.

[3] Alexander Seymour Hooe, born in Virginia, was graduated from West Point in 1827. Appointed to the Fifth Infantry, he served in a number of frontier garrisons, including Fort Howard (1828–31) and Fort Winne-

bago (1831–37). He lost an arm in the Mexican War and was brevetted major for gallantry in 1846. He died at Baton Rouge in 1847, aged forty-one (Cullum, *Biographical Register*, I, 395).

[4] The instructions regarding whiskey have not been found but apparently are those discussed in 1:259.

[5] George Gibson (sketch, 1:179, *n.* 2).

ABSTRACT

1:234

Senate Resolution

In the Senate of the United States, February 28, 1831

The Senate confirms the promotion of, among others, "Brevet 2. Lieut Jefferson Davis to be. 2d. Lieut 1s. July 1828."[1]

WALTER LOWRIE[2]
Secretary.

LbC (NA, RG 94 Records of the Adjutant General's Office, Records of the Appointment, Commission, and Personnel Branch, Register of Confirmations of Officers, United States Army, Senate Resolutions of Consent to Promotions and Appointments, I, 75–79), 3. Printed: *Senate Executive Journal*, IV, 131–33, 166, variant version.

[1] Davis' nomination appears on the promotions and appointments list of December 14, 1830 (1:222).

[2] Walter Lowrie (sketch, 1:136, *n.* 2).

ABSTRACT

1:235

Report of Persons and Articles Employed and Hired

Fort Winnebago,[1] Michigan Territory[2]
February [28,] 1831

Lieutenant J. F. Davis, acting assistant quartermaster, certifies that he paid $30 during the month of February for the hire of a clerk[3] in the Quartermaster Department.

DS (NA, RG 92 Records of the Office of the Quartermaster General, Reports of Persons and Articles Hired), 2. Signed: "J. F. Davis L[ieutenant] a[cting] a[ssistant] Q. M." Acknowledged: The Office of the Quartermaster General to Davis, April 19, 1831 (NA, RG 92 Records of the Office of the Quartermaster General, Letters Sent, XV, 410).

[1] See 1:144, *n.* 1.

[2] See 1:149, *n.* 2.

[3] P. G. Hambaugh was the clerk hired (see 1:176, *n.* 4).

ABSTRACT

Post Return 1:236

Fort Winnebago,[1] Michigan Territory[2]
February [28,] 1831

Lists Second Lieutenant J. F. Davis, Company C, First Infantry, present at the post. Remarks: "On Extra duty."

Printed form, filled in and signed (NA, RG 94 Records of the Adjutant General's Office, Post Returns, Fort Winnebago, 1828–45), 2. Signed: "D. E. Twiggs Major 1 Ifty." Endorsed: "Entd. recd. 18th. April."

[1] See 1:144, *n.* 1.
[2] See 1:149, *n.* 2.

ABSTRACT

Company Muster Roll 1:237

Fort Winnebago,[1] Michigan Territory[2]
February 28, 1831

Lists Brevet Second Lieutenant J. F. Davis of Captain Thomas J. Beall's[3] Company C, First Regiment of Infantry commanded by Colonel Willoughby Morgan,[4] as present. Remarks: "On Extra duty. Actg Ass[istant] Quarter Master." Report covers January and February 1831.

Printed form, filled in and signed (NA, RG 94 Records of the Adjutant General's Office, Muster Rolls of Regular Army Organizations, First Infantry, Company C), 2. Signed: "A. S. Miller Lieut D. E. Twiggs Major 1 Ifty." Endorsed: "Proves Recd. *April 18th. 1831.* Entered."

[1] See 1:144, *n.* 1.
[2] See 1:149, *n.* 2.
[3] Thomas J. Beall (sketch, 1:151, *n.* 2).
[4] Willoughby Morgan, born in Virginia, entered the army a captain of the Twelfth Infantry in 1812 and was retained at the end of the war as captain of a rifle regiment. In the summer of 1816, Morgan was placed in charge of the construction of Fort Crawford at Prairie du Chien. He served in various garrisons in the Northwest from 1817 until his return to Fort Crawford in 1822. Promoted to colonel of the First Infantry in 1830, Morgan was still commander at Prairie du Chien when he died there in April 1832. He was replaced by Zachary Taylor ([Thwaites (ed.)], "The Fur-Trade in Wisconsin, 1815–1817," Wisconsin Historical *Collections*, XIX, 479–80*n.*; Heitman, *Historical Register*, I, 726).

1:238 To George Gibson

Fort Winnebago[1] March 2nd. 1831

SIR[2]

I have the honor of inclosing a return of provisions received and issued at this Post during the month of Feby. 1831. Verry respectfully Your Mo. Obt Sert.

J. F. DAVIS

L[ieutenant] a[cting] a[ssistant] C[ommissary] S[ubsistence]

LS (NA, RG 192 Records of the Office of the Commissary General of Subsistence, Letters Received, D-1044, 1831). Addressed: "Genl. Geo. Gibson Com[missary] Genl. U. S. A. Washington, D. C." Endorsed: "Recd. 18 April." Enclosure missing.

[1] See 1:144, *n.* 1.

[2] George Gibson (sketch, 1:179, *n.* 2).

1:239 Commission as Second Lieutenant

[Washington, March 15, 1831]

THE PRESIDENT
of the
UNITED STATES of AMERICA,
To all who shall see these presents greeting:

Know Ye: That reposing special trust and confidence in the patriotism, valor, fidelity, and abilities of *Jefferson Davis* I have nominated, and by and with the advice and consent of the Senate,[1] do appoint him *Second Lieutenant in the First Regiment of Infantry* in the service of the United States: to rank as such from the *first* day of *July* eighteen hundred and *twenty eight.* He is therefore carefully and diligently to discharge the duty of *Second Lieutenant* by doing and performing all manner of things thereunto belonging.

And I do strictly charge, and require all Officers and Soldiers under his command, to be obedient to his orders as *Second Lieutenant*. And he is to observe and follow such orders, and directions, from time to time, as he shall receive from me, or the future President of the United States of America, or the General, or other superior Officers set over him, according to the rules and discipline of War. This Commission to continue in force during the pleasure of the President of the United States, for the time being.

GIVEN under my hand, at the City of Washington, this *fifteenth* day of *March* in the year of our Lord, one thousand eight hundred and *thirty one* and in the *fifty fifth* year of the Independence of the United States.

By the President, *Andrew Jackson*[2]

Jno H Eaton[3]
Secretary of War.

Printed form, filled in and signed, copy (American Antiquarian Society, Worcester, Massachusetts); printed form, filled in, retained copy (NA, RG 94 Records of the Adjutant General's Office, Records of the Appointment, Commission, and Personnel Branch, Register of Army Commissions, VII, 316). An unidentifiable seal is affixed. Endorsed: "Adj. Gens. Office R Jones Adjt. Genl."

[1] Davis' appointment as second lieutenant in the First Infantry was confirmed by the Senate on February 28, 1831 (1:234).

[2] Andrew Jackson (1767–1845), seventh President, was known personally to Davis from an 1816 visit to "The Hermitage," Jackson's Tennessee home (see 1:2, lxx for Davis' memory of the Jacksons). Jackson had been elected in 1828 and retired to "The Hermitage" in 1837 (*DAB*). Davis was a newly elected congressman at the time of Jackson's death, and delivered a memorial address in Vicksburg (Vicksburg *Sentinel and Expositor*, July 15, 1845).

[3] John Henry Eaton (1790–1856) had, like Andrew Jackson, adopted Tennessee as his home while a young man and served in the War of 1812. He married a ward of Jackson and completed a biography of the general in 1817. Appointed to the Senate in 1818, he was elected to hold the same position until 1829, when Jackson appointed him secretary of war. In 1829 Eaton remarried, and his second wife, Peggy O'Neale Timberlake, was found unacceptable to some of Washington society, resulting in a scandal and reorganization of the cabinet in 1831. Eaton resigned his post, failed to win a Senate seat in 1833, and so was made governor of Florida, and later minister to Spain. Eaton lost favor with Jackson in 1840 when he declined to support Van Buren for President. He died in Washington (*DAB*; *Biographical Directory of the American Congress*, 844).

From the Office of the Quartermaster General[1] 1:240

SIR, March 21st. 1830 [2]

I have received your letter dated the 30th. of December.[3] The full compensation of an Officer of the Commissary's Department acting as Commissary and Quarter Master is twenty dollars per month–if you have received that amount it is all that can be legally paid. As to the per diem authorized by the Regulation of June 1828,[4] if you will forward your account, with those of the other officers claiming that allowance, I will submit the question to the Treasury for decision; but as the Auditor[5] has disallowed the payment made to Major Twiggs[6] I think it doubtful whether he will admit the account of others.

The expenditures for Barracks at Fort Winnebago[7] have been so great as to occasion great inconvenience. The original appropriation, which Major Twiggs considered sufficient, was exhausted sometime ago, and I am apprehensive that the accounts outstanding will have exhausted the additional appropriation made last Session[8] before this reaches you.

LbC (NA, RG 92 Records of the Office of the Quartermaster General, Letters Sent, XV, 342). Addressed: "Lieut. J. F. Davis, Acting asst. Quarter Master, Fort Winnebago, Michigan Territory."

[1] The quartermaster general was Thomas S. Jesup (sketch, 1:174, *n.* 4).

[2] The date should read 1831.

[3] See 1:224 for Davis' letter of December 30.

[4] See 1:197 for the regulation of June 1828. Davis submitted his claim as requested (1:264) and it was allowed (1:276).

[5] Peter Hagner (sketch, 1:199, *n.* 5).

[6] David E. Twiggs (sketch, 1:149, *n.* 4).

[7] See 1:144, *n.* 1 for Fort Winnebago.

[8] An act passed March 2, 1829, provided $10,000 for the erection of barracks at Fort Winnebago (*Statutes at Large of the United States*, IV [1846], 356); an additional $5,000 for completion of the work was provided March 2, 1831 (*ibid.*, 466). Davis sent his estimate of funds needed to complete the construction in October 1830 (1:212).

1:241

To Thomas S. Jesup

Fort Winnebago[1] M[ichigan] T[erritory][2]
March 30th. 1831

SIR[3]

I have the honor of inclosing Some corrected vouchers and Statement of explanations as required by official Statement of remarks[4] from the Treasury Department on my a/cs for 2 & 3 quarters of 1830. I am respectfully Your Mo. Obt. Sert. J. F. DAVIS
L[ieutenant] ac[ting] A[ssistant] Q. M.

[Encl] Statement of explanations required by the accounting Officers at Washington City on Lt. Davis a/cs for 2. & 3. qr. 1830

2 qr. Vo. 1 B. Francis Roy's[5] a/c "Witness wanting" I inclose his a/c & Voucher *witnessed*	262.00
3 qr. Vo. 2 A. J. P. Arndt.[6] a/c "receipt incorrect." I forward his a/c with *Correct* receipt	50.00
Same qr. Vo. 3 B. J. Barbour "Witness wanting" Same. as F. Roy's a/c	15.00
Same qr. Vo. 6 B. Roll Extra Duty men "Over added $11.00" On examining the duplicate of the above Voucher filed in this office I find it adds $651.50 in place of $640.50. I herewith inclose an attested copy.	11.00
Same qr. Vo. 7 B Roll Extra Duty men "*William* Patterson Signed *Samuel* Patterson" [7] Private *Samuel* Patterson of "B" Comp. 1st. Inf was mustered while employed by me on "Extra Duty" as *William* Patterson. The error arose from a wrong discriptive roll having been left by the Officer Comdg. the detacht. of recruits.	11.40
Same qr. Vo. 8 B. Roll Extra Duty men *William* Patterson Signed. *Samuel* Patterson Same circumstances & remarks as made to vo. 7.	8.40
This Sum is $10. more than the neat amt. Suspended by official Statement for want of explanations and proper Vos. (arising from roll 8. added short & due my cr.)	$357.80

I forward an A/Current of disbursements at this Post on account of Contingencies for the 3rd. qr. of 1830 as required by official Statement. If that amt. could be transferred to my cr. in the Qr mrs. Dept. it would Save Some trouble in the adjustment of my accounts.

Attention will be paid to the articles noticed in your Statement of remarks (as not borne on that return) in my next property return. The Condemned Horses, oxen and Boats,[8] will also be Sold and accounted for in my next return.

J. F. Davis
L. ac. A. Q. M.

LS (NA, RG 217 Records of the United States General Accounting Office, Third Auditor's Office, Third Auditor's Accounts, Account 11,263). Addressed: "Genl. T. S. Jesup Q M Genl. U. S. A. Washington." Endorsed: "Referred to 3d. Aud. with papers wh[ich] accompanied it. Q. M. Gen. Office July 9. 1831."; in a different hand, "Recd May 19th. 1831." Enclosure: DS (NA, RG 217 Records of the United States General Accounting Office, Third Auditor's Office, Third Auditor's Accounts, Account 11,263).

[1] See 1:144, *n.* 1.

[2] See 1:149, *n.* 2.

[3] Thomas S. Jesup (sketch, 1:174, *n.* 4).

[4] The third auditor sent Davis a "sheet of remarks" on his second and third quarter returns in 1:225; the sheet has not been found.

[5] François Roy (sketch, 1:176, *n.* 3).

[6] John P. Arndt (1780–1861) was born in Pennsylvania. He was concerned with merchandising and shipbuilding in Wilkes-Barre before he moved to Green Bay in 1824. In 1825 he operated the first ferry across the Fox River and in 1827 opened a sawmill on the shore of Green Bay, twenty miles north of Fort Howard. Two years later he built a steamboat to run on the Fox River and was given a government contract for making and furnishing brick for Fort Winnebago. By 1834 he was able to ship a raft of seasoned lumber from his mill on the Devil River to Chicago. Arndt was a probate judge, a member of the Territorial Council, and the contractor for provisions at several Indian councils (Carpenter, "Report on the Picture Gallery," Wisconsin Historical *Collections*, III, 47–49; [Thwaites (ed.)], "The Fur-Trade in Wisconsin, 1812–1825," *ibid.*, XX, 381*n.*; Arndt, "Pioneers and Durham Boats," Wisconsin Historical *Proceedings, 1912*, pp. 185–89, 214–15).

[7] Samuel Patterson enlisted March 28, 1829, for five years. He was recruited by Lieutenant [William L.?] Harris in Philadelphia (Muster Roll, April 30, 1831 [NA, RG 94, First Infantry, Company B]).

[8] See 1:214, 223.

EXTRACT

1:242

The Office of the Quartermaster General to the Third Auditor

SIR,[1] March 31st. 1831

Herewith you will receive a statement of the Officers acting in my Department in the 4th. quarter of the last year, who had accounts to render for that quarter. . . .

81. Lieut. Jef. Davis Acting asst. Qr. Master Fort Winnebago[2]
Accounts not received. . .

In regard to the accounts of Lieutenant J. Davis, it is proper to state, that the severity of the winter,[3] rendering the communication from his station uncertain, and the remoteness of the post at which he is on duty, are sufficient to account for their not having been received. . . . QUARTER MASTER GENERAL'S[4] OFFICE

LbC (NA, RG 92 Records of the Office of the Quartermaster General, Letters Sent, XV, 361–63), 2. Addressed: "3rd. Auditor."

[1] Peter Hagner was the third auditor (sketch, 1:199, *n.* 5).

[2] See 1:144, *n.* 1.

[3] The winter of 1830–31 was one of

unusual severity and in after years was referred to as the "winter of the deep snow" (Nicolay and Hay, *Abraham Lincoln*, I, 47).

[4] The quartermaster general was Thomas S. Jesup (sketch, 1:174, *n.* 4).

ABSTRACT

Report of Persons and Articles Employed and Hired 1:243

Fort Winnebago,[1] Michigan Territory[2]
March [31,] 1831

Lieutenant J. F. Davis, acting assistant quartermaster, certifies that he paid $30 during the month of March for the hire of a clerk[3] in the Quartermaster Department.

DS (NA, RG 92 Records of the Office of the Quartermaster General, Reports of Persons and Articles Hired), 2. Signed: "J. F. Davis L[ieutenant] a[cting] a[ssistant] Q. M." Enclosed: Davis to Jesup, April 10, 1831 (1:247).

[1] See 1:144, *n.* 1.
[2] See 1:149, *n.* 2.
[3] The clerk was P. G. Hambaugh (see 1:176, *n.* 4).

EXTRACT

Peter Hagner to James B. Thornton 1:244

SIR,[1] April 2nd. 1831

In accordance with instructions heretofore rec'd from the Secy of the Treasury[2] to report the names of each Officer or agent who has omitted to render his accounts as required by the second section of the Act. of the 31st. January 1823 [3] "concerning the disbursement of public money" I hereby report the following names of persons whose accounts should have been rendered to this office to be audited— viz . . . .

Lieut. Jef. Davis The Qr. Mr. Genl.[4] remarks "In regard to the a/cs of Lt Davis, it is proper to state that the severity of the winter rendering the communication from his station uncertain & the remoteness of the post, Fort Winnebago,[5] are sufficient to account for their not being rendered. . . ." [6] Respectfully Your obt. St

PETER HAGNER[7]
Aud.

LbC (NA, RG 217 Records of the United States General Accounting Office, Third Auditor's Office, Miscellaneous Letters Sent, LVI, 247–48), 2. Addressed: "J. B. Thornton Esq. 2d. Comptroller of the Treasury."

[1] James B. Thornton, from Merrimac, New Hampshire, was second comptroller from May 1830 until June 1836, when President Jackson appointed him chargé d'affaires to Peru. He evidently died there since he was replaced in June 1838 (*Senate Executive Journal*, IV, 109–11, 560–61; *ibid.*, V, 118). The second comptroller was responsible for all War and Navy Department accounts and for examining accounts from the second, third, and fourth auditors' offices (*American Almanac* [1832], 129).

[2] The secretary of the treasury was Louis McLane.

[3] The act of January 31, 1823, is printed in *Statutes at Large of the United States*, III [1861], 723.

[4] The quartermaster general was Thomas S. Jesup (sketch, 1:174, *n.* 4).

[5] For Fort Winnebago, see 1:144, *n.* 1.

[6] See 1:242 for the remarks of Jesup.

[7] Peter Hagner (sketch, 1:199, *n.* 5).

1:245

To George Gibson

Fort Winnebago[1] M[ichigan] T[erritory][2]
April 2nd. 1831

SIR[3]

Herewith I have the honor of inclosing a return of provisions received and issued during the month of March 1831 and also an Account Current of money received and expended by me in the Sub. Dept. during the first Quarter of 1831.

Yours of the 25th. Nov. last[4] was received on the 18th. March ultimo, in conformity with which I inclose a corrected return for the month of September 1830. I have also corrected the error in the present return by adding the amt. of issues during the month of August 1830, to the issues of March 1831. Please inform me if corrected returns are required for the intervening months.

For the want of funds I have not paid the contractor[5] for the amount of Beef issued during the last quarter. I am verry respectfully Your Mo. Obt. Sert.

J. F. DAVIS
L[ieutenant] ac[ting] A[ssistant] C[ommissary] S[ubsistence]

LS (NA, RG 192 Records of the Office of the Commissary General of Subsistence, Letters Received, D–1051, 1831). Addressed: "Genl. Geo. Gibson Com[missar]y Genl. U. S. A. Washington." Endorsed: "Recd. 9 May." Enclosures missing.

[1] See 1:144, *n.* 1.

[2] See 1:149, *n.* 2.

[3] George Gibson (sketch, 1:179, *n.* 2).

[4] See 1:218 for Gibson's letter of November 25.

[5] Wallace Rowan (sketch, 1:184, *n.* 1).

From George Gibson 1:246

SIR, 9 April 1831

The troops at Fort Winnebago[1] will, in pursuance of general order of the 31st. of March,[2] be relieved by those at Fort Howard.[3] A Contract has been made for supplying both posts by a delivery of provisions at the latter: if these arrive in time, you will take to your new station enough to subsist the three companies for twelve months: but if the provisions should not reach you before the removal, the regular supply will be sent over. There will then be no necessity of furnishing an additional supply at Prairie du Chien,[4] by way of the Mississippi.

The gentlemen who have the Contract for Forts Howard and Winnebago are old and approved Contracters,[5] so that there is every assurance of their provisions being of a good quality. G. G.[6]

LbC (NA, RG 192 Records of the Office of the Commissary General of Subsistence, Letters Sent, VIII, 261). Addressed: "Lt. J. F. Davis a[cting] a[ssistant] c[ommissary] s[ubsistence] Fort Winnebago."

[1] See 1:144, *n.* 1.

[2] War Department General Order No. 5 of March 31, 1831, stated that "1. The Post of Chicago will be evacuated as early as practicable, and the garrison, consisting of two companies of the 5th regiment of infantry will proceed to Green Bay, and occupy Fort Howard. 2. The four Companies of the Fifth Regiment, now at Fort Howard, will, on being relieved, proceed to Fort Winnebago, and relieve the three Companies of the 1st Regiment of Infantry stationed at that Post. 3. The three Companies of the 1st Regiment, on being relieved, will repair to the Head Quarters of the Regiment at Prairie du Chien" (NA, RG 94, General Orders [Printed], I, 1825–33). It was expected that such an arrangement would not only strengthen the line between Green Bay and the Mississippi along which the Indians had lately been restless, but also have the effect of preventing them from entering into open hostility (*American State Papers*, Class V, Military Affairs, IV, 717).

[3] See 1:231, *n.* 5 for Fort Howard.

[4] Prairie du Chien was the location of Fort Crawford (1:231, *n.* 12).

[5] See 1:233 for mention of "Messrs. Gidings & Co.," the contractors.

[6] George Gibson (sketch, 1:179, *n.* 2).

To Thomas S. Jesup 1:247

Fort Winnebago[1] M[ichigan] T[erritory][2]

SIR[3] April 10th. 1831

I have the honor of inclosing to you my property returns and accounts current for the first quarter of 1831. I also forward a muster roll of "Extra Duty" men and a report of persons and articles employed and hired at this Post during the month of March 1831.

Previously I have informed you that I could not learn by the records of my predecessor,[4] the State of the "Barracks Appropn." [5] at the time I entered on duty in the Qr. Mrs. Department, and as no Statement of the cost of purchases made in compliance with requisitions on the Quarter Masters, at St Louis and Detroit,[6] has been furnished, it was impossible for me to know the amount in dollars thus drawn for by myself. It is thus that I have made expenditures beyond the "Appropriation" and in <–further–> justification allow me to remark that quarters have been built for our company more than (I am informed) was intended when the appropriation was made.

The amount of $166.55/100 was disbursed on a/c of "New Barracks" at this Post during the quarter, as will appear by reference to the inclosed accounts. These disbursements were made previous to my receipt of the letter (from the Treasury Department)[7] informing me that the Appropriation was exhausted.

The error in the application of the 1200 Dollars, received per draft on Capt. J. B. Brant,[6] arose from Supposing that it was drawn chargeable to the "Barracks Appropriation". Please inform me whether or not the amount of money I report on hand belonging to the "New Barracks" Shall be transfered to the Qr. Mrs. Department, towards accounting for the amount expended in the wrong Department. I am respectfully Your Mo. Obt. Sert J. F. Davis

L[ieutenant] a[cting] a[ssistant] Q. M.

LS (NA, RG 217 Records of the United States General Accounting Office, Third Auditor's Office, Third Auditor's Accounts, Account 11,263). Addressed: "Genl. T. S. Jesup Qr. Mr. Genl. U S A Washington D. C." Endorsed: "Referred to 3d. aud. with accounts. Q M. Gen. Office. July 9. 1831"; in a different hand, "Recd. May 28th. 1831." Enclosure: Report of Persons and Articles Employed and Hired, March 31, 1831 (1:243); other enclosures missing.

1 See 1:144, *n.* 1.

2 See 1:149, *n.* 2.

3 Thomas S. Jesup (sketch, 1:174, *n.* 4).

4 Davis' predecessor in the position of acting assistant quartermaster was Thomas P. Gwynn (sketch, 1:148, *n.* 1). See 1:174 and 1:177.

5 For mentions of the barracks appropriation, see 1:232, 240.

6 The assistant quartermasters at St. Louis and Detroit were Joshua B. Brant (sketch, 1:192, *n.* 6) and Henry Whiting (sketch, 1:208, *n.* 2), respectively.

7 The letter from the Treasury Department has not been found.

From William B. Lewis 1:248

SIR, 20 April 1831

Your letters of the 23 February and 3 March last[1] have been received, together with your recruiting account[2] on the adjustment of which a balance is found to be due the U. States of $17.—corresponding with your own Statement.

Such accounts are only required of you every two months, corresponding with the periods for which musters are taken—and when no expenditure is made in the two past months, a letter to that effect is all that is necessary. W. B. L[3]

LbC (NA, RG 217 Records of the United States General Accounting Office, Second Auditor's Office, Letters Sent, XV, 445–46). Addressed: "Lieut. J. F. Davis, 1 Inf. Ft. Winnebago, via Greenbay."

[1] Davis' letters to Lewis have not been found.

[2] The recruiting account is missing.

[3] William B. Lewis (sketch, 1:166, *n.* 1).

From the Office of the Quartermaster General[1] 1:249

SIR, April 25th. 1831

Your money and property accounts,[2] for the Fourth quarter of the last year, after the usual examination at this office, are transmitted to the Third Auditor[3] of the Treasury for settlement.

Vouchers 1. 4. 5 and 8 of your Abstract C. should have been entered in abstract B, they being properly chargeable to the Quarter Master's Department. The two vouchers to your abstract A. on account of New Barracks, and the one voucher to your Abstract B, on the same account, amounting, together, to $1.164.75, are marked "charge to Qr. Mrs. Department."

LbC (NA, RG 92 Records of the Office of the Quartermaster General, Letters Sent, XV, 414). Addressed: "Lieut. J. F. Davis, Acting Asst. Qr. Master, Fort Winnebago."

[1] The quartermaster general was Thomas S. Jesup (sketch, 1:174, *n.* 4).

[2] The cover letter for Davis' money and property accounts for the fourth quarter of 1830 is printed as 1:227. The accounts and vouchers are missing.

[3] The third auditor was Peter Hagner (sketch, 1:199, *n.* 5).

1:250 From Peter Hagner

SIR, April 30th. 1831

Your a/c for disbursements in the 4th qr of 1830,[1] has been audited and reported to the 2d Comptroller[2] for his decision thereon, by whom it has been returned to this office, exhibiting the following balances due from you viz on a/c Barracks at Fort Winnebago[3] $780.36 & on a/c qm Dpt $248.39—differing from your statement in the aggregate $611.20, which the enclosed sheet of remarks made on your money and property accounts will explain. Vo 1. B. 4 qr 1830, is herewith returned Respectfully Your obt. St

PETER HAGNER[4]
Aud.

LbC (NA, RG 217 Records of the United States General Accounting Office, Third Auditor's Office, Miscellaneous Letters Sent, LVI, 332). Addressed: "Lt. J. F. Davis a[cting] a[ssistant] qm Fort. Winnebago." Enclosure missing.

[1] Davis' accounts for the fourth quarter were sent to the third auditor from the quartermaster general April 25 (NA, RG 92, Letters Sent, XV, 414).

[2] The second comptroller was James B. Thornton (sketch, 1:244, *n.* 1).

[3] See 1:144, *n.* 1.

[4] Peter Hagner (sketch, 1:199, *n.* 5).

ABSTRACT

1:251 Report of Persons and Articles Employed and Hired

Fort Winnebago,[1] Michigan Territory[2]
April [30,] 1831

Lieutenant J. F. Davis, acting assistant quartermaster, certifies that he paid $30 during the month of April for the hire of a clerk[3] in the quartermaster's office.

DS (NA, RG 92 Records of the Office of the Quartermaster General, Reports of Persons and Articles Hired), 2. Signed: "J. F. Davis L[ieutenant] a[cting] a[ssistant] Q. M." Transmitted: Davis to Jesup, May 2, 1831 (NA, RG 92 Records of the Office of the Quartermaster General, Letters Received, D–118, 1831). Acknowledged: The Office of the Quartermaster General to Davis, May 30, 1831 (NA, RG 92 Records of the Office of the Quartermaster General, Letters Sent, XV, 455).

[1] See 1:144, *n.* 1.

[2] See 1:149, *n.* 2.

[3] The clerk was P. G. Hambaugh (see 1:176, *n.* 4).

ABSTRACT

Post Return

1:252

Fort Winnebago,[1] Michigan Territory[2]
April [30,] 1831

Lists Second Lieutenant J. F. Davis, Company B,[3] First Infantry, present at the post. Remarks: "For Duty A[cting] A[ssistant] C[ommissary] S[ubsistence] &. Qr. Mr."

Printed form, filled in and signed (NA, RG 94 Records of the Adjutant General's Office, Post Returns, Fort Winnebago, 1828–45), 2. Signed: "D. E. Twiggs Major 1 Infty." Endorsed: "Submitted for the Inspection of the Genl in Chief. R[oger] J[ones]."; in a different hand, "Entd. Recd. 28 May."

[1] See 1:144, *n.* 1.

[2] See 1:149, *n.* 2.

[3] See 1:253 for evidence that Davis joined and assumed command of Company B on April 16, 1831.

ABSTRACT

Company Muster Roll

1:253

Fort Winnebago,[1] [Michigan Territory][2]
April 30, 1831

Lists Second Lieutenant[3] J. F. Davis of Captain G. C. Spencer's[4] Company B, First Regiment of Infantry commanded by Colonel Willoughby Morgan,[5] as present. Remarks: "Joined company the 16th Ap. 1831 Commanding Company. Assumed command–the 16th April 1831." Report covers March and April 1831.

Printed form, filled in and signed (NA, RG 94 Records of the Adjutant General's Office, Muster Rolls of Regular Army Organizations, First Infantry, Company B), 2. Signed: "J. F. Davis Lt. D E Twiggs Major 1 Ifty." Endorsed: "Proves Recd. *May 29th. 1831.* Entered."

[1] See 1:144, *n.* 1.

[2] See 1:149, *n.* 2.

[3] See 1:252 for first use of Davis' new rank, and 1:239 for Davis' commission as second lieutenant.

[4] George C. Spencer (sketch, 1:193, *n.* 3).

[5] Willoughby Morgan (sketch, 1:237, *n.* 4).

1:254

To William B. Lewis

Fort Winebago[1] M[ichigan] T[erritory][2]

SIR[3]

May 1st 1831

Herewith I have the honor to enclose you my accts. as Recruiting offr. for this post for the month of april 1831. Very Respectfully yr. obt. Servt.

J. F. DAVIS

Lt. 1 Inf. Recruting

ALS (NA, RG 217 Records of the United States General Accounting Office, Second Auditor's Office, Second Auditor's Accounts, Account 15,233). Addressed: "To W. B. Lewis 2nd Auditor U. S. Treasury." Enclosure missing.

[1] See 1:144, *n.* 1.

[2] See 1:149, *n.* 2.

[3] William B. Lewis (sketch, 1:166, *n.* 1).

1:255

To George Gibson

Fort Winnebago[1] M[ichigan] T[erritory][2]

SIR[3]

May 2nd. 1831

Inclosed herewith I have the honor of forwarding a return of Provisions received and issued at this Post during the month of April 1831. I am respectfully Your Mo. Obt. Sert.

J. F. DAVIS

L[ieutenant] 1. Inf.

a[cting] a[ssistant] C[ommissary] S[ubsistence]

LS (NA, RG 192 Records of the Office of the Commissary General of Subsistence, Letters Received, D–1056, 1831). Addressed: "Genl. Geo. Gibson Com[missar]y Genl. U. S. A. Washington *D. C.*" Endorsed: "Recd. 30 May." Enclosure missing.

[1] See 1:144, *n.* 1.

[2] See 1:149, *n.* 2.

[3] George Gibson (sketch, 1:179, *n.* 2).

ABSTRACT

1:256

Pay Voucher

Fort Winnebago,[1] May 8, 1831

Lieutenant J. F. Davis, First Infantry, acknowledges that he has received $649.10 from Paymaster W. Piatt.[2] Amount includes pay, allowance for one servant,[3] and forage for two horses, for October

1830 through April 1831, and additional pay for duty as acting assistant quartermaster during the same period. The servant is described as "James Pemberton A Slave."

[AE] "Disallow—The Regulation requiring *acting* ass[istant] qr mrs. to be paid from the contingent fund of the qr. M. Gen. Dept. had the charge have been for an a[cting] ass[istant] C[ommissary] Sub[sistence] in addition, without forage, it would have been admitted, but the forage is allowed when the officer acts with doubl capacity." [4]

Printed form, filled in and signed (NA, RG 217 Records of the United States General Accounting Office, Paymasters' Accounts, Piatt 1537, Voucher 18), 3. Signed: "J. F. Davis L[ieutenant] 1 Inf. a[cting] a[ssistant] Q. M." Endorsed: "and acting a[ssistant] c[ommissary] s[ubsistence] J. H. Hook Comm[issar]y Dept."

[1] See 1:144, *n.* 1.

[2] William Piatt (sketch, 1:185, *n.* 2).

[3] James Pemberton (sketch, 1:5, *n.* 4).

[4] These confusing and apparently contradictory remarks seem to say that when an officer acts as both acting assistant commissary of subsistence and acting assistant quartermaster, the forage is allowed in kind and no money charge will be admitted.

ABSTRACT

Register of Payments to Officers 1:257

[Washington, D.C.,] May 8, 1831

Lists payment by Paymaster W. Piatt[1] to Second Lieutenant Jefferson Davis, First Infantry, $649.10. Amount includes pay and allowance for Davis and one servant,[2] and allowance for two horses, from October 1830 through April 1831. Remarks: "*Actg.* Asst. Qr. Mr. (disallowed)." [3]

D (NA, RG 99 Records of the Office of the Paymaster General, Register of Payments to Officers, IV, 27), 1.

[1] William Piatt (sketch, 1:185, *n.* 2).

[2] James Pemberton (sketch, 1:5, *n.* 4) was the servant.

[3] See the endorsement of 1:256 for evidence of the fact that Davis' claim ($112) for forage for two horses for seven months was disallowed.

ABSTRACT

1:258 Register of Fresh Beef Contracts

[Washington, D.C.,] May 15, 1831

Records that Lieutenant J. F. Davis contracted with Hiram G. Eads to supply Fort Winnebago[1] with fresh beef at 4.49 cents per pound for the period September 1831 through August 1832.

D (NA, RG 192 Records of the Office of the Commissary General of Subsistence, Register of Fresh Beef Contracts, 1820–56), 1.

[1] See 1:144, *n.* 1.

1:259 To George Gibson

Fort Winnebago[1] M[ichigan] T[erritory][2]

SIR[3] May 21st. 1831

In compliance with your "Circular" of the 7th. last,[4] I have consulted the Comdg. Officer[5] at this Post respecting the amount of whiskey which may be required for issues to men on daily duty &c. for one year commencing on the 1st. June next. The probable amount required will be about 300 gallons. There will be on hand at the end of this month about 684 gallons, from which, deduct 300 gallons (the amt. required for next year) and it will leave a Surplus of 384 gallons.

Indian Traders, <—illegible—> who are prohibited Keeping Spiritous liquors, are the only merchants near this Post, except the Sutler,[6] and as he has heretofore purchased and transported to this place whiskey of a better quality, for a less price, it is not presumable he will give the contract price for that on hand. If the Surplus be retained by the Comy. part of it may be disposed of per Sales to Officers, the leekage and evaporation of the remainder would (I think) occasion less loss to government than would accrue from Selling it at Such price as could probably be obtained.

I have the honor of inclosing a contract[7] between the united States & H. G. Eads for Supplying the Troops at this post with Fresh Beef for one year commencing 1st. Sept. 1831. The contract has been made this early on account of the advantages afforded thereby to the contractors. I am respectfully Your Mo. Obt. Sert. J. F. DAVIS

L[ieutenant] 1 Inf.

a[cting] a[ssistant] C[ommissary] S[ubsistence]

Fort Crawford, 1816–1830

Fort Crawford, 1830–56

LS (NA, RG 192 Records of the Office of the Commissary General of Subsistence, Letters Received, D–1069, 1831). Addressed: "Genl. Geo Gibson Com[missar]y Genl. U. S. A. Washington D. C." Endorsed: "Recd. 9 July." Enclosure missing.

[1] See 1:144, *n.* 1.

[2] See 1:149, *n.* 2.

[3] George Gibson (sketch, 1:179, *n.* 2).

[4] The circular of March 7, signed by Gibson, asked commanding officers of posts to estimate the quantities of whiskey required for "daily duty men" for the year beginning June 1, 1831; it also asked the post commanders to state probable whiskey surpluses and suggest means of disposal (NA, RG 92, Letter Book, VIII, 231).

[5] David E. Twiggs (sketch, 1:149, *n.* 4) was the commanding officer at Fort Winnebago.

[6] The sutler at Fort Winnebago was Satterlee Clark (Calkins, "William Hull and Satterlee Clark," Wisconsin Historical *Collections*, IX, 417).

[7] See 1:258 for the register of Eads's fresh beef contract.

From James Eakin 1:260

SIR, 23 May 1831

Your accounts for expenditures at Fort Winnebago[1] in the 3d. & 4th. Quarters of 1830,[2] have been examined and adjusted, and $139.60 found due you; which Sum has been carried to your Credit on the Books of the 3d. Auditor,[3] and your accounts closed in this office.

I return you four Vouchers with the necessary remarks made on them.

J. E.[4]
A[cting] A[uditor]

LbC (NA, RG 217 Records of the United States General Accounting Office, Second Auditor's Office, Letters Sent, XV, 492). Addressed: "Lieut. J. F. Davis, Act[ing] A[ssistant] Q. Mr. Ft. Winnebago, via Greenbay." Enclosures missing.

[1] See 1:144, *n.* 1.

[2] Davis transmitted his third and fourth quarter commissary accounts in 1:207, 227.

[3] Peter Hagner was the third auditor (sketch, 1:199, *n.* 5).

[4] James Eakin (see 1:165, *n.* 1).

From George Gibson 1:261

SIR, 24 May 1831

The balance due to the United States on the settlement of your accounts for the 1st. quarter of the year[1] is $15.30/100 in lieu of $14.96/100 which differs from your statement 34 cents, and which arises from your calculating 68 lbs of Candles sold to officers at 14 instead of 14½ cents pr lb. the contract price being 12½ in lieu of 12 cts & the transportation 2 cts p lb. On receipt of this you can correct the error.[2]

G. G.[3]

LbC (NA, RG 192 Records of the Office of the Commissary General of Subsistence, Letters Sent, VIII, 292). Addressed: "Lt. J. F. Davis A[cting] A[ssistant] C[ommissary] S[ubsistence] Prairie du Chien."

[1] See 1:245 for Davis' letter of transmittal.

[2] Davis did not receive this letter until September (1:281).

[3] George Gibson (sketch, 1:179, *n.* 2).

1:262

From Peter Hagner

SIR, May 1831[1]

The Comy Genl of Sub[2] has transmitted to this office, your a/c and vouchers for the quarter ending the 30th December last[3]—and the Same have been by me audited and reported to the Second Comptroller[4] of the Treasury for his decision thereon, by whom they have been returned to this office with the following result. A balance is found to be due you from the u. S of Seventy one Dollars and twenty cents—differing from your statement 7. cents, being the difference on Settlement of your a/c the 19th August last[5] which has not Since been noticed in your accounts. Respectfully Your obt. St

PETER HAGNER[6]
Aud

LbC (NA, RG 217 Records of the United States General Accounting Office, Third Auditor's Office, Miscellaneous Letters Sent, LVI, 343). Addressed: "Lt. J. F. Davis Fort. Winnebago."

[1] The dating of other items in the letterbook from which this document was taken makes it probable that this letter was written May 5 or 6, 1831.

[2] The commissary general of subsistence was George Gibson (sketch, 1:179, *n.* 2).

[3] See 1:227 for Davis' letter transmitting his fourth quarter account current.

[4] The second comptroller was James B. Thornton (sketch, 1:244, *n.* 1).

[5] Hagner's letter regarding the seven cents was dated August 25 (1:199).

[6] Peter Hagner (sketch, 1:199, *n.* 5).

1:263

From William B. Lewis

SIR, 1 June 1831

Your account for recruiting disbursements made at Fort Winnebago[1] to the 30 April last[2] has been received and adjusted, and a balance of $34.00 found to be due the U. States, as represented by your own Statement.[3]

Permit me to refer you to the Circular of the Adjutant Genl.[4] dated the 26 July 1825,[5] respecting the endorsement of your inlistments.

W. B. L.[6]

LbC (NA, RG 217 Records of the United States General Accounting Office, Second Auditor's Office, Letters Sent, XV, 505). Addressed: "Lieut. J. F. Davis, 1 Inf., Ft. Winnebago, via Greenbay."

[1] See 1:144, *n.* 1.

[2] See 1:254 for the letter transmitting Davis' April recruiting account.

[3] Davis forwarded a receipt for $34 from Lieutenant J. J. Abercrombie (1:283), which closed his recruiting account (1:299).

[4] Roger Jones (sketch, 1:123, *n.* 6).

[5] The first paragraph of the circular of July 26, 1825, provided that enlistment documents were to be endorsed "duplicate"; one copy to be sent to the adjutant general and the other to be retained by the recruiting officer and submitted with his accounts to the second auditor (NA, RG 94, War Department Orders and Circulars, General Orders, I [1825–33]).

[6] William B. Lewis (sketch, 1:166, *n.* 1).

To Thomas S. Jesup 1:264

Fort Winebago[1] M[ichigan] T[erritory][2]

SIR[3]

June 1st 1831

I have the honor to acknowledge the receipt of your communication of the 21st March 1831[4]

I had not been informed of an additional appropriation for this Post before the receipt of yours of the above date and have made no expenditures on account of new Barracks since I learned that the appropriation originally made to that object was exhausted,[5] Consequently no picketing timber or hair for plaistering has been procured, as I expected they would when I made my last report on the state of the Barracks.[6] Since the receipt of your letter above referred to I have written to Maj. H Whiting[7] A[ssistant] Q. M at Detroit informing him of the quantity of hair which would be necessary to finish the buildings erected at this Post and <requested>[8] him if he had any disposible funds appropiated for that purpose to purchase and forward the amount required or a less quantity if the whole could not be procured.[9]

I herewith enclose (as instructed by your letter) my accts. and those of Capt Harney[10] embracing our claims for "Extra duty services" at this post.[11] My claim is made in two accts. the 1st includes the amount due me up to the 1st of May 1830 from which date I have drawn pay for "staff services" should this fact in your opinion render the second acct. objectionable you will oblige me by destroying it in your office.[12] Very Respectfly. I have the honor to be yr. mo. obt. servt J. F. Davis

L[ieutenant] 1 Inf. A[cting] A[ssistant] Q. M.

ALS (NA, RG 92 Records of the Office of the Quartermaster General, Consolidated Correspondence File, "Ft. Winnebago," D–147, 1831). Addressed: "Maj. genl. T. S. Jesup Q. M. genl. U. S. A. Washington City D. C." Endorsed: "Recd July 9. 1831." Enclosures missing.

[1] See 1:144, *n.* 1.

[2] See 1:149, *n.* 2.

[3] Thomas S. Jesup (sketch, 1:174, *n.* 4).

[4] See 1:240 for Jesup's letter of March 21.

[5] The additional appropriation of which Davis writes was made on March 2, 1831 (see 1:240, *n.* 6). See also 1:232 for further reference to the money difficulties encountered in the building of the new barracks.

[6] See 1:247 for Davis' last extant report to Jesup on the barracks.

[7] Henry Whiting (sketch, 1:208, *n.* 2).

[8] Interlined.

[9] Davis' letter to Whiting has not been found.

[10] William Selby Harney (1800–89) was born in Tennessee (Warner, *Generals in Blue*, 208) or Louisiana (Heitman, *Historical Register*, I, 502) and was appointed a second lieutenant in the First Infantry in 1818. He was promoted to captain in 1825 and served at Fort Winnebago, 1828–31, earning a reputation as an able officer and firm disciplinarian (Clark, "Fort Winnebago," Wisconsin Historical *Collections*, VIII, 310–11). Harney distinguished himself in the Black Hawk, Seminole, and Mexican wars, being brevetted brigadier general in 1847 for gallantry at Cerro Gordo. Because of birthplace and family connections, Harney was suspected of pro-Southern feelings at the outbreak of the Civil War and was relieved of command. Brevetted major general in 1865, he lived in retirement in the South and died in Florida (Warner, *Generals in Blue*, 208–209; Reavis, *William Selby Harney*). In after years Davis wrote of Harney: "At that period of his life he was, physically, the finest specimen of a man I ever saw. Tall, straight, muscular, broad-chested and gaunt-waisted, he was one of the class which Trelawney describes as 'natures noblemen' . . . . Captain Harney was also a bold horseman, fond of the chase, a good boatman, and skillful in the use of the spear as a fisherman. Neither drinking nor gaming, he was clear of those rocks and shoals of life in a frontier garrison, and is no doubt indebted to this abstinence for much of the vigor he has possessed to his present advanced age" (Davis to Reavis, January 1878, printed in Reavis, *William Selby Harney*, iv). See also V. Davis, *Memoir*, I, 73, for confirmation of Harney's attitude toward drinking and other vices common to frontier posts.

[11] Davis wrote to George W. Jones January 5, 1872, of his role in the construction of the Fort Winnebago barracks: "In 1829 I went to Fort Winnebago, then a stockade, and was put in charge of the working parties, to ob-

tain material for the construction of blockhouses, barracks and stores. Gen. (then Capt.) W. S. Harney was sent with his company to the pine forest high up the Wisconsin river, another party was sent to the maple, ash and oak forest on the Baraboo river, both parties used the whip saw, and being among wild Indians were doubtless objects of wonder. When the timber procured on the Ouisconsin was brought down to the portage of the Wisconsin and Fox, the former river was so full that its waters flowed over its bank, and ran in a broad sheet into the Fox river. Taking advantage of the fact, we made rafts suited to the depth of the water and floated the lumber across to the site of the fort, on the east bank of the Fox river" (Milwaukee *Sentinel*, February 3, 1891, p. 2). The exact dates of Davis' supervision are not known, although further proof of his having been in charge of the construction is found in an 1835 letter from David E. Twiggs to Thomas S. Jesup (1:451).

12 The rule which clouded Davis' and Harney's claims for extra duty payment is that of August 16, 1830 (1:197). Davis questioned the validity of these claims (1:224), but was told to submit them (1:240). They were eventually accepted (1:276).

To George Gibson

1:265

Fort Winnebago[1] M[ichigan] T[erritory][2]

SIR[3]

June 2nd. 1831

I have the honor of inclosing a return of provisions received and issued at this Post during the month of May 1831.

The articles condemned in Voucher no. 5. have been sold at public auction and will be accounted for in my next A/Current. I am Verry respectfully Your Mo Obt Sert. J. F. DAVIS

L[ieutenant] a[cting] a[ssistant] C[ommissary] S[ubsistence]

LS (NA, RG 192 Records of the Office of the Commissary General of Subsistence, Letters Received, D–1064, 1831). Addressed: "Genl. Geo. Gibson Com[missary] Genl. U. S. A. Washington." Endorsed: "Recd. 27 June."

Enclosure missing.

1 See 1:144, *n*. 1.

2 See 1:149, *n*. 2.

3 George Gibson (sketch, 1:179, *n*. 2).

From Peter Hagner

1:266

SIR,

June 4th. 1831

The Commissary Genl of Subs[1] has transmitted to this office your a/c and vouchers for the quarter ending the 31st. March last,[2] and the same have been by me audited and reported to the Second Comptroller[3] of the Treasury for his decision thereon, by whom they have been returned to this office with the following result.

A Balance is found to be due from you to the u. S. of Fifteen Dollars and twenty three cents. Differing from your a/c current 27 cents, which you will find explained in the statement of Differences enclosed. Respectfully Your obt. St

PETER HAGNER[4]
Aud.

LbC (NA, RG 217 Records of the United States General Accounting Office, Third Auditor's Office, Miscellaneous Letters Sent, LVII, 26). Addressed: "Lt. J. F. Davis Act. As-s[istant] Comy of Sub at. Fort. Winnebago." Enclosure missing.

1 The commissary general was George Gibson (sketch, 1:179, *n.* 2).

2 Davis' letter of transmittal for his account current for the first quarter of 1831 is printed as 1:245.

3 James B. Thornton (sketch, 1:244, *n.* 1) was the second comptroller.

4 Peter Hagner (sketch, 1:199, *n.* 5).

ABSTRACT

1:267

Post Return

Fort Crawford,[1] Michigan Territory[2]
June [30,] 1831

Lists Second Lieutenant J. F. Davis, Company B, First Infantry, absent on special duty at Rock Island.[3] Remarks: "Majr. Twiggs[4] with Compys. B. & K. arrived 26th.[5] Col. Morgan[6] relinquished the Command to Capt Barker[7] 27th. and departed same day with the F[ield] & Staff. and Compy "*A.*" *B. G.* & *K.* and all the efficient men of *D.* & *F.* for Fort Armstrong." [8]

Printed form, filled in and signed (NA, RG 94 Records of the Adjutant General's Office, Post Returns, Fort Crawford, 1817–34), 2. Signed: "T. Barker Capt 1 Infy." Endorsed: "Ent[ered] Recd. 6 August."

1 See 1:231, *n.* 12.

2 See 1:149, *n.* 2.

3 Rock Island: an island in the Mississippi River opposite the Rock River in Illinois. Fort Armstrong, one of a chain of forts built after the War of 1812 to defend the Northwest Territory, was established on the southern end of the island in 1816 and was abandoned twenty years later (Prucha, *Guide to Military Posts*, 57).

4 David E. Twiggs (sketch, 1:149, *n.* 4).

5 See 1:246, *n.* 2 for an explanation of why troops were transferred from Fort Winnebago to Fort Crawford.

6 Willoughby Morgan (sketch, 1:237, *n.* 4).

7 Originally from New York, Thomas Barker entered the army a first lieutenant in 1813 and was discharged in

1815. He returned to the service in 1819 and was a captain, First Infantry, from 1829 until his death in 1839 (Heitman, *Historical Register*, I, 191).

8 Colonel Willoughby Morgan with soldiers of the First Infantry, including Davis' Company B, left Fort Crawford for Fort Armstrong at the orders of General E. P. Gaines, who was attempting to persuade, or, if necessary, to force Black Hawk, the Sauk Indian leader, to retire from his ancestral lands east of the Mississippi, which he was then occupying in defiance of the treaty of 1804 (Thwaites, "The Black Hawk War," *How George Rogers Clark Won the Northwest*, 115–30). The campaign, which resulted in no bloodshed, has often, particularly in contemporary accounts, been called the first campaign of the Black Hawk War; Davis thus described it in later years when he wrote, "in the summer of 1832 [1831], the garrison at Fort Winnebago was ordered to Rock Island to join in the first Black Hawk campaign . . ." (Davis, "Indian Policy of the United States," *North American Review*, CXLIII, 455; see also 1:Appendix II, 482 for a Davis reference to the second Black Hawk campaign). A treaty signed in June 1831 forced Black Hawk and the members of his band to agree never to return to the eastern bank of the Mississippi (Thwaites, "The Black Hawk War," *How George Rogers Clark Won the Northwest*, 131).

ABSTRACT

Semiannual Company Muster Roll 1:268

Fort Armstrong[1] [Illinois,] June 30, 1831

Lists Second Lieutenant J. F. Davis of Captain G. C. Spencer's[2] Company B, First Regiment of Infantry commanded by Colonel Willoughby Morgan,[3] as present, and remarks that he "Assumed comd of Compy. 16th. April 1831. Relinquished Command of Compy 27th. June 1831."[4] Further remarks indicate that "Compy. B. left Fort Winnebago on the 24, arrived at Fort Crawford 26th. left Fort Crawford 27th. and arrived at Fort Armstrong 28th. June 1831."[5] Report covers January through June 1831.

Printed form, filled in and signed (NA, RG 94 Records of the Adjutant General's Office, Muster Rolls of Regular Army Organizations, First Infantry, Company B), 2. Signed: "Th. P. Gwynn Lt Wy Morgan. Col 1st I[nfantr]y Com[mandin]g." Endorsed: "Proves. Recd. August *13th. 1831.* Entered."

1 See 1:267, *n.* 3 for Fort Armstrong.

2 George C. Spencer (sketch, 1:193, *n.* 3).

3 Willoughby Morgan (sketch, 1:237, *n.* 4).

4 See 1:274 for evidence that Davis commanded Company B, April 17–June 26.

5 See 1:267, *n.* 8 for explanation of the various troop movements mentioned here.

1:269 From the Office of the Quartermaster General[1]

SIR, July 9th. 1831

Your money and property accounts, for the First quarter of the present year,[2] after the usual examination at this office, are transmitted to the Third auditor[3] of the Treasury for settlement.

On Voucher 1 of your abstract A. and Voucher 1 of your abstract B. New Barracks, is this remark, charge to Quarter Master's Department–item $226.800."

Your letter dated March 30th.,[4] with the papers which accompanied it, is referred to the Third Auditor. Your letter of April 10th.[2] is referred to him also

LbC (NA, RG 92 Records of the Office of the Quartermaster General, Letters Sent, XVI, 58). Addressed: "Lieut. J. F. Davis, Acting Asst. Qr. Master, Fort Winnebago."

[1] Thomas S. Jesup (sketch, 1:174, *n.* 4) was the quartermaster general.

[2] The April 10 cover letter for Davis' money and property accounts for the first quarter of 1831 is printed as 1:247.

[3] Peter Hagner (sketch, 1:199, *n.* 5) was the third auditor.

[4] See 1:241 for Davis' letter of March 30.

1:270 To George Bomford

Fort Crawford[1] M[ichigan] T[erritory,][2] July 20th 1831

SIR[3]

Herewith I have the honor to enclose to you my return of ordnance and ordnance Stores received and issued during the 2nd Quarter of 1831, accompanied by the invoices of the officer from whom received and the receipt of the officer to whom transferred.

The Bayonet Scabbards reported worn out must have been an error in Capt. Spencer's[4] Invoice they belonged to the old set of accoutrements and were worn out previous to the time when I relieved him Very Respectfly I am yr. mo. obt. Servt.

J. F. DAVIS
2. L[ieutenant] 1. Inf. Co. "B"

ALS (NA, RG 156 Records of the Office of the Chief of Ordnance, Letters Received, D–90, 1831). Addressed: "To Col. G. Bomford Ordnance officer Washington D. C." Endorsed: "Recd. <–Augt.–> Sept. 3d an[swere]d Sept 8." Enclosures missing.

[1] See 1:231, *n.* 12.
[2] See 1:149, *n.* 2.
[3] George Bomford (sketch, 1:155, *n.* 3).
[4] George C. Spencer (sketch, 1:193, *n.* 3).

EXTRACT

The Cutting Marsh[1] Diary 1:271

Wed <–27–> 25 July [1831][2]

Wrote to Lieut. Davis Ft. Winnebago.[3] Contents of t[he] letter.[4] First the Bill of t[he] Bibles &c Se[co]nd urged t[he] importance of his inquiring whether he could not do something for t[he] moral renovation of t[he] soldiers at t[he] Ft. Love & gratitude to t[he] Sav[ior] sh[oul]d induce it. immediately. Altho' alone he sh[oul]d not feel a sufficient excuse for declining to make an effort.[5] David went alone against his foe & t[he] defier of the army of Israel, but in t[he] name of t[he] Ld. of hosts, & he conquered. God has without doubt something for you to do in thus bringing you as you hope to t[he] knowledge & to t[he] acknowledgement. of t[he] truth as it is in Jesus. It was but a few years ago when christians began to make t[he] inquiry respecting seamen[6] as a very few do now respecting our Military Posts, and Behold t[he] results!

MS, diary (State Historical Society of Wisconsin, Madison), 2. Printed: W. L. Fleming, "Religious Life of Davis," *Methodist Quarterly Review*, LIX, 329; Quaife, "Northwestern Career of Davis," *Journal of the Illinois State Historical Society*, XVI, 7–8; Davidson, *In Unnamed Wisconsin*, 127.

[1] Cutting Marsh (1800–73), a native of Vermont, was educated at Phillips Academy, Dartmouth, and Andover Theological Seminary. He was licensed to preach by the Congregational church and ordained a foreign missionary in 1829. He arrived at the Grand Kakalin on the Fox River (now Kaukauna, Wisconsin) to minister to the Stockbridge Indians May 1, 1830. The mission house he established was known as "almost the only house of entertainment between Green Bay and Fond du Lac" (A. J. M'Call, "[J.] M'Call's Journal," Wisconsin Historical *Collections*, XII, 189*n.*). Marsh opened a day school as well as a church and ran the school with Reverend Chauncey Hall (Kemper, "Journal of an Episcopalian Missionary's Tour," *ibid.*, XIV, 421*n.*). As a result of the Black Hawk War treaty, the Stockbridges moved to new lands east of Lake Winnebago, and Marsh accompanied them. He remained until 1848, when the American Board of Commissioners for Foreign Missions discontinued its work with the tribe. In 1851 Marsh moved to Waupaca, and preached there and in neighboring communities until his death (Chapin, "Sketch of Cutting Marsh," *ibid.*, XV, 25–38).

[2] The date of this entry appears to have been originally Wednesday, July

27, which would be correct.

[3] See 1:144, *n.* 1 for Fort Winnebago.

[4] The Cutting Marsh letter has not been found. If Marsh wrote on July 27, 1831, Davis may never have received the letter, since he left Fort Winnebago for Fort Crawford on June 24, 1831 (see 1:268).

[5] See W. L. Fleming, "Religious Life of Davis," *Methodist Quarterly Review*, LIX, 328–30, for an interpretation of Davis' religious convictions and activities during his army career.

[6] Marsh may be referring to the American Seamen's Friend Society, which was founded in New York in 1826 and was active especially in the Northeast, where Marsh had been reared and educated. For a discussion of the society and others like it, see Langley, *Social Reform in the United States Navy*, 48–67.

ABSTRACT

1:272

Post Return

Fort Crawford,[1] July [31,] 1831

Lists Second Lieutenant Jeff. F. Davis, Company B, First Infantry, as absent on special duty superintending a sawmill on the Yellow River.[2] Remarks: "Comps. A. B. & G. returned from Fort Armstrong[3] 5th. Inst." [4]

Printed form, filled in and signed (NA, RG 94 Records of the Adjutant General's Office, Post Returns, Fort Crawford, 1817–34), 2. Signed: "G. Loomis, Cap. 1st. Infy Commandg." Endorsed: "Ent[ered] Recd 26 Augst."

[1] See 1:231, *n.* 12.

[2] The government sawmill used in construction of the second Fort Crawford was built by soldiers on the Yellow River, about twelve miles above Prairie du Chien on the Iowa side of the Mississippi River, and was operating by October 1829 (Scanlan, *Prairie du Chien*, 138; Mahan, *Old Fort Crawford*, 134). Davis explained on January 5, 1872, in a letter to George W. Jones (Milwaukee *Sentinel*, February 3, 1891, p. 2), that he was sent to the sawmill after his return from Rock Island, July 5; he was back at Fort Crawford by August 31 (1:278). See also Freeman, "Two Local Questions," Dunn County [Wisconsin] *News*, October 14, 1909, p. 10.

[3] See 1:267, *n.* 3 for Fort Armstrong.

[4] Six companies of the First Infantry were ordered to Fort Armstrong on June 27 to aid in the forced eviction of Black Hawk (see 1:267, *n.* 8).

1:273

From Peter Hagner

SIR August 2d. 1831

Your account for disbursements in the 1st Quarter 1831,[1] has been audited and reported to the 2d Comptroller[2] for his decision thereon by whom it has been returned to this office exhibiting an aggregate balance due from you of $147.05—differing from your statement $88.20, which the enclosed sheet will explain[3] Respectfully Your Obt Sevt

PETER HAGNER[4]
A[uditor]

LbC (NA, RG 217 Records of the United States General Accounting Office, Third Auditor's Office, Miscellaneous Letters Sent, LVII, 184). Addressed: "Lieut J. F Davis Actg Asst Qr Mr Fort Winebago." Enclosure missing.

[1] The cover letter for Davis' account for disbursements in the Commissary Department for the first quarter of 1831 is printed as 1:245.

[2] James B. Thornton (sketch, 1:244, *n.* 1) was the second comptroller.

[3] See 1:297 for Davis' reply.

[4] Peter Hagner (sketch, 1:199, *n.* 5).

ABSTRACT

Pay Voucher 1:274

Fort Crawford,[1] August 15, 1831

Second Lieutenant J. F. Davis, First Infantry, acknowledges that he has received $209.13 from Paymaster Thomas Biddle.[2] Amount includes pay, allowance for one servant,[3] and forage for two horses, for May and June, and additional pay for duty as acting assistant quartermaster during the same period. It also includes pay for duty as commanding officer of Company B from April 17 to June 26.[4] The servant is described as "James a Slave."

Printed form, filled in and signed (NA, RG 217 Records of the United States General Accounting Office, Paymasters' Accounts, Biddle 15, 877, Voucher 45), 3. Signed: "J. F. Davis L[ieutenant] 1. Inf."

[1] See 1:231, *n.* 12.

[2] Thomas Biddle (sketch, 1:134, *n.* 1).

[3] James Pemberton (sketch, 1:5, *n.* 4).

[4] See 1:268 which shows that Davis commanded the company, April 16–June 27.

ABSTRACT

Register of Payments to Officers 1:275

[Washington, D.C.,] August 15, 1831

Lists payment by Paymaster T. Biddle[1] to Second Lieutenant Jefferson Davis, First Infantry, $209.13. Amount includes pay and allowance for Davis and one servant,[2] and forage for two horses, for May and June. Remarks: "*Actg.* Asst. Qr. Mr. Com[mandin]g 'B' Co. 17 Apl. to 26 June." [3]

D (NA, RG 99 Records of the Office of the Paymaster General, Register of Payments to Officers, IV, 27), 1.

[1] Thomas Biddle (sketch, 1:134, *n.* 1).
[2] James Pemberton (sketch, 1:5, *n.* 4).
[3] See also 1:268, 274.

1:276 From the Office of the Quartermaster General[1]

SIR, August 23rd. 1831

I return two accounts received under cover of your letter dated the 1st. of June of this year,[2] viz: One for per diem to yourself, from the 1st. of January to the 30th. of April 1830 amounting to Eighty five dollars and sixty cents, and one for per diem to Captain Harney[3] the 26th. of June to the 16th. of August 1830, being forty one dollars and sixty cents—both of which have been allowed by the Comptroller[4] of the Treasury, as you will perceive by the enclosed copy of his letter to me on the subject. Your account for the time you were paid as a Staff Officer has been disallowed by the Comptroller and is filed in this Office with his letter.[5]

LbC (NA, RG 92 Records of the Office of the Quartermaster General, Letters Sent, XVI, 152). Addressed: "Lieut. J. F. Davis, Acting Asst. Qr. Master, Prairie du Chien, Michigan Territory." Enclosures missing.

[1] Thomas S. Jesup (sketch, 1:174, *n.* 4) was the quartermaster general.
[2] See 1:264 for Davis' letter.
[3] William S. Harney (sketch, 1:264, *n.* 10).
[4] James B. Thornton was second comptroller (sketch, 1:244, *n.* 1).
[5] Davis' and Harney's claims seemed to be disallowed by the rule of August 16, 1830 (1:197). Davis requested clarification (1:224) and was told to submit the claims (1:240), which he did (1:264).

ABSTRACT

Post Return 1:277

Fort Crawford,[1] Michigan Territory[2]
August [31,] 1831

Lists Second Lieutenant Jeff. F. Davis, Company B, First Infantry, present at the post. Remarks: "For Duty."

Printed form, filled in and signed (NA, RG 94 Records of the Adjutant General's Office, Post Returns, Fort Crawford, 1817–34), 2. Signed: "G. Loomis Cap. 1st. Infy. Commanding." Endorsed: "Entd. Recd. 1st. Octr."

[1] See 1:231, *n.* 12.
[2] See 1:149, *n.* 2.

ABSTRACT

Company Muster Roll 1:278

Fort Crawford,[1] August 31, 1831

Lists Second Lieutenant J. F. Davis of Captain G. C. Spencer's[2] Company B, First Regiment of Infantry commanded by Colonel Willoughby Morgan,[3] as present. Remarks that "Company B. left Fort Armstrong on the 2d. of July and arrived on the 5th. of July 1831."[4] Report covers July and August 1831.

Printed form, filled in and signed (NA, RG 94 Records of the Adjutant General's Office, Muster Rolls of Regular Army Organizations, First Infantry, Company B), 2. Signed: "Th P Gwynn 1st Infy G. Loomis Cap. 1. Infy." Endorsed: "Proves. (Recd. Octr. 3d. 1831.) Entered."

[1] See 1:231, *n.* 12.
[2] George C. Spencer (sketch, 1:193, *n.* 3).
[3] Willoughby Morgan (sketch, 1:237, *n.* 4).
[4] See 1:267, *n.* 8 and 1:272 for movements of Davis' company to and from Fort Armstrong.

To Thomas S. Jesup 1:279

Fort Crawford[1] Prairie du Chien
M[ichigan] T[erritory,][2] Sept 5th 1831

SIR[3]

Herewith I have the honor to forward my Quarterly return for the 2nd Quarter of 1831. The delay which exists was occasioned by my having left Fort Winebago suddenly and a neglect on the part of my agent at that place to perform such services as I required to close my accounts in due time. I left Fort Winebago before having regularily closed my accts. because I was *Commanding* Co. "B." 1. Inf. which was ordered to proceed to Rock Island Ill. to oppose the hostile Sac & Fox Indians.[4] Maj. Twiggs having left the Regt. sooner than I expected[5] I failed in procuring his signature to the abstract of expenditures and two muster Rolls but have requested him to sign them at Head Quarters of the Dept[6] Very Respectfully I remain yr. mo. obt. Servt.

J. F. DAVIS
L[ieutenant] A[cting] A[ssistant] Q. M.
at Fort Winebago in the 2nd Quarter of 1831

ALS (NA, RG 217 Records of the United States General Accounting Office, Third Auditor's Office, Third Auditor's Accounts, Account 11,527). Addressed: "To Maj. Genl. T. S. Jessup Q. M. genl. Washington D. C." Endorsed: "Referred to the 3d. Auditor. Q M Gen. Office Oct. 8. 1831."; in a different hand, "Recd Oct 8th. 1831." Enclosures missing.

[1] See 1:231, *n.* 12.

[2] See 1:149, *n.* 2.

[3] Thomas S. Jesup (sketch, 1:174, *n.* 4).

[4] Davis left Fort Winnebago with Company B June 24, arrived at Fort Crawford June 26, and was ordered to Rock Island the next day (1:268). He returned with Company B to Fort Crawford July 5 (1:278). See also Scanlan, *Prairie du Chien*, 146.

[5] David E. Twiggs (sketch, 1:149, *n.* 4) was promoted to lieutenant colonel in the Fourth Infantry July 15 (Heitman, *Historical Register*, I, 976) and, having received a furlough, was on his way to New York by the end of July (Post Return, July 1831 [NA, RG 94, Fort Crawford, 1817–34]).

[6] Whether Davis has reference to the headquarters of the Western Department of the army, which was at Memphis (Gordon, *Compilation of Registers of the Army*, 454), the headquarters of the Right Wing of the department at St. Louis (Nichols, *Atkinson*, 146), or the headquarters of the Quartermaster Department at Washington is unknown.

1:280

To Thomas S. Jesup

Fort Crawford,[1] Prairie du Chien Sept 6th 1831

SIR[2]

Herewith I have the honor to transmit my Quarterly Return[3] (<Fort Winebago>[4] new Barracks) for the 2nd Quarter of 1831 accompanied by Lieut Hooe's[5] receipts for the property and funds on hand.

The cause of delay the same as stated in my communication of the 5th Inst.[6] Very respectfully yr. mo. obt. Servt. J. F. DAVIS

L[ieutenant] 1. Inf—

A[cting] A[ssistant] Q. M. Fort Win[nebago]

ALS (NA, RG 217 Records of the United States General Accounting Office, Third Auditor's Office, Third Auditor's Accounts, Account 11,688). Addressed: "To Maj. Genl. T. S. Jesup Qr. master genl Washington D. C." Endorsed: "Referred to the 3d. Aud. Q. M. Gen. office Decr. 2 1831"; in a different hand, "Recd Novr. 19th. 1831." Enclosures missing.

[1] See 1:231, *n.* 12.

[2] Thomas S. Jesup (sketch, 1:174, *n.* 4).

[3] Trueman Cross acknowledged the receipt of Davis' money and property accounts for the second quarter on December 2, 1831 (NA, RG 92, Letters Sent, XVI, 313), and forwarded them to the third auditor on the same day (*ibid.*).

[4] Interlined. See 1:144, *n.* 1 for Fort Winnebago.

[5] Alexander S. Hooe (sketch, 1:233, *n.* 3).

[6] See 1:279 for Davis' letter of September 5.

To George Gibson

1:281

Fort Crawford[1] M[ichigan] T[erritory,][2] Sept 14th 1831

SIR[3]

Your's of May 24th 1831[4] has been forwarded to me at this place. Having closed my accts. I cannot make the correction you suggest in the account of Sales to officers. I have nothing to which I can refer for confirmation but I feel certain that the price at which the Candles were sold was nearly correct and that the *division* was erroneous, contract price being—12½ transportation 1½ nearly (I think 1 47/100) cost 14—if however I am incorrect in my recollections please inform me to whom I shall pay the amount due the United States. Very Respectfully I am yr. mo. obt Servt. J. F. DAVIS

L[ieutenant] 1. Inf.

ALS (NA, RG 192 Records of the Office of the Commissary General of Subsistence, Letters Received, D–1088, 1831). Addressed: "To Genl. Geo. Gibson Comy. Genl U. S. Army Washington D. C." Endorsed: "Recd. 8 Octr."

[1] See 1:231, *n.* 12.

[2] See 1:149, *n.* 2.

[3] George Gibson (sketch, 1:179, *n.* 2).

[4] Gibson's letter of May 24 is printed as 1:261.

ABSTRACT

1:282

Post Return

Fort Crawford,[1] Michigan Territory[2]
September [30,] 1831

Lists Second Lieutenant Jeff. F. Davis, Company B, First Infantry, as absent on furlough.[3] Remarks: "By order of Capt Loomis." [4]

Printed form, filled in and signed (NA, RG 94 Records of the Adjutant General's Office, Post Returns, Fort Crawford, 1817–34), 2. Signed: "G. Loomis Capn 1t. Infy, Com[mandin]g Post." Endorsed: "Recd. Novr. 6 1831."

1 See 1:231, *n.* 12.
2 See 1:149, *n.* 2.
3 Just where Davis went during this furlough is unknown. That the furlough was a short one is attested to by the fact that Davis wrote official letters from Fort Crawford on September 14 (1:281) and October 1, 1831 (1:283).
4 Gustavus Loomis, born in Vermont, was graduated from West Point in 1811 and served in the War of 1812, being taken prisoner at Niagara in 1813. He had been in the Quartermaster Department and Artillery Corps before his transfer to the First Infantry in 1821. Brevetted major in 1829, he later participated in the Florida and Mexican wars. He retired in 1863, was brevetted brigadier general two years later, and died in 1872, aged eighty-three (*Register of Graduates* [1964], 203; Heitman, *Historical Register*, I, 641).

1:283

To William B. Lewis

Fort Crawford[1] M[ichigan] T[erritory,][2] Oct 1st 1831

SIR[3]

Herewith I have the honor to enclose to you 1st. Lt. Abercrombie's[4] receipt for thirty four Dollars—(recruiting fund) being the amount for which I was accountable to the U. S. Treasury as a recruiting offr. of the 1st Infantry.[5] Very Respectfully yr. mo. obt. Servt.

J. F. DAVIS
2. L[ieutenant] 1. Inf.

[Encl] Received at Fort Crawford (M. T.) 19th. Septr. 1831, of Lieut. Jeff. F. Davis 1st. Infy. Thirty four Dollars Recruiting fund.

J J ABERCROMBIE
Adjt 1st Inf Rectg Off.

ALS (NA, RG 217 Records of the United States General Accounting Office, Second Auditor's Office, Second Auditor's Accounts, Account 15,663). Addressed: "To W. B. Lewis Esq. 2 Auditor U. S. Tresy." Endorsed: "recd

5 Nov ans[wered]." Enclosure: ADS (NA, RG 217 Records of the United States General Accounting Office, Second Auditor's Office, Second Auditor's Accounts, Account 15,663). Endorsed: "Duplicates."

1 See 1:231, *n.* 12.

2 See 1:149, *n.* 2.

3 William B. Lewis (sketch, 1:166, *n.* 1).

4 John Joseph Abercrombie, adjutant at regimental headquarters, 1825–33, was born in Tennessee and graduated from the Military Academy in 1822. Abercrombie was a first lieutenant, First Infantry, in 1831, and later served in the Black Hawk, Florida and Mexican wars, being brevetted lieutenant colonel for gallantry at Monterrey. During the Civil War, he was a brigadier general of volunteers, Union Army, and saw service mostly in the Virginia campaigns. He retired from active service as a brevet brigadier general in 1865, and died at Roslyn, New York, in 1877 at the age of seventy-nine (Cullum, *Biographical Register*, I, 297–98).

5 Davis had informed the second auditor that he owed $34 on his recruiting account (1:263); the receipt enclosed here closed the account (1:299).

EXTRACT

Peter Hagner to Enoch Reynolds

1:284

Oct. 4th. 1831

SIR,[1]

In pursuance of the directions heretofore recd from the Secy of the Treasury[2] to report to the proper Comptroller the names of each Officer or agent, who has omitted to render his accounts as required by the 2d Section of the Act of the 31 January 1823 "concerning the disbursement of public money",[3] I hereby report the following names . . . .

Quarter Masters Department

Lt. J. F. Davis, actg. ass[istant] Q. M. . . .

Very respectfully Your obt St

PETER HAGNER[4]
Aud.

LbC (NA, RG 217 Records of the United States General Accounting Office, Third Auditor's Office, Miscellaneous Letters Sent, LVII, 357), 1. Addressed: "Enoch Reynolds Esq Actg 2d. Comptroller."

1 Enoch Reynolds was appointed a justice of the peace for the District of Columbia in 1821. He served two full five-year terms and was reappointed by President Jackson. Reynolds was a deacon of the Baptist church in Washington and, with others, founded the Columbian College in Washington in 1822. He was a trustee of the school, which was established for the training of Baptist ministers. He died in 1834 (*Senate Executive Journal*, III, 236, 242, 449, 456, IV, 154, 169; Wilkinson, "Early Baptists in Washington, D.C.," Columbia Historical *Records*, XXX, 232, 240).

2 The secretary of the treasury was

Louis McLane.

[3] The second section of the act of January 31, 1823, required that every officer should render his accounts quarterly to the Treasury (*Statutes at Large of the United States*, III [1846], 723).

[4] Peter Hagner (sketch, 1:199, *n.* 5).

1:285 From the Office of the Quartermaster General[1]

SIR, October 8th. 1831

Your money and property accounts, on account of this Department proper, for the second quarter of the present year,[2] after the usual examination at this office, are transmitted to the proper offices of the Treasury[3] for settlement.

A remark is made on Voucher 1 of your abstract G. Forage for public animals for April, May and June, 1831, viz: "In addition to the certificate which Lieutenant Davis has signed, he should have certified that the forage was necessarily and absolutely *fed* to the public animals in his charge."

On your account current for the first quarter of this year,[4] on account of New Barracks at Fort Winnebago,[5] you stated as being due to the United States on the 31st. of March $251. which balance you have not noticed in the accounts, for the second Quarter, as received at this office. Your attention is called to this subject.

LbC (NA, RG 92 Records of the Office of the Quartermaster General, Letters Sent, XVI, 228). Addressed: "Lieut. J. F. Davis, 1st. Regt. Infantry, Fort Crawford."

[1] The quartermaster general was Thomas S. Jesup (sketch, 1:174, *n.* 4).

[2] Davis' money and property accounts were transmitted in 1:279.

[3] Davis' accounts were sent to both the second and the third auditors' offices (October 8, 1831 [NA, RG 92, Letters Sent, XVI, 227–28]).

[4] See 1:247 for the letter transmitting Davis' account current for the first quarter of 1831.

[5] For Fort Winnebago, see 1:144, *n.* 1.

1:286 From the Office of the Quartermaster General[1]

SIR 11th. Octr. 1831

Your Clothing Return, for issues in the 2d. qr. of the present year, to Company B. 1st. Regt. Infy has been received and examined at this Office and sent to the Treasury[2] for settlement.

LbC (NA, RG 92 Records of the Office of the Quartermaster General, Letters Sent Relating to Clothing, III, 461). Addressed: "Lt. J. F. Davis 1st. Regt. Infy. Fort Crawford Prairie du Chien M[ichigan] T[erritory]."

[1] Thomas S. Jesup was the quartermaster general (sketch, 1:174, *n.* 4).

[2] The office of the quartermaster general transmitted Davis' return to the second auditor October 11 (NA, RG 92, Letters Sent Relating to Clothing, III, 460).

Special Order No. 45 1:287

Head Quarters, 1st Infy. Fort Crawford,[1]
Oct. 11. 1831

Lieut. Davis will proceed to the position[2] occupied by Lt. Burbank[3] and relieve him in his duties there, upon being relieved Lt. Burbank will Secure his stores and boat untill they can be brought to this post (which must be done by the first Steam boat), after which he will with his Command return to his proper station.

Lt. Davis will report to Col. Morgan[4] for further instructions previous to his departure. By order of Col. Morgan

J J Abercrombie.[5]
Adjt. 1st Inf

ADS (NA, RG 49 Records of the Bureau of Land Management, Lead Mine Records).

[1] See 1:231, *n.* 12.

[2] Until Davis relieved him, Burbank was stationed at the Dubuques Mines. See 1:291, *n.* 2.

[3] Sidney Burbank (sketch, 1:195, *n.* 6).

[4] Willoughby Morgan (sketch, 1:237, *n.* 4), colonel of the First Infantry, who had been on furlough since July 21, 1831, returned to Fort Crawford on October 10 (Post Returns, July, October, 1831 [NA, RG 94, Fort Crawford, 1817–34]).

[5] John J. Abercrombie (sketch, 1:283, *n.* 4).

From Peter Hagner 1:288

Sir, Oct 15th. 1831

Your a/c, as late a[cting] a[ssistant] qm at Fort Winnebago,[1] for disbursements in 2 qr 1831[2] has been audited and reported to the 2d Compr[3] for his decision thereon, by whom it has been returned to this office exhibiting an aggregate balance due from you of $161 90/100 differing from your statement $198.90, which the enclosed sheet of remarks, made on your money and property accounts will explain.

Two muster Rolls, to wit, for May and June 1831—of men on extra duty, are returned to be countersigned.[4] Respectfully Your obt St

PETER HAGNER[5]
Aud.

LbC (NA, RG 217 Records of the United States General Accounting Office, Third Auditor's Office, Miscellaneous Letters Sent, LVII, 389). Addressed: "Lt. J. F. Davis now at Fort Crawford." Enclosures missing.

[1] See 1:144, *n.* 1.

[2] The letter transmitting Davis' account current for the second quarter of 1831 is printed as 1:279 and receipt is acknowledged in 1:285.

[3] The second comptroller was James B. Thornton (sketch, 1:244, *n.* 1).

[4] Davis acknowledged receipt of this letter and its enclosures and reported return of the muster rolls in December (1:307).

[5] Peter Hagner (sketch, 1:199, *n.* 5).

1:289

From William B. Lewis

SIR

October 22, 1831

Your Clothing return for 2d. Quarter 1831 has been received[1] with the following remarks noted thereon. ("Remarks Noted.")

You therefore stand charged with $21.04 as per A/c enclosed.

You receipted on 4th. of March last[2] to Major Twiggs[3] for 1 Wall Tent & fly—to Capt. Spencer[4] 16th. April following[2] for 3 Wall Tents & flies, and you afterwards (12th. July 1831)[2] turn over to Major Garland[5] 3 Wall Tents & flies, and 10 Com[mo]n Tents, leaving you chargeable with 1 Wall Tent and fly and 4 Comn. Tents, which when accounted for, will close this A/c. by the receipt of Lt. Gwynn[6] 30th. June 1831.[2]

W. B. L.[7]

LbC (NA, RG 217 Records of the United States General Accounting Office, Second Auditor's Office, Letters Sent, Property Division, Volume F, 76). Addressed: "Lt. J. F. Davis [Company] B: 1st Infy. Fort Crawford."

[1] The receipt of Davis' clothing return for the second quarter of 1831 was acknowledged by the quartermaster general October 11 and sent to the second auditor the same day (1:286, *n.* 2).

[2] The receipts have not been found.

[3] David E. Twiggs (sketch, 1:149, *n.* 4).

[4] George C. Spencer (sketch, 1:193, *n.* 3).

[5] John Garland, brevet major and assistant quartermaster, was a Virginian who served in the War of 1812 and the Mexican War. He was brevetted colonel and brigadier general in 1846 and 1847, respectively, and died as a colonel, Eighth Infantry, in 1861 (Heit-

man, *Historical Register*, I, 447).

[6] Thomas P. Gwynn (sketch, 1:148, *n.* 1).

[7] William B. Lewis (sketch, 1:166, *n.* 1) was second auditor of the Treasury Department.

From William B. Lewis

1:290

SIR, 27 October. 1831

Your accounts for expenditures at Fort Winnebago[1] between the 1 April and 30 Septr. 1831 [2] have been examined and adjusted–and $137.63 found due you; which Sum has been carried to your Credit on the Books of the 3d. Auditor,[3] and your accounts as Acting Asst. Qr. Mr. closed in this Office.

In this Settlement the suspended vouchers 2, 3, 4 & 7 returned per your letter of the 7 August last have been admitted–and Vos. 1 &. 3–have been taken from your Abstract and handed to the 3d. Auditor.

W. B. L.[4]

LbC (NA, RG 217 Records of the United States General Accounting Office, Second Auditor's Office, Letters Sent, XVI, 131). Addressed: "Lieut. J. F. Davis, Act. A[ssistant] Q. M. Fort Winnebago, Mic[higan] T[erritor]y."

[1] See 1:144, *n.* 1.

[2] Davis' accounts for the second quarter were sent to the quartermaster general in September. Davis ceased to act as assistant quartermaster at Fort Winnebago in June (1:279).

[3] The third auditor was Peter Hagner (sketch, 1:199, *n.* 5).

[4] William B. Lewis (sketch, 1:166, *n.* 1).

To Willoughby Morgan

1:291

SIR[1] October 31st. 1831

On arriving at Du Buques Mines[2] I received intelligence which rendered it probable that intruders were at that time on the district of country Known as Du Buque's Mines. I examined that part of it which I supposed was the seat of intrusion and my <observations>[3] at this as well as subsequent examinations convence me that during the persent and past seasons persons have been frequently on the Indian lands designated as above. seeking lead Mineral. from information the best to be obtained I have come to the conclusion that persons are now preparing to go into the above mentioned Indian lands. The Mineral if any be "raised" will probably be brought down the Maccokaztah River[4] and carried to a furnace on Platte river.[5]

If I had possessed a force sufficient I would have thrown such obstructions in the former of these Rivers as to destroy its Navigation. Beleiving it necessary to the protection of the Country I was ordered to guard that a force as great as that heretofore Kept at the same place should be continued there. I have the honor to submit to you my opinion.

Capt Legate[6] Superintendant of the lead Mines. concurs with me in the foregoing views. Very respectfully Your Obt Sevt (signed)

J F DAVIES
2nd. Leut 1st. Infy

L, copy (NA, RG 94 Records of the Adjutant General's Office, Letters Received, A–151, 1831). Addressed: "To Col. Wy Morgan Comdg 1st Infy." Endorsed: "A. Copy (Signed) Wly. Morgan Col 1st Infy Comdg Recd. Decr. 17th 1831." Enclosed: Morgan to Acting Assistant Adjutant General Right Wing Western Department, November 1, 1831 (1:294), which was in turn enclosed in Atkinson to McCall, November 29, 1831 (1:301). All three items were enclosed in Atkinson to Jones, November 29, 1831 (NA, RG 94 Records of the Adjutant General's Office, Letters Received, A–151, 1831).

1 Willoughby Morgan (sketch, 1:237, *n.* 4).

2 Davis was assigned October 11 to duty at Dubuques Mines (1:287), near the present site of Dubuque, Iowa. Julien Dubuque had obtained a permit in 1788 from the Sauk and Fox Indians to work the rich lead mines in the area. He became wealthy from the mines and cooperated with the Indians and the Spanish until the territory was purchased by the United States. With the opening of mineral lands by government leases in 1822, a flood of emigrants came from the east; by 1830 the area was well settled, especially in the region of the Fever River and Galena, Illinois. By an unratified treaty made with General Edmund P. Gaines July 1, 1831, the Sauks and Foxes agreed to remain on the west side of the river, and the white settlers were to be evicted from what was then Indian territory. In 1833 the Spanish and Indian titles were cleared, and mining began on a larger scale west of the river ([Thwaites], "Notes on Early Lead Mining," Wisconsin Historical *Collections,* XIII, 279–92; Van der Zee, "Early History of Lead Mining," *Iowa Journal of History and Politics*, XIII, 7–50; Davidson, *In Unnamed Wisconsin,* 186–95). Davis recalled in an 1882 letter to George W. Jones: "In 1831 the Sauks sent a war party against the Sioux, and this breach of the peace, they feared would bring upon them punishment by the U. S., such at least was then understood to be the cause of their abandonment of their settlement at the lead mines of DuBuque. I was sent there by Col. W. Morgan in the fall of that year, to watch the Indians who were semi hostile, and to prevent trespassing on the Indian territory. . . . I remained on duty there until the spring of 1832, and though I made frequent reconnaissance into the country, never saw an Indian, or any indication of their presence in that neighborhood" (August 8, 1882 [Charles Aldrich Collection, Iowa State Department of History and Ar-

chives, Des Moines]; see also the reminiscences related in V. Davis, *Memoir*, I, 87–89, 150–52).

[3] In the margin.

[4] "Maccokaztah" is presumably the present Maquoketa River, about 30 miles south of Dubuque, which flows 150 miles from northeast Iowa into the Mississippi. In January 1888, Charles Aldrich interviewed Davis and afterwards reported that Davis "mentioned his service in the United States Army at Dubuque, remarking that he was often sent out west of that point in command of scouting parties for the purpose of watching the Indians. 'How far were you in the habit of going?' I asked. 'Often to the Maquoketa River, or about as far as we could march and return the same day'" (Frank E. Stevens Collection, Illinois State Historical Library, Springfield).

[5] The Platte River is about five miles northeast of Dubuque in Grant County, Wisconsin. In 1829 there were at least two lead furnaces on the Platte, Hough's and Detandebaratz's ([Thwaites], "Narrative of Morgan L. Martin," Wisconsin Historical *Collections*, XI, map facing p. 400).

[6] Thomas C. Legate (sketch, 1:35, *n.* 3).

ABSTRACT

Post Return

1:292

Fort Crawford,[1] Michigan Territory[2]
October [31,] 1831

Lists Second Lieutenant Jeff. F. Davis, Company B, First Infantry, as absent on special duty. Remarks: "On Det[ached] Service at Dubuques Mines[3] order[4] of Col. Morgan."[5]

Printed form, filled in and signed (NA, RG 94 Records of the Adjutant General's Office, Post Returns, Fort Crawford, 1817–34), 2. Signed: "Wy Morgan Col 1st Inf Com[mandin]g." Endorsed: "Entd Recd. 3 Decr."

[1] See 1:231, *n.* 12.

[2] See 1:149, *n.* 2.

[3] See 1:291, *n.* 2 for Dubuques Mines.

[4] Special Order No. 45 is 1:287.

[5] Willoughby Morgan (sketch, 1:237, *n.* 4).

ABSTRACT

Company Muster Roll

1:293

Fort Crawford,[1] October 31, 1831

Lists Second Lieutenant J. F. Davis of Captain G. C. Spencer's[2] Company B, First Regiment of Infantry commanded by Colonel Willoughby Morgan,[3] as absent "on detached service.[4] By Order Col Morgan dated Oct 11. 1831."[5] Report covers September and October 1831.

Printed form, filled in and signed (NA, RG 94 Records of the Adjutant General's Office, Muster Rolls of Regular Army Organizations, First Infantry, Company B), 2. Signed: "Th P Gwynn Lt 1 Infy Wy Morgan (col 1st Infty." Endorsed: "Proves Recd *Decr. 6th. 1831.* Entered."

1 See 1:231, *n.* 12.

2 George C. Spencer (sketch, 1:193, *n.* 3).

3 Willoughby Morgan (sketch, 1:237, *n.* 4).

4 Davis was at Dubuques Mines (1:291, *n.* 2).

5 See 1:287 for the order of October 11, 1831.

1:294 Willoughby Morgan to the Acting Assistant Adjutant General of the Right Wing Western Department

Head Quarters 1st. Infantry
Fort Crawford[1] Novr. 1st. 1831

SIR[2]

Herewith is a letter[3] from Lt Davis a young Officer in whom I have much confidence. I am apt to think that an attempt will be made to occupy Dubuques Mines[4] in violation of law, or perhaps under those who claim the country including those mines by a Spanish grant. I hope that you will have done me the favour to have pressed for Such an order as the law requires, for though I have the Secretary's[5] order[6] on the subject, yet I shall be loth to use force until the proper authority is given by the President[7] according to the suggestions heretofore made. Very respectfully Your Obdt Servt. (Signed)

WLY MORGAN[8]
Col. 1st. Inf. Commdg

[PS] I have sent Lieut Davis down with a party perhaps his presence may deter from intrusions.[9] (Signed) WLY. MORGAN
Commdg

L, copy (NA, RG 94 Records of the Adjutant General's Office, Letters Received, A–151, 1831). Addressed: "The Actg A[ssistant] A[djutant] Genl. Right Wing West. Dept. Jeffn. Barracks Mo." Endorsed: "Submitted. R[oger] J[ones]. [Received] Dec. 17. 1831." Enclosure: Davis to Morgan, October 31, 1831 (1:291). Enclosed: Atkinson to McCall, November 29, 1831 (1:301), which was in turn enclosed in Atkinson to Jones, November 29, 1831 (NA, RG 94 Records of the Adjutant General's Office, Letters Received, A–151, 1831).

1 See 1:231, *n.* 12.

2 First Lieutenant George A. McCall (sketch, 1:301, *n.* 2) was the acting assistant adjutant general.

3 Davis' letter is 1:291.

4 See 1:291, *n.* 2 for Dubuques Mines.

[5] Lewis Cass (sketch, 1:349, *n.* 5) was secretary of war.

[6] The order is most likely General Order No. 16 of May 5, 1831, from the Adjutant General's Office regarding trespassing by whites on Indian lands, presumably the lead mining region west of the Mississippi where Davis was stationed. The commanding officers of frontier posts were enjoined to see that "unlawful settlers" were removed (NA, RG 94, General Orders [Printed], I, 1825–33).

[7] Andrew Jackson (sketch, 1:239, *n.* 2) was President.

[8] Willoughby Morgan (sketch, 1:237, *n.* 4).

[9] See 1:287 for the order sending Davis to Dubuques Mines.

Order No. 79

1:295

Head Quarters, 1st Infty Fort Crawford,[1]
1st. Novr. 1831

Sergt Welch[2] of "*D*", Privates Bates[3] of "*A*", Hayes[4] of "*B.*", Boman[5] of "*D*", Andrews[6] of "*F*" and Daines[7] of "*G*" Companies are hereby detailed for Detached Service—they will report this afternoon at retreat to Lt. Davis who will proceed to Morrow morning to the position occupied by Mr. Du bois (opposite to Du buques Mines)[8]

The A[cting] A[ssistant] Qr. Mr.[9] will furnish Lt Davis with a Mackinac[10] boat and oars.

The "A[ssistant] C[ommissary] S[ubsistence]"[9] will furnish Lt. Davis with provisions for two months.

Lt. Davis will rent Quarters from Mr. Du bois for himself and party (if they can be obtained upon reasonable terms) by the month.

He will be governed by the instructions both written, and verbal, given him by the Col. By order of Col Morgan[11]

J J Abercrombie[12]
Adjt—1st. Inf

[PS]

Sir.

The Col directs you will take charge of the boat[13] left at Galena by Lt. Burbank[14] and send it to this post by the first opportunity together with any other public property left by him that may not be useful to yourself & party.

J J Abercrombie
Adjt 1 Inf

DS (NA, RG 49 Records of the Bureau of Land Management, Lead Mine Records).

[1] See 1:231, *n.* 12.

[2] William Welsh was enlisted at Cantonment Clinch, Florida, in 1827 for five years. He was from Detroit, aged thirty-four in October 1827, and was listed as a soldier by profession (NA, RG 94, Register of Enlistments, XXXVII).

[3] John Bates, a baker, was twenty years old when he was recruited in 1829 in Philadelphia by Major James M. Glassell. Bates deserted from Fort Crawford in 1832 but was quickly apprehended. He was discharged in 1834 (NA, RG 94, Register of Enlistments, XXXVIII).

[4] Michael Hayes was enlisted August 17, 1829, for five years, by Lieutenant Alexander H. Morton in New York (Muster Roll, October 31, 1831 [NA, RG 94, First Infantry, Company B]).

[5] Edward Bowman, from Vinyard, Vermont, was thirty-one when he enlisted for five years in Whitehall [New York?] in 1830. Recruited by Gustavus Loomis, Bowman was a shoemaker, and was discharged at Fort Crawford in 1832 on a surgeon's certificate (NA, RG 94, Register of Enlistments, XXXVIII).

[6] William Andrews, a hatter, was twenty-five when he enlisted in Philadelphia in 1829; Major James M. Glassell was the recruiting officer. Andrews was to serve five years but evidently deserted in May 1832 and was not apprehended (NA, RG 94, Register of Enlistments, XXXVIII).

[7] Elias K. Daines, from Stockbridge, Vermont, was recruited by Gustavus Loomis in 1830 for five years. Daines was twenty-seven when he enlisted and gave his profession as farmer. He was discharged at Fort Crawford in 1835 (NA, RG 94, Register of Enlistments, XXXVIII).

[8] See 1:291, *n.* 2 for Dubuques Mines.

[9] Major Richard B. Mason (sketch, 1:375, *n.* 8) was serving as acting assistant quartermaster and First Lieutenant James W. Kingsbury (sketch, 1:213, *n.* 2) as assistant commissary of subsistence at Fort Crawford (Post Returns, October, November, 1831 [NA, RG 94, Fort Crawford, 1817–34]).

[10] For mackinac, see 1:214, *n.* 7.

[11] Willoughby Morgan (sketch, 1:237, *n.* 4).

[12] John J. Abercrombie (sketch, 1:283, *n.* 4).

[13] See 1:287 for evidence of the fact that the boat formerly in Burbank's charge had not been sent to Fort Crawford.

[14] Sidney Burbank (sketch, 1:195, *n.* 6).

1:296

From John J. Abercrombie

Head Quarters, 1st. Infty.
Fort Crawford,[1] Novr. 2d. 1831

SIR

Col. Morgan[2] directs you will in addition to the duties assigned you perform those of Actg. "A[ssistant] C[ommissary] S[ubsistence]" to the Detachment under your command.[3] Respectfully Your obt. Servt.

J J ABERCROMBIE.[4]
Adjt. 1 Inf

ALS (NA, RG 49 Records of the Bureau of Land Management, Lead Mine Records). Addressed: "Lieut. Jeff. F. Davis Comdg. Det. 1st Infty. Dubuques Mines."

[1] For Fort Crawford, see 1:231, *n.* 12.

[2] Willoughby Morgan (sketch, 1:237, *n.* 4).

[3] See 1:287 for the order sending Davis to the Dubuques Mines. See also 1:291, *n.* 2 for the reasons he was assigned there.

[4] John J. Abercrombie (sketch, 1:283, *n.* 4).

To the Third Auditor 1:297

Galena Ill.[1] Nov 6th 1831

SIR[2]

I have just received your letter of Aug 2nd 1831 accompanying a statement of differences[3] arising on the settlement of my accts. for the 1st Quarter of 1831

In the beginning of that statement I notice a misnomer, by referring to my a/cts. Current it will be seen that it is to the new Barracks appropriation I acknowledge a debt of 251.00 Dollars and that my claim is on the Qr. master's Dept. not the reverse as stated.

The two oxen you require me to sell and which were reported "expended" were a part of the public property returned sold in the Quarter, without them the bill of sale would have been but of *five oxen*

There was no auctioncer at Fort Winebago[4] at the sale above alluded to, I officiated as such myself, I enclose the duplicate bill of sale retained in my possession, if an *Auctioneer's* bill is required I have only to say it is not in my power to furnish it.[5] Vy. Respctfly. yr. mo. obt. Scvt.

J. F. DAVIS

(ex A[cting] A[ssistant] Q. M.) L[ieutenant] 1. Inf

ALS (NA, RG 217 Records of the United States General Accounting Office, Third Auditor's Office, Third Auditor's Accounts, Account 11,688). Addressed: "To the 3rd Auditor U. S. Tresy." Endorsed: "Referred to the 3d. Auditor. Q. M. Gen office, Decr. 6. 1831."; in a different hand, "Recvd 6th"; in a third hand, "Recd Decr. 5th. 1831." Enclosure missing.

[1] Near Dubuques Mines where Davis was stationed (see 1:291, *n.* 2 and 1:231, *n.* 18).

[2] Peter Hagner was the third auditor (sketch, 1:199, *n.* 5).

[3] The Hagner letter of August 2 is 1:273; the "statement of differences" has not been found.

[4] See 1:144, *n.* 1 for Fort Winnebago, the post Davis left in June 1831 (1:268).

[5] Davis refers here to paragraph 1002 of the regulations which requires that the autioneer's bill from a sale of government property be sent, along with a duplicate of the board of survey report, to the quartermaster general (*General Army Regulations* [1825], 219).

1:298

To Thomas S. Jesup

SIR Du Buque's mines[1] near Galena Ill.[2] Nov 6th 1831

In the first Quarter of the current year I sold at public sale condemned property belonging to the Qr. Master's Dept. for 192.00 Dollars and appropriated the money to the payment of claims on the Dept. not finding a suitable person to bid off the property I done so myself. The 3rd Auditor[3] now requires of me a certificate from the Bank in which the nett proceeds of the sale were deposited, and the auctioneers bill of the sale—as there was neither Bank nor auctioneer in the country the Auditor's decision seems to be founded on an illiberal construction of the Reg. of the Department[4] I have therefore taken the liberty to address to you this communication and to request <—you request—> your attention to the subject matter of it.[5] I have the honor to be yr. mo. obt. Servt. J. F. DAVIS

L[ieutenant] 1. Inf. & formerly A[cting] A[ssistant] Q. M. at Fort Winebago[6]

[AE] Dcr. 7th 1831

Respectfully referred to the 3d Auditor—a certified statement, would, it is believed, be a sufficient substitute for the usual acct of sales, under the circumstances of the case—and with respect to the deposite of the proceeds, this, it is believed, is dispensed with by the Comptroller's last instructions on that subject which authorized the application of the proceeds of property purchased within the next preceding two years, to the currant service.

Q M GENERAL'S[7] OFFICE

ALS (NA, RG 217 Records of the United States General Accounting Office, Third Auditor's Office, Third Auditor's Accounts, Account 11,688). Addressed: "To Maj. Genl. T. S. Jesup Q. M. Genl. U. S. Army Washington D. C." Endorsed: "Recd Decr. 5th. 1831."; in a different hand, "Recd 7th Decr 1831."

1 For Dubuques Mines, see 1:291, *n.* 2.

2 For Galena, see 1:231, *n.* 18.

3 The third auditor was Peter Hagner (sketch, 1:199, *n.* 5). His cover letter to Davis is 1:273; Davis' reply is 1:297.

4 For regulations concerning the bank certificate and the auctioneer's bill of sale, see paragraphs 1000 and 1002, *General Army Regulations* (1825), 218–19. See also 1:297, *n.* 5.

5 See 1:304 for the reply of Trueman Cross.

6 See 1:144, *n.* 1 for Fort Winnebago.

7 Thomas S. Jesup (sketch, 1:174, *n.* 4).

From William B. Lewis 1:299

SIR, 7 November 1831

Your account for Bounties and premiums has been closed[1] on the Books of this office by the receipt of Lieut. J. J. *Abercrombie*[2] for $34.00 paid over to him the 19 Septr. last.[3] W. B. L.[4]

(P. S.) An A/Current ought to have been prepared and forwarded by you.[5]

LbC (NA, RG 217 Records of the United States General Accounting Office, Second Auditor's Office, Letters Sent, XVI, 144). Addressed: "Lieut. J. F. Davis, 1 Inf. Prairie du Chien."

[1] See 1:290 for notice of the closing of Davis' account as acting assistant quartermaster.

[2] John J. Abercrombie (sketch, 1:283, *n.* 4).

[3] Davis transmitted Abercrombie's receipt in 1:283, after the second auditor had agreed with Davis' statement of the account (1:263).

[4] William B. Lewis (sketch, 1:166, *n.* 1).

[5] Whether Davis forwarded an account current as here requested is unknown.

ABSTRACT

Register of Payments to Officers 1:300

[Washington, D.C.,] November 20, 1831

Lists payment by Paymaster A. Phillips[1] to Second Lieutenant Jefferson Davis, First Infantry, $127. Amount includes pay and allowance for Davis and one servant,[2] for July and August.

D (NA, RG 99 Records of the Office of the Paymaster General, Register of Payments to Officers, IV, 27), 1.

[1] Asher Phillips, a native of Ohio, enlisted in the army as an ensign in 1812. He remained in the Third Infantry at the close of the war, and was commissioned a first lieutenant in 1816 and paymaster in 1821, to rank from 1815. In 1831 he was major and paymaster at Detroit. He resigned three years later, and died in 1843 (Heitman, *Historical Register*, I, 788; Edwards, "A Western Reminiscence," Wisconsin Historical *Collections*, V, 158; *Senate Executive Journal*, III, 524, 530, IV, 96, 106).

[2] James Pemberton (sketch, 1:5, *n.* 4) was probably the servant.

EXTRACT

1:301 ## Henry Atkinson to George A. McCall

Head Qur. right wing West. dept.
Jefferson Barracks,[1] [Missouri,] Nov. 29th. 1831

SIR,[2]

I have the honor to enclose herewith, for the information of Major General Gaines,[3] a copy of a letter from Col. Morgan,[4] of the . . . 1st. inst. relative to a supposed intention of some of our Citizens to force an intrusion on the mineral land near Du Buques Mines.[5] Also a copy of a letter from Lt. Davis to Col. Morgan on the same subject.[6] . . .

In reference to the supposition of Lt. Davis & Col. Morgan that an unlawful, or rather a forcable attempt will be made by some of our citizens to procure lead mineral from the lands about the De Buques mines, I can hardly think such a course will be adopted. Yet such may be the result. With great respect Sir. Your Mo. ob. [Sert?] (Signed)

H. ATKINSON[7]
Br. Gn. u. S. Army

L, copy (NA, RG 94 Records of the Adjutant General's Office, Letters Received, A–151, 1831), 4. Addressed: "To Lt. Mc. Call act. asst. adjt. Genl. West. dept. Jeff. Barracks." Endorsed: "(Copy) [Received] 17. Decr. 1831." Enclosures: Davis to Morgan, October 31, 1831 (1:291); Morgan to Acting Assistant Adjutant General Right Wing Western Department, November 1, 1831 (1:294). Enclosed: Atkinson to Jones, November 29, 1831 (NA, RG 94 Records of the Adjutant General's Office, Letters Received, A–151, 1831).

1 See 1:123, *n.* 3 for Jefferson Barracks.

2 George Archibald McCall, a Pennsylvanian born in 1802, was graduated from West Point in 1822. He served in various garrisons, and was aide-de-camp to General Edmund P. Gaines, 1831–36. After duty in the Florida, Texas, and Mexican wars, he was twice brevetted for gallantry in 1846, and served as General Robert Patterson's chief of staff, 1846–47. Appointed inspector general and promoted to colonel in 1850, he resigned in 1853, but commanded the Pennsylvania Volunteers from 1861 to 1862, when he was captured and briefly imprisoned at Richmond. He retired from the service in 1863 and died five years later on his farm in Pennsylvania (Heitman, *Historical Register*, I, 653; Cullum, *Biographical Register*, I, 293–94; Warner, *Generals in Blue*, 289–90).

3 Edmund Pendleton Gaines (1777–1849) was born in Virginia, the son of a Revolutionary War soldier. The family moved to Tennessee in 1789, and Gaines entered the army as an ensign in 1797. He saw active service in the War of 1812, was seriously wounded at Fort Erie where he was adjutant general, and was promoted to brigadier general and brevetted major general in 1814. Gaines served with Andrew Jackson in the 1817–19 Seminole War, and alternated command of the Western and Eastern departments with

Winfield Scott, 1821–31. After engagements in the Black Hawk and Seminole wars, Gaines's and Scott's failures in the latter war were investigated by a court of inquiry; both were cleared, although criticized. The two men were never friends, and during the inquiry were openly hostile. Gaines participated in the war for Texas independence and submitted several reports on the defense of the western frontier to the War Department (1838–46). At the outbreak of the Mexican War, Gaines illegally called up volunteers, was censured by the secretary of war, and was called before another court of inquiry in the summer of 1846. Although he was found guilty of transcending his authority, it was recommended that no disciplinary action be taken. He asked to serve in the war, but Scott was sent to lead the Vera Cruz expedition. Gaines died of cholera in New Orleans (Silver, *Gaines*; *DAB*). Davis served as Henry Dodge's adjutant under the command of Gaines in 1833, and was praised by Gaines in 1845 as "An incomparable adjutant, and the most fearless and dashing young soldier of his day" (V. Davis, *Memoir*, I, 202).

[4] Willoughby Morgan (sketch, 1:237, *n.* 4).

[5] See 1:291, *n.* 2 for a sketch of Dubuques Mines.

[6] See 1:291 for Davis' letter to Morgan advising him of his fear that intruders would enter the lead mining region; see 1:294 for Morgan's letter expressing the same fears.

[7] Henry Atkinson (1782–1842), a North Carolinian, entered the army in 1808 and after the War of 1812 retained the rank of colonel. In 1819 Atkinson was ordered by Secretary of War John C. Calhoun to command the Missouri Expedition, the purpose of which was to establish military posts on the Missouri River for defense against Indians and to wrest the Northwest from British traders' influence. After having successfully established Cantonment Missouri (above Omaha), Atkinson returned to St. Louis and his command of the Ninth Military Department, being promoted to brigadier general in 1820. Atkinson declined appointment as adjutant general with the rank of colonel in the army reorganization of 1821, and was appointed colonel of the Sixth Infantry and commander of the Right Wing of the Western Department. Atkinson led the Yellowstone Expedition of 1825 to treat with Indians on the northern plains, and in 1826 supervised the construction of Jefferson Barracks, becoming first commander of the infantry school there. He conducted several campaigns against the Indian tribes of the Northwest, 1826–32, and in 1832 commanded the expeditions against Black Hawk. The last ten years of his life were spent mainly at Jefferson Barracks in administrative tasks and attempts to prevent Indian wars (*DAB*; Nichols, *Atkinson*; Heitman, *Historical Register*, I, 174).

ABSTRACT

Post Return

1:302

Fort Crawford,[1] Michigan Territory[2]
November [30,] 1831

Lists Second Lieutenant Jeff. F. Davis, Company B, First Infantry, as absent on special duty. Remarks: "At Dubuques Mines,[3] order of Col. Morgan[4] 1st. Nov. 1831." [5]

Printed form, filled in and signed (NA, RG 94 Records of the Adjutant General's Office, Post Returns, Fort Crawford, 1817–34), 2. Signed: "G. Loomis Capt Inf." Endorsed: "Recd. 21st. May."

1 See 1:231, *n.* 12.
2 See 1:149, *n.* 2.
3 See 1:291, *n.* 2.
4 Willoughby Morgan (sketch, 1:237, *n.* 4).
5 See 1:287 for the order sending Davis to Dubuques Mines.

1:303

To George Gibson

Du Buque's mines[1]—near Galena Ill[2] Dec. 2nd 1831

SIR[3]

Herewith I have the honor to transmit a return of Provisions received and issued to the Detachment of the 1st U. S. Infantry Stationed at this place during the month of November 1831. Very Respctfly. yr. mo. obt. Servt. J. F. DAVIS

L[ieutenant] 1. Inf. ac[ting] Asst. Com. Sub.

ALS (NA, RG 192 Records of the Office of the Commissary General of Subsistence, Letters Received, D–1104, 1831). Addressed: "To Genl. Geo. Gibson Com[missary] Genl. U. S. Army." Endorsed: "Recd. 3 Jany."

Enclosure missing.

1 See 1:291, *n.* 2.
2 See 1:231, *n.* 18.
3 George Gibson (sketch, 1:179, *n.* 2).

1:304

From Trueman Cross

SIR: December 7th 1831

Your letter of the 6th. Ultimo[1] has been received at this office, and referred to the 3rd. Auditor[2] of the Treasury, with the suggestion, that a certified statement from you, should, under the circumstances of the case, be a sufficient substitute for the usual account of sales, and that the last instructions of the Comptroller,[3] on the subject of depositing the proceeds of the sales of public property, dispensed, it was believed with that formality in your case, as the property sold, was, in all probability, purchased within the two years preceeding the sale.[4] (Signed) T CROSS[5]

Major & Actg Qr Mr Genl.

LbC (NA, RG 92 Records of the Office of the Quartermaster General, Letters Sent, XVI, 320). Addressed: "Lt. J. F. Davis 1st. Infantry, Galena, Illinois."

[1] Davis' letter of November 6 is printed as 1:298.

[2] Peter Hagner was the third auditor (sketch, 1:199, *n.* 5).

[3] James B. Thornton (sketch, 1:244, *n.* 1) was the second comptroller.

[4] See 1:297 for previous mention of Davis' sale of property.

[5] Trueman Cross, born in Maryland, was an ensign in the army in 1814 and became a regimental quartermaster in 1816. He was promoted to captain, was assistant deputy quartermaster general and assistant inspector general, then was promoted to major and quartermaster in 1826. Cross was colonel and assistant to Thomas S. Jesup, quartermaster general, from 1838 until his murder by Mexican bandits in 1846 (Heitman, *Historical Register*, I, 341; Risch, *Quartermaster Support of the Army*, 182–246 *passim*; *Appleton's*).

To Thomas S. Jesup 1:305

Near Galena Du Buque's mines[1] Ill. Dec 12th 1831

SIR[2]

I have the honor to acknowledge the receipt of your letter of Oct. 8th. 1831.[3] The money which I acknowledged to be due New Barracks appropiation for Fort Winebago[4] in my acct. Current for 1st Quarter of 1831 [5] was delivered to the officer who relieved me Lt. Hooe.[6]

For reasons which I have once stated and with which I will not again trouble you my papers were brought to me at Fort Crawford and forwarded from that place.[7] Lt. Hooe's receipt had been lost I sent the return for the 2nd Quarter New Barracks to that officer at Fort Winebago, requesting him to add his receipt and forward the whole to your office supposing it would arrive near the same time as the Return for Q. M. Dept.[8] Very Respctfully yr. mo. obt. Servt.

J. F. DAVIS
L[ieutenant] 1. Inf.

ALS (NA, RG 92 Records of the Office of the Quartermaster General, Consolidated Correspondence File, Lead Mines, D–22, 1832). Addressed: "To Genl. Jesup Q. M. Genl. U. S. A. Washington D. C." Endorsed: "Recd Jany 23d 1832."

[1] See 1:291, *n.* 2 and 1:231, *n.* 18.

[2] Thomas S. Jesup (sketch, 1:174, *n.* 4).

[3] Jesup's letter of October 8 is printed as 1:285.

[4] See 1:144, *n.* 1 for Fort Winnebago.

[5] Davis' account current for the first quarter of 1831 was transmitted in 1:247.

[6] Alexander S. Hooe (sketch, 1:233, *n.* 3).

[7] Davis' reasons for delay are ex-

plained in 1:279, 280.

[8] Davis' letter to Hooe and the mentioned receipt and return have not been found.

1:306

From Peter Hagner

SIR, December 13. 1831

A supplementary statement of your a/c as late a[cting] a[ssistant] qm,[1] has been made and reported to the 2d Comptroller[2] for his decision thereon—by whom it has been returned, exhibiting a balance due from you of $11 15/100. For particulars you are referred to the inclosed sheet. Respectfully Your obt. St. PETER HAGNER[3]
Audr

LbC (NA, RG 217 Records of the United States General Accounting Office, Third Auditor's Office, Miscellaneous Letters Sent, LVIII, 141). Addressed: "Lt J. F. Davis (late a[cting] a[ssistant] q m) now at Fort Crawford Prairie du Chien." Enclosure missing.

[1] Davis transmitted his account current for the second quarter of 1831—the last quarter for which he served as acting assistant quartermaster at Fort Winnebago—on September 5. The letter of transmittal is printed as 1:279.

[2] James B. Thornton was the second comptroller (sketch, 1:244, *n.* 1).

[3] Peter Hagner (sketch, 1:199, *n.* 5).

1:307

To Peter Hagner

Du Buque's Mines near Galena[1] Ill. Dec 22nd 1831

SIR[2]

I have the honor to acknowledge the receipt of your communication of Oct. 15th 1831.[3]

I have taken those measures which will probably soonest possess you of the Muster Rolls (countersigned) which were returned from your office. By reference to my Quarterly returns (new Barracks and Q. M. Dept.) for the 1st Quarter of 1831 [4] (I think) you will find "what disposition was made" of six paint-brushes two Iron-wedges and one Spade invoiced by Maj. Whiting[5] and Capt. Harney.[6] You have probably received *through the Q. M. Genl's.*[7] *office* the returns of new Barracks appropriation (Fort Winebago)[8] for the 2nd Quarter of the present year.[9] Not having been charged with the money received ($192) by sale of condemned property,[10] I will place that amount in the first office of Deposit I can reach, though I cannot give you any assurance that your caution against "unnecessary delay" will expedite the event. Very Respctfly. yr. mo. obt. servt.

J. F. DAVIS
L[ieutenant] 1. Inf.

ALS (NA, RG 217 Records of the United States General Accounting Office, Third Auditor's Office, Third Auditor's Accounts, Account 11,688). Addressed: "To P. Hagnor Esq. 3rd Auditor U. S. Trsy." Endorsed: "Recd 23 Jany 32. Ansd"; in a different hand, "Same Day."

1 See 1:291, *n.* 2 and 1:231, *n.* 18.

2 Peter Hagner (sketch, 1:199, *n.* 5).

3 Hagner's letter of October 15 is printed as 1:288.

4 See 1:247 for Davis' letter transmitting his quarterly returns for the first quarter of 1831.

5 Henry Whiting (sketch, 1:208, *n.* 2).

6 William Selby Harney (sketch, 1:264, *n.* 10).

7 The quartermaster general was Thomas S. Jesup (sketch, 1:174, *n.* 4).

8 For Fort Winnebago, see 1:144, *n.* 1.

9 Davis' cover letter for the return of the new barracks appropriation, second quarter, was transmitted on September 6, 1831, and is printed as 1:280.

10 See 1:297, 298, 304 for reference to the sale of condemned property.

ABSTRACT

Semiannual Company Muster Roll 1:308

Fort Crawford,[1] [Michigan Territory][2]
December 31, 1831

Lists Second Lieutenant J. F. Davis of Captain G. C. Spencer's[3] Company B, First Regiment of Infantry commanded by Colonel Willoughby Morgan,[4] as absent "On detached Service by Order col Morgan dated Novr. 1st. 1831."[5] Report covers July through December 1831.

Printed form, filled in and signed (NA, RG 94 Records of the Adjutant General's Office, Muster Rolls of Regular Army Organizations, First Infantry, Company B), 2. Signed: "Th P Gwynn Lt 1 Infty Wy Morgan Col 1st Infty Com[mandin]g." Endorsed: "Proves Recd. Janry. 28. 1832. Entered."

1 See 1:231, *n.* 12.

2 See 1:149, *n.* 2.

3 George C. Spencer (sketch, 1:193, *n.* 3).

4 Willoughby Morgan (sketch, 1:237, *n.* 4).

5 Morgan's order of November 1 is 1:295.

ABSTRACT

1:309

Register of Pay Stoppages

[Washington, D.C.,] January 3, 1832

The paymaster general[1] reports a stoppage in the pay of Second Lieutenant J. F. Davis in the amount of $252.[2]

D (NA, RG 99 Records of the Office of the Paymaster General, Register of Pay Stoppages, I, 17), 1.

[1] Nathan Towson was the paymaster general.

[2] Because of this stoppage, and one of January 23, 1832 (1:314), Davis returned $324 to the government on March 31, 1832 (1:323), which cleared his pay account (1:326).

1:310

From George Gibson

SIR, 6 January 1832

Your return for November[1] has been examined in this office and an error found of six pounds of pork, in substracting total issued from quantity to be accounted for, on hand 1 bbl. 65 lbs. in place of 1 bbl. 59 lbs.

Make the correction in your next return after you receive this.

G. G.[2]

LbC (NA, RG 192 Records of the Office of the Commissary General of Subsistence, Letters Sent, VIII, 449). Addressed: "Lt. J. F. Davis a[cting] a[ssistant] c[ommissary] s[ubsistence] Dubuques Mines."

[1] Davis' November return was transmitted in 1:303.

[2] George Gibson was the commissary general (sketch, 1:179, *n.* 2).

1:311

Special Order No. 3

Head Qrs 1 Inf Fort Crawford[1] Jany 7th 1832

Private Benjn. Sutterel[2] of B Company 1st Inf will proceed with Lieut Davis to the position occupied by him near Debuques Mines[3] & remain in place of Privt Hays[4] of the same Compy who will be Ordered to return with the train[5] (employed to transport Subsistence

Stores to that place) and report to the Officer in Command of his Company[6] for duty. By Order of Col Morgan[7]

J J ABERCROMBIE[8]
Adjt 1 Inf

DS (NA, RG 49 Records of the Bureau of Land Management, Lead Mine Records).

[1] See 1:231, *n.* 12.

[2] Benjamin Suttrull was enlisted for a five-year term November 15, 1827, at Jefferson Barracks by Lieutenant Thomas Barber. He was discharged at the end of his enlistment (Muster Roll, December 31, 1832 [NA, RG 94, First Infantry, Company B]).

[3] See 1:291, *n.* 2.

[4] Michael Hayes (sketch, 1:295, *n.* 4) was ordered to Dubuques Mines November 1 (1:295).

[5] Presumably the reference is to a mule or wagon train.

[6] George C. Spencer (sketch, 1:193, *n.* 3) was the commander of B Company, although he was on furlough. Thomas P. Gwynn (sketch, 1:148, *n.* 1), the company's first lieutenant, was listed as present for duty (Post Return, January 1832 [NA, RG 94, Fort Crawford, 1817–34]).

[7] Willoughby Morgan (sketch, 1:237, *n.* 4).

[8] John J. Abercrombie (sketch, 1:283, *n.* 4).

To George Gibson 1:312

Du Buques mines[1] Jany 8th 1832

SIR[2]

Herewith I have the honor to enclose my returns as A[cting] A[ssistant] Com[missary] Subsistence for the Quarter ending 31st December 1831. Very respectfully yr. mo. obt. servt. J. F. DAVIS
L[ieutenant] 1. Inf. a. a. C. S.

ALS (NA, RG 192 Records of the Office of the Commissary General of Subsistence, Letters Received, D–1118, 1832). Addressed: "To Genl. Geo. Gibson Com[missary] Genl. U. S. A. Washington D. C." Endorsed: "Recd. 7 March." Enclosures missing.

[1] See 1:291, *n.* 2.

[2] George Gibson (sketch, 1:179, *n.* 2).

Special Order No. 1 1:313

Asst. Adjt. Genls. Office, West. Dept.
Memphis, Ten. 15th. January, 1832

A furlough for Sixty days, with permission to apply for an extension of four additional months,[1] is hereby granted to 2nd. Lieut. Jef. Davis of the 1st. Infantry, to take effect the day he leaves his post.[2]

At the expiration of his furlough Lieut. Davis will join his Company.[3] By order of Major General Gaines[4]

GEO. A. MCCALL[5]

A[ide-] D[e-] C[amp]–actg. Asst. Adj. Genl.

LbCS (NA, RG 94 Records of the Adjutant General's Office, Western Department Orders, CCLXXI, 573); DS (NA, RG 393 Records of United States Army Continental Commands, 1821–1920, Orders and Special Orders Received from the Adjutant General's Office, Headquarters Western Department, Order Book VII, 227–28). Endorsed: "(Recd. Febry. 8th. 1832.)"

[1] See 1:327 for Davis' request for a four-month extension and 1:329 for the order granting the request.

[2] Davis left on furlough March 26, 1832 (1:317, 325); see V. Davis, *Memoir*, I, 91, for Davis' statement that he requested a furlough to attend to "private matters" in Mississippi.

[3] On August 18, 1832, Davis rejoined his company (1:332).

[4] Edmund P. Gaines (sketch, 1:301, *n.* 3).

[5] George A. McCall (sketch, 1:301, *n.* 2).

ABSTRACT

1:314

Register of Pay Stoppages

[Washington, D.C.,] January 23, 1832

The paymaster general[1] reports a stoppage in the pay of Second Lieutenant J. F. Davis in the amount of $72.[2]

D (NA, RG 99 Records of the Office of the Paymaster General, Register of Pay Stoppages, I, 17), 1.

[1] The paymaster general was Nathan Towson.

[2] Because of this stoppage and an earlier one of January 3, 1832 (1:309), Davis reimbursed the government $324 on March 31, 1832 (1:323) and cleared his pay account (1:326).

1:315

From Peter Hagner

SIR, Jany. 23d. 1832

I have received your letter of the 22d ultimo,[1] and in reply have to state, that your return of property for 2d quarter of 1831,[2] belonging to the Fort Winnebago[3] Barrack <—account—> appropriation, was duly received through the office of the Q. M. Genl.[4]

The wedges and Spade alluded to by you, are found to have been accounted for in the returns of your property account for the 1. quarter of 1831.[5]

In relation to the $192 proceeds of public property sold,[6] and which you were requested to deposit &c &c I have to state, that in a settlement made of your account on the 13th ultimo,[7] the *$192* in question, was brought to *your debit* (leaving a balance on that Settlement due from you of $11.15 as mentioned in my letter to your address of that date)

This course was adopted in consequence of its being ascertained that you had ceased to act in the q m Dept[8] and that you had turned over to your successor[9] at Fort Winnebago[3] the balance of public moneys in your hands belonging to the quarter Masters Department and Barrack account.

Consequently the necessity for making the deposite is obviated.

Your property a/c as late, a[cting] a[ssistant] qm at Fort Winnebago is closed Respectfully Your obt St PETER HAGNER[10]
Aud.

LbC (NA, RG 217 Records of the United States General Accounting Office, Third Auditor's Office, Miscellaneous Letters Sent, LVIII, 332). Addressed: "Lieut J. F. Davis Du Buques Mines near Gallena Illinois."

[1] Davis' letter of December 22 is printed as 1:307.

[2] The property accounts for the second quarter of 1831 were transmitted in 1:280.

[3] See 1:144, *n.* 1.

[4] Thomas S. Jesup (sketch, 1:174, *n.* 4) was quartermaster general.

[5] Davis' property accounts for the first quarter of 1831 were transmitted to the quartermaster general in 1:247.

[6] The sale of public property, proceeds of which were $192, took place in the first quarter (see 1:297).

[7] Hagner's letter of December 13 is printed as 1:306.

[8] Davis left Fort Winnebago June 24 (1:268).

[9] Alexander S. Hooe (sketch, 1:233, *n.* 3) was Davis' successor as acting assistant quartermaster at Fort Winnebago (1:305).

[10] Peter Hagner (sketch, 1:199, *n.* 5).

To George Gibson 1:316

Du Buque's Mines[1] Feby. 4th 1832

SIR[2]

Herewith I have the honor to transmit a monthly return of Subsistence stores received and issued at this post during the month of January 1832 Very Respectfully yr. mo. obt. Servt.

J. F. Davis
L[ieutenant] 1. Inf.
A[cting] A[ssistant] C[ommissary] S[ubsistence]

ALS (NA, RG 192 Records of the Office of the Commissary General of Subsistence, Letters Received, D-1120, 1832). Addressed: "To Genl G. Gibson Com[missary] Genl. U. S. A." Endorsed: "Recd. 17 March." Enclosure missing.

[1] See 1:291, *n*. 2.

[2] George Gibson (sketch, 1:179, *n*. 2).

1:317 Order No. 65[1]

Head Quarters 1st Inf
Fort Crawford[2] March 26th 1832

Lt Davis <—havig—> having obtained a furlough[3] is hereby relieved from duty at Dubuques Mines[4] he will turn over to Lt Gardenier[5] (by whom he will be relieved) such instructions as may have been recievd from Time to time from Col Morgan.[6]

Lt Gardenier will proceed forth with to the position occupied by Lt Davis, assume command of the Detacht at that place & act under the instructions turned over by Lt Davis

Three men will be detailed immediately to accompany Lt Gardenier who will compose a part of his command & be reported on detach'd service

The A[ssistant] C[ommissary] Sub[sistence][7] will furnish the Detacht consisting of one N. C. off & five privats with provisions for two months

Lt Gardenier will act as Asst Comy of Sube to his command By order of Col Morgan Signed

J J Abercombie[8]
adjt 1st If

D, copy (NA, RG 49 Records of the Bureau of Land Management, Lead Mine Records). Endorsed: "(A true Copy) J Randolph B Gardenier Lt 1st U. S. Inf."

[1] The order number is nearly illegible and may be 85.

[2] See 1:231, *n*. 12.

[3] See 1:313 for Special Order No. 1 granting Davis a sixty-day furlough. Davis left his post on March 26 (1:325).

[4] Davis was sent to Dubuques Mines by Special Order No. 45 (1:287). See 1:291, *n*. 2 for a description of the lead

mining area.

[5] John R. B. Gardenier (sketch, 1:102, *n.* 8).

[6] Willoughby Morgan (sketch, 1:237, *n.* 4).

[7] James W. Kingsbury (sketch, 1:213, *n.* 2), assistant commissary of subsistence at Fort Crawford, is listed as being on leave March 26, but returned to his duties by April 30 (Post Returns, March, April, 1832 [NA, RG 94, Fort Crawford, 1817–34]).

[8] John J. Abercrombie (sketch, 1:283, *n.* 4).

From William B. Lewis

1:318

SIR March 28, 1832

Your letter of 19th. January last,[1] enclosing the receipt of Major Twiggs[2] and deposition of B. Suttrull,[3] has been received and referred to the Q. M. General.[4] You are relieved from the charges raised against you for the Tents, and the following remarks present themselves in relation to lost property. ("Remarks Noted.")

You therefore stand charged with $21.04 as before informed, per my letter of 22d. October last, for which you are requested to forward the Paymaster's receipt, or otherwise settle to the satisfaction of the Q. M. General.[5] W. B. L.[6]

LbC (NA, RG 217 Records of the United States General Accounting Office, Second Auditor's Office, Letters Sent, Property Division, Volume F, 148). Addressed: "Lt. J. F. Davis U. S. A. Galena."

[1] Davis' letter of January 19 and its enclosures have not been found.

[2] David E. Twiggs (sketch, 1:149, *n.* 4).

[3] Benjamin Suttrull (sketch, 1:311, *n.* 2).

[4] The quartermaster general was Thomas S. Jesup (sketch, 1:174, *n.* 4).

[5] See 1:289 for Lewis' letter of October 22 for further information as to the charges raised against Davis.

[6] William B. Lewis (sketch, 1:166, *n.* 1).

From Peter Hagner

1:319

SIR, March 29th 1832

I have received under cover of a letter[1] from Lieut Col D. E. Twiggs[2] at New York two muster Rolls of men on extra duty at Fort Winnebago[3] for the months of May and June 1831—on the adjustment of your account for the 2d quarter of 1831,[4] as late a[cting] a[ssistant] qm[5] at Fort Winnebago, in October last, three items in Vo 3. B. amounting to $26 10/100, being payments to John Simmonds,[6] James Carouso[7] and T. Michaels,[8] for extra duty in May and June 1831, were suspended, in consequence of the Muster Rolls for those months not being countersigned by the Commanding Officer,[9] as required by the regulations[10]—the requisition being now complied with, a supplementary statement[11] of your account for the 2d qr of 1831, has been made for the purpose of bringing to your credit the above Stated sum of $26 10/100, and reported to the Second Comptroller[12] for his decision thereon, by whom it has been returned to this office, exhibiting a balance due you on account of qm Dpt of $14.95, which will be carried to your credit on account of Subsistence, under which head of appropriation you <are>[13] charged with $15.23, per settlmt. of the 3d June last, leaving an aggregate balance due from you of 28/100.[14] Respectfully Your obt. Servt

PETER HAGNER[15]
Aud.

Note

Settt. of 3 June 1831,[16] due <—you—> U S. on a/c Subs.	$15.23
Settt. of 13. Decr. '31[17] due u. S. on a/c qm Dpt	11.15
	$26.38
Credit items now admitted	$26.10
Due U. S	28/100.

LbC (NA, RG 217 Records of the United States General Accounting Office, Third Auditor's Office, Miscellaneous Letters Sent, LIX, 231–32). Addressed: "Lt. J. F. Davis 1st. Infantry Dubuques Mines via Fort Crawford, Prairie du Chien."

1 The letter and its enclosures have not been found.

2 David E. Twiggs (sketch, 1:149, *n.* 4).

3 For Fort Winnebago, see 1:144, *n.* 1.

4 Davis' account for the second quarter of 1831 was transmitted to the quartermaster general in 1:279. Receipt of Davis' accounts by Jesup was acknowledged in 1:285.

5 Davis left Fort Winnebago June 24 (1:268).

6 Most likely John Simmons, private in Company C, who was recruited at Baton Rouge by Captain Thomas Barker in 1826 for five years. Born in Pennsylvania, Simmons was twenty-seven in 1826 and listed his trade as blacksmith (NA, RG 94, Register of Enlistments, XXXVII).

7 James Carouse, a private in Company C, was enlisted for five years in 1829 in Philadelphia by Second Lieutenant William L. Harris (Muster Roll, February 28, 1831 [NA, RG 94, First Infantry, Company C]).

8 Theophilus B. Michaels, a private in Company K, was born in Pennsylvania, and in 1830, when he enlisted, was twenty-nine years old. He was recruited and re-enlisted at the end of the five-year term (NA, RG 94, Register of Enlistments, XXXVIII).

[9] See 1:279 for Davis' reasons for having failed to get Twiggs's signature, and see 1:307 for indication of Davis' efforts to obtain that signature.

[10] Paragraph 875 and article of war 19 of the regulations are undoubtedly referred to (*General Army Regulations* [1825], 165, 411).

[11] The supplementary statement has not been found.

[12] James B. Thornton was second comptroller (sketch, 1:244, *n.* 1).

[13] Interlined.

[14] Davis evidently did not receive this letter until another copy was sent him under cover of a letter from Hagner dated March 1, 1833 (1:348).

[15] Peter Hagner (sketch, 1:199, *n.* 5).

[16] The settlement of June 3, 1831, was transmitted in 1:266.

[17] The settlement of December 13, 1831, was transmitted in 1:306.

ABSTRACT

Pay Voucher 1:320

Fort Crawford,[1] March 31, 1832

Second Lieutenant J. Davis, First Infantry, acknowledges that he has received $638.82 from Paymaster Thomas Wright.[2] Amount includes pay, and allowance for one servant,[3] for September 1831 through March 1832, and additional pay for duty as acting assistant commissary of subsistence. The servant is described as "James a Slave. Black." Remarks: "Acting Ass[istan]t Commissary of Subsistence to more than three Companies from the 1 Oct 1830 to the 30 June 1831 and to a Detachment from the 5 Nov 1831 to the 25 March 1832."[4]

Printed form, filled in and signed (NA, RG 217 Records of the United States General Accounting Office, Paymasters' Accounts, Wright 16,484, Voucher 1), 3. Signed: "J. F. Davis L[ieutenant] 1. Infantry."

[1] See 1:231, *n.* 12.

[2] Thomas Wright, paymaster at St. Louis, was a Pennsylvanian who enlisted in the army in 1812, and became a regimental paymaster for the Eighth Infantry in 1815. He was retained in the army reorganization of 1821 as major and paymaster, and was paymaster at Pensacola, 1821–31. He died in 1834 (Heitman, *Historical Register*, I, 1063; Gordon, *Compilation of Registers of the Army, passim*).

[3] James Pemberton (sketch, 1:5, *n.* 4).

[4] Davis served as acting assistant commissary of subsistence for three companies at Fort Winnebago from May 1, 1830 (1:175), and not from October 1, 1830, as would appear from the remarks on this pay voucher. The reason for discrepancy in dates is that he had previously been paid for acting as assistant commissary of subsistence for the period of May through September (see 1:186, 209). Davis left Fort Winnebago June 24 (1:268); the detachment mentioned was at Dubuques Mines (see 1:287, 307).

ABSTRACT

1:321 Register of Payments to Officers

[Washington, D.C.,] March 31, 1832

Lists payment by Paymaster T. Wright[1] to Second Lieutenant Jefferson Davis, First Infantry, $638.82. Amount includes pay and allowance for Davis and one servant,[2] for September 1831 through March 1832. Remarks: "$20 A[ssistant] C[ommissary] S[ubsistence] QM 1 Oct 1830 to 30 June 1831. $10* 5 Nov '31 to 25 Mch '32." [3]

D (NA, RG 99 Records of the Office of the Paymaster General, Register of Payments to Officers, IV, 27), 1.

[1] Thomas Wright (sketch, 1:320, *n.* 2).

[2] James Pemberton was undoubtedly the servant (sketch, 1:5, *n.* 4).

[3] For serving as acting assistant commissary of subsistence at Fort Winnebago from October 1, 1830, to June 30, 1831—a total of nine months—Davis was paid $20 a month. He was paid $10 a month for the period November 5, 1831–March 25, 1832 (1:320).

ABSTRACT

1:322 Post Return

Fort Crawford,[1] Michigan Territory[2]
March [31,] 1832

Lists Second Lieutenant J. F. Davis, Company B, First Infantry, as absent on furlough.[3] Remarks: "Order dated A[djutant] G[eneral's] O[ffice] W[estern] D[epartment] 15 January 1832, untill 26 May 1832." [4]

Printed form, filled in and signed (NA, RG 94 Records of the Adjutant General's Office, Post Returns, Fort Crawford, 1817–34), 2. Signed: "G Loomis Cap. 1st. Infy, Commg." Endorsed: "Recd. 4th. <—April—> May 1832."

[1] See 1:231, *n.* 12.

[2] See 1:149, *n.* 2.

[3] See 1:313 for the order granting Davis' furlough.

[4] Davis left Fort Crawford on March 26, 1832 (1:325), and by the end of the month was at St. Louis (see the receipt of Paymaster Thomas Wright, 1:323). On April 14 he posted a letter to William B. Lewis from Natchez, Mississippi (1:323), and by May 26 (1:327) was at Woodville, his home town in Wilkinson County, Mississippi. That he was still at Woodville as late as July 9 may be inferred from the Joseph Emory Davis letter to him of that date (see 1:328, *n.* 3). Just when Davis left Woodville to return to his post is unknown, but that he did return prior to the expiration of his furlough (see 1:329 for the granting of a

furlough extension to Davis) is confirmed by the muster roll of his company which lists him as having joined on August 18, 1832 (1:332). The question of whether or not Davis gave up his furlough to return to his regiment is now undisputed; whether he returned in time to take an active part in the second campaign of the Black Hawk War has been much discussed but never fully resolved (see 1:267, *n.* 8 for the distinction between the first and second campaigns; see also 1:334, *n.* 6 for the Black Hawk War). Although the August muster roll of Davis' company (1:332) lists him as having joined sixteen days after the last battle of the war, a number of sources maintain that he was in the war from its beginning to its close (Eckenrode, *President of the South*, 31; Flagler, *Rock Island Arsenal*, 21; McElroy, *The Unreal and the Real*, I, 25–29; Stevens, *Black Hawk War*, 294). Stevens goes even further and maintains that although the records list Davis as having joined his company on August 18, "he was present in flesh and blood from start to finish, delaying that perfunctory duty [reporting himself as having returned from furlough] until he was once more back to quarters . . ." (*Black Hawk War*, 295). Other sources assert that, although on furlough, Davis returned and took an active part in most of the campaign (Armstrong, *Sauks and the Black Hawk War*, 421; W. P. Johnston, *Life of Gen. Albert Sidney Johnston*, 36; Strode, *American Patriot*, 71–77); still others, either unaware of Davis' furlough or choosing to ignore the matter, so relate the incidents about Davis and the war that the questions raised by his furlough are altogether avoided (Cutting, *Political Soldier*, 27–28; Dodd, *Jefferson Davis*, 37; Tate, *Jefferson Davis*, 65–66). The truth as to when Davis returned may never be known, but assuming—and the assumption is not a tenuous one—that Davis left Mississippi shortly or immediately after July 9, he could not have reached the seat of the war before July 14 or 15. The steamboats of the period—and it was by steamboat that he undoubtedly travelled—were incapable, even if they travelled non-stop, which, of course, they did not, of covering the 1,550 miles between Natchez and Galena, Illinois, in anything less than four and a half or five days (see Donovan's statement in *River Boats of America*, 117, that in the prewar years "Fifteen miles an hour against the current was good speed for a Mississippi boat . . . ."). Under optimum conditions and travelling non-stop, Davis could not have arrived at Galena—Fort Crawford was even farther up the river—before July 21 or 22. Further, the army was in the field, and it would have taken a number of additional days for Davis to locate his regiment in order to take part in the campaign. Given these facts, it is most unlikely that Davis had any part in the second campaign of the Black Hawk War prior to the last of July, which means that, if he fought at all, he fought on August 2, 1832, in the Battle of Bad Axe and not in any earlier battles.

Although most of the evidence (see Stevens, *Black Hawk War*, 290–308) purporting to prove that Davis took an active part in the war may be doubted, the statements of Davis himself must be given greater consideration. In 1896 Charles Aldrich published an article based upon an interview with Davis entitled "Jefferson Davis and Black Hawk," in which he wrote that Davis "said in substance if not in words: 'We were one day pursuing the Indians, when we came close to the Wisconsin River. Reaching the river bank the Indians made so determined a stand, and fought with such desperation, that they held us in check. During this time the squaws tore bark from the trees, with which they made little shallops, in which they floated their papooses and other impedimenta across to an island, also swimming over the ponies. As soon as this was accomplished, half of the warriors plunged in and swam across, each holding his gun in one hand over his head and swimming with the other. As soon as they reached the opposite bank they also opened fire upon us, under cover of which the other half slipped down the bank and swam over in like manner. This,' said Mr. Davis, 'was the most brilliant exhibition of military tactics that I ever witnessed—a feat of most consummate management and bravery, in the face of an enemy of greatly superior numbers. I never read of anything that could be compared with it. Had it been performed by white men, it would have been immortalized as one of the most splendid achievements in military history' " (*Midland Monthly*, V, 408–409). According to Aldrich, Davis did not name the battle, although the circumstances described so closely resemble those of the Battle of Wisconsin Heights that none other could have been intended (see Black Hawk, *An Autobiography*, ed. Jackson, 155, for Black Hawk's description of the battle). Whatever the intention, Aldrich wrote of the battle as if Davis had been there; yet it would have been almost impossible for Davis to have been at Wisconsin Heights July 21. The same incident was related by Davis to William P. Johnston, and again, Davis did not name the battle (Sibley [ed.], "Davis Recalls the Past," *Journal of Mississippi History*, XXXIII, 170). In addition to the time factor, the battle was fought, as Davis himself wrote (1:Appendix II, 483), by volunteer forces only (Armstrong, *Sauks and the Black Hawk War*, 449–64; Black Hawk, *An Autobiography*, ed. Jackson, 155; Reynolds, *My Own Times*, 263; Stevens, *Black Hawk War*, 221). Thus, the Aldrich article and the Johnston reminiscence cannot be fully reconciled to the facts presented above. The same is true of a letter written by Davis to President James Buchanan May 1, 1858, in which he recommends Warner Lewis for reappointment as surveyor general of Wisconsin and Iowa, noting that he and Lewis served in the 1832 Black Hawk campaign (NA, RG 48, Wisconsin Territory Appointment Papers, 1849–1907).

1:323

To William B. Lewis

SIR[1] April 14th 1832

Herewith I have the honor to enclose you a receipt from Pay-Master Tho. Wright[2] for three hundred and twenty four Dollars paid to cover a stoppage which he informed me had been made in my pay accts. for May & June 1831 also a stoppage which I was indirectly informed had been made in my pay-accts. from the 1st oct. to 30th april 1830–31[3]

address Woodville Mississippi[4] Very Respctfly yr. mo. obt. Servt.

J. F. DAVIS
L[ieutenant] 1. Inf.

[Encl] Army Pay Office St Louis Mo. March 31. 1832

Received of Lieut J F Davis 1. Regt of Infantry three Hundred twenty four dollars, on account of the Pay and Forage of the Army.

Pay—180
Forage 144
$324.

For which I am accountable having signed duplicates hereof.

THO WRIGHT
Pay Master

ALS (NA, RG 217 Records of the United States General Accounting Office, Second Auditor's Office, Second Auditor's Accounts, Account 16,173). Addressed: "To W. B. Lewis Esq. 2nd Auditor U. S. Treasury Washington D. C." Postmarked: "Natchez Apl 19." Endorsed: "rec 15 May ans[wered]." Enclosure: ADS (NA, RG 217 Records of the United States General Accounting Office, Second Auditor's Office, Second Auditor's Accounts, Account 16,173).

[1] William B. Lewis (sketch, 1:166, *n.* 1).

[2] Thomas Wright (sketch, 1:320, *n.* 2).

[3] The amount of Davis' payment to Wright, $324, equals that of the two pay stoppages registered January 3, 1832 (1:309), and January 23, 1832 (1:314). Davis' payment cleared his pay account, as indicated in Lewis to Davis, May 10, 1832 (1:326).

[4] Davis left Fort Crawford on furlough March 26, 1832 (1:325), and applied for a furlough extension from his home town, Woodville, Mississippi, on May 26 (1:327). For Woodville, see 1:22, *n.* 5.

From George A. McCall 1:324

Asst. Adjt. Genl's. Office, West. Dept.
Memphis, Ten., April 30th, 1832

SIR,

Your letter of the 14th Inst.[1] applying for an extension of the furlough granted you by virtue of Dept. "Special Order" No. 1, of 1832,[2] has been received at this office.

By reference to the S. Order above cited, you will perceive that, permission is thereby granted you to apply for an extension of four months; which application should be made at General Head. Quarters.[3] I am, Sir, Very respectfully, Your obt. Servt.

GEO. A. MCCALL[4]
A[ide-] D[e-] C[amp]—actg. ass[istant] adj. Genl.

LbCS (NA, RG 393 Records of United States Army Continental Commands, 1821–1920, Western Department, Letters Sent, VI, 113). Addressed: "To: Lt. J. F. Davis, 1st Inf. Woodville, Wilkinson Co., Mississippi."

[1] Davis' letter of April 14 requesting a furlough extension has not been found.

[2] See 1:313 for Special Order No. 1.

[3] General headquarters at Washington, D.C. (*General Army Regulations*

[1825], 364). Davis applied, as directed, in May (1:327).

[4] George A. McCall (sketch, 1:301, *n.* 2).

ABSTRACT

1:325

Company Muster Roll

Fort Crawford,[1] April 30, 1832

Lists Second Lieutenant J. F. Davis of Captain S. MacRee's[2] Company B, First Regiment of Infantry, as absent "On Furlough for 60. days. Order dated, A[djutant] G[eneral's] O[ffice] W[estern] D[epartment] 15 Jany 1832 [3] left his post 26 March 1832." Report covers March and April 1832.[4]

Printed form, filled in and signed (NA, RG 94 Records of the Adjutant General's Office, Muster Rolls of Regular Army Organizations, First Infantry, Company B), 2. Signed: "S. MacRee Capt G. Loomis Capt. 1s In[fantry]." Endorsed: "Proves (Recd. June 8th. 1832.) Entered."

[1] See 1:231, *n.* 12.

[2] Samuel MacRee (also spelled McRee) was born in North Carolina, graduated from West Point in 1820, and served briefly at the Academy as an assistant instructor of tactics and in several garrisons before his appointment as General Henry Atkinson's aide-de-camp, 1824–31. MacRee served in the Black Hawk War, and at Fort Crawford, 1832–33 and 1834–37. While stationed at Prairie du Chien, he became involved in Davis' courtship of Zachary Taylor's daughter Sarah Knox. Taylor had forbidden Davis to court Sarah Knox; ill feeling between the two men increased until Davis asked MacRee to serve as his second in a challenge to Taylor. MacRee refused, telling Davis "how absurd it was to plan the death of the man whom he wished as a father-in-law" (McElroy, *The Unreal and the Real*, I, 23). MacRee's wife helped arrange rendezvous for the young couple at Fort Crawford, and in 1835 MacRee booked passage for Sarah Knox to Louisville for her wedding to Davis (W. L. Fleming, "Davis' First Marriage," Mississippi Historical *Publications*, XII, 26–30). MacRee found himself an object of contention between Generals Atkinson and E. P. Gaines in 1837 when, although MacRee was ordered to Florida, Atkinson decided to retain him at Jefferson Barracks (Nichols, *Atkinson*, 205–206). MacRee served in the Seminole wars and later became Winfield Scott's chief quartermaster in the Mexican War, being brevetted lieutenant colonel in 1847. He died in St. Louis, aged forty-eight, in 1849 (Cullum, *Biographical Register*, I, 257–58).

[3] See 1:313 for the order granting Davis a sixty-day furlough and 1:324 which states Davis requested a four-month extension.

[4] The muster roll does not list the commanding officer, as was usual, because Willoughby Morgan, colonel of the First Infantry, died on April 4, 1832 (Post Return, April 1832 [NA, RG 94, Fort Crawford, 1817–34]). Zachary Taylor, the new commander of the regiment, arrived at Fort Crawford to take command from the temporary commander, Gustavus Loomis,

on August 5 (Post Return, August 1832 [NA, RG 94, Fort Crawford, 1817–34]). Taylor had been at Fort Armstrong May 7 with the troops of the First Infantry who were beginning their campaign against Black Hawk and his warriors (Hamilton, *Zachary Taylor*, 87).

From William B. Lewis 1:326

SIR, 10 May 1832

You have been relieived from the debits raised against you the 30 Novr. & 18 January last, by crediting your account with the Sum of $324.00 which you refunded paymr. T. *Wright*[1] the 31 of March of the present year.[2]

W. B. L.[3]

LbC (NA, RG 217 Records of the United States General Accounting Office, Second Auditor's Office, Letters Sent, XVI, 350). Addressed: "Lieut. J. F. Davis, 1 Inf. Prairie du Chien, Mic[higan] T[erritor]y."

[1] Thomas Wright (sketch, 1:320, *n.* 2).

[2] See 1:323 for evidence of Davis' having refunded $324. See also pay stoppages of January 3 (1:309) and January 23 (1:314).

[3] William B. Lewis (sketch, 1:166, *n.* 1).

To Alexander Macomb 1:327

May 26th 1832 Woodville Mississippi[1]

SIR[2]

With the permission of the Comdg. Genl. of the Western Dept.[3] granted in Special Order No. 1[4]—issued at Memphis Tenn. 16th January 1832 I have the honor to forward this my application for an extension of my furlough by four additional months[5] Very Respectfully yr. mo. obt. Servt.

J. F. DAVIS
L[ieutenant] 1. Infantry

ALS (NA, RG 94 Records of the Adjutant General's Office, Letters Received, D–42, 1832, filed with 38051, Adjutant General's Office, 1896). Addressed: "To Maj. Genl. A. Macomb Comdg. U. S. Army Head Qrs. Washington D. C." Endorsed: "Submitted R[oger] J[ones] Granted A[lexander] M[acomb] *July 20th*."

[1] See 1:22, *n.* 5 for Woodville, Mississippi.

[2] Alexander Macomb (sketch, 1:38, *n.* 10).

[3] The commanding general of the Western Department was Edmund P. Gaines (sketch, 1:301, *n.* 3).

[4] See 1:313 for Special Order No. 1.

[5] See 1:324 for mention of Davis' misdirected request for a furlough extension; see 1:329 for the granting of the requested extension.

1:328 ## From Joseph Emory Davis[1]

MY DEAR BROTHER Hurricane[2] July 9th '32[3]

This is the first hour since the receipt of your letters of the 22nd ult.[4] that I could devote to a subject of the greatest interest, and difficulty a difficulty increased by the consequene you seem to attach to my opinion, and though I am sure it is of no value I am fearful you may allow <–the of–> <it to>[5] influene your conduct in a Matter that deeply concer[n]s your future life. No One can judge for an other and the worst of all reasons is that such a one *said so* in determining upon a plan of life we should look to the end and take the <not>[5] shortest route but the surest that which is beset with the fewest difficulty and the most pleasant to travel

of this Rail Road[6] I have no high opinion and as you know have always regarded it as a failure sooner or later I had therefore a desire that you should rather have Comd[7] Engineer under the authority of the Govt. than in the employ of a small Comy. but of this you are better able than I am to form an opinion it is now probably too late to visit Washington which I regret tho' it been of no other use than to form some acquaintane the working of the machine of Govt.[8]

You know my views of a profesion and other things Conneceted with it. I will Close by repeating that I wish you to decide for yourself and any [thing?] I can render you in carrying into effect your own plan [it is?][9] useless to say shall be afforde[d.][9]

I have been out at two or More meetings of the [people?] and made as many stump speeches and have to attend an other on Saturday it said they have had an effect but I doubt whether it is such as to Change the popular Current which you probaby saw was for electing every thing[10]

Say to mother[11] I hope to see her this summer and will write to her if I do not.

I have felt great uneasiness about the Children and sincerely regret we had not brought them home.

I hope to hear from you soon I would say see you but fear it would be inconvenent or objectionable on other accts I have to visit Natchez next week for a day or so I think about wednesday when I hope at least to hear from you perhaps you could come home with us and see the Claibone Spings[12]

AL (Jefferson Hayes-Davis, Colorado Springs, 1969). Addressed: "J. F. Davis Esqr. Woodville Mississippi." Endorsed: "J. E. Davis."

[1] Joseph E. Davis (sketch, 1:19, *n.* 1; 1:Appendix IV, Entry 15).

[2] Comprising some 3,000 acres in Warren County, Mississippi, "Hurricane," the plantation home of Joseph E. Davis, was located on a bend in the Mississippi River twelve or fifteen miles south of Vicksburg. The area has been known variously as Palmyra Peninsula, Davis Bend, and, after the river cut through the narrowing finger of land, as Davis or Palmyra Island. "Hurricane," "Brierfield," and several other plantations were carved out of the land Joseph bought from the government in 1818. For at least a few years after the purchase, while Joseph practiced law in the vicinity of Vicksburg, a younger Davis brother, Isaac, managed the property. After a particularly violent storm in which Isaac was seriously injured and his son killed, Isaac and his wife Susannah left Warren County and settled near Canton, Mississippi (1:9, *n.* 12). Apparently undeterred by the storm, Joseph named his plantation "Hurricane" and moved there with his family sometime in the 1820's to become a full-time cotton planter (J. E. Davis to Johnson, September 22, 1865, Davis *v.* Bowmar, 3–4, 441 [Mississippi Department of Archives and History, Jackson]; Strode, *American Patriot*, 50).

The home Joseph eventually built there was a huge three-story, brick and stucco structure which "presented an air of isolated grandeur. Part of it . . . [was] swept away by a terrific storm . . . [and] new buildings gave it a rambling misshapen appearance . . ." (E. Rowland, *Varina Howell*, I, 65). Windows on the third story afforded vistas of the river and the surrounding woodlands. "Above the heavy roof numerous sharp-pointed dormers glistened in the sun like so many spires" (*ibid.*, I, 65). Varina Howell Davis gives a detailed description of the main house (*Memoir*, I, 192–93): "'The Hurricane' house stood in many acres of splendid oaks, and the main part of the building had low ceilings; a wide hall with four rooms on the lower floor, as many on the second story, and the same number in the attic. The windows were small, the walls were thick, and the doors were panelled below, and had six small panes of glass above. On the right-hand side of the hall were the drawing-room and the 'tea-room,' where the ladies sat; on the other, was a bedchamber and the 'office.' . . . The house was surrounded by wide galleries that ran nearly all around it, upstairs and down. Below, the floor was paved with bricks, which were reddened industriously. To the west was a large annex of two rooms forty-three feet long and twenty-five wide. The lower one was a dining-room, paved also and cemented. The upper one was arched and called the 'music-room' . . . . There was a little store-room adjoining Mr. Davis's bed-room below stairs . . . . This little closet was an ark, of which Mr. J. E. Davis kept the key, and made provision for the accidental needs of 'each one after his kind.'" An especially interesting feature of the house was that its bathrooms had running water. Cincinnati artisans hired by Joseph had installed a large tank in the attic, which the Negroes pumped full of water (White, "Interludes," 167 [Mrs. Betty White Wills, Tulsa, Oklahoma, 1968]).

Careful attention was also given the grounds immediately around "Hurricane." At the front of the house, in the area extending toward the river, "the native trees had been thinned to make finer specimens." Here also were magnolias, camellias, and many varieties of plants from foreign countries. Joseph later employed an English gardener who fashioned "a curving band of green meadow three miles long . . . cropped like turf" between the river and the park in front of the house (Strode, *American Patriot*, 101–102). Behind the main house was a large rose garden which adjoined the eight-acre orchard of peach, apple, and fig trees.

"Immediately back of the house was a two-story brick and stucco building . . . with an enormous kitchen, store rooms, etc., and six bedrooms for servants above, very nice rooms they were too, ceiled and plastered, with large windows. There was another building [called the commissary] in back of this one where plantation stores were kept, with an office for the overseer and two bedrooms above. Grandpa [Joseph E.] Davis's office and library were in a separate building a short distance from the main house. There were only two rooms with huge fireplaces and French windows. At the end of each room was a large recessed bay. Heavy cornices were around the roof and large white columns completely surrounded the building" (White, "Interludes," 167 [Mrs. Betty White Wills, Tulsa, Oklahoma, 1968]). This building, referred to as the library or garden cottage, was described as "a replica of a Greek temple with square Doric columns." It was spared in 1863 when Federal troops razed the main house (Strode, *American Patriot*, 101). Among other outbuildings were a stable east of the mansion containing thirty stalls for horses, a large barn, a cotton gin, a blacksmith shop, a hospital, and "a small hamlet of white-washed cabins" for the Negroes (V. Davis, *Memoir*, I, 194; 1:439; E. Rowland, *Varina Howell*, I, 65).

[3] That Davis was at Woodville, Mississippi, on July 9, 1832, and not with his regiment in the Black Hawk War may fairly be inferred from this letter. It is unlikely that Davis would have left Woodville without seeing or informing his brother of his departure, and, as may be seen in the last paragraph, Joseph was hoping to visit with his brother at Natchez on Wednesday, July 18.

[4] Davis' letters of June 22 have not been found.

[5] Interlined.

[6] The railroad here discussed was probably the ill-fated West Feliciana Railroad Company, chartered in 1831 by the Mississippi General Assembly, to run from Woodville to St. Francisville, Louisiana (D. Rowland, *Mississippi, Heart of the South*, I, 563–64). It was a standard gauge road, and a bank was operated in connection with it at Woodville (*Biographical and Historical Memoirs of Mississippi*, I, 183).

[7] "Commissioned" is probably intended.

[8] Davis did not make a trip to Washington until 1836. See V. Davis, *Memoir*, I, 165–66, where, although the events are confused, the dates are correct.

[9] Manuscript damaged and illegible.

[10] The election here referred to was probably that for delegates to the new state constitutional convention which met in September 1832 (D. Rowland, *Mississippi, Heart of the South*, I, 565 *ff*).

[11] Jane Cook Davis (sketch, 1:22, *n.* 4; 1:Appendix IV, Entry 14) was living at "Rosemont," her home near Woodville.

[12] Undoubtedly a reference to the natural chalybeate springs in Claiborne Parish, northwest Louisiana, known for their medicinal qualities ("Northwest Louisiana," *De Bow's Review*, XI, 89; "North Louisiana," *ibid.*, XXVI, 602).

Special Order No. 108 1:329

Adjutant Genl's. Office Washington 21st July. 1832

On the recommendation of the Commanding General of the Western Department,[1] the furlough granted to 2nd. Lieut. Davis of the 1st Infantry in Virtue of his Special Order No. 1.[2] of the present year, is hereby extended four additional Months.[3] On its expiration, Lieut. Davis will join his proper Station.[4] By order of Major Genl. Macomb[5] (Sgd)

R. JONES[6]
Adjt Genl.

LbC (NA, RG 94 Records of the Adjutant General's Office, War Department Orders and Circulars, Special Orders, II, 337).

[1] The commanding general of the Western Department was Edmund P. Gaines (sketch, 1:301, *n.* 3).

[2] See 1:313 for Special Order No. 1.

[3] See 1:324, 327 for Davis' requested extension.

[4] According to the company muster roll of August (1:332), Davis rejoined his regiment August 18.

[5] Alexander Macomb (sketch, 1:38, *n.* 10).

[6] Roger Jones (sketch, 1:123, *n.* 6).

To George Bomford 1:330

Prairie du Chien[1] M[ichigan] T[erritory][2]
August 18th 1832[3]

SIR[4]

Herewith I have the honor to transmit to you an Invoice and receipt of ordinance received by me from G. W. Campbell[5] at Galena[6] Ills. and this day "turned over" to Lt Abbercrombie[7] acg. ordinance officer at this post Very respectfully yr. mo. obt. Servant

J. F. DAVIS
L[ieutenant] 1. Inf.

ALS (NA, RG 156 Records of the Office of the Chief of Ordnance, Letters Received, D–62, 1832). Addressed: "To Col G. Bomford Comdg. Ordinance." Endorsed: "Recd. Octr. 12." Enclosures missing.

[1] Location of Fort Crawford (1:231, *n.* 12).

[2] See 1:149, *n.* 2.

[3] If the company muster roll for August (1:332) is to be believed, Davis had just returned from furlough.

[4] George Bomford (sketch, 1:155, *n.* 3).

[5] Probably George W. Campbell, briefly mentioned in LeBron, "Col. James W. Stephenson," *Journal of the Illinois State Historical Society*, XXV, 356–57.

[6] See 1:231, *n.* 18.

[7] John Joseph Abercrombie (sketch, 1:283, *n.* 4).

ABSTRACT

1:331

Post Return

Fort Crawford,[1] Michigan Territory[2]
August [31,] 1832

Lists Second Lieutenant Jeff. F. Davis, Company B, First Infantry, present at the post. Remarks: "For duty." [3]

Printed form, filled in and signed (NA, RG 94 Records of the Adjutant General's Office, Post Returns, Fort Crawford, 1817–34), 2. Signed: "Z. Taylor Col, 1st Infy." Endorsed: "Recd. 11th. Octr."

[1] See 1:231, *n.* 12.

[2] See 1:149, *n.* 2.

[3] According to the August muster roll of Company B, Davis had returned from furlough August 18 (1:332).

ABSTRACT

1:332

Company Muster Roll

Fort Crawford,[1] August 31, 1832

Lists Second Lieutenant J. F. Davis of Captain S. MacRee's[2] Company B, First Regiment of Infantry commanded by Colonel Z. Taylor,[3] as present. Remarks: "Joined Co. August 18. 1832." [4] Report covers July and August 1832.

Printed form, filled in and signed (NA, RG 94 Records of the Adjutant General's Office, Muster Rolls of Regular Army Organizations, First Infantry, Company B), 2. Signed: "S. MacRee Capt Z. Taylor, Col 1st Infy." Endorsed: "Proves (Recd. Octr 9. 1832.) Entered."

[1] See 1:231, *n.* 12 for Fort Crawford.

[2] Samuel MacRee (sketch, 1:325, *n.* 2).

[3] Zachary Taylor (1784–1850), twelfth President of the United States, was born in Virginia but moved to Kentucky at an early age. He had little formal education and began military service as a volunteer in 1806. He served in the War of 1812 as a captain and major, was retained as an infantry captain at the end of the war, and served at several garrisons before he succeeded Willoughby Morgan as commander of the First Infantry April 4, 1832, at which time he was promoted to lieutenant colonel. Taylor led his regiment in the Black Hawk War, and it was after the war, at Fort Crawford, that he probably first made the acquaintance of Davis. Their association was not pleasant at first because Taylor opposed Davis' courtship of his daughter Sarah, but in later years they were reconciled (V. Davis, *Memoir*, I, 199). Taylor's successes in the Mexican War paved his way to the White House as the 1848 Whig candidate; he died in office (*DAB*; Hamilton, *Zachary Taylor*). Of the Davis-Taylor quarrel, Mrs. Davis, quoting H. Dous-

man, wrote that "When Lieutenant Davis proposed for the hand of Miss Knox Taylor, Colonel Taylor said to Mr. Dousman that 'While he had nothing but the kindliest feeling and warmest admiration for Mr. Davis, he was in a general way opposed to having his daughter marry a soldier. Nobody knew better than he the trials to which a soldier's wife was subjected. His own wife and daughter had complained so bitterly of his almost constant absence from home, and of their own torturing anxieties for his safety, he had once resolved that his daughter should never marry a soldier with his approval. . . . Some time after this, a court-martial was being held, composed of Taylor, [Captain Thomas Floyd] Smith, Davis, and a lieutenant whose name Mrs. McRee [Mrs. Samuel MacRee] had forgotten. There was an angry feud between Taylor and Smith. By the rules of the army, then and now, each officer sitting on such a court was bound to appear in full uniform. The lieutenant had left his uniform at Jefferson Barracks, near St. Louis. He asked the court to excuse him from wearing it. Taylor voted no, Smith voted yes, and Davis voted with Smith. Colonel Taylor became highly incensed. One thing led to another, until he swore, as an officer only in those days could swear, that no man who voted with 'Tom Smith' should ever marry his daughter. He forbade Davis from entering his quarters as a guest, and repudiated him utterly' " (*Memoir*, I, 95–96; see also Wood, "Jefferson Davis' First Marriage," New Orleans *Daily Picayune*, August 28, 1910; statement of Dandridge to "D. B. C.," New York *Times*, October 20, 1906; W. L. Fleming, "Davis' First Marriage," Mississippi Historical *Publications*, XII, 21–36). Years later, Davis wrote of his estrangement with Taylor: "In the controversy with my Col. at Prairie du Chien I was right as to the principle from which it arose, but impolitic in the manner of asserting it. A mean fellow misrepresented me, the Col. believed him and assailed me harshly, imputing to me motives the reverse of those by which I was actuated. Then I became wrong as angry men are apt to be; and the smoldering fire kindled your wrath as my friend. In after years the Col. and I knew each other and I grew to love and honor him, 'despite my wrongs, by hasty wrath and slanderous tongues' " (Davis to Northrop, April 25, 1879, D. Rowland, *Papers*, VIII, 383). See 1:325, *n.* 2 for MacRee's part in the Davis-Taylor quarrel and 1:483, *n.* 8 for George W. Jones's reminiscence of the Davis-Taylor feud. Although the estrangement between Davis and Taylor was not healed during the life of Davis' first wife, their differences were later reconciled. According to Mrs. Davis, Taylor and her husband-to-be met on a steamboat in the spring of 1845, when Davis was on his way to Natchez to be married for the second time. "An entire reconciliation took the place of the unexpressed but friendly regard which had never ceased to exist in all those years of mutual grief and separation" (*Memoir*, I, 199).

[4] Davis had been on furlough since March 26 (1:317). See 1:322, *n.* 4 for a discussion of Davis and the Black Hawk War.

1:333 To George Gibson

Fort Crawford[1] 1st Sept 1832

GENERAL,[2]

With this I transmit an a/c current to close my a/cts in your Dept[3]

I Remain With great Respect Yr Obt Sevt J. F. DAVIS

L[ieutenant] 1. Inf.

ac[ting] A[ssistant] C[ommissary] S[ubsistence]

LS (NA, RG 192 Records of the Office of the Commissary General of Subsistence, Letters Received, D–1162, 1832). Addressed: "Brig Genl Geo Gibson Comsy Genl of Subst." Endorsed: "Recd 22 Sept." Enclosure missing.

[1] See 1:231, *n.* 12.

[2] George Gibson (sketch, 1:179, *n.* 2).

[3] See 1:296 for Davis' appointment as the acting assistant commissary of subsistence at Dubuques Mines.

1:334 Receipt for Quartermaster's Stores

Fort Crawford[1] 3d. Sept. 1832

List of Qr. Master' Stores Delivered to Lt. <—Davis—> <Anderson[2]>[3] of the 1st. <—Infy—> <Artillery>[3] by Lt. Th. P. Gwynn[4] A[cting] A[ssistant] Qr. Master U. S. Army at Fort Crawford the 3d. Sept. 1832.

(Viz)

1 One Ball & Chain
1 One pair of Hand Cuffs
1 One Shackle[5]

TH P GWYNN

Lt A A Q M

[AE] On my leaving the Post with the guard escorting Black Hawk's[6] party[7]

DS (Black Hawk War Collection, Illinois State Historical Library, Springfield).

[1] See 1:231, *n.* 12.

[2] Robert Anderson (1805–71) was a Kentuckian, a graduate of West Point (1825), and was, in September 1832, serving as colonel and assistant inspector general of the Illinois volunteers, being actually a second lieutenant, Third Artillery. Anderson recalled the circumstances of escorting Black Hawk and other Sauk prisoners to Rock Island more than three decades later: "The last duty I performed in that war was when I was sent by Gen. [Winfield] Scott from Prairie du

Chien with Black Hawk and some other prisoners who had been surrendered to Col. Zachary Taylor, then commanding that post. The cholera broke out in the Camp at Rock Island the day I left, and soon afterward among my guard. When I left Prairie du Chien we were all suffering from that disease, in consequence of which Colonel Taylor sent Lieutenant Jefferson Davis with another detachment to act under me as an additional guard over the prisoners. As the cholera was raging at Rock Island, when we reached there on our return, General Scott ordered me to take the party to Jefferson Barracks, which I did" (Anderson to Arnold, March 16, 1869 [typescript in Black Hawk War Collection, Illinois State Historical Library, Springfield]; for another account, see Anderson to Washburne, May 10, 1870, in Armstrong, *Sauks and the Black Hawk War*, 372–76; see also Anderson, "Reminiscences of the Black Hawk War," Wisconsin Historical *Collections*, X, 167–76). Anderson was later to win attention as the commander of Fort Sumter in April 1861, and by the time of the Civil War, had been twice brevetted for gallantry, in the Seminole and Mexican wars. He served as a brigadier general in the Union Army until his retirement from active service in 1863. He died in Nice, France (Cullum, *Biographical Register*, I, 347–52; Warner, *Generals in Blue*, 7–8; *DAB*).

[3] Interlined.

[4] Thomas Page Gwynn (sketch, 1:148, *n.* 1).

[5] Whether or not Davis actually fought in the Black Hawk War is a moot question (see 1:322, *n.* 4), but that he escorted Black Hawk to Jefferson Barracks is unquestioned. See 1:Appendix II, 483 for Davis' account of the capture; see also 1:386, *n.* 10. William B. Street, in a biography of his father, General Joseph M. Street, also confirms that Davis was in charge of the troops escorting the Indian prisoners and further states that "Black Hawk had been delivered to Colonel Taylor and held for several days in the guard house of the fort till the party should be ready to start. While in custody Black Hawk had been put in irons, and was so delivered to Lieutenant Davis. When General Street went on the boat he walked around the deck taking each Indian by the hand, until he came to Black Hawk. Seeing the irons on his wrists, he turned to Lieutenant Davis and said: 'Lieutenant Davis, have these irons removed.' Davis suggested that it might not be safe. Then Mr. Street, facing him, said 'Sir, I hold myself personally responsible for this man's safety and good conduct.' Lieutenant Davis replied, 'If you direct it, General,' and turning to his orderly sent for a blacksmith belonging to the boat to file them off. The irons were made from a small half round bar bent around each wrist and riveted. The iron was cutting into the flesh" ("General Joseph M. Street," *Annals of Iowa*, 3rd Ser., II, 92). Contrary to the above, Black Hawk does not mention anything about being shackled until after he arrived at Jefferson Barracks (*An Autobiography*, ed. Jackson, 165). That he was in irons at Jefferson Barracks is confirmed by Washington Irving who was at St. Louis when Davis and his prisoners arrived (McDermott [ed.], *Western Journals of Washington Irving*, 83; Sibley [ed.], "Davis Recalls the Past," *Journal of Mississippi History*, XXXIII, 170). Mrs. Davis states the two men met at Fort Gibson (*Memoir*, I, 148), but Davis did not go to Fort Gibson until December 1833 (1:397), and Irving's visits were in October and November of the previous year (McDermott [ed.], *Western Journals of Washington Irving*, 23–33, 150–51). Whether Black Hawk was first shackled at Fort Crawford or at Jefferson Barracks cannot be finally determined, but from this document it would appear that the authorities were

prepared to shackle him, if necessary.

[6] Black Hawk (1767–1838), named Ma-ka-tai-me-she-kia-kiak, a Sauk war chief, was born near the present town of Rock Island, Illinois, at Saukenuk, and served with the British in the War of 1812. Believing an 1804 treaty between the United States and the Sauk and Fox nations to be invalid, Black Hawk allied himself to a Winnebago medicine man, "the Prophet" (see 1:335, *n.* 13), and conspired against white encroachment on Indian lands in northwestern Illinois and southwestern Wisconsin (then part of Michigan Territory). In June 1831, Black Hawk crossed the Mississippi into United States territory on the eastern side, but withdrew because federal authorities made a show of force at Rock Island (see 1:267, *n.* 8). But in April 1832 he recrossed the river with about 200 warriors and their families on the way to the tribe's ancestral lands on the Rock River. When General Henry Atkinson arrived at the frontier late in April 1832, and the Winnebago tribes were found to be disunited in their attitude and support for Black Hawk, the Sauk leader realized further opposition was useless, and decided to turn back. But on May 14, when several Indians were killed by a mounted volunteer company at Stillman's Run (see 1:Appendix II, 483), the Sauks retaliated, killed about twelve militiamen, and the Black Hawk War began. After a series of ill-managed campaigns, the war ended August 2 at the Bad Axe River where most of the Indians were killed or captured by Atkinson's troops (see 1:Appendix II, 483). Black Hawk had left his band August 1 or 2, but gave himself up to the Winnebagoes, and to Indian agent Joseph M. Street at Prairie du Chien August 27. After a visit to Washington and a short imprisonment in Fortress Monroe, he was returned to Iowa, where he died in his lodge near the Des Moines River (*DAB*; Black Hawk, *An Autobiography*, ed. Jackson; Nichols, *Atkinson*, 156–73; C. Cole, *I am a Man*; 1:386). In a letter to Crafts J. Wright, Davis answered the charge that he was cruel to prisoners during the Civil War by citing his treatment of Black Hawk: "Did you ever read the life of Black Hawk? If so you may remember that he mentioned gratefully the courtesy with which I treated him, when he was a prisoner under my charge [1:386], an Indian would not be more apt to excite sympathy, and should not be more willing to acknowledge having received it, than one of our own people" (February 12, 1876, D. Rowland, *Papers*, VII, 496).

[7] The endorsement, although unsigned, is probably by Robert Anderson.

EXTRACT

1:335 Robert Anderson's Muster Roll Book

[Rock Island, Illinois,][1] Sept. 5th. 1832

Names of some of the Prisoners brought down from Prairie du Chien[2] by Lt R. Anderson[3] & by order of Brig. Genl Atkinson[4]—Lt. J. Davis—Comdg. guard from the Prairie.

Pu-she-pa-hoe—The stabber—or little stabbing Chief[5]

<Black Hawk —>[6] (Muck-ca-ta-me-che-ca-ca) —Black sparrowhawk—<or (Mucca-ta-micha-ca-keg)[7]>[6]

A-che-way-schuk <Na-cre-as-kuck[?]>[8]—1st. son of B. Hawk[9]
Way-sah-me-saw <Ah-tam-ma-sah>[6]—2nd. son of B. Hawk
A-sin-ne-ke—Little rock—Lt. Davis
Kush-ca-na—Little bird—Lt. Davis
Ma-me-wa-ne-ca—Bear—Lt. Davis
Me-tha-hay
Pash-qua-yah
Shu-kuck
Mah-nee-as-qua—Deer
Wa-ha-she-kah
Prisoners Continued—[10]
A-pa-ta-ha-ne
Che-a-muck-quo—Little bear
Pah-me-ah-cha-skuk
Mah-nah-quet
Muk-qua-tah-an-quit
Kish-ca-nah
Tah-qua-me
Tuc-quo
A-pah-tis-tah
Ta-koo-schuck
Pas-que
Tsho-kuk
Mu-kas-an-nu me
Wa-chu-ku-ne qua Pottawattamies
A-co-mu Pottawattamies
Sons of Ta-o-me—Some women & children of this party not embraced on the list. These were landed at the mouth of the Ioway with instructions to proceed to Keo-Kuck's[11] village.[12]

R. ANDERSON

<In addition to the names here given were brought down—Wa-he-ke-shuk—the Prophet[13] two of his sons—his brother—one of the sons of Win-no-shick[14]—& a few others whose names I have lost.

R ANDERSON
Lt & A[ssistant] I[nspector] G[eneral]>.[6]

ADS (Black Hawk War Collection, Illinois State Historical Library, Springfield), 6.

[1] Site of Fort Armstrong (1:267, *n.* 3).

[2] Location of Fort Crawford (1:231, *n.* 12).

[3] Robert Anderson (sketch, 1:334, *n.* 2).

[4] Henry Atkinson (sketch, 1:301, *n.* 7).

[5] The Pashepaho (Patchipao, Pahchippeho, Pashepauko, Pashepahaw) mentioned here is the younger of two Sauk chiefs of the same name, the elder having signed the 1804 treaty at St. Louis which ceded Indian lands to the United States. The younger was one of Black Hawk's warriors and later, in 1834, was recognized by the Sauks as head chief, but was not so recognized by the whites (Hagen, *Sac and Fox Indians*, 25; Catlin, *North American Indians*, II, 212; Wight and [Thwaites], "Documents Relating to the Stockbridge Mission, 1825–48," Wisconsin Historical *Collections*, XV, 113–14). The name "Pashepaho" is also translated as the "Giger" or "He who touches lightly in passing" (McKenney and Hall, *Indian Tribes*, I, 195*n.*).

[6] In the margin.

[7] Black Hawk (sketch, 1:334, *n.* 6).

[8] Interlined.

[9] Nasheakuk (Nah-se-us-kuk, Nasheakusk, Loud Thunder, Tommy Hawk) accompanied his father on an enforced tour of eastern cities in 1833 where he became a favorite of the crowds and journalists. In 1839 he was accused of slaying Keokuk, his father's chief Sauk rival, but was found innocent; according to another source (*DAB*), Keokuk lived until 1848 (Black Hawk, *An Autobiography*, ed. Jackson, 4, 171; Catlin, *North American Indians*, II, 211; Jordan, "Life and Works of James Gardiner Edwards," *Journal of the Illinois State Historical Society*, XXIII, 476).

[10] Page heading.

[11] Keokuk (*ca.* 1780–1848), or the Running Fox, was acknowledged chief of the Sauks and Foxes by Winfield Scott in 1833 after Black Hawk's defeat and capture. Keokuk, with the majority of the Sauks and Foxes, had remained at peace during the Black Hawk War. He was born near Rock Island, Illinois, and early became a respected member of the tribal council. When Black Hawk left the Sauk village to fight with the British in the War of 1812, Keokuk took over tribal leadership. In 1829 the Sauks were forced to move from their tribal lands to the western side of the Mississippi; Keokuk consented to the move, Black Hawk opposed it vigorously, and from that time on, as Black Hawk related: "There was no more friendship existing between us" (*An Autobiography*, ed. Jackson, 113). After the Black Hawk War, Keokuk and his followers were given a reservation in Nebraska, and Keokuk was made Black Hawk's guardian from 1833 until the latter's death in 1838. In 1833 and 1837, he and Black Hawk went on sight-seeing tours in the East, at the request of the government and attended a conference in Washington in 1837 to reconcile differences between the Sioux and Sauk and Fox nations. In 1845 Keokuk moved with his tribe to Kansas and he died there (*DAB*; McKenney and Hall, *Indian Tribes*, II, 115–49; Catlin, *North American Indians*, II, 210–12).

[12] In 1832 Keokuk's village was on the western side of the Mississippi, near the Iowa River, where he had consented to move in 1829 (see *n.* 11 above and Black Hawk, *An Autobiography*, ed. Jackson, 111–12).

[13] Wabokieshiek (Wapesheka, Waubakeeshik, Wawhekashick, White Cloud, Light Cloud), most commonly called the Prophet, was half Sauk and half Winnebago, and was believed to be a man of great insight, in contact with the spirit world. He was one of Black Hawk's chief advisers at the time of the 1832 war, and was called both his "right arm" and his "evil genius" (Washburne, "Col. Henry Gratiot," Wisconsin Historical *Collections*, X, 252; [Thwaites], "Story of the Black Hawk War," *ibid.*, XII, 224). He was captured with Black Hawk and accompanied him to Washington in 1833; he died among the Winnebagoes in 1840 or 1841, at approximately age fifty (Catlin, *North American Indians*,

II, 211; McKenney and Hall, *Indian Tribes*, II, 80; Black Hawk, *An Autobiography*, ed. Jackson, 113*n. et passim*).

14 Winneshick (Winneschick, Winnesheck, Winnosheek) was the name of two Winnebago chiefs, one of whom fought in the War of 1812 and was the leader of the tribe in 1829, and the younger who was the leader of the Winnebagoes in Iowa by 1855 (W. R. Smith and others, "Report," Wisconsin Historical *Collections*, I, 11; Grignon, "Seventy-two Years' Recollections," *ibid.*, III, 287). The younger Winneshick was taken prisoner by Henry Dodge in the summer of 1827 and detained at Galena for two weeks because of Indian troubles around Prairie du Chien. It was undoubtedly he who aided Black Hawk and made the trip to Washington with him in 1837 (Parkinson, "Pioneer Life," *ibid.*, II, 331; De La Ronde, "Personal Narrative," *ibid.*, VII, 359). He returned to Wisconsin from the Winnebago reservation in Nebraska in 1872 or 1873, had his own farm on the Black River, and died in 1887 ([Thwaites], "The Wisconsin Winnebagoes: An Interview with Moses Paquette," *ibid.*, XII, 431).

ABSTRACT

Pay Voucher 1:336

Fort Crawford,[1] Michigan Territory[2]
September 17, 1832

Second Lieutenant Jefferson Davis, First Infantry, acknowledges that he has received $315.50 from Paymaster Major Thomas Wright.[3] Amount includes pay, and allowance for one servant,[4] for April through August 1832. The servant is described as "James A Slave."

Printed form, filled in and signed (NA, RG 217 Records of the United States General Accounting Office, Paymasters' Accounts, Wright 17,538, Voucher 46), 3. Signed: "Jeffn Davis 2. L[ieutenant] 1. Inf."

1 See 1:231, *n.* 12.

2 See 1:149, *n.* 2.

3 Thomas Wright (sketch, 1:320, *n.* 2).

4 James Pemberton (sketch, 1:5, *n.* 4).

ABSTRACT

Register of Payments to Officers 1:337

[Washington, D.C.,] September 17, 1832

Lists payment by Paymaster T. Wright[1] to Second Lieutenant Jefferson Davis, First Infantry, $315.50. Amount includes pay and allowance for Davis and one servant,[2] for April through August.

D (NA, RG 99 Records of the Office of the Paymaster General, Register of Payments to Officers, IV, 27), 1.

[1] Thomas Wright (sketch, 1:320, *n.* 2).
[2] James Pemberton was the servant (sketch, 1:5, *n.* 4).

1:338

From Trueman Cross

SIR, September 21st, 1832

Your letter of the 8th instant, and the Invoice and receipts of public property which accompanied it,[1] are referred to the Third Auditor.[2] (Signed) T CROSS.[3]
Major & Actg Qr Mr Gen.

LbC (NA, RG 92 Records of the Office of the Quartermaster General, Letters Sent, XVII, 471). Addressed: "Lieut. J. F. Davis, 1st. Regt. Infantry, Jefferson Barracks, Missouri." Endorsed: "(Returned as a Dead Letter May 29th, 1833.)."

[1] Davis' letter of September 8 and its enclosed invoice and receipts have not been found.
[2] The third auditor was Peter Hagner (sketch, 1:199, *n.* 5).
[3] Trueman Cross (sketch, 1:304, *n.* 5).

ABSTRACT

1:339

Post Return

Fort Crawford,[1] [September 30,] 1832 [2]

Lists Second Lieutenant Jeff. F. Davis, Company B, First Infantry, as absent on special duty. Remarks: "Detachd. to Rock Island, order of Col. Taylor[3] 3 Sep. 1832." [4]

Printed form, filled in and signed (NA, RG 94 Records of the Adjutant General's Office, Post Returns, Fort Crawford, 1817–34), 2. Signed: "Z. Taylor. Col." Endorsed: "Entd Recd. 8 Decr."

[1] See 1:231, *n.* 12.
[2] The date given this post return may be incorrect. It carries an October 1832 date on its face, indicates a furlough begun October 2 by the commander of Company F, and lists orders received at Fort Crawford between October 4 and October 31. However, there are two reports (not duplicates) for October and none for September, and docketing indicates that this one was accepted by the Adjutant General's Office as the September return. The October return shows the same leave begun by the same company commander (by virtue of an order of a later date), and the same orders received (but all on October 4). It seems likely that some administrative con-

fusion was created by the Black Hawk War, and that both September and October reports were actually made out some time after they should have been. Post returns from Fort Crawford were almost invariably received by the Adjutant General's Office within the first week or two of the second month following that of the return date—sometimes earlier, but seldom later. This report, however, was received December 8, and the October report was not received until June 19, 1833. (The November post return, by contrast, was received January 7, 1833, within the normal time [1:342].) In any event, Davis is listed as performing the same duty by the same order on both reports.

[3] Zachary Taylor (sketch, 1:332, *n.* 3).

[4] On September 3, 1832, Colonel Zachary Taylor ordered Davis to escort Black Hawk and the other captives from Fort Crawford to Jefferson Barracks. Robert Anderson, who was first assigned the task, fell ill and was unable to fully perform his duties, hence the appointment of Davis as the commander of the troops escorting the captives (see 1:334, *n.* 2 for Anderson's account of the circumstances surrounding the escorting of Black Hawk). Notice of the fact that Davis commanded the troops escorting Black Hawk is found in the *Galenian* of September 5, 1832, wherein it says, "Gen. [Joseph M.] Street, the Indian Agent at Prairie du Chien, arrived today, on board the steam boat Winnebago, with about 100 Sac prisoners, guarded by an escort of troops under command of Lt. Jefferson Davis. Among the prisoners, are the celebrated Black Hawk, the Prophet, and La-ce-o-scuck-ka (the Thunder) son of Black Hawk; the latter was delivered up on the night of the 3d. The prisoners were brought in by the Winnebagoes, and the Sioux."

To Edmund P. Gaines 1:340

SIR[1] Memphis Tenn. Oct. 3rd 1832

My services being no longer required with my Regiment I have been permitted to avail myself of the remainder of a furlough granted,[2] and as that furlough will terminate during the winter when I cannot return to my Post (Fort Crawford)[3] without much exposure and difficulty, I would respectfully ask an extension of the indulgence until the 31st of March next.[4] With great respect yr. mo. obt. Servt.

J. F. DAVIS

2d. L[ieutenant] 1. Inf.

[AES 1] Approved by the Genl. Comdg. W[estern] Dept. By Order, *Geo. A. M.Call*[5] A[ide-] D[e-] C[amp] &c. Hd. Qr. W[estern] D[epartment] Oct. 4th. 1832.

[AES 2] State the Length of his furlough. R[oger] J[ones].[6]

[ES 3] Furloughed for 60 days by W[estern] Dept. S[pecial] Order No. 1, dated 15 Jany. 1832. Left his Post on the 26th. March. *Extended*

for 4 additional months by *S[pecial] Order* No. 108. from the adjt. General's office dated 21. July. R. Jones.
[AES 4] Submitted. R[oger] J[ones] Novr. 13th.

ALS (NA, RG 94 Records of the Adjutant General's Office, Letters Received, D–80, 1832, filed with 38051, Adjutant General's Office, 1896). Addressed: "To Genl. E. P. Gaines, Com[mandin]g W[estern] Dept. U. S. Army Memphis T[ennessee]." Endorsed: "Thro[ugh]. W[estern] Dept 23 Oct 1832."

[1] Edmund P. Gaines (sketch, 1:301, *n.* 3).

[2] See 1:313 for the furlough granted; see 1:329 for the granting of a four-month extension.

[3] See 1:231, *n.* 12.

[4] Davis returned to his regiment August 18, 1832 (1:332), and since he had received a four-month extension (1:329), he had about six weeks' leave remaining. He was granted the extension, although not of the requested length, as he is listed for duty on the muster rolls for January and February 1833 (NA, RG 94, First Infantry, Company B; 1:347).

[5] George A. McCall (sketch, 1:301, *n.* 2).

[6] Roger Jones (sketch, 1:123, *n.* 6).

ABSTRACT

1:341 Company Muster Roll

Fort Crawford,[1] October 31, 1832

Lists Second Lieutenant J. F. Davis of Captain Samuel MacRee's[2] Company B, First Regiment of Infantry commanded by Colonel Z. Taylor,[3] as absent on "detached Service, Jeff Barracks,[4] Order of Col Taylor Sept 3, 1832." [5] Report covers September and October 1832.

Printed form, filled in and signed (NA, RG 94 Records of the Adjutant General's Office, Muster Rolls of Regular Army Organizations, First Infantry, Company B), 2. Signed: "S. MacRee Capt. Z. Taylor. Col. 1st Regt. U. S. Infy." Endorsed: "Proves. (Recd. Decr. 6th. 1832.) Entered."

[1] See 1:231, *n.* 12.

[2] Samuel MacRee (sketch, 1:325, *n.* 2).

[3] Zachary Taylor (sketch, 1:332, *n.* 3).

[4] For Jefferson Barracks, see 1:123, *n.* 3.

[5] Davis was on detached service for the purpose of escorting Black Hawk and other Indian prisoners to Jefferson Barracks (1:335).

ABSTRACT

Post Return

1:342

Fort Crawford,[1] Michigan Territory[2]
November [30,] 1832

Lists Second Lieutenant Jeff. F. Davis, Company B, First Infantry, as absent on furlough.[3]

Printed form, filled in and signed (NA, RG 94 Records of the Adjutant General's Office, Post Returns, Fort Crawford, 1817–34), 2. Signed: "Z Taylor, Col, 1st. Regt, U. S. Infy." Endorsed: "Entd Recd Jany. 7th 1833."

[1] See 1:231, *n.* 12.

[2] See 1:149, *n.* 2.

[3] See 1:340, *n.* 4 for an explanation of why Davis was on furlough at this time.

ABSTRACT

Semiannual Company Muster Roll

1:343

Fort Crawford,[1] December 31, 1832

Lists Second Lieutenant Jeff Davis of Captain Samuel MacRee's[2] Company B, First Regiment of Infantry commanded by Colonel Z. Taylor,[3] as being on furlough.[4] Report covers June through December 1832.

Printed form, filled in and signed (NA, RG 94 Records of the Adjutant General's Office, Muster Rolls of Regular Army Organizations, First Infantry, Company B), 2. Signed: "Saml MacRee Capt Z. Taylor. Col. 1st Regt. U. S. Infy." Endorsed: "Proves. Recd. Febry. 15th. 1833. Entered."

[1] See 1:231, *n.* 12.

[2] Samuel MacRee (sketch, 1:325, *n.* 2).

[3] Zachary Taylor (sketch, 1:332, *n.* 3).

[4] See 1:340, *n.* 4 for an explanation of Davis' furlough.

ABSTRACT

Register of Payments to Officers

1:344

[Washington, D.C.,] January 5, 1833

Lists payment by Paymaster T. Wright[1] to Second Lieutenant Jefferson Davis, First Infantry, $252. Amount includes pay and allowance for Davis and one servant,[2] for September through December 1832.

D (NA, RG 99 Records of the Office of the Paymaster General, Register of Payments to Officers, IV, 27), 1.

[1] Thomas Wright (sketch, 1:320, *n.* 2).
[2] The servant was James Pemberton (sketch, 1:5, *n.* 4).

ABSTRACT

1:345

Order No. 5

Assistant Adjutant General's Office
Western Department
Memphis, Tennessee, February 22, 1833

Second Lieutenant Jeff. Davis is ordered to sit on a court martial which will convene at Fort Crawford[1] April 22, 1833, or as soon thereafter as possible.[2] By order of Major General Gaines.[3]

GEO. A. MCCALL[4]
A[ide-] D[e-] C[amp], actg. ass[istant] adj[utant] gen[eral]

LbCS (NA, RG 94 Records of the Adjutant General's Office, Western Department Orders, CCLXXII, 555), 1. Endorsed: "(Recd. March 13th. 1833)."

[1] For Fort Crawford, see 1:231, *n.* 12.
[2] By April 22 Davis had received his appointment as a second lieutenant of Dragoons and had left Fort Crawford (1:349, 353).
[3] Edmund P. Gaines (sketch, 1:301, *n.* 3).
[4] George A. McCall (sketch, 1:301, *n.* 2).

ABSTRACT

1:346

Post Return

Fort Crawford,[1] Michigan Territory[2]
February [28,] 1833

Lists Second Lieutenant Jeff. F. Davis, Company B, First Infantry, present at the post. Remarks: "For duty."

Printed form, filled in and signed (NA, RG 94 Records of the Adjutant General's Office, Post Returns, Fort Crawford, 1817–34), 2. Signed: "Z. Taylor.

Col, 1st Regt. U. S. Infy. Com[man]d-[ing]." Endorsed: "Entd Recd. 30th. March."

[1] See 1:231, *n*. 12.
[2] See 1:149, *n*. 2.

ABSTRACT

Company Muster Roll

1:347

Fort Crawford,[1] February 28, 1833

Lists Second Lieutenant Jeff. Davis of Captain Samuel MacRee's[2] Company B, First Regiment of Infantry commanded by Colonel Z. Taylor,[3] as present. Report covers January and February 1833.

Printed form, filled in and signed (NA, RG 94 Records of the Adjutant General's Office, Muster Rolls of Regular Army Organizations, First Infantry, Company B), 2. Signed: "S. MacRee Capt Z. Taylor. Col 1st Regt U S Infy." Endorsed: "Proves Recd. 13th. April 1833. Entered."

[1] See 1:231, *n*. 12.
[2] Samuel MacRee (sketch, 1:325, *n*. 2).
[3] Zachary Taylor (sketch, 1:332, *n*. 3).

From Peter Hagner

1:348

SIR. March 1st. 1833

I have received your letter of the 26th. January last,[1] wherein you request information as to the State of your public Accounts. In reply, I herewith enclose a Copy of a letter addressed to you on the 29th. March last,[2] which appears to be the last communication made to you from this office, and by which you may perceive that a balance of 28 Cents is due from you per Settlement of that date, which sum you can pay over to any Officer now disbursing in the Subsistence Department, and forward his receipt to this Office. Respectfully, Your Obd. Servt. PETER HAGNER[3]
Audr.

LbC (NA, RG 217 Records of the United States General Accounting Office, Third Auditor's Office, Miscellaneous Letters Sent, LXI, 369). Addressed: "Lieut. Jeffn. Davis. Fort Crawford. Praire du Chien." Enclosure missing.

[1] Davis' letter of January 26 has not been found.
[2] The Hagner letter of March 29, 1832, is printed as 1:319.
[3] Peter Hagner (sketch, 1:199, *n*. 5).

1:349 From Lewis Cass

SIR: WAR DEPARTMENT *4. March 1833*

You are hereby informed, that on the *fourth instant* the President[1] of the United States appointed you a *Second Lieutenant* in the *U. S.* regiment of *Dragoons*[2] in the service of the United States: should the Senate, at their next session, advise and consent thereto, you will be commissioned accordingly.[3]

You will, immediately on receipt hereof, please to communicate to this Department, through the Adjutant General's Office,[4] your acceptance or non acceptance of said appointment; and, in case of accepting, you will <—report yourself—> *repair without delay to Jefferson Barracks, and there await further orders.*

Lewis Cass[5]
Secretary of War

Printed form, filled in and signed (Lewis Cass Collection, Illinois State Historical Library, Springfield); printed form, filled in and signed, copy (Abraham Lincoln Collection, Chicago Historical Society); printed form, filled in, retained copy (NA, RG 94 Records of the Adjutant General's Office, Records of the Appointment, Commission, and Personnel Branch, Letters of Army Appointments, I, 54). Addressed: "For Second Lieutenant Jefferson Davis U. S. Regiment of Dragoons Fort Crawford."

[1] The President was Andrew Jackson (sketch, 1:239, *n.* 2).

[2] The Regiment of Dragoons, comprising ten companies and some 1,832 men, was established by act of Congress, March 2, 1833, to replace the Battalion of Mounted Rangers which had been recruited to patrol the upper Mississippi Valley in the summer of 1832. Dragoons were to serve on horse or foot, receive equal pay and allowances with the regular army (*Statutes at Large of the United States*, IV [1846], 533, 652; Weigley, *United States Army*, 159–60), and were to be commanded by Colonel Henry Dodge, who had led the six-company Mounted Ranger Battalion (*DAB*). Jefferson Barracks was selected as the regiment's assembly post, and Louisville as its recruiting headquarters (Weigley, *United States Army*, 159).

[3] Davis did not receive this notification until late July 1833, according to his letter of acceptance (1:366). However, his appointment was twice announced to the army, in Order No. 14, Headquarters of the Army, March 6, 1833 (1:350), and in Order No. 40, Headquarters of the Army, May 4, 1833 (1:354). Because of the protest against his rank contained in his acceptance, and apparently because of his forthcoming staff service (see 1:370), when the Senate met for its next session (December 2, 1833–June 30, 1834), Davis was nominated for appointment as a first lieutenant of Dragoons (1:404).

[4] Roger Jones was the adjutant general (sketch, 1:123, *n.* 6).

[5] Lewis Cass (1782–1866), secretary of war, 1831–36, was born in New Hampshire, educated at Exeter Academy, and practiced law in Ohio, 1802–12. He served in the War of 1812, beginning as a colonel of volunteers and

was, in 1813, appointed governor of Michigan Territory. Cass was named as John Eaton's successor in the War Department after a particularly distinguished career as governor, and in 1836 was sent to France as minister plenipotentiary. Resigning that post in 1842, Cass hoped to be named the Democratic presidential nominee in 1844, but was not, and instead was elected to the Senate in 1845. A strong nationalist, Cass was the unsuccessful 1848 Democratic presidential candidate and remained an influential member of Congress until his resignation in 1860 (*DAB*).

EXTRACT

Order No. 14

1:350

Head Quarters of the Army.

Adjutant Genls. Office, Washington, 6th. March, 1833

I. The following lists of appointments in the United States Regiment of Dragoons,[1] has been received from the War Office, and is published for general information

War Department
5th. March, 1833

II. The President[2] has made the following appointments in the Regiment of United States Dragoons, to be raised under the Act of Congress, approved 2nd. March, 1833. . . .

Jeff. Davis 4 Mar. 1833. 2d. Lieut. 1st Infy. 1. July, 1828.[3]. . .

III. The organization of the Regiment of Dragoons will be perfected hereafter by the selection of such Officers from the Battalion of Rangers,[1] as may be deemed qualified for the Service. The Mounted Rangers will be continued in service until relieved by the regular Cavalry. By order of Major General Macomb.[4] (Signed)

R. JONES.[5]
Adjt. Genl.

LbC (NA, RG 94 Records of the Adjutant General's Office, War Department Orders and Circulars, Orders, VI, 164–66), 2. Endorsed: "printed."

[1] See 1:349, *n.* 2 for information about both the Mounted Rangers and the Dragoon Regiment.

[2] The President was Andrew Jackson (sketch, 1:239, *n.* 2).

[3] Davis left Fort Crawford by the end of April (1:353), and since the letter notifying him of his appointment (1:349) did not reach him until July (1:366), he undoubtedly learned of his appointment to the Dragoons by this order. Davis' appointment was also announced in the order of May 4, 1833 (1:354).

[4] Alexander Macomb (sketch, 1:38, *n.* 10).

[5] Roger Jones (sketch, 1:123, *n.* 6).

1:351

From William B. Lewis

Sir March 6, 1833

Agreeably to your request, per your letter of 26th. January last,[1] I now enclose you a copy of my letter, addressed you at Galena[2] 28th. March 1832,[3] to which I beg leave to call your attention.

W.B.L.[4]

LbC (NA, RG 217 Records of the United States General Accounting Office, Second Auditor's Office, Letters Sent, Property Division, Volume F, 305). Addressed: "Lt. Jef. Davis 1st Infy. Fort Crawford." Enclosure missing.

[1] Davis' letter of January 26 has not been found.

[2] Galena was near Dubuques Mines, where Davis had been stationed (1:231, *n.* 18; 1:291, *n.* 2).

[3] The Lewis letter of March 28, 1832, is printed as 1:318. Davis was on furlough on March 28 (1:325).

[4] William B. Lewis (sketch, 1:166, *n.* 1).

ABSTRACT

1:352

Post Return

Fort Crawford,[1] Michigan Territory[2]
March [31,] 1833

Lists Second Lieutenant Jeff. F. Davis, Company B, First Infantry, present at the post. Remarks: "Sick."

Printed form, filled in and signed (NA, RG 94 Records of the Adjutant General's Office, Post Returns, Fort Crawford, 1817–34), 2. Signed: "Z. Taylor. Col." Endorsed: "Entd Recd 27th. April."

[1] See 1:231, *n.* 12.

[2] See 1:149, *n.* 2.

ABSTRACT

1:353

Post Return

Fort Crawford,[1] Michigan Territory[2]
April [30,] 1833

Lists Second Lieutenant J. F. Davis, Company B, First Infantry, as transferred.[3] Remarks: "Appointed 2nd Lieut. of Dragoons, Mar. 4. 1833."[4]

Printed form, filled in and signed (NA, RG 94 Records of the Adjutant General's Office, Post Returns, Fort Crawford, 1817–34), 2. Signed: "Z. Taylor Col 1st. Regt. U. S. Infy." Endorsed: "Recd. May. 23d."

1 See 1:231, *n.* 12.

2 See 1:149, *n.* 2.

3 Davis has not been located on post returns for either Fort Crawford or Jefferson Barracks for May or June 1833, apparently because he was quickly ordered into recruiting duty for the Dragoons at Lexington, Kentucky (see 1:357).

4 See 1:349 for evidence of Davis' appointment to the Dragoons.

ABSTRACT

Order No. 40 1:354

Headquarters of the Army
Adjutant General's Office, Washington, May 4, 1833

The appointment of Second Lieutenant Jefferson Davis, First Regiment of Infantry, as second lieutenant of Dragoons effective March 4, 1833, "is published for general information." [1] By order of Major General Macomb.[2] (Signed) R. JONES,[3]
Adjutant General.

LbC (NA, RG 94 Records of the Adjutant General's Office, War Department Orders and Circulars, Orders, VI, 217–23), 4. Endorsed: "Printed."

1 By the time this order was published, Davis had already left Fort Crawford (1:353). He evidently learned of his appointment by War Department Order No. 14, March 6, 1833 (1:350), since the letter of appointment from Secretary of War Lewis Cass, March 4, 1833 (1:349), did not reach him until July (1:366).

2 Alexander Macomb (sketch, 1:38, *n.* 10).

3 Roger Jones (sketch, 1:123, *n.* 6).

ABSTRACT

Register of Payments to Officers 1:355

[Washington, D.C.,] May 8, 1833

Lists payment by Paymaster A. D. Steuart[1] to Second Lieutenant Jefferson Davis, First Infantry,[2] $124. Amount includes pay and allowance for Davis and one servant,[3] for January and February.

D (NA, RG 99 Records of the Office of the Paymaster General, Register of Payments to Officers, IV, 27), 1.

1 Adam D. Steuart, a Virginian commissioned paymaster in January 1833, was stationed at Charleston in 1833 and

later at St. Louis, 1834–36 (Gordon, *Compilation of Registers of the Army*, 486, 516, 546, 576). Brevetted for meritorious conduct in 1848, he was promoted to lieutenant colonel and deputy paymaster general in 1854, and resigned in 1855. When the Civil War began, he reentered the service, and was commissioned major and paymaster in 1861. He died in 1867 (Heitman, *Historical Register*, I, 921–22).

[2] Davis had been transferred to Dragoons (1:349, 353).

[3] The servant was James Pemberton (sketch, 1:5, *n.* 4).

ABSTRACT

1:356

Register of Payments to Officers

[Washington, D.C.,] May 18, 1833

Lists payment by Paymaster E. Kirby[1] to Second Lieutenant Jefferson Davis, Dragoons,[2] $126. Amount includes pay and allowance for Davis and one servant,[3] for March and April. Remarks: "Dragoons."

D (NA, RG 99 Records of the Office of the Paymaster General, Register of Payments to Officers, IV, 27), 1.

[1] Edmund Kirby (1794–1849), paymaster at Brownsville, New York (Gordon, *Compilation of Registers of the Army*, 486), enlisted in the army in Connecticut in 1812, was retained as a second lieutenant in 1815, and became major and paymaster in 1824. Kirby was Winfield Scott's chief paymaster in the Mexican War (J. H. Smith, *War with Mexico*, II, 366), was brevetted lieutenant colonel for gallantry in the battles of Contreras and Churubusco, and colonel for gallantry at Molino del Rey (*Appleton's*; Heitman, *Historical Register*, I, 603).

[2] Davis was appointed to the Dragoons March 4 (1:349).

[3] The servant was James Pemberton (sketch, 1:5, *n.* 4).

ABSTRACT

1:357

Register of Contracts for Rations for Recruits &c

[Washington, D.C.,] June 1, 1833

Records that Lieutenant Jeff Davis, U.S. Dragoons, recruiting officer in Lexington, Kentucky, contracted on June 1, 1833, with Benjamin C. Blincoe[1] to provide rations for recruits, between June 5 and November 30, 1833, at 12.75 cents per ration, and filed the contract with the second comptroller's[2] office.

D (NA, RG 192 Records of the Office of the Commissary General of Subsistence, Register of Contracts, IV [1831–34]), 1.

[1] Perhaps Benjamin C. Blinco, who was the keeper of the Columbus coffee-house in Lexington, 1838–39 (MacCabe, *Directory of the City of Lexington*, 41).

[2] The second comptroller was James B. Thornton (sketch, 1:244, *n.* 1).

To George Gibson

1:358

SIR[1] Lexington Ky. June 14th 1833

I received this spring from the 3rd Auditor[2] a letter[3] closing as follows.

"due you on account of Q. M. Dpt. of $14.95 which will be carried to your credit on account of Subsistence, under which head of appropiation you are charged with $15.23 per settlement of the 3rd. June last," referring to June 1831.[4]

I then believed that the Auditor was at fault but nevertheless took from the A. Com. of Subsitence[5] where I was serving a receipt for the balance claimed as due the Subsistence Dept. (as enclosed;) whereby I have paid to the Subsistence Department fifteen 23/100 Dollars. With great respect yr. mo. obt. Servant JEFFN. DAVIS

2d. L[ieutenant] U. S. Dragoons

ALS (NA, RG 192 Records of the Office of the Commissary General of Subsistence, Letters Received, D–1251, 1833). Addressed: "To Genl. Geo. Gibson Com[missar]y Gen[era]l U. S. Army Washington D. C." Endorsed: "Recd. 25 June." Enclosure missing.

[1] George Gibson (sketch, 1:179, *n.* 2).

[2] The third auditor was Peter Hagner (sketch, 1:199, *n.* 5).

[3] The letter from the third auditor to which Davis refers and from which he quotes is printed as 1:319.

[4] The "settlement of the 3rd. June last" was probably that enclosed in 1:266.

[5] Possibly James W. Kingsbury, assistant commissary at Fort Crawford until April 24, by which time Davis was probably on his way to Lexington (Post Return, April 1833 [NA, RG 94, Fort Crawford, 1817–34]).

To George Gibson

1:359

SIR[1] Lexington Ky. June 21st 1833

Herewith enclosed I transmit you a contract for furnishing the Recruits[2] at this Rendezvous. I could not sooner obtain the bond accompanying. Vy. Respectfully yr. mo. obt. Servt.

JEFFN. DAVIS

Lt. U. S. Dragoons

ALS (NA, RG 192 Records of the Office of the Commissary General of Subsistence, Letters Received, D–1213, 1833). Addressed: "To Genl. Geo. Gibson Com[missary] Gen[era]l Sub-[sistence] U. S. Army Washington D. C." Endorsed: "Recd. 29 June." Enclosures missing.

[1] George Gibson (sketch, 1:179, *n.* 2).

[2] The mentioned contract may be the rations contract noted in 1:357.

1:360 To William B. Lewis

SIR[1] Lexington June 30th 1833

Herewith I have the honor to transmit to you a monthly acct. current for the recruiting Rendezvous at Lexington Kentucky accompanied by the Vouchers referred to therein Very Respectfully yr. mo. obt. Servt.

JEFFN DAVIS
L[ieutenant] U. S. Drgs.

ALS (NA, RG 217 Records of the United States General Accounting Office, Second Auditor's Office, Second Auditor's Accounts, Account 17,593). Addressed: "To W. B. Lewis Esq. 2nd Auditor Treasy. Washington D. C." Enclosures missing.

[1] William B. Lewis (sketch, 1:166, *n.* 1).

1:361 From Florida A. Davis McCaleb

["Hurricane,"[1] June 30, 1833][2]

Once more My Dearest Uncle, I enter on my long cherished employment. Yet so lately have I arisen from a sick bed, that I fear I shall send you but a poor and incoherent letter. Illness takes from our hearts too much of their buoyancy, and enfeebles our constitutions too much, to render us even tolerably agreeable even to our dearest friends. Fever and very <–ob–> unkind inflammation in the eyes have kept me shut up, nearly all the Spring—and dull, very dull and cheerless does every object appear when viewed with the eyes of sorrow and ill health.

My employments since your absence have been as usual. My music, when I am able to see the keys, is still a source of inexhaustable amusement. Le jeune malade[3] sounds somewhat, feebly though, now.

You are I fear in the midst of a disease which has proved truly melancholy in its effects, in our own land.[4] Thank God, we are still untouched, by its destructive hand. Do you take[5] of yourself my Dear Uncle? I have my fears! But surely one, with high hopes, and bright prospects, might be persuaded, to shield himself from the evil day, and if he did not, why should the miserable and obscure, seek to prolong suffering.

July. 1—I commenced this, yesterday, and have been so unwell all the morning, that I have not been able to finish it. My eyes, are growing worse and, I know not when my general health will be restored.

You think me very forgetful, Dear Uncle, that I have not written to you, before, but my heart must be cold indeed, when I remember you no more. Indeed I have cause to complain of you, for all your friends have been favoured with Some mark of remembrance but myself[6]—not a word, not a line to tell me you were well, or—but I trust you have more agreeable pastimes. I am too dull and common-place, too unwearied in my perseverence, to be highly appreciated, and you have grown weary of receiving the stupid letters of a very stupid friend. So I am risking much in sending you another. Throw it aside, if too long, but do not tell me of it when I see you. I cannot hope for an answer.

I am on a visit to the Hurricane for some days, as Papa[7] leaves to morrow for Jackson, and I have promised to remain with Mama,[8] until he returns. She speaks of you frequently, and with affection, and says, she would write to you, but thinks you would not care for her letters.

Our friends are generally well. I have seen but few of them since your departure and I have become so poor a correspondent, that I seldom write.

I anticipate a visit to Woodville[9] in a few weeks, if my health will allow me to accomplish the trip. You are not here to go with us now. Will we ever meet again? If not, I know My Dear Uncle too well to think he will forget me, even though the world should smile fondly on him, and his Country hold out fair rewards to <—the—> <his>[10] ambitions. [that?][11] you will never forget me, and that some[time?][11] you will desire to see me again. Cherish Ambition, cherish pride, and <—alw—> run from excitement to excitement, it will prevent that ever preying *viper* melancholy, it will blunt your sensibilities, and cause you to be unmoved amidst all afflictions. You have cause to look for happiness, and that you may gather it sweet blossoms to your bosom at last, do I fondly pray. But—I, who am the very type of all obscurity whose life has been but a tissue of misfortune from my very birth, and that the greatest, should sleep in <the>[10] [unsunned?], <and>[10] most secret vale of Earth Then let it be. Write to me, et prenez garde, prenez garde, si vous ne voulez pas me rendre miserable a la mort. Your Sister. FLORIDA[12]

ALS (Jefferson Davis Papers, University of Alabama Library, Tuscaloosa). Addressed: "To, Lieut. J. F. Davis <—Lexington Kentucky—> Jefferson Barracks Mo." Printed: Strode, *Private Letters*, 8–9, variant version.

[1] See 1:328, *n.* 2 for "Hurricane."

[2] Both place and date were supplied from internal evidence. The envelope bears a handwritten postmark indicating that the letter was posted on July 5, 1833, from Rocky Spring, Mississippi. "Rocky Spring" was no doubt Rocky Springs, "a post-hamlet of Claiborne county, 25 miles northeast of Port Gibson, the county seat" (*Encyclopaedia of Mississippi History*, II, 572).

[3] Possibly a song title but, in spite of the confused gender, more likely a reference to herself.

[4] Cholera was raging in many parts of the nation when Mrs. McCaleb wrote this letter. *Niles' Weekly Register*, June 22, 1833 (p. 265), reported 169 persons had died at Lexington, Kentucky, during the first eleven days of June. Of Davis' experience during the epidemic, Mrs. Davis wrote, "Lieutenant Davis was sent on recruiting service, and went to Louisville and Lexington, Ky. The cholera broke out while he was at the latter place, and people fled from it in numbers. . . . he remained at his post, took care of his recruits, attended to their diet, and, as ever, did his best regardless of consequences" (*Memoir*, I, 145). The total number of deaths from cholera in Lexington between June 1 and August 1 was 502 (*Niles' Weekly Register*, August 24, 1833, p. 417). See 1:357, 360 for evidence that Davis was in Lexington; see also 1:2, *n.* 10.

[5] The word "care" has obviously been omitted.

[6] None of Davis' letters to his friends have been found.

[7] "Papa" was Joseph Emory Davis (sketch, 1:19, *n.* 1; 1:Appendix IV, Entry 15).

[8] Eliza Van Benthuysen Davis (1:Appendix IV, Entry 25), Florida's stepmother, came from a New York family of Dutch origin (Van Benthuysen and Hall, *Van Benthuysen Genealogy*, 71). One of twelve children, Eliza was born January 23, 1811 (Gravestone ["Hurricane" and "Brierfield" plantations cemetery, near Vicksburg, Mississippi]), and was living with her widowed mother in New Orleans when she met Joseph E. Davis (Strode, *American Patriot*, 51). After their marriage on October 5, 1827 (Marriage Records [Mississippi Department of Health, Jackson]), they made their home at "Hurricane," Joseph's plantation in Warren County, Mississippi, where Eliza devoted herself to caring for Joseph's three daughters by a previous marriage (Strode, *American Patriot*, 51). Always somewhat frail, Eliza's health declined markedly when, after the fall of New Orleans in 1862, the family left "Hurricane." She died October 4, 1863, at Fort Lauderdale Springs, Mississippi (Mitchell, Journal, 50–51 [Southern Historical Collection, University of North Carolina Library, Chapel Hill]).

[9] Davis' mother and his sister, Lucinda Stamps, lived near Woodville,

county seat of Wilkinson County, in extreme southwestern Mississippi. See 1:22, *n.* 5.
[10] Interlined.
[11] Seal damage.
[12] Florida A. Davis McCaleb Laughlin (sketch, 1:19, *n.* 9; 1:Appendix IV, Entry 28) was Davis' niece, not his sister.

From Lucinda Farrar Davis Davis Stamps 1:362

MY DEAR BROTHER Heatherdon[1] July 7th 1833

It has been long since I have written to you not because I had not the inclination for that has never been wanting my health since you left here has been verry bad and for six weeks past I have been confined to my bed[2] I am now mutch better and hope soon to be in perfect health I have felt great concern for you While the cholera was rageing in Lexington[3] and was verry mutch relieved by the receit of your letter of the 14th of June[4] do Write to us often or as often as you have time while the Cholera remains there but I fervently hope it will have left there before you receive this Our Country has seffered greatly from it perticularly New Orleans on the coast and in the Attacapas[5] a part of our State has allso suffered from it in Adams County the farmers have sustained great loss from the loss of slaves I think we had two cases on our place but both recovered[6]

the health of our family at present is good allso mothers[7] and her children[8] are in verry good health our friend in Louisanna are allso well the last letter from Eliza[9] says they were all well except Florida[10] who had the sore eyes We expect them in August to stay some time Mary[11] still remains with me she has not been verry well she will rite to you soon Mr Stamps[12] says every day he will rite the next but you know how lazy he is about writeing I fear you will not be able to read what I have writen my eyes are verry weak. I wished to say something on the subject of Hughs[13] education to ask you what you thought of Trancelvania in its pesent situaion[14] write to me what you think of it Or if he was to go there have you any friend to whose care he could be intrusted or that would take charge of him It is a matter of great importance to me and I think of it with great concern Write to me soon and tell me what you think of it I had mutch to say about your future prospecs but must delay for the next letter my eyes are so weak that it is painful to write in a short time I hope to be able to write you a better letter   do write too us often there is nothing gives me more pleasure than your letters and Mother is verery unhappy when she does not hear from you often   The children[15] all wish to be remembered to their Uncle   Farewell my dear brother believe me as ever your tru<l>[16]ly affectionate sister

LUCINDA STAMPS[17]

ALS (Jefferson Davis Papers, University of Alabama Library, Tuscaloosa). Addressed: "To Left J. F. Davis <–Lexington Ky–> Jefferson Barracks Mo."

1 Possibly William Stamps's plantation, which a sales notice in the November 24, 1834, issue of the Woodville (Mississippi) *Republican* described as being of 1,500 acres and lying some three miles east of Woodville.

2 Lucinda had recently had a miscarriage (see 1:363).

3 For a discussion of the cholera epidemic in Lexington, see 1:2, *n.* 10 and 1:361, *n.* 4.

4 Davis' letter of June 14 has not been found.

5 The Attakapas region consisted of St. Mary, St. Martin, and Lafayette parishes in south central Louisiana (Prichard [ed.], "Glimpses of Louisiana a Century Ago," *Louisiana Historical Quarterly*, XXIV, 39). Another source includes Iberia and Vermilion parishes (Dimitry, *Lessons in the History of Louisiana*, 158).

6 Asiatic cholera raged in Mississippi and Louisiana in May, June, and most of July. During the first three weeks of June, 1,032 deaths were reported in New Orleans; St. Martinville, in southern Louisiana, was nearly abandoned; the epidemic had abated at Natchez (*Niles' Weekly Register*, July 13, 1833, pp. 321–22). The disease seemed to affect mainly the black population of both states (*ibid.*, July 6, p. 305, July 13, p. 322, August 3, p. 369; Duffy [ed.], *History of Medicine*, II, 142).

7 Jane Cook Davis (sketch, 1:22, *n.* 4; 1:Appendix IV, Entry 14).

8 The reference here is probably to Jane Lucinda (sketch, 1:363, *n.* 35; 1:Appendix IV, Entry 90) and Ellen Mary (sketch, 1:363, *n.* 36; 1:Appendix IV, Entry 92), daughters of Mary Ellen Davis, who were reared by their grandmother, Jane Cook Davis, after their mother's death in 1824. Lucinda may also mean to include Mary Jane Bradford (sketch, 1:363, *n.* 20; 1:Appendix IV, Entry 74) who was visiting her grandmother (see 1:363).

9 Eliza Van Benthuysen Davis (sketch, 1:361, *n.* 8; 1:Appendix IV, Entry 25), Lucinda's sister-in-law.

10 Florida A. Davis McCaleb Laughlin (sketch, 1:19, *n.* 9; 1:Appendix IV, Entry 28), Lucinda's niece. See also 1:361.

11 Probably Mary Lucinda Davis Mitchell (1:Appendix IV, Entry 26). Niece of Lucinda Stamps, she was the daughter of Joseph E. Davis and his first wife, whose identity is not known (1:Appendix IV, *n.* 25). Born in 1816, Mary Lucinda married Dr. Charles Jouett Mitchell in 1838 and went with him to Paris, where he attended medical school (1:521; Mitchell to E. Davis, December 5, 1838, Mitchell, Journal, 1–7 [Southern Historical Collection, University of North Carolina Library, Chapel Hill]). By 1845, when living in Louisiana, Mary Lucinda's health began to fail, and she travelled to Bermuda and Cuba in hopes of restoring her strength. She died the following year, leaving three children—Mary Elizabeth, Hugh, and Joseph—who were reared by Eliza and Joseph E. Davis at "Hurricane" (Gravestone ["Hurricane" and "Brierfield" plantations cemetery, Davis Island, near

Vicksburg, Mississippi]; E. Davis to Mitchell, February 17, 1846, Mitchell, Journal, 18–21 [Southern Historical Collection, University of North Carolina Library, Chapel Hill]; Strode, *American Patriot*, 213).

[12] William Stamps (1:Appendix IV, Entry 63), second husband of Lucinda Farrar Davis Davis, was born *ca.* 1797–99 and died in March 1878 (H. A. Davis, *The Davis Family*, 84; More, Genealogical Data [Jefferson Davis Association, Rice University, Houston]). He married Lucinda March 5, 1820 (Marriage Records [Wilkinson County Courthouse, Woodville, Mississippi]), and by her had four children —Jane Davis, Anna Aurelia, William, Jr., and Isaac Davis. A prominent citizen of Woodville, William Stamps was appointed a director of the Planters' Bank in 1833, was selected in 1834 as delegate to the state rights convention in Jackson, and in 1842 served as secretary of the temperance meetings (Woodville [Mississippi] *Republican*, March 23, 1833, May 10, 1834, October 1, 1842). As a landowner and businessman, Stamps seems to have been a victim of bad fortune, for notices in the local newspaper during the 1830's and 1840's indicate that his considerable holdings were progressively diminished through sale, often necessitated by litigation: announcements in 1836 stated that property belonging to William Stamps—1,500 acres near Woodville—was to be sold to satisfy the "debts and costs" incurred in legal cases; similar notices appeared in 1838 and 1845 (*ibid.*, April 2, June 4, 1836, September 22, 1838, June 28, 1845). Stamps himself advertised still other property, including four lots in Woodville and fifty slaves, for sale in 1836 (*ibid.*, May 28, 1836). By that time the family had moved from Woodville to land bordering the Mississippi River above Fort Adams (1:395, 496, 513). Their plantations there, "Artonish" and "Lochleven," as well as some other property, which Stamps had apparently used as security for promissory notes, were lost in 1839 (Woodville *Republican*, April 27, 1839). The Stampses then moved back to Woodville (1:529) and resided at "Rosemont," Jane Cook Davis' home (H. A. Davis, *The Davis Family*, 84).

[13] Hugh Robert Davis (1:Appendix IV, Entry 61), son of Lucinda Stamps by her first husband, was born in 1818 in Wilkinson County, Mississippi (H. A. Davis, *The Davis Family*, 173). On March 26, 1845, he married Anne Jane Boyle of West Feliciana Parish, Louisiana; they had five children. Hugh Robert apparently was a planter until his death on March 1, 1871 (More, Genealogical Data [Jefferson Davis Association, Rice University, Houston]; H. A. Davis, *The Davis Family*, 173).

[14] Davis had attended Transylvania University, 1823–24, while Horace Holley was president (1:5, *n.* 8). The university, which had had an excellent reputation under Holley's leadership, went into a period of decline after his resignation in 1827 (Miller, "Transylvania University as the Nation Saw It," *Filson Club History Quarterly*, XXXIV, 309–12). A fire in May 1829 destroyed the main building and the law library with a loss of $30,000. Only the medical department continued to prosper, as successive presidents resigned almost annually. In 1839 most of the prestigious medical faculty left to form the Medical Institute of Louisville, and by 1840 almost all state aid had been withdrawn from Transylvania (Townsend, "Transylvania University," in Kerr [ed.], *History of Kentucky*, II, 1055–58).

[15] For Lucinda's children, see 1:Appendix IV, Chart Ten.

[16] Interlined.

[17] Lucinda Farrar Davis Davis Stamps (sketch, 1:19, *n.* 3; 1:Appendix IV, Entry 20).

1:363

From David Bradford

Abeyville, West Feliciana,[1] Loua.

DEAR BROTHER July 7th. 1833

Your very acceptable letter[2] from Lexington we recd. a day or two ago and it afforded us great pleasure to find you were in good health and had escaped the Cholera which appears to have raged with excessive destruction at Lexington.[3] I saw an account of the death of Dr. Challen[4] and have great fears for my brother-in-law, the Revd. Jas. Challen[5] who is now or was lately in Lexington. Certainly St. Francisville and the whole section of Country watered by Bayou Sara[6] and Thompson's Creek[7] has been unaccountably favored by not being visited by the pestilence.[8] It has been very fatal on the Homochitto.[9] I was at Mr. Stamps[10] this day Week; his last news from brother Jo.[11] was that they were all well but that the Cholera was at the adjoining plantations; he advised Mr. Stamps to pull up every melon vine and cut down the fruit trees. I have not tho't it requisite to adopt these precautions; fearing that some of my children or black people might meet with fruits and melons abroad and eat so greadily as to make themselves sick, but having them at home I could have them used in moderation. Thus far we have used garden vegetables and roasting ears without any detriment.

I went to N[ew] O[rleans] last Jany. many of my most experienced friends thinking it requisite to obtain the [Shffty?][12] I was very sanguine. I found my Competetor[13] had pledged himself to my brother James[14] not to be an aplicant at that time but to support me; and to Dr. Smith[15] he had done the same thing; and had Dr. S. been alive no one doubted but that I would have been appointed. I considered myself injured and demanded gentlemanly satisfaction but the mean wretch[13] would not nor could not be made, fight. Brother James outraged him in the public ballroom. I never laid eyes on him after his appointment in N. O. and since my return I have been requested to let him alone.

I moved to this place about the last of March and Contemplate improving and residing on my land adjoining (a small tract of 80 or 90 acres) and perhaps resuming my profession[16] after I get fixed so as to attend to it without inconvenience to myself or family.

I have an interesting young Kentuckian living with me, learning French and Spanish and reading law and teaching school. David[17] &

Ben,[18] and Ann[19] go to school to him. Mary Jane[20] is at Mothers[21] going to Miss Calders.[22] Hugh[23] is at home, not in good health. I wanted him to come down and stay with me and read Spanish with Mr. Martin the Schoolmaster; and I hope we will have Joseph[24] and Luther,[25] (who are at home attending to plantation affairs as Mr. Smith[26] has no overseer) alternately week about with us. Sister Lucinda[27] had the misfortune of having a miscarriage and it was tho't it would benefit her to have an infant at the breast and we have left her namesake our dear little Lucinda[28] with her. Amanda[29] misses her very much; but we are in hopes it will benefit both, as Amanda's milk had become somewhat injurious to the child. We have a number of Candidates for Congress, brother James, J. M. Bradford[30] Dr. Chinn[31] and Alexr. Penn,[32] Recr. of the Land Office; the Election will be 1st. monday in next July.[33]

John Stafford's wife died lately and he is in low health himself. Matilda Vaughan[34] came down with Amanda to see him in his distress, and is with us still.

Mr. Smith is in statu quo. Your Cousins the little girls are doing finely as school. Lucinda[35] plays very handsomely and Ellen[36] also and their manners are very lady-like.

As usual with me I have written this at various times having been called off and not much to communicate, however I know you will make every allowance for me. Your letters are truly favors to us continue them notwithstanding our remissness in answering them and making any thing like an equivalent return for them and accept from us all our Love and axious solicitude for your health and welfare Yr Brother DAVID BRADFORD[37]

ALS (Jefferson Davis Papers, Frances Carrick Thomas Library, Transylvania University, Lexington, Kentucky). Addressed: "Lieut. J. F. Davis <—Lexington Kentucky—> Jefferson Barracks Mo."

1 "Abeyville," a tract of land in West Feliciana Parish originally granted by the Spanish government to David Bradford's father, was a short distance north of St. Francisville and fronted the road running from that town to Woodville, Mississippi. Portions of this property were later acquired by Bradford (Notarial Record B, October 10, 1822, p. 545 [West Feliciana Parish Courthouse, St. Francisville, Louisiana]); he may have called that part on which he first resided "Variety" (see 1:419).

First settled by whites *ca.* 1712–13, West Feliciana Parish was a part of Spanish West Florida, 1779–99; veterans of the French and Indian War and the Revolution were the majority of the earliest immigrants to the region. Representatives of the District of New Feliciana and the other Florida parishes declared themselves independent of the United States in September 1810, but were annexed by December of the same year. Feliciana was divided into two parishes in 1824 and by 1830 was believed to be one of the wealthiest districts in the South (Writers of the W.P.A., *Louisiana,* 509; L. Butler, "West Feliciana," *Louisiana Historical Quarterly*, VII, 93–99). See also *n.* 6 below.

[2] Davis' letter to Bradford has not been found.

[3] See 1:361, *n.* 4 for a discussion of cholera in Lexington where Davis was on recruiting duty (see 1:357).

[4] Dr. John Challen, brother-in-law of Bradford's sister, was born in New York in 1800. He married Mary Kavanaugh of Lexington in 1822, and moved to central Illinois in 1830 (Challen family folder [The Filson Club, Louisville, Kentucky]).

[5] James Challen, born in New Jersey in 1802, was educated at Transylvania University, and became a Baptist minister before he was twenty-one. By 1825 he was preaching in Cincinnati, where he and the congregation of Evon Baptist Church formed the First Church of Disciples of Christ. He established several churches and chapels in the area, was later pastor of churches in Philadelphia, Lexington, Davenport, and Covington, travelled widely, wrote many books and essays, and was a founder of the American Missionary Society. Married to Eliza Bradford in Lexington in 1827, they had five children—four sons and one daughter. Challen died in Cincinnati in 1878 (Challen family folder [The Filson Club, Louisville, Kentucky]; Clift, *Kentucky Marriages*, 49; *In Memoriam: Cincinnati, 1881*, pp. 128–33).

[6] Bayou Sara, named for an unidentified old woman who lived on its banks, was first named Clay's Bayou. The town of Bayou Sara (population 523 in the 1850 census) was located near the mouth of the creek at the Mississippi River, and was the shipping and commercial center of West Feliciana Parish. St. Francisville, parish seat of West Feliciana, is located just north of the town of Bayou Sara and the Mississippi River junction with Bayou Sara. Once terminus of the short-lived West Feliciana Railroad, St. Francisville is older than neighboring Bayou Sara and during the Spanish occupation was called New Valencia. Both towns were settled largely by businessmen and wealthy planters; by 1860 the parish wealth was assessed at more than $30 million. During the Civil War, St. Francisville, reportedly a Confederate stronghold, was largely destroyed by a Union gunboat; Bayou Sara was not shelled because of the citizens' Union sympathies (L. Butler, "West Feliciana," *Louisiana Historical Quarterly*, VII, 97–98; E. A. Davis, *Plantation Life*, 7–10; Seebold, *Old Louisiana Plantation Homes*, I, 249–55).

[7] Thompson's Creek, located less than ten miles east-southeast of Bayou Sara and St. Francisville, is the dividing line between East and West Feliciana parishes (L. Butler, "West Feliciana," *Louisiana Historical Quarterly*, VII, 108).

[8] See 1:362, *n.* 6 for a discussion of the cholera epidemic in Louisiana and Mississippi.

[9] The Homochitto is a river in southwestern Mississippi that flows into the Mississippi (Writers of the W.P.A., *Mississippi*, 35).

[10] William Stamps (sketch, 1:362, *n.* 12; 1:Appendix IV, Entry 63).

[11] Joseph Emory Davis (sketch, 1:19, *n.* 1; 1:Appendix IV, Entry 15).

[12] Possibly sheriffcy or sherifty.

[13] For more on Bradford's efforts to obtain the position of sheriff, see 1:419, in which he mentions two competitors, Ratliff and Parkinson. Since the latter was ultimately appointed, he may be "the mean wretch" referred to here.

[14] James Bradford was the owner of a large (1,500–2,000 acres) plantation in West Feliciana Parish, adjoining the

town of St. Francisville, and on the right of way of the West Feliciana Railroad Company, a holding offered for sale in 1833 and 1835 (Woodville [Mississippi] *Republican*, November 9, 1833, January 24, 1835).

15 Probably Dr. Isaac A. Smith, an early settler at St. Francisville, who was a member of the state senate until his death in 1831. He was an incorporator of the St. Francisville library and the Baptist church, and was a trustee and at one time president pro tem of Louisiana College at Jackson (E. Robinson, *Early Feliciana Politics*, 106).

16 David Bradford was an attorney.

17 The Bradfords had two sons named David; one died in 1831 and the other was born *ca.* 1835 (1:Appendix IV, *nn.* 99, 115). Thus, the schoolboy referred to as David in this letter and again in 1:419 cannot be their child.

18 Benjamin Franklin Bradford (1:Appendix IV, Entry 73), second son of David and Amanda Bradford, was born about 1822/23. During the Civil War, he served in the Confederate Army. He never married and died in 1885 in Louisiana (H. A. Davis, *The Davis Family*, 88; Ganier, Davis Family Tree [Alfred F. Ganier, Nashville, 1968]).

19 Anna Matilda Bradford Miles (1:Appendix IV, Entry 77), fourth child and second daughter of David and Amanda Bradford, was born about 1826/27 and attended school for a time in Nazareth, Kentucky (McGill, *Sisters of Charity*, 130). Also called Nannie or Nancy, Anna Matilda married Edward L. Miles; their marriage bond is dated May 17, 1848 (O'Neill, "Warren County Marriages," *Journal of Mississippi History*, XXIX, 214). They went to live in New Hope, Kentucky; evidently there were no children (H. A. Davis, *The Davis Family*, 88). She died in 1904 (Ganier, Davis Family Tree [Alfred F. Ganier, Nashville, 1968]).

20 Mary Jane Bradford Brodhead Sayre (1:Appendix IV, Entry 74), eldest daughter of David and Amanda Bradford, was born in Louisiana in 1825 (H. A. Davis, *The Davis Family*, 88) and for a time attended a boarding school managed by the Sisters of Charity in Nazareth, Kentucky (McGill, *Sisters of Charity*, 130). Fondly known as "Malie" to her family, Mary Jane was about the same age as Davis' second wife, Varina, and was invited to accompany the Davises to Washington in the fall of 1845 (Strode, *American Patriot*, 142). While living with them in the national capital, she met Representative Richard Brodhead of Easton, Pennsylvania. They signed a marriage bond in Warren County, Mississippi, on April 3, 1849 (O'Neill, "Warren County Marriages," *Journal of Mississippi History*, XXIX, 215; see 1:Appendix IV, *n.* 102). The Brodheads had two sons (H. A. Davis, *The Davis Family*, 88). During the Civil War, Mary Jane Brodhead lived in Pennsylvania, where her husband died September 16, 1863 (*Biographical Directory of the American Congress*, 601). In April 1866 she joined Varina Davis in New York and, when permission was secured, went with her to Fort Monroe (Strode, *Private Letters*, 245; Strode, *Tragic Hero*, 297). Mary Jane married Robert Sayre in 1872 and died in 1877 (Ganier, Davis Family Tree [Alfred F. Ganier, Nashville, 1968]).

21 "Mother" is probably Jane Cook Davis (sketch, 1:22, *n.* 4; 1:Appendix IV, Entry 14), David Bradford's mother-in-law, who lived near Woodville.

22 The Misses Amanda and Anna Theodosia Calder notified the public that classes at the Young Ladies' Academy would resume September 1, 1833, at Mount Hope, one and a half miles east of Woodville (Woodville [Mississippi] *Republican*, August 10, 1833). Their school first opened in January 1832 at a location adjoining William Stamps's property and was the second school operated by the Misses Calder, who were already well known to the

citizens of Wilkinson County as the directors of the Pine Grove Academy in nearby St. Francisville, Louisiana (*ibid.*, December 27, 1831). The name and location of the school in Mississippi changed several times; by 1835 it had moved into the town of Woodville and was most frequently referred to as the Wilkinson Female Academy (*ibid.*, January 18, 1834, August 22, 1835, January 7, 1837, September 7, 1838). An announcement in 1834 noted that the annual cost of tuition and board was $150 with additional charges for special instruction in music and art (*ibid.*, January 18, 1834).

[23] Hugh Robert Davis, Bradford's nephew (sketch, 1:362, *n.* 13; 1:Appendix IV, Entry 61), whose home was at Woodville, Mississippi, with his mother and stepfather, Lucinda and William Stamps. See also 1:362.

[24] Joseph Davis Smith (1:Appendix IV, Entry 45), Bradford's nephew and son of Luther L. and Anna Eliza Davis Smith, was born April 6, 1817, on "Locust Grove" plantation, West Feliciana Parish, Louisiana. On April 24, 1839, he married Marie Coralie Guibert, and they made their home at "Solitude" plantation, also in West Feliciana Parish, where at least ten of their twelve children were born. A physician by profession, Joseph remained in Louisiana during the Civil War and died in New Orleans on January 13, 1876 (Watts and De Grummond, *Solitude*, 24, Family Record).

[25] Luther L. Smith, Jr. (1:Appendix IV, Entry 47), Bradford's nephew, was born to Anna Eliza Davis and Luther Smith in 1818. Little is known of him beyond the fact that he, like his father, became a planter. He apparently never married, and in 1850 was living in Warren County, Mississippi (H. A. Davis, *The Davis Family*, 83).

[26] Luther L. Smith (1:Appendix IV, Entry 44), Bradford's brother-in-law, was a wealthy planter in West Feliciana Parish, Louisiana, where his grandfather, an Episcopal minister loyal to the British crown, had settled when it was under Spanish rule (Strode, *American Patriot*, 20). Luther Smith's second marriage in 1816—to Davis' eldest sister, Anna Eliza—produced seven children (Probate Box 81 [West Feliciana Parish Courthouse, St. Francisville, Louisiana]; H. A. Davis, *The Davis Family*, 82–83). He died at his plantation, "Locust Grove," in 1833 at the age of sixty-three after a prolonged illness (Gravestone ["God's Acre," "Locust Grove" plantation cemetery, near St. Francisville, Louisiana]; Woodville [Mississippi] *Republican*, January 18, 1834).

[27] Lucinda Farrar Davis Davis Stamps (sketch, 1:19, *n.* 3; 1:Appendix IV, Entry 20), Bradford's sister-in-law.

[28] Lucinda Bradford Mitchell (1:Appendix IV, Entry 82), David Bradford's daughter, became Dr. Charles Jouett Mitchell's second wife, probably in late December 1850; their marriage bond is dated December 13, 1850 (O'Neill, "Warren County Marriages," *Journal of Mississippi History*, XXIX, 217). They apparently had seven children, several of whom did not reach maturity (H. A. Davis, *The Davis Family*, 89; Ganier, Davis Family Tree [Alfred F. Ganier, Nashville, 1968]). In 1862 the Mitchells moved to Crockett, Texas (Mitchell, Journal, 36 [Southern Historical Collection, University of North Carolina Library, Chapel Hill]); by 1870 they had returned to Vicksburg (H. A. Davis, *The Davis Family*, 89). Lucinda, born *ca.* 1831, lived long after her husband's death in 1886, dying in 1919 (V. Davis to Mitchell, February 7, 1886 [Lise Mitchell Papers, Howard-Tilton Memorial Library, Tulane University, New Orleans]; Ganier, Davis Family Tree [Alfred F. Ganier, Nashville, 1968]).

[29] Amanda Davis Bradford (1:Appendix IV, Entry 21), Bradford's wife, was Jane and Samuel Davis' third daughter, born in 1799 while they were living in Christian County, Kentucky.

Amanda married *ca.* 1820 David Bradford, a Louisiana planter and lawyer (H. A. Davis, *The Davis Family*, 88); they had nine children (Ganier, Davis Family Tree [Albert F. Ganier, Nashville, 1968]). When her husband was assassinated in 1844 (see 1:Appendix IV, *n.* 98), Amanda and the children went to live with her brother Joseph's family at "Hurricane" plantation near Vicksburg, Mississippi. Joseph E. Davis is thought to have seen to the education of the Bradford children. By 1870 Amanda was residing in Vicksburg; she died in 1881 (H. A. Davis, *The Davis Family*, 88).

30 James Morgan Bradford, David Bradford's brother-in-law, from a family of printers, learned the printing trade in Kentucky as a young man, but moved to New Orleans in 1804 and purchased a newspaper which he named the Orleans *Gazette*. Bradford was made territorial printer until he and Governor W. C. C. Claiborne had political differences (D. Rowland [ed.], *Official Letter Books of W. C. C. Claiborne*, IV, 314, 372–73, V, 14–15; Phelps, *Louisiana*, 232–33, 243). When Claiborne revoked the patronage in February 1809, Bradford sold his interest in the paper and moved to St. Francisville, where he practiced law, engaged in politics, and established the town's first newspaper, *The Time Piece*, in April 1811. Except for a year's absence in 1826 in New Orleans, where he was the state printer, and editor and publisher of the *Louisiana State Gazette*, Bradford was involved in the publication of St. Francisville papers until his death there in 1837 or 1838 (E. Robinson, *Early Feliciana Politics*, 55, 107–109; Padgett [ed.], "Official Records of the West Florida Revolution and Republic," *Louisiana Historical Quarterly*, XXI, 709*n.*).

31 Thomas Withers Chinn (1791–1852), a native of Kentucky, served briefly in the War of 1812, moved to Woodville, Mississippi, and then to St. Francisville, where he began practicing medicine in 1817. He was admitted to the bar in 1825, practiced at St. Francisville, and was appointed first parish judge of West Feliciana in 1826. Because of alleged irregularities, Chinn was impeached by the Louisiana house in 1826, but was acquitted by the senate. In 1827 or 1831, he moved to West Baton Rouge Parish, practiced law, and had a sugar plantation. He was a member of the Louisiana legislature in 1833 and was elected as a Whig to the Congress of 1839–41. Preferring not to run for a second term because of ill health, Chinn returned to his plantation, "Cypress Hall." He was commissioned chargé d'affaires to the Two Sicilies by President Zachary Taylor in 1849, but served at Naples only five months before returning to his home (E. Robinson, *Early Feliciana Politics*, 9–11, 33–51; *Biographical Directory of the American Congress*, 688; *Who Was Who*; Aucoin, "The Political Career of Isaac Johnson," *Louisiana Historical Quarterly*, XXVIII, 942*n.*).

32 Alexander G. Penn (1799–1866), born in Virginia, was educated at Henry and Emory College in Marion, Virginia, moved to St. Tammany Parish, Louisiana, in 1821, and served in the state legislature. Penn was postmaster in New Orleans, 1843–49, and was elected as a Democrat to the House of Representatives in 1850. In 1853, he returned to his plantation and the operation of a lumber mill near Covington. He died in Washington (*Who Was Who*; *Biographical Directory of the American Congress*, 1442).

33 See 1:419 for additional information on the Louisiana elections of July 1834.

34 Of Matilda Davis Vaughan (1:Appendix IV, Entry 22), Bradford's sister-in-law, less is known than about any of Davis' other sisters. She was born *ca.* 1800 (see 1:Appendix IV, *n.* 21) and died March 16, 1834 (1:419). That her husband may have predeceased her and that they may have had a child are suggested by a notice

in the Woodville (Mississippi) *Republican* of April 12, 1834, in which Jane Cook Davis (Davis' mother) states that, as guardian of Sarah Matilda Vaughan, she will present her account at the May term of the Wilkinson County Probate Court.

[35] Jane Lucinda Davis Farish (1:Appendix IV, Entry 90), David Bradford's niece, was reared by her grandmother. One of Mary Ellen and Robert Davis' two children, Jane Lucinda was born *ca.* 1820 and married Hazlewood M. Farish, a lawyer, on May 3, 1842 (Woodville [Mississippi] *Republican*, May 7, 1842). She was widowed in May 1851, and died at the age of thirty-one in November of the same year (Gravestone ["Rosemont" plantation cemetery, near Woodville, Mississippi]). Their three children—William Stamps, Robert Davis, and Fannie —were reared by Jane Lucinda's sister, Ellen Mary Davis Anderson (H. A. Davis, *The Davis Family*, 94–95).

[36] Ellen Mary Davis Anderson (1:Appendix IV, Entry 92), Bradford's niece and Mary Ellen and Robert Davis' younger daughter, was born in 1824 (H. A. Davis, *The Davis Family*, 95; Ganier, Davis Family Tree [Alfred F. Ganier, Nashville, 1968]). Upon the death of her parents, she was reared by her grandmother, Jane Cook Davis. Ellen Mary assumed responsibility for her sister's three children after the deaths of Jane Lucinda and Hazlewood M. Farish in 1851. She married, *ca.* 1852, Thomas Anderson, a widower with four children. The Andersons later had two children of their own, and lived on a prosperous plantation near Jackson, Mississippi. Ellen Mary survived her husband by many years, dying in New Orleans *ca.* 1915 (H. A. Davis, *The Davis Family*, 95).

[37] David Bradford, Davis' brother-in-law (sketch, 1:5, *n.* 10; 1:Appendix IV, Entry 71).

ABSTRACT

1:364

Register of Payments to Officers

[Washington, D.C.,] July 13, 1833

Lists payment by Paymaster T. Wright[1] to Second Lieutenant Jefferson Davis, Dragoons, $110.96. Amount includes pay and allowance for Davis and one servant,[2] and allowance for one horse, for May.

D (NA, RG 99 Records of the Office of the Paymaster General, Register of Payments to Officers, IV, 27), 1.

[1] Thomas Wright (sketch, 1:320, *n.* 2).
[2] The servant was James Pemberton (sketch, 1:5, *n.* 4).

1:365

From James H. Hook

SIR; 15th. July 1833

Mr. Blincoe's[1] Special Contractor's accounts for issues to Recruits[2]

last month are received this day. In future let the Abstract of issues correspond with the accompanying form. J. H. HOOK[3]
Acting C[ommissary] G[eneral] S[ubsistence]

LbC (NA, RG 192 Records of the Office of the Commissary General of Subsistence, Letters Sent, IX, 519). Addressed: "Lieut. Jeff. Davis U. S. Dragoons Lexington, Ky." Enclosure missing.

[1] Benjamin C. Blincoe (see 1:357, *n.* 1).

[2] See 1:357 for the register of contracts for rations.

[3] James Harvey Hook, born in Maryland, enlisted in the army in 1812, and was promoted to captain by the end of the war. He was serving as a commissary of subsistence in 1829, and by 1838 was lieutenant colonel and assistant commissary general, a post he held until his death in 1841 (Heitman, *Historical Register*, I, 540).

To Lewis Cass 1:366

Jefferson Barracks[1] Mo. July 24th 1833

SIR[2]

Your letter of "4 March 1833" [3] (twice forwarded) [4] has just been received, I accept the appointment of second Lieutenant of Dragoons, in which capacity I have been serving since the receipt of gnrl. order no. 15 (present series) [5] withdrew me from the first Regiment of Infantry.

I am as an Officer ever ready to render my best services wherever the Government may require them, not doubting but that I shall receive all to which I am entitled.

Your letter refers it to my option to refuse or accept an assignment to dragoon service, having communicated by acceptance above, allow me to say, that as Cadets the three first Lieutenants were but one year my seniors, as second Lieutenants of Infantry my regimental position (on the last Army register) was higher than two of them, and that serving as at present with another corps my appointment to Dragoons of 4th March 1833 places me subordinate to officers formerly much my juniors.[6] Very Respectfully yr. mo. obt. Servt.

JEFFN. DAVIS
2. L[ieutenant] U. S. Dragoons

[AES 1] Mr. Williams.[7] Examine. Report. R[oger] J[ones].[8]
[AE 2] 2 Lt Jefferson Davis 1st Infy 1st July 1828 when appointed 2 Lt of Dragoons his regimental rank was No. 5.

2 Lt Abram Van Buren[9] 2d Infy 1st. July 1827 when appointed 1 Lt of Dragoons his regimental rank was No. 6.[10]

2 Lt P. St. George Cooke[11] 6 Infy 1st July 1827 when appointed 1 Lt of Dragoons his regimental rank was No. 6.

ALS (NA, RG 94 Records of the Adjutant General's Office, Letters Received, D-65, 1833). Addressed: "To the Honble. Lewis Cass Secretary of War Washington D. C." Endorsed: "[Received] Augt. 6. 1833."

1 For Jefferson Barracks, see 1:123, *n.* 3.

2 Lewis Cass (sketch, 1:349, *n.* 5).

3 Cass's letter of March 4 is printed as 1:349.

4 Cass's letter was no doubt forwarded from Fort Crawford to Lexington to Jefferson Barracks.

5 Section 3 of General Order No. 15, March 11, 1833, reads in part that the general-in-chief "would remark, that the President expects every Officer will repair to his post without delay, and that all will immediately assume their respective duties, and proceed with alacrity in the discharge of them" (NA, RG 94, War Department Orders and Circulars, Orders, VI, 166–68). Davis' appointment was announced for the information of the army in Order No. 14, March 6, 1833 (1:350) and Order No. 40, May 4, 1833 (1:354).

6 The three first lieutenants in the Regiment of Dragoons were David Perkins, Philip St. George Cooke and Abraham Van Buren. Cooke and Van Buren were, prior to their appointment to the Dragoons, inferior to Davis in rank, being numbers six and eight in their respective regiments while Davis was number five. Although Davis was inferior to both in date of rank, he is complaining about the fact that two officers of lesser regimental rank were promoted before he was (Gordon, *Compilation of Registers of the Army*, 462, 463, 465). The protest was evidently effective, for when Davis was nominated to the Senate in February 1834, he was recommended for the rank of first lieutenant (see 1:404).

7 Probably Brook(e) Williams, clerk in the Adjutant General's Office (*American Almanac* [1835–42], *passim*).

8 Roger Jones, adjutant general (sketch, 1:123, *n.* 6).

9 Abraham Van Buren, son of the eighth President, was born in 1807 in New York and was graduated from West Point in 1827. He served two years on the frontier, and seven years as General Alexander Macomb's aide before his resignation in 1837, when he became his father's private secretary. When the Mexican War began, he reentered the army as major and paymaster, served on Generals Zachary Taylor's and Winfield Scott's staffs and was brevetted lieutenant colonel for gallantry in 1847. Van Buren remained on paymaster duty after the war until 1854, when he retired to his wife's inherited plantation in South Carolina. In 1859 he moved to New York City, where he died in 1873 (*Appleton's*; Cullum, *Biographical Register*, I, 403–404).

10 Although Van Buren's rank is given as six in the endorsement, the register lists him as eighth (Gordon, *Compilation of Registers of the Army*, 463).

11 Philip St. George Cooke (1809–95) was a Virginian and an 1827 graduate of the Military Academy. A veteran of the Black Hawk War, Cooke served at several frontier garrisons and in many expeditions against the Indians. He commanded a volunteer battalion (1846–47) and a regiment (1848) in the Mexican War and was brevetted lieutenant colonel in 1847. Involved in the Kansas disturbances of 1856–57, Cooke later prepared a system of cavalry tactics which was accepted for service in

1861. He was promoted to brigadier general in 1861, saw no active service after 1862, but remained on the army list until 1873. He was the author of two books on his army life: *Scenes and Adventures in the Army* (Philadelphia, 1857) and *The Conquest of New Mexico and California* (New York, 1878). For a detailed biography, see Young, *The West of Philip St. George Cooke*; also Cullum, *Biographical Register*, I, 397–98, and Warner, *Generals in Blue*, 89–90.

ABSTRACT

Post Return 1:367

Jefferson Barracks,[1] Missouri, July [31,] 1833

Lists Second Licutenant Jefferson Davis, U.S. Dragoons, present at the post.[2] Remarks: "For Duty, Joined Company 11th. July 1833." [3]

Printed form, filled in and signed (NA, RG 94 Records of the Adjutant General's Office, Post Returns, Jefferson Barracks), 2. Signed: "Albert S. Johnston A[ide-] D[e-] C[amp] & A[ssistant] A[djutant] Gen[eral]. H. Atkinson Br[igadier] Gen. U. S. Army." Endorsed: "Entd Recd 16 Augst."

[1] See 1:123, *n.* 3.

[2] Davis returned to Jefferson Barracks from Lexington, Kentucky, where he had been on recruiting duty (1:357, 360).

[3] A member of the Dragoon Regiment recalled seeing Davis at Jefferson Barracks: "My memory is bad, but I very distinctly remember the first time I saw you on horseback. It was at Jefferson Bks., and you rode a brown—rather dark brown—horse, which was, I believe, a favorite with you. It was the summer of 1833, and you wore white drill Pants, made quite narrow at the boot, and quite wide at the thigh, and undress coat, and as you rode through the Parade ground, I think even Charley O'Malley would not have made a more gallant and dashing Dragoon" (Doran to Davis, June 11, 1886 [Museum of the Confederacy, Richmond]).

From William B. Lewis 1:368

SIR August 31, 1833

Your letter of 21th., June last,[1] which was referred to the Q. M. Genl.[2] has been returned with the following remarks noted thereon. ("Remarks Noted.")

You are therefore requested to forward the Paymaster's receipt for $21.04, so as to enable me to close this A/c. on the books of this office. W. B. L.[3]

LbC (NA, RG 217 Records of the United States General Accounting Office, Second Auditor's Office, Letters Sent, Property Division, Volume F, 401). Addressed: "Lt. Jef. Davis U. S. A. Lexington Ky." Endorsed: "Paid to p[ay]m[aste]r Phillips Septr. 18. 1833."

[1] The reference may be to 1:359.

[2] The quartermaster general was Thomas S. Jesup (sketch, 1:174, *n.* 4).

[3] William B. Lewis (sketch, 1:166, *n.* 1).

ABSTRACT

1:369

Post Return

Jefferson Barracks,[1] Missouri, August [31,] 1833

Lists Jefferson Davis, adjutant[2] U.S. Dragoons, present at the post. Remarks: "For Duty. Transferred from Compy C to Staff 30th Augt. 1833."

Printed form, filled in and signed (NA, RG 94 Records of the Adjutant General's Office, Post Returns, Jefferson Barracks), 2. Signed: "H. Atkinson Br[igadier] Gen. U. S. Army." Endorsed: "Recd. 4th. Novr Corrected as pointed out by the Adjt. Genl."

[1] See 1:123, *n.* 3.

[2] Davis was appointed adjutant on August 29 or 30 (1:371, *n.* 4). He recalled the occasion of his appointment as adjutant in an 1878 letter to George W. Jones: "In the beginning of 1833 I was one of the two officers selected from the First Infantry for promotion into the newly created regiment of dragoons, and left Prairie du Chien under orders for recruiting service in Kentucky. As soon as the Kentucky company was raised I returned to Jefferson Barracks, the rendezvous of the regiment. The first field officer who joined was Major [Richard B.] Mason . . . and by him I was appointed adjutant of the squadron, composed of the first companies which reported. After other companies had joined, the colonel, Henry Dodge, came . . . and by him I was appointed adjutant of the regiment" (V. Davis, *Memoir*, I, 149).

ABSTRACT

1:370

Field and Staff Muster Roll

Jefferson Barracks,[1] August 31, 1833

Lists Adjutant Jefferson Davis of the field and staff, U.S. Regiment of Dragoons commanded by Colonel Henry Dodge,[2] as present. Remarks: "Appointed Adjutant 29th August[3] 1833." Report covers July and August 1833.

Printed form, filled in and signed (NA, RG 94 Records of the Adjutant General's Office, Muster Rolls of Regular Army Organizations, First Dragoons [Company A], Field and Staff), 2. Signed: "Jeffn Davis H. Dodge." Endorsed: "Entered Recd. Septr 18th. 1833."

[1] See 1:123, *n.* 3.

[2] Henry Dodge (1782–1867) was born at Post Vincennes (now Indiana) and was reared in Illinois, Kentucky, and Louisiana. He received little formal education, was sheriff in the Ste. Genevieve district of the Louisiana Purchase for sixteen years (1805–21), and migrated in 1827 to Michigan Territory where the rich lead mining lands were being opened. Having led a force of volunteers in the Black Hawk War, Dodge was appointed major of the Battalion of Mounted Rangers who patrolled the upper Mississippi Valley frontier, and became colonel of the newly-formed Regiment of Dragoons in March 1833. Dodge resigned from the army in 1836 to enter politics and was Democratic governor, then senator, from Wisconsin for two decades, until his retirement (*DAB*; Salter, *Henry Dodge*). Although Dodge had appointed Davis his adjutant, the two quarrelled later (see 1:409). It was Dodge's daughter Mary who was rumored to be Davis' first love, largely on the evidence of a letter Davis wrote to her in 1883: "Widely and long we have been separated, but your image has not been dimmed by time and distance. . . . If you have preserved enough of the pleasant memories of one springtime to care for one who flitted with You over the flowers of youth's happy garden, it will give me sincere gratification to hear from you . . ." (to Mrs. John Dement, February 4, 1883, D. Rowland, *Papers*, IX, 203; Rugg, *Dement Dodge Patterson Williams*, 20–21; see also W. L. Fleming, "Davis' First Marriage," Mississippi Historical *Publications*, XII, 22–23).

[3] See 1:371, *n.* 4 for a discussion of the date of Davis' appointment.

ABSTRACT

Company Muster Roll

1:371

Jefferson Barracks[1] August 31, 1833

Lists Second Lieutenant Jefferson Davis of Captain R. Holmes's[2] Company C, U.S. Dragoons commanded by Colonel Henry Dodge,[3] as present. Remarks: "Joined July 11th. 1833. Appointed Adjutant 30th. of August 1833."[4] Report covers July and August 1833.

Printed form, filled in and signed (NA, RG 94 Records of the Adjutant General's Office, Muster Rolls of Regular Army Organizations, U. S. Dragoons, Company C), 2. Signed: "R. Holmes Capt. H C Dodge Col of U S Dragoons." Endorsed: "Recd. Septr 18th. 1833. Entered."

[1] See 1:123, *n.* 3.

[2] Reuben Holmes, born in Connecticut, was an 1823 West Point graduate who served first at Fort Atkinson, Iowa, then on commissary duty in St. Louis (1827–33). He was a veteran of the Black Hawk War, having been colonel and chief quartermaster for the

Illinois volunteers. Appointed to the Dragoons, as Davis was, March 4, 1833, he died at Jefferson Barracks at the age of thirty-three in November 1833 (Cullum, *Biographical Register*, I, 303).

[3] Henry Dodge (sketch, 1:370, *n.* 2).

[4] The difference between this muster roll and that of the field and staff (1:370) in dating Davis' appointment as adjutant cannot be authoritatively explained. Possibly Davis was appointed adjutant on August 29 and assumed his duties the next day.

ABSTRACT

1:372

Pay Voucher

Jefferson Barracks,[1] September 1, 1833

Second Lieutenant Jefferson Davis, Dragoons, acknowledges that he has received $305.40 from Paymaster Thomas Wright.[2] Amount includes pay, allowance for one servant,[3] and forage for two horses[4] for June through August, and additional pay for duty as acting assistant commissary of subsistence at Dubuques Mines from November 1831 through March 1832.[5] The servant is described as "James A Slave."

Printed form, filled in and signed (NA, RG 217 Records of the United States General Accounting Office, Paymasters' Accounts, Wright 18,178, Voucher 26), 3. Signed: "Jeffn. Davis 2. L[ieutenant] Dragoons."

[1] See 1:123, *n.* 3.

[2] Thomas Wright (sketch, 1:320, *n.* 2).

[3] James Pemberton (sketch, 1:5, *n.* 4).

[4] As adjutant Davis was paid an extra $10 per month, and compensated for forage for two horses, a privilege captains and first and second lieutenants were not allowed (*General Army Regulations* [1825], 287).

[5] For evidence of the fact that Davis served as acting assistant commissary of subsistence from November 2, 1831, to March 26, 1832, see 1:296, 317. For Dubuques Mines, see 1:291, *n.* 2.

ABSTRACT

1:373

Register of Payments to Officers

[Washington, D.C.,] September 1, 1833

Lists payment by Paymaster T. Wright[1] to Second Lieutenant Jefferson Davis, Dragoons, $305.50. Amount includes pay and allowance for Davis and one servant,[2] and allowance for two horses, for June through August. Remarks: "Ch[arge]d an arrear of $5.* p[er] mo

1 Nov. '31 to 31 March '32 actg a[ssistant] c[ommissary] s[ubsistence][3] <chd but $10.>[4]"

D (NA, RG 99 Records of the Office of the Paymaster General, Register of Payments to Officers, IV, 27), 1.

[1] Thomas Wright (sketch, 1:320, *n.* 2).

[2] James Pemberton was the servant (sketch, 1:5, *n.* 4).

[3] See 1:296, 317 for Davis' assignment as acting assistant commissary.

[4] Interlined.

Henry Dodge to Roger Jones 1:374

Head Qrs. Regt. of Dragoons Jeffn. Bks.[1] Sepr. 3 1833

SIR[2]

In conformity with paragraph 1469 <G. Army Regulations[3]>[4] I herewith inform you that on the 29th Augt 1833,[5] Lieut Jefferson Davis was appointed Adjutant of Dragoons Very Respectfully Yr Mo. Ob. Servt.

H. DODGE[6]
Col of U S Dragoons

ALS (NA, RG 94 Records of the Adjutant General's Office, Letters Received, D–86, 1833). Addressed: "To Col. R Jones Adjt General U S Army Washington D. C." Endorsed: "[Received] Sepr. 18. 1833."

[1] See 1:123, *n.* 3.

[2] Roger Jones (sketch, 1:123, *n.* 6).

[3] Paragraph 1469 states: "The date of appointment and removal of all aides-de-camp, adjutants, quartermasters, assistant-commissaries, and details of officers for ordnance duties, will be forthwith reported to the adjutant-general . . ." (*General Army Regulations* [1825], 403).

[4] Interlined.

[5] See 1:371, *n.* 4 for Davis' appointment as adjutant.

[6] Henry Dodge (sketch, 1:370, *n.* 2).

Henry Dodge to Roger Jones 1:375

Hd. Qrs Regt Dragoons Jeffn Bar'ks[1] 13. Septr. 1833

SIR,[2]

In obedience to par. 1496 Army Regulations,[3] I have the honor to report that, on the 29th ult. 2d Lieut Jefferson Davis was appointed the Adjutant[4] of the Regiment of Dragoons,

The law creating this Corps [au]thorizes one additional Lieut. for an Adjutant but is silent as to what grade he shall be,[5]

Lieut Davis having been appointed the Adjutant he therefore becomes the additional Lieut authorized by law, & I have the honor to request that he may be promoted to a first Lieut, to take rank from the date of his appointment as Adjutant, believing it due to his Merit & perfectly within the power of the Department of War to make the promotion in this case,

Lt Davis was first for promotion in his Regt. at the time of his transfer to the Dragoons, & should a vacancy occur in that Regt. before Lt Davis is promoted in the Dragoons, then an officer who has always been his junior will get the rank of him & Lt. D. will have lost rank by the transfer,[6] I have the honor to be Sir Very Respely Yr Obt Srt H. DODGE[7]

Col. U S Dragoons

[Encl] Jeffn Bar'ks 13 Sept 1833

I most cheerfully concur with Col. Dodge in Soliciting the promotion of Lt Davis, he is every way worthy of it, and as the law is silent as to what grade (wheather 1st. or 2d. Lieut.) the Adjutant shall be, I indulge the hope that the opportunity will be embraced to give Lt. Davis promotion. I have the honor to be Sir Very Respectfully Yr obt Sert R. B. MASON[8]

Maj. Dragoons

LS (NA, RG 94 Records of the Adjutant General's Office, Letters Received, D–90, 1833). Addressed: "Col. R. Jones Adjt. Genl U. S. A. Washington." Endorsed: "Mr. Williams, to note, R[oger] J[ones]"; in a different hand, "Appd 1st Lt of Dragoons 4 March 1833"; in a third hand, "[Received] Sepr 26. 1833."

1 See 1:123, *n.* 3.

2 Both this letter and the enclosure printed below were addressed to Roger Jones (sketch, 1:123, *n.* 6).

3 Paragraph 1469 is undoubtedly intended (see 1:374, *n.* 2).

4 See 1:371, *n.* 4 for Davis' appointment as adjutant.

5 "An act for the more perfect defence of the frontiers," March 2, 1833, provided for "one adjutant, who shall be a lieutenant" (*Statutes at Large of the United States*, IV [1846], 652).

6 Davis wrote to Cass (1:366) noting his seniority in rank to two of the first lieutenants appointed to the Dragoons; he was recommended for the rank of first lieutenant in February 1834 (1:404).

7 Henry Dodge (sketch, 1:370, *n.* 2).

8 Richard Barnes Mason (1797–1850) was a Virginian and son of Revolutionary patriot George Mason. He was privately educated and commissioned a second lieutenant in 1817, being promoted to captain two years later. Mason served with Zachary Taylor in the Black Hawk War, and in 1833 was appointed major in the Dragoon Regiment. Colonel of the First Regiment of United States Cavalry in 1846, Mason accompanied Stephen Watts Kearny to New Mexico and California and became military commander of the region in 1847. In 1849 Mason was relieved and returned to Jefferson Barracks, where he died of Asiatic cholera (*DAB*). Mason had appointed Davis adjutant of the first companies that arrived at St. Louis in the spring of 1833, but in 1834 he preferred charges against

Davis that led to a court martial (1:369, *n.* 2; C. T. Foreman, "Mason," *Chronicles of Oklahoma*, XIX, 14–36; 1:454–58).

Roger Jones to Henry Dodge

1:376

SIR,[1] Adjt. Genl's. office, Washington, Sept. 26th. 1833

In answer to your letter of the 13th. inst.[2] referring to *2d. Lt. Davis*, the Adjutant of your Regiment, I have the pleasure to inform you, that your suggestions will be taken into consideration, at the final organization of the Regiment.[3] I am sir, Very respectfully Your obt. Servt. (Signed) R. JONES[4]
Adjt. Genl.

LbC (NA, RG 94 Records of the Adjutant General's Office, Letters Sent, X, 322). Addressed: "Col. H. Dodge U S. Dragoons Jefferson Bks Missouri."

[1] Henry Dodge (sketch, 1:370, *n.* 2).

[2] Dodge's letter of September 13 is printed as 1:375.

[3] Davis was recommended for promotion in February 1834 (1:404).

[4] Roger Jones (sketch, 1:123, *n.* 6).

To William B. Lewis

1:377

Jeffn. Bks.[1] Mo. Sept 27th 1833

SIR[2]

Herewith I have the honor to transmit to you an account current with vouchers covering the amount of funds acknowledged to be the U. States in my last recruitg. account[3] Very. Respectfly yr. mo. obt. Servt. JEFFN. DAVIS
L[ieutenant] Rgt. Dragoons

ALS (NA, RG 217 Records of the United States General Accounting Office, Second Auditor's Office, Second Auditor's Accounts, Account 17,593). Addressed: "To W. B. Lewis 2. Aud. U. S. Treasy." Endorsed: "Recd. 10 Octr. Ansd." Enclosures missing.

[1] See 1:123, *n.* 3.

[2] William B. Lewis (sketch, 1:166, *n.* 1).

[3] See 1:360 for the letter transmitting Davis' last recruiting account.

30 SEPTEMBER 1833

ABSTRACT

1:378 # Post Return

Jefferson Barracks,[1] Missouri, September [30,] 1833

Lists Jefferson Davis, adjutant Dragoons,[2] present at the post. Remarks: "For Duty."

Printed form, filled in and signed (NA, RG 94 Records of the Adjutant General's Office, Post Returns, Jefferson Barracks), 4. Signed: "H. Atkinson Br[igadier] Genl. U. S. army." Endorsed: "Recd. Novr. 11th. Corrected, as pointed out by the Adjt. Genl."

[1] See 1:123, *n.* 3.

[2] Davis was appointed adjutant August 29 or 30 (see 1:371, *n.* 4).

1:379 # Special Order No. 22

Brigade Head Quarters Jeff. Bks[1] 2d Octr 1833

Colonel Henry Dodgde[2] U S. Dragoons assumes command of this Post <2d Lt. Davis Adjutant U. S. Dragoons will perform the duties of Staff officer to the Command[3]>[4] By order of Col. Dodge

JEFFN. DAVIS
L[ieutenant] Adjt. Drgs

ALbCS (NA, RG 393 Records of United States Army Continental Commands, 1821–1920, Jefferson Barracks, Orders and Special Orders, March 1831–November 1837).

[1] For a description of Jefferson Barracks, see 1:123, *n.* 3.

[2] Henry Dodge (sketch, 1:370, *n.* 2).

[3] Davis was adjutant of Dragoons from August 1833 to February 1834 (1:370, 403).

[4] Interlined.

1:380 # Order No. 25

Brigade Head Quarters Jeff Bks[1] 2d Octr 1833

Private J. Ellis[2] of K. Compy 6th Infy is excused from morning drills till further orders By order of Col. Dodge[3]

JEFFN. DAVIS
L[ieutenant] Adjt. Dragoons

ALbCS (NA, RG 393 Records of United States Army Continental Commands, 1821–1920, Jefferson Barracks, Orders and Special Orders, March 1831–November 1837).

[1] See 1:123, *n.* 3 for Jefferson Barracks.

[2] John Ellis, born in Massachusetts, gave his age as thirty-one and his occupation as laborer when he enlisted in 1831 for five years. He was recruited at Newport, Kentucky, and joined Company K, Sixth Infantry, in February 1832. Ellis served as a clerk at Jefferson Barracks during most of his service, which ended with his discharge in 1836 (Muster and Descriptive Roll of a Detachment of United States Recruits, February 14, 1832 [NA, RG 94, Sixth Infantry, Company K]; Muster Rolls and Semiannual Muster Rolls, June 30, 1832–October 31, 1836 [NA, RG 94, Sixth Infantry, Company K]).

[3] Henry Dodge (sketch, 1:370, *n.* 2).

Order No. 26

1:381

Brig. Head Qrs. Jeffn Bks.[1] 4th Oct. 1833

By virtue of authority delegated in Dept. order No. 30 [2] Sept. 6th 1833—1st Lieut Cooke[3] Regt. of Dragoons is detailed a member of the Genl. Court Martial now in session at this post, to supply a vacancy occasioned by the illness of Brvt. 2d Lieut Van Derveer.[4] Brvt 2nd Lieut J. S. Williams[5] 6th Infy. will perform the duties of Special Judge Advocate to the Court, Capt Wharton[6] Regt. Dragoons who was designated for that duty in Brig Order No. 18 [7] of the 25th Ult. being sick By order of Col. Dodge[8] JEFFN. DAVIS

L[ieutenant] Adjt. Drgs. & Brig Staff offr.

ALbCS (NA, RG 393 Records of United States Army Continental Commands, 1821–1920, Jefferson Barracks, Orders and Special Orders, March 1831–November 1837).

[1] For Jefferson Barracks, see 1:123, *n.* 3.

[2] Departmental Order No. 30 provided for a general court martial of nine officers to assemble at Jefferson Barracks September 20. The order authorized the post commander to detail officers at or near Jefferson Barracks to fill vacancies (NA, RG 393, Department of the West, Orders and Special Orders, July 1832–October 1833, NA XXVII, 391–92—formerly Volume VIII).

[3] Philip St. George Cooke (sketch, 1:366, *n.* 11).

[4] John Suthpin Vanderveer (or Van Derveer) was born in New Jersey and was graduated in the 1830 West Point class. He served at Jefferson Barracks, Rock Island, and in the Black Hawk War before his appointment to the Dragoons as a second lieutenant. Stationed at Fort Gibson intermittently, 1833–39, Vanderveer resigned from the army in 1840 with the rank of captain of Dragoons. He died in Kansas City, Missouri, in 1876, aged sixty-nine (Cullum, *Biographical Register*, I, 465).

[5] James S. Williams, born in Georgia, was graduated from the Military Academy in 1831. He served in the Black Hawk War and was at Jefferson Barracks, 1832–34. Williams resigned in 1837 as a first lieutenant, Sixth Infantry, and became a civil engineer—employed by the federal government to survey Cumberland Sound, 1843–44, and as a commissioner to trace the western

boundary of Arkansas in 1857. Williams served in the Confederate Army, 1861–65, and died in New York, aged sixty, in 1871 (Cullum, *Biographical Register*, I, 494).

[6] Clifton Wharton, born in Pennsylvania, was first commissioned a second lieutenant in light artillery in 1818 and had served as assistant quartermaster, 1826–30. He was a captain in the Sixth Infantry when he was assigned to the Dragoons in 1833; he died in 1848 as lieutenant colonel (Heitman, *Historical Register*, I, 1022).

[7] Brigade Order No. 18 ordered a general court martial to assemble September 25, and filled two vacancies in the original court (NA, RG 393, Jefferson Barracks, Orders and Special Orders, March 1831–November 1837). See also *n.* 2 above.

[8] Henry Dodge (sketch, 1:370, *n.* 2).

1:382 Special Order No. 23

Brig Head Qrs. Jeffn. Bks.[1] 4 Octr 1833

On the application of Major J. B. Brant[2] <Q. M.>[3] U. S. A. a board of survey to consist of Capts. Sumner[4] & Holmes[5] Regt. Dragoons is instituted to examine and report on certain public Horses recently turned over to Maj. Brant Q. Master <—at St. Louis—> and will proceed to St. Louis and commence the examination to morrow morning By order of Col. Dodge[6]

JEFFN DAVIS
L[ieutenant] Adjt. Drgs

ALbCS (NA, RG 393 Records of United States Army Continental Commands, 1821–1920, Jefferson Barracks, Orders and Special Orders, March 1831–November 1837).

[1] See 1:123, *n.* 3.

[2] Joshua B. Brant (sketch, 1:192, *n.* 6).

[3] Interlined.

[4] Edwin V. Sumner (1797–1863), born in Massachusetts, was commissioned a second lieutenant in 1819 and appointed a captain of Dragoons in 1833, serving mostly on the frontier. Brevetted lieutenant colonel and colonel in the Mexican War, Sumner became colonel of the First Cavalry in 1855. He was given command of the United States Second Corps in 1861, and served with distinction in the Peninsular campaign and the Battles of Seven Pines, Sharpsburg, and Fredericksburg. Sumner died en route to an assignment as commander of the Department of Missouri (Warner, *Generals in Blue*, 489–90).

[5] Reuben Holmes (sketch, 1:371, *n.* 2).

[6] Henry Dodge (sketch, 1:370, *n.* 2).

1:383 Order No. 27

Brig. Head Qrs. Jeffn. Bks.[1] 5 Oct. 1833

Three Privates will be detailed from the Regt of Dragoons for

"Extra duty" and ordered to report to the A[ssistant] Q. Master[2] of the Post.

Privates Davenport[3] of "E" and Thomas[4] of "G." Companies 6th Infy. are relieved from "Extra duty" and will join their Companies. By Order of Col Dodge[5]

JEFFN DAVIS
L[ieutenant] Adjt. Drgs Brig. Staff offr.

ALbCS (NA, RG 393 Records of United States Army Continental Commands, 1821–1920, Jefferson Barracks, Orders and Special Orders, March 1831–November 1837).

1 For Jefferson Barracks, see 1:123, *n.* 3.

2 George H. Crosman, first lieutenant of the Sixth Infantry, was assistant quartermaster (Post Return, October 1833 [NA, RG 94, Jefferson Barracks]).

3 Joel Davenport was enlisted March 1829 at Newport, Kentucky, by Captain Andrew Lewis for five years. He was discharged in 1834 at Jefferson Barracks (Muster Rolls, August 31, 1829, and April 30, 1834 [NA, RG 94, Sixth Infantry, Company E]).

4 John Thomas was born in Philadelphia and enlisted January 1833 for five years. He gave his occupation as piano maker and was twenty-four years old when he was recruited at Philadelphia. He was discharged in 1838 at Fort Basinger, Florida (Muster and Descriptive Roll of a Detachment of United States Recruits, March 21, 1833 [NA, RG 94, Sixth Infantry]; Semiannual Muster Roll, June 30, 1838 [NA, RG 94, Sixth Infantry, Company G]).

5 Henry Dodge (sketch, 1:370, *n.* 2).

ABSTRACT

Order No. 28 1:384

Brigade Headquarters
Jefferson Barracks,[1] October 7, 1833

The commander approves the proceedings of the court presided over by Lieutenant Colonel Baker,[2] and orders its dissolution. By order of Colonel Dodge[3]

JEFFN. DAVIS
L[ieutenant] Adjt.

LbCS (NA, RG 393 Records of United States Army Continental Commands, 1821–1920, Jefferson Barracks, Orders and Special Orders, March 1831–November 1837).

1 See 1:123, *n.* 3.

2 Daniel Baker, lieutenant colonel of the Sixth Infantry, 1829–36, was born in New Hampshire and enlisted as an ensign, Sixteenth Infantry, in 1799. Discharged in 1800, he was commissioned a second lieutenant the next year, and served in the War of 1812, being brevetted major at the Battle of Brownstown. Baker died in 1836 (Heitman, *Historical Register*, I, 183).

3 Henry Dodge (sketch, 1:370, *n.* 2).

1:385 Order No. 29

Brig Head Qrs. Jeffn Barracks[1] 9. Oct. 1833

The Troops at this post will be assembled at the usual hour of "evening parade" to witness the execution of the sentence[2] of the General Court Martial of which Capt. Noel[3] 6th Infantry was President, in the case of Private Jno. Dawson[4] Compy. "C." 6th Infantry

Fatigue duties will cease one hour previous to the time designated for the assembly of the Troops. By order of Col. Dodge[5]

JEFFN DAVIS
L[ieutenant] Adjt.

ALbCS (NA, RG 393 Records of United States Army Continental Commands, 1821–1920, Jefferson Barracks, Orders and Special Orders, March 1831–November 1837).

[1] See 1:123, *n.* 3.

[2] John Dawson, a deserter, was sentenced to be publicly flogged and confined to a cell on bread and water for sixty days, to work at hard labor for six months with ball and chain, and to forfeit all pay during the time of his sentence (Western Department Order No. 23, July 28, 1833 [NA, RG 393, Western Department, Orders and Special Orders, July 1832–October 1833, NA XXVII, 341–42—formerly Volume VIII]).

[3] Thomas Noel, born in Maryland, was graduated from West Point in 1820 and served in the Sixth Infantry twenty-six years. He was assigned mainly to garrisons on the frontier and was promoted to captain in 1827. Noel participated in the Black Hawk and Seminole wars, being brevetted major for gallantry in 1837. He was on sick leave when he died in 1848 in Maryland, at the age of forty-seven (Cullum, *Biographical Register*, I, 258).

[4] Dawson was enlisted by Captain Joseph Van Swearingen at Jefferson Barracks, on November 25, 1831, for the usual term of five years (Semiannual Muster Roll, December 31, 1831 [NA, RG 94, Sixth Infantry, Company K]). Dawson evidently did not find army life agreeable, for he was in confinement within eleven months of his enlistment (Muster Roll, October 31, 1832 [NA, RG 94, Sixth Infantry, Company K]), and spent a considerable portion of his remaining service in arrest. He deserted at least three times (Muster Rolls, February 28, 1833–February 28, 1835 [NA, RG 94, Sixth Infantry, Company C]). Dawson's final downfall was due to drunkenness and desertion. After a court martial he was sentenced to "fifty lashes on his bare back with a raw hide well laid on in presence of the prisoners of the Post. To forfeit all pay and allowances that are or may be due him. To be indelibly marked on the hip with the word 'Deserter.' To be tarred and feathered from the top of his head to his hips and to be drummed out of service with the rogues march" (Western Department Order No. 29, May 9, 1835 [NA, RG 393, Western Department, Orders and Special Orders, NA XXIX, 167–78—formerly Volume X]).

[5] Henry Dodge (sketch, 1:370, *n.* 2).

16 OCTOBER 1833

EXTRACT

Autobiography of Black Hawk

1:386

Editorial Note: In April 1832 Black Hawk[1] and a small band of warriors crossed to the eastern side of the Mississippi, in defiance of an 1804 treaty; they were defeated at the Battle of Bad Axe, August 2, by General Henry Atkinson's forces. Black Hawk escaped and took refuge with the Winnebagoes at Prairie La Cross until August 27, when he surrendered to Joseph M. Street, the Indian agent at Prairie du Chien (see 1:334, *n.* 6 for the part played by Davis in the capture of Black Hawk).

Dictated by Black Hawk at Rock Island, Illinois, after August 1833 to Antoine LeClaire, a halfbreed interpreter, and first prepared for publication by a young journalist, J. B. Patterson, the following extract describes the first weeks of Black Hawk's imprisonment, August–September 1832.

Rock Island,[2] Illinois October 16, 1833

I was now given up by the agent[3] to the commanding officer[4] at fort Crawford,[5] (the White Beaver[6] having gone down the river.) We remained here a short time, and then started to Jefferson Barracks,[7] in a steam boat,[8] under the charge of a young war chief, [Lieut. Jefferson Davis] [9] who treated us all with much kindness. He is a good and brave young chief, with whose conduct I was much pleased. On our way down, we called at Galena,[10] and remained a short time. The people crowded to the boat to see us; but the war chief would not permit them to enter the apartment where we were—knowing, from what his own feelings would have been if he had been placed in a similar situation, that we did not wish to have a gaping crowd around us.

We passed Rock Island without stopping. The great war chief, [Gen. Scott,[11]] [9] who was then at fort Armstrong,[2] came out in a small boat to see us; but the captain of the steam boat would not allow any body from the fort to come on board of his boat, in consequence of the cholera raging among the soldiers. . . .

On our arrival at Jefferson barracks,[12] we met the great war chief, [White Beaver,] [9] who had commanded the American army against my little band. I felt the humiliation of my situation: a little while before, I had been the leader of my braves, now I was a prisoner of war! but had surrendered myself. He received us kindly, and treated us well.

We were now confined to the barracks, and forced to wear the *ball and chain*![13] This was extremely mortifying, and altogether useless.

MS not found. Text from Black Hawk, *Life of Ma-ka-tai-me-she-kia-kiak or Black Hawk*, edited by J. B. Patterson (Boston: Russell, Odiorne, & Metcalf, 1834), 137–39.

[1] Black Hawk (sketch, 1:334, *n.* 6).

[2] Rock Island was the site of Fort Armstrong (1:267, *n.* 3).

[3] Joseph M. Street (1782–1840) was a Virginian who immigrated in 1812 to Shawneetown, Illinois, via Kentucky. He was appointed Indian agent in 1827 and the next year moved to Prairie du Chien. Street established good relations with the Winnebagoes, who had been exploited and controlled by local traders, and saw to the establishment of schools, farms, and religious groups for the tribe. He participated in the council which led to the September 15, 1832 treaty with the Winnebagoes, and attempted to have the lands west of the Mississippi reserved forever for them. In 1834 Street was appointed agent for the Sauks and Foxes and in 1835 moved to Rock Island. By 1837 he had returned to Fort Crawford, and accompanied a group of Indians on a tour of the Northeast to treat with the government for the sale of Indian land west of the Mississippi. He died at his home on the Des Moines River, Wapello County, Iowa (W. B. Street, "General Joseph M. Street," *Annals of Iowa*, 3rd Ser., II, 81–105; "Prairie du Chien in 1827," Wisconsin Historical *Collections*, XI, 356–57*n.*).

[4] Zachary Taylor (sketch, 1:332, *n.* 3).

[5] For Fort Crawford, see 1:231, *n.* 12.

[6] Henry Atkinson (sketch, 1:301, *n.* 7) had left Fort Crawford before August 27 and assumed command at Jefferson Barracks September 13 (Street to Blair, September 3, 1832, in *Niles' Weekly Register*, September 29, 1832, p. 78; Post Return, September 1832 [NA, RG 94, Jefferson Barracks]).

[7] See 1:123, *n.* 3 for Jefferson Barracks.

[8] The steamboat was the *Winnebago* ([Galena, Illinois] *Galenian*, September 5, 1832).

[9] The brackets appear in the original text.

[10] For Galena, see 1:231, *n.* 18. The steamer conveying Davis and Black Hawk arrived there September 4 ([Galena, Illinois] *Galenian*, September 5, 1832).

[11] Winfield Scott (sketch, 1:124, *n.* 2).

[12] They arrived at St. Louis September 10 on their way to Jefferson Barracks (*Missouri Republican*, September 11, 1832, cited in Stevens, *Black Hawk War*, 240*n.*).

[13] See 1:334, *n.* 5 for a discussion of the shackling of Black Hawk.

1:387

Order No. 30

Brigade Head Quarters Jeffn Barrack[1] 18th Oct. 1833

A fatigue party to consist of a commissioned officer and ten privates will be detailed for the purpose of erecting a temporary shed to serve as a Market house.

Lieut. Blake[2] 6th Infy. is designated for the above duty and will

apply to the Asst. Qr. Master[3] of the post for the means necessary to execute the purpose By Order of Col. Dodge[4] JEFFN DAVIS
L[ieutenant] Adjt.

ALbCS (NA, RG 393 Records of United States Army Continental Commands, 1821–1920, Jefferson Barracks, Orders and Special Orders, March 1831–November 1837).

[1] See 1:123, *n.* 3.

[2] Jacob Edmund Blake, a Pennsylvanian, was an 1833 graduate of West Point and was assigned to Jefferson Barracks, 1833–34. After service as quartermaster at the Academy, duty in the Subsistence Department and Adjutant General's Office, he transferred to the Corps of Topographical Engineers in 1838. Blake was on General William J. Worth's staff, 1842–44, and served in the Mexican War. He accidentally shot himself and died at Palo Alto, Texas, in 1846, at the age of thirty-four (Cullum, *Biographical Register*, I, 559).

[3] First Lieutenant George H. Crosman, Sixth Infantry, was assistant quartermaster (Post Return, October 1833 [NA, RG 94, Jefferson Barracks]).

[4] Henry Dodge (sketch, 1:370, *n.* 2).

Order No. 31 1:388

Brigade Head Qrs. Jefferson Bks[1] 21st. Oct 1833

The Command of the Post of Jefferson Barracks having divolved on Lt Col D Baker[2] 6th Inf the usual reports and returns required at Head Quarters will be made to him[3]

Adjt Brooke[4] of the 6th Inf will relieve Adjt Davis of the Dragoons in the duties of Staff Officer to the Command[5] By order of Lt Col Baker F J BROOKE
Lt & Post Adjt

ALbCS (NA, RG 393 Records of United States Army Continental Commands, 1821–1920, Western Department, Orders and Special Orders, March 1831–November 1837).

[1] See 1:123, *n.* 3.

[2] Daniel Baker (sketch, 1:384, *n.* 2).

[3] The commander of the post, Henry Atkinson, was absent on leave October 21–November 15 (Post Returns, October, November, 1833 [NA, RG 94, Jefferson Barracks]).

[4] Francis J. Brooke was born in Virginia and graduated from West Point in 1826. He served in various frontier and southern garrisons, and in the Black Hawk War. Brooke was adjutant at Jefferson Barracks, 1833–36, and was killed in 1837 in Florida at the age of thirty-five (Cullum, *Biographical Register*, I, 380).

[5] Davis was appointed adjutant of the post October 2 (1:379).

ABSTRACT

1:389 ## Post Return

Jefferson Barracks,[1] Missouri, October [31,] 1833

Lists Jefferson Davis, adjutant Dragoons,[2] present at the post. Remarks: "For Duty, Acting Staff officer to the Brigade from 2d Octr. to 21st Rel[ieve]d by Brig[ade] Order No. 31." [3]

Printed form, filled in and signed (NA, RG 94 Records of the Adjutant General's Office, Post Returns, Jefferson Barracks), 2. Signed: "F J Brooke Lt & Adjt 6th Inf Actg Post Adjt D Baker Lt Col 6th. Infy." Endorsed: "Recd. 19 Novr."

[1] See 1:123, *n.* 3.

[2] Davis was appointed adjutant on August 29 or 30 (see 1:371, *n.* 4).

[3] See 1:388 for Brigade Order No. 31.

1:390 ## To Aeneas Mackay

Head Qrs. Regt. Dragoons Jefferson Bks.[1] 2d Novr. 1833

SIR[2]

Herewith enclosed I have the honor to transmit to you duplicate receipts for the Books furnished to the Staff, to Companies "A", "B", "C", "D", & "E" Regiment of Dragoons.[3] Those sent for the remaining Companies will be delivered to those Companies when organized[4] By order—Very Respectfully Yr Mo obt. Servt. (signed)

JEFFN. DAVIS
L[ieutenant] Adjt. Dragoons

LbC (NA, RG 393 Records of United States Army Continental Commands, 1821–1920, Regimental Headquarters, First Dragoons, Letters Sent, 1833–39, p. 12). Addressed: "To Capt. Aeneas MacKay Qr. Master. U. S. Army Philadelphia Pa." Enclosures missing.

[1] See 1:123, *n.* 3.

[2] Aeneas Mackay, born in New York, was in the Ordnance Department from 1813 until 1816, when he was transferred to artillery. Mackay was promoted to captain in 1822, and became an assistant quartermaster two years later. During the Mexican War, he was lieutenant colonel and deputy quartermaster general, and was brevetted colonel in 1848. He died in 1850 (Heitman, *Historical Register*, I, 670).

[3] For a list of the books in the adjutant's charge, see *General Army Regulations* (1825), 57–60.

[4] A total of ten companies was provided for by the act establishing the Regiment of Dragoons (*Statutes at Large of the United States*, IV [1846], 652).

From William B. Lewis 1:391

SIR, 6 November 1833

Your account for recruiting expenditures made at Lexington in June[1] & July last, has been adjusted, and is found to be balanced by the receipt of Lt. Col. *Kearney*[2] for $275.38, paid over to him the 9th. of September of the present year. W. B. L.[3]

LbC (NA, RG 217 Records of the United States General Accounting Office, Second Auditor's Office, Letters Sent, XVII, 446). Addressed: "Lieut. Jeffn. Davis, U S. Dragoons, Fort Gibson, Ark. T[erritory]."

1 Davis' recruiting account for June was transmitted in 1:360.

2 Stephen Watts Kearny, commander of the Army of the West on its famed march to California in 1846–47, was born in Newark in 1794 and joined the army in 1812. He served most of his early career on the western frontier: on the 1825 Yellowstone expedition, at Fort Crawford (1828–29), at Jefferson Barracks (1829–33), and at the first Fort Des Moines. Lieutenant colonel of Dragoons from March 1833 until 1836, he was promoted to brigadier general in 1846, having been commander of the Third Military District for four years. Kearny's Mexican War service in California and Mexico won him a brevet as major general, but he contracted yellow fever in Vera Cruz in April 1848 and died later that year in St. Louis (*DAB*; see also Clarke, *Stephen Watts Kearny*).

3 William B. Lewis (sketch, 1:166, *n.* 1).

ABSTRACT

Pay Voucher 1:392

Jefferson Barracks,[1] November 7, 1833

Lieutenant Jefferson Davis, U.S. Dragoons, acknowledges that he has received $188.46 from Paymaster Major T. Wright.[2] Amount includes pay, allowance for one servant,[3] and forage for two horses, for September and October, and additional pay for duty as adjutant[4] during the same period. The servant is described as "James a Slave."

Printed form, filled in and signed (NA, RG 217 Records of the United States General Accounting Office, Paymasters' Accounts, Wright 1,878[?], Voucher 12), 3. Signed: "Jeffn. Davis L[ieutenant] & Adjt. Dragoons." Endorsed: "[Received] 7 Novr 1833."

1 See 1:123, *n.* 3.

2 Thomas Wright (sketch, 1:320, *n.* 2).

3 James Pemberton was the servant (sketch, 1:5, *n.* 4).

4 Davis was appointed adjutant on August 29 or 30 (1:371, *n.* 4).

ABSTRACT

1:393
Register of Payments to Officers

[Washington, D.C.,] November 7, 1833

Lists payment by Paymaster T. Wright[1] to Second Lieutenant Jefferson Davis, Dragoons, $188.46. Amount includes pay and allowance for Davis and one servant,[2] and allowance for two horses, for September and October. Remarks: "Adjutant."[3]

D (NA, RG 99 Records of the Office of the Paymaster General, Register of Payments to Officers, IV, 27), 1.

[1] Thomas Wright (sketch, 1:320, *n.* 2).

[2] The servant was James Pemberton (sketch, 1:5, *n.* 4).

[3] Davis was appointed adjutant on August 29 or 30 (1:371, *n.* 4).

1:394
To Jesse Bean

Head Qrs. Regt Dragoons Jeffn Bks.[1] Novr. 12th. 1833

SIR[2]

Col. Dodge[3] directs that you will proceed with the least delay to this Post and report yourself to Lieut. Col. Kearny,[4] Superintending the recruiting of Dragoons, for orders and instructions Very Respy. Yr. Mo. ob. Servt. (Signed) JEFFN DAVIS

L[ieutenant] Adjt. Dragoons

LbC (NA, RG 393 Records of United States Army Continental Commands, 1821–1920, Regimental Headquarters, First Dragoons, Letters Sent, 1833–39, p. 20). Addressed: "To Capt. Jesse Bean Regt. Dragoons Batesville Ark."

[1] See 1:123, *n.* 3.

[2] Jesse Bean, a Tennesseean who raised a company of mounted rangers in 1832, became a captain of the Dragoons when the regiment was organized in 1833 (Heitman, *Historical Register*, I, 203). Bean had served under Andrew Jackson in the Battles of Horse Shoe Bend (Basset [ed.], *Correspondence of Andrew Jackson*, I, 491) and New Orleans and later commanded a company of spies in the Indian wars in Florida (McDermott [ed.], *Western Journals of Washington Irving*, 28). In an 1817 petition which Congress refused, Bean requested the right to work a silver mine he had discovered in Missouri Territory (*Congressional Debates*, 14th Cong., 2nd Sess., 133, 218). He and his mounted rangers achieved considerable fame through Washington Irving's *A Tour on the Prairies* (ed. McDermott, 48), an account of an expedition from Fort Gibson which Irving and other notables joined in 1832. Irving described Bean as about forty and as an excellent woodsman and hunter. Another source reported him a poor disciplinarian (Young, "United States Mounted Ranger Battalion," *Mississippi Valley*

Historical Review, XLI, 467). Captain Bean resigned from the army in 1835, but two years later was involved in military operations against the Seminoles in Florida (C. T. Foreman, "The Bean Family," *Chronicles of Oklahoma*, XXXII, 325). For a comment on Davis' acquaintance with Bean, see V. Davis, *Memoir*, I, 134–35.

[3] Henry Dodge (sketch, 1:370, *n.* 2).

[4] Stephen W. Kearny (sketch, 1:391, *n.* 2).

From Eliza Van Benthuysen Davis 1:395

Poplar Grove,[1] Nov 20th 1833

My Dear Brother will not be surprised at My Writing When he is informed that Mother[2] requested it, I have Sometimes felt unpleasantly that I shared so little of your affection, as to make it a matter of indifference to you Wether or not you ever heard from me, I expected you Would Write to us Much oftener knowing that your Brother[3] Seldom Writes, & would receive great pleasure in hearing from one he loves so dearly.

I find Mother complaining of your silence & immagining that some calamity had befallen you. I quieted her fears, as we received a letter[4] from you a few days previous to my leaving home,[5] You perceive I am here With out My husband, do not immagine Me the same foolish creature as heretofore, I am anxious to get home or rather to My husband, but I think of your remarks concerning silly people & am quite composed, I have been absent ten days from the Hurricane[5] & expect to be five More, Florida[6] came With me as far as Natches but has returned. My Brother[7] accompanied me down yesterday & we return in the Morning, the visit is short but I feel it my duty & 'tis also a pleasure to come & see Mother whenever circumstances permit. Caroline[8] has been here for some months past, & I fear is a trouble to Mother, at least More than Ellen[9] & Jane,[10] We think of sending her to Mrs Thayer who has recently established a school in Clinton[11] & has sent to the North for Teachers to assist her, it probably will be the best institution the state <can>[12] afford, I wish very much Jane & Ellen would accompany her, but Mother is opposed both to moving & having the children removed,

I look forward to change in some form as regards our Mode of living I cannot say I am discontented, but I am not satisfied, but I suppose this is not of Much importance, as it is seldom we find any one who is perfectly content with their lot if so it may be called,

Mr Stamps[13] has purchased on or near the river,[14] about twenty five Miles from where he now resides,[15] he removes his negroes next Week, They do not think of it as a residence at least for the present, if they should we must seek some place where we can have Mother & the children reside with us as it would never do to leave her alone.

Mr Bradford[16] came up to day, & reports all well, they have suffered Much in both families, but fortunately lost none.[17] Mother's health has been unusually good, she is cheerful at least for her, says she is resolved upon paying you a visit if you do not write to her & I have promised to accompany her, & force you to come home, but I think it would be wrong as you seem More disposed to remain where you are, It is useless to tell you that all of us have a great wish to see you, I cannot immagine <why>[12] but yet it is so, & even Basto would have a welcome, far greater than any of his tribe he receives a consequence from his Master,

The Hurricane is not much improved since you last saw it although Mr Davis continues to take the same interest, We have not built a house, but hope to have one commenced before summer, I do not know that we shall remain at home during the Next summer, but if we leave we shall surely see you before our return, I suppose you will retain Mary[18] as you pro[posed?] she should remain with you when she left school, [torn] if she is disposed, she is much company for us dividing her time between Florida & Myself,

Your Horses are beautiful I Wish you had them to train, you Would prefer them to Leon, although the latter is much admired. You must come & take them,

I have written you a Miserable scrawl but hope you will excuse it, the paper ruled pen bad & My poor brain deficient, but it would all be nothing at least to Me, if I thought it would be received as from *a dearly loved sister*,

Mother's love as a Matter of course, also that of your Would be Sister

ELIZA[19]

Charity[20] wishes when you write to Mother to send her some information from Jim,[21] Julia Ann[22] & child are well.

ALS (Jefferson Hayes-Davis, Colorado Springs, 1969). Addressed: "Lieut J. F. Davis <—Jefferson Barracks Missouri—> Fort Gibson A[rkansas] T[erritory]." Endorsed: "Forwarded."

1 "Poplar Grove," later called "Rosemont," the Davis homestead about one mile east of Woodville, Mississippi, was more a farm than a plantation, and contained some forest and cleared land where it is said the Davises "camped out" while building their home. Ellen Mary Davis Anderson, Davis' niece

who lived there for a time, described it years later: " 'a comfortable brown cottage with servant's outhouses . . . a plain but comfortable frame dwelling, one and a half stories high, of six rooms, four on the ground floor and two on the second, large brick chimneys, glass windows, and verandas the full length of the house. The ground on one side sloped down to the purest of springs with its crystal stream rippling through the forest.' " Around the house, Davis' mother had a flower garden which was divided from the vegetable garden and orchard by rose bushes. "A huge pear tree in one corner of the yard is said to have been the delight of young Jefferson Davis and his nephews and nieces" (W. L. Fleming, "Early Life," Mississippi Valley Historical *Proceedings, 1915–16*, IX, 158).

[2] Jane Cook Davis (sketch, 1:22, *n.* 4; 1:Appendix IV, Entry 14), Eliza's mother-in-law.

[3] Joseph Emory Davis (sketch, 1:19, *n.* 1; 1:Appendix IV, Entry 15), Eliza's husband.

[4] The Davis letter mentioned here has not been found.

[5] "Hurricane" was Joseph Emory Davis' plantation on the Mississippi River just south of Vicksburg (1:328, *n.* 2).

[6] Florida A. Davis McCaleb Laughlin, Eliza's stepdaughter (sketch, 1:19, *n.* 9; 1:Appendix IV, Entry 28).

[7] Watson Van Benthuysen, Eliza's brother, edited the New York *American*, owned by Charles King (Van Benthuysen and Hall, *Van Benthuysen Genealogy*, 71; Spooner [ed.], *Historic Families of America*, III, 70–72), and had family ties in New York, where his brother operated a prosperous printing firm, and in Natchez (Howell and Tenney, *History of the County of Albany*, 701; see 1:361, *n.* 8; 1:517, 523). Van Benthuysen was a proprietor of the New Orleans *Jeffersonian* for a time, and after the departure of J. F. H. Claiborne in September 1846, sole proprietor and editor (Kosciusko [Mississippi] *Chronicle*, February 21, 1846; Van Benthuysen to Walker, August 21, 1846 [Robert J. Walker Papers, Library of Congress]; Vicksburg *Tri-Weekly Whig*, October 1, 1846).

[8] Caroline Davis Robins Leonard (1:Appendix IV, Entry 31), Eliza's stepdaughter, was born in 1823. She first married Thomas E. Robins (also spelled Robbins); their marriage bond is dated December 17, 1842 (O'Neill, "Warren County Marriages," *Journal of Mississippi History*, XXIX, 146). They reportedly had two sons who died in infancy (H. A. Davis, *The Davis Family*, 81; Van Benthuysen, "Supplement to the Van Benthuysen, Conklin-Dally and Seaward Genealogies," 8 [New York State Library, Albany]); this is partially verified by a tombstone in the Davis Island cemetery which reads "Jack, son of Thos E. & Caroline Robins," who lived from August 18, 1844, to August 21, 1846, and by a letter from Varina Davis to her mother, November 26, 1847, in which she mentions the serious illness of Caroline's child (Jefferson Davis Papers, University of Alabama Library, Tuscaloosa). Caroline Robins and Abram F. Leonard signed a marriage bond in Warren County, Mississippi, on December 3, 1856; she was apparently living in Virginia as late as 1901 (O'Neill, "Warren County Marriages," *Journal of Mississippi History*, XXX, 152; Lise Mitchell's journal entry of June 1, 1862, and Leonard to Harper, March 21, 1901 [Lise Mitchell Papers, Howard-Tilton Memorial Library, Tulane University, New Orleans]). Her death date is unknown.

[9] Ellen Mary Davis Anderson (sketch, 1:363, *n.* 36; 1:Appendix IV, Entry 92).

[10] Jane Lucinda Davis Farish (sketch, 1:363, *n.* 35; 1:Appendix IV, Entry 90).

[11] Caroline Matilda Warren Thayer was a noted author and pedagogue. Before moving to Clinton, she had directed the Elizabeth Female Academy

in Washington, Mississippi, and at the time of her death in 1844 she was teaching in Harrisonburg, Louisiana. As the granddaughter of General Joseph Warren, who was mortally wounded at the Battle of Bunker Hill, and reportedly the mother of one of the doomed defenders of the Alamo, Mrs. Thayer was closely associated with the history about which she wrote (Vicksburg *Sentinel and Expositor*, April 9, 1844). Among her published works are a didactic novel, printed in 1805, a book of letters and poems on religious themes (1818), and a text on American history (1828). In an 1835 entry in the Clinton *Gazette* Mrs. Thayer gave notice of an examination of students in the Female Department of Mississippi College, Clinton. During that academic year the school had sixty-eight pupils, and the curriculum included English, music, and art (Clinton [Mississippi] *Gazette*, November 21, 1835, January 16, July 16, 1836).

[12] Interlined.

[13] William Stamps, Eliza's brother-in-law (sketch, 1:362, *n.* 12; 1:Appendix IV, Entry 63).

[14] Stamps's new land was undoubtedly located near Fort Adams on the Mississippi (see 1:513).

[15] Possibly "Heatherdon." See 1:362, *n.* 1.

[16] David Bradford, Eliza's brother-in-law (sketch, 1:5, *n.* 10; 1:Appendix IV, Entry 71).

[17] See 1:363 for Bradford's comments on the cholera epidemic in Louisiana.

[18] Probably Mary Lucinda Davis Mitchell, Eliza's stepdaughter (sketch, 1:362, *n.* 11; 1:Appendix IV, Entry 26).

[19] Eliza Van Benthuysen Davis (sketch, 1:361, *n.* 8; 1:Appendix IV, Entry 25), Davis' sister-in-law.

[20] Charity was undoubtedly the slave owned by Jane Cook Davis and originally owned by Davis' father (1:528; Stamps to Davis, July 3, 1874 [Jefferson Davis Papers, Frances Carrick Thomas Library, Transylvania University, Lexington, Kentucky]). See also 1:419.

[21] "Jim" was James Pemberton (sketch, 1:5, *n.* 4).

[22] Julia Ann is probably the same slave called "Julyan" and "Julian" in other letters and, from context, may be the wife of James Pemberton, Davis' plantation manager-to-be (1:496, 528).

1:396

From Peter Hagner

SIR. November 29th. 1833

I have received your letter of the 13th. Instant,[1] wherein you mention that in a letter received by you from the 2d. Auditor,[2] dated 27. Octo. 1831,[3] you were informed that $137.63—had been transferred to your credit on the Books of this office—and you add—that you do not find in the Statements received from this office, that you have received credit for the same. In reply, I have to state, that in a Settlement made of your account on the *13th. Decr. 1831*[4]—you received credit for the amount in question. On reference to the Sheet of "differences" [5] enclosed to you in a letter from this office, of that date, may be seen the following words, "and amounts allowed by 2d. auditor & brot. by transfer to Lt. Davis' credit on the Books of the 3d. Auds. office, $277.23;" this aggregate sum was made up of two separate transfers from the office of the 2d. Audr. viz. One in may 1831[6] for $139.60, the other in October 1831, for 137.63;[7] the first (139.60.) you received a credit in a settlement made 1. August 1831.[8] Respectfully, Your Obd. Svt. PETER HAGNER[9]

Audr.

LbC (NA, RG 217 Records of the United States General Accounting Office, Third Auditor's Office, Miscellaneous Letters Sent, LXIII, 125). Addressed: "Lieut. Jefferson Davis, U. S. Dragoons. Jefferson Barracks. via St. Louis, Mo."

[1] Davis' letter of November 13 has not been found.

[2] William B. Lewis was the second auditor (sketch, 1:166, *n.* 1).

[3] The letter from the second auditor is printed as 1:290.

[4] The letter transmitting the settlement of December 13, 1831, is printed as 1:306.

[5] The sheet of differences is missing.

[6] See 1:260 for Eakin's letter of May 23 advising Davis of the credit of $139.60.

[7] Notice of Davis' credit of $137.63 was transmitted in 1:290.

[8] The settlement of August 1831 has not been found.

[9] Peter Hagner (sketch, 1:199, *n.* 5).

ABSTRACT

Post Return

1:397

Fort Gibson,[1] December [31,] 1833

Lists Jefferson Davis, adjutant Dragoons,[2] present at the post. Remarks: "For duty." Further remarks note that "The Dragoons left Jefferson Barracks on the 20th. of November and arrived at Camp Jackson[3] in the vicinity of this Post on the 14th. of Decemb. 1833."[4]

DS (NA, RG 94 Records of the Adjutant General's Office, Post Returns, Fort Gibson), 2. Signed: "D. S. Miles. Post. Adjutant. M. Arbuckle Colo. 7th Infy Commdg." Endorsed: "Recd. 19th Feby 1834."

[1] Fort Gibson was located about fifty miles northwest of Fort Smith, Arkansas Territory, on land ceded to the Cherokees in an 1828 treaty. The site of Fort Gibson had been in Arkansas Territory (1824–28) and was to be in Indian Territory in 1834 (*Statutes at Large of the United States*, IV [1846], 40, 729, 733, V [1846], 50, VII [1846], 311; F. K. Van Zandt, *Boundaries of the United States and the Several States*, 78, 191–93, 225). The fort was first established in 1824 to protect roads and control the Indians. It was abandoned, 1857–63, and finally closed in 1890 (Prucha, *Guide to Military Posts*, 76).

[2] Davis had been appointed adjutant August 29 or 30 (1:371, *n.* 4).

[3] Camp Jackson, about one mile west of Fort Gibson, was established by the Dragoons in mid-December 1833 ([Hildreth], *Dragoon Campaigns*, 59–

85; Young, *The West of Philip St. George Cooke*, 72–74) and became the permanent regimental winter quarters. "Large barracks of oak shingles quartered the troops but afforded poor protection from the cold. The roofs were leaky, but buffalo robes kept the water from the saddles, knapsacks, and clothing, and preserved a dry sleeping place for the night" (Pelzer, *Marches of Dragoons*, 27).

[4] General Order No. 88, Washington, October 11, read in part: "Colonel Dodge of the Dragoons, will, as early as practicable march the 5 companies of his Regiment, now at Jefferson Barracks to Fort Gibson, and in the vicinity of that place establish the Head Quarters of his Regiment and winter the 5 companies" (NA, RG 94, War Department Orders and Circulars, Orders, VI [1832–34]). The order was received at Jefferson Barracks October 26 (Post Return, October 1833 [NA, RG 94, Jefferson Barracks]), and by November 20 the expedition was underway. Travelling in a southwesterly direction over uncharted land, the march of the Dragoons was a difficult one. Both Dodge and the War Department were criticized for attempting the march at that time of the year: "Convinced by the experience of late years, of the necessity of a mounted force, to cope with mounted and other Indians, Congress passed the bill to raise a regiment of dragoons, on the 2d of March, 1833. . . . Five companies were soon completed and concentrated at Jefferson Barracks. The recruits had generally disposed of nearly all their clothing, in anticipation of their uniforms, on their arrival at that station. In this they were destined to be sadly disappointed. At the approach of winter,—in November,—before any clothing or their proper arms had been received; before two companies had received their horses; just at that season when all civilized, and, I believe, barbarous nations, even in a state of war, suspend hostilities and go into winter quarters, these five companies received an order to march out of theirs,—to take the field! . . . The march to Fort Gibson was commenced on the 20th of November. On the third day, they encountered a severe snow-storm. On the 14th of December, they reached their destination, having marched five hundred miles. Here they found no comfortable quarters, but passed a severe winter for any climate in tents; the thermometer standing more than one day at 8° below zero. There were of course no stables, and but very little corn, and the horses were of necessity turned loose to sustain a miserable existence on cane in an Arkansas bottom.

"In what originated this march? Was any important public end to be attained? Was it to repel an invading foe? Was it to make a sudden and important attack upon a foreign enemy? Did the good of the service in any way call for it? To these questions there is but one answer—No!" (Cooke, *Scenes and Adventures in the Army*, 219–20).

Whether or not such criticism was justified, Dodge felt obliged to defend himself, and did so in a letter to Adjutant General Roger Jones wherein he said, "The great anxiety I had to place the Corps in a situation to be servicable to the Country was the reason I recommended the marching the five Companies now under my Orders from Jefferson Barracks to this place. I was strongly impressed with the Belief <[the?] horses> would be in a Better situation to sustain themselves on the Grass of the prairies than to march them from Jefferson Barracks in the Spring when the roads were bad <—and—> the water slight and Forage scarce, I am still of this Opinion, <that> the movement made was a proper one and that the Dragoon Horses will be better able to perform the contemplated march the next season than if they had remained at Jefferson Barracks" (February 15, 1834 [Henry Dodge Order Book, Iowa State Department of History and Archives, Des Moines]). Whatever the validity of Dodge's reasons, the men who made the trip and endured its hardships were slow to forget the discomfort that they believed was unnecessary. One of the enlisted men wrote, in speaking of the difficuty of the journey, "truly I believe no dragoons of the command will ever forget the day of our arrival there [Fort Gibson]; weariness and extreme fatigue were depicted upon every countenance; and now, indeed, (as we have since experienced during our stay here,) we would willingly have drained our pockets of the last copper for a morsel of bread. I never before saw so many half-starved men together; the greater portion of us had eaten scarce a mouthful since our departure from the Illinois river two days previous . . ." ([Hildreth], *Dragoon Compaigns*, 78).

ABSTRACT

Field and Staff Muster Roll 1:398

Camp Jackson, Arkansas Territory,[1] December 31, 1833

Lists Adjutant[2] Jefferson Davis of the field and staff, U.S. Regiment of Dragoons commanded by Colonel Henry Dodge,[3] as present. Report covers November and December 1833.

Printed form, filled in and signed (NA, RG 94 Records of the Adjutant General's Office, Muster Rolls of Regular Army Organizations, First Dragoons [Company A], Field and Staff), 2. Signed: "Jefferson Davis 2 L[ieutenant] H. Dodge Col Com[mandin]g." Endorsed: "Entered Recd Febry. 18th. 1834."

1 Camp Jackson was not actually in Arkansas Territory, but on Cherokee land (see 1:397, *n.* 3).

2 Davis was appointed adjutant August 29 or 30 (see 1:371, *n.* 4).

3 Henry Dodge (sketch, 1:370, *n.* 2).

From William B. Lewis 1:399

Jany. 10, 1834

SIR,

Your letter of 19 November last[1] has been referred to the Q. M. General,[2] as the papers contained therein, are not usually acted on in this Office.

The Charge of $21.04 [3] raised against you on account of property, has been settled by your paying said amount over to Pay Master Phillips,[4] and this A/C. is now closed on the books of this Office.

W. B. L.[5]

LbC (NA, RG 217 Records of the United States General Accounting Office, Second Auditor's Office, Letters Sent, Property Division, Volume F,

453). Addressed: "Lt. J. Davis A[cting] A[ssistant] Qr. Mr. U. S. A. Jeff[erson] Barracks."

[1] Davis' letter of November 19 has not been found.

[2] The quartermaster general was Thomas S. Jesup (sketch, 1:174, *n.* 4).

[3] See 1:368 for evidence of $21.04 having been charged against Davis; see also the endorsement that indicates payment.

[4] Asher Phillips (sketch, 1:300, *n.* 1), paymaster at Jefferson Barracks until his resignation January 17, 1834.

[5] William B. Lewis (sketch, 1:166, *n.* 1).

1:400 To James W. Stephenson[1]

[Fort Gibson,][2] January 17, 1834

Before leaving St. Louis, Mo.,[3] I authorized Mr. Hempstead[4] of that place to call on you for whatever money you owed me, and to hold it subject to my order, intending to inform you immediately of what I had done, which of course, I wished you to understand as merely an arrangement by which, when it was convenient for you to pay it, I could receive the amount without incurring the hazard of transportation. I pursued the same course towards Mr. Bennet[5] for whatever he might have received for the horse I left with him, and also omitted to inform him of it. Please explain to him, and give him my assurances of my friendly regard for him.

I understand some time since that you agreed that your friends should name you for an appointment in the Rgt. of Dragoons,[6] and it would, I hope, be superfluous to assure you of my desire to be associated thus with you. Should this, however, not be the case, and should Michigan pass into a state government,[7] I will look with interest to the organization of the Territory of Ouisconsin,[8] in which you must appear conspicuously. How is our friend Redding?[9] Does he talk of "Tish," by the way, I wish he would get married, or become settled otherwise, for he has equally the head and the heart to be distinguished and his welfare will always be a matter of solicitude to me.

MS not found. Text from Jeanne LeBron, "Colonel James W. Stephenson: Galena Pioneer," *Journal of the Illinois State Historical Society*, XXXV (1942), 351–52. Originally filed with the estate papers of Colonel Stephenson in the vault of the county clerk's office in Jo Daviess County, Illinois, this letter, along with others of the Stephenson papers, was or should have been transferred to the Illinois State Historical Library at Springfield upon the resolution of the Board of Supervisors (Eggleston to McIntosh, July 18, 1967 [Jefferson Davis Association, Rice University, Houston]). However, a search of their holdings has failed to locate the letter. According to the curator of manuscripts, it was not among the Stephenson letters sent to the Illinois Library (Spence to McIntosh, June 4, 1968 [Jefferson Davis Association, Rice University, Houston]).

[1] James W. Stephenson was the son of a Kentuckian who had come to Illinois in 1809 and for whom Stephenson County is named. James was clerk of the commissioners' court, clerk of the circuit court, and recorder for Jo Daviess County when he was elected captain of a band of mounted rangers, organized in Galena for local defense in the Black Hawk War. He participated actively in the war and was elected lieutenant colonel of Henry Dodge's division in July 1832 (Stevens, *Black Hawk War*, 209). At the end of the war in August 1832, Stephenson returned to his county jobs. Evidently he was hoping for an appointment to the Dragoons or a position as surveyor when he was elected to the Illinois senate in August 1834. He was appointed register of lands at Galena and Chicago in 1835, and was the Democratic candidate for governor in December 1837. Having withdrawn from the campaign before the election because of ill health, the thirty-two-year-old Stephenson remained in Galena until his death from tuberculosis in 1838 (LeBron, "James W. Stephenson," *Journal of the Illinois State Historical Society*, XXXV, 347–67; Bateman and Selby [eds.], *Historical Encyclopedia of Illinois*, 507; Pease, *Frontier State*, 249–50). Davis probably had met Stephenson and the others mentioned in this letter on one of his earlier trips to Galena, while he was stationed at Dubuques Mines (November 1831–March 1832).

[2] See 1:397, *n.* 1.

[3] Davis left Jefferson Barracks near St. Louis on November 20 (1:397).

[4] Of the several Hempsteads that figure prominently in the early history of Galena, Illinois, and St. Louis, the "Mr. Hempstead" referred to here is probably William Hempstead. Born in Connecticut into the large family of Stephen Hempstead, William (1800–54) began his merchant career in Galena before moving to St. Louis. Although the date of this move cannot be fixed exactly, there are extant letters written to him in St. Louis by his sister, Susan Hempstead Gratiot, between 1831 and 1837. By 1835 he was well established in business and was venturing into new fields. In 1837 he joined five other citizens as an original stockholder in the St. Louis theater, and during the 1840's he was part owner of the steamboat *Uncle Toby* (Bale, "Packet of Old Letters," *Wisconsin Magazine of History*, XI, 153–68; Carson, "Night Life in St. Louis a Century Ago," Missouri Historical *Bulletin*, II, 4; Ferris [ed.], "Captain Thomas Hawkes Griffith," *ibid.*, V, 302).

[5] William Bennet (or Bennett) was a native of New Jersey who had immigrated to Galena in 1827, attracted, as many were, by the local discovery of rich lead mines. He owned the Galena Hotel where James Stephenson lived for a short time. Bennet also had a farm north of town, where he was living at the time of his death (*Portrait and Biographical Album of Jo Daviess and Carroll Counties*, 394; LeBron, "James W. Stephenson," *Journal of the Illinois State Historical Society*, XXXV, 348).

[6] The Dragoon Regiment was established in March 1833 and headquartered at Jefferson Barracks near St. Louis (*Statutes at Large of the United States*, IV [1846], 652).

[7] Michigan was admitted to the Union in 1837.

[8] The act creating Wisconsin Territory had been first proposed in 1824 by congressional delegate James D. Doty, Wisconsin then being a part of Michigan Territory (Thwaites, *Story of Wisconsin*, 195–97). The act establishing the new territory was finally

passed April 20, 1836, and went into effect July 4 of that year (*Statutes at Large of the United States*, V [1846], 10–16).

[9] Charles Redding Bennet (also Reading, Bennett) was born in New Jersey in 1807, educated in Illinois and Kentucky, and sometime after 1827 joined his family in Galena where his father (see *n.* 5 above) owned the hotel. The younger Bennet was approximately the same age as James W. Stephenson and Davis and was best man at Stephenson's wedding. Having first studied law, Bennet turned to civil engineering in Illinois, and was one of the surveyors who laid out the towns of Dixon and Galena. He was later Jo Daviess County surveyor and commissioner of schools, and resided in Galena until 1875, three years before his death in Collinsville, Illinois (*Portrait and Biographical Album of Jo Daviess and Carroll Counties*, 394–95; *History of Jo Daviess County*, 627; Stevens, "Hazelwood," *Journal of the Illinois State Historical Society*, XXXII, 326; LeBron, "James W. Stephenson," *ibid.*, XXXV, 348, 355; *History of Lee County*, 101). In a letter to T. C. Reynolds, Davis spoke of having known Bennet when he was stationed near Galena (December 12, 1882, in St. Louis *Globe-Democrat*, January 3, 1883).

1:401

To Lewis Cass

Camp Jackson Near Fort Gibson[1]
A[rkansas] Ter 27th January 1834

SIR[2]

I am directed by the Colonel commanding Regiment[3] to transmit to You the enclosed communication from Brevet 2 Lieut. Vanderveer[4] on the Subject of his Regimental position in the Dragoons. Very Respectfully Yr. Mo. Obt. Servt JEFFN. DAVIS

Lt. & Adjutant of Dragoons

LbC (NA, RG 393 Records of United States Army Continental Commands, 1821–1920, Regimental Headquarters, First Dragoons, Letters Sent, 1833–39, p. 25). Addressed: "To the Honble Lewis Cass Secretary of War Washington D C." Enclosure missing.

[1] See 1:397, *nn.* 1, 3.

[2] Lewis Cass (sketch, 1:349, *n.* 5).

[3] The colonel commanding the Dragoon Regiment was Henry Dodge (sketch, 1:370, *n.* 2).

[4] John S. Vanderveer (sketch, 1:381, *n.* 4).

1:402

To Lewis Cass

Head Q. Regt. Dragoons
Camp Jackson (Near Fort Gibson)[1] 29th. Jany 1834

SIR[2]

I am directed by the Colonel Comdg Regiment,[3] to transmit to the Secretary of War, the enclosed Protest made by Brevet 2nd Lieut.

Northrop[4] Serving with Dragoons, against a decision as to his Regimental Position. Very Respectfully Yr. Mo. Obt Servt. (Signed)

JEFF. DAVIS
Lt. & Adjutant

LbC (NA, RG 393 Records of United States Army Continental Commands, 1821–1920, Regimental Headquarters, First Dragoons, Letters Sent, 1833–39, p. 26). Addressed: "To the Hon. Lewis Cass Secretary of War Washington D. C." Enclosure missing.

[1] See 1:397, *nn.* 1, 3.

[2] Lewis Cass (sketch, 1:349, *n.* 5).

[3] Colonel Henry Dodge commanded the Dragoon Regiment (sketch, 1:370, *n.* 2).

[4] Lucius B. Northrop (1811–94) was a South Carolinian and an 1831 graduate of the Military Academy. He first made the acquaintance of Davis at West Point, and they remained friends and correspondents until Davis' death. Severely wounded in the 1839 Seminole War, Northrop was retired from active service and studied medicine in Philadelphia. He was dropped from the army rolls in January 1848 for practicing medicine on charity patients in Charleston. Davis, as chairman of the Senate Committee on Military Affairs, seems to have been instrumental in his reinstatement by August of the same year (Warner, *Generals in Gray*, 225; Davis to Polk, June 23, 1848, D. Rowland, *Papers*, I, 205–206). Northrop was promoted to captain in 1848 and resumed the practice of medicine until his appointment as colonel and commissary general for the Confederacy in 1861. As food became more and more scarce, Northrop was severely criticized—for his being a favorite of Davis, as well as for the alleged inefficiency of his department. Davis was forced to relieve him in February 1865, and he was arrested by Federal authorities in June. Soon released, he spent twenty-five years on his farm in Virginia and died in the Confederate Home, Pikesville, Maryland (*DAB*; Warner, *Generals in Gray*, 225–26).

Henry Dodge to Roger Jones 1:403

Head Qrs. Regt. Dragoons
Camp Jackson[1] 11th. Feby 1834

SIR[2]

I have the honor to inform you that on the 4th. Inst. I received and accepted the resignation[3] of the Staff appointment, held by 2nd Lieut Jeffn. Davis of Dragoons and that on the 5th. Inst. I appointed 1st. Lieut James W Hamilton[4] Adjutant of the Regiment of Dragoons[5] I have the honour To be yr mo Obt. Servt. H DODGE[6]

Col Commg. U S Dragoons

LS (NA, RG 94 Records of the Adjutant General's Office, Letters Received, D–21, 1834); LbC (NA, RG 393 Records of United States Army Continental Commands, 1821–1920, Regimental Headquarters, First Dragoons, Letters

Sent, 1833–39, p. 27). Addressed: "Col R Jones Adjt Genl U S Army Washington D. C." Endorsed: "[Received] Mar. 30. 1834."

[1] See 1:397, *n.* 3.

[2] Roger Jones (sketch, 1:123, *n.* 6).

[3] Davis' recommendations for promotion to first lieutenant were based on his position as adjutant, for the law organizing the Dragoons specified only that this staff position was to be held by a lieutenant without mention of what grade (see 1:375, *n.* 5). It was hoped that the ambiguity of the law could be utilized to secure the promotion. Although Davis had a good case for advancement on other grounds (1:366), his resignation as adjutant did erode his position and weaken his claims.

[4] James W. Hamilton (sketch, 1:77, *n.* 18).

[5] A copy of this letter was sent by Dodge to William S. Harney, the United States Army paymaster at St. Louis (February 11, 1834 [NA, RG 393, Regimental Headquarters, First Dragoons, Letters Sent, 1833–39, p. 28]).

[6] Henry Dodge (sketch, 1:370, *n.* 2).

ABSTRACT

1:404

Promotions and Appointments List[1]

Headquarters of the Army
Adjutant General's Office
Washington, February 13, 1834

Jefferson Davis, "late of the 1st Infantry," is recommended for appointment as first lieutenant, Regiment of Dragoons, to be ranked from March 4, 1833.

MS not found. Text from *Journal of the Executive Proceedings of the Senate of the United States of America* (90 vols., Washington: Duff Green, Government Printing Office, 1828–1948), IV, 350–56. Signed: "R. Jones, Adj. General." Transmitted: Cass to the President, February 13, 1834 (*Senate Executive Journal*, IV, 350).

[1] This list was transmitted to the Senate by letter of President Jackson dated February 13, and appears under the proceedings of February 21, 1834. The nominations of Davis and the other officers were referred to the Committee on Military Affairs on February 21, and those of the officers of Dragoons were reported back to the Senate and confirmed on May 8, 1834. See *Senate Executive Journal*, IV, 350–56, 358, 401, and 1:414.

ABSTRACT

Post Return 1:405

Fort Gibson,[1] February [28,] 1834

Lists Second Lieutenant Jefferson Davis, Company F, Dragoons, present at the post. Remarks: "for duty (not organized company & not included in the face of the <Return>[2]." [3]

DS (NA, RG 94 Records of the Adjutant General's Office, Post Returns, Fort Gibson), 2. Signed: "D. S. Miles. Post. Adjutant M. Arbuckle Colo. 7th. Infy and Commanding officer." Endorsed: "Recd. April 12th."

[1] See 1:397, *n.* 1.

[2] Interlined.

[3] Company F was not one of the five companies to march from Jefferson Barracks to Fort Gibson (1:390). Evidently Davis had been assigned to Company F in anticipation of the arrival of the remaining five companies of Dragoons who were still at Jefferson Barracks. "The march of the last five companies to Fort Gibson was not made in one echelon, as had been the case with Companies A, B, C, D and E. Each moved out alone, in general following their alphabetical order, although H, I and K were grouped roughly in the final movement. . . . First to arrive at Fort Gibson was Company F, late in April, 1834, having been 24 days en route. Company G reported in a few days later. Companies H, I and K reached Camp Jackson on June 12" (Gardner, "The March of the First Dragoons," *Chronicles of Oklahoma*, XXXI, 33).

From the Office of the Quartermaster General[1] 1:406

SIR 28th. Mar. 1834

Your Clothing Return for the 4th. qr. of last year, has been received and examined at this. Office and sent to the Treasury[2] for settlement.

LbC (NA, RG 92 Records of the Office of the Quartermaster General, Letters Sent Relating to Clothing, V, 131). Addressed: "Lt. Jeffn. Davis of Dragoons Camp Jackson near Fort Gibson Arks."

[1] The quartermaster general was Thomas Jesup (sketch, 1:174, *n.* 4).

[2] The return was sent to the second auditor of the Treasury (see 1:407).

1:407 The Office of the Quartermaster General[1] to the Second Auditor

SIR[2] 28th. Mar. 1834

Herewith I transmit the Clothing Return of Lt. Jeffn. Davis for the Non-Com[missione]d. Staff of the Regt. of Dragoons at Camp Jackson[3] in the 4th. qr. of last year.

LbC (NA, RG 92 Records of the Office of the Quartermaster General, Letters Sent Relating to Clothing, V, 131). Addressed: "2d. Auditor." Enclosure missing.

[1] Thomas S. Jesup (sketch, 1:174, *n.* 4) was quartermaster general.

[2] William B. Lewis (sketch, 1:166, *n.* 1) was second auditor.

[3] Camp Jackson, near Fort Gibson (see 1:397, *n.* 3).

ABSTRACT

1:408 Post Return

Fort Gibson,[1] March [31,] 1834

Lists Second Lieutenant Jefferson Davis, Company F, U.S. Dragoons, present at the post. Remarks: "Compy. not organized. doing duty in Compy. 'A' and not included *<in the face of the Return>*[2]."[3]

DS (NA, RG 94 Records of the Adjutant General's Office, Post Returns, Fort Gibson), 2. Signed: "D. S. Miles. Post Adjt. M. Arbuckle Colo. 7th. Infy. & Commdg. Officer." Endorsed: "Recd. May 8th."

[1] See 1:397, *n.* 1.

[2] Interlined.

[3] Company F was not one of the five companies to march from Jefferson Barracks to Fort Gibson; see 1:405, *n.* 3.

EXTRACT

1:409 Henry Dodge to George W. Jones

Camp Jackson Near Fort Gibson[1]

DEAR JONES[2] April 18th. 1834

. . . The profession of arms is a dull one in a time of peace and suits those who has been many years on the peace Establishment and

I find More treachery and deception practised in the Army than I ever expected to find with a Body of Men who Call themselves Gentlemen My Situation is unpleasant Davis who I appointed my adjt.[3] was among the first to take a Stand against me Major Mason[4] and Davis are Now two of My Most inveterate enemies the desire of these Gentlemen appears to be to Harrass <me>[5] in Small Matters they dont want to fight if Mason would Say fight I would go to the field with him with Great pleasure and indeed unless Harmony and good feeling exists in a Corps the public Service Cannot be promoted and to undertake an Expedition with Such Men I should run the risque of Loosing what Little reputation I have acquired and there is no prospect of War with the Indians the Pawnes[6] are a distant rising nation of Indians without any fixed place of residence and the greater part of them within the Limit of the Mexican Government. . . . Most truly your friend H. DODGE[7]

ALS (Correspondence of Henry Dodge, Iowa State Department of History and Archives, Des Moines), 3. Addressed: "Col. George W. Jones Iowa Michigan Territory." Printed: Salter (ed.), "Letters of Henry Dodge to Gen. George W. Jones," *Annals of Iowa*, Ser. 3, III, 221–22, variant version.

1 See 1:397, *nn.* 1, 3.

2 George Wallace Jones (1804–96), born in Vincennes, Indiana, was a lifetime friend of Davis; their acquaintance dated from college days at Transylvania University. Jones migrated to Sinsinawa Mound, Michigan Territory, in 1831, where he was a storekeeper and miner. Having served as Dodge's aide in the Black Hawk War, Jones was elected as a delegate to Congress (1835–39). Appointed surveyor of public lands for Iowa and Wisconsin in 1840, he was removed the next year and reappointed in 1846, serving until his election as Democratic senator from Iowa in 1848. After his defeat in the 1858 election, Jones was made minister to New Granada but served only two years. He was arrested and briefly imprisoned in 1861 because of his friendly correspondence with Davis, after which he retired from public life to Dubuque, Iowa (*DAB*; *Biographical Directory of the American Congress*, 1136; for biography, see Parish, *George Wallace Jones*).

3 Davis was appointed adjutant August 29 or 30, 1833 (1:371, *n.* 4) and resigned February 4, 1834 (1:403).

4 Richard Barnes Mason (sketch, 1:375, *n.* 8).

5 Interlined.

6 The Kiowa and Wichita Indians, then referred to as Comanches and Pawnee Picts, had their villages some two hundred miles from Fort Gibson in what is now southwestern Oklahoma (Shirk, "Peace on the Plains," *Chronicles of Oklahoma*, XXVIII, 6). See also 1:420, *n.* 6.

7 Henry Dodge (sketch, 1:370, *n.* 2).

ABSTRACT

1:410 ## Company Muster Roll

Camp Jackson, Arkansas Territory,[1] April 30, 1834

Lists First Lieutenant[2] Jefferson Davis of Captain David Perkins'[3] Company E,[4] U.S. Regiment of Dragoons commanded by Colonel Henry Dodge,[5] as present. Remarks: "Joined April 25th. 1834. by virtue of Regtl. Order No. 80."[6] Report covers March and April 1834.

Printed form, filled in and signed (NA, RG 94 Records of the Adjutant General's Office, Muster Rolls of Regular Army Organizations, U. S. Dragoons, Company E), 2. Signed: "D. Perkins Capt. Dragoons H Dodge Col Comdg U S Dragoons." Endorsed: "Proves Entered Recd. June 9th. 1834."

[1] See 1:397, *n.* 3.

[2] Davis is listed here as first lieutenant for the first time. See 1:415 for his commission.

[3] David Perkins, born in Pennsylvania, was graduated from the Military Academy in 1827 and served at Jefferson Barracks and Forts Snelling, Howard, and Winnebago before his appointment to the Dragoons in 1833. Perkins went on various Indian expeditions and served on recruiting and paymaster duties before he resigned in 1839. He died at New Orleans in 1848, at the age of forty-three, having been a merchant and captain of the citizens' guard in Tampico, Mexico, 1846–47 (Cullum, *Biographical Register*, I, 396).

[4] Davis had previously been attached to Companies F (not organized) and A (1:405, 408).

[5] Henry Dodge (sketch, 1:370, *n.* 2).

[6] Regimental Order No. 80 has not been found. NA, RG 393, Orders and Special Orders, Jefferson Barracks, March 1831–November 1837, filed with Western Department Orders, includes orders numbered to 77. The records in the volume are badly kept and not consecutively entered (Trever to McIntosh, May 18, 1970 [Jefferson Davis Association, Rice University, Houston]).

ABSTRACT

1:411 ## Register of Payments to Officers

[Washington, D.C.,] May 1, 1834

Lists payment by Paymaster W. S. Harney[1] to Second Lieutenant Jefferson Davis, Dragoons, $267.10. Amount includes pay and allowance for Davis and one servant,[2] and allowance for two horses in November 1833, and for one horse December 1833 through January 1834. Remarks: "Adjutant[3] 2 horses in Nov.[,] 1 after."

D (NA, RG 99 Records of the Office of the Paymaster General, Register of Payments to Officers, IV, 27), 1.

[1] William S. Harney (sketch, 1:264, *n.* 10).

[2] James Pemberton (sketch, 1:5, *n.* 4).

[3] Davis was adjutant August 29 or 30, 1833 (1:371, *n.* 4) to February 4, 1834 (1:403).

To George Gibson 1:412

May 5th 1834 Fort Gibson Cherokee Nation[1]

SIR[2]

I have received from the third Auditor[3] U. S. Treasy. a statement of differences in my acts.[4] as actg. asst. Com. Sub. at Fort Winebago[5] and at Du Buque's mines.[6] differing from the statement received from you on the same accts. under date of 31st May 1833 [7] by the sum of fifty four Dollars and forty cents, to which allow me to request your attention and to be your much obliged and verry obt. servt.

JEFFN. DAVIS
L[ieutenant] Drgs.

ALS (NA, RG 192 Records of the Office of the Commissary General of Subsistence, Letters Received, D–1283, 1834). Addressed: "To Genl G. Gibson Subsistence Dpt. Washington D. C." Endorsed: "Recd 9 June."

[1] See 1:397, *n.* 1.

[2] George Gibson (sketch, 1:179, *n.* 2).

[3] The third auditor was Peter Hagner (sketch, 1:199, *n.* 5).

[4] Hagner's statement of differences is missing.

[5] See 1:224 for evidence of Davis' service as acting assistant commissary of subsistence at Fort Winnebago. For Fort Winnebago, see 1:144, *n.* 1.

[6] For evidence that Davis served as acting assistant commissary of subsistence at Dubuques Mines, see 1:296, 317. See 1:291, *n.* 2 for Dubuques Mines.

[7] Gibson's statement of differences has not been found.

To Peter Hagner 1:413

Fort Gibson[1] May 6th 1834

SIR[2]

I have the honor to acknowleage the receipt of your letter of the 29th nov. last[3] forwarded from Jeffn. Barracks Mo.

The letter[4] of the 2d Auditor[5] which (I believe) I quoted to you led me to believe that the amount with regard to which I inquired (137 63/100 Dolls.) had been transferred from his office to yours after a settlement of my accts. proper in that office, I infer from your "Statement" that it was partly composed of vouchers originally sent to your office and referred to that of the 2d Auditor.

Also I have the honor to acknowledge the receipt of your letter of March 6th 1834 [6] in which you say that on the settlement of my accts. as acting asst. Com. Subsistence at Fort Winebago,[7] and at Du Buque's mines;[8] I have been found indebted to the United States Fifty five Dollars & seventy cents, differing from your Statement in a letter of March 29th 1832 [9] which read thus "balance due you on account of q. m. Dpt. of $14.95 which will be carried to your credit on account of Subsistence, under which head of appropriation you are charged with $15.23 per Settl. of the 3rd June last" differing also from statement of Comy. Genl.[10] of 31st May 1833 [11] in which I am informed "The balance due to the United States on the Settlement of your account is $1 30/100.

allow me to suggest the possibility of my accts. having been confounded with some other officer's of the same surname. Very Respectfully yr. mo. obt. Servt.

JEFFN. DAVIS
L[ieutenant] Drgs.

ALS (NA, RG 217 Records of the United States General Accounting Office, Third Auditor's Office, Third Auditor's Accounts, Account 2,740). Addressed: "To Peter Hagnar 3d Aud. U. S. Tresy. Washington D. C." Endorsed: "Recd 9 Ansd 10"; in a different hand, "Sub[sistence] a/c letter 4 June 1831, due 15.23 Q M D March 29, 32 due him 14.95 [illegible] Sub[traction] leaves 28/100 due Sub[sistence] Sub[sistence] March 6.34 due U. S. 55.70."

1 See 1:397, *n.* 1.

2 Peter Hagner (sketch, 1:199, *n.* 5).

3 Hagner's letter of November 29 is printed as 1:396.

4 See 1:290 for the letter of the second auditor in regard to $137.63 carried to the books of the third auditor.

5 William B. Lewis was the second auditor (sketch, 1:166, *n.* 1).

6 The Hagner letter of March 6 has not been found.

7 See 1:224 and 1:144, *n.* 1.

8 See 1:296, 317, and, for Dubuques Mines, 1:291, *n.* 2.

9 Hagner's letter of March 29, 1832, is printed as 1:319.

10 The commissary general was George Gibson (sketch, 1:179, *n.* 2).

11 The commissary general's statement of May 31, 1833, has not been found.

ABSTRACT

Senate Resolution 1:414

In the Senate of the United States, May 8, 1834

The Senate confirms the appointment of, among others, "Jefferson Davis, late of the 1s. Infantry, to be 1s. Lieutenant 4. March 1833."[1]

WALTER LOWRIE[2]
Secy.

LbC (NA, RG 94 Records of the Adjutant General's Office, Records of the Appointment, Commission, and Personnel Branch, Register of Confirmations of Officers, United States Army, Senate Resolutions of Consent to Promotions and Appointments, I, 108–10), 2. Printed: *Senate Executive Journal*, IV, 401, variant version.

[1] Davis and the others were recommended for appointment in February (1:404). Davis' appointment was in the Regiment of Dragoons.

[2] Walter Lowrie (sketch, 1:136, *n.* 2).

Commission as First Lieutenant 1:415

[Washington, May 10, 1834]

THE PRESIDENT
OF THE
UNITED STATES OF AMERICA,
TO ALL WHO SHALL SEE THESE PRESENTS GREETING:

Know Ye, That reposing special trust and confidence in the patriotism, valor, fidelity and abilities of *Jefferson Davis* I have nominated, and by and with the advice and consent of the Senate,[1] do appoint him *First Lieutenant in the Regiment of Dragoons* in the service of the UNITED STATES:[2] to rank as such from the *Fourth* day of *March* eighteen hundred and *thirty three*. He is therefore carefully and diligently to discharge the duty of *First Lieutenant* by doing and performing all manner of things thereunto belonging.

And I do strictly charge, and require all Officers and Soldiers under his command, to be obedient to his orders as *First Lieutenant*. And he is to observe and follow such orders, and directions, from time to time, as he shall receive from me, or the future President of the United States of America, or the General or other superior Officers set over him, according to the rules and discipline of War. This Commission to continue in force during the pleasure of the President of the United States, for the time being.

GIVEN under my hand, at the City of Washington, this *tenth* day of *May* in the year of our Lord, one thousand eight hundred and *thirty four* and in the *fifty eighth* year of the Independence of the United States.

By the President, *Andrew Jackson*[3]

Lew Cass[4]
Secretary of War.

Printed form, filled in and signed (Samuel Richey Confederate Collection, Miami University, Oxford, Ohio); printed form, filled in, retained copy (NA, RG 94 Records of the Adjutant General's Office, Records of the Appointment, Commission, and Personnel Branch, Register of Army Commissions, VII, 537). Seal affixed. Endorsed: "R. Jones Adjt. Genl."

1 Davis' appointment as first lieutenant of Dragoons was confirmed by the Senate on May 8, 1834 (1:414).

2 Davis is first listed as being a first lieutenant on the muster roll printed as 1:410. For other documents relating to Davis' promotion to first lieutenant, see 1:366, 375, 404, 414.

3 Andrew Jackson (sketch, 1:239, *n.* 2).

4 Lewis Cass (sketch, 1:349, *n.* 5).

ABSTRACT

1:416

Register of Payments to Officers

[Washington, D.C.,] May 31, 1834

Lists payment by Paymaster T. Wright[1] to Second Lieutenant[2] Jefferson Davis, Dragoons, $327.33. Amount includes pay and allowance for Davis and one servant,[3] and allowance for one horse, for February through May 1834.

D (NA, RG 99 Records of the Office of the Paymaster General, Register of Payments to Officers, IV, 27), 1.

1 Thomas Wright (sketch, 1:320, *n.* 2).

2 Although Davis is listed as a second lieutenant here, his first lieutenant's commission had been approved (1:414).

3 James Pemberton (sketch, 1:5, *n.* 4).

From George Gibson

1:417

SIR 9 June 1834

Yours of the 5th ultimo[1] is received. Upon reference to the 3d Auditors[2] books, it appears that the difference between his statement & that from this office of $54 40/100 on the Settlement of your accounts arises from a charge against you of the following provisions unaccounted for at the expiration of your duties at Fort Winnebago[3]

3 Bbls 127 lbs pork	@	$8.75	$31.81	
115 14/100 galls whiskey	@	.25	$28.86	
64 8/32 " Vinegar	@	.15	$ 9.64	$70.31
Short calculation in provisions sold to Officers at Fort Winnebago per Settlement for 2d Qr 1831				.34
				$70.65
deduct				
This sum transferred from his quarter Master to Subsistence accounts 30th March 1832				14.95[4]
				$55.70

The difference from this office previous to above settlement by the auditor was $1 30/100 which makes the difference of $54 40/100 between the statement of the two officers.

The difference of $55 70/100 as exhibited by the 3d Auditor you are requested to pay over to the Assistant Commissary[5] at the Post and forward his receipt in order that your accounts may be closed.[6]

G. G.[7]

LbC (NA, RG 192 Records of the Office of the Commissary General of Subsistence, Letters Sent, X, 322). Addressed: "Lt Jeff. Davis U S Dragoons Fort Gibson." Endorsed: "Duplicate sent to Fort Leavenworth."

[1] Davis' letter of May 5 is printed as 1:412.

[2] The third auditor was Peter Hagner (sketch, 1:199, *n.* 5).

[3] See 1:144, *n.* 1 for Fort Winnebago.

[4] See 1:319 for notice of the transfer of $14.95 from the Quartermaster Department to that of the commissary of subsistence.

[5] Lawrence F. Carter (sketch, 1:426, *n.* 3) was assistant commissary (Post Return, June 1834 [NA, RG 94, Fort Gibson]).

[6] Davis forwards the requested receipt in 1:425.

[7] George Gibson (sketch, 1:179, *n.* 2).

1:418

From Peter Hagner

SIR. June 10th. 1834

I have received your letter of the 6th. ultimo,[1] the object of which appears to be, to ascertain the situation of your Accounts on the Books of this Office. In reply, I have to state, that the only charge against you on the Books of this Office, is $55.70. arising on Settlement of your Subsistence Account the 6. March last,[2] In further explanation & in reply to your remarks relating to the previous Settlements of your Accounts, I have to remark that on the *4. June 1831* your Subsistence Account was adjusted and $15.23 found due the U. States.[3]

On the 29. March 1832, your qr. Master's Account was adjusted, and $14.95 found due to you,[4] which was transferred to your credit on Account of Subsistence, thereby closing your qr. Master's Account, & reducing the balance due the U. S. to *28 Cents*, on a/c. of Subs. On the 6. March last another Settlement was made of your Subsistence Account and $55.70 found due the U. States, (as above stated) all the particulars which gave rise to these Several results, were communicated to you at the different dates of Settlement, and it would seem from your letter, now under consideration, that my letters were received by you; your apparent misapprehension, most likely, arises from confounding the dates of the several Settlements; it is presumed the explanations contained in this letter will prove satisfactory. Respectfully. Your Obd. Svt. PETER HAGNER[5]
Audr.

LbC (NA, RG 217 Records of the United States General Accounting Office, Third Auditor's Office, Miscellaneous Letters Sent, LXIV, 141–42). Addressed: "Lieut. Jeff. Davis. Regt. Dragoons, Fort Gibson, Arkansas."

[1] Davis' letter of May 6 is printed as 1:413.

[2] Neither the settlement of March 6 nor its letter of transmittal has been found.

[3] Notice of the June 4 settlement of $15.23 was sent to Davis in 1:266.

[4] Notice of the adjustment of Davis' quartermaster's account, made on March 29, 1832, was sent to him in 1:319.

[5] Peter Hagner (sketch, 1:199, *n.* 5).

18 JUNE 1834

From David Bradford

1:419

DEAR BROTHER, West Feliciana,[1] June 18th. 1834

I have had the pleasure of reading your letter to mother[2] of the 19th. Apl.[3] which was not recd. till a few days since, and mother requests me to answer it for her. I have the melancholy event to communicate of the death of sister Matilda Vaughan[4] which occurred on the 16th. of March, and has affected mother greatly; she wishes to see you above all things, and to hear from you frequently if you cannot come to see her before another summer elapses. Mother has been with us 8 or 10 days. Amanda[5] is about to lay in, and I hope to have to open this letter to inform you that you have a young namesake[6] in my family, which might occur before the closing of the mail.

We moved from Variety to Abeyville[7] in March last year, and last Novr. I bought this place (which we have not yet dignified with a name) adjoining Dr. Bartons,[8] and about a mile and a quarter from St. Francisville,[9] consisting of 25 arpens[10] and a new frame house 50 feet long and kitchen &c where we moved on last New Years day and which I would fondly make my home for life; as I have 100 acres of land adjoining and opposite to our residence and can buy 200 more. Last May our Shff. Courteny resigned. I applied with two others for the appointment, Ratliff and Parkinson, the latter was Depy. Shff. and I was very sangine in getting the appointment but someone had possessed the Govr.[11] with the idea that I was a desperate kind of character "un homme emporté" and he appointed Parkinson. Ratliff had got the signatures of the greatest number to his recommendation, by the usual means, promptness and importunity, I have tho't it due to myself and my friends to elicit some public expression to Confute the erroneous impression under which the Govr. acted as regards myself and for that purpose I have proposed running for the Legislature and thus far have met with very encouraging support. Our Election comes on the 7th. 8th. & 9th. of next month. It was tho't I was too late, but it is now expected one of the Candidates originally announced will decline, in which event my election[12] is almost certain. We are to have an animated Election. Dawson[13] & White[14] are the Cand'. for Govr. The first the Jackson the latter the anti-Jackson Cand'. Ripley,[15] Bradford James M.[16] and also brother James,[17] Jackson Cad'. for Congress, Woodrooff[18] &

Chinn[19] the anti-Jackson Cand'. one of the two first will I think be elected. It is said that three states have nominated Genl. Ripley for the Presidency at the next election. I would far prefer him to Van Buren[20] or either of the Jackson Candidates I have heard spoken of. The three states they say are Kentucky Tennessee and Mississippi—I have not seen any thing in the news papers about it. And it may be all a mere election trick to opperate at the approaching election for Congress in this District; if so and it be a mistake, it will cause James M. Bradford to be elected.

Mr. Stamps[21] has had a harassing time this year on account of the death of Dr. Farish[22] for whom he had endorsed extensively, but I hear he has a fine Crop at Old River[23] and at home[24] which I hope will extricate him. Hugh,[25] Joseph[26] & Luther[27] have been going to College at Jackson the last session which ended last week.[28] Jo. & L. spoke very creditably, Hugh excused himself and went home before the exhibition, They all boarded with Genl. Ripley who lived in Jackson, but is now moving back to his plantation on Redwood.[29]

I have great pleasure in saying we are all in excellent health here, at sister Anns[30] and at Mr. Stamps

Mother says Jims[31] wife and son[32] are in good health also Aunt Charity and all his friends.[33]

I have little time for scientific or litterary reading I have had to sell my Laplace[34]—I have a volume of Jacotot's "Enseignment Universel" [35] with which I am greatly taken. He says that he could instruct a regiment of Tartars in a month thoroughly in the artilery service. In one year he fits his Eléves for the Universities of Germany. &c. &c. He certainly is the Newton of Instruction.

Dr. Brother I write this with a very sore finger on my right hand and fear it will be hardly legible and to it you must also attribute the poorness of my letter. Let us hear often from you. I will write you whenever I have any thing worthy of communicating

Mother & Amanda and all the family send you their Love. David[36] wants you to come or to get leave to go and stay with you. Yr. Affect Brother (in-law) DAVID BRADFORD[37]

ALS (Jefferson Davis Papers, University of Alabama Library, Tuscaloosa). Addressed: "Lieut. Jefferson F. Davis Fort Gibson Arkansas."

[1] See 1:363, *n*. 1.

[2] "Mother" was Jane Cook Davis, Bradford's mother-in-law (sketch, 1:22, *n*. 4; 1:Appendix IV, Entry 14).

[3] Davis' letter of April 19 has not been found.

[4] Matilda Davis Vaughan, Brad-

ford's sister-in-law (sketch, 1:363, *n.* 34; 1:Appendix IV, Entry 22).

[5] Amanda Davis Bradford (sketch, 1:363, *n.* 29; 1:Appendix IV, Entry 21).

[6] The child born in 1834 was probably Sarah D. (1:Appendix IV, Entry 85). Davis' namesake, Jefferson Davis Bradford, was not born until 1838 (Strode, *American Patriot*, 87*n.*).

[7] See 1:363, *n.* 1 for "Abeyville" and "Variety."

[8] Edward H. Barton, an outstanding figure in the Louisiana public health movement, was appointed professor of *materia medica* at the Medical College of Louisiana in 1835 and was dean of the New Orleans school, 1836–37. He was a prolific writer—mostly on disease in southern Louisiana—founder of the New Orleans Temperance Society in 1842, chairman of the city board of health, president of the Louisiana State Medical Society, 1851–55, and chairman of the Sanitary Commission which reported on the 1853 yellow fever epidemic in New Orleans. He died in 1859 (Duffy [ed.], *History of Medicine*, II, *passim*).

[9] St. Francisville (1:363, *n.* 6).

[10] Arpent: a French unit of land measurement equal to about .85 acre (*Webster's Seventh Collegiate*).

[11] The governor of Louisiana, 1831–35 and 1839–43, was André B. Roman.

[12] See also Bradford's November 1833 letter to Davis concerning the election (1:363).

[13] John Bennett Dawson (1798–1845), born in Tennessee, attended Centre College in Danville, Kentucky, then moved to Louisiana where he became a planter and newspaper publisher. He was an unsuccessful Democratic candidate for governor in 1834, but was later elected to the Louisiana legislature, then to the United States House of Representatives in 1841, where he served until his death (*Who Was Who*; *Biographical Directory of the American Congress*, 789; E. Robinson, *Early Feliciana Politics*, 57–65).

[14] Edward D. White (1795–1847) was born in Tennessee and was a graduate of the University of Nashville. He was admitted to the bar and practiced in Donaldsonville, Louisiana, before being appointed judge of the city court of New Orleans in 1825. Elected to the United States House of Representatives in 1828, he was successful as the Whig candidate for governor in 1834 and served one term before returning to the House in 1839. From 1843 to 1847, he practiced law and had a sugar plantation in Lafourche Parish. His youngest child, Edward Douglass, became chief justice of the Supreme Court in 1910 (*DAB*).

[15] Eleazar Wheelock Ripley (1782–1839), grandson of the founder of Dartmouth College, was born in New Hampshire and graduated from Dartmouth in 1800. Admitted to the bar, he became active in politics and, at the outbreak of the War of 1812, was commissioned a lieutenant colonel. He was severely wounded at Lundy's Lane and promoted to brigadier general in 1814; after the war he was voted a gold medal by Congress for gallantry. He resigned from the army in 1820, practiced law at New Orleans, and then moved to West Feliciana Parish. An ardent Jacksonian, Ripley was elected to the Louisiana senate in 1832, and to the United States House in 1834, where he served until his death (*DAB*). Ripley's second wife was Davis' sister-in-law Aurelia, widow of Davis' brother Benjamin; Ripley is buried at "Locust Grove," home of Davis' sister Anna Davis Smith (H. A. Davis, *The Davis Family*, 40).

[16] James M. Bradford (sketch, 1:363, *n.* 30).

[17] James Bradford (sketch, 1:363, *n.* 14).

[18] Clark Woodrooff (1791–1851), Bradford's brother-in-law, was born in Connecticut, but moved to St. Francisville as a young man, and established an academy there in 1811. He served in the Battle of New Orleans and evidently knew Andrew Jackson well,

for the Woodrooffs spent their honeymoon at "The Hermitage." He was an incorporator of the St. Francisville library and Baptist and Presbyterian churches and studied law in Bradford's office. He was successful in his campaign for the Louisiana legislature in 1827, and in 1828 was appointed judge of the eighth judicial district and St. Francisville. Sometime in the 1830's, he moved to New Orleans and changed the spelling of his name to Woodruff. Appointed auditor of public accounts in 1846, he served one four-year term before retiring to his home, five miles above New Orleans (E. Robinson, *Early Feliciana Politics*, 53–56).

[19] Thomas W. Chinn (sketch, 1:363, *n.* 31).

[20] Martin Van Buren (1782–1862), Andrew Jackson's chosen successor, was the successful Democratic candidate for President in 1836. A New York lawyer long active in politics, Van Buren was elected to the United States Senate in 1821 and became leader of the "Albany regency," a group of influential politicians. Although he opposed Jackson's nomination in the 1824 election, he was appointed secretary of state in 1829 and gained the President's confidence. He resigned from the cabinet in 1831 during the Eaton affair, but was elected vice president in 1832. He was opposed in the 1836 Democratic convention by John Bell of Tennessee and by the followers of Virginian William C. Rives, but clearly won the nomination. His one-term administration was plagued with abolitionist agitation, economic instability, and disturbances in Canada and Mexico, and the Democrats were easily defeated in 1840. Van Buren retired to his estate, actively sought the 1844 Democratic presidential nomination, and became the Free Soil party candidate in 1848 (*DAB*; Van Deusen, *Jacksonian Era*, 111–49).

[21] William Stamps, Bradford's brother-in-law (sketch, 1:362, *n.* 12; 1:Appendix IV, Entry 63).

[22] Dr. Edward T. Farish had had a medical practice with a Dr. Stone in Woodville, Mississippi. Farish was appointed, with William Stamps, a director of the Planters' Bank (Woodville *Republican*, January 12, March 23, 1833). He had previously been a representative of Wilkinson County in the state legisature (1830) and a member of the 1832 state constitutional convention (D. Rowland, *Official and Statistical Register, 1908*, p. 81; D. Rowland, *Mississippi, Heart of the South*, I, 566). Farish died in October 1833, and Stamps was one of the estate administrators (Woodville, *Republican*, October 19, November 9, 1833). Farish had sizable holdings, consisting of slaves, horses, and several pieces of land—he owned about seventy acres in Wilkinson County, tracts on Old River, and two houses and some office buildings in Woodville (*ibid.*, January 4, March 1, 1834). Sale of his property was postponed, however, and an investigation of the estate was made in August 1834, because of reports of insolvency (*ibid.*, April 26, August 16, 1834).

[23] Old River, earlier called Ancienne Rivière, had been a channel of the Mississippi, but was, by 1834, a lake which lay in Adams and Wilkinson counties, Mississippi (Woodville *Republican*, August 16, 1834).

[24] See 1:362, *n.* 1 for Stamps's home; at this time he was evidently living near Woodville, but trying to sell his property.

[25] Hugh Robert Davis, Bradford's nephew (sketch, 1:362, *n.* 13; 1:Appendix IV, Entry 61).

[26] Joseph Davis Smith, Bradford's nephew (sketch, 1:363, *n.* 24; 1:Appendix IV, Entry 45).

[27] Luther L. Smith, Jr., Bradford's nephew (sketch, 1:363, *n.* 25; 1:Appendix IV, Entry 47).

[28] The College of Louisiana at Jackson in East Feliciana Parish was established in 1825 as part of an attempt by the legislature to promote public edu-

cation. The region was too sparsely populated to furnish many students, and the college did not prosper until 1845, when the Methodists of Mississippi moved Centenary College there from Brandon Springs. With support from patrons in both states, the school began to expand and improve and has survived—it is now located in Shreveport. In the 1830's the school year was divided into two sessions, the first of which opened in mid-July (Shaw, "Rampant Individualism in an Ante-Bellum Southern College," *Louisiana Historical Quarterly*, XXXI, 877–79, 882–83).

[29] Redwood, a creek in East Feliciana Parish ("Statistical and Historical Collections of Louisiana: Parish of East Feliciana," *De Bow's Review*, XI, 267).

[30] Anna Eliza Davis Smith (1:Appendix IV, Entry 18), Bradford's sister-in-law, was the oldest of Jane and Samuel Davis' five daughters. Born in Wilkes County, Georgia, in 1791, Anna Eliza married Luther L. Smith, a wealthy planter, in 1816. They lived at "Locust Grove" in West Feliciana Parish, Louisiana, and had seven children, six of whom lived to maturity. Anna Eliza died in 1870 and was buried in the cemetery at "Locust Grove" (H. A. Davis, *The Davis Family*, 82–83; Gravestone ["God's Acre," "Locust Grove" plantation cemetery, near St. Francisville, Louisiana]).

[31] "Jim" is James Pemberton (sketch, 1:5, *n.* 4).

[32] See 1:395, *n.* 22 for the possible identity of Pemberton's wife, and 1:528, *n.* 7 for his son.

[33] "Aunt Charity and all his friends" —probably slaves. For Charity, see 1:395, *n.* 20.

[34] Pierre Simon, marquis de Laplace (1749–1827), was a friend of d'Alembert and a graduate of the École Militaire. By 1816 he was a member of the Académie Française in charge of reorganizing the prestigious École Polytechnique. He was author of forty-one works in the fields of physics, pure and applied mathematics, and astronomy, his best-known treatises being *Exposition du Système du Monde* (2 vols., Paris, 1808) and *Traité de Mécanique Céleste* (5 vols., Paris, 1798–1823). See (Michaud and Desplaces [eds.]), *Biographie Universelle*.

[35] Jean Joseph Jacotot (1770–1840) was a 1794 graduate of the École Polytechnique and taught languages at Dijon and Louvain. Influenced by Fénélon's *Télémaque*, Jacotot came to the conclusion that schoolmasters were not indispensable, and in 1818 proposed his theory of "universal instruction" with its three principles of learn, repeat, and compare to one basic work. Jacotist schools were established all over Europe by 1840, and used Jacotot's two basic books—*L'Enseignement Universel: Langue Maternelle* (Louvain, 1822) and *Enseignement Universel: Langue Etrangère* (Louvain, 1823) —as texts ([Michaud and Desplaces (eds.)] *Biographie Universelle*).

[36] For "David," see 1:363, *n.* 17.

[37] David Bradford, Davis' brother-in-law (sketch, 1:5, *n.* 10; 1:Appendix IV, Entry 71).

ABSTRACT

Semiannual Company Muster Roll 1:420

Camp near F[alse] Wachita,[1] June 30, 1834

Lists First Lieutenant Jefferson Davis of Captain David Perkins'[2] Company E, U.S. Regiment of Dragoons commanded by Colonel

Henry Dodge,[3] as present. Remarks: "Joined April 25th. 1834 by virtue of Regtl. order No. 80.[4] Dated, April 25th. 1834. <Prest. Commanding Compy F.>"[5] Further remarks indicate that "The Company left Camp Jackson 'near Fort Gibson' for the Pawnee Towns on the 18th. of June 1834."[6] Report covers January through June 1834.

Printed form, filled in and signed (NA, RG 94 Records of the Adjutant General's Office, Muster Rolls of Regular Army Organizations, U. S. Dragoons, Company E), 2. Signed: "D. Perkins Capt Dragoons." Endorsed: "Proves Entd Recd. March 30th. 1835."

1 Camp Washita, located about a mile and a half east of the False Washita River, thirty miles above its junction with the Red River, is presently in Bryan County, Oklahoma (Frazer, *Forts of the West*, 125–26).

2 David Perkins (sketch, 1:410, *n.* 3).

3 Henry Dodge (sketch, 1:370, *n.* 2).

4 For Order No. 80, see 1:410, *n.* 6.

5 Interlined.

6 For Camp Jackson and Fort Gibson, see 1:397, *nn.* 1, 3. According to the official journal of the expedition (Wheelock, "Journal of Colonel Dodge's expedition from Fort Gibson to the Pawnee Pict village," *American State Papers*, Class V, Military Affairs, V, 378–82), the nine companies of approximately 500 men chosen to make the campaign—Company A, the tenth company in the regiment, had been previously sent to escort a wagon train to Santa Fe—began their movement from Camp Jackson near Fort Gibson on June 15. The regiment assembled five days later at Camp Rendezvous (near the present town of Oktaka, Muskogee County, Oklahoma) and prepared to march for the villages of the Kiowa and Wichita Indians. The expedition had been proposed in the annual report of the secretary of war, November 29, 1833 (*American State Papers*, Class V, Military Affairs, V, 170), its purposes being to establish friendly relations with the Indians, to invite them to a conference, and to secure the release of two white prisoners. General Henry Leavenworth originally planned to lead the troops, but on July 4, the command was assigned to Henry Dodge, colonel of Dragoons, General Leavenworth having been seriously injured in a fall. On July 7, having marched almost 200 miles from Fort Gibson, the men were reorganized into six companies of forty-two men each; provisions and ammunition were issued, and on July 9 the march began again. It was a week before any Indians were seen, and two weeks before a council was organized with the Toyash tribe at their village, in what is now the extreme southwest corner of Kiowa County, Oklahoma. Dodge obtained the release of one of the white prisoners (the other was reported dead) and convinced some representatives of the Kiowa, Comanche, and Toyash tribes to accompany him to Fort Gibson for a formal conference. The Comanches did not go as far as the fort, but the other representatives were amenable, and in September met not only with the government representatives, but also with those of the Creek, Osage, Cherokee, and Choctaw tribes (Shirk, "Peace on the Plains," *Chronicles of Oklahoma*, XXVIII, 6–39). The march was long and difficult, made worse by scarcity of provisions, summer heat, and disease. Davis, who later recalled the hardships of the trip—mostly in terms of lack of food and water (V. Davis, *Memoir*, I, 146, 153–57)—seems to have escaped the typhus and dysentery which killed about 150 men,

including General Leavenworth (Busby, "Buffalo Valley," *Chronicles of Oklahoma*, XL, 29). There are at least five extant journals of the expedition, including the official one edited in Shirk, "Peace on the Plains," *ibid.*, XXVIII, 8–39. See also Perrine (ed.), "Journal of Hugh Evans," *ibid.*, III, 175–212; [Hildreth], *Dragoon Campaigns*, 116–82; Pelzer (ed.), "A Journal of Marches," *Iowa Journal of History and Politics*, VII, 331–78; and Catlin, *North American Indians*, II, 45–86. For a map of the route taken, see Shirk, "Peace on the Plains," *Chronicles of Oklahoma*, XXVIII, facing page 10.

Richard B. Mason to Thomas S. Jesup 1:421

Fort Gibson[1] 30th. Aug. 1834

GENL.[2]

The three Companies of Dragoons assigned to my Command,[3] & to be stationed in this vicinity, will be located near the Arkansas River in the Creek Nation about twenty Miles above this post,[4] they will move to that point on Tuesday next,[5] and commence the erection of Log Cabins, with Clapboard roofs for Men & officers, & clapboard Sheds for the Horses, these buildings will cost nothing More than the extra pay of the men engaged in the work, the cost of two <ox>[6] waggons & teams, and a few tools suitable for throwing up such huts, the greater part of the tools I am enabled to get from the asst. Qr. Master[7] here, My Command is very sickly, there are now 62 out of 156 on the sick report,[8] & only one officer for duty in the three companies, but still I hope to be able to complete all my Cabins before the end of October.

The position I shall occupy has been selected on account of its health, the abundance of water, building Materials, forage, & the extensive range both in winter & Summer, & the cheaper rate at which it is believed forage can be had than at this post. Mechanics & Laborers cannot be obtained to construct suitable Quarters & Stables at this post, except at a great cost, & the building Materials are so distant, that with my command I could not erect them during the whole of next Winter, indeed the fire wood is so distant that the Command Could do nothing more than look to thier horses & keep themselves in fuel, Under these circumstances, and after Consulting with Col. Dodge[9] and Lt. Col. Kearny,[10] I have deemed it More to the intrest of the service to occupy the position above Mentioned, than to attempt to locate here, not withstanding hay for the three Companies has been provided at this place,

The selection of my position Col. Dodge has left to myself, and I am aware of the responsibility I am about to assume in abandoning the hay already provided, but with my sickly Command & under the existing Circumstances, I believe it due to the best intrests of the Service that I should do so.[11]

I have appointed 1st. Lt. Jefferson Davis to perform the duties of actg. asst. Qr. Master to my Command, & have to request that the necessary funds May be placed in his hands. I am Respectfully yr. obt. Sert.

R. B. MASON[12]
Maj. Dragoons

ALS (NA, RG 92 Records of the Office of the Quartermaster General, Consolidated Correspondence File, Fort Gibson, M–206, 1834). Addressed: "Majr. Genl. Jesup Qr. Mr. Genl U. S. Army Washington City." Endorsed: "Recd Oct. 13. 1834."

[1] See 1:397, *n.* 1.

[2] Thomas S. Jesup (sketch, 1:174, *n.* 4).

[3] The three companies assigned to Mason's command were E, F, and K (Dodge to Mason, September 2, 1834 [NA, RG 153, Court Martial Records, CC–219, 1837, Document (F)]).

[4] The camp subsequently established by Mason was named Camp Jones (see 1:425, 426, 428, 429).

[5] September 2, 1834.

[6] Interlined.

[7] The assistant quartermaster was Thomas Johnston (Post Return, September 1834 [NA, RG 94, Fort Gibson]).

[8] See 1:420, *n.* 6 for a mention of the typhus and dysentery contracted by many soldiers on an expedition during the summer.

[9] Henry Dodge (sketch, 1:370, *n.* 2).

[10] Stephen W. Kearny (sketch, 1:391, *n.* 2).

[11] A letter written November 28, 1889, by John Doran to Davis recalled their early association in the Dragoons and the removal from Fort Gibson to Camp Jones: "Once when there was much sickness prevailing among the 1st. Dragoons, at Fort Gibson, and when I was very sick in the Hospital, the Regt. was ordered, for the benefit of its health, to remove from the Cherokee Nation to the Creek Nation; but the surgeon refused to allow me to be removed with the Regt. However, you came to my aid, and had me taken to the Creek Nation, where I rapidly recovered . . ." (Museum of the Confederacy, Richmond).

[12] Richard B. Mason (sketch, 1:375, *n.* 8).

ABSTRACT

1:422 Pay Voucher

Fort Gibson,[1] August 31, 1834

Lieutenant Jefferson Davis, U.S. Dragoons, acknowledges that he has received $268.16-2/3 from Paymaster A. D. Steuart.[2] Amount includes pay, and allowance for one servant,[3] and forage for two horses, for June through August 1834. It also covers additional pay for commanding Company F for fourteen days. The servant is described as "James a Slave."

DS (NA, RG 217 Records of the United States General Accounting Office, Paymasters' Accounts, Steuart 19,197, Voucher 134), 3. Signed: "Jeffn. Davis L[ieutenant] Dr[a]g[oon]s."

[1] See 1:397, *n.* 1.

[2] Adam D. Steuart (sketch, 1:355, *n.* 1).

[3] James Pemberton (sketch, 1:5, *n.* 4).

[4] Davis commanded Company F June 17–30, 1834 (1:423).

ABSTRACT

Register of Payments to Officers

1:423

[Washington, D.C.,] August 31, 1834

Lists payment by Paymaster A. D. Steuart[1] to Second Lieutenant[2] Jefferson Davis, Dragoons, $268.16. Amount includes pay and allowance for Davis and one servant,[3] and allowance for two horses, for June through August 1834. Remarks: "Com[mandin]g F Co. 17 to 30 June."

D (NA, RG 99 Records of the Office of the Paymaster General, Register of Payments to Officers, IV, 27), 1.

[1] Adam D. Steuart (sketch, 1:355, *n.* 1).

[2] Davis was by this time a first lieutenant (see 1:415).

[3] The servant was James Pemberton (sketch, 1:5, *n.* 4).

ABSTRACT

Company Muster Roll

1:424

Camp near Fort Gibson,[1] August 31, 1834

Lists First Lieutenant Jefferson Davis of Captain D. Perkins'[2] Company E, U.S. Regiment of Dragoons commanded by Colonel Henry Dodge,[3] as present. Remarks: "Acting Adjt, Acting Asst. Qr. Master[4] & Acting Asst Commissary of Subs." Further remarks indicate that "The Company left Camp Jackson for the Pawnee Towns on the 18th. of June, and returned to Fort Gibson on the 16th. of August 1834." [5] Report covers April through August 1834.

Printed form, filled in and signed (NA, RG 94 Records of the Adjutant General's Office, Muster Rolls of Regular Army Organizations, U. S. Dragoons, Company E), 2. Signed: "D Perkins Capt. Dragoons H Dodge Col Comdg U S Dragoons." Endorsed: "Recd Octor. 13th R[oger] J[ones]"; in a different hand, "Proves Entered."

[1] The camp referred to here is probably Camp Jackson (1:397, *n.* 3). See 1:397, *n.* 1 for Fort Gibson.

[2] David Perkins (sketch, 1:410, *n.* 3).

[3] Henry Dodge (sketch, 1:370, *n.* 2).

[4] For evidence of Davis' having been appointed acting assistant quartermaster by Mason, see 1:421.

[5] See 1:420, *n.* 6 for a discussion of the expedition to the Pawnee towns.

1:425

To George Gibson

Camp Jones Creek Nation[1] Sept 22d 1834

SIR[2]

Enclosed I send you a receipt from the A[cting] C[ommissary] S[ubsistence][3] at Fort Gibson[4] for the amount of money claimed in your letter of June last[5] to be due from me

On the faith of the letters received at the original settlement of my accounts I destroyed the copies of my returns, and the only reason I can extract from the third <auditor[6]>[7] to account for the great augmentation in the demand made against me is the *different dates of settlement*, a circumstance I should have deemed of very little importance whilst the accounts to be settled remained the same.

Vy. Respectfully yr. mo. obt. Servt. JEFFN. DAVIS

1. L[ieutenant] Regt. Drgs.

ALS (NA, RG 192 Records of the Office of the Commissary General of Subsistence, Letters Received, D-1309, 1834). Addressed: "To Genl. Geo. Gibson Com[missar]y Genl. U. S. A. Washington D. C." Endorsed: "Recd 27 Octr." Enclosure missing.

[1] See 1:421 for a discussion of the establishment of Camp Jones.

[2] George Gibson (sketch, 1:179, *n.* 2).

[3] Lawrence F. Carter (sketch, 1:426, *n.* 3) was assistant commissary of subsistence at Fort Gibson (Post Return, September 1834 [NA, RG 94, Fort Gibson]).

[4] See 1:397, *n.* 1 for Fort Gibson.

[5] Gibson's letter to Davis of June 9, 1834, is printed as 1:417.

[6] The third auditor was Peter Hagner (sketch, 1:199, *n.* 5). Hagner's letter of June 10 (1:418) contains a detailed explanation of Davis' accounts.

[7] Interlined.

ABSTRACT

Provision Book

1:426

[Washington, D.C.,] September 30, 1834

Records that Lieutenant Jefferson Davis, Dragoons, acting assistant commissary of subsistence[1] at Camp Jones,[2] had pork, flour, rice, beans, candles, soap, salt, vinegar, coffee, and sugar charged to his account, but no beef, bacon, cornmeal, or whiskey. Remarks indicate that Davis received his initial provisions from Lieutenant Carter.[3]

D (NA, RG 192 Records of the Office of the Commissary General of Subsistence, Provision Book, Volume 1833–42, p. 83), 1.

1 Davis was appointed acting assistant commissary of subsistence in August (1:424).

2 Camp Jones (1:421).

3 Lawrence F. Carter, assistant commissary of subsistence at Fort Gibson, was born in Virginia and graduated from West Point in 1825. He served at Fort Towson, Indian Territory, 1826–27, and at Fort Gibson from 1827 until his death there in 1837, at age thirty-three. He was a first lieutenant, Seventh Infantry, in 1834 (Cullum, *Biographical Register*, I, 358).

ABSTRACT

Post Return

1:427

Fort Gibson,[1] September [30,] 1834

Lists First Lieutenant Jefferson Davis, Company E, U.S. Dragoons, present at the post,[2] and performing the duties of acting assistant quartermaster and acting assistant commissary of subsistence.[3]

Printed form, filled in and signed (NA, RG 94 Records of the Adjutant General's Office, Post Returns, Fort Gibson), 2. Signed: "D. S. Miles. Post Adjt. Jas. B. Many B[reve]t Col. U. S. A." Endorsed: "Entd Recd. 10 Nov. 1834."

1 See 1:397, *n.* 1.

2 Davis was actually at Camp Jones, twenty miles north of Fort Gibson, with a detachment of three companies commanded by Richard B. Mason (1:421).

3 Davis was appointed acting assistant quartermaster and acting assistant commissary of subsistence in August (1:421, 424).

1:428 To George Gibson

Camp Jones Creek Nation[1] October 5th 1834

SIR,[2]

Herewith I transmit to you a Return with the necessary accompanying papers for the month of September 1834 being the last of a Quarter but the first of my issuing as a Comry. Subsistence[3]

The wastage on Sugar has probably been increased by the exposure to which it was necessarily subjected after I received it. Vy. Respectfully yr. mo. obt. Servt. JEFFN. DAVIS

L[ieutenant] Drgs.

A[cting] A[ssistant] C[ommissary] S[ubsistence]

P. S. But one bid was made for the delivery of fresh Beef. Vy. Respectfly J. DAVIS

L. A. A. C. S.

ALS (NA, RG 192 Records of the Office of the Commissary General of Subsistence, Letters Received, D–1313, 1834). Addressed: "To Genl. Gibson Com[missar]y Genl. U. S. A Washington D. C." Endorsed: "Recd. 10 Nov." Enclosures missing. Acknowledged: Gibson to Davis, November 11, 1834 (NA, RG 192 Records of the Office of the Commissary General of Subsistence, Letters Sent, X, 528).

[1] Camp Jones (see 1:421).

[2] George Gibson (sketch, 1:179, *n.* 2).

[3] Indication of Davis' appointment as acting assistant commissary of subsistence first appears in the muster roll for August 1834 (1:424).

1:429 To Thomas S. Jesup

Camp Jones Creek Nation[1] October 5th 1834

SIR[2]

Herewith I transmit to you my return and accounts for the 3d Quarter of 1834. The uncertainty of the time we should remain here prevented me from originally proposing for a contract to furnish corn until the issues should commence from that for which the Asst. Qr. Master[3] at Fort Gibson[4] had issued proposols, the corn has been received in the Field or I should have been compelled to give one third (at least) higher for it. Fatigue parties have furnished Grass without expence to the government, and no notice has been taken

therefore of the Hay part of the Ration which it may be proper to add could not have been furnished by purchase Vy. Respecfly. yr. mo. obt. Servt.
JEFFN. DAVIS
1. L[ieutenant] A[cting] A[ssistant] Q. M.

ALS (NA, RG 92 Records of the Office of the Quartermaster General, Consolidated Correspondence File, Camp Jones, Creek Nation, D–344, 1834). Addressed: "Maj. Genl. T. S. Jesup Qr. Mr. Genl. U. S. A. Washington D. C." Endorsed: "Recd. Novr. 10. 1834." Enclosures missing.

[1] Camp Jones (see 1:421).

[2] Thomas S. Jesup (sketch, 1:174, *n.* 4).

[3] The assistant quartermaster at Fort Gibson until October 24 was First Lieutenant Thomas Johnston, Seventh Infantry (Post Returns, September, October, 1834 [NA, RG 94, Fort Gibson]).

[4] See 1:397, *n.* 1 for Fort Gibson.

From Peter Hagner 1:430

SIR— Oct. 29th 1834

The Commissary General of Subsistence[1] has transmitted to this office a receipt of Lt. L. F. Carter[2] for $55.70—paid over to him by you—and the same has been passed to your credit, opposed to a like amount standing against you, which closes your <Subsistence>[3] account, on the Books of this office.[4] Respectfully, Yr. ob. Ser.
PETER HAGNER.[5]
Aud

LbC (NA, RG 217 Records of the United States General Accounting Office, Third Auditor's Office, Miscellaneous Letters Sent, LXV, 76). Addressed: "Lt. J. F. Davis of U. S. Dragoons, Fort Gibson, Ark. Ty."

[1] The commissary general of subsistence was George Gibson (sketch, 1:179, *n.* 2).

[2] Lawrence F. Carter was the assistant commissary of subsistence at Fort Gibson (sketch, 1:426, *n.* 3).

[3] Interlined.

[4] See 1:417, 418, 425 for further reference to the $55.70 that Davis owed the Subsistence Department.

[5] Peter Hagner (sketch, 1:199, *n.* 5).

ABSTRACT

Provision Book 1:431

[Washington, D.C.,] October 31, 1834

Records that Lieutenant Jefferson Davis, Dragoons, acting assistant commissary of subsistence[1] at Camp Jones,[2] had pork, rice, beans, candles, soap, coffee, and sugar, plus much-depleted stores of flour, salt, and vinegar charged to his account, but no beef, bacon, cornmeal, or whiskey.

D (NA, RG 192 Records of the Office of the Commissary General of Subsistence, Provision Book, Volume 1833–42, p. 83), 1.

[1] Davis had been acting assistant commissary since August 31 (1:424).
[2] For Camp Jones, see 1:421.

ABSTRACT

1:432

Company Muster Roll

Camp near Fort Gibson,[1] October 31, 1834

Lists First Lieutenant Jefferson Davis of Captain D. Perkins'[2] Company E, U.S. Regiment of Dragoons commanded by Colonel Henry Dodge,[3] as present. Report covers September and October 1834.

Printed form, filled in and signed (NA, RG 94 Records of the Adjutant General's Office, Muster Rolls of Regular Army Organizations, U.S. Dragoons, Company E), 2. Signed: "D Perkins Capt. Dragoons R. B. Mason Maj Dragoons." Endorsed: "Proves Entered Recd. 12th. Decr. 1834."

[1] Camp Jones; see 1:421 for a discussion of the camp and its establishment. For Fort Gibson, see 1:397, *n.* 1.
[2] David Perkins (sketch, 1:410, *n.* 3).
[3] Henry Dodge (sketch, 1:370, *n.* 2).

1:433

To Thomas S. Jesup

Camp Near Ft. Gibson[1] Nov. 2d 1834

SIR[2]

Herewith I have the honor to transmit to you a Muster Roll and summary Statement for the mont of Oct. 1834.[3] Vy. Respectfly yr. mo. obt servt.

JEFFN. DAVIS
1. Lt. Drgs. Act. Q. M.

ALS (NA, RG 92 Records of the Office of the Quartermaster General, Letters Received, D–6, 1835). Addressed: "To Genl T. S. Jesup Q. M. Genl. U. S. A. Washington D. C." Endorsed: "for acknowledgt"; in a different hand, "Recd. Decr. 9th. 1834." Enclosures missing. Acknowledged: Office of the Quartermaster General to Davis, December 10, 1834 (NA, RG 92 Records of the Office of the Quartermaster General, Letters Sent, XXI, 157).

[1] Camp Jones near Fort Gibson. See 1:421. See 1:397, *n.* 1 for Fort Gibson.
[2] Thomas S. Jesup (sketch, 1:174, *n.* 4).
[3] Probably a muster roll of extra duty men and not a bimonthly company muster roll such as 1:432.

To George Gibson 1:434

Camp Near Ft. Gibson[1] Nov. 3d 1834

SIR[2]

Herewith I have the honor to transmit to you a Return of Subsistence with the accompanying Abstracts for the month of October 1834 Vy. Respectfully yr. mo. obt. Servt. JEFFN. DAVIS
L[ieutenant] Drgs. A[cting] A[ssistant]
C[ommissary] S[ubsistence] Squadron Dragoons

ALS (NA, RG 192 Records of the Office of the Commissary General of Subsistence, Letters Received, D–1321, 1834). Addressed: "To Maj. Genl Geo. Gibson Com[missar]y Genl. U. S. A. Washington D. C." Endorsed: "Recd. 9 Dec." Enclosures missing.

[1] Camp Jones (1:421). For Fort Gibson, see 1:397, *n.* 1.
[2] George Gibson (sketch, 1:179, *n.* 2).

From George Gibson 1:435

SIR 10 November 1834

Yours, enclosing a fresh beef Contract and Bond is this day received.[1]

These instruments are Satisfactorily executed G G[2]

LbC (NA, RG 192 Records of the Office of the Commissary General of Subsistence, Letters Sent, X, 527). Addressed: "Lt Jeff Davis a[cting] a[ssistant] c[ommissary] s[ubsistence] Camp Jones, near Fort Gibson."

[1] The mentioned beef contract and bond along with their letter of transmittal have not been found.
[2] George Gibson (sketch, 1:179, *n.* 2).

ABSTRACT

Provision Book 1:436

[Washington, D.C.,] November 11, 1834

Records that Lieutenant Jefferson Davis, Dragoons, turned over the commissary stores charged to his account to Lieutenant William Eustis,[1] the succeeding acting assistant commissary of subsistence[2] at Camp Jones.[3]

D (NA, RG 192 Records of the Office of the Commissary General of Subsistence, Provision Book, Volume 1833–42, p. 83), 1.

1 Second Lieutenant William Eustis, born in Rhode Island, was graduated from the Military Academy in 1830 and transferred from infantry to Dragoons in August 1833. He served in various frontier garrisons, at the French cavalry school, on several army expeditions, and in the Mexican War. After resigning from the army in 1849, he became a farmer in Mississippi and was later civil engineer and city surveyor at Natchez (1863–75). He died in 1889 (Cullum, *Biographical Register*, I, 467; Heitman, *Historical Register*, I, 409).

2 For evidence of Davis' having been made the acting assistant commissary of subsistence at Camp Jones, see 1:424.

3 See 1:421 for Camp Jones.

1:437

To Thomas S. Jesup

Camp Near Fort Gibson[1] Nov. 16th 1834

SIR[2]

Herewith I have the honor to transmit to you a "Return" &C. closing my accts. as actg. Asst. Qr. Master[3] for the Squadron of Dragoons commanded by Maj. R. B. Mason[4]

By the new regulations of the Quarter Master's Department[5] I perceive that additional compensation is allowed to *actg.* Asst. Qr. Master's, should the account be made and presented to the Qr. Masters Dept. for payment? You will oblige me by answering my question. Vy. Respectfly. yr. mo. obt. Servt. JEFFN. DAVIS

1. Lieut. Dragoons

ALS (NA, RG 92 Records of the Office of the Quartermaster General, Letters Received, D–14, 1835). Addressed: "To Maj. Genl. T. S. Jesup Qr. Mr. Genl. U. S. A. Washington D. C." Endorsed: "Recd. Decr. 23d. 1834." Enclosures missing.

1 Camp Jackson (1:397, *n.* 3). For Fort Gibson, see 1:397, *n.* 1.

2 Thomas S. Jesup (sketch, 1:174, *n.* 4).

3 Davis was made the acting assistant quartermaster at Camp Jones sometime prior to August 30, 1834 (1:421).

4 Richard B. Mason (sketch, 1:375, *n.* 8).

5 Paragraph 108 of the revised army regulations, printed August 28, 1834, reads as follows: "Officers temporarily in the quartermaster's department, will be allowed extra compensation according to the duties performed, not exceeding the extra pay provided by law for assistant quartermasters" (Trever to McIntosh, May 18, 1970 [Jefferson Davis Association, Rice University, Houston]).

To George Gibson 1:438

Camp near Fort Gibson A[rkansas Territory][1]
Nov. 16th 1834

SIR[2]

Herewith I have the honor to transmit to you a "Return" &C of Subsistence received and issued in the 4th Qr. up to the 10th of Nov. 1834 closing my accts. as acting asst. Com. Subsistence[3] Vy. Respectfly. yr. mo. obt. Servt.

JEFFN. DAVIS
1. Lieut. Dragoons

ALS (NA, RG 192 Records of the Office of the Commissary General of Subsistence, Letters Received, D-1325, 1834). Addressed: "To Maj. Genl Geo. Gibson Com[missar]y Genl. U. S. A. Washington D. C." Endorsed: "Recd. 23 Decr." Enclosure missing.

[1] Camp Jackson (1:397, *n.* 3); Fort Gibson (1:397, *n.* 1).

[2] George Gibson (sketch, 1:179, *n.* 2).

[3] Davis was replaced by Second Lieutenant William Eustis as acting assistant commissary of subsistence at Camp Jones (1:436).

From Eliza Van Benthuysen Davis 1:439

Hurricane[1] Nov 17th 1834

I have Not received an answer My Dear Brother to a scrawl I sent you some time since[2]—but I *Shall* not be detered in consequence—of Writing again I have nothing to communicate, but that you are already in possession of—Namely the strong desire we have to see you. It is made some of us gay other's sad—as good tidings effect people very differently—here is Mary[3]—now by My Chair the very picture of happiness—although she says she has such a head ache that she cannot write to night—poor child her thoughts are on you so much that she cannot withdraw them long enough to date a letter—she says all the love she has is for you—but of this I am inclined to be jealous—again she says you have not treated her with any confidince as her advice was to be asked before you entered into *engagements* of any kind.[4] You see I am her deputy—but take the opportunity of saying a word now & then for Myself.

To-Morrow Mr Davis[5] goes to Vicksburg & Mary Will accompany him as far as Mr McCaleb's.[6] Florida[7] sent for her this evening—as Miss Apthorpe[8] has arrived from New Haven to spend the Winter with her—she wishes to shew her some civility. It is Miss Emily I believe. I very seldom leave home & have not been at Diamond Place[9] for three Months although the last visit I made was there.

Our improvements progress very slowly—& I fear Brother Jeff will think Me indolent so far as I could have contributed—but indolent I am—& likely to continue. I sometimes feel as if I had No motive to exertion—that this life is but a dream that will soon pass away. You will say let it be a dream of pleasure—even so would I have it—but the pleasure Must be confered, by My friends if any I have. I am willing to see all happy. Yes! as happy as it is in the Nature of persons to be—but I cannot make them so—<e'en>[10] if my indolence was cured.

Our House is unfinished—perhaps will get into it before March—therefore if you, come which we all desire—you will feel perfectly at home—in this little house where you have been with us all—it is much the worse of Time of this you will Not think—if the inhabitants are not changed.

I have put your room in oder with My own hands—it does n[ot] look as neatly as I could desire although I have a scrap of New Carpetting in it—the doors are fastened & I wish when they are opened it would be for yourself—& one equally as dear to you. We expect you before Christmas   Mr Davis has written to Mother[11] to come & remain the winter with—we fear the Summers & will have to change.[12] If Mr Stamps[13] goes to Old River[14] she will be very lonely and I fear it will require much persuasion to get her to come with us.[15] When our house is finished she can be very comfortable.

I must write to Mother & Ma[16]—& as I could not wait another Mail to write you fearing you would not receive it—(I venture this)—*as the loss* would *be great* if you did not. My Dearie[5] & Mary are both to Much occupied this Morning—for Morning it is & they will take leave—& I knew you would forgive me the Manner when you knew My intentions were good. My pen is bad but no time to Mend it.

We have quite a Colony here—seven Carpenters two brick layers & one *Physician* so he calls himself—& *then and then* Mr Mills his wife two grown daughters & one *lovely son*   I know your aversion to good company & have established all the *good* people at the Hospital—even the Physician—but it is his place. The dogs being a pleasure to you are detained. I will not say with My consent. Mr Davis has some twenty or thirty in & out of the house—the poor things will have to live untill you pass sentence upon them—when I expect at least half will be committed to the Waves.

Arab[17] is well, but one of My Match Pacolds[18] are dead—it was a great loss to me as I intended to set out on My travels as soon as they could be made to yield to harness.

Robert Adams is at home the school having been dismissed—he is so fond of dogs that the house is not much more than a kennel. I like the child—but his return to school I will not regret—he asked us yesterday how old was that Jeff we spoke of so often & was quite surprised to hear that you were a Man

Love to you with a desire that you will soon be with us—yours affectionately ELIZA[19]

Bring Basto—as well as your pretty wild horse *I* remind you of this—fearing a more precious charge[4] Might occupy all your thoughts. ED

ALS (Jefferson Davis Papers, Frances Carrick Thomas Library, Transylvania University, Lexington, Kentucky). Addressed: "Lt J F Davis Fort Gibson Arkansas."

1 "Hurricane" was Joseph E. Davis' plantation south of Vicksburg. See 1:328, *n.* 2.

2 See 1:395 for the last extant letter from Eliza to Davis.

3 Mary Lucinda Davis Mitchell, Eliza's stepdaughter (sketch, 1:362, *n.* 11; 1:Appendix IV, Entry 26).

4 The reference is no doubt to Sarah Knox Taylor, Davis' intended, about whom he had evidently written home.

5 Joseph E. Davis, Eliza's husband (sketch, 1:19, *n.* 1; 1:Appendix IV, Entry 15).

6 David McCaleb (1:Appendix IV, Entry 29), Eliza's stepson-in-law, was born October 21, 1803, in Pendleton District, Saluda River, South Carolina, the son of David and Matilda Prince Farrar McCaleb, later of Claiborne County, Mississippi. After attending Jefferson College and Bowdoin College, McCaleb became a cotton planter. On October 21, 1830, he married Florida Davis (Woodville [Mississippi] *Republican*, November 3, 1830). They moved to "Diamond Place," a plantation given Florida by her father (Strode, *American Patriot*, 117). The Port Gibson (Mississippi) *Correspondent* (October 10, 1835) noted that McCaleb was president of the Board of the Claiborne County Police. One account states that McCaleb died September 7, 1849 (unidentified newspaper clipping, *ca.* 1906, Kerrigan, Genealogical Data [Jefferson Davis Association, Rice University, Houston]); that he died earlier is affirmed by a marriage bond between his widow and Edmund C. Laughlin, dated July 17, 1848 (O'Neill, "Warren County Marriages," *Journal of Mississippi History*, XXIX, 214).

7 Florida A. Davis McCaleb Laughlin, Eliza's stepdaughter (sketch, 1:19, *n.* 9; 1:Appendix IV, Entry 28).

8 Emily Sophia Apthorp, daughter of Charles W. and Elizabeth D. Apthorp of New Haven, Connecticut, was born sometime after 1805, the fifth of six daughters. Her father evidently died before 1840, and her mother had a girls' boarding school in New Haven by 1844. Emily married Joseph Sampson of New York in 1846; she died in

1870 (Carhart, *Genealogy of the Morris Family*, ed. Nelson, 154–55; Davenport to Lasswell, April 16, 1970 [Jefferson Davis Association, Rice University, Houston]).

[9] "Diamond Place," a plantation of about 1,200 acres, thirteen miles north of "Hurricane," which Joseph Davis had given to his daughter Florida for a wedding present (Strode, *American Patriot*, 117, 125; Strode, *Private Letters*, 8; V. Davis, *Memoir*, I, 188; J. E. Davis' will, Exhibit D, Davis *v.* Bowmar, 29 [Mississippi Department of Archives and History, Jackson]).

[10] Interlined.

[11] "Mother" was Jane Cook Davis, who lived at "Rosemont," near Woodville (sketch, 1:22, *n.* 4; 1:Appendix IV, Entry 14).

[12] See 1:124, *n.* 3.

[13] William Stamps, Eliza's brother-in-law (sketch, 1:362, *n.* 12; 1:Appendix IV, Entry 63).

[14] See 1:419, *n.* 23 for Old River.

[15] Stamps's land, some 1,500 acres three miles east of Woodville, was offered for sale November 24 (Woodville [Mississippi] *Republican*, December 20, 1834).

[16] "Ma" may be Eliza's mother, or Lucinda Farrar Davis Davis Stamps, Eliza's sister-in-law (sketch, 1:19, *n.* 3; 1:Appendix IV, Entry 20; see also 1:529, *n.* 4).

[17] Arab, foal of the thoroughbred Sir Archie, won several races during the 1823–24 seasons. Since it was not unusual to call a horse by its sire's name, the Arab mentioned here may well have been one of the famous racer's offspring (Blanchard and Wellman, *Life and Times of Sir Archie*, 201–203).

[18] Since several horses seem to have borne the name Pacolet, including a famous gray racer owned by Andrew Jackson, it can only be surmised that Eliza here has reference to a pair of thoroughbreds, matched in size and color, descended from one of the distinguished horses named Pacolet (*American Turf Register*, I, 178, II, 299).

[19] Eliza Van Benthuysen Davis, Davis' sister-in-law (sketch, 1:361, *n.* 8; 1:Appendix IV, Entry 25).

1:440 From the Office of the Quartermaster General[1]

SIR 20th. Nov. 1834

Your Clothing Return for Company F. of Dragoons in the 2d. qr. of the present year,[2] closed by the receipt of Capt. Trenor[3] has been received and examined at this Office and sent to the Treasury[4] for settlement.

LbC (NA, RG 92 Records of the Office of the Quartermaster General, Letters Sent Relating to Clothing, V, 288). Addressed: "Lt. Jeffn. Davis of Dragoons Fort Gibson Arks."

[1] Thomas S. Jesup was the quartermaster general (sketch, 1:174, *n.* 4).

[2] The return has not been found.

[3] Eustace Trenor, an 1822 graduate of the Military Academy, was born in Virginia. After graduation he served in Florida and in the Creek Nation and was appointed captain in the Dragoons in 1833. He accompanied several Indian expeditions and was garrisoned on the frontier for most of his career. He was a major, First Dragoons, on sick leave

in New York City when he died at age forty-four in 1847 (Cullum, *Biographical Register*, I, 287–88).

[4] The return and receipt were transmitted to the second auditor November 20 (NA, RG 92, Letters Sent Relating to Clothing, V, 288).

ABSTRACT

Post Return 1:441

Fort Gibson,[1] November [30,] 1834

Lists First Lieutenant Jefferson Davis, Company E, U.S. Dragoons, present at the post. Remarks: "For duty."

DS (NA, RG 94 Records of the Adjutant General's Office, Post Returns, Fort Gibson), 3. Signed: "W. Seawell 1st Lieut 7th Infy. Aid de Camp M. Arbuckle Brigdr. Genl. U. S. Army & Commdg. Officer."

[1] See 1:397, *n.* 1.

From George Gibson 1:442

SIR 10 Decr 1834

Your Return for October[1] has been examined in this office 830½ pounds of sugar was reported on hand to 30th September, the quantity brought on the October Return is only 803½. Make the Correction in your next return after you receive this G G[2]

LbC (NA, RG 192 Records of the Office of the Commissary General of Subsistence, Letters Sent, X, 563). Addressed: "Lt Jeff Davis a[cting] a[ssistant] c[ommissary] S[ubsistence] Camp Jones."

[1] Davis' October return was transmitted in 1:434.

[2] George Gibson (sketch, 1:179, *n.* 2).

To Sarah Knox Taylor 1:443

Fort Gibson[1] Dec 16th 1834

Tis strange how superstitious intense feeling renders us. but stranger still what aids chance sometimes brings to support our superstition, dreams my dear Sarah[2] we will agree are our weakest thoughts, and yet by *dreams* have I been latly almost crazed, for they were of you and the *sleeping* immagination painted you not such as I left you, not such as I could like and see you, for you seemed a sacrifice to your parents desire the bride of a wretch that your pride and sense equally compelled you to despise, and a <–illegible–> creature here, telling the on dits[3] of the day at St Louis said you were "about to be married to a Doctor Mc[Laraine?]"[4] a poor devil who served with the Battalion of Rangers[5] possibly you may have seen him—but last night the vision was changed you were at the house of an Uncle in Kentucky,[6] Capt McCree[7] was walking with you when I met you he left you and you told me of your Father[8] and of yourself almost the same that I have read in your letter[9] to night. Kind, dear letter, I have kissed it often and it has driven many mad notions from my brain. Sarah whatever I may be hereafter I will ascribe to you. Neglected by you I should be worse than nothing and if the few good qualities I possess shall under your smiles yield a fruit it will be your's as the grain is the husbandman's.

It has been a source productive of regret with me that our union must seperate you from your earliest and best friends, a test to which the firmness of very few are equal, though giddy with passion or bouant by the hope of reconciliation there be many who brave it, from you I am prepared to expect all that intellect and dignified pride brings, the question as it has occured to you is truly startling Your own answer is the most grattifying to me, is that which I should expected from you, for as you are the first with whom I ever ought to have one fortune so you would be the last from whom I would expect desertion. When I wrote to you I supposed you did not intend soon to return to Kentucky. I approve entirely of your preference to a meeting elsewhere than at Prarie-du-Chien[10] and your desire to avoid any embarrassment might widen the breach made already cannot be greater than my own,[11] did I know when you would be at St Louis I could meet you there. At all events we meet in Kentucky.[12] Shall we not soon meet Sarah to part no more? oh! how I long to lay my head upon that breast which beats in unison with my own, to turn from the sickening sights of worldly duplicity and look in those eyes so eloquent of purity and love. Do you remember the "hearts ease"[13] you gave me, it is bright as ever—how very gravely you ask leave to ask me a question. My dear girl I have no secrets from you, have a right to ask me any question without an apology. Miss Bullitt did not give me a guard for a watch but if she had do you supose I would have given it to *Capt* Mccree. But Ill tell you what she did give me, [torn] most beautifell and lengthy lecture on my and your charms, the which combined, once upon an evening at a "fair" in Louisville, as she was one of the few subjects of conversation we had apart from ourselves on that evening you can & I have left you to guess what beside a sensibility to your charms constituted my offence. the reporters were absent and the speech I made is lost.

<Pray what manner of messages could la belle Elvin have sent you concerning me? I supose no attempt to destroy harmony. I laughed at her demonstrations against the attachment existing between myself a subaltern of Dragoons but that between you and I is not fair, gains it is robbing to make another poor, but No! She is too discerning to attempt a thing so difficult and in which sucess would be valueless. "Miss Elizabeth one very handsome; lady" Ah; Knox what did you put that semicolon between handsome and lady for? I hope you find in the society of the Prarie enough to amuse if not to please The griefs over which we weep are not those to be dreaded. It is the little pains the constant falling of thy drops of care which wear away the heart, I join you in rejoicing that Mrs McCree[14] is added to your society. I admire her more than any one else you could have had Since I wrote to you we have abandoned the position in the Creek Nation[15] and are constructing quarters at Ft Gibson

My lines like the beggars days are dwindling to the shortest span. Write to me immediately My dear Sarah My betrothed No formality is proper between us. Adieu Ma chere tres chere amie adieu au Recrire[16]

JEFFN.>[17]

ALS (From the collection of Elsie O. and Philip D. Sang, Chicago, 1969). Addressed: "To. Miss Sarah K. Taylor Prairie du Chien M[ichigan] T[erritory]." Printed: Strode, *Private Letters*, 10–12, variant version; Strode, *American Patriot*, 87–89, variant version; Hamilton, *Zachary Taylor*, 104–105, variant version; W. L. Fleming, "Davis' First Marriage," Mississippi Historical *Publications*, XII, 28–29, variant version.

1 See 1:397, *n.* 1.

2 Sarah Knox Taylor, second daughter of Zachary Taylor, was born at Vincennes, Indiana, in 1814 or 1815 (1:Appendix IV, *n.* 129), and was named for her paternal grandmother and for the fort where she was born. Educated by Thomas Elliott in Kentucky and at Pickett School in Cincinnati, she joined her parents in 1831 in Louisville, where her father was on furlough. The family moved to Fort Crawford, Prairie du Chien, in August 1832, and it was there she first met Davis. Taylor opposed the match from the start because of the hardships of army life; his objections were partly personal, too, there having been some friction between the two on a military

matter (statement of Dandridge to "D. B. C.," New York *Times*, October 20, 1906; V. Davis, *Memoir*, I, 94–96). Davis was transferred to St. Louis in 1833 and probably did not see Sarah Knox again until they married June 17, 1835, at her aunt's home near Louisville. After the ceremony Davis took his bride to "Hurricane," his brother's home in Mississippi, then to his sister's home in West Feliciana Parish, Louisiana. At "Locust Grove," both fell ill with malaria; Sarah Knox died on September 15, 1835 (W. L. Fleming, "Davis' First Marriage," Mississippi Historical *Publications*, XII, 23–34; Hamilton, *Zachary Taylor*, 57, 100–108; V. Davis, *Memoir*, I, 163).

[3] The French phrase "on dit" is undoubtedly intended.

[4] Adam Neill McLaren, a Scotsman, was appointed assistant surgeon March 2, 1833, and was stationed at Fort Crawford, 1833–36 (Gordon, *Compilation of Registers of the Army*, 487, 517, 547, 577). Promoted to major and surgeon in 1839, he was brevetted lieutenant colonel in 1865 and died in 1874 (Heitman, *Historical Register*, I, 674).

[5] The Battalion of Mounted Rangers provided for by Congress in June 1832 is presumably what Davis refers to here. Established for the defense of the upper Mississippi Valley, the battalion was relieved by the Regiment of Dragoons in 1833 (*Statutes at Large of the United States*, IV [1846], 533, 652).

[6] Sarah's uncle, Hancock Taylor, lived near Louisville. See 1:484, *n.* 1.

[7] Samuel MacRee (sketch, 1:325, *n.* 2).

[8] Zachary Taylor (sketch, 1:332, *n.* 3).

[9] Sarah Knox Taylor's letter to Davis has not been found. See *n.* 16 below.

[10] Prairie du Chien, Michigan Territory, site of Fort Crawford (see 1:231, *n.* 12).

[11] See 1:332, *n.* 3 for a further mention of the breach between Zachary Taylor and Davis.

[12] Davis and Sarah Knox were married near Louisville June 17, 1835 (1:485).

[13] Heartsease is the name given to any of various garden hybrids "with solitary white, yellow, or purple often variegated flowers resembling but smaller than typical pansies" (*Webster's Seventh Collegiate*).

[14] Mrs. Samuel MacRee was a good friend of Davis and his fiancée at Fort Crawford; it was at her home that the two met after Davis was forbidden to call on Sarah Knox (W. L. Fleming, "Davis' First Marriage," Mississippi Historical *Publications*, XII, 26–67; V. Davis, *Memoir*, I, 94–95).

[15] Davis left Camp Jones approximately November 10–11 (1:436).

[16] All the correspondence between Davis and Sarah Knox Taylor, save this letter, has apparently been lost. As Davis explained to Miss Lee H. Willis, April 13, 1889: "The package containing all our correspondence was in a writing desk, among the books and papers I left in Missi. when called to Alabama [in 1861], and it would be to me a great solace to recover the letters Miss Taylor wrote to me, and which were <with> the one you graciously offer to restore" (Jefferson Davis Association, Rice University, Houston). For the two known letters written by Sarah Knox Taylor Davis, see 1:483 and 1:Appendix I, 475.

[17] In the margin.

ABSTRACT

Post Return 1:444

Fort Gibson,[1] December [31,] 1834

Lists First Lieutenant Jefferson Davis, Company E, Dragoons, present at the post. Remarks: "In arrest."[2]

DS (NA, RG 94 Records of the Adjutant General's Office, Post Returns, Fort Gibson), 3. Signed: "W. Seawell 1st Lieut. 7th Infy. Aid de Camp. M. Arbuckle Brigdr. Genl. U. S. Army Commdg." Endorsed: "Recd. 18 Feby. 1835."

[1] Fort Gibson (1:397, *n.* 1).

[2] Davis was held in arrest on charges brought against him by R. B. Mason (see 1:454).

ABSTRACT

Semiannual Company Muster Roll 1:445

Camp near Fort Gibson,[1] December 31, 1834

Lists First Lieutenant Jefferson Davis of Captain D. Perkins'[2] Company E, U.S. Regiment of Dragoons commanded by Colonel Henry Dodge,[3] as "Present in arrest."[4] Report covers July through December 1834.

Printed form, filled in and signed (NA, RG 94 Records of the Adjutant General's Office, Muster Rolls of Regular Army Organizations, U. S. Dragoons, Company E), 4. Signed: "D Perkins Capt. Dragoons M. Arbuckle Brigdr. Genl. U. S. Army." Endorsed: "Proves Entd Recd. Febry. 6th. 1835 different changes of Stations to be noted."

[1] Camp Jackson (1:397, *n.* 3); Fort Gibson (1:397, *n.* 1).

[2] David Perkins (sketch, 1:410, *n.* 3).

[3] Henry Dodge (sketch, 1:370, *n.* 2).

[4] Davis was held in arrest on charges brought against him by R. B. Mason (see 1:454).

ABSTRACT

Register of Payments to Officers 1:446

[Washington, D.C.,] January 1, 1835

Lists payment by Paymaster A. D. Steuart[1] to Second Lieutenant[2] Jefferson Davis, Dragoons, $400.45. Amount includes pay and allowance for Davis and one servant,[3] and forage for two horses, from

September through December 1834. Remarks: "Com[mandin]g E. Co. 11 Nov to 24 Dec. $20 A[cting] C[ommissary] S[ubsistence] 1 Sept <to 10 Nov.>[4]."[5]

D (NA, RG 99 Records of the Office of the Paymaster General, Register of Payments to Officers, IV, 27), 1.

[1] Adam D. Steuart, paymaster at St. Louis (sketch, 1:355, *n.* 1).

[2] Davis was a first lieutenant (1:415).

[3] James Pemberton was undoubtedly the servant (sketch, 1:5, *n.* 4).

[4] Interlined.

[5] For confirmation of Davis' term of office as acting assistant commissary of subsistence, see 1:428, 438.

1:447

Order No. 1

Head Quarters West. Dept.
Asst. Adjutant General's office
Memphis Tennessee January 15th. 1835

I. A general Court Martial to consist of thirteen members, will convene at Fort Gibson, A[rkansas Territory][1] on the 2nd. February 1835, or as soon thereafter as practicable, for the trial of 2nd. Lieut. L. B. Northrop,[2] of the US. Dragoons, and such other persons as may be properly brought before it.

Bt Brigr. General M. Arbuckle[3] President

Members

Bt. Major Geo. Birch[4] 7th. Inf.
Captain F Lee,[5] 7th. Inf.
1st. Lieut J Davis, Dragoons
2nd. Lieut. S Kinny,[6] 7th. Inf.
2nd. Lieut R S Dix[7] 7th. Inf.
Bt 2nd. Lt. F Britton,[8] 7th. Inf.
Captain J. Bean,[9] Dragoons
1st. Lieut. J F Izard,[10] Dragoons
2nd. Lieut T H Holmes,[11] 7th. Inf.
2nd. Lieut R H Ross[12] 7th Inf.
2nd. Lieut R. C Gatlin[13] 7th. Inf.
Bt. 2nd. Lt A Montgomery[14] 7th. Inf.

1st. Lt and Adjt. D S Miles,[15] 7th. Inf. Special Judge Advocate.

II. General Arbuckle is hereby authorized to fill any vacancy, except that of President which may occur in the foregoing detail, either at the organization of the court or during its session, by a detail from the officers of his command present for duty at Fort Gibson. By order of Major General Gaines[16] GEO. A. MCCALL[17]
A[ide-] D[e-] C[amp]—actg. asst. adj genl

LbCS (NA, RG 94 Records of the Adjutant General's Office, Western Department Orders, CCLXXIV, 439); D, copy (NA, RG 153 Records of the Office of the Judge Advocate General [Army], Court Martial Records, CC–47, 1835); D, copy (NA, RG 153 Records of the Office of the Judge Advocate General [Army], Court Martial Records, CC–54, 1835). Endorsed: "Recd. Feby. 4th. 1835."

1 See 1:397, *n.* 1.

2 Lucius B. Northrop (sketch, 1:402, *n.* 4).

3 Matthew Arbuckle (1776–1851), a Virginian, entered the army as an ensign in 1799 and advanced through the ranks to major by the beginning of the War of 1812. He served throughout the war, then accompanied Generals Andrew Jackson and E. P. Gaines in the Seminole campaigns, and was promoted to colonel, Seventh Infantry, in 1820. From April 1824 he was commander at Fort Gibson, attempting to maintain peace with the Indians. Brevetted brigadier general in 1830, he served in the Mexican War and died in 1851 (*Appleton's*; F. Robinson, *Organization of the Army*, I, 315–16).

4 George Birch, born in England, enlisted in the Light Dragoons in 1808 and fought in the War of 1812. He was transferred to the Seventh Infantry in 1815, brevetted major in 1826 for ten years' service in one grade, and was major, Seventh Infantry, at the time of his death in 1837 (Heitman, *Historical Register*, I, 219).

5 Francis Lee, an 1822 graduate of West Point and a native of Pennsylvania, had served at Forts Jesup and Leavenworth before his appointment to Fort Gibson in 1834. He was on duty in several southern garrisons and in the Mexican War, being brevetted lieutenant colonel and colonel in 1847 for gallantry at Contreras, Churubusco, and Molino del Rey. As colonel of the Second Infantry, he commanded the Department of the West for several months in 1858, and died the following year in St. Louis, aged fifty-five (Cullum, *Biographical Register*, I, 294–95).

6 Samuel Kinney was born in Illinois and graduated from the Military Academy in 1830. He served only at Fort Gibson and Camp Arbuckle, Indian Territory, before his death at Fort Gibson in 1835, at the age of thirty (Cullum, *Biographical Register*, I, 458).

7 Roger Sherman Dix, born in New Hampshire, was graduated from West Point in 1832 and served in the Black Hawk expedition and at Fort Smith and Little Rock, before being briefly assigned to Fort Gibson in 1835. After assignments to topographical, recruiting, and quartermaster duties, he participated in the Mexican War as major and paymaster, and was brevetted lieutenant colonel for gallantry at Buena Vista in 1847. He died in Pennsylvania, aged thirty-eight, in 1849 (Cullum, *Biographical Register*, I, 523).

8 Forbes Britton was graduated from West Point in 1834, and was first assigned to Fort Gibson. A Virginian, Britton was in the Seventh Infantry until his resignation in 1850, serving with the unit in the Florida wars, the occupation of Texas, and the Mexican War. He became a Texas merchant and farmer in 1850, and was a member of the state senate and brigadier general of the state militia when he died in 1861, aged forty-nine (Cullum, *Biographical Register*, I, 585).

9 Jesse Bean (sketch, 1:394, *n.* 2).

10 James F. Izard, a Pennsylvanian and son of War of 1812 general George Izard, was graduated in the same West Point class as Davis, and served at Jefferson Barracks, in the Black Hawk War, on the so-called Pawnee Pict expedition in 1834, and at Fort Gibson, 1834–35. He died in 1836, at the age of twenty-six, of wounds received in a skirmish at Camp Izard, Florida (Cullum, *Biographical Register*, I, 414).

11 Theophilus H. Holmes (1804–80) was born in North Carolina. Graduated

from West Point in 1829, Holmes served at many southern garrisons, in the Florida and Mexican wars, and was brevetted major in 1846. He resigned in 1861 and was appointed brigadier general in the Confederate Army. He commanded a brigade at the first Battle of Bull Run, and was for a time commander of the Trans-Mississippi Department. After the war he lived on a farm in Fayetteville, North Carolina, until his death (Cullum, *Biographical Register*, I, 446–47; Warner, *Generals in Gray*, 141).

[12] Richard H. Ross, a native of Maryland, was on his second tour of duty at Fort Gibson in 1835, having been graduated from West Point in 1830. He served at various frontier and southern forts and in the Florida War (1840–42) before his unit was called to the Mexican War. Brevetted major in 1846 and lieutenant colonel in 1847 for gallantry at Monterrey and Contreras, Ross was wounded in the latter battle, and served after the war on recruiting service and in the 1849–50 campaigns against the Seminoles. He was on sick leave in Boston when he died, at age forty-five, in 1851 (Cullum, *Biographical Register*, I, 468).

[13] Richard Caswell Gatlin (1809–96), born in North Carolina, attended the state university and was graduated from the Military Academy in 1832. He served with the Seventh Infantry in several southern and frontier posts, in the 1839–42 Florida War, and in the Mexican War, where he was wounded and brevetted major at Monterrey. He participated in the Seminole campaigns of 1849–50, and served in various garrisons before resigning his major's commission in 1861. Appointed adjutant general of North Carolina, he served in that capacity for the duration of the war, and was a brigadier general in the Confederate Army, 1861–62. After the war he retired to a farm in Sebastian County, Arkansas (Cullum, *Biographical Register*, I, 525; Warner, *Generals in Gray*, 102–103).

[14] Alexander Montgomery, an 1834 Academy graduate from Pennsylvania, was at Fort Gibson, 1834–35, and later served in the Florida and Mexican wars. On quartermaster duty, 1861–63 and 1866–74, Montgomery retired as lieutenant colonel and deputy quartermaster general and died in 1893 (Cullum, *Biographical Register*, I, 586; Heitman, *Historical Register*, I, 719).

[15] Dixon Stansbury Miles, cadet at the Military Academy from Maryland (1819–24), was regimental adjutant, 1830–36, and later served in Florida and in the Mexican War, when he was twice brevetted for gallant conduct. Miles commanded two Indian expeditions in New Mexico before the Civil War. A colonel in the United States Second Infantry, he was mortally wounded in the defense of Harpers Ferry in 1862, and died there at the age of fifty-eight (Cullum, *Biographical Register*, I, 334–35).

[16] Edmund P. Gaines (sketch, 1:301, *n.* 3).

[17] George A. McCall (sketch, 1:301, *n.* 2).

1:448 From the Office of the Quartermaster General[1]

SIR, January 20th, 1835

Your money and property Accounts, for the Third Quarter of the last year,[2] after the usual examination at this Office, are transmitted to the Third Auditor[3] for settlement. You will find herewith a Statement of remarks.

[Encl] 3rd. Quarter 1834.

Quarterly return. "Clothing, Camp and Garrison equipage should be borne on a return separate from that of quarter Master's stores proper."

Abstract E. "*Two* Invoices of Camp equipage are withdrawn from this abstract and will be sent to the Second Auditor" [4]

Abstract E. Voucher. Lieut Collins,[5] Invoice of tents, tent Poles, and tent flies.

"This Invoice is withdrawn from Lieut. Jefferson Davis's abstract E, 3rd. quarter 1834 and will be send to the Second Auditor."

Voucher. Lieut Thomas Johnston's[6] Invoice of tents, tent flies, and tent poles.

"Same remark as on Lieut. Collins' Invoice of Camp equipage"

Abstract G. Voucher. Lieut J. Davis—requisition for forage for eight daught oxen the month of September.

"Lieut. Davis has omitted to certify that the forage was necessarily fed to the public oxen in his charge."

LbC (NA, RG 92 Records of the Office of the Quartermaster General, Letters Sent, XXI, 230). Addressed: "To, Lieut. Jeff. Davis, Regt. of Dragoons, Camp Jones, near Fort Gibson, Arkansas." Enclosure: LbC (NA, RG 92 Records of the Office of the Quartermaster General, Remarks on Officers' Accounts, I, 195). Addressed: "Lieut Jefferson Davis, Acting Asst. Qr. Master, Jones Camp, near Fort Smith. Arkansas."

1 The quartermaster general was Thomas S. Jesup (sketch, 1:174, *n.* 4).

2 Davis' letter of transmittal for his money and property accounts for the third quarter is printed as 1:429.

3 The third auditor was Peter Hagner (sketch, 1:199, *n.* 5); the returns were sent to him January 20 (NA, RG 92, Letters Sent, XXI, 230).

4 William B. Lewis was the second auditor (sketch, 1:166, *n.* 1).

5 Richard D'Cantillon Collins, a native of New York, was on quartermaster duty in Little Rock in the autumn of 1834. Collins was graduated from West Point in 1823 and served mainly in Florida and Indian Territory before his dismissal from the service in 1841. He died later that year at Little Rock, aged forty-six (Cullum, *Biographical Register*, I, 311).

6 Thomas Johnston was an assistant quartermaster at Fort Gibson from July to December 1834 when he was dismissed from the service. Johnston was born in Pennsylvania and graduated from West Point in 1822. He served at garrisons in Arkansas and Indian territories and died at Little Rock in 1835, aged thirty-three (Cullum, *Biographical Register*, I, 296).

1:449

George A. McCall to Matthew Arbuckle

Asst. Adjt. Genls office. W[estern] D[epartment]
Memphis Tennessee Janu. 22nd. 1834[1]

SIR[2]

Your letter of the 28th. Ult[3] enclosing a charge and Specification[4] preferred by Major R B Mason[5] of the Dragoons, against 1st. Lieut. J Davis, of the same Regt. has been received at this office and Submitted to the General,[6] who directs that you cause the Lieutenant to be brought before the Court[7] ordered for the trial of Lieut Northrop;[8] At the same time he would recommend to you the arrangement by the Commanding officer of the post, of a difference of the nature which this appears to be, when Such a course is practicable, in preference to a resort to trial by a general Court Martial I am Sir with great respect Your Mo Obt Sert G. A. McC[9]
A[ide-] D[e-] C[amp]

LbCS (NA, RG 393 Records of United States Army Continental Commands, 1821–1920, Western Department, Letters Sent, VII, 108). Addressed: "To General M Arbuckle Commdg S[outh] W[estern] Frontier. Fort Gibson Arkansas."

[1] Clerical error no doubt accounts for the date being written 1834 rather than 1835 as it should be.

[2] Matthew Arbuckle (sketch, 1:447, *n.* 3).

[3] Arbuckle's letter of December 28 has not been found.

[4] See 1:454 for the charge and specification.

[5] Richard B. Mason (sketch, 1:375, *n.* 8).

[6] Edmund P. Gaines, commander of the Western Department (sketch, 1:301, *n.* 3).

[7] See 1:447 for the order authorizing the trial of Northrop.

[8] Lucius B. Northrop (sketch, 1:402, *n.* 4).

[9] George A. McCall (sketch, 1:301, *n.* 2).

[10] A letter of the same date and of similar import was sent by G. A. McCall to Dixon S. Miles (NA, RG 393, Western Department, Letters Sent, VII, 107–108).

ABSTRACT

1:450

Post Return

Fort Gibson,[1] January [31,] 1835

Lists First Lieutenant Jefferson Davis, Company E, Dragoons, present at the post. Remarks: "For duty."

DS (NA, RG 94 Records of the Adjutant General's Office, Post Returns, Fort Gibson), 2. Signed: "W. Seawell 1st Lieut. 7th Infy. Aide de Camp. M. Arbuckle Brigdr. Genl. U. S. Army Commdg." Endorsed: "Entd Recd. March 19."

[1] See 1:397, *n.* 1.

David E. Twiggs to Thomas S. Jesup 1:451

SIR.[1] New Orleans 7 Febr. 1835

Major Clark[2] informs me that he is very much in want of an experienced officer to assist him at the Barracks below the City.[3] allow me to recommend, as well qualified Liet Jefferson Davis of the Dragoons. he was with me at Ft Winebago & had the entire Superintendence of the werking partes at that fort.[4] I have no hesitation in Saying that he is as well, *if not bettor* qualified for that duty, than any officer of my acquaintance. I do not know Mr Davis' wishes on the Subject but he is so perfect a Soldier that he is ready for any duty. I am Sir Vy Resp yr ob Svr D. E. TWIGGS[5]

Lt Col C[omman]d[in]g

ALS (NA, RG 92 Records of the Office of the Quartermaster General, Consolidated Correspondence File, Col. J. Davis, T-35, 1835). Addressed: "Genl Th. S. Jesup U S. A Washington D. C." Endorsed: "Recd. Feb. 23d. 1835."

[1] Thomas S. Jesup (sketch, 1:174, *n.* 4).

[2] Isaac Clark, Jr., entered the army as an ensign from Vermont in 1812, was discharged, then reinstated, in the Fifth Infantry at the close of the War of 1812. By 1835 he was brevet major, Sixth Infantry; he died by drowning in 1842 (Heitman, *Historical Register*, I, 304).

[3] The appropriation for barracks, quarters and storehouses at New Orleans had been made in June 1832 (*Statutes at Large of the United States*, IV [1846], 594–95). Twiggs had been scheduled for duty at New Orleans, but was diverted to Augusta, Georgia, during the nullification crisis, and selection of a site was delayed (Jesup to Cass, February 26, 1833, *American State Papers*, Class V, Military Affairs, V, 167). Work was begun in 1834 and completed in less than three years. New Orleans Barracks were situated on the river front adjacent to the Mereaux plantation, and plans were furnished by Second Lieutenant Frederick Wilkinson; after the Civil War the post was known as Jackson Barracks. For a detailed description and plan of the finished buildings, see Curtis, *New Orleans*, 222–27; see also Prucha, *Guide to Military Posts*, 94.

[4] The dates of Davis' supervision are uncertain (see 1:197, *n.* 3). See 1:144, *n.* 1 for Fort Winnebago.

[5] David E. Twiggs (sketch, 1:149, *n.* 4).

1:452

Order No. 5

Head Quarters South Western Frontier
Fort Gibson,[1] February 11th. 1835

The General Court Martial ordered to convene at this post on the 2d. instant by Department order No. 1,[2] will convene at 11 O'clock A. M. tomorrow.

The following officers are detailed as members of the court to fill vacancies in the original detail Viz. Bvt. Lieut. Col. Burbank[3] 7th Inf. Capt. Perkins[4] Regiment U. S. Dragoons and 1st. Lieut. Rains[5] 7th. Inf. By order of Bt. Brigd. Genl. Arbuckle[6] Signd.

W. Seawell[7]
A[ide-] D[e-] C[amp] & A[cting] A[ssistant] Adjt. Genl

D, copy (NA, RG 153 Records of the Office of the Judge Advocate General [Army], Court Martial Records, CC–47, 1835); D, copy (NA, RG 153 Records of the Office of the Judge Advocate General [Army], Court Martial Records, CC–54, 1835).

1 See 1:397, *n.* 1.

2 Department Order No. 1 is printed as 1:447.

3 Sidney Burbank (sketch, 1:195, *n.* 6).

4 David Perkins (sketch, 1:410, *n.* 3).

5 Gabriel J. Rains, born in North Carolina in 1803, was an 1827 graduate of the Military Academy. Rains was first assigned to Jefferson Barracks, and later to commissary duty, 1831–34. Brevetted major for gallantry in the Seminole wars, he served with the Seventh Infantry in the military occupation of Texas and briefly in the Mexican War. He resigned his commission as lieutenant colonel, Fifth Infantry, in 1861 and was appointed a brigadier in the Confederate Army. In 1862 Rains, who had experimented for years with explosives, invented "land torpedoes" (antipersonnel mines), which caused large numbers of Union casualties. Relieved from field service after the Battle of Seven Pines, Rains concentrated on developing mines and torpedo defenses after May 1863. He was a clerk in the United States Quartermaster Department at Charleston, 1877–80, and died in Aiken, South Carolina, in 1881 (Cullum, *Biographical Register*, I, 393; Warner, *Generals in Gray*, 249–50).

6 Matthew Arbuckle (sketch, 1:447, *n.* 3).

7 Washington Seawell, a Virginian, was graduated in 1825 from the Military Academy and served as Matthew Arbuckle's aide-de-camp, 1834–36. He participated in the Florida wars, 1839–42, and for his services was brevetted major. After the Mexican War, Seawell was in command of the Department of Texas, then was retired from active service in 1862 for disability. He continued to serve as a mustering and disbursing officer during the Civil War and was brevetted brigadier general in 1865. He was residing in San Francisco at the time of his death, at age eighty-six, in 1888 (Cullum, *Biographical Register*, I, 357–58).

From the Office of the Quartermaster General[1] 1:453

SIR, February 12th, 1835

Your return of Horses, &c, and its vouchers, of Company F, Regiment of Dragoons, for part of the Second quarter—from 17th to 30th June—of the last year,[2] after examination at this Office, are transmitted to the Third Auditor[3] for settlement.[4] These papers were in the first instance sent to the Second Auditor,[5] but were subsequently returned to this Office.[6]

LbC (NA, RG 92 Records of the Office of the Quartermaster General, Letters Sent, XXI, 281). Addressed: "To, Lieut. Jeff. Davis, Regiment of Dragoons, Fort Gibson." Endorsed: "Returned as a Dead Letter from General Post Office, October 9th, 1835."

1 Thomas S. Jesup was the quartermaster general (sketch, 1:174, *n.* 4).

2 Davis' return for June 17–30, 1834, has not been found.

3 The third auditor was Peter Hagner (sketch, 1:199, *n.* 5).

4 Davis' "return of Horses" was transmitted from the quartermaster general to the third auditor February 12 (NA, RG 92, Letters Sent, XXI, 281).

5 William B. Lewis was the second auditor (sketch, 1:166, *n.* 1).

6 Evidently this letter reached Fort Gibson after Davis had left, as witness the clerical endorsement in the descriptive footnote. See 1:474 for evidence of Davis' having left Fort Gibson on furlough.

Proceedings of a General Court Martial—First Day Trial of Jefferson Davis 1:454

Fort Gibson[1] February 12, 1835

The court met pursuant to the above order.[2]

Present.

Bt. Brigd. Genl. M. Arbuckle[3] President.

Members

Bt. Lieut. Col. Burbank[4] 7th. Inf.
Capt. J. Bean[5] Dragoons
Captain F. Lee[6] 7th. Inf.
2d. Lieut. T. H. Holmes[7] 7th. Inf.
2d. Lieut. R. S. Dix[8] 7th Inf.
Bt. 2d. Lieut. F. Britton[9] 7th. Inf.
Bt. Majr. Geo. Birch[10] 7th Inf.
Captain Perkins[11] Dragoons
1st. Lieut. Rains[12] 7th. Inf.
2d. Lieut. R. H. Ross[13] 7th. Inf.
2d. Lieut. R. C. Gatlin[14] 7th. Inf.
Bt. 2d. Lieut. A. Montgomery[15] 7th. Inf

1st. Lieut. & Adjt. D. S. Miles[16] 7th. Inf. Special Judge Advocate

The court being duly sworn in the presence of the accused, proceeded to the trial of 1st. Lieut. Jefferson Davis of the Regiment of Dragoons, who being previously asked if he had any objections to the members named in the above orders, and replying in the negative, was arraigned on the following charge & specification prefered against him by Major R. B. Mason[17] of the Dragoons.

Charge—Conduct subversive of good order and Military decipline.

Specification. In this that 1st. Lieut. Jefferson Davis of the Regiment of Dragoons, on or about the morning of the 24th. day of December 1834, at the Dragoon Camp near Fort Gibson, upon being sent for by Majr. Mason his immediate Commanding Officer, and spoken to as to his abscence on that morning from the Reve<i>[18]llie roll call of his company, did reply, in these words, or words of like meaning, "because I was not out of my tent, and the Regulations[19] require when it rains that the roll shall be call'd in quarters by Chiefs of squads," and upon Major Mason's saying to him, "You know it is my order that all officers of this command attend the Revellie roll call of their respective companies," the said Lt. Davis did, in a highly disrespectful, insubordinate, and contemptuous manner abruptly turn upon his heel and walk off, saying at the same time, Hum! and furthermore, being ordered back by Major Mason & told that he (Major Mason) was not in the habit of receiving such treatment from officers when speaking to them upon a point of duty, and that he (Lieut. Davis) would consider himself in arrest and go to his quarters, whereupon the said Lt. Davis stared Majr. Mason full in the face, without showing any intention of obeying the order of arrest, and upon Majr. Mason's repeating the order of arrest, the said Lt. Davis, still staring Major Mason in the face, did in a disrespectful and Contemptuous manner, ask: "Now are you done with me?" And did not obey the order to go to his quarters in arrest until after Major Mason had peremptorily repeated it a third time. Signd. R. B. Mason
Majr. Dragoons.

The accused before pleading to the charge & Specification requested the opinion of the Court; whether the charge & specification embraced any criminality.

The court was cleared and decided that the charge & Specification prefered against 1st. Lt. J. Davis of Regt. of Dragoons embraced a Military offence and therefore direct it shall be investigated.

The accused pleaded Not Guilty to the specification and Not Guilty to the charge.

Major R. B. Mason of the Regt. of Dragoons a witness for the prosecution being duly sworn, says: on or about the morning of the 24th. of December last, Company (E) Regiment of Dragoons, (one of the companies composing my command) turned out as usual upon its parade at Reve<i>[18]llie roll call. The accused who commanded the company at the time, was absent at the calling of the Roll. I sent the orderly for him, to learn the cause of his abscence; he came and upon being spoken to upon the subject, replied: "because I was not out of <my>[18] tent, and the Regulations require when it rains that the Rolls shall be called in quarters by Chiefs of Squads,"[19] upon my saying to him, you know it is my order that all the officers of this command shall attend the Revellie roll call of their respective companies! Hum! says he, and turned upon his heel in an abrupt, disrespectful and contemptuous manner and walked off. I immediately ordered him back; and said to him, I was not in the habit of receiving such treatment from officers, when speaking to them on a point of duty; that he would consider himself in arrest and go to his Quarters. Whereupon he stared me full in the face and showed no intention of obeying the order. I repeated, it is my order that you go to your quarters in arrest and confine yourself to them: he still, showed no intention of obeying the order and continued to stare me in the face, and asked in a disrespectful and contemptuous manner; "now are you done with me," and did not obey the order to go to his quarters in arrest until after I had repeated it in the most positive and peremptory manner a third time.

Question by the Accused. Did I not say that in bad weather the Regulations[19] prescribed that the rolls should be called in Quarters? and that the custom of service justified Officers on such occasions in staying away?

Answer. No.

Question by the accused. Did you send the orderly to inquire the cause of my abscence from Reve<i>[18]llie, or did you send to require my presence before you?

Answer. To require his presence and so intended to be understood in the first part of my testimony.

Question by the accused. Did you say, "it is my order that all officers of this command attend the Revellie roll call: it is my order that you attend the Reve<i>[18]llie roll call rain or <no>[18] rain: it is my order and you know it." and did I not then and not till then turn to leave you: and was it not after having turned and commenced walking off that I used the interjection of which you speak: and had you not finished speaking to me before I turned to leave you?

Answer. I said to Lieut. Davis as near as I can recollect, you know it is my order that all officers of this command attend the Reve<i>[18]llie roll call of their respective companies: I think these are the identical words used. I said nothing to him about rain or no rain, that I recollect. he immediately turned upon his heel and walked off. He made use of the interjection, I believe at the moment of turning and turn'd off immediately at my telling him, he knew it was my order that all officers attend the Revellie Roll Call. and he did turn off before I had said to him all I intended.

Question by the Accused. Did any such order exist, as you mentioned relative to attendance at Revellei roll call?

Answer. I do not recollect there was any written order, particularly requiring the presence of officers at the Reve<i>[18]llei Roll call, but it was well understood by the officers of my command, that their presence was required at the Roll call at Reveillei. The accused well knew it, besides I had once given him the order myself and had occasion repeatedly to send for him on account of a breach of it.

Question by the accused. Had you ever given me an order to attend Reve<i>[18]llei roll call in bad weather? and had I ever been absent from the Revellei roll call during the time I had been on company duty?

Answer. I never gave an order in relation to attending Roll call in bad weather. Mr. Davis had been repeatedly absent from the Reve<i>[18]llei roll call previous to that time. I cannot say positively that he had been absent before while on Company duty. The weather on that occasion (I allude to the 24th. Decbr.) was a little rainy, his company paraded as usual at the Reve<i>[18]llei roll call and I well recollect that several of his men stood in the ranks in their shirt sleeves: previous to the Reve<i>[18]llei a short time, it had been raining very hard, and the accused was the only absentee I observed that morning.

Question by the accused. Can you recollect that I suffered from the effect of this climate in the winter of 1833, & 34, and that I expressed to you a desire to leave this post for fear of a like effect from the present winter?

Answer. Whilst we were encamped last winter or spring at Camp

Jackson,[20] Lieut. Davis was sick with an affection of the lungs as I understood and beleived. And he spoke to me sometime this winter about getting a Surgeon's Certificate and said he could get one, and he wished to go away. I expressed some surprise at it, and since have heard no more of it.

Question by the Accused. Did you not know of a reason why I might be silent under censure, though I should have an excuse?

Answer. I know of no reason.

Question by the accused. Did you not after calling me back *harshly*, and informing me that my conduct was not such as could be permitted under such circumstances say—you will confine yourself to your quarters—you will confine yourself to your quarters strictly, and when the company I commanded approached within hearing, say—I order you to your Quarters in arrest! And did I not then immediately go?

Answer. When the accused turned upon his heel and walked off, in the first instance as I have stated, I peremptorily ordered him back and said to him, I was not in the habit of receiving such treatment from officers when speaking to them upon a point of duty: that he would consider himself in arrest and go to his quarters. After pausing a moment or two, sufficiently long for him to have obeyed the order, I repeated, it is my order, you will go to your quarters in arrest and that you confine yourself to them. And it is very probable that I may have repeated the latter more than once, although I have no recollection of it. It was then that the accused asked the question, "now are you done with me," My reply was a repitition of the order to go to his quarters in arrest and confine himself to them. About which time I believe the company, he commanded approached: how near I do not recollect, and only recollect that it did approach from the accused's question bringing it to my recollection. The time between my first order and the last, occupied but a short time, probably not more than a minute or two.

Question by the accused. Do you recollect whether or not you were excited in the interview with the accused on the morning of the 24th. Decbr. 1834?

Answer. I was not at all excited with the accused when I sent for him. But the disres<pe>[18]ctful and contemptuous manner in which I felt myself treated and non obedience of the peremptory order I have given him, did Excite me.

The evidence on the part of the prosecution here closed.

The court adjourned to meet again on the 13th. instant at 10 o'clock A. M.

DS (NA, RG 153 Records of the Office of the Judge Advocate General [Army], Court Martial Records, CC–47, 1835).

[1] See 1:397, *n.* 1.
[2] See 1:447 for Order No. 1.
[3] Matthew Arbuckle (sketch, 1:447, *n.* 3).
[4] Sidney Burbank (sketch, 1:195, *n.* 6).
[5] Jesse Bean (sketch, 1:394, *n.* 2).
[6] Francis Lee (sketch, 1:447, *n.* 5).
[7] Theophilus H. Holmes (sketch, 1:447, *n.* 11).
[8] Roger S. Dix (sketch, 1:447, *n.* 7).
[9] Forbes Britton (sketch, 1:447, *n.* 8).
[10] George Birch (sketch, 1:447, *n.* 4).
[11] David Perkins (sketch, 1:410, *n.* 3).
[12] Gabriel J. Rains (sketch, 1:452, *n.* 5).
[13] Richard H. Ross (sketch, 1:447, *n.* 12).
[14] Richard C. Gatlin (sketch, 1:447, *n.* 13).
[15] Alexander Montgomery (sketch, 1:447, *n.* 14).
[16] Dixon S. Miles (sketch, 1:447, *n.* 15).
[17] Richard B. Mason (sketch, 1:375, *n.* 8).
[18] Interlined.
[19] The regulation to which Davis refers provided: "At the dawn of day, a signal or call will be made for the music to repair to the regimental parade, and five minutes after the call, the whole will commence the *reveillé*, when both officers and men will rise. As soon as the music ceases, the first sergeants will call their rolls in front (when the weather will permit) of the tents or quarters of the respective companies, each company being in the habitual order of formation. In bad weather, permission may be given to the chiefs of squads, to make the call in tents or quarters" (*General Army Regulations* [1825], 40).
[20] Davis and Mason were stationed at Camp Jackson near Fort Gibson, December 14, 1833–June 18, 1834 (1:397, 420). See 1:397, *n.* 3 for a description of the camp.

1:455 Proceedings of a General Court Martial—Second Day Trial of Jefferson Davis

Fort Gibson[1] 13th. Feby. 1835

The Court convened pursuant to adjournment.

Present.

Bvt. Brigd. Genl. M. Arbuckle[2] President

Members.

Bt. Lieut. Col. Burbank[3] 7th. Inf.
Capt. J. Bean[4] Dragoons
Capt. F. Lee[5] 7th. Inf.
2d. Lieut. T. H. Holmes[6] 7th. Inf.
2d. Lieut. R. S. Dix[7] 7th. Inf.
Bt. 2d. Lieut. F. Britton[8] 7th. Inf.
Bt. Majr. Birch[9] 7th. Inf.
Captain Perkins[10] Drags.
1st. Lieut. Rains[11] 7th. Inf.
2d. Lieut. R. H. Ross[12] 7th. Inf.
2d. Lieut. R. C. Gatlin[13] 7th. Inf.
Bt. 2d. Lieut. A. Montgomery[14] 7th. Inf.

1st. Lieut & Adjt. D. S. Miles[15] 7th. Inf. Specl. Judge Advocate.

Captain D. Perkins Regt. of Dragoons a witness for the accused being duly sworn; answered as follows.

Question by the accused. Did you ever hear of an order by Major Mason,[16] that officers should attend revellei?

Answer. I never did.

Question by the accused. Did you beleive that officers were required to be present at the Reve<i>[17]llei roll call in bad weather?

Answer. I would have expected if I was not present to be sent for.

Question by the accused. Have you not been absent on account of bad weather and not sent for; and do you not beleive that Majr. Mason Commdg. saw you standing in your Quarters?

Answer. I was absent one morning when it rained or snowed, I dont recollect which. The Company was paraded in front of its quarters for the Reve<i>[17]llei roll call, and I was standing in my door; the orderly came to me, and said that Major Mason directed the rolls to be call'd in quarters. I told the orderly to give the order to the Sergeant and I went to my room. I do not know whether Major Mason the Comdg. officer saw me in my door, but I was under the impression at the time that he did.

Question by the accused. Have you found Major Mason in his official intercourse uniformily courteous, or at times harsh and disregardful of the feelings of those under him?

Answer. I recollect distinctly on three occasions, when Major Mason spoke to me on points of duty, when I thought he was rather harsh and I did not think he had a proper regard for my feelings.

Question by the accused. Have you had an opportunity of observing me as an officer, if so; state the circumstances and whether I have frequently neglected or habitually attended to my duties?

Answer. Lieut. Davis has been in my company since May 1834[18] part of which time he was acting Adjutant, acting asst. Commissary and actg. Asst. quarter master,[19] and served with the command to which my company belonged; and I never<knew>[17] him to neglect his duty. He has habitually attended to his duties as far as I know.

Lieut. Bowman[20] of the Regiment of Dragoons a witness for the Accused being duly sworn, answered as follows.

Question by the accused. Have you never heard Major Mason of Drags. reply to an officer (who gave him an excuse for what Majr. Mason censured him) in terms which would prevent any man of pride who knew the circumstances from subjecting himself to like treatment?

Answer. I have.

Question by the accused. Have you not reason to beleive, that I knew of the circumstance just refered to, previous to the morning of the 24th. Decemb. 1834?

Answer. Yes.

Question by the accused. Have you observed in the course of our service together, whether I was habitually attentive to all duties incumbent on me, or reverse?

Answer. He has been habitually attentive to duty. I have had a long time to observe him; ever since I have been in the Regiment.

Question by the accused. Whether from your observation do you suppose Majr. Mason Drags. or myself have been oftenest absent from Reve<i>[17]llei since Majr Mason Commanded the Squadron in which we both serve?

Answer. I should say Major Mason has been absent the oftenest; as far as I have been able to observe.

Private Decons[21] Regiment of Dragoons a witness for the accused being duly sworn. answer'd as follows.

Question by the accused. Were you orderly to Majr. Mason on or about the morning of the 24th. Decembr. 1834, and were you sent for the accused (Lieut Davis) immediately after Reve<i>[17]llei?

Answer. I was orderly to Majr. Mason on or about the 24th. of Decbr. 1834, and was sent by him for the accused immediately after Reve<i>[17]llei.

Question by the accused. Did you find the accused (Lieut. Davis) in his front tent, or where he slept?

Answer. I found him in his front tent.

Question by the accused. Did you hear any remarks of Majr. Mason on that morning, when speaking to the accused, and if so, what were they?

Answer. I heard but one distinctly and that was, "go to your tent and consider yourself under arrest.

Question by the accused. Were you during the interview in the same relative position, to Majr. Mason and the accused (Lieut. Davis)?

Answer. What I heard, I heard while passing and afterwards stationed myself sixteen or eighteen paces from the parties.

Major Mason Regt. of Dragoons was called as a witness for the accused. and answered as follows.

Question by the accused. What did you state to the accused relative to the manner in which the Guard Reports of the Squadron had been transmitted to you, when on the morning of the 25th. Jany. 1835, he told you that non commissioned officers of the guard had under other officers carried the Guard reports to you?

Answer. Some short time since, in a conversation with the accused in relation to the Guard reports, I stated that they had never been handed to me, except by the old offic. of the Day, that I had not the smallest recollection nor have I yet, of ever having received a report by a messenger of the officer of the Day. I think I also stated to the accused, although I am not very positive, that I sometimes found the report laying on my table & always presumed it had been left there by the officer himself.

Question by the accused. Do you recollect during the spring of 1834, when exercising in the school of the Trooper[22] to have supposed you were disrespectfully treated by Lt. Davis; (the accused) and whether you were correct in your supposition or not?

Answer. I well recollect the time to which I presume the accused alludes; I thought at the moment, that the words the accused made use of, was a reply to an order that I gave. The accused said they were not; he said so afterwards, I then was perfectly satisfied, they were not a reply and no disrespect intended. The accused & myself at the time, were upon terms of warm friendship, we messed together and this affair produced so far as I know, not the smallest change in that Friendship and intimacy that previously existed and I thought it was to be forever forgotten.

Question by the accused. Was your reason for anticipating disrespectful conduct on official matters, better founded, on the morning of the 24th. Decbr. 1834, than in the spring of that year, and <do you think>[17] that on your part, conduct equally courteous in the latter case, as in the first, would not have produced a like effect?

Answer. I had no reason to anticipate disr<—a—>espectful conduct from any one at any time, more especially on official matters, and consider my conduct on the morning of the 24th. towards the accused in sending for him and reminding him of his abscence from the Reve<i>[17]llei roll call, as perfectly proper, decorous and corteous; and if the <conduct of the>[17] accused upon that occasion (disrespectful and insubordinate as I considered it to have been) drew from me an uncorteous or improper remark or reply, I acknowledge it to have been unworthy of me.

Question by the Court. Might not the usual manner of the accused be considered disrespectful or even contemptuous by one not well acquainted with him?

Answer. Far from it in my opinion, the general conduct of the accused is that of a corteous gentleman.

Question by the court. Has the accused been habitually attentive to his duty, or the reverse; since he joined the Regiment of Dragoons?

Answer. I cannot answer the question so satisfactorily either to myself or the court; (previous to the seperation of the Regiment of Dragoons in Septbr. last,) (when the accused became immediately under my command.)[23] Since that time I have had in repeated instances to call the attention of the accused to his duty. I recollect of no dereliction of duty of the accused before coming under my command; but frequently heard him complain of it in others and expressed a great <deal>[17] of soldierly feeling in relation to the welfare of the Regiment of Dragoons.

Question by the accused. Will you state between what dates the derelictions (on the part of the accused) you speak of, occured?

Answer. I do not recollect the particular dates, but it was both at Camp Jones in the Creek Nation[24] and after our return to this place.

Question by the accused. What was the nature of the derelictions, and who knows them besides yourself?

Answer. They were generally abscence from Roll Calls & neglect of stable duties, I can't say who knows <them>[17] besides myself, the attention of the accused was generally call'd to them at the time: and I kept no account of dates nor did I charge my memory with them.

Captain Perkins Regt. of Dragoons a witness for the Accused was again call'd & answerd.

Question by the Accused. Do you know for whom my remark was made in the spring of 1834, when exercising in the School of the Trooper, and do you not know that it had no bearing on the instructor of the Squad Majr. Mason Drags?

Answer. <I think>[17] I know for whom the remark was made and <I think>[17] it was not made for Major Mason. <however at the moment it was made I did think it was made for Majr. Mason.>[17]

Question by the accused. Do you not from intercourse with Major Mason beleive, that a calm, collected bearing before him is likely to irritate him?

Answer. I think it would. at the time he was reproving a person.

Sergeant Sample[25] of the Regiment of Dragoons a witness for the accused being duly sworn: answered as follows.

Question by the accused. Did you hear any remarks which passed between Majr. Mason and Lieut. Davis (the accused) in an interview between them on the morning of the 24 Decbr. 1834, and if so, what were they?

Answer. I heard some remarks on that morning that passed between Lt. Davis and Majr. Mason as I was passing from the Company parade to the stables, I heard Majr. Mason tell Lt. Davis "Mr. Davis you shall not turn your back to me in that manner. Majr. Mason then made a remark concerning an order. I do not recollect the words. He then said "go to your Quarters in arrest."

Question by the accused. Did you see when Lieut. Davis left Majr. Mason, if so, state how soon after Majr. Mason's order?

Answer. I did not see him when he left Majr. Mason and dont know how soon after Majr. Mason's order.

Question by the accused. Did you march immediately past Majr. Mason and the accused after hearing the order?

Answer. At that time; I was passed them, and were too far past them to observe whether Mr Davis went to his tent or not.

Question by the accused. Did you observe anything contemptuous and disrespectful in the action of Lt. Davis (the accused) towards Majr. Mason Comdg.?

Answer. I did not.

Quest. by S. J. Advocate. How far was it from Majr. Mason & Lieut. Davis, that you march'd the Company?

Answer. Passed within six feet of the two.

Quest. by S. Judge Advocate. If Lieut. Davis had been disrespectful to Majr. Mason while you were passing, would you have noticed it?

Answer. If there had been any disrespectful conduct on the part of Lieut. Davis, I would have been in a favourable position to notice it, but I did not perceive any.

Quest. by Spl. Judge Advocate. How long were you passing the accused & Majr. Mason? And do you know what took place either before or after you passed, or were they standing together before you passed?

Answer. I observed them from the time I turned the corner of the Tent, and was in sight until I was so far passed, as to be unable to see them without turning my head. They were standing together before I approached, I do not know what took place either before or after I passed them.

Question by the accused. Have you when the accused commanded the Company of which you are orderly Sergeant, found him neglectful of his duties as a company officer or otherwise; and how <has>[17] his attention compared with other officers who have commanded the same company?

Answer. Lieut. Davis has been as attentive <as much so>[17] as any other officer, I ever was under.

Lieut. Izard[26] of the Regiment of Dragoons a witness for the accused, after being duly sworn answered as follows.

Question by the accused. Were you absent from Reve<i>[17]llei on the morning of the 24th. Decbr. 1834, and if so, were you required to explain the cause of your abscence?

Answer. I was absent from reveillie that morning and was not required to explain the cause of my abscence.

Question by the Accused. Had Majr. Mason appeared to you, since under his command: vexatiously exacting or otherwise?

Answer. I should think, that the manner in which Major Mason required duty to be done in camp was unnecessarily strict. By being unnecessarily strict I mean that the requirements of Majr. Mason to perform minute duties was unnecessary and to me vexatious.

Quest. by Spl. Judge Advocate. Had you not permission to be absent from Reve<i>[17]llei on account of your previous indisposition?

Answer. I had been for some time on the sick report and when I reported to Majr. Mason for duty in camp, he told me I need not expose myself, when the weather was inclement, but this was sometime previous to the date of the accused's charge. I conceived that the indulgence had expired, from <having>[17] being sent for, on being absent from Reve<i>[17]llei once before.

Question by Spl. Judge Advocate. What duties were required of you by Majr. Mason, that you considered unnecessarily rigid?

Answer. The attendance of all the officers throughout the day at the Quarters which were in process of Building: the requiring of the actual presence and superintendance of the officers during the operation of cleaning and grooming the horses and cleaning out the stables &c. when as far as I could judge they were of no possible use.

Quest. by Spl. Judge Advocate. Did you ever know of an officer having been refused leave of abscence by Majr. Mason, when he requested one?

answer. I do not.

The Court adjourned to meet Tomorrow at 10 o'clock A. M.

DS (NA, RG 153 Records of the Office of the Judge Advocate General [Army], Court Martial Records, CC-47, 1835).

1 See 1:397, *n.* 1.

2 Matthew Arbuckle (sketch, 1:447, *n.* 3).

3 Sidney Burbank (sketch, 1:195, *n.* 6).

4 Jesse Bean (sketch, 1:394, *n.* 2).

5 Francis Lee (sketch, 1:447, *n.* 5).

6 Theophilus H. Holmes (sketch, 1:447, *n.* 11).

7 Roger S. Dix (sketch, 1:447, *n.* 7).

8 Forbes Britton (sketch, 1:447, *n.* 8).

9 George Birch (sketch, 1:447, *n.* 4).

10 David Perkins (sketch, 1:410, *n.* 3).

11 Gabriel J. Rains (sketch, 1:452, *n.* 5).

12 Richard H. Ross (sketch, 1:447, *n.* 12).

13 Richard C. Gatlin (sketch, 1:447, *n.* 13).

14 Alexander Montgomery (sketch, 1:447, *n.* 14).

15 Dixon S. Miles (sketch, 1:447, *n.* 15).

16 Richard B. Mason (sketch, 1:375, *n.* 8).

17 Interlined.

18 Davis joined Perkins' company April 25, 1834 (1:410).

19 Davis was acting adjutant, acting assistant quartermaster, and acting assistant commissary in August 1834 (1:424) and acting assistant commissary, September 1–November 10, 1834 (1:446).

20 James Monroe Bowman, an 1832 West Point graduate from Pennsylvania, had served at Jefferson Barracks and on two Indian expeditions before his second tour at Fort Gibson, 1835–36. He was later with the Dragoons at Nacogdoches, Texas, and died in 1839, aged thirty-one, at Fort Wayne (Cullum, *Biographical Register*, I, 528).

21 Francis G. Decons had been enlisted April 19, 1833, for three years in New York by First Lieutenant David Perkins (Semiannual Muster Roll, December 31, 1834 [NA, RG 94, U.S. Dragoons, Company E]).

22 The "school of the Trooper" was presumably Jefferson Barracks where the Dragoons received their preliminary training, and Davis undoubtedly intended to say the spring of 1833 because neither he nor Mason was at St. Louis in the spring of 1834. For Jefferson Barracks, see 1:123, *n.* 3.

23 Davis came under Mason's direct command in late August 1834, as his company was one of the three assigned to establish Camp Jones (1:421).

24 Camp Jones (see 1:421).

25 David Sample was appointed orderly sergeant September 12, 1834. He was enlisted by First Lieutenant David Perkins in New York in May 1833 for three years (Semiannual Muster Roll, December 31, 1833 [NA, RG 94, U.S. Dragoons, Company E]). Sample later moved to Texas, obtained a commission in the Texas army, and was reportedly killed in a duel (Doran to Davis, October 13, 1882 [Museum of the Confederacy, Richmond]).

26 James F. Izard (sketch, 1:447, *n.* 10).

1:456 Proceedings of a General Court Martial—Third Day Trial of Jefferson Davis

Fort Gibson[1] 14th. Feby. 1835

The Court met pursuant to adjournment.

Present.

Bt. Brig. Genl. M. Arbuckle[2] President

Members

Bt. Lieut. Col. Burbank[3] 7th. Inf
Capt. J. Bean[4] Dragoons
Capt. F. Lee[5] 7th. Inf
2d. Lieut. Th. H. Holmes[6] 7th. Inf.
2d. Lieut. R. S. Dix[7] 7th Inf.
Bt. 2d. Lieut. F. Britton[8] 7th Inf.
Bt. Majr. Geo. Birch[9] 7th. Inf.
Capt. Perkins[10] Dragoons
1st. Lieut. Rains[11] 7th. Inf.
2d. Lieut. R. H. Ross[12] 7th. Inf.
2d. Lieut. R. C. Gatlin[13] 7th Inf.
Bt. 2d. Lieut. A. Montgomery[14] 7th. Inf.

1st. Lieut & Adjt. D. S. Miles[15] 7th Inf. Special Judge Advocate.

The Court was cleared and the following question, "Whether the accused has the right to inquire into the general conduct of Major Mason[16] of Dragoons towards his officers similarly situated as the accused was, on the morning of the 24th. of Decbr. 1834." <& which>[17] was, decided in the affirmative.

Majr. Mason of Dragoons appeared and requested of the court to make an addition to his answer to the question of the accused of yesterday. "Wat was the nature of the derelictions and who knows them besides yourself"? which was granted, and he stated as follows.

"And I further answer, that on or about the middle of December last, I directed the accused to take all the men of the Company he commanded, (not otherwise employed) and go to work and have the floor of his company quarters fixed and put down. After giving this order I for several days paid daily and repeated visits to this party, I almost invariably found the accused absent; <from his party, idle & the work progressing slowly>[17] so repeatedly was this the case, together with the fear of the immediate setting in, of the winter and being exceedingly anxious to get the men out of their Tents and into their houses: and feeling it was the duty of every grade both commissioned and enlisted to use their utmost exertion in accomplishing so desirable an object (as that of getting them into their Quarters.) I therefore on or about the 19th. of the month ordered verbally through Lieut. Eustis[18] the then actg. Adjutant, that a Commissioned officer of each Company (they being all engaged in similar duties) should remain constantly with those working parties: this is one of the duties and one of the orders that has been considered unnecessarily rigid and vexatious.

Lieut. Northrop[19] of the Regiment of Dragoons a witness for the accused, after being duly sworn, answered as follows.

Question by the accused. Were you at the Reve<i>[17]llei roll call on the 24th. December 1834?

Answer. Yes.

Question by the accused. What was the nature of the weather on that morning?

Answer. It was rainy, cold, much rain had fallen and the ground very wet.

Quest. by the Accused. How long were you at your company parade?

Answer. About the time it would take to call the roll of a small company (as F Company was.) I can't tell exactly.

Question by the accused. Did you pass the quarters of Lieut. Davis, in going to, and returning from your company parade?

Answer. I passed going and stop'ed in returning.

Question by the accused. Did you see Lieut. Davis before going to his tent, either when proceeding to your Company parade or when returning from it?

Answer. I saw Lieut. Davis as I was returning from my company ground, he was coming from the direction of Major Mason's quarters, and I followed him, into his tent.

Question by the accused. Did Lieut. Davis appear excited when you saw him, or as from you knowledge of him he probably would have appeared, just after an angry discussion?

Answer. Lieut. Davis did not appear excited. In the habit of examining counten<an>[17]ces, I can infallibly detect any irritation in any man of Lieut. Davis's character; (from what I know of him.): he was calm and under no irritation and smilingly described to me, the occur<a>[17]ence that had happened between him and Majr. Mason.

Question by the accused. Did not Lieut. Davis consider the conduct of Majr. Mason as merely irritation on the part of Majr. Mason and that such must be the result of Major Mason's reflection?

Answer. He did. I recollect that when speaking of it, that neither of us supposed that any thing would follow <more than>[17] the immediate action of Majr. Mason, which was, his arrest. And I remarked to Lieut. Davis, that Majr. Mason could not have reflected, for he had nothing tangible to lay hold of him and had he waited until Lt. Davis was in a passion he would have committed himself.

Question by the accused. How long have you served with the accused (Lieut. Davis) and under what circumstances?

Answer. I have served with Lieut Davis ever since I joined at Jefferson Barracks (I beleive in Sepbr. 1833) [20] except the interval when we were separated on duty. I have seen him in various capacities as Adjutant[21] & in the line.

Question by the accused. What is your opinion of the general conduct of the accused during the time you have had an opportunity to observe it, and what opinion has that conduct led you to form of his character as an officer?

Answer. My opinion is, that it has been strictly and rigidly military; (so far as my notions go of military decipline.) and I have frequently remarked to him in conversations, that I thought him too rigid in the minutiae of the Service. While we were up at Camp Jackson[22] in 1834 and in this Camp near Fort Gibson it has been a subject of general remark that Lieut. Davis confined himself to the Camp, when other officers were away—that is left it seldom or comparitively so: for the reason that he assigned to me at Camp Jackson in 1834, which was, that he thought it wrong for officers to be frequently away from the command to which they were attached and being out of the way of any duty that might arise.

When Lieut. Davis commanded (E) Company,[23] I was struck with his attention to his stable duties and in the other duties of his company (as far as I had an opportunity of judging.) A short time however before he was arrested, the weather was cold and all the officers collected at a fire which was near E company and only paid occasional visits to their stables.

Question by the accused. What has been the general conduct of the accused Lieut. Davis, towards officers under whose orders his service placed him, since you have served with him?

Answer. I have believed that conduct; with regard to all the officers he has served under, (I know but of two, he has served with) highly becoming of a Soldier and a man of honor.

The Court adjourned to meet on Monday Morning at 10' O clock.

DS (NA, RG 153 Records of the Office of the Judge Advocate General [Army], Court Martial Records, CC–47, 1835).

1 See 1:397, *n.* 1.
2 Matthew Arbuckle (sketch, 1:447, *n.* 3).
3 Sidney Burbank (sketch, 1:195, *n.* 6).
4 Jesse Bean (sketch, 1:394, *n.* 2).
5 Francis Lee (sketch, 1:447, *n.* 5).
6 Theophilus H. Holmes (sketch, 1:447, *n.* 11).
7 Roger S. Dix (sketch, 1:447, *n.* 7).
8 Forbes Britton (sketch, 1:447, *n.* 8).
9 George Birch (sketch, 1:447, *n.* 4).
10 David Perkins (sketch, 1:410, *n.* 3).
11 Gabriel J. Rains (sketch, 1:452, *n.* 5).
12 Richard H. Ross (sketch, 1:447, *n.* 12).
13 Richard C. Gatlin (sketch, 1:447, *n.* 13).
14 Alexander Montgomery (sketch, 1:447, *n.* 14).
15 Dixon S. Miles (sketch, 1:447, *n.* 15).
16 Richard B. Mason (sketch, 1:375, *n.* 8).
17 Interlined.
18 William Eustis (sketch, 1:436, *n.* 1).
19 Lucius B. Northrop (sketch, 1:402, *n.* 4).
20 Northrop was transferred to the Dragoons in August 1833 (Heitman, *Historical Register*, I, 751).
21 Davis served as acting adjutant in August 1834 (1:424) and August 1833–February 1834 (1:370, 403).
22 Camp Jackson (1:397, *n.* 3).
23 Davis commanded Company E November 11 to December 24, 1834 (1:446).

Proceedings of a General Court Martial—Fifth Day Trial of Jefferson Davis 1:457

Editorial Note: The court met February 16, but because of the indisposition of Lieutenant R. S. Dix adjourned until February 17, 1835 (NA, RG 153, Court Martial Records, CC–47).

Fort Gibson[1] 17th. Feby. 1835

The court met pursuant to adjournment.

Present.

Bt. Brigd. Genl. M. Arbuckle[2] President.

Members.

Bt. Lt. col. Burbank[3] 7th Inf.
Capt. J. Bean[4] Drags.
Capt. F. Lee[5] 7th. Inf.
2d. Lt. T. H. Holmes[6] 7th. Inf.
2d. Lt. R. S. Dix[7] 7th. Inf.
Bt. 2d. Lt. F. Britton[8] 7th. Inf.
Bt. Majr. Geo. Birch[9] 7th. Inf.
Captain Perkins[10] Drags
1st. Lt. Rains[11] 7th Inf.
2d. Lt. R. H. Ross[12] 7th Inf
2d. Lt. R. C. Gatlin[13] 7th. Inf.
Bt. 2d. Lt. A. Montgomery[14] 7th. Inf.

1st. Lt & Adjt. D. S. Miles[15] 7th Inf. Special Judge Advocate.

Sergeant Budd[16] of the Regiment of Dragoons a witness for the accused, after being duly sworn, answered as follows.

Question by the accused. Were you in charge of the Party of Company "E" Regt. of Dragoons, ordered to lay the floor of the Quarters of that company, about the middle of Decbr. last?

Answer. Yes.

Question by the accused. Did Lieut. Davis appear neglectful and careless as to whether the work should be completed, or otherwise?

Answer. He appeared to encourage it, as much as possible.

Question by the accused. Did Majr. Mason[17] ever find the party or any portion of it idle to your knowledge?

Answer. He found part of it, idle one day, on account of the want of Tools. we had no saw to work with.

Quest. by the Accused. Do you know whether or not application had been made for the necessary Tool to the Quarter Master,[18] from whom Tools were received?

Answer. Yes. I went myself.

Quest. by the accused. Do you know what duty Lieut. Davis was on, in addition to his company duties, on the day refered to?

Answer. I am not positive as to that, but beleive he was officer of the Day.

Question by the accused. Do you beleive that Lieut. Davis's presence with the party at work on the Quarters was required oftener than he gave it or, that his constant presence would have caused the work to advance more rapidly?

Answer. No sir, I dont beleive we would have done any more work, if had been present all the time.

Question by the accused. How did the progress of the work in the quarters of company "E" compare with that of the other companies of the Squadron?

Answer. Company K commenced ten days before we did and finished at the same time, Company F, commenced at the same time & did not finish for three or four days after we did: although they were assisted by Citizens.

Asst. Surgeon Porter[19] a witness for the accused being duly sworn answered as follows.

Question by the accused. Do you recollect whether or not I applied to you for medical aid about the middle of Decemb. last?

Answer. I do.

Question by the accused. What was the nature of my complaint and the probable cause of it?

Answer. The complaint was an affection of the lungs, a chronic complaint, which Mr. Davis is subject; the probable cause, at that time the vicissitudes of the weather—the changible climate.

Question by the accused. What was the probable effect of the Morning's duties as they were described to you?

Answer. They were injurious to the health of Lt. Davis.

Quest. by the accused. Had any change taken place in the health of Lt. Davis previous to the 24th. of Decbr. 1834, to diminish his liability to suffer from these causes?

Answer. They had not.

Question by the accused. Did I ever explain the reason why I was unwilling to urge an application for leave of abscence for the benifit of my health.

Answer. Yes: the reason was, that Dr. Hales[20] had attended on Lt. Davis more than on any other physician; and his illness rendered it unadviseable at that time.

Quest. by accused. Did I ever repeat to you a conversation I held with my immediate commander on the subject of sick leave?

Answer. Yes.

Question by the accused. Will you state the general course and effect of it, as you understood it?

Answer. Lt. Davis told me he had spoken to his Commanding officer about a leave of abscence for his ill health and that the reply was such that it induced him to think at the time he would say nothing more about it.

Question by Special Judge Advocate. Was the accused reported on the sick report of his company, at the time to which you allude (about 24th. Decbr. last) and previous?

Answer. I do not know my impression <—was—> is that he was not.

Here ended the testimony for the accused, who requested one day to prepare his Defence; which being granted the court adjourned to meet on Thursday Morning at 10' o'clock.

DS (NA, RG 153 Records of the Office of the Judge Advocate General [Army], Court Martial Records, CC–47, 1835).

1 See 1:397, *n.* 1.

2 Matthew Arbuckle (sketch, 1:447, *n.* 3).

3 Sidney Burbank (sketch, 1:195, *n.* 6).

[4] Jesse Bean (sketch, 1:394, *n.* 2).
[5] Francis Lee (sketch, 1:447, *n.* 5).
[6] Theophilus H. Holmes (sketch, 1:447, *n.* 11).
[7] Roger S. Dix (sketch, 1:447, *n.* 7).
[8] Forbes Britton (sketch, 1:447, *n.* 8).
[9] George Birch (sketch, 1:447, *n.* 4).
[10] David Perkins (sketch, 1:410, *n.* 3).
[11] Gabriel J. Rains (sketch, 1:452, *n.* 5).
[12] Richard H. Ross (sketch, 1:447, *n.* 12).
[13] Richard C. Gatlin (sketch, 1:447, *n.* 13).
[14] Alexander Montgomery (sketch, 1:447, *n.* 14).
[15] Dixon S. Miles (sketch, 1:447, *n.* 15).
[16] John J. Budd, sergeant, Company E, was enlisted for three years in New York, June 10, 1833, by First Lieutenant David Perkins (Semiannual Muster Roll, December 31, 1834 [NA, RG 94, U.S. Dragoons, Company E]).
[17] Richard B. Mason (sketch, 1:375, *n.* 8).
[18] William Eustis (sketch, 1:436, *n.* 1) was acting assistant quartermaster (Post Return, December 1834 [NA, RG 94, Fort Gibson]).
[19] John B. Porter, born in Connecticut, was appointed an assistant surgeon in 1833, and promoted to major and surgeon in 1846. He retired in 1862 and died seven years later (Heitman, *Historical Register*, I, 799).
[20] Samuel W. Hales, assistant surgeon of the Dragoons since July 1833, died at Fort Gibson, January 30, 1835 (Heitman, *Historical Register*, I, 488; Gordon, *Compilation of Registers of the Army*, 487, 517, 566).

1:458

Proceedings of a General Court Martial—Sixth Day Trial of Jefferson Davis

Fort Gibson[1] 19th. Feby. 1835

The Court met pursuant to adjournment.

Present.

Bt. Brig. Genl. M. Arbuckle[2] President.

Members.

Bt. Lieut. Col. Burbank.[3] 7th. Inf.
Capt. J. Bean[4] Dragoons
Capt. F. Lee[5] 7th. Inf.
2d. Lieut. T. H. Holmes[6] 7th Inf.
2d. Lieut. R. S. Dix[7] 7th Inf.
Bt. 2d. Lt. F. Britton[8] 7th. Inf.
Bt Majr Geo. Birch[9] 7th. Inf.
Captain Perkins[10] Drags.
1st. Lieut. Rains[11] 7th. Inf.
2d. Lt. R. H. Ross.[12] 7th Inf.
2d. Lieut. R. C. Gatlin[13] 7th. Inf.
Bt. 2d. Lt. A. Montgomery[14] 7th Inf.

1st. Liet, & Adjt. D. S. Miles[15] 7th. Inf. special Judge Advocate.

The accused being asked if he was ready to proceed made the following. Defense marked (A.)

19 FEBRUARY 1835

A

Mr. President and Gentlemen of the Court.

Called on to answer a charge the subject matter of which could be fully Known to none beside myself and him who has appeared before you in the triple character of the offended, the accuser, and the witness.[16] I could but anticipate difficulty in the management of my defence, so circumstanced I must consider myself fortunate that the feeling of accuser, has led the witness for the prosecution into irrelevant statements, against which I could introduce opposing testimony; and I anxiously ask of the Court to give the wide field of evidence which has been opened before them, that patient inquiry which will enable them closely to estimate, how far feeling may have warped the judgement and influenced the reminiscence of the only witness for the prosecution.

The origin of the charge under which I am arraigned was absence from the company parade at Reveillee roll call on the 24th of Dec. 1834. I have shown by Prvt. Decons[17] the orderly who came for me, that I had risen and left my sleeping apartment when he was <sent>[18] to me by Maj. Mason immediately after Reveillee; I have shown by Asst. Surg. <–illegible–> Porter[19] that my health was <–illegible–> broken at that time, that exposure in the discharge of my mornings duties had been injurious; and by Lieut. Northrop[20] I have shown that the weather on that morning was bad; further it has appeared by the evidence of Maj. Mason, that I had in a previous winter suffered from the influence of this climate & feared a like result from the present winter; <–I–> and therefore had a right to expect from my commander, a care similar to that by which he attempted to account for not noticing the absence of Lt. Izard[21] from the Reveillee roll call of the same morning, but when differently treated, and called on to account for my absence from Reveillee, I prefered to defend my course by the Genl. Army Regulations[22] rather than to give an individual explanation, for reasons shown by the evidence of Capt. Perkins and Lieut. Bowman,[23] on the harshness of Maj. Mason's manner to subordinates, and the wounding reception he gave officer's explanations of conduct which <he>[24] (Maj. Mason) deemed censurable, and how was the defence I offered for my conduct received, as far as the recorded testimony shows without any attention being paid to the distinction between good and bad weather, I am answered "it is my order that all officers attend reveillee," though I have shown by Capt. Perkins that no such order existed, and when the witness for the prosecution was questioned as to the order he spoke of, it shrinks in his own hand to an individual requirement of me, though he could not say that I ever had been absent from a Reveillee roll call before whilst on Company duty, and is then left in the no enviable situation of a Commander making a distinction against one officer under him, though in the present case there is before the Court (the assertions of my accuser opposing only) a great weight of evidence to show that my previous con<duct>[24] should have pointed me out rather as an exception to, than as a fit subject for exaction, not that I acknowledge the right to except more than to exact, on the day when I learn that the caprice of a commander can increase or decrease the obligations of my commission, can magnify or diminish the quantum of military offence contained in military acts, I shall cease to consider myself a freeman and no longer feel proud of my sword.

After having received Maj. Mason's reply to the reason I gave him for his not seeing me at Reveillee, though I knew too well the state of his orders to have found any difficulty in giving an answer I forbore to do so, and instead of giving me credit for my silence which my acquaintance will readily believe resulted from military subordination, my accuser seizes upon an isolated meagre interjection as little expressive as any of it's class, and magnifies it into an importance worthy the most significant word in the English language.

In such a word as "hum" the tone and manner with which it is used must det<ermine>[24] entirely the signification, to be mistaken as to the tone and manner is therefore to be mistaken in the meaning, and that the witness for the prosecution has probably mistaken the tone and manner is to be infered from his uncertainty as to the time and position when the word was used, for in the specification to the charge against <me>[18] preferred by the witness for the prosecution, it is stated that I walked off saying "hum," when first called as a witness before the court he states that I said hum immediately after his addressing me and then whirled upon my heel, and when questioned by the accused he states that the interjection was used whilst turning, if then the witness is uncertain as to the time & position, points, on which he might naturally be positive, how much more uncertain must he be as to the tone and manner, points, on which all men are liable (even under the most favorable circumstances) to err.

The very short time between the period of my being required to appear before my immediate commander, and my return from him, together with the silence of the witness on the part of the prosecution which can hardly be supposed to have resulted from any desire to shield the accused, is probably sufficient evidence that his summons to the presence of his commander was promptly obeyed, as well as the order to return to that presence when first leaving it, and who can believe that an officer who obeys with alacrity a summons to the presence of his commander, can go with any other intention than to hear the communication intended for him, and if I left Mj. Mason as appears by his testimony before he had finished speaking to me, does not my unhesitating compliance with his order to return, show that I left him because my presence seemed no longer required, and afford a fair and natural explanation to the question now are you done with me, asked before leaving a second time, a question so well belonging to what had gone before it that the witness to make out his case has been compelled to dwell upon the manner, which as well as the manner of turning round, he has been able to construe into contempt and disrespect, and this too at the very time when he has acknowledged himself to be excited; he who has acknowledged at least in one case to have imagined disrespect, and which case could have been more fully shown if the court had thought proper. If an officer shown to be harsh and disregardful of the feelings of others, irritable and forgetful, which last the court will recollect I offered more fully to show, if such an officer can with the jaundiced eye of passion see in simple questions, and facings about, contemptuous and disrespectful conduct, there can be little security for his subordinates in his official intercourse, the next point in the prosecution was for looking at my accuser, when angrily addressing me, or to adopt his own language staring him full in the face, can it be required of a Gentleman, is it part of the character of a soldier to humble him self beneath the haughty tone, or quail before the angry eye of any man.

The witness for the prosecution has further stated, that I delayed to obey his order of arrest until it was given the third time, and I here particularily feel the embarrassment of my situation; I, the accused, and the witness for the prosecution, my accuser, are the only persons who could fully know the conversation which passed, and as I am compelled by circumstancial evidence to oppose positive testimony, I must ask of the Court that lenity in their comparison which all civilized custom gives to the accused. Sergt. Sample[25] heard Maj. Mason object to the manner I turned from him, then indistinctly heard Maj.

Mason say something, and then heard Maj. Mason order me into arrest, Sergt. Sample though favorably situated saw no disrespectful action, and heard no word of mine. Pvt. Decons also once heard Maj. Mason order me into arrest, it is not probable, had the order been repeated three times in a conversation as short as that which occurred between Maj. Mason and myself, that it would have been heard by one near us, once, and but once, for if that order had been three times <repeated,>[18] at least twice it would have been uttered in a voice sufficiently loud, for all bystanders or passers by that heard it once to hear it twice; again if I was braving the authority of my superior, why was no action seen, no word heard to prove it, there are members on this court who know me too well to believe, that had I been a party to an angry discussion, that mine would have been the only voice unheard; and the calm mood in which Lieut. Northrop found me immediately after the interview with Maj. Mason, forbids the belief even were my character worse than I hope it is considered, that in such a temper, I would forget my own safety so far, as to have withheld obedience from my commander, and to have treated him with contempt and disrespect.

To the general reflections which the witness for the prosecution has made against me I have brought I trust sufficient evidence to refute his accusations, and to show by the peculiarity of his opinions the strong bias of his mind in whatever concerns me, my accuser was asked to state the nature of the derelictions with which he had in general terms charged me, on a subsequent day, he appeared and made a statement relative to the laying of floors in the company Quarters, as this statement was made after due deliberation it must be supposed to have been his strongest case; the evidence of Sergt. Budd[26] places the matter in a light so positively favorable that it cannot fail to have left an impression on the mind of all who heard it, and recollected the testimony of my accuser on the same subject. It may be proper here to state in scrutinizing the evidence of the witness against me, I mean no reflection upon his <—character—> further than as a man biassed by strong feelings, and standing in the attitude of a party to my trial; and I probably do him no more nor less than justice in saying, that I believe his irritation committed him to the course he has taken against me, and that had my self respect allowed me to make to him those explanations which through witnesses I have made to the court, that his course would have been different; and it is but equal justice to myself to say that I felt and feel that his conduct previous to the 24th Dec. 1834 required me to adopt the guarded manner I used on that occasion, and that his illegally confining me to my Quarters, his refusing to extend those limits when I made an application, driving me into complaint to our common superior the presiding officer of this court, gave me little reason to adopt a course of greater confidence.

An experienced officer[27] to whom for the interest he has evinced in me, I shall always acknowledge myself grateful spoke to me a short time before the commencement of my trial, with a view to save me the investigation, I then felt that an examination into the charges should wipe away the discredit which belonged to my arrest, the humble and narrow reputation which a subaltern can acquire by years of the most rigid performance of his duty, is little worth in the wide world of Fame, but yet is something to himself. If I have complied with the first part of the 11th paragraph of the 2d Article Genl. Army Regulations, and my commander has shown a disregard to last part of the same paragraph,[28] then have I by my arrest and charges been injured, and I look to the court for redress. JEFFN DAVIS

1. Lt. Drgs. U. S. A.

The Court being ordered to be cleared, and the whole of the proceedings read over to the Court by the special Judge Advocate, the following sentence was pronounced.

Sentence.

The court, after mature deliberation on the testimony adduced, find the Accused 1st. Lieutenant Jefferson Davis of the Regiment of Dragoons *Guilty* of the Specification exhibited against him, except the words, "highly disrespectful, insubordinate and contemptuous conduct," wherever they occur in the specification. and attach no criminality to the facts of which he is found Guilty.

Not Guilty of the *Charge*, and do therefore acquit *him*.[29]

M. ARBUCKLE

Brigdr. Genl. U. S. Army Presidt. of the Court.

D. S. MILES.

1st. Lieut & Adjt. 7th. Inf. & Special Judge Advocate.

DS, proceedings, ADS, defense (NA, RG 153 Records of the Office of the Judge Advocate General [Army], Court Martial Records, CC–47, 1835); D, typed copy (Walter Lynwood Fleming Collection, New York Public Library). Endorsed: "(Confirmed E. P Gaines) Recd. April 6th. R. Jones."

1 See 1:397, *n.* 1.

2 Matthew Arbuckle (sketch, 1:447, *n.* 3).

3 Sidney Burbank (sketch, 1:195, *n.* 6).

[4] Jesse Bean (sketch, 1:394, *n.* 2).

[5] Francis Lee (sketch, 1:447, *n.* 5).

[6] Theophilus H. Holmes (sketch, 1:447, *n.* 11).

[7] Roger S. Dix (sketch, 1:447, *n.* 7).

[8] Forbes Britton (sketch, 1:447, *n.* 8).

[9] George Birch (sketch, 1:447, *n.* 4).

[10] David Perkins (sketch, 1:410, *n.* 3).

[11] Gabriel J. Rains (sketch, 1:452, *n.* 5).

[12] Richard H. Ross (sketch, 1:447, *n.* 12).

[13] Richard C. Gatlin (sketch, 1:447, *n.* 13).

[14] Alexander Montgomery (sketch, 1:447, *n.* 14).

[15] Dixon S. Miles (sketch, 1:447, *n.* 15).

[16] Richard B. Mason (sketch, 1:375, *n.* 8).

[17] Francis Decons (sketch, 1:455, *n.* 21). See 1:455, p. 364 for his testimony.

[18] Interlined.

[19] John B. Porter (sketch, 1:457, *n.* 19). For his statements, see 1:457, p. 374.

[20] Lucius B. Northrop (sketch, 1:402, *n.* 4). For his testimony, see 1:456, p. 371.

[21] James F. Izard (sketch, 1:447, *n.* 10). See 1:455, p. 368 for his testimony.

[22] For the army regulation on reveille, see 1:454, *n.* 19.

[23] James M. Bowman (sketch, 1:455, *n.* 20). For his testimony, see 1:455, p. 363.

[24] In the margin.

[25] David Sample (sketch, 1:455, *n.* 25). See 1:455, p. 367 for his statements.

[26] John J. Budd (sketch, 1:457, *n.* 16). See 1:457, p. 374 for his testimony.

[27] Probably Matthew Arbuckle (see 1:507).

[28] Article 2, paragraph 11 reads as follows: "In all that concerns the good of the service, the government requires that the superior shall always find in the inferior a passive obedience; and that all orders given, shall be executed with alacrity and good faith; but, in prescribing this kind of obedience, it is understood that orders shall not be manifestly against law or reason; and every superior is strictly enjoined not to injure those under him, by abusive or unbecoming language, or by capricious or tyrannical conduct" (*General Army Regulations* [1825], 15).

[29] The sentence of the court was approved March 15 (1:471).

1:459

Proceedings of a General Court Martial—Sixth Day Trial of Lucius B. Northrop

Editorial Note: With the exception of this, the first day of the Northrop trial, only those days wherein Davis is mentioned or testifies will be printed. An exception has been made of the first day because the charges and specifications made against Northrop are necessary to understand the subsequent Davis involvement.

Fort Gibson[1] 19th. February 1835

The Court met in continuation of its Session.

Present.

Bt. Brigd. Genl. M. Arbuckle[2] President.

Members.

Bt. Lieut. Col. Burbank[3] 7th Inf. Captain J. Bean[4] Drags.

Captain F. Lee[5] 7th Inf.
2d. Lt. T. H. Holmes[6] 7th Inf.
2d. Lt. R. S. Dix[7] 7th Inf.
Bt. 2d. Lt. F. Britton[8] 7th Inf.
Bt. Majr. Geo. Birch[9] 7th Inf.
Captain Perkins[10] Drags.

1st. Lieut. Rains[11] 7th Inf.
2d. Lieut. R. H. Ross[12] 7th Inf.
2d. Lieut. R. C. Gatlin[13] 7th Inf.
Bt. 2d. Lt. A. Montgomery[14] 7th Inf.

1st Lieut & Adjt. D. S. Miles[15] 7th Inf. Special Judge Advocate.

2d. Lieut. L. B. Northrop[16] of Dragoons was brought before the court and asked if he objected to any of the members named in the above orders and replying in the affirmative: that he objected to Capt. Perkins of Dragoons. for the following reason. "I object to Capt. Perkins for this reason, that he has several times expressed himself to me with much warmth relative to certain treatment which has been received by him from Major Mason[17] in interviews connected with points of duty. He last sunday took occasion to remark to me, that he had no irritable recollections of Majr. Mason and had entirely forgiven him, that it was with great pain he found himself compelled to give evidence relative to this subject or say anything injurious to him. This evinces an influence of feeling which I do not wish in any judge of my affairs."

The Court was cleared & the objection over-ruled.

The Court was then <duly>[18] Sworn in the presence of the accused and proceeded to the trial of 2d. Lieut. L. B. Northrop of Dragoons on the following charges & Specifications and "Additional Charges & Specifications, prefered against him by Maj. R. B. Mason of Drags.

Charge 1st.
Disobedience of Orders.

Specification. In this that 2d. Lieut. L. B. Northrop of the Regiment of Dragoons did, on or about the 20th. day of December 1834, absent himself from a working party,[19] of which he had the immediate command, engaged in completing the Quarters, near Fort Gibson, of Company F, Regt. Dragoons, contrary to a verbal order duly communicated to him the day previous by his commanding officer Majr. R. B. Mason through Lt. W. Eustis[20] the Actg. Adjt.

Charge 2d.
Breach of Arrest.

Specification. In this that the said 2d. Lieut. L. B. Northrop after having been, on or about the 20th. day of December 1834, duly arrested and ordered to confine himself to his quarters, situated in the Dragoon Camp near Fort Gibson,[21] did, on the same day without any authority or permission, leave his quarters and go off beyond the limits of the aforesaid camp.[22]

By order of Majr. R. B. Mason
Sig[ned] W. Eustis
Lt & A[cting] Adjt.

Witnesses
Majr. Mason Dragoons.
Lt. Eustis

Additional Charges & Specifications.

Charge 1st.

Conduct unbecoming an Officer and a Gentleman.

Specification. In this, that 2d. Lieut. L. B. Northrop of the Regiment of Dragoons, did, at the Dragoon Camp near Fort Gibson, continue on the sick report, when he was able to do duty, from about the 8th. to the 24th. of Jany. 1835 inclusive, thereby avoiding his duty and throwing upon his Brother Officers that part which he himself should have performed.

Charge 2d.

Disobedience of Orders.

Specification 1st. In this that the said 2d. Lieut. L B. Northrop, having been ordered on or about the afternoon of the 24th. of January 1835, at the Dragoon Camp near Fort Gibson, by Majr. R. B. Mason through Lt. Bowman[23] the Actg. Adjt. to report for duty in his (Lt. Northrop's) company, the next morning; did disobey said order.

Specification 2d. In this, that the said 2d. Lieut. L. B. Northrop, at the Dragoon Camp near Fort Gibson, when ordered to duty by Majr. R. B. Mason through Lt. Bowman the Actg. Adjt. on or about the 25th. of January 1835, and when in like manner he was detailed to go on duty on or about the 25th. of Jany. 1835, as the Officer of the day, did, refuse obedience to the said order & said detail.

signed. R. B. Mason.
Majr. Dragoons

To which the accused pleaded as follows.
To the specification 1st. charge, Not Guilty,
To 1st. Charge Not Guilty.
To the specification of 2d. Charge Not Guilty,
To 2d. Charge—Not Guilty.
To specification of the 1st. additional charge Not Guilty.

To 1st. Additional charge Not Guilty.
To the 1st. specification of 2d. additional charge I admit this fact.
To the 2d. Specification of 2d. additional Charge I admit the latter part.
To 2d. additional Charge–Not Guilty.

The Court adjourned to meet at 10 o'clock tomorrow morning.

DS (NA, RG 153 Records of the Office of the Judge Advocate General [Army], Court Martial Records, CC–54, 1835), 106.

[1] See 1:397, *n.* 1.
[2] Matthew Arbuckle (sketch, 1:447, *n.* 3).
[3] Sidney Burbank (sketch, 1:195, *n.* 6).
[4] Jesse Bean (sketch, 1:394, *n.* 2).
[5] Francis Lee (sketch, 1:447, *n.* 5).
[6] Theophilus H. Holmes (sketch, 1:447, *n.* 11).
[7] Roger S. Dix (sketch, 1:447, *n.* 7).
[8] Forbes Britton (sketch, 1:447, *n.* 8).
[9] George Birch (sketch, 1:447, *n.* 4).
[10] David Perkins (sketch, 1:410, *n.* 3).
[11] Gabriel J. Rains (sketch, 1:452, *n.* 5).
[12] Richard H. Ross (sketch, 1:447, *n.* 12).
[13] Richard C. Gatlin (sketch, 1:447, *n.* 13).
[14] Alexander Montgomery (sketch, 1:447, *n.* 14).
[15] Dixon S. Miles (sketch, 1:447, *n.* 15).
[16] Lucius B. Northrop (sketch, 1:402, *n.* 4).
[17] Richard B. Mason (sketch, 1:375, *n.* 8).
[18] Interlined.
[19] Northrop and Davis left the construction site and went to a race track behind the quarters to watch a horse race (1:467, p. 391).
[20] William Eustis (sketch, 1:436, *n.* 1).
[21] Camp Jackson (see 1:397, *n.* 3).
[22] Northrop left his quarters and went, as was his custom, to Fort Gibson to eat dinner (1:467, p. 392).
[23] James M. Bowman (sketch, 1:455, *n.* 20).

EXTRACT

Proceedings of a General Court Martial—Eighth Day Trial of Lucius B. Northrop 1:460

Editorial Note: Northrop[1] attempts to demonstrate by questioning Mason[2] that other officers disobeyed orders and were absent from the construction site, but that they, unlike himself, were not arrested.

Fort Gibson[3] 21st February 1835

Question by the Accused. At the time you observed my abscence: did you not see that Capt. Bean[4] and Lt. Davis were absent from their parties, looking at the race?

Answer. I only observed the abscence of the officers of Company's

E & F[5] and I sent an order to arrest them both, but the Commandant of Company E excused himself, to the Adj't. Lt. Eustis,[6] by saying he had left an officer[7] in charge of the party, which I deemed an ample & sufficient excuse, as that was all my order required: though when I spoke to that officer, about his abscence he acknowledged that he was there, when the Commandant of Company E, went away, but that he did not know he was left in charge of the party, and therefore said nothing more to him on the subject. If the officers of company K[8] were absent it escaped my observation, which I hardly think it would have done, if both of them had been absent at the same time on that occasion. I think there were two officers for duty in Company K, at that time and it is therefore probable that Capt. Bean was on the race ground for aught I know.

DS (NA, RG 153 Records of the Office of the Judge Advocate General [Army], Court Martial Records, CC–54, 1835), 106.

1 Lucius B. Northrop (sketch, 1:402, *n.* 4).

2 Richard B. Mason (sketch, 1:375, *n.* 8).

3 See 1:397, *n.* 1.

4 Jesse Bean (sketch, 1:394, *n.* 2).

5 Davis commanded Company E from November 11 to December 24, 1834 (1:446). Northrop commanded Company F (NA, RG 153, Court Martial Records, CC–54, 1835, p. 22).

6 William Eustis (sketch, 1:436, *n.* 1).

7 James M. Bowman (sketch, 1:455, *n.* 20) was the officer that Davis left in charge (NA, RG 153, Court Martial Records, CC–54, 1835, p. 24).

8 The commander of Company K was Captain Jesse Bean; First Lieutenant James F. Izard was the other officer (Post Return, December 1834 [NA, RG 94, Fort Gibson]).

EXTRACT

1:461 Proceedings of a General Court Martial—Ninth Day Trial of Lucius B. Northrop

Editorial Note: Lieutenant Eustis,[1] a witness for the prosecution, testifies as to Northrop's[2] disobedience of orders and his subsequent arrest.

Fort Gibson[3] 23d. Feby. 1835

Quest. by the accused. What directions did you receive relative to Lt. Davis and what reply did he make to you?

Answer. I was directed to say to Lieut. Davis and Lieut. Northrop, that they disobeyed the order which was given the day previous, requiring a commissioned officer to be constantly present with the working parties, that they therefore would consider themselves in arrest and confine themselves to their quarters; when I communicated the first part of the order to Lieut. Davis, namely, "That he disobeyed the orders of the day before," he replied that he did not disobey them, having left Lieut. Bowman[4] with the party.

DS (NA, RG 153 Records of the Office of the Judge Advocate General [Army], Court Martial Records, CC-54, 1835), 106.

[1] William Eustis (sketch, 1:436, *n.* 1).
[2] Lucius B. Northrop (sketch, 1:402, *n.* 4).
[3] See 1:397, *n.* 1.
[4] James M. Bowman (sketch, 1:455, *n.* 20).

EXTRACT

Proceedings of a General Court Martial—Tenth Day Trial of Lucius B. Northrop 1:462

Editorial Note: In testimony relating to the charge that Northrop[1] had been on sick report when he should have been on duty, Assistant Surgeon Porter[2] mentioned Davis.

Fort Gibson[3] 24th. Feby. 1835

I attended on Mr. Northrop during some of the last days in December and until the 5th. of Jany. I visited Lieut. Northrop last on the 5th. of January and found him in the tent of either Lieut. Izard[4] or Lt. Davis. at that time I told him, that he wanted no more attendance, and that I should not see him again unless sent for; but that he better take good care of himself for some days, or for some time I dont recollect exactly the expression.

DS (NA, RG 153 Records of the Office of the Judge Advocate General [Army], Court Martial Records, CC-54, 1835), 106.

[1] Lucius B. Northrop (sketch, 1:402, *n.* 4).
[2] John B. Porter (sketch, 1:457, *n.* 19).
[3] See 1:397, *n.* 1.
[4] James F. Izard (sketch, 1:447, *n.* 10).

25 FEBRUARY 1835

EXTRACT

1:463 Proceedings of a General Court Martial—Eleventh Day—Trial of Lucius B. Northrop

Editorial Note: Lieutenant Bowman,[1] a witness for the prosecution, testifies as to the arrest of Northrop[2] and as to whether or not he (Bowman) had been left in charge of Davis' company.

Fort Gibson[3] 25th. Feby. 1835

Quest. by Accused. On the 20th. Decemb. 1834, when Major Mason[4] sent after Lt. Davis and myself were you at the quarters or not at that time?

Answer. I was there that day, I dont know what time Major Mason sent for him.

Quest. by the accused. Describe the whole conversation between you and major Mason, when he sent for you and asked you about being at the quarters on the 20th. when he sent for Lieut Davis & myself?

Answer. Major Mason sent for me and asked me if I considered myself left by Lt. Davis in charge of the working party. I told him at first I did not, but on reflecting I had had a conversation with Lieut. Davis that morning about <one>[5] or the other being absent from the quarters, from which I had no doubt Lieut. Davis did consider me in command of the party.

DS (NA, RG 153 Records of the Office of the Judge Advocate General [Army], Court Martial Records, CC-54, 1835), 106.

[1] James M. Bowman (sketch, 1:455, *n.* 20).

[2] Lucius B. Northrop (sketch, 1:402, *n.* 4).

[3] See 1:397, *n.* 1.

[4] Richard B. Mason (sketch, 1:375, *n.* 8).

[5] Interlined.

ABSTRACT

1:464 Post Return

Fort Gibson,[1] February [28,] 1835

Lists First Lieutenant Jefferson Davis, Company E, Dragoons, present at the post. Remarks: "In arrest." [2]

Meeting of Commanches and Dragoons

I Jefferson Davis of the state of Mississippi appointed a First Lieut. in the Regiment of Dragoons in the Army of the United States, do solemnly swear, or affirm, that I will bear true allegiance to the United States of America, and that I will serve them honestly and faithfully against all their enemies or opposers whatsoever; and observe and obey the orders of the President of the United States, and the orders of the Officers appointed over me, according to the Rules and Articles for the government of the Armies of the United States.

Sworn to and subscribed before me, at Port Gibson this 26 day of March 1835

Jeffn. Davis
1 L. Drgs. U. S. A.

Jas H. Maury Justice of the Peace

Oath of Allegiance

DS (NA, RG 94 Records of the Adjutant General's Office, Post Returns, Fort Gibson), 3. Signed: "W. Seawell 1st Lieut. 7th Infy. Aid de Camp. M. Arbuckle Brigdr Genl. U. S. Army Commdg." Endorsed: "Recd 2 April 1835."

[1] See 1:397, *n.* 1.

[2] See 1:454 for charges brought against Davis.

To Richard B. Mason

1:465

Dragoon Quarters Fort Gibson[1] 1st. March 1835

SIR[2]

During the Suspension from the duties of my Commission which necessarily follows my late trial before a Court Martial,[3] I wish to obtain a leave of absence from the Commanding General of this District,[4] and respectfully ask your Sanction to such an application I am Sir Your Most obt. Servt (Signed) JEFFERSON DAVIS
1st. Lieut. Drags. U. S. A.

[E] There is no objection on my part to granting the indulgence to Lieut. Davis that he asks, his application to the Commanding General will therefore meet with my approbation[5] (Signed)

R. B. MASON
Majr. Dragoons *Comdg.*

L, copy (NA, RG 393 Records of United States Army Continental Commands, 1821–1920, Letters Received, 2nd and 7th Military Departments, January–May, 1835). Addressed: "To Majr. R. B. Mason Comdg. Squadn. Drags. near Fort Gibson." Endorsed: "True Copy W. Seawell Aid de Camp & Actg. Asst. Adjt. Genl. Received 2d. March 1835." Enclosed: Arbuckle to Jones, March 10, 1835 (1:470).

[1] Probably Camp Jackson (1:397, *n.* 3).

[2] Richard B. Mason (sketch, 1:375, *n.* 8).

[3] See 1:454–58 for the court martial proceedings.

[4] The commanding general was Matthew Arbuckle (sketch, 1:447, *n.* 3).

[5] The decision of the court was made February 19 (1:458) but was not approved by the Western Department commander until March 15 (1:471).

To Matthew Arbuckle

1:466

Fort Gibson Arks.[1] 2d. March 1835

SIR[2]

That I may give that attention, to individual interests, which my future welfare requires, and which family transactions imperiously demand of me to render; I respectfully solicit from you the indulgence of a leave of absence for forty days.[3] I have the honor to be Your Mo. obt. Servt (Signed) JEFFERSON DAVIS

1st. Lieut. Drgs. U. S. A.

L, copy (NA, RG 393 Records of United States Army Continental Commands, 1821–1920, Letters Received, 2nd and 7th Military Departments, January–May, 1835). Addressed: "To Genl. M. Arbuckle Comdg. S[outh] W[estern] Frontier Fort Gibson A[rkansas]." Endorsed: "True Copy W. Seawell Aid de Camp & Actg. Asst. Adjt. Genl. Received 2d. March 1835." Enclosed: Arbuckle to Jones, March 10, 1835 (1:470). Printed: G. Foreman, *Advancing the Frontier*, 47.

[1] See 1:397, *n.* 1.

[2] Matthew Arbuckle (sketch, 1:447, *n.* 3).

[3] See 1:474 for the granting of Davis' requested leave of absence.

EXTRACT

1:467

Proceedings of a General Court Martial—Fourteenth Day—Trial of Lucius B. Northrop

Fort Gibson[1] 2d. March 1835

Lieut. Davis Regt. of Dragoons a witness for the accused[2] after being duly sworn answered as follows.

Quest. by Accused. What do you know of the charge of Disobedience of orders and of the circumstances connected with my abscence?

Answer. About the time specified in the 1st. Charge[3] I received a verbal order from the Actg. Adjt. Lt. Eustis,[4] to take charge of the men off duty and set them to laying the floor of their Company quarters and was also directed that one officer of each company should remain constantly with the men, until the quarters were completed. I considered it, as a standing order or a Regulation, enjoining certain duties upon officers during certain circumstances and that a failure to perform those duties, with proper zeal & fidelity would have subjected the party to an accusation of neglect, though unless accompanied by a refusal I should not have considered it, a disobedience. Just before Lieut. Northrop was sent for by the Adjt. he approached me from the direction of Co. F.'s quarters, (which he then commanded) I being just in rear of the quarters now occupied by officers and invited me to go with him to the race track, proposing as a reason why we should go there, instead of looking at the race where we stood, that he wished to make a trial of skill with me in selecting the fleeter horse, from the conversation and manner (for I dont recollect exactly what words were spoken) I infered his intention to return in a short time. As I was returning with him from the track, he told me he had left a book in the company quarters which he had taken there, to read whilst he remained with the party at work upon those quarters. That he would return with me to the quarters and get it.

Quest. by Accused. Did not Lt. Eustis come to us almost immediately after we got on the race track?

Answer. Very soon. I dont think we had been there over ten minutes.

Quest. by accused. On going to get this book was I not returning to my quarters in arrest?

Answer. He informed me that he had been arrested by Lieut. Eustis, while on the race track, that he would go by the Company Quarters and get the book referred to, before going to his own quarters.

Quest. by Accused. Were the officers in the habit of remaining in the immediate presence of the working men? was it not considered a compliance with the order to be about in the neighborhood of the quarters?

Answer. The officers were not in the habit of remaining constantly in the rooms, where the men were working; by remaining about the quarters, that were about being built I should infer from their conduct, that they considered the letter of the order complied with.

Quest. by accused. What do you know of my reason for declining Major Mason's[5] offer to withdraw the charges which he first prefered against me? state the grounds of those reasons?

Answer. I recollect that Lt. Northrop told me, that the Commandg. Officer of the Squadron of Dragoons (Majr. Mason) who had prefered charges against him, had sent the actg. Adjt. Lt. Eustis, to say to him Lt. Northrop, that if he Majr. Mason, had known that he Lt. Northrop did not intend to break his arrest, that he would not have prefered the charges against him, that he had not intended to prefer charges against him for the first offence alone and that if he Lt. Northrop would now state that the breach of arrest of which he was charged had not been wilfully and knowingly committed he would withdraw the charges made against him. Lieut. Northrop told me, that he had sent a message to the effect, that he did not consider it a breach of arrest, when he went to Dinner and that he considered Major Mason's requirement for a reiteration as exacting from him Lt. Northrop an act of self humiliation, or words to that effect. I can add after the conversation refered to, Lieut. Northrop told me that he would answer Majr. Mason that he had fully given his reply and that he had no other to give. And I also recollect when returning from the race track on the day Lieut. Northrop was arrested, that a conversation took place between us, upon the nature of an arrest: that it was my opinion and I believe his, that except in most flagrant cases an officer could not be subjected to close confinement and that Lieut. Northrop's was not one of the cases which appeared as exceptions in the order of the President prohibiting such close confinements.[6]

DS (NA, RG 153 Records of the Office of the Judge Advocate General [Army], Court Martial Records, CC–54, 1835), 106.

[1] For Fort Gibson, see 1:397, *n.* 1.

[2] Lucius B. Northrop (sketch, 1:402, *n.* 4).

[3] The time specified in the first charge was on or about December 24, 1834 (see 1:454, p. 358).

[4] William Eustis (sketch, 1:436, *n.* 1).

[5] Richard B. Mason (sketch, 1:375, *n.* 8).

[6] General Order No. 37, Headquarters of the Army, April 28, 1832, stated: "The President of the United States has had under consideration and review the proceedings of the General Court Martial in the case of Lieut. [Charles L. C.] Minor of the 3rd. Regiment of Infantry, Assistant Quarter Master who was tried at Jefferson Barracks in January last on charges preferred against him by Brevet Brigadier General [Henry] Atkinson, then commanding at Jefferson Barracks and on which charges Lieut. Minor was most honorably acquitted by the Court.

"The President in the examination of these proceedings has seen with regret, a severity on the part of General Atkinson towards Lieut. Minor, while under arrest and awaiting the assembling of the Court, wholly unprecedented in the American Service, in allowing Lieut. Minor to remain *in close confinement* for the long period of one hundred and eight days and this too without any apparent necessity for such extraordinary rigor towards him. . . . Under a full view of the facts disclosed in the trial the President has Commanded the General-in-Chief to make known his dissatisfaction, as above expressed and to direct that in cases where Officers may in future be put in arrest that *close* confinement is not to be resorted to unless under circumstances of an aggravated character and when the arrested Officer should exhibit evidence of an utter disregard to the station he holds" (NA, RG 94, General Orders, VI, 37–38).

9 MARCH 1835

From Peter Hagner 1:468

Sɪʀ, March 5th 1835

Your account for disbursements during the 3d. qr. 1834[1] has been audited and reported to the 2d. Comptroller[2] for his decision thereon, by whom it has been returned, exhibiting a balance of $1280.09 due from you to the U. States—agreeing with your own a/c current.

Respectfully, Yr. ob. St PETER HAGNER,[3]
Aud.

LbC (NA, RG 217 Records of the United States General Accounting Office, Third Auditor's Office, Miscellaneous Letters Sent, LXV, 302). Addressed: "Lt. *Jeffn. Davis* a[cting] a[ssistant] q[uarter] m[aster], Camp Jones, near Fort Gibson, Ark."

[1] Davis' account for disbursements was transmitted to the quartermaster general in 1:429.

[2] The second comptroller was James B. Thornton (sketch, 1:244, *n.* 1).

[3] Peter Hagner (sketch, 1:199, *n.* 5).

EXTRACT

Proceedings of a General Court Martial—Nineteenth Day—Trial of Lucius B. Northrop 1:469

Fort Gibson[1] 9th. March 1835

Lt. Davis Regt. Drags. a witness for the accused was again call'd.

Quest. by Accused.[2] Did you, or not tell me a short time previous to this trial that Dr. Porter[3] had sometime before taken occasion to speak to you, on the subject of his report to Major Mason[4] concerning me? if so, state what he said to you on the subject of his having made an examination of me previous to this report?

Answer. I did inform Lieut. Northrop that when on a visit to Dr. Porter, he spoke to me in a friendly manner of a report he had made to Majr. Mason relative to the health of Lieut. Northrop and said to the effect that he had been call'd by Major Mason, about the 24th. Jany. last, to state whether Lieut. Northrop's health was such, that he should report <him>[5] for duty, he said he had replied that Lieut. Northrop was fit for duty: that his reply was founded on the observations he had made of Lieut. Northrop when passing about the post; that he had not examined him (Lt. Northrop) when he made the report, and that his written report to Mjr. Mason showed that he had made no such examination: that he had subsequently examined Lieut. Northrop and that his professional opinion formed after the examination, was the reverse of that expressed in the report he had made to Majr. Mason and which was founded upon grounds too loose for a medical opinion. I think it probable I did tell Lieut. Northrop, before his trial commenced of this conversation.

Quest. by Accused. How many wolf fights were there at the Dragoon Camp? [6]

Answer. I know but of two.

Quest. by Accused. State whether I was at the first? also whether I was at the second?

Answer. I saw Lieut. Northrop at the first, of the only two wolf fights I have known to take place at the Camp. I am quite positive he was not at the second. My recollection of his abscence being confirmed by the account I gave him of incidents which occur'ed at that fight.

Quest. by accused. How long have you known me & what do you know of my readiness and efficiency in performing duty of any sort?

Answer. I have known Lieut. Northrop since the Fall of 1833. I have never seen him avoid duty & I recollect his voluntary performing a hard service which with such general observations, have induced me, in believing him a very active and Effecient Officer.

Quest. by Accused. What do you know of that part of my character which relates to the compromising of opinion? or the feigning of what did not exist?

Answer. I have always thought Lieut. Northrop rather pertinacious than yeilding in his opinions and his strict adherence to veracity I have considered a marked trait in his character, from my opinion of his character for veracity, which I have just stated, I consider him incapable of feigning anything.

Quest. by Spl. Judge Advocate,[7] *(suggested by the accuser).*[4] Have you or have you not known the accused to avoid duty, on the last summers expidition,[8] under the plea of sickness and at the same time, engage in sports, much more arduous than the duties required of him as an officer and did you not make remarks upon it, at the time or shortly thereafter to Major Mason and to Capt. Perkins? [9]

Answer. I recollect on the Campaign last summer either Capt. Perkins or Majr. Mason told me that Lieut. Northrop had left the Column, as he said, because he was sick; that I saw Lieut. Northrop turn out into the prairie after a Deer as I supposed, that I then thought that if Lieut. Northrop was able to hunt Deer, he was able to ride in the column: from the manner in which his leaving it, was reported to me, I supposed it <to>[5] have been the result of pique against Capt. Perkins.[10] My opinion of Lieut. Northrop then, was much the same that it is now and had he then told me he was sick, I should have believed him as soon as I would now.

Quest. by accused. Did you see me hunt, or had I my Gun, when I left the Column? did I go any distance from the column? at the time refered to in the previous question?

Answer. The first time I recollect of seeing Lieut. Northrop on that occasion he was turning off from the rear of the column: I was riding near the head of it, I have no recollection now, whether he had a Gun or not, nor do I know how far he went from the column, though I recollect that an orderly Bugler was sent after him, that the orderly Bugler was sometime absent and that Lieut. Northrop did not return with the Bugler. I saw him for a very short time after leaving the column and did not see him hunt.

Quest. by Accused. Was not this <the>[5] day that Private Loper[11] of E. Company, kill'd a fat buck? did your informant state that I left the head of the column to hunt or for what other cause? or did he say that I said I was <on the>[5] sick report and therefore took advantage of the custom of the sick, which was to ride separate?

Answer. I think private Loper of Company E, of which I was a Subaltern, kill'd a deer on the day of the occurrence above refered to, and that he kill'd it near the trace of our Column. I do not recollect that any thing was said about hunting, as a reason why Lieut. Northrop left the Column, but that he left it (ostensibly) because he was on the sick report, though perhaps, the real reason, so ran my information was the pique against Capt. Perkins. The custom of the sick Officers was to ride separate.

Quest. by Accused. Do you know of any of the arduous sports refered to by the accuser in his question, as enjoyed by me, while indisposed?

Answer. Hunting was the only sport, I knew of on the Campaign, chasing Buffalo on horse back was the most common. I do not recollect to have seen Lieut Northrop chasing Buffalo, when he was either sick or well. and I think from what I know of Lieut. Northrop's attention to his horses, that he seldom if he ever did, join in a Buffalo chase.

DS (NA, RG 153 Records of the Office of the Judge Advocate General [Army], Court Martial Records, CC–54, 1835), 106.

[1] See 1:397, *n.* 1.

[2] Lucius B. Northrop (sketch, 1:402, *n.* 4).

[3] John B. Porter (sketch, 1:457, *n.* 19).

[4] Richard B. Mason (sketch, 1:375, *n.* 8).

[5] Interlined.

[6] Camp Jackson (see 1:397, *n.* 3).

[7] The special judge advocate was First Lieutenant Dixon S. Miles (sketch, 1:447, *n.* 15).

[8] The expedition to the Pawnee Picts (see 1:420, *n.* 6).

[9] David Perkins (sketch, 1:410, *n.* 3).

[10] For Northrop's relationship with Perkins, see also 1:459, p. 383.

[11] Darius Loper of Company E was enlisted by First Lieutenant David Perkins July 7, 1833, in Buffalo, New York, for a period of three years (Semiannual Muster Roll, December 31, 1834 [NA, RG 94, U.S. Dragoons, Company E]).

1:470

Matthew Arbuckle to Roger Jones

Head Quarters South Western Frontier
Fort Gibson,[1] March 10th. 1835

SIR,[2]

I have the honor to report, that I have this day granted a leave of Absence for forty days, to 1st Lieut. Jefferson Davis of the Regiment of U. S. Dragoons, to take effect from this date. His application and Major Mason's[3] approval are herewith enclosed.

Lieut. Davis has recently been tried by the General Court martial[4] which is now in session at this post, and as the leave of absence[5] I have granted him, will, in any event not much exceed the period when the result of his trial can be received for publication here and being convinced of the necessity of his attention to his private concerns, will, I trust, be sufficient excuse for the responsibility I have taken in granting him this indulgence He has placed his resignation[6] in my hands, to be forwarded to you, in the event of his not returning here at the expiration of his leave of Absence. I am Sir, Very respectfully. Your Obdt. Srvt. (Signed) M. ARBUCKLE[7]
Brig Gen U S A

LbC (NA, RG 393 Records of United States Army Continental Commands, 1821–1920, Headquarters, Southwestern Frontier, Letters Sent, November 1834–May 1836, NA LIII, 63—formerly Fort Gibson, Southwestern Frontier, Letters Sent, November 1834–May 1836, Book 110). Addressed: "To, Brgdr. Genl. R. Jones, Adjt Genl. Washington City." Enclosures: Davis to Mason, March 1, 1835 (1:465); Davis to Arbuckle, March 2, 1835 (1:466).

[1] See 1:397, *n.* 1.

[2] Roger Jones (sketch, 1:123, *n.* 6).

[3] Richard B. Mason (sketch, 1:375, *n.* 8).

[4] The court martial of Davis was concluded February 19 (1:458), but the sentence of the court was not approved until March 15 (1:471).

[5] See 1:474 for further evidence of Davis' leave of absence.

[6] Davis' resignation is 1:476, Enclosure 1, and was transmitted to the Adjutant General's Office May 12.

[7] Matthew Arbuckle (sketch, 1:447, *n.* 3).

Order No. 10

1:471

Head Quarters West. Dept. Asst. Adjt. General's office
Memphis Tennessee March 15th. 1835

I. At a General Court Martial, which convened at Fort Gibson,[1] pursuant to West. Dept. order No "1"[2] of the present year, and of which Brig. General M Arbuckle,[3] is president, was arraigned 1st. Lieut. Jefferson Davis, of the Regt. of Dragoons, on the following charge and specification viz:

Charge

Conduct subversive of good order and military discipline: Spec—I[n] this, that 1st. Lieut. Jefferson Davis, of the Regt. Dragoons on or about the morning of the 24th. day of December 1834, at the Dragoon camp,[4] near Fort Gibson, upon being sent for by Major Mason,[5] his immediate commanding officer; and Spoken to as to his absence on that morning from the Revielee roll call of his compy, did reply in these words, or words of like meaning—Because I was not out of my tent, and the Regulation requires when it raines the rolls shall be called in quarters by chiefs of Squads"[6]—and upon "Major Mason's saying to him, you know it is my orders that all officers of this command attend the Revielee roll call of their respective companies" the said Lieut. Davis did in a highly disrespectful, insubordinate and contemptuous manner, abruptly turn upon his heel and walk off "saying at the same time Hum" and furthermore, being ordered back by Major Mason and told that he (Major Mason) was not in the habit of receiving Such treatment from officers when speaking to them on a point of duty, and that he (Lieut. Davis) would consider himself in arrest and go to his Quarters; whereupon the said Lieut Davis stared Major Mason, full in the face, without showing any intention of obeying the order of arrest, and upon Major Masons repeating the order of arrest, the said Lieut. Davis still staring Major Mason in the face, did in a disrespectful and contemptuous manner ask, Now, are you done with me, and did not obey the order to go to his quarters in arrest, untill after Major Mason had peremptorily repeated it the third time

To the Specification the accused pleaded "Not guilty"

To the charge he pleaded "Not guilty"

The Court after the most mature deliberation on the testimony adduced, find the accused, 1st. Lieut. Jefferson Davis of the Regiment of Dragoons, guilty of the specification exhibited "against him except the words highly disrespectful insubordinate and contemptuous conduct" wherever they occur in the specification; and attach no criminality to the facts of which he is found guilty"

Not guilty of the charge

And do therefore acquit him

II. The General[7] confirms the decision of the Court in the case of 1st. Lieut. Jefferson Davis; he will resume his sword and return to duty with his company By order of Major General Gaines

G. A. McC[8]

A[ide-] D[e-] C[amp]

LbCS (NA, RG 393 Records of United States Army Continental Commands, 1821–1920, Orders and Special Orders Received from the Adjutant General's Office, Headquarters Western Department, Order Book X, 35–37); DS, printed (NA, RG 94 Records of the Adjutant General's Office, Western Department Orders, CCLXXIV, 471); DS, printed (NA, RG 153 Records of the Office of the Judge Advocate General [Army], Court Martial Records, CC–47, 1835); D, typed copy (Walter Lynwood Fleming Collection, New York Public Library).

1 See 1:397, *n.* 1.

2 Order No. 1 is printed as 1:447.

3 Matthew Arbuckle (sketch, 1:447, *n.* 3).

4 See 1:397, *n.* 3.

5 Richard B. Mason (sketch, 1:375, *n.* 8).

6 See 1:454, *n.* 19 for the regulation.

7 Edmund P. Gaines (sketch, 1:301, *n.* 3).

8 George A. McCall (sketch, 1:301, *n.* 2).

ABSTRACT

1:472

Proceedings of a General Court Martial— Twenty-second Day—Trial of Lucius B. Northrop

[Fort Gibson,[1]] March 16, 1835

Second Lieutenant Lucius B. Northrop[2] answers to the charge of disobedience of orders[3] and refers to Davis' testimony[4] as evidence that there was no willful intention to disobey. Although Northrop—

the only officer in his company for duty—was ordered to remain with the men of his company who were on a working detail, he left his post and went to the race track. Davis' testimony supports, by inference, Northrop's contention that although he went to the track as charged, he intended to be absent for only a short time. While Northrop was gone, Major R. B. Mason,[5] the commanding officer, noted his absence and ordered his arrest. Davis' testimony seemed to prove that Northrop's arrest was ordered without proper investigation. Davis' statements of March 2 are also used by Northrop to support his claim that no breach of arrest was intended when Northrop left his quarters to go to dinner. In response to the charge of conduct unbecoming an officer and a gentleman,[3] Northrop cites Davis' testimony of March 9[6] to prove that before he reported for duty he was not fully examined by Surgeon John B. Porter,[7] that he was not present at a wolf fight while on sick call in January 1835, and that although he left the Dragoon column while on sick call in the summer of 1834, he did not go hunting.

The court finds Northrop guilty of neglect of duty, breach of arrest and disobedience of orders, but not guilty of unbecoming conduct. He is sentenced to be cashiered, but the court recommends the sentence be remitted.

DS (NA, RG 153 Records of the Office of the Judge Advocate General [Army], Court Martial Records, CC–54, 1835), 106. Signed: "M. Arbuckle Brigdr. Genl. U. S. Army Presidt. of the Ct. D. S. Miles 1st. Lt & Adj. 7. Inf. & Sp[ecia]l Judge Ad vocate G[eneral] C[ourt] Martl." Endorsed: "Recd. April 27th. 1835. Respectfully Submitted. R. Jones Adjt. Sentence approved but remitted. L[ewis] C[ass] War Dept. Apl. 30. 1835 Returned with the proceedings of the Ct. of Inq[uiry] in the case of [torn] Col. Mason this 20th. Mar. 37." Transmitted: Miles to McCall, March 22, 1835 (NA, RG 153 Records of the Office of the Judge Advocate General [Army], Court Martial Records, CC–54, 1835).

1 See 1:397, *n.* 1.

2 Lucius B. Northrop (sketch, 1:402, *n.* 4).

3 See 1:459 for the charges and specifications brought against Northrop.

4 See 1:467 for Davis' testimony.

5 Richard B. Mason (sketch, 1:375, *n.* 8).

6 See 1:469.

7 John B. Porter (sketch, 1:457, *n.* 19).

Oath of Allegiance 1:473

[Port Gibson,[1] Mississippi, March 26, 1835]

I Jefferson Davis of the state of *Mississippi*[2] appointed a First Lieut.

in the Regiment of Dragoons in the Army of the United States, do solemnly swear, or affirm, that I will bear true allegiance to the United States of America, and that I will serve them honestly and faithfully against all their enemies or opposers whatsoever; and observe and obey the orders of the President of the United States,[3] and the orders of the Officers appointed over me, according to the Rules and Articles for the government of the Armies of the United States.

Jeffn. Davis 1. L [ieutenant] *Drgs. U. S. A.*[4]

Sworn to and subscribed before me, at *Port Gibson* this *26* day of *March* 18*35* *Jas H Maury*[5] Justice of the Peace[6]

Printed form, filled in and signed (NA, RG 94 Records of the Adjutant General's Office, Letters Received, D-59, 1835). Endorsed: "Received. April. 15th."

[1] Port Gibson, some twenty-eight miles south of Vicksburg in Claiborne County, was and is a town supported by cotton growing. Established by Samuel Gibson about 1788, it was the scene of a Civil War battle, and is now well known for its antebellum homes (Writers of the W.P.A., *Mississippi*, 327–29).

[2] In a third hand, probably that of James H. Maury.

[3] Andrew Jackson (sketch, 1:239, *n.* 2).

[4] Filled in and signed by Davis.

[5] James H. Maury (1798–1876) was born and educated in Kentucky. Moving to Port Gibson, Mississippi, in 1826, he set up a law practice, which, in partnership with his brother, continued until the war (Gravestone [Wintergreen Cemetery, Port Gibson, Mississippi]; J. H. Maury to J. F. Maury, 1863–64 [Mary Sessions Morehead Godwin, Port Gibson, Mississippi, 1970]). Maury represented Claiborne County in the Mississippi legislature in 1831 and served as state senator, 1837–40 (D. Rowland, *Official and Statistical Register, 1908*, pp. 55, 98). In 1835 he was secretary of the board of directors of the Grand Gulf Railroad and Banking Company (Port Gibson [Mississippi] *Correspondent*, January 17, 1835). At this time he was also editor of the Port Gibson *Correspondent*, a position he relinquished at the end of 1835, notifying his readers that his other duties prevented his giving the editorship the care it required (Woodville [Mississippi] *Republican*, November 28, 1835).

[6] Why Davis did not sign this document before leaving Fort Gibson is not known.

ABSTRACT

1:474

Post Return

Fort Gibson,[1] March [31,] 1835

Lists First Lieutenant Jefferson Davis, Company E, Dragoons, as absent with leave. Remarks: "Until 20th. Apl. 35. . . . Specl. Ord. No. 8 S[outh] W[estern] Frontier date 10th. March '35."[2]

DS (NA, RG 94 Records of the Adjutant General's Office, Post Returns, Fort Gibson), 2. Signed: "W. Seawell 1st Lieut. 7th Infr. Aid de camp. M. Arbuckle Brigdr. Genl. U S. Army Comdg." Endorsed: "Entd Recd. May 6th."

[1] See 1:397, *n.* 1.

[2] Davis applied for leave March 2 (1:466); see also 1:476.

ABSTRACT

Company Muster Roll 1:475

Dragoon Quarters near Fort Gibson,[1] April 30, 1835

Lists First Lieutenant Jefferson Davis of Captain David Perkins'[2] Company E, U.S. Regiment of Dragoons commanded by Colonel Henry Dodge,[3] as "Absent without leave since 19th. Apl. 1835."[4] Report covers March and April 1835.

Printed form, filled in and signed (NA, RG 94 Records of the Adjutant General's Office, Muster Rolls of Regular Army Organizations, U.S. Dragoons, Company E), 2. Signed: "D Perkins Capt. Dragoons M. Arbuckle Brigdr. Genl. U. S. Army." Endorsed: "Proves. Entered Recd. June 17th. 1835."

[1] Camp Jackson (see 1:397, *n.* 3). For Fort Gibson, see 1:397, *n.* 1.

[2] David Perkins (sketch, 1:410, *n.* 3).

[3] Henry Dodge (sketch, 1:370, *n.* 2).

[4] See 1:474 for Davis' having been granted leave until April 20.

Matthew Arbuckle to Roger Jones 1:476

Head Quarters South West. Frontier
Fort Gibson[1] 12th. May 1835

SIR.[2]

I have the Honor herewith to Transmit the Resignation of 1st. Lieut. Jefferson Davis of the Regiment of United States Dragoons.

I took the responsibility of granting to Lieut. Davis a Leave of abscence on the 10th. of March last for forty days,[3] at a time he was awaiting the publication of the sentence of a General Court Martial, before which he had been tried.[4] In consequence of this indulgence appearing to be very material to Lieut. Davis & being approved by his Commanding officer Major Mason;[5] and it not being probable that the sentence of the Court in his case would be received at this post more than a few days before his leave of abscence would expire;[6] I regarded it however proper, to conditionally receive, his resignation, which, if my recollection is correct, he proposed leaving with me. It is herewith enclosed with a copy of a note he left with it, authorizing me to fill up the date and Transmit the same for acceptance <provided he did not return at the expiration of his Leave of abscence.>[7] You will note that I have dated it at the period, his Leave of abscence Expired. I am sir Very respectfully yr. obt. Sert.

M. ARBUCKLE[8]

Brigdr. Genl. U S. Army Comdg

[Encl 1]

SIR,[8] Fort Gibson Arks. 20th April 1835

My individual interests interfering with my duties as an officer of the Army, I respectfully tender to you my resignation of the Commission of First Lieutenant of Dragoons, with which I have had the honor to be entrusted. I remain vy. Respectfully yr. mo. obt. Svt.

JEFFN DAVIS

1. L[ieutenant] Drgs. U. S. A.

[Encl 2] Genl. Arbuckle is authorized to date and Transmit the enclosed resignation drawn up by me this 2d. day of March 1835. Sigd.

JEFF. DAVIS

1st. Lt. Drgs. U. S. A.

LS (NA, RG 94 Records of the Adjutant General's Office, Letters Received, A–104, 1835); LbC (NA, RG 393 Records of United States Army Continental Commands, 1821–1920, Headquarters, Southwestern Frontier, Letters Sent, November 1834–May 1836, NA LIII, 86–87—formerly Fort Gibson, Southwestern Frontier, Letters Sent, November 1834–May 1836, Book 110). Addressed: "To Brigd. Genl. R. Jones. Adjt Genl. Washington City." Endorsed: "[Received] June 17. 1835." Enclosure 1: ALS (NA, RG 94 Records of the Adjutant General's Office, Letters Received, D–107, 1835, filed with 38051, Adjutant General's Office, 1896). Addressed: "To the Adjutant Genl. U. S. Army Washington D. C." Endorsed: "[Received] June 17. 1835 Submitted. R[oger] J[ones] Recommended to take effect 30 June 1835 inclusive. Al Macomb M[ajor] Gen Approved 23 June 1835 C. A. Harris Actg. Secy. War Done 'order' 37. June 24.' R[oger] J[ones]." Enclosure 2: D, copy (NA, RG 94 Records of the Adjutant General's Office, Letters Received, D–107, 1835, filed with 38051, Adjutant General's Office, 1896). Endorsed: " 'True copy' D. S. Miles. A[cting] A[ide-] D[e-] C[amp] & a[cting] ass[istan]t Adj. Genl. S[outh] W[estern] F[rontier]."

[1] See 1:397, *n.* 1.

[2] Roger Jones (sketch, 1:123, *n.* 6).

[3] See 1:470 for further evidence of

Davis' having been granted a forty-day leave of absence.

[4] The court martial was concluded February 19 (1:458).

[5] Richard B. Mason (sketch, 1:375, *n.* 8).

[6] The sentence of the court martial was approved March 15 (1:471).

[7] Interlined.

[8] Matthew Arbuckle (sketch, 1:447, *n.* 3).

Matthew Arbuckle to George A. McCall 1:477

Head Quarters S. Western Frontier
Fort Gibson,[1] May 12th. 1835

SIR[2]

You will herewith receive the resignation of 1st. Lieut. Jefferson Davis[3] of the Regiment of Dragoons which I have reason to believe he desires to be accepted as I have not received a line from him since he left this post.[4] Yet as Lieut. Davis is a young officer of much intelligence and great promise I have regarded it proper to transmit his resignation through your office believing it possible that the Commanding General[5] may have recieved such information from him as would induce him to recommend that it should not be accepted. I am Sir Very respectfully Your Obt. Servt (Signed)

M. ARBUCKLE[6]
Brig Gen. U. S. A.

LbC (NA, RG 393 Records of United States Army Continental Commands, 1821–1920, Headquarters, Southwestern Frontier, Letters Sent, November 1834–May 1836, NA LIII, 87—formerly Fort Gibson, Southwestern Frontier, Letters Sent, November 1834–May 1836, Book 110). Addressed: "To Lieut. Geo. A Mc.Call A[cting] A[ssistant] Adjt. Gen. W[estern] Dept Memphis Tennessee." Enclosure: Arbuckle to Jones, May 12, 1835, Enclosure 1 (1:476).

[1] See 1:397, *n.* 1.

[2] George A. McCall (sketch, 1:301, *n.* 2).

[3] Arbuckle wrote to the adjutant general the same day, enclosing Davis' resignation (1:476).

[4] Davis left Fort Gibson approximately March 10 (1:470).

[5] Edmund P. Gaines (sketch, 1:301, *n.* 3) was commander of the Western Department.

[6] Matthew Arbuckle (sketch, 1:447, *n.* 3).

From the Office of the Quartermaster General[1] 1:478

SIR, May 21st, 1835

Your money and property Accounts, for the fourth quarter of the last year, to November 11th,[2] after the usual examination at this Office, are transmitted to the proper Treasury Offices for settlement.[3] Vouchers 1. 2. 3. 4. 5. 6, and 9, of abstract C, are withdrawn from that abstract and sent to the third Auditor[4]—they should have been entered on abstract C. You will find herewith a statement of remarks.

All vouchers for purchases should show when each article was purchased, by inserting the date of purchase in the margin opposite the item charged, as well as the date of payment by inserting it in the receipt. In all matters of business dates are important and should not be omitted.

[Encl] Part of 4th Quarter 1834.

Quarterly Return. "Clothing, Camp and Garrison equipage of all description, Should be borne on the return of those articles, and not on that of Quarter Master's Stores proper."

LbC (NA, RG 92 Records of the Office of the Quartermaster General, Letters Sent, XXI, 470). Addressed: "To, Lieut. Jeff. Davis, Regiment of Dragoons, Dragoon Camp, near Fort Gibson." Enclosure: LbC (NA, RG 92 Records of the Office of the Quartermaster General, Remarks on Officers' Accounts, I, 217). Addressed: "Lieut Jefferson Davis, Act. Asst. Qr. Master, Fort Gibson, Ark."

1 Thomas S. Jesup was the quartermaster general (sketch, 1:174, *n.* 4).

2 Davis transmitted his money and property accounts to the quartermaster general in 1:437.

3 The accounts and vouchers were sent to the offices of the second and third auditors May 21 (NA, RG 92, Letters Sent, XXI, 470).

4 The third auditor was Peter Hagner (sketch, 1:199, *n.* 5).

1:479

From James Eakin

SIR, 25 May 1835

I enclose herewith two Vouchers[1] for disbursements made by you on account of the pursuit of deserters, received from the Quarter Mr. General,[2] in order that their names, the company & regiment, to which they belong may be stated.

J. E.[3]
A[cting] A[uditor]

LbC (NA, RG 217 Records of the United States General Accounting Office, Second Auditor's Office, Letters Sent, XIX, 151). Addressed: "Lieut. Jeffn. Davis, Drags. Fort Gibson, Ark. Ty." Enclosures missing.

1 The vouchers were transmitted by the quartermaster general May 21, 1835 (1:478, *n.* 3).

2 Thomas S. Jesup was the quartermaster general (sketch, 1:174, *n.* 4).

3 James Eakin (sketch, 1:165, *n.* 1).

George A. McCall to Matthew Arbuckle 1:480

Asst. Adjt. Genl's. office W[estern] D[epartment]
SIR,[1] Memphis, Ten. June 1st. 1835

Your letter of the 12th. Ult.[2] enclosing the resignation of Lt. J. Davis, of the Dragoons, was received by the last mail.

These papers have, in accordance with the wishes of Lt. Davis, expressed in a letter[3] to Lt. & A[ide-] D[e-] C[amp] Miller,[4] this day been mailed for Washington. I have the honor to be &c.

GEO. A. MCCALL[5]
A. D. C. &c.

P. S. Your letter of the 19th Ult.[6] has been recd. & submitted to the Genl.,[7] by whom your preparatory measures in relation to the reported intention of the Mexican Govr. are approved GAM

LbCS (NA, RG 393 Records of United States Army Continental Commands, 1821–1920, Western Department, Letters Sent, VII, 176). Addressed: "To Genl. M. Arbuckle, Com[mandin]g S[outh] W[estern] Frontier, Fort Gibson."

1 Matthew Arbuckle (sketch, 1:447, *n.* 3).

2 Arbuckle's letter of May 12 is printed as 1:477. See 1:476, Enclosure 1, for Davis' letter of resignation.

3 Davis' letter to Miller has not been found.

4 Albert S. Miller, aide-de-camp to General E. P. Gaines, 1833–35, was a first lieutenant, First Infantry. A graduate of West Point in 1823, he had been in the Black Hawk War and assigned to various garrisons, and later served in the Florida and Mexican wars. He was brevetted major for gallantry in 1846 and was major, Second Infantry, when he died in California at age fifty-two, in 1859 (Cullum, *Biographical Register*, I, 318).

5 George A. McCall (sketch, 1:301, *n.* 2).

6 Arbuckle's letter of May 19 has not been found.

7 Edmund P. Gaines, commander of the Western Department (sketch, 1:301, *n.* 3).

ABSTRACT

Register of Payments to Officers 1:481

[Washington, D.C.,] June 3, 1835

Lists payment by Paymaster A. D. Steuart[1] to Second Lieutenant[2] Jefferson Davis, Dragoons, $343.33. Amount includes pay and allowance for Davis and one servant,[3] and forage for two horses, from January through April 1835. Remarks: "1 horse to 28 Feb."

D (NA, RG 99 Records of the Office of the Paymaster General, Register of Payments to Officers, IV, 27), 1.

[1] Adam D. Steuart, paymaster at St. Louis (sketch, 1:355, *n.* 1).

[2] Although Davis is listed here as a second lieutenant, he had been a first lieutenant since May 10, 1834 (1:415).

[3] James Pemberton was undoubtedly the servant (sketch, 1:5, *n.* 4).

1:482 To Peter Hagner

SIR,[1] Louisville June 17th 1835

Since I left Fort Gibson[2] in March last I have been so circumstanced as not to have received any letters addressed to me at that place.[3]

Please inform what has been the result of the final examinati[on][4] of my accounts as a[cting] a[ssistant] Q. M. 1834[5] Address to me at Warrenton[6] Mi.[7] Vy. Respectfully yr. mo. obt. Svt.

JEFFN. DAVIS

ALS (NA, RG 217 Records of the United States General Accounting Office, Third Auditor's Office, Third Auditor's Accounts, Account 3,185). Addressed: "To P Hagnar Esq. 3d Audr U. S. Tres. Washington D. C." Endorsed: "Recd 26 Ansd 26."

[1] Peter Hagner (sketch, 1:199, *n.* 5).

[2] See 1:397, *n.* 1.

[3] Davis' furlough from Fort Gibson began on March 10 (1:470), and by March 26 (1:473) he was at Port Gibson, Mississippi. On the eve of his departure from Fort Gibson, he reportedly gave the Dragoons a champagne party (Northrop to Davis, December 15, 1879, D. Rowland, *Papers*, VIII, 433).

[4] Torn.

[5] Davis was acting assistant quartermaster at Camp Jones from September to *ca.* November 10, 1834 (1:427, 437).

[6] Warrenton was made county seat of Warren County, Mississippi, when the county was organized in 1809; as the result of a plebiscite in 1836, the county seat was moved to Vicksburg. Although Warrenton suffered from the loss of the county administration, cotton exports contributed to the town's prosperity until the Civil War. The competition of Vicksburg, the gradual change in course of the Mississippi beginning in the 1840's, and finally, the shelling and burning of the town by Federal troops in 1863 marked the demise of the once busy port (*Encyclopedia of Mississippi History*, II, 932; Writers of the W.P.A., *Mississippi*, 325).

[7] See 1:487 for Hagner's reply.

1:483 Sarah Knox Taylor to Margaret Mackall Smith Taylor

Louisville June 17th. 1835

You will be much surprised, no doubt my dear Mother[1] to hear of my being married[2] so soon, when I wrote to you last[3] I had no idea of leaving here before fall, but hearing the part of the Country to which I am going is quite healthy[4] I have concluded to go down this summer and will leave here this afternoon at 4 o'clock.

Will be married as you advised <—illegible—> in my bonnet and travelling dress. I am very much gratified that Sister Ann[5] is here[6] this time having one member of the family present I shall not feel so entirely destitute of friends. But you my dearest mother I know will still return some feelings of affection for a child who has been so unfortunate as to form [su][7]ch a connexion without the sanction of her parents;[8] but who will always feel the deepest affection for them whatever may be their feelings towards her. Say to my dear Father I have received his kind and affectionate letter.[9] <—illegible—> and thank. him for the liberal supply of money sent me. Sister will tell you all that you will want to know about me. I will write as soon as I get down and as often as my Mother may wish to hear from me. and do my kind ma write I shall feel so much disappointed and mortified if you do not. I send a bonnet by Sister. the best I could get. I tried to get you some cherries to preserve but could not. Sally[10] has kindly offered to make your preserves this summer

[Farew]ell my dear Mother give my best love to Pa and Dick[11]
Believe me always your affectionate DAUGHTER KNOX[12]

ALS, facsimile (New Orleans *Daily Picayune*, August 28, 1910). Addressed: "To Mrs. Margaret Taylor Prairie du Chien M[ichigan] T[erritory]." Printed: New Orleans *Daily Picayune*, August 28, 1910; Strode, *American Patriot*, 96–97; W. L. Fleming, "Davis' First Marriage," Mississippi Historical *Publications*, XII, 31–32.

1 Margaret Mackall Smith Taylor (1787/88–1852), daughter of Maryland planter Walter Smith, was educated at home and married Captain Zachary Taylor in Kentucky in 1810. She travelled with him to various frontier garrisons and, during the Seminole wars, worked diligently in the army hospital in Tampa. When Taylor was elected President in 1848, Mrs. Taylor, being in poor health, surrendered the social duties of the White House to her youngest daughter, Mary Elizabeth. She moved to Pascagoula, Mississippi, after the death of her husband in 1850 (*Appleton's*; Bixby [ed.], *Letters of Zachary Taylor*, ix–x).

2 The wedding ceremony took place June 17 near Louisville, at "Beechland," home of Sarah Knox's widowed aunt, Mrs. John Gibson Taylor. None of Davis' family were able to attend, so his best man was Nicholas L. Taylor, Sarah Knox's first cousin. The ceremony was performed by the rector of Christ Church, Louisville, and a reception was held in Mrs. Taylor's home. The Davises later drove to Ohio, and took steamboat passage to Vicksburg (Wood, "Jefferson Davis' First Marriage," New Orleans *Daily Picayune*, August 28, 1910).

3 Sarah Knox's previous letter to her mother has not been found.

[4] A report that unfortunately proved to be untrue. The Davises visited Davis' sister at "Locust Grove," West Feliciana Parish, Louisiana, in late summer 1835. "Very soon after their arrival Mr. Davis was taken very ill with malarial fever, and, the day after, Mrs. Davis became ill also. They were both suffering greatly, but he was considered very dangerously ill, and they were nursed in different rooms. He was too ill to be told of her peril, and delirium saved her from anxiety about him. Soon after the fever set in she succumbed to it, and hearing her voice singing loud and clear a favorite song, 'Fairy Bells,' [possibly a song of that name by Mrs. Caroline Sheridan Norton (Lichtenwanger to McIntosh, June 20, 1968, Jefferson Davis Association, Rice University, Houston)] he struggled up and reached her bedside—to find her dying. The poor young creature drew her last sigh September 15, 1835, and was burried in his sister's family burying-ground" (V. Davis, *Memoir*, I, 164). There has been some disagreement on the questions of whether the Davises were ill when they arrived at "Locust Grove," and whether the disease was malarial or yellow fever. For a brief discussion, see Evans, "Davis, His Diseases and His Doctors," reprint from *Mississippi Doctor*, XX, 2–3. See also 1:443, *n.* 2 for a sketch of Sarah Knox Taylor.

[5] Ann Mackall Taylor Wood was born near Louisville in 1811. She married army surgeon Robert C. Wood in 1829 at Fort Crawford, where he was also stationed in 1835. He remained in the army until his death in 1869; she survived him by six years and died in Germany (Bixby [ed.], *Letters of Zachary Taylor*, x–xi).

[6] Possibly the word "at" has been omitted.

[7] Ink blot.

[8] Years later, Davis' friend George W. Jones wrote publicly of the quarrel between Taylor and Davis: "Col. H. L. Dousman, of Prarie du Chien, who was an intimate friend of Gen. Taylor, told me that the general said to him on one occasion, when speaking of Davis' desire to marry his daughter Knox that the only objection he had to his marriage with her was because he belonged to the army, as his son-in-law Surgeon [Robert C.] Wood did, and knew from his own experience the anxieties which Mrs. Taylor and Mrs. Wood [Ann Mackall Taylor] suffered because of the frequent absence of their husbands as army officers. He said, what I know was the fact, that he held Lieut. Davis in high regard, and he gave his consent to his marriage with his daughter Knox" (to Hempstead, December 18, 1882, in Dubuque [Iowa] *Daily Telegraph*, December 19, 1882). Sarah Taylor's younger sister Elizabeth stated that "there was never any estrangement" between Zachary Taylor and his daughter (statement of Dandridge to "D. B. C.," New York *Times*, October 20, 1906). See also 1:332, *n.* 3 for further information about the Davis-Taylor quarrel.

[9] Zachary Taylor (sketch, 1:332, *n.* 3). His letter has not been found.

[10] "Sally" may be Sally (Sarah, Sallie) Strother Taylor (1814–88), Sarah Knox's first cousin, who was maid of honor (Hamilton, *Zachary Taylor*, 107; Taylor family folder [The Filson Club, Louisville, Kentucky]; "L. H. L.," "Youthful Romance of Jefferson Davis," *Confederate Veteran*, XVII, 388).

[11] Richard Taylor (1826–79), only son of Zachary and Margaret Taylor, was born near Louisville on the family estate, and first educated in Massachusetts and Europe. He entered Harvard in 1843, but transferred to Yale and was graduated in 1845. A Louisiana sugar planter, Taylor became active in politics, and was a Democratic member of the state senate, 1856–61. Appointed a brigadier general by Davis in 1861, Taylor commanded the District of Louisiana and later was assigned to the Department of East Louisiana,

Mississippi, and Alabama. His was one of the last armies to surrender, in May 1865. After the war Taylor worked for the release of Confederate prisoners, made a tour of Europe, served as a trustee of the Peabody Education Fund, and wrote his memoirs, *Destruction and Reconstruction* (New York, 1879). He died in New York City (*DAB*).

12 Sarah Knox Taylor Davis (sketch, 1:443, *n.* 2; 1:Appendix IV, Entry 94). For a fragment of Sarah Davis' last extant letter to her mother, see 1:Appendix I, 475.

Bond for Marriage License 1:484

[Louisville, Kentucky, June 17, 1835]

KNOW ALL MEN BY THESE PRESENTS, That we, *Jefferson J Davis and Hancock Taylor*[1] of the County of Jefferson, and Commonwealth of Kentucky, are held and firmly bound unto the said Commonwealth in the full and just sum of fifty pounds, (equal to one hundred and sixty-six dollars and sixty-six and two-third cents,) current money, for the payment whereof well and truly to be made to the said Commonwealth, we bind ourselves, our heirs, executors and administrators, jointly and severally, firmly by these presents, sealed with our seals, and dated this *17th* day of *June 1835*

The condition of the above obligation is such, that whereas, there is a marriage shortly intended to be had and solemnized between the above bound *Jefferson Davis and Sarah Knox Taylor*[2] *daughter of Col. Zachariah Taylor*[3] *and of lawful age* for which purpose a license has been this day issued by the Clerk of the County Court of Jefferson County, in the State of Kentucky. Now therefore, in case there shall be no lawful cause to obstruct the said marriage, then the above obligation shall be void, otherwise the same shall be and remain in full force and virtue.

TEST.

Jeffn. Davis (SEAL.)
Hancock Taylor (SEAL.)

[AES] Hancock Taylor Made Oath before me that Sarah Knox Taylor daughter of Zachariah Taylor as Mentioned in the Within bond is of lawful age <—and—> to the best of his Knowledge & belief[4]—this 17th day of June 1835

ALEXR H POPE[5]
D. C. Jeffn County Court

Printed form, filled in and signed (Papers of Jefferson Davis and Family, Library of Congress); printed form, filled in and signed (The Filson Club, Louisville, Kentucky). Printed: Scanlan, "Jefferson Davis in Wisconsin," *Wisconsin Magazine of History*, XXIV, 182.

[1] Hancock Taylor (1781–1841), eldest brother of Zachary Taylor, served in the War of 1812 as a quartermaster sergeant, and afterwards managed the Taylor family farms in Kentucky. He lived near Louisville and was married twice; his second wife, whom he married sometime before 1824, was Annah Hormsby (Taylor family file [The Filson Club, Louisville, Kentucky]; Hamilton, *Zachary Taylor*, *passim*).

[2] Sarah Knox Taylor Davis (sketch, 1:443, *n.* 2; 1:Appendix IV, Entry 94).

[3] Zachary Taylor (sketch, 1:332, *n.* 3).

[4] According to secondary sources, Davis had taken out a license prior to the wedding, but the clerk had withdrawn it because of Zachary Taylor's reported antagonism to the match and the uncertainty of the bride-elect's age. Before another license could be issued, Pope required Hancock Taylor's oath as to the age of Sarah Knox Taylor (New York *Times*, November 12, 1933, Sec. E, p. 7; Wood, "Jefferson Davis' First Marriage," New Orleans *Daily Picayune*, August 28, 1910).

[5] Most likely Alexander Hamilton Pope (1815–94), a member of the Pope family which held the clerkship in Louisville for about sixty years. Pope was deputy clerk, 1831–35, and in approximately 1836 began to study law. He became a prominent attorney and served in the state legislature. Delegate to the Union Democratic conventions in Chicago and Philadelphia, he was active for many years in local politics. When the Civil War began, Pope was placed in charge of the Louisville militia (Union) until it was organized for active service (Bentley to Lasswell, April 9, 1970 [Jefferson Davis Association, Rice University, Houston]; *Biographical Encyclopaedia of Kentucky*, 173; Rogers Index [The Filson Club, Louisville, Kentucky]).

ABSTRACT

1:485

Marriage Register

[Louisville, Kentucky, June 17, 1835][1]

Lists the marriage of Jefferson Davis and Sarah Knox Taylor,[2] "Daughter of Colo. Zachariah Taylor[3] and of lawful age as proved by the Oath of Hancock Taylor."[4]

D (County Clerk's Office, Jefferson County Courthouse, Louisville, Kentucky), 2.

[1] Of the marriages registered on this page of the county clerk's records, the Davis entry is the only one which does not record the date of the marriage and the return of the license.

[2] Sarah Knox Taylor Davis (sketch, 1:443, *n.* 2; 1:Appendix IV, Entry 94).

[3] Zachary Taylor (sketch, 1:332, *n.* 3).

[4] Hancock Taylor (sketch, 1:484, *n.* 1).

1:486

Order No. 37

Adjutant Genl's. Office Washington 24 June. 1835

The Resignation[1] of First Lieut. Jefferson Davis, of the Regiment of Dragoons, has been accepted by the President[2] to take effect on the 30th. day of June 1835. By order of Major General Macomb.[3]

R. JONES[4]
A[djutant] G[eneral]

LbCS (NA, RG 94 Records of the Adjutant General's Office, War Department Orders and Circulars, Orders, VII, 82); DS (NA, RG 99 Records of the Office of the Paymaster General, Letters Received); LbC (NA, RG 393 Records of United States Army Continental Commands, 1821–1920, Orders and Special Orders Received from the Adjutant General's Office, Headquarters Western Department, Order Book X, 207–208).

[1] Davis' resignation was submitted May 12, 1835 (1:476).
[2] Andrew Jackson (sketch, 1:239, *n.* 2) was the President.
[3] Alexander Macomb (sketch, 1:38, *n.* 10).
[4] Roger Jones (sketch, 1:123, *n.* 6).

From Peter Hagner 1:487

SIR June 26th 1835

I have received your letter of the 17th. Instant,[1] making inquiry as to the state of your quarter masters account. In reply I have to inform you, that your account for Disbursement in the 4 quarter 1834,[2] which was Audited and reported to the 2d. Comptroller[3] for his decision, on the 22nd. Instant, has this day been returned, exhibiting a balance of $27.01 due from you to the U. States–differing that amount, from your own Acct. Current, arising from Abstract C. (with the exception of Vouchers 1. 2. 3. 4. 5. 6. & 9. which were withdrawn & admitted to your credit in this Office) having been referred to the Office of the 2nd. Auditor[4] to be acted on for that amount ($27.01)[5] Respectfully Your obdt Servt

PETER HAGNER[6]
Aud

LbC (NA, RG 217 Records of the United States General Accounting Office, Third Auditor's Office, Miscellaneous Letters Sent, LXVI, 72). Addressed: "*Lt Jeff. Davis* now at Warrenton Mi[ssissippi]."

[1] Davis' letter to Hagner of June 17 is printed as 1:482.
[2] Davis' letter advising the quartermaster general of the closure of his accounts is printed as 1:437. Acknowledgment of receipt is 1:478.
[3] James B. Thornton was second comptroller (sketch, 1:244, *n.* 1).
[4] The second auditor was William B. Lewis (sketch, 1:166, *n.* 1).
[5] Davis' accounts were referred to the Treasury May 21 (NA, RG 92, Letters Sent, XXI, 470).
[6] Peter Hagner (sketch, 1:199, *n.* 5).

1:488 From William B. Lewis

SIR, 26 June 1835

I have received your letter of the 17th. Inst.[1] which, relating to your accounts as Acting Assistt. Comy. of Subsistence, has been referred to the 3d. Auditor.[2] W. B. L.[3]

(P. S.) I beg leave to refer <—you—> to a letter addressed you at Fort Gibson,[4] from this Office dated 25th. last month,[5] enclosing two vouchers which were incomplete.

LbC (NA, RG 217 Records of the United States General Accounting Office, Second Auditor's Office, Letters Sent, XIX, 197). Addressed: "Lieut. Jeffn. Davis, Drags., Warrenton, Mi[ssissippi]."

[1] Davis' letter to Lewis has not been found.

[2] The third auditor was Peter Hagner (sketch, 1:199, *n.* 5).

[3] William B. Lewis (sketch, 1:166, *n.* 1).

[4] See 1:397, *n.* 1 for Fort Gibson.

[5] 1:479 is the May 25 letter to Davis.

ABSTRACT

1:489 Semiannual Company Muster Roll

Camp Holmes, West of the Cross Timbers between the Canadian and Little River,[1] June 30, 1835

Lists First Lieutenant Jefferson Davis of Captain David Perkins'[2] Company E, U.S. Regiment of Dragoons commanded by Colonel Henry Dodge,[3] as "Absent without leave."[4] Report covers January through June 1835.

Printed form, filled in and signed (NA, RG 94 Records of the Adjutant General's Office, Muster Rolls of Regular Army Organizations, U.S. Dragoons, Company E), 3. Signed: "D. Perkins Capt. Drgs R. B. Mason Maj. Drags." Endorsed: "Proves Entered Recd. Octr. 13th. 1835."

[1] Camp Holmes was located on Chouteau Creek, north of the South Canadian River and about five miles northeast of the present town of Purcell, Oklahoma. It was the site of a council in the summer of 1835 which led to two treaties: between the Wichita and their allies and the Cherokee, Creek, Choctaw, Osage, Seneca, and Quapaw tribes; and between the western Indians and the United States (G. Foreman, *Advancing the Frontier*, 137–38, 232*n.*).

[2] David Perkins (sketch, 1:410, *n.* 3).

[3] Henry Dodge (sketch, 1:370, *n.* 2).

[4] Davis' resignation was accepted effective June 30 (1:486).

From James Thompson 1:490

August 19th 1835

The Commissary General of Subsistence[1] has transmitted to this office your accounts & vouchers for the 3d & 4th qrs of 1834[2]—and they have been audited and reported to the Second Comptroller[3] of the Treasury for his decision thereon, by whom they have been returned to this office Balanced. Your Account for subsistence consequently stands closed on the Books of this office Respy Your Obdt Servt

J. THOMPSON[4]
Acting Aud

LbC (NA, RG 217 Records of the United States General Accounting Office, Third Auditor's Office, Miscellaneous Letters Sent, LXVI, 182). Addressed: "*Lt. Jefferson Davis* of the U. S. Army Warrenton Mi[ssissippi]."

[1] George Gibson was commissary general of subsistence (sketch, 1:179, *n.* 2).

[2] Davis transmitted his accounts in 1:428, 438.

[3] The second comptroller was James B. Thornton (sketch, 1:244, *n.* 1).

[4] James Thompson, from Maryland, was chief clerk and, occasionally, acting auditor, *ca.* January 1811–March 1853 (Trever to McIntosh, May 8, 1970 [Jefferson Davis Association, Rice University, Houston]).

To Roger Jones 1:491

Warrenton,[1] Mi[ssissippi,] Aug. 21st 1835

SIR,[2]

Not having received any communication from Army Head Quarters since I left Fort Gibson[3] with leave of absence during last spring,[4] my anxiety induces me to send you my address, as in the Caption of this letter. Very Respectfully yr. mo. obt. Servt.

JEFFN. DAVIS
from Dragoons U. S. A.

ALS (NA, RG 94 Records of the Adjutant General's Office, Letters Received, D–169, 1835). Addressed: "To Genl R. Jones Adjt. Genl. U. S. Army Washington D. C." Endorsed: "[Received] Sepr. 11. 1835."

[1] See 1:482, *n.* 6 for Warrenton.

[2] Roger Jones (sketch, 1:123, *n.* 6).

[3] See 1:397, *n.* 1 for Fort Gibson.

[4] Davis left Fort Gibson on or about March 10 (see 1:470).

ABSTRACT

1:492
Company Muster Roll

Camp near the North Fork of the
Canadian River, August 31, 1835

Lists First Lieutenant Jefferson Davis of Captain D. Perkins'[1] Company E, U.S. Regiment of Dragoons commanded by Colonel Henry Dodge,[2] as resigned. Remarks: "To take effect from June 30th. 1835. O[rder] No. 38. A[djutant] G[eneral's] O[ffice] Dated Washington July 1st 1835."[3] Report covers July and August 1835.

Printed form, filled in and signed (NA, RG 94 Records of the Adjutant General's Office, Muster Rolls of Regular Army Organizations, U.S. Dragoons, Company E), 3. Signed: "D Perkins Capt. Dragoons R. B. Mason Maj. Drags." Endorsed: "Proves Entered. Recd. Octr 13th. 1835."

[1] David Perkins (sketch, 1:410, *n.* 3).

[2] Henry Dodge (sketch, 1:370, *n.* 2).

[3] Order No. 37 (1:486) announces Davis' resignation effective June 30.

1:493
To William B. Lewis

Warrenton[1] Mi[ssissippi,] Nov 17th 1835

SIR,[2]

After some delay I have procured the names of the Deserters required in your letter of May 25th 1835[3] (letter from your *office*) and retransmit the vouchers interlined with the information called for.[4]

It will not fail to occur to you that it is only where a Qr. Master gives information of payment made on account of Deserters, that he has any use for their names, and the within accounts when offered for payment were deemed perfect; I therefore have been compelled to wait until I could write to Fort Gibson[5] and receive an answer before I could give you the names required as above referred to. Vy Respectfully yr. mo. obt. Svt. JEFFN. DAVIS

ALS (NA, RG 217 Records of the United States General Accounting Office, Second Auditor's Office, Second Auditor's Accounts, Account 20,643). Addressed: "To W. B. Lewis 2d. Aud. U. S. Tres. Washington." Endorsed: "recd 14 decr ansd." Enclosures missing.

[1] See 1:482, *n.* 6 for Warrenton.

[2] William B. Lewis (sketch, 1:166, *n.* 1).

[3] The letter of May 25 is printed as 1:479.

[4] The names of the deserters and the vouchers have not been found.

[5] See 1:397, *n.* 1 for Fort Gibson. Davis' letter to Fort Gibson has not been found.

ABSTRACT

Lewis Cass[1] to the President of the United States[2] 1:494

Washington, D.C., December 18, 1835

Second Lieutenant John H. K. Burgwin[3] is recommended for promotion to first lieutenant, Regiment of Dragoons, to be ranked from June 30, 1835, "vice Davis, resigned."[4]

MS not found. Text from *Journal of the Executive Proceedings of the Senate of the United States of America* (90 vols., Washington: Duff Green, Government Printing Office, 1828–1948), IV, 490–95.

[1] Lewis Cass (sketch, 1:349, *n.* 5).

[2] The President was Andrew Jackson (sketch, 1:239, *n.* 2).

[3] John H. K. Burgwin, a North Carolinian and 1830 West Point graduate, was appointed to the Dragoon Regiment, as Davis was, in March 1833. He was promoted to captain in 1837, served in a number of frontier posts, and was killed in 1847 at the age of thirty-six in the assault on Pueblo-de-Taos, New Mexico (Cullum, *Biographical Register*, I, 461).

[4] This letter was transmitted to the Senate by letter of President Jackson December 18, 1835. The nominations of Burgwin and others were referred December 22 to the Committee on Military Affairs, which reported them back to the Senate May 30, 1836, at which time they were confirmed. See *Senate Executive Journal*, IV, 490–95, 496, 553.

ABSTRACT

Register of Pay Stoppages 1:495

[Washington, D.C.,] February 29, 1836

The paymaster general[1] reports a stoppage in the pay of Lieutenant J. Davis in the amount of $27.01.[2]

D (NA, RG 99 Records of the Office of the Paymaster General, Register of Pay Stoppages, I, 29), 1.

[1] The paymaster general was Nathan Towson.

[2] See 1:487 for Hagner's statement that Davis owed the Quartermaster Department $27.01.

1:496 From Jane Cook Davis

MY DEAR SON Artornish[1] April 8th. 1836

I received your kind letter[2] by the girls and your kind favor was joyfully <—received—> <accepted>[3] by your Mother. I am very anxious to see you indeed and hope I shall have that pleasure before long, or as soon as you find it convenient. My Children[4] are gone to school.[5] when they return I shall bring them up to see you, as they are desirous of so doing, and spend some time with you.

I have planted a small crop of corn and have a fine stock of Cattle, I have Charles[6] employed in cutting cord wood

As regards your kind offer we will arrange it when I visit in the fall—this Summer I intend Spending the most of my time with my Daughters Anna[7] and Amanda.[8] I will stay here untill it gets warm and disagreable.[9] Mr Stamps[10] and Lucinda[11] are as kind to me as children could be, and were they in a better Situation themselves I should be better contented, They are very well their Children[12] are all School, as to my own health it is as good <as I>[13] could expect at my time of life. I must conclude this Short letter with the Sincere love of your affectionate Mother JANE DAVIS[14]

[PS] Tell James[15] Julian[16] lost her trunk on the Boat. perhaps he may See the Boat if he does he had better try and get it—his Mother and other relations are well

ALS (Jefferson Davis Papers, University of Alabama Library, Tuscaloosa). Addressed: "To Jefferson Davis Warrenton Mississippi." Printed: Strode, *American Patriot*, 108, variant version; Strode, *Private Letters*, 13, variant version.

1 Artonish was a tiny (population fifty-one in 1900) post-village in Wilkinson County, about twenty miles west of Woodville on the Mississippi River (*Encyclopedia of Mississippi History*, I, 171), near "Artonish," the home of Davis' sister Lucinda Stamps (1:362, *n.* 12).

2 Davis' letter has not been found.

3 Interlined.

4 "My Children": Jane Lucinda Davis Farish and Ellen Mary Davis Anderson (sketches, 1:363, *nn.* 35, 36; 1:Appendix IV, Entries 90, 92).

5 The school was probably the academy run by the Misses Calder in Woodville (see 1:363, *n.* 22), or possibly Nazareth, a female academy in Kentucky (1:526, *n.* 7).

6 Charles was possibly a slave originally owned by Samuel Davis, Davis' father (Stamps to Davis, July 3, 1874 [Jefferson Davis Papers, Frances Carrick Thomas Library, Transylvania University, Lexington, Kentucky]).

7 Anna Eliza Davis Smith (sketch, 1:419, *n.* 30; 1:Appendix IV, Entry 18).

8 Amanda Davis Bradford (sketch, 1:363, *n.* 29; 1:Appendix IV, Entry 21).

9 Anna and Amanda lived with their

families in West Feliciana Parish, Louisiana.

10 William Stamps, Mrs. Davis' son-in-law (sketch, 1:362, *n.* 12; 1:Appendix IV, Entry 63).

11 Lucinda Farrar Davis Davis Stamps, Mrs. Davis' daughter (sketch, 1:19, *n.* 3; 1:Appendix IV, Entry 20).

12 Their children were: Jane Davis Stamps Alexander (sketch, 1:528, *n.* 14; 1:Appendix IV, Entry 64); Anna Aurelia Stamps Farish (sketch, 1:529, *n.* 2; 1:Appendix IV, Entry 66); Isaac Davis Stamps (1:Appendix IV, Entry 69); and William Stamps, Jr. (sketch, 1:535, *n.* 11; 1:Appendix IV, Entry 68).

13 In the margin.

14 Jane Cook Davis, Davis' mother (sketch, 1:22, *n.* 4; 1:Appendix IV, Entry 14).

15 James Pemberton (sketch, 1:5, *n.* 4).

16 Julian (see 1:395, *n.* 22).

To William B. Lewis 1:497

Warrenton[1] Mi[ssissippi,] Aug. 7th 1836

SIR,[2]

Some time since I forwarded to you two vouchers (for disbursements made by me as ac[ting] a[ssistant] qr. Master in the 4th Qr. 1834)[3] which had been returned as incomplete—since which I have not had the satisfaction of hearing from you.

You will oblige me by giving information of the final adjustment of my accounts at your office. Vy. Respectfly. yr. mo. obt. Servt.

JEFN. DAVIS
late a Lt. U. S. Drags.

ALS (NA, RG 217 Records of the United States General Accounting Office, Second Auditor's Office, Second Auditor's Accounts, Account 20,643). Addressed: "To W. B. Lewis Esq. 2d Aud. U. S. Treasy. Washington D. C." Endorsed: "Recd 5 Sept Ansd."

1 See 1:482, *n.* 6 for Warrenton.

2 William B. Lewis (sketch, 1:166, *n.* 1).

3 Davis transmitted the vouchers in November 1835 (1:493). He was acting assistant quartermaster September–November 1834 at Camp Jones near Fort Gibson (1:427, 437).

From Samuel Lewis 1:498

SIR, Sept. 7. 1836

Your letter of the 7th. ulto.[1] has been received, & in reply I have to inform you that a Statement has this day been made of your A/cs. & the two suspended vouchers referred to the[rein?][2] for expenses incurred in pursuing deserters in 1834, have been admitted & the amount thereof $27. carried to your credit on the Books of the 3d. Auditor,[3] which again closes your A/cs. in this Office. S. L.[4]

A[cting] A[uditor]

LbC (NA, RG 217 Records of the United States General Accounting Office, Second Auditor's Office, Letters Sent, XX, 327–28). Addressed: "Jefferson Davis Esq. late Lieut. & Actg. A[ssistant] Q. Mr Warrenton, Miss."

[1] Davis' letter to the second auditor is printed as 1:497.

[2] Ink blot.

[3] The third auditor was Peter Hagner (sketch, 1:199, *n.* 5).

[4] Samuel Lewis was first employed by the War Department in 1802 as an accountant, a position he held until 1817. The office of second auditor being created in the same year, Lewis was transferred and was a clerk until his dismissal in 1845. In 1846 he was reappointed and was still working in the auditor's office as late as 1849 (NA, RG 56, Personnel Records, 1789–1945).

EXTRACT

1:499

Proceedings of a Court of Inquiry—Fifth Day Case of Richard B. Mason

Editorial Note: The court, having been officially convened at Fort Gibson, December 20, 1836, by General Order No. 66 of October 10, 1836 (NA, RG 153, Court Martial Records, CC–219, 1837, p. 1), met[1] to hear accusations made against Lieutenant Colonel R. B. Mason[2] by First Lieutenant L. B. Northrop,[3] both of the Regiment of Dragoons. The charges, specifications, and statements from the proceedings which follow (1:499–511) are the only ones which mention or concern Davis.[4]

Fort Gibson[5] Thursday Jan 5th 1837

Charges and Specifications against Major[6] R. B. Mason of the Regiment of Dragoons U. S. A. prefered by 2d Lieutenant[6] L. B. Northrop of the Regiment of Dragoons U. S. A.

Charge 1st Disobedience of General Order and Regulations. . . .

Specification 2d In this that Major R. B. Mason of the Regiment of Dragoons U. S A. did at Camp Near Fort Gibson[7] on or about the 24th Dec 1834 in Disobedience of General order No 37 of April 28th 1832[8] confine to his quarters, 1st Lieutenant Jefferson Davis, of the Regiment of Dragoons U. S. A. No act of the said Lieut Davis, having given reason to believe that he (Lieut Davis) was one of those Cases in which close confinement was by the order referred to permitted, and did so retain the said (Lieut Davis) in close confinement until the 27th of Dec 1834 and after the said Lieut Davis had appealed to Bvt Brig Genl. Arbuckle[9] for protection against the oppression under which he (Lieut Davis) was suffering.[10] The aforesaid Lieut Davis having previously applied to the aforesaid Major Mason for relief from Close Confinement.[11]...

Charge 2d Arbitrary and oppressive Conduct.

Specification 1st In this that Major R. B. Mason of the Regiment of Dragoons U. S A on or about the 20th December 1834 on visiting the new Quarters Near Fort Gibson did not see a single officer present with the working parties or about the buildings and only noticing the absence of Lieuts. Davis & Northrop of Dragoons, sent Lieut Eustice[12] of the Regiment of Dragoons Acting Adjutant to arrest them both, thus making a distinction in his conduct to the officers under his command, or watching some and passing over others . . . .

Specification 4th In this that Major R. B. Mason U S Dragoons at the Dragoons stables Near Fort Gibson on or about the 7th Dec 1834 directed 1st Lieut Jefferson Davis U. S. Dragoons Commanding (E) Company U. S Dragoons to send Corporal Harrison[13] and Bugler Reid[14] of (E) Company U S Dragoons to the officer of the day to be put on the wooden horse[15] Lieut Davis aforesaid previously in the presence of Major Mason as aforesaid ascertained by enquiries that the breaking loose of the horse which the aforesaid Corporal Harrison was leading (on which account Major Mason had ordered him under guard was unavoidable The said Major Mason after this ordered Lieut Northrop officer of the day U S Dragoons to place Corporal Harrison and Bugler Reid aforesaid on the wooden horse and on the officer of the day asking if the non-commissioned officer should be put on, the said Major Mason replied Yes. non commissioned officers and all. Thus violating Paragraph 129 General Army Regulations[16] and subjecting the said Corporal Harrison one of the best non-commissioned officers in the squadron to a degrading punishment without a trial. . . .

Charge 3d Conduct unbecoming a Gentleman and a Commanding Officer . . . .

Specification 6th In this that Major R. B. Mason of the Regiment of Dragoons U. S. A. when in full charge of the interior poliece of the Dragoon Camp in the vicinity of Fort Gibson which constituted him the immediate commanding officer of Camp, was engaged in an association with one or more individuals, and established a Faro Bank of Joint Stock of which the said Major Mason was genneraly dealer, and counters being prepared, and notice given when the Bank would open.[17] The aforesaid Major Mason did deal in the months of Jan and Feb 1835 both within the garrison and at the public house attached to Fort Gibson

Witnesses Lt Northrop Lt Davis Lt Eustice . . . .

DS (NA, RG 153 Records of the Office of the Judge Advocate General [Army], Court Martial Records, CC–219, 1837), 179.

[1] The court had convened on four previous occasions but had adjourned because of the absence of one of its members.

[2] Richard B. Mason (sketch, 1:375, *n.* 8).

[3] Lucius B. Northrop (sketch, 1:402, *n.* 4).

[4] Although Davis was not present at this court of inquiry (see 1:476 for evidence of his resignation), his testimony as previously given in his own and Northrop's courts martial (1:454–63, 467, 469, 472) was received in absentia.

[5] See 1:397, *n.* 1.

[6] The ranks of major and second lieutenant were those held at the time the events mentioned in the charges and specifications took place, December 1834–February 1835.

[7] Camp Jackson (1:397, *n.* 3).

[8] For General Order No. 37, see 1:467, *n.* 6.

[9] Matthew Arbuckle (sketch, 1:447, *n.* 3).

[10] See also 1:507 for Arbuckle's testimony.

[11] See 1:504.

[12] William Eustis (sketch, 1:436, *n.* 1).

[13] W. H. Harrison was enlisted April 20, 1833, in New York by First Lieutenant David Perkins for three years (Semiannual Muster Roll, December 31, 1834 [NA, RG 94, U.S. Dragoons, Company E]).

[14] James Reed was enlisted in New York June 21, 1833, by First Lieutenant David Perkins for three years (Semiannual Muster Roll, December 31, 1834 [NA, RG 94, U.S. Dragoons, Company E]).

[15] The wooden horse, long a form of military and civil punishment, was usually a sort of saw horse which the man was forced to sit astride, often with weights tied to his feet and unable to touch the ground (Earle, *Curious Punishments of Bygone Days*, 128–31).

[16] Paragraph 129 of *General Army Regulations* [1825], page 35, reads as follows: "The appointment of every non-commissioned officer will be announced in regimental orders; after which, he cannot be degraded, except for incapacity, or misconduct proven before a court, and if found guilty of a slight offence, the punishment shall not exceed reduction to the ranks."

[17] Staff officers who participated in games of chance were violating paragraph 1500 of *General Army Regulations* for 1825, page 407.

ABSTRACT

1:500

Proceedings of a Court of Inquiry—Tenth Day Case of Richard B. Mason

Fort Gibson,[1] January 14, 1837

After First Lieutenant L. B. Northrop's[2] testimony that he had conferred with Davis December 20, 1834, about breaking the terms of his (Northrop's) arrest, Lieutenant Colonel R. B. Mason[3] states that he arrested Davis and confined him to quarters from December 24 until December 26 or 27.[4] Davis applied for an extension of the limits of confinement, but Mason refused.[5] Mason also admits that he ordered Corporal W. H. Harrison[6] and Bugler James Reed[7] on the wooden horse[8] and that Davis' inquiries about the punishment were unsatisfactory to Mason.

DS (NA, RG 153 Records of the Office of the Judge Advocate General [Army], Court Martial Records, CC–219, 1837), 179.

[1] See 1:397, *n.* 1.

[2] Lucius B. Northrop (sketch, 1:402, *n.* 4).

[3] Richard B. Mason (sketch, 1:375, *n.* 8).

[4] For the specifications and charges to which Mason is answering, see 1:499.

[5] See testimony in 1:504, 510.

[6] W. H. Harrison (sketch, 1:499, *n.* 13).

[7] James Reed (sketch, 1:499, *n.* 14).

[8] See 1:499, *n.* 15 for the wooden horse.

ABSTRACT

Proceedings of a Court of Inquiry—Twelfth Day Case of Richard B. Mason 1:501

Fort Gibson,[1] January 17, 1837

First Lieutenant L. B. Northrop[2] testifies that on December 20, 1834, while he and Davis had charge of working parties of Companies E and F at the new barracks at Fort Gibson, Northrop proposed they leave their details to watch a horse race, judging "the work would not be effected by this absence."[3] Northrop's absence led to his arrest by Major R. B. Mason.[4]

DS (NA, RG 153 Records of the Office of the Judge Advocate General [Army], Court Martial Records, CC–219, 1837), 179.

[1] See 1:397, *n.* 1.

[2] Lucius B. Northrop (sketch, 1:402, *n.* 4).

[3] For the circumstances which followed Davis' and Northrop's absence from the working parties, see 1:504 and the proceedings from Northrop's court martial in February 1835 (1:459–63, 467, 469, 472).

[4] Richard B. Mason (sketch, 1:375, *n.* 8).

ABSTRACT

1:502 ## Proceedings of a Court of Inquiry—Thirteenth Day Case of Richard B. Mason

Fort Gibson,[1] January 18, 1837

The commanding officer of Company E, Captain David Perkins,[2] testifies he returned from New Orleans about December 27, 1834,[3] and found Davis in arrest and confined to his tent[4] by order of Major R. B. Mason.[5]

DS (NA, RG 153 Records of the Office of the Judge Advocate General [Army], Court Martial Records, CC–219, 1837), 179.

[1] See 1:397, *n.* 1.

[2] David Perkins (sketch, 1:410, *n.* 3).

[3] Perkins resumed command of Company E December 28, 1834 (Post Return, December 1834 [NA, RG 94, Fort Gibson]).

[4] Davis was held in arrest at Mason's order as a result of an incident on December 24, and was later brought before a general court martial (see 1:454–58 for proceedings).

[5] Richard B. Mason (sketch, 1:375, *n.* 8).

ABSTRACT

1:503 ## Proceedings of a Court of Inquiry—Fourteenth Day Case of Richard B. Mason

Fort Gibson,[1] January 19, 1837

Captain David Perkins,[2] commanding Company E in the winter and spring of 1835, states that he believed Davis was acquitted of charges brought against him by Major R. B. Mason[3] in December 1834.[4]

DS (NA, RG 153 Records of the Office of the Judge Advocate General [Army], Court Martial Records, CC–219, 1837), 179.

[1] See 1:397, *n.* 1.

[2] David Perkins (sketch, 1:410, *n.* 3).

[3] Richard B. Mason (sketch, 1:375, *n.* 8).

[4] Davis was acquitted (see 1:458, 471).

ABSTRACT

Proceedings of a Court of Inquiry—Fifteenth Day 1:504
Case of Richard B. Mason

Fort Gibson,[1] January 21, 1837

Second Lieutenant William Eustis,[2] acting adjutant of the Regiment of Dragoons in December 1834, testifies that he remembered Davis' application to Major R. B. Mason[3] for relief from close confinement, and that no reason was given in Mason's refusal. Eustis did not remember a similar appeal having been made by Davis to General Matthew Arbuckle.[4] Eustis, who was ordered by Mason to arrest both second lieutenants, L. B. Northrop and Davis, because of their absence from company working parties December 20, arrested only Northrop because Davis said he had left another officer of his company in charge.[5]

DS (NA, RG 153 Records of the Office of the Judge Advocate General [Army], Court Martial Records, CC–219, 1837), 179.

1 See 1:397, *n.* 1.

2 William Eustis (sketch, 1:436, *n.* 1).

3 Richard B. Mason (sketch, 1:375, *n.* 8).

4 Matthew Arbuckle (sketch, 1:447, *n.* 3). An appeal was made by Davis to Arbuckle to extend the limits of his confinement (see 1:507); the letter has not been found.

5 Davis was confined to his quarters December 24 for about three days (see 1:500). He was tried before a general court martial February 12–19, 1835, on charges brought against him by Mason (1:454–58).

EXTRACT

Proceedings of a Court of Inquiry—Seventeenth Day 1:505
Case of Richard B. Mason

Fort Gibson,[1] Tuesday Jan the 24th, 1837

Lt. R. H. Ross[2] of the 7th Regiment of Infantry being duly sworn testified as follows in relation to the 2d Specification of 1st Charge.[3] I know that Lt. Davis was arrested and tried by a Genl. Court Martial. I think the Court acquitted him of a greater portion of the Specifications, and of the Charge.[4]. . .

Ques by Court Was or <was>[5] not Lt Davis tried for an offence which no one but he and Major Mason[6] had knowledge of, which the latter alone testified on, and was not Lieut Davis acquitted of the accusations for which he was <—tried—> confined to his tent

Ans Lieut Davis as I have already stated was acquitted by the Court of the offence for which he was tried. that offence as set forth in the charge. to the best of my reccollection, was some contemptuous words or actions towards Major Mason. when he spoke to him of his (Lieut Davis) absence from reviellee Roll Call. At the time he was spoken to by Major Mason, I believe so far as the testimony went on that trial of Lieut Davis by Genl. Court Martial there was no one present but Lieut Davis and Major Mason. I do not reccollect whether there was any other witness called upon to testify to that particular charge and specification besides Major Mason. I was a member of the Court which tried Lieuts Davis and Northrop.[7]

Ques by accused—Dont you reccollect of Sargt Sample,[8] who was called on to state what passed between Lieut Davis, and myself, also the orderly, Private Decons[9]

Ans—I reccollect that the orderly was called, the nature of his testimony I cannot give. I think also that there was a sargt called on who was marching his company past when Major Mason was speaking to Lieut Davis

DS (NA, RG 153 Records of the Office of the Judge Advocate General [Army], Court Martial Records, CC–219, 1837), 179.

1 See 1:397, *n.* 1.

2 Richard H. Ross (sketch, 1:447, *n.* 12).

3 See 1:499 for "2d Specification of 1st Charge."

4 Davis was acquitted. For the proceedings and decision of Davis' general court martial held in February 1835, see 1:454–58.

5 Interlined.

6 Richard B. Mason (sketch, 1:375, *n.* 8).

7 Lucius B. Northrop (sketch, 1:402, *n.* 4).

8 David Sample (sketch, 1:455, *n.* 25) testified in Davis' defense (see 1:455, p. 367).

9 Francis J. Decons (sketch, 1:455, *n.* 21); for his testimony, see 1:455, p. 364.

ABSTRACT

1:506 Proceedings of a Court of Inquiry—Eighteenth Day Case of Richard B. Mason

Fort Gibson,[1] January 25, 1837

First Lieutenant Sidney Burbank,[2] First Infantry, a member of the general court martial which heard Davis' case in February 1835, states that he thought Davis was acquitted[3] and that he (Davis) had clearly been confined to his tent by Major R. B. Mason[4] for the offense.

DS (NA, RG 153 Records of the Office of the Judge Advocate General [Army], Court Martial Records, CC-219, 1837), 179.

[1] See 1:397, *n.* 1.

[2] Sidney Burbank (sketch, 1:195, *n.* 6).

[3] For the proceedings and decision of the general court martial, see 1:454–58. Davis was acquitted.

[4] Richard B. Mason (sketch, 1:375, *n.* 8).

EXTRACT

Proceedings of a Court of Inquiry—Nineteenth Day Case of Richard B. Mason 1:507

Fort Gibson,[1] Friday Jan 27th, 1837

Bvt Brig. Gen Arbuckle[2] being duly sworn testified as follows in relation to the 2d Specification of 1st. Charge.[3] Lt Davis was arrested and confined to his quarters, and addressed a letter to me on the subject.[4] How long he was in confinement I cannot say,[5] it was not very long however I think I wrote to Major Mason[6] respecting Lt Davis confinement, requesting him, to give him the usual limits.[7] My rec collection is bad on this subject.

Ques by Court—Was you request to Major Mason to allow Lt Davis the usual limits given as command of the post, and did you desire him to grant these limits, because you considered he had a right to them?

Ans—I think I wrote, or spoke, to Major Mason on this subject, because I thought the crime for which Lt Davis was closely confined was not one for which it was customary to keep officers in close confinement[8]

Ques by Court—Did, or did not you offer to withdraw the charges against Lt Davis a short time before he was tried, this by the desire of Major Mason?

Ans—There was something said respecting the withdrawal of those charges, it was proposed by Genl. Gaines.[9] I mentioned this proposition to Lt Davis, and Major Mason the condition was as well as I reccollect, that Lt Davis should make a suitable appology to Major

Mason, which he did not think proper to do.[10] Col Mason told me he had no desire to pr<o>[11]ssecute Lt Davis if he would make a suitable apology for the outrage which he had committed.

DS (NA, RG 153 Records of the Office of the Judge Advocate General [Army], Court Martial Records, CC–219, 1837), 179.

[1] See 1:397, *n.* 1.

[2] Matthew Arbuckle (sketch, 1:447, *n.* 3).

[3] See 1:499 for "2d Specification of 1st Charge."

[4] The letter has not been found.

[5] Davis was confined to his tent for about three days (see Mason's testimony, 1:500).

[6] Richard B. Mason (sketch, 1:375, *n.* 8).

[7] Arbuckle's letter to Mason has not been located.

[8] See 1:467, *n.* 6 for an order concerning confinement of officers.

[9] Edmund P. Gaines (sketch, 1:301, *n.* 3). The proposal referred to was evidently the suggestion mentioned in McCall to Arbuckle, January 22, 1835 (1:449).

[10] Davis did not apologize to Mason and so was brought before a general court martial in February 1835 (see 1:454–58).

[11] Interlined.

EXTRACT

1:508

Proceedings of a Court of Inquiry Twenty-second Day—Case of Richard B. Mason

Editorial Note: First Lieutenant L. B. Northrop[1] testifies as to whether or not he engaged in "arduous sports" while on sick call. The incident he describes in the testimony below occurred in the fall of 1834. Northrop had been ill, was under a doctor's care, and was recovering at Auguste P. Chouteau's trading post, some forty miles north of Fort Gibson.

Fort Gibson,[2] Friday Feb 3d, 1837

While there I received one morning[3] an order by a Dragoon comming through Lt Davis the Act adjt.[4] directing me to return to Fort Gibson. I took the letter, and told the man very well, that he could go I had felt bad for a day or two back. I did not start that day. I told Col Chautau[5] that I would have to go. The next day it rained I however started in the evening, and went part of the way, the next <—day—> morning about fifteen miles from this place in the Road I saw three men approaching me. they were Lt. Davis and two armed Dragoons[6] before the Dragoons came up Lt Davis saw me and turned them back, he asked me as well as I can reccollect why I had not started at once on receiving the order, I told him that

I had not felt well, we then returned togeather to this place. he told me that he had been ordered to take two armed Dragoons and go after me he said that he had enquired of Major Mason[7] whether there was any necessity for them to take arms, it was however directed so I understood. I do not reccollect the particulars of this information this is <the amount of>[8] what gathered from what he said. When we arrived here he told me that Major Mason wanted me. I stopped for a few minutes here as I lived here. he asked me if I wa[s]nt agoing then I told him I would in a few minutes. I went up that night, whether I saw Major Mason that night or the next morning I am not certain.

DS (NA, RG 153 Records of the Office of the Judge Advocate General [Army], Court Martial Records, CC–219, 1837), 179.

[1] Lucius B. Northrop (sketch, 1:402, *n.* 4).

[2] See 1:397, *n.* 1.

[3] The date of this incident is uncertain. Northrop is listed as present at Fort Gibson, but on sick call September 30, 1834, and as being absent without leave October 31, 1834. By the end of November, he was present for duty (Post Returns, September–November 1834 [NA, RG 94, Fort Gibson]).

[4] Davis was serving as acting adjutant on August 31, 1834 (1:424). He may have acted in that capacity through September and October, although the post returns for those months do not so indicate. By November 30 William Eustis was acting adjutant (Post Returns, August–November 1834 [NA, RG 94, Fort Gibson]).

[5] Auguste P. Chouteau (1786–1838), an 1806 graduate of West Point, was of a prominent St. Louis family. He served briefly as General James Wilkinson's aide on the frontier and resigned in 1807 to move permanently to Indian territory. By 1834 he had two trading posts, one at the mouth of the Verdigris River near Fort Gibson, and a homestead and post at the Grand Saline some forty miles from the fort. In 1832 he acted as guide to Washington Irving's party and entertained them at his home (McDermott [ed.], *Western Journals of Washington Irving*, *passim*). Chouteau was a well-known trader and friend of the Indians, and in 1837 was appointed a United States Indian commissioner. Chouteau built a stockade fort on the site of Camp Holmes near the South Canadian River after the 1835 treaty with the western tribes was signed there. He traded extensively with the Comanches until his death, after which the fort was abandoned (Cullum, *Biographical Register*, I, 69; G. Foreman, *Advancing the Frontier*, 26, 232*n.*; H. F. Van Zandt, "History of Camp Holmes and Chouteau's Trading Post," *Chronicles of Oklahoma*, XIII, 316–37; G. Foreman, "The Three Forks," *ibid.*, II, 43–44).

[6] One of the dragoons who accompanied Davis was Private Francis Gunnell; see his testimony, 1:509, and sketch, 1:509, *n.* 4.

[7] Richard B. Mason (sketch, 1:375, *n.* 8).

[8] Interlined.

EXTRACT

1:509 Proceedings of a Court of Inquiry Twenty-fourth Day—Case of Richard B. Mason[1]

Fort Gibson,[2] Wednesday Feb 8th, 1837

<Pvt.>[3] Francis Gunnel[4] of (K) Company U. S. Dragoons being duly sworn testified as follows.

Ques by Court Were you, or were you not one of the <two>[5] men who went with Lt Davis in the fall of 1834 when he went after Lt Northrop[6] up towards Col Cheautau's[7]

Ans I was

Ques by Court How far off from Lt Northrop were you when you were turned back by Lt Davis.

Ans To the best of my <–recollection–> <knowledge>[5] between three fourths of a mile and a mile.

Ques by Court Were or were not these two men without arms of any kind?

Ans. We had no arms.

DS (NA, RG 153 Records of the Office of the Judge Advocate General [Army], Court Martial Records, CC–219, 1837), 179.

[1] Richard B. Mason (sketch, 1:375, *n.* 8).

[2] For Fort Gibson, see 1:397, *n.* 1.

[3] In the margin.

[4] Francis Gunnell was recruited by Captain Jesse Bean February 1, 1834, for three years. From Gloster [Gloucester] City, Virginia, Gunnell was listed as a hammerman by trade and was thirty-two years old in 1834 (NA, RG 94, Muster and Descriptive Roll of Detachment of Recruits, U.S. Dragoons, April 27–28, 1834).

[5] Interlined.

[6] Lucius B. Northrop (sketch, 1:402, *n.* 4).

[7] Auguste P. Chouteau (sketch, 1:508, *n.* 5).

EXTRACT

1:510 Proceedings of a Court of Inquiry Twenty-sixth Day—Case of Richard B. Mason

Editorial Note: The following extract, which concerns Davis and the 1st Charge, 2nd Specification,[1] is from Lieutenant Colonel R. B. Mason's[2] formal statement to the court.

Fort Gibson,[3] Friday Feb 10th, 1837

In relation to the arrests of Lieuts Davis & Northrop[4] I claim the full benefit of the 190th. paragraph Genl Regulations of the Army,[5] which leaves it discretionary with a Commander to extend the limits of an arresed officer, or not—I go further, & contend that, as the law points out the limits of an arrested officer, that strictly speaking, no one has a right to set aside the injunctions of the law & extend those limits. The 77th. Article of War is in these words, "Whenever any officer shall be charged with a crime, he *shall* be arrested and *confined* in his barracks, quarters, or tent, & deprived of his sword, by the commanding officer. And any officer who shall leave his confinement before he shall be set at liberty by his commanding officer, or by a superior officer, shall be cashier[e]d."[6] Now I contend that order No. 37 of 28 April 1832[7] is an illegal order, & cannot set aside the above named article of war, if any one article of war can be renderd null & void by an order, so can another, in that case the president might order a Genl Court Martial to consist of less than five members.[8]

DS (NA, RG 153 Records of the Office of the Judge Advocate General [Army], Court Martial Records, CC–219, 1837), 179.

[1] See 1:499 for the charge and specification.

[2] Richard B. Mason (sketch, 1:375, *n.* 8).

[3] See 1:397, *n.* 1.

[4] Lucius B. Northrop (sketch, 1:402, *n.* 4).

[5] Paragraph 190 reads as follows: "An arrested officer may have larger limits than his tent or quarters assigned to him, on written application to that effect, addressed to the commander, at the discretion of the latter" (*General Army Regulations* [1825], 45).

[6] The italics in Mason's quote of article 77 are his; there is no ampersand (*General Army Regulations* [1825], 418).

[7] For Order No. 37, see 1:467, *n.* 6.

[8] Mason here no doubt refers to article 64 of the "Rules and Articles of War," which states that general courts martial shall consist of not less than five nor more than thirteen members (*General Army Regulations* [1825], 416).

EXTRACT

Proceedings of a Court of Inquiry Twenty-seventh Day—Case of Richard B. Mason 1:511

Fort Gibson,[1] Saturday Feb 11th, 1837

The Court finds in reference to the 2d specification, 1st charge,[2] that Lt Davis was arrested and closely confined from the 24th to the 27th Dec 1834, that, in that time he applied to Lt Col Mason[3] for relief from close confinement which was refussed, and that an appeal was also made by him to Genl. Arbuckle;[4] and for its opinion in relation to the authority of <Lt>[5] Col Mason to closely confine Lieut Davis, the court refers to that which has already been expressed in relation to a similar case found in the 1st specification to the 1st Charge.[6] In reference to the refusal of Lt Col Mason to release Lt Davis from close confinement on his application, the court is of the opinion, that in the exercise of the discretion given him by the 190th paragraph Genl Regulations,[7] he did not violate duty, or propriety.[8]...

The Court finds that Lieut Eustis[9] Act adjt. was sent by Lt Col Mason to arrest Lieuts Davis & Northrop,[10] as set forth in the 1st specification 2d Charge,[2] and that the remainder of the specification is not proved....

The court in reference to the 4th Specification 2d Charge finds, that the only material point in the Specification, Viz, the placing of Corpl. Harrison[11] on the *wooden horse*[12] is proved—that, although the statement made in explanation of the cause of this punishment may have been satisfactory to Lt Davis, it would seem it had not been so to Lt Col Mason, the common commander—that the punishment of Corpl. Harrison was a violation of the 129th paragraph of Genl. Regulations,[13] and for that reason the court deems it reprehensible.

DS (NA, RG 153 Records of the Office of the Judge Advocate General [Army], Court Martial Records, CC–219, 1837), 179. Signed: "S. G. Simmons Lt 7th Inft Recorder S. Burbank Lt. Col. 5th. Infy. President of the Court." Endorsed: "Recd. March 20th. 1837." Enclosure: Northrop to Macomb, February 13, 1837 (1:512).

[1] See 1:397, *n.* 1.

[2] See 1:499 for the statement of charges and specifications.

[3] Richard B. Mason (sketch, 1:375, *n.* 8).

[4] Matthew Arbuckle (sketch, 1:447, *n.* 3).

[5] Interlined.

[6] The court found that Mason was "not only empowered, but imperatively required by the language of the 77 art. of War, to confine [Lt. Davis] . . . an opinion sustained by the provisions of paragraph 190th Genl. Regulations" (NA, RG 153, Court Martial Records, CC–219, 1837, p. 10).

[7] For paragraph 190 of army regulations, see 1:510, *n.* 5.

[8] For testimony concerning Davis' confinement, see 1:500, 504, 505, 507, 510.

[9] William Eustis (sketch, 1:436, *n.* 1).

[10] Lucius B. Northrop (sketch, 1:402, *n.* 4).

[11] W. H. Harrison (sketch, 1:499, *n.* 13).

[12] See 1:499, *n.* 15 for the wooden horse.

[13] For paragraph 129 of army regulations, see 1:499, *n.* 16.

ABSTRACT

Lucius B. Northrop to Alexander Macomb[1] 1:512

Fort Gibson,[2] February 13, 1837

First Lieutenant L. B. Northrop[3] appeals the decision of the court of inquiry held at Fort Gibson (October 20, 1836–February 14, 1837),[4] which found that Northrop's accusations against Lieutenant Colonel Richard B. Mason[5] were, for the most part, untenable. Northrop cites previous courts martial and testimony, including that of Davis in February 1835,[6] in support of his appeal.

ALS (NA, RG 153 Records of the Office of the Judge Advocate General [Army], Court Martial Records, CC–219, 1837), 4. Addressed: "For, the Genl in Chief Comdg U S. A." Signed: "L B Northrop 1st Lt U S D[ragoons]." Enclosed: Proceedings of a Court of Inquiry, Case of Richard B. Mason (NA, RG 153 Records of the Office of the Judge Advocate General [Army], Court Martial Records, CC–219, 1837).

1 Alexander Macomb (sketch, 1:38, *n.* 10).

2 See 1:397, *n.* 1.

3 Lucius B. Northrop (sketch, 1:402, *n.* 4).

4 The proceedings of the court of inquiry which concern Davis are 1:499–511. It appears that Northrop was being unduly prompt in protesting the decision of this court of inquiry, since his letter is dated the day before the last meeting of the court. However, the verdict had been reached, and at the final session, the court concerned itself only with the reading of the proceedings.

5 Richard B. Mason (sketch, 1:375, *n.* 8).

6 For Davis' testimony in Northrop's 1835 court martial, see 1:467, 469.

From Lucinda Farrar Davis Davis Stamps 1:513

MY DEAR BROTHER May 14th 1837

I will not say how mutch pleasure I felt on once more receiveing a letter from my brother[1] it had been so long since I saw you or received a letter form you that I had given up the hope of ever geting one

I hope I shall see you before long and the rest of our friends there[2] but it is some what uncirtin I may not be able to come it depends verry mutch on mother[3] if she goes to spend the sommer below[4] I will come while she is absent if she remains at home I will not leave her Should that be the case I hope you will come down <—in the course of the—> <and Mary[5] must come with>[6] you as the promised to come home with me

I scarcely know what to say on the subject of my poor Hugh[7] it is one verry near my heart and at times I feel all most hopeless I had thought of his going to France and converced with him about it before he was up there and your approbation if possible makes me more anxious than before. But ther is one obsticle and it seems a most important one at persent We cannot raise money sufficient to send him with

He thinks at present (if possible) of going to [Oushilla?] springs[8] the water is said to be of service in cases like his God know if any thing will be of service to him I fear not tho I will hope there is some remedy We are all in good health at present and the prospect for a cop is beautiful

I have been expecting a letter from Mary but none has arrived yet I should have writen to you a week sooner but my feelings have been so mutch affected by the burning of the Steam boat Ben Sherod on Monday night it hapened before our house I have never witnessed any thing so dreadful it would be in vain for me to attempt any thing like a discription We were told by the few we are able to save that at least tw[o][9] hundred persons were lost[10]

Write to me often my dear brother your letters are ever welcom for my own part I will write to you when I can My letters have but little to recommend them and I should not write but I know you will take an inerest in all that nearly concerns me and I know that you will not think of the bad writing and still worse composition (that is if you can read it) of a Sister that time nor circumstance can never change Your Sister LUCINDA[11]

ALS (Jefferson Davis Papers, Frances Carrick Thomas Library, Transylvania University, Lexington, Kentucky). Addressed: "To Mr. Jefferson F. Davis Warrenton Mississippi." Postmark: "Fort Adams Mi[ssissippi] May 17th."

[1] Davis' letter to his sister has not been found.

[2] Davis was either at "Brierfield," his plantation near Warrenton, Mississippi, or at "Hurricane," the adjacent plantation home of his brother, Joseph E. Davis.

[3] Jane Cook Davis (sketch, 1:22, *n.* 4; 1:Appendix IV, Entry 14).

[4] In April 1836 Davis' mother had mentioned spending the summer in West Feliciana Parish, Louisiana, with her daughters Anna and Amanda (1:496). Perhaps the same vacation is mentioned here.

[5] "Mary" is probably Mary Lucinda Davis Mitchell, Lucinda's niece (sketch, 1:362, *n.* 11; 1:Appendix IV, Entry 26). See also 1:395, *n.* 18 and 1:439, *n.* 3.

[6] Interlined.

[7] Hugh Robert Davis, Lucinda's eldest son (sketch, 1:362, *n.* 13; 1:Appendix IV, Entry 61). See 1:362 for further evidence of Lucinda Stamps's concern for her son.

[8] Probably a reference to the cele-

brated warm springs in Ouachita Parish, northwest Louisiana ("Louisiana Ouachita Region," *De Bow's Review*, III, 229; "North-western Parish," *ibid.*, IV, 228).

[9] Ink blot.

[10] The steamer *Ben Sherrod* had been racing from New Orleans with the *Prairie* when it passed by the Stampses' home, some fourteen miles above Fort Adams, Mississippi, early in the morning of May 9. Firewood lying near the boilers caught fire, and the craft filled with water. It quickly sank, killing almost all the passengers aboard. William Stamps was mentioned as having helped some of the survivors (Vicksburg *Register*, May 17, 1837). For a detailed description of the disaster and a further mention of Stamps's assistance, see Lloyd, *Steamboat Directory*, 95–101.

[11] Lucinda Farrar Davis Davis Stamps (sketch, 1:19, *n.* 3; 1:Appendix IV, Entry 20), Davis' sister.

From James Thompson

1:514

SIR 19th August 1837

I received this morning your letter of the 28th of June last,[1] asking to be furnished with a certificate that your accounts have been finally adjusted in the office.

In reply I have to state, that in September last, the sum of $27 was transferred to your credit on the books of this office, from the 2nd. Auditor's[2] office, which Sum closed your accounts on the books of this office, with the exception of one cent.[3]

It appears that a balance of $27 1/100 was reported from this office, in February 1836, to the 2d. Comptroller[4] for stoppage,[5] and as only $27 was transferred to your credit from the 2nd Auditors office as above stated, it is presumed that only that sum was stopped from your pay by the Paymaster. I am very Respy. Your most Ob St.

J. T.[6]
A[cting] Aud.

LbC (NA, RG 217 Records of the United States General Accounting Office, Third Auditor's Office, Miscellaneous Letters Sent, LXX, 98). Addressed: "Jeffn. Davis Esq. late Lt. U S. Dragoons Warrenton Missi."

[1] The June 28 letter from Davis has not been found.

[2] The second auditor was William B. Lewis (sketch, 1:166, *n.* 1).

[3] The September 1836 letter advising Davis of the closing of his account is printed as 1:498. See also 1:515.

[4] James B. Thornton (sketch, 1:244, *n.* 1) was second comptroller.

[5] The $27.01 balance was reported in the pay stoppage of February 29, 1836 (1:495).

[6] James Thompson (sketch, 1:490, *n.* 4).

1:515 From William B. Lewis

SIR, 28 August 1837

In reply to your letter of the 28 June last,[1] received the 18th. Inst., I have to inform you, that your accounts stand closed on the Books of this office. W. B. L.[2]

LbC (NA, RG 217 Records of the United States General Accounting Office, Second Auditor's Office, Letters Sent, XXI, 392). Addressed: "Mr. Jeff. Davis, late Lieut. Drags. Warrenton, Missi."

1 Davis' letter of June 28 has not been found.

2 William B. Lewis (sketch, 1:166, *n.* 1).

1:516 To Joseph Emory Davis

DEAR BROTHER,[1] Washington D. C. 2d Jany. 1838

You have probably learned through the correspondence[2] of Mr. Van Benthuysen[3] of my arrival at and departure from New York— when I reached Baltimore I was too unwell to proceed, a Surgeon of the Army[4] who was travelling from Philad. with me stopped and attended to me the next day was much better, went a few miles into the country to see some late importations of the "Short Horned Durhams" very superior to any I had seen before, & on the following morning continued my journey to this place.[5] I arrived here <Dec. 26th>[6] with a severe cough and considerable fever, which latter became intermittent and has confined me to my room until yesterday, I believe I am now free of disease but the unfavorable weather renders me fearful of exposure and I am to day a prisoner. I have therefore as you will suppose little news. Yesterday the President's rooms were thrown open to "all the world" I went up the house was closely crowded and being weak of body and luke warm of spirit I hung like a poor boy at a frolick about the empty corners for a short time and left the House without being presented.[7]

I have been disappointed at not hearing from you at this place and if you had been in time past a punctual correspondent should be very anxious on account of silence.

It is expected that three Regiments of Infantry will be added to the Army this year[8]—tomorrow I hope I shall be able to call on such persons as I know in public life here and adding the Missi. delegation to whom I must become known, review the whole & then endeavor to estimate what influence I can bring to bear on my purpose.

The Mississippi Election[9] is before the house of Rep. the committee to whom the question was referred will probably report to day—it is said that courtesy required the reference &c but that no change can be anticipated, to-morrow Mr. Calhoun[10] will introduce his resolution denying the right of the abolitionists to petition the senate[11] as they have done and Mr. Morris[12] will follow with his counter resolutions[13] which you will probably see in the paper of last week—the Vermont Senators also on the part of the Vermont Legislature will present memorials of like character,[14] they are said to be unfavorably disposed to the documents themselves—and altogether it is hoped that the discussion will be calmly conducted at least more so than heretofore.

My love to all the family. Remember me to James.[15] Write to me when you can affectionately your Brother JEFFN

ALS (Jefferson Davis Association, Rice University, Houston). Addressed: "J. E. Davis Esqr. Warrenton Mississippi."

1 Joseph Emory Davis, Davis' eldest brother (sketch, 1:19, *n.* 1; 1:Appendix IV, Entry 15).

2 Van Benthuysen's correspondence has not been found.

3 Watson Van Benthuysen, Joseph Davis' brother-in-law (sketch, 1:395, *n.* 7).

4 Probably Willison Hughey (see 1:522).

5 The dates of Davis' departure from Mississippi, arrivals and departures from New York and Baltimore are unknown.

6 Interlined.

7 The President was Martin Van Buren (sketch, 1:419, *n.* 20). Reportedly, Davis had breakfast at the executive mansion on this trip to Washington (V. Davis, *Memoir*, I, 169).

8 One regiment of infantry was added to the army by an act of July 5, 1838 (*Statutes at Large of the United States*, V [1846], 256).

9 Davis, as a Democrat, was hopeful the two Mississippi representatives sitting in the House would be retained. They were not. "Mississippi elected its Representatives in November of odd numbered years . . . as Congress had been called to meet in September, the governor issued writs for a special election to fill vacancies until the regular election; John F. H. Claiborne and Samuel J. Gholson presented credentials and were seated September 4, 1837, when, at their request, the question of the validity of their election was referred to the Committee on Elections; on October 3, 1837, the House decided they had been elected for the full term; Sergeant S. Prentiss and Thomas J. Word presented credentials on December 27, 1837, and on February 5, 1838, the House rescinded its former decision and declared the seats vacant; Prentiss and Word were subsequently elected, and took their seats May 30, 1838" (*Biographical Directory of the American Congress*, 126*n.*). For sketches of Prentiss and Word, see 1:518, *nn.* 16, 17.

10 John C. Calhoun (sketch, 1:8, *n.* 2).

11 For Calhoun's resolution, see *Congressional Globe*, 25th Cong., 2nd Sess., 73.

12 Thomas Morris (1776–1844), sen-

ator from Ohio, was born in Pennsylvania and settled in Ohio in 1804. He was admitted to the bar and in 1806 began serving in the state legislature. Defeated for Congress in 1832, he was elected senator, 1833–39. An ardent Union Democrat, he denounced nullification and secession, and opposed slavery, remaining an active abolitionist until his death (*DAB*).

[13] For Morris' resolution in answer to Calhoun's, see *Congressional Globe*, 25th Cong., 2nd Sess., 73.

[14] The senators from Vermont, Samuel Prentiss and Benjamin Swift, did not present the resolutions of the state legislature until January 16 (*Congressional Globe*, 25th Cong., 2nd Sess., 74, 107–109).

[15] James Pemberton, a slave (sketch, 1:5, *n.* 4).

1:517 From Watson Van Benthuysen

DEAR SIR New York Jan 16. 1838

I Received your letter[1] on Saturday last but having been very unwell since that time I have not answerd you as soon as otherwise I should have done. I feel uneasy about your being so ill & think you done very wrong in leaving us as soon as you did—cannot you arrange your matters in Washington[2] so that you can return here immediately—I think we can take better Care of you here than it is possible for you to find in a public house You Cane have the room you occupied when here—*with a Stove in it*—so that you may be as private as you have a desire to & at the Same time be among friends who will, <& do>[3] take <–Some–> <an>[3] interest in your welfare. If you Can make arrangements to leave Washington do so immediately & be with us the first of next week or sooner if possible. If I was well enough I should go (to Washington)[4] myself <for you>[3] & not take *no* for an answer

I received a letter from the Hurricane[5] this morning your brother[6] is gradually improving—the residue of the family are as well as usual—don't you think it would <–do–> be a good thing for your brother to take a trip to Havana[7]—I think the *sea trip* would of great advantage to him

The late *Cotton* accounts from Europe are favorable & I think will improve much more. Watson[8] is getting better but he is wonderfully altered—being but a mere skeleton. Let me know if you can come & Stay with us Your friend WATSON VAN BENTHUYSEN[9]

ALS (Jefferson Davis Papers, Frances Carrick Thomas Library, Transylvania University, Lexington, Kentucky). Addressed: "Mr Jefferson Davis Washington City D. C."

1 Davis' letter to Van Benthuysen has not been found.

2 Davis arrived in Washington December 26 (1:516).

3 Interlined.

4 Van Benthuysen left for Washington April 11 (1:523).

5 "Hurricane," plantation home of Van Benthuysen's sister and brother-in-law; see 1:328, *n.* 2.

6 Joseph E. Davis (sketch, 1:19, *n.* 1; 1:Appendix IV, Entry 15), Van Benthuysen's brother-in-law.

7 Havana was the spot chosen for Davis' winter travel in 1835–36 after the death of his first wife (V. Davis, *Memoir*, I, 165–66).

8 Watson Van Benthuysen, son of the writer, was born in Brooklyn in 1832 and died in New Orleans in 1901. He moved to New Orleans with his family in the 1840's and was associated with his father in the newspaper business. During the Civil War, he and two of his brothers served in the Confederate Army and accompanied the Davises on their flight from Richmond. Van Benthuysen was captured and confined for a time at Fort St. Philip, Louisiana. After his release, he returned to New Orleans, engaged in the wholesale tobacco business, and was president of the New Orleans and Carrollton and Crescent City Railways. About 1885 he moved to New York and became president of the Poughkeepsie Bridge Company (Van Benthuysen, "Supplement to the Van Benthuysen, Conklin-Dally and Seaward Genealogies," 9 [typescript in New York State Library, Albany]).

9 Watson Van Benthuysen, brother of Davis' sister-in-law (sketch, 1:395, *n.* 7).

From Joseph Emory Davis 1:518

Jackson Mi[ssissippi] Jany 19th '38

On my way to this place I found at the Office in Warrenton[1] the letter of my Brother of Decr. 4th[2] this letter relieved me from the fears I had entertained of Some disaster the letter at any time would have been of interest, but more So under the Circumstances Your letter informs me of Some intressting matter of which I was previously ignorant and if—I would set out immediately for this Island of enchantment but more of this when we meet. I am here for the purpose of Closing Some old business with but little prospect of effecting it.

The Election of Senator to Supply the vacancy by the resignation of Judge <Black[3]>[4] Seems to occupy the attention of the Legislature and Seems Still doubtful upon whom the Choice will fall Judge Trotter[5] is thought most likely to be chosen he is Administration John Gildart[6] is also thought to have Some prospects. Judge Bodley[7] and A. L. Bingaman[8] are Candidates on the Side of the opposition with I Should judge pretty equal Chance of Success. The Legislature have Prays Code[9] under Consideration or rather under trial whether they will Consider it for there Seems a dread of the undertaking few have read it perhaps none and I think it quite probable they will reject it after the labor of four or five years without examination the old Lawyers are opposed to any inovation they with those who from indolence or the urgency of business at home will in all probability make a majority. The Union Bank bill[10] was before the house yesterday I think it will Scarcely pass without amendments if amended will never pass as it will be necessary to delay it an other year & by that time public opinion on the Subject of Banks (So far as the value of the Stock will influence opinion) will change, there is now near forty million of Bank Capital in the State chartered & near thirty million in or about to go into opperation, this amt. together with the revolution in trade will be quite as much as can for a long time be used to advantage & much more than Can be so used if a national Bank is created, But in all these measures I am "*but a passenger*" and mean not trouble myself about the Safety of the Ship

Our little affairs at home have been nearly as you left them you people have been occasionly sick the worst case was Fanny[11] who had a fellon[12] on the thumb I think before you left which has been attended with loss of her Service and I am Sorry to add a portion of the bone, it <was>[4] thought advisable to amputate but her objections were so great that I thought proper to <leave>[4] Nature to her Own Cure, and <it>[4] now appears to getting well, Jim[13] thinks he will be able to pick all the Cotton in ten days of good weather I left him gathering the Corn The business of Gining was So delayed as render it impossible to get the Crop Gined in time to use the horses in the ploughing Season I therefore determined to build one at the Steam Mill and have Comncd & now So employed I cannot tell the amt you have out but think it must be more than you expected mine was 1.228.000 which (with what has Still to be picked) will make 800 bales or perhaps Something more I Shall not be ready to Send yours to market for Some time to Come and in the mean time Something w[ill][14] develope itself in regard to the Solvency of the H[ouse][14] we Spoke of–I have heard Since I came here that the house of W. M. Lambeth & Co had failed if So I Shall most probably dispose of mine to the Bank with which I can make the best bargain including yours if you wish it. On my return I hope I Shall be able to prepare my papers in Such a way as to enable you to understand them I have Suffered as much from indolenc[e] as disease Since you left us Some times thinking myself almost well and at others falling back a dread of Confinement or of writing especially has become almost a disease.

I am now at the house our friend George Work[15] whose Situation for long life is but little better than my own he says he derived great advantage from his Short Stay in Cuba but Since his return has been Subject to Chills & fevers. could he get the appointment of Consul at Havana Or Matanza he would go there to live or die as fate might determine he thinks the appointment worth $20000 per. an.

Report is here that Prentiss[16] & word[17] have obtained their Seats[18] Send me any reports or Speeches that you may think worth the postage and any others that our members will Frank I may not write you again untill I get home Yr Brother J E D[19]

ALS (Jefferson Hayes-Davis, Colorado Springs, 1969). Addressed: "Jefferson Davis Esq Washington City D. C."

1 See 1:482, *n.* 6 for Warrenton.

2 The December 4 letter has not been found.

3 John Black, born in Massachusetts, had practiced law in Louisiana and Mississippi and served as judge of the fourth circuit and state supreme courts, 1826–32. He was a member of the United States Senate, filling vacancies, 1832–38. Affiliated with the Whig party, Judge Black retired to Winchester, Virginia, to practice law and died there in 1854 (*Who Was Who*).

4 Interlined.

5 James Fisher Trotter (1802–66) was born in Virginia. He attended private schools and, although admitted to the bar in 1820, did not begin his practice in Mississippi until 1823. A member of the state legislature, 1827–33, he was appointed a circuit judge in 1833, and in 1838 a United States senator, filling a vacancy caused by the resignation of Senator John Black. Judge of the Mississippi Supreme Court, 1839–42, vice-chancellor of the northern district of Mississippi, 1855–57, and professor of law at the University of Mississippi, 1860–62, Trotter was a circuit judge at the time of his death in Holly Springs, Mississippi (*Biographical Directory of the American Congress*, 1729).

6 In 1821 John W. Gildart resigned as justice of the peace (Governors Papers, Series E, V [Mississippi Department of Archives and History, Jackson]) and by 1833 had become a practicing attorney in Woodville, Mississippi (Woodville *Republican*, April 6, 1833).

7 William Stewart Bodley (also spelled Bodely, Boadley) was born in Lexington, Kentucky, in 1806. Salutatorian of the 1821 Transylvania University class, he studied law and began practice at Maysville, Kentucky. Later he moved to Natchez and Vicksburg, where he was appointed to the first circuit court in 1833. He was unsuccessful in his bid for the United States Senate in 1838 and in 1849 moved to Louisville where he practiced law until his death in 1877 (Bodley family folder [The Filson Club, Louisville, Kentucky]; Dorman, "Descendants of General Jonathan Clark," *Filson Club History Quarterly*, XXIII, 129–30; Foote, *Bench and Bar of the South and Southwest*, 75; D. Rowland, *Courts, Judges and Lawyers of Mississippi*, 257).

8 Adam L. Bingaman, scion of an old Mississippi family whose estate was near Natchez, was graduated from Harvard and volunteered for a rifle company which fought in the Battle

of New Orleans. He was a leader of the Whig party, speaker of the Mississippi house, 1833–35, and president of the Mississippi senate, 1838–39. Defeated for election to the United States Senate in 1839, Bingaman retired from active public life, although it was he who spoke at the June 1847 welcoming celebration at Natchez for Davis and the Mississippi Rifles. He died about 1867 (*Encyclopedia of Mississippi History*, I, 243–44; D. Rowland, *Mississippi: Heart of the South*, I, 579, 678).

[9] P. Rutilius R. Pray, a native of Maine, had a college education and some experience as a teacher in New York before moving to Mississippi. He served in the state legislature, 1827–29, and in 1832 was president of the state constitutional convention. In 1833 Pray was authorized by the state convention to prepare a new digest of state laws which was found by the Mississippi bar to be too "ambitious of originality, and . . . too much flavored with the civil law. Mr. Pray resided at Pearlington, near the seaboard, where lands were chiefly held under old French and Spanish grants, and he had occasion to study the civil law, and, like many others, became enamored with it." The code was not accepted (Claiborne, *Mississippi as a Province, Territory and State*, 473). In 1837 Pray was elected to the high court of errors and appeals but died in 1839 at the age of forty-five, before completing his term (*Encyclopedia of Mississippi History*, II, 463–64; D. Rowland, *Mississippi: Heart of the South*, I, 566, 569, II, 447).

[10] The Mississippi Union Bank was chartered January 21, 1837, and by late 1839 had issued almost $7 million in demand and post notes, with liabilities of over $4 million. The Union Bank bonds, along with those of the Planters' Bank, were repudiated by the state in 1840 (D. Rowland, *Mississippi: Heart of the South*, I, 592, 600–24).

[11] Probably a slave.

[12] Felon—a deep inflammation of the finger (or toe), usually around the nail (*Webster's Seventh Collegiate*).

[13] "Jim" was James Pemberton, Davis' slave and plantation manager (sketch, 1:5, *n.* 4).

[14] Seal damage.

[15] According to the 1850 census of Hinds County, Mississippi, Volume I, George Work was listed as an attorney, born in Kentucky, and aged forty-nine.

[16] Seargent S. Prentiss (1808–50), a noted Whig orator in Mississippi, was born in Maine, graduated from Bowdoin College in 1826, and admitted to the Mississippi bar in 1829. He formed a law partnership in Natchez, then in 1832 moved to Vicksburg and became John I. Guion's partner in a very successful office. Elected to Congress in November 1837, he was not seated until May 1838 because of a controversy over the seating of the Mississippi delegation. He was defeated in the Senate race of 1839 and held no more public offices, although he remained active in politics. In 1843, during the course of Davis' unsuccessful campaign for the Mississippi legislature, he debated with Davis on the bond repudiation issue. Because of financial difficulties, Prentiss moved from Vicksburg to New Orleans where he opened a successful practice with Pierre Soulé. Prentiss delivered a welcoming speech to Davis and the Mississippi regiment in June 1847 in New Orleans and was active in his law office until the month before his death (*DAB*; Lynch, *Bench and Bar of Mississippi*, 216–45; see also Dickey, *Prentiss: Whig Orator of the Old South*).

[17] Thomas Jefferson Word, born in North Carolina, was a member of the state legislature in 1832. He moved to Pontotoc, Mississippi, and was elected to Congress in 1837. He did not take his seat until May 1838 and served until March of the next year (*Biographical Directory of the American Congress*, 1849).

[18] For a brief explanation of the con-

troversy over the disputed seats of the Mississippi representatives, see 1:516, *n.* 9.

[19] Joseph E. Davis (sketch, 1:19, *n.* 1; 1:Appendix IV, Entry 15) was Davis' eldest brother.

From Peter Hagner

1:519

SIR February 8. 1838

Your accounts for Property on file in this office have been examined, found correct and now stand closed.[1] Respectfully Your obt. Servt.

P. H.[2]
Aud.

LbC (NA, RG 217 Records of the United States General Accounting Office, Third Auditor's Office, Miscellaneous Letters Sent, LXXI, 60). Addressed: "Lieut. Jefferson Davis Late U. S. Dragoons Washington D. C[olumbi]a."

[1] Davis' subsistence accounts were closed in August 1835 (1:490).

[2] Peter Hagner (sketch, 1:199, *n.* 5).

ABSTRACT

Register of Payments to Officers

1:520

[Washington, D.C.,] February 10, 1838

Lists payment by Paymaster T. P. Andrews[1] to Second Lieutenant[2] Jefferson Davis, Dragoons, $180.66. Amount includes pay and allowance for one servant,[3] and forage for two horses, for May and June 1835. Remarks: "Resigned 30 June 1835."[4]

D (NA, RG 99 Records of the Office of the Paymaster General, Register of Payments to Officers, IV, 27), 1.

[1] Timothy P. Andrews, born in Ireland, became major and paymaster in 1822. He was colonel of Voltigeurs, 1847–48, and was brevetted brigadier general for gallantry at Chapultepec. Deputy paymaster general in 1851, he became paymaster general in 1862 and retired in 1864. He died four years later (Heitman, *Historical Register*, I, 167).

[2] Although Davis is listed as a second lieutenant, he had attained the rank of first lieutenant in the spring of 1834 (1:415), and at the time of this payment had been a civilian for over thirty-one months.

[3] Most likely James Pemberton (sketch, 1:5, *n.* 4).

[4] Davis' resignation was dated April 20, submitted May 12, and accepted June 24, 1835 (1:476, 486).

1:521 From Joseph Emory Davis

DEAR BROTHER Hurricane[1] Feby 19th '38

I am fearful your health has been Seriouly affected, by your long Silence and your attack at Baltimore[2] I fear the winter at Washington which has been a Severe one here, may have been too much for your feeble Condition. The winter as before mentioned has uncommon the ground has been covered with Snow for a week past and Still frozen we have not been able to Start a plough this Season nor indeed to do any thing for the last three weeks except to Cut wood and Such like hard labor and a few little jobs in doors Your people are about as usual they have done as well as they Could but like mine have been hindered by the weather from effecting much. Mary[3] wrote You by the aid of Jim Some particulars She was maried to Doctr Mitchell[4] on the 6th inst and they are now on a visit to our relations, with Caroline,[5] the presen[t] plan is to leave here in the Spring for Paris[6] and Caroline I think will go with them as far as Bards Town Kentucky.[7]

Poor Stamps[8] had the misfortune to have his Gin burned as learn from the newspape[r] of the 7th.[9] You recollect I ordered two Gin Stands from Id[illegible][10] of Phila. they turn out a failure, the delay in geting my crop out has been increased by this Circumstance but all may be for the best, the price may rise it Some times happens that luck attends our failures to do as we wish and our best fortune is the result of Such failure. My health is much improved Since I wrote you from Jackson[11] indeed I may almost Say I am well

The Legislature have passed the Union Bank Bill and were laboring to pass a Suplement to it the last information I have Some idea of taking Stock and would like to have Your opinion & wishes the Charter is a Clumsey performanc[e] in Some respects wholey uninteligabe but it may work with an inteligent Board.[12]

Rumor says Prentiss[13] & Word[14] have obtained their Seats[15] this I did not expect <though>[16] I thought them entitled to them. I have to Close this letter in haste and without time to look over it. Your Brother J E DAVIS[17]

ALS (Jefferson Hayes-Davis, Colorado Springs, 1969). Addressed: "Jefferson Davis Esq Washington City D. C."

[1] See 1:328, *n.* 2 for "Hurricane."

[2] Davis' last known letter to his brother is printed as 1:516; in it Davis mentions his illness while in Baltimore.

[3] Mary Lucinda Davis Mitchell, Joseph Davis' daughter (sketch, 1:362, *n.* 11; 1:Appendix IV, Entry 26).

[4] Dr. Charles Jouett Mitchell (1:Appendix IV, Entry 27). Shortly after his marriage to Mary Lucinda Davis, the couple went to Paris where they lived for over a year while Dr. Mitchell attended medical school (Mitchell to E. Davis, December 5, 1838, Mitchell, Journal, 1–7 [Southern Historical Collection, University of North Carolina Library, Chapel Hill]). Mary Lucinda died in 1846, and in 1850 Dr. Mitchell married his first wife's cousin, Lucinda Bradford (Ganier, Davis Family Tree [Albert F. Ganier, Nashville, 1968]). The dislocations of war induced Dr. Mitchell to move with his family to Crockett, Texas, in the fall of 1862 (Mitchell, Journal, 36 [Southern Historical Collection, University of North Carolina Library, Chapel Hill]). He apparently died early in 1886 (V. Davis to Mitchell, February 7, 1886 [Lise Mitchell Papers, Howard-Tilton Memorial Library, Tulane University, New Orleans]).

[5] Caroline Davis Robins Leonard, Joseph Davis' daughter (sketch, 1:395, *n.* 8; 1:Appendix IV, Entry 31).

[6] Davis seems to have been a particular favorite of Mary Lucinda (see 1:439). For some correspondence from the Mitchells in Paris, France, in the winter of 1838–39, see Mitchell, Journal, 1–7 (Southern Historical Collection, University of North Carolina Library, Chapel Hill). See also *n.* 4 above.

[7] There was an academy at Nazareth, near Bardstown, where Caroline and some of Davis' other nieces attended school (see 1:526, *n.* 7).

[8] William Stamps, Davis' brother-in-law (sketch, 1:362, *n.* 12; 1:Appendix IV, Entry 63).

[9] The Vicksburg *Daily Register*, February 5, reported the burning of Stamps's gin house and 200 bales of cotton at an estimated loss of $10 thousand–$12 thousand. The exact date of the disaster was not given, although the Woodville *Republican* of January 27 reports it occurred "a few nights" prior to January 27.

[10] Ink blot.

[11] A letter postmarked Jackson from Joseph E. Davis to his brother is printed as 1:518.

[12] See 1:518, *n.* 10 for the Mississippi Union Bank. A bill was signed by the governor February 5, and a supplementary bill passed February 15 which made the State of Mississippi surety and partner in the bank. The board elected by the 1838 legislature as managers of the bank was comprised of Hiram G. Runnels, president, J. A. Grimball, J. L. Irwin, R. M. Williamson, John S. Gooch, John J. McRae, Jacob B. Morgan, G. M. Barnes, Thomas Land, and James McLaren (D. Rowland, *Mississippi: Heart of the South*, I, 600–603).

[13] Seargent S. Prentiss (sketch, 1:518, *n.* 16).

[14] Thomas J. Word (sketch, 1:518, *n.* 17).

[15] For Prentiss' and Word's claim to the Mississippi congressional seats, see 1:516, *n.* 9.

[16] Interlined.

[17] Joseph E. Davis (sketch, 1:19, *n.* 1; 1:Appendix IV, Entry 15) was Davis' eldest brother.

To Willison Hughey 1:522

DOCTOR HUGHEY[1] Washington March 7th 1838

My dear Sir, I have expecting to hear from you for some days and am not without fears lest the enclosure I made to you of a draft to cover your pay account[2] should have missed it's destination.

Receive my thanks for the attention you gave to wishes expressed on the subject of shooting Irons or rather Steels, one good turn deserves another, would be convenient to take the five pair of 11 inch pistols for *trial* and bring them over with you to this place, I think they might suit me.

You have of course examined the amendments of the Military committee of the house of Reps. attached to the senate Bill for the increase of the Army, will your feelings as regards your profession be affected if those amendments relative to the Medical Staff be adopted?[3]

Speaking of guns how long would the ajent for steel barrels require to execute an order for a pair of pistols? Sincerely yours &c

JEFFN. DAVIS

ALS (William P. Palmer Collection, Western Reserve Historical Society, Cleveland). Addressed: "Willison Hughey M. D. Surgeon U. S. Army Baltimore Maryland."

[1] Willison Hughey is presumably the surgeon who travelled with Davis from Philadelphia to Baltimore (see 1:516). A native of Pennsylvania, Hughey was appointed an assistant surgeon in 1833 and was killed in the explosion of the steamer *Moselle* at Cincinnati in April 1838 (Heitman, *Historical Register*, I, 553).

[2] Davis' previous letter and draft to Hughey have not been found.

[3] "A Bill to increase the present military establishment of the United States, and for other purposes" was read, amended, and ordered to be printed January 24, 1838 (*Congressional Globe*, 25th Cong., 2nd Sess., 133–34). It was finally passed July 5, 1838; the amendment Davis refers to is presumably section 24 wherein officers of the pay and medical departments were to receive "the pay and emoluments of officers of cavalry of the same grades respectively . . ." (*Statutes at Large of the United States*, V [1846], 257–60).

1:523 From Watson Van Benthuysen

DEAR FRIEND New York April 18/38

Your letter dated Washington April 4th[1] reached me on the 5th. I immediately, on the same day, wrote to Washington that, in consequence of Mr King[2] being out of town, I would Start for Washington on the Wednesday following (11th) which I did accompanied <—both—> by my wife—and lo when we arrived in Washington *friend Jeff* had gone—I set myself to work to find you out—commenced by introducing myself to your friend *Jones*,[3] who by the way appears to be a very fine fellow & I hope to See him in New York when congress adjourns, from him I learned that you had left for Phila the Thursday previous to proceed via pittsburg for home—this was a damper—being obliged to spend the day ("a'la Havana") Mrs V & I made the best use of our time in visiting the various places worth seeing & at ¼ before 5 p. m. started for Baltimore—remained in B. over night & next morning took flight for Phila in hopes of overtaking the *fugitive*—but alas nothing so sure as disappointment again friend Jeff had the start of us <—for—> <by>[4] several days—& not being able to find out positively which way he had gone we gave up the pursuit—passed a very pleasant Sabbath in Phila & came home on Monday a little tired <—we—> & a little chagrinned that we had missed you—but never mind we console ourselves with the hope that ere long we shall again have the pleasure of your Company—judging from What your friend Jones said I expect that ere many months you will be on the *northern way* to Secure the Western promise.

We were much startled to hear of your Serious accident in Washington[5]—I hope the <—effects—> injury has been overcome & that you are enjoying good health in fact Genl Jones Said he thought you in better health when you arrd in Washington.

I had a great deal to say to you before you left for home & among the rest I designed to give you a commission which might have given you some trouble—I believe I will venture on the last even now—so here it is—Iin accordance with a request of Wadsworth I obtained in this City 267 dollars worth of goods & shipped them to him in January last—since when although I have written to him several times, I have not heard from him or the goods. (I saw the arrival of the vessel in N. Orleans) being obliged to become responsible for the goods *myself*, I begin to feel a little uneasy in the matter—and therefore beg of you if you <should>[4] be going to Natchez anytime in the course of 2 or 3 months—to make some inquiries of or about Mr Wadsworth & let me know the result of your inquiries—if not too much trouble.

There is but little news stirring here   We are just becoming calm, after our great Contest, the Whigs have achieved a great victory—the [battle][6] has no parralell in the annals of our political history.[7] Our banks will resume specie payments on the 10th prox[8]—specie is arriving in very large quantities and there are no fears on our part[9]—

notwithstanding *Emperor Nicks Manifesto*[10]–Mr Biddle[11] has fallen considerably in the estimation of the *New York public* and from present appearances will have to come into our Measures instead our driving us into his plans. The last Lpool cotton market had declined a little <(¼d per lb.)>[4] in consequence of the heavy arrivals of cotton at that port–but was considered good & supposed it would again advance

The steam ship Sirius[12] from Liverpool Apl 2 is hourly expected–our latest dates now are 18 Ma–I will send you her news in the paper

Write to me soon and let me know how your health is–give my love to brother Joseph.[13] Eliza[14] & the rest. & believe me with Sincere regards Your friend W Van Benthuysen[15]

ALS (Jefferson Davis Papers, Frances Carrick Thomas Library, Transylvania University, Lexington, Kentucky). Addressed: "Jefferson Davis Esq Care of Joseph E. Davis Esq *Hurricane* Warrenton *Mississippi*."

1 Davis' letter of April 4 has not been found.

2 Charles King (1787–1867) was the owner of the New York *American*, a newspaper for which Watson Van Benthuysen was at one time an editor (see 1:395, *n.* 7). Born in New York City the son of Rufus King, Charles began his career as a merchant. More scholarly than businesslike, he turned to journalism when, in 1823, his business firm failed. After competition had forced a merger of the *American* with the *Courier and Enquirer*, he resigned his position as associate editor of the newly amalgamated papers in 1848. The next year he was elected president of Columbia College, where, during his fifteen-year tenure as president, he inaugurated the schools of law, medicine, and mining (*DAB*).

3 George Wallace Jones (sketch, 1:409, *n.* 2).

4 Interlined.

5 Davis' accident in Washington is described in an undated memorandum of George W. Jones: "On one occasion, that winter, Davis and I accompanied Dr. [Lewis F.] Linn, the Senator from Missouri, and Senator [William] Allen, of Ohio, to a reception given by the Secretary of War [Joel R. Poinsett]. Dr. Linn and I returned home, leaving Senator Allen and Davis to return with [Senator] John J. Crittenden, of Kentucky, at Crittenden's request. After Dr. Linn and I got to bed, we heard the voice of Allen at a distance. He and Davis soon entered our room. Mr. Davis was bleeding profusely from a deep cut in his head, and the blood was streaming down over his face, and upon his white tie, shirt-front, and white waistcoat. Mr. Allen, who had been drinking champagne freely, was somewhat intoxicated, and missing the bridge (Mr. Allen being supposed to be familiar with the road) Davis had followed him, and they had both fallen into the Tiber, a small stream which they had to cross. Allen had alighted on his feet, but Mr. Davis, who was perfectly sober, had endeavored to save himself, and had pitched head foremost into the creek and cut his head badly. He was covered with blood, and his clothes were drenched with water and stained with mud. He was on the verge of fainting from the loss of blood when Dr. Linn and myself applied the proper restoratives. In the morning I went to his room and found him again uncon-

scious. I informed Dr. Linn of his condition, and after several hours' hard work we restored him to consciousness. Dr. Linn remarked that he would have been dead had I been five minutes later in reaching him the morning after the accident" (V. Davis, *Memoir*, I, 167–68; see also G. W. Jones, "A Tribute from a Classmate," in Daniel [ed.], *Life and Reminiscences of Davis*, 119–20).

[6] Paper fold.

[7] The Whigs had swept the November 1837 elections in New York, winning 101 of 126 assembly seats and six of the eight senatorial contests, largely on the strength of feeling against the Democrats, who were held responsible for the Panic of 1837 (Alexander, *Political History of New York*, II, 17–18).

[8] A convention of 143 bankers chaired by Samuel Hubbard of Boston met in New York April 11 and adjourned April 16, resolving that banks should resume specie payments no later than January 1839. Mississippi's two representatives and New York's forty voted against the resolution: Mississippi wanted a deferment to July 1839, when the proceeds of another cotton crop would be in; New York bankers resumed payment May 10 because a state law which legalized payments expired May 15 (*Niles' National Register*, April 14, 21, 28, 1838, pp. 97, 113, 129–31).

[9] Arrangements were made with the Bank of England to obtain approximately $10 million in specie, scheduled to arrive in New York by June 1 (*Niles' National Register*, April 21, 1838, p. 128; Seaman, *Essays on the Progress of Nations*, 242).

[10] Nicholas Biddle, president of the Bank of the United States of Pennsylvania, made public an April 5 letter to John Quincy Adams in which he stated the banks should not yet resume payment, but should be ready to do so; after repeal of the Specie Circular in May, he reversed his position (*Niles' National Register*, April 14, June 9, 1838, pp. 98–100, 226; see also McGrane [ed.], *Correspondence of Nicholas Biddle*, 299–317).

[11] Nicholas Biddle (1786–1844), of an old, established Quaker family, was born and died in Philadelphia. Valedictorian of the 1801 Princeton class, Biddle studied law and made an extended trip to Europe before being chosen as James Monroe's secretary in London in 1806. Biddle was admitted to the bar in 1809 but did not practice full time. Preferring a literary life, he contributed to the periodical *Port Folio* and was the author of several monographs. He became active in state politics and aided the administration in obtaining needed loans for the War Department. In 1819 Monroe appointed him a director of the Bank of the United States; three years later, Biddle became president and retained the position until expiration of the charter in 1836. He remained president of the Philadelphia bank until his retirement in 1839 (*DAB*; see also Govan, *Biddle: Nationalist and Public Banker*).

[12] The *Sirius*, built by Menzies of Leith, Scotland, was a 703-ton steamer which usually traded between Cork and London, and was the first steamship to cross the Atlantic without recoaling. She sailed from Cork to New York in eighteen days, arriving April 22, one day before the *Great Western*, a larger, more famous English steamship, which made the trip from Bristol to New York in fifteen days (Fry, *History of North Atlantic Steam Navigation*, 38–41).

[13] Joseph Emory Davis, Van Benthuysen's brother-in-law (sketch, 1:19, *n.* 1; 1:Appendix IV, Entry 15).

[14] Eliza Van Benthuysen Davis (sketch, 1:361, *n.* 8; 1:Appendix IV, Entry 25), Van Benthuysen's sister.

[15] Watson Van Benthuysen (sketch, 1:395, *n.* 7), brother of Davis' sister-in-law.

1:524 From Florida A. Davis McCaleb[1]

My Dear Uncle, The Hot Springs–July 19th. 1838

Do you not wonder whether your friends are still in the land of the living, after all the trials by land and sea, which they must necessarily have under-gone, since they parted with you? Has it not been a subject of serious consideration with you, how and where they are in this hot summer month, when you are necessarily burnt to a cinder?

Well I can tell you that if you have [n][2]ever been in this <State of>[3] Arkansas, you have [n][2]o idea of the variety of "out-cast humans" which infest it, nor have you an idea of the benefits of hot-water and "rare meats" bread the same, if you have not stopped at these hot-Springs–I should be glad to know if Texas can bear a comparison. We have existed here for four weeks, and the more I reflect upon it, the more am I astonished that I still survive. I even begin to doubt the fact. I look on this Month of July as an "aching void" in my life, which time can never fill! It is really awful to think of.

I hope My Dear Uncle that you are well mentally an physically, and that you have not found the time hang heavily on your hands. How could it, when you are at home? You are not at the Hot-Springs.

Papa[4] has been quite ill, but is better now than he has been previous to his last indisposition. I suppose you knew from my letter to Mr. MCaleb[5] of his attack. I do not know what could have caused it, or even what it was. It was something like a fainting fit, or as a, very learned and precise gentleman physician here calls it a syncope.[6] Papa had been as well as usual, and at the moment was conversing with a gentleman with great animation. He rose suddenly in the midst of a remark, and made one step towards the room, when his strength failing he fell on his knee and would have been much injured by the fall had not Mr. Lewis caught him. The fall was <–illegible–> <arrested>,[3] but in a moment more Papa was quite insensible. I was absent bathing at the time, but arrived just as they were attempting to bleed him. After that had been accomplished, he gradually recovered his recollection, though the loss of blood and its consequent debility kept him confined to his bed for a day or two. At present he appears to be tolerably well, but I fear the singularity of his illness has made an unfavourable impression, and <upon>[3] his mind. He tries to forget it, or laugh at it but it evidently distresses him. I am very sorry you are not here to amuse him, I should say entertain, for he feels I am sure the loss of Society that is agreeable to him. We live as secluded here, as if there was no one within fifty miles of here, so far as an intercourse with the visitors is concerned.

There are a few Mississippians here, but none whose acquaintance is very creditable. I at first tried to amuse myself with my books and guitar, but the latter attracted so much attention, that in the evening when it is most agreeable, I am compelled to lay it aside or shut myself up, in a very hot room, with no company, but my own Sad thoughts. I have been reading some french novels which a friend of Papa's, who is here for his son's health, has been kind enough to lend me. You have heard Papa speak of Mr. Garnier, with whom he boarded in Natchez Several years since eh bien c'est lui.

I hope Dear Uncle Jeff to see you with Mr. M'Caleb in Louisville. Be sure you do not disappoint me, I feel as much alone as if I were in the deserts of Arabia. Le betises de cette femme m'ennui tellement, que quelquesfois, j'ai envie de [illegible] tuer. I hope to hear from you at Little Rock be sure I shall be outragiously angry if I am disappointed. I wish I could meet you and Mr. M'Caleb there. It would certainly put off an attack of fever for two years. Adieu To yet have it heureux comme je desire, et vous aurez rien a plaindre.

Give my love to Mr. M'Caleb and tell him I never wished to see him so much [as] I do now.

[illegible] My chere Mama,[7] desires me to ask you how succeed in house-keeping. She hopes you find yourself well.

Papa is anxious for your health—speaks of you often and hopes to hear from you at Little Rock and to see you at Louisville. Moi aussi—adieu—Ne manquez pas di venir.

AL (Jefferson Davis Papers, University of Alabama Library, Tuscaloosa). Addressed: "To, J. F. Davis Esqr. Warrenton Mississippi." Endorsed: "Recd. 31st Aug. 1838."

[1] Florida A. Davis McCaleb Laughlin, Davis' niece (sketch, 1:19, *n.* 9; 1:Appendix IV, Entry 28).

[2] Torn.

[3] Interlined.

[4] Joseph E. Davis (sketch, 1:19, *n.* 1; 1:Appendix IV, Entry 15). Davis' brother had written of his previous illness in January (see 1:517 and 1:518).

[5] David McCaleb (sketch, 1:439, *n.* 6; 1:Appendix IV, Entry 29), Florida's husband. Her letter to him has not been found.

[6] Syncope: "a partial or complete temporary suspension of respiration and circulaton due to cerebral ischemia" (*Webster's Seventh Collegiate*).

[7] Eliza Van Benthuysen Davis, Florida's stepmother (sketch, 1:361, *n.* 8; 1:Appendix IV, Entry 25).

1:525
From Joseph Emory Davis

S[team] B[oa]t Pavilion[1] Augt. 27th '38

My Dear Brother

We are now on the way to St Louis having Since we left Arkansas[2] visited BardsTown[3] Harodsburg Lexington &c the Stay was necessarily Short at any of them having been only three weeks from the time we lef Louisville until our return, I went to See Mr. Taylor[4] on our first arrival at Louisville, Mr. [Jeut?][5] & Miss Taylor[4] called on us the next day and we promised to See them on our return but on our return the Pavilion was on the eve of Starting and the opportunty thought better than would [likely? occer?] again in a Short time <we determeid to go>[6] the morning after I purchased Some linsey &c for the Supply of the people Sufficient for yours & mine[7] tho I fear it may be late before they Can be got down as the river is low and Such delay attending it that I purchased nothing <in the provision way>[6] for ourselves or Mr. Payne[8] thinking they may be had at St Louis with a better prospect of getting them home or if they Cannot be had there will order them from Louisville in time for the rise. I hope the Castings & baging & rope has arrived Safe.

My anxciety was increased when I learnt by David McCaleb[9] that you had determend to Stay at home[10] for the Season[11] I expected you although I knew the necessity of Some one of Competent authority yet I had made up my mind to the risk. My greatest fear now is that you may Suffer from the influence of the Season & the increased exposure as to any thing relating to the business of the place You Can judge better being on the Spot than I can, I will however Caution you against an error that I have too often committed & which you I think are Some what liable to an attempt at *too much*. Several pieces of work that I spoke of, <—that—> if I had thought you would continue at home Should have omited, the Clearing up the new ground & planting the Oat land in Corn though work that I wished done might have been omited if the Season Should be wet and increase the labor of Cultivation. The preparation for paking baskets Sacks &c are matters that may give you Some trouble but hope your health may enable you give a general direction to these and all other affairs about the premises <—I—>

I think I See now (as Mr. Biddle[12] would Say) "what till now I could not See" the prospect of geting well my health has greatly improved & I now announce myself as well.[13]

At Lexington I made a visit to *Tranby*[14] one of Natures Nobles, it Cost me a ride of 8 miles <–of–> on a very warm day but felt no regret at having done So I Saw three of his Colts of last Spring they were haulter broke the 2 olst Say 4 mo for the exhibition they were all fine with this peculiarity perfectly black feet. Todhunter[15] we found a friendly kind Sort of a man Said he knew of but one Buzzard mare[16] that had been put a Mare of Bradley[17] who keeps a Training Stable the next day he Came to Town and offered to go with me, I accepted, and found the young Tranby had lost its dam at 4 weeks old and was reared by hand, it looked So much like young Snap under Simerlar Circumstances that I made no further inquires, he Said to Mr. T.[15] that he would not take one Cent less than $500. After viewing his Stud we went to Mr. [Heys?] and here a little Circumstance occur, which led to an engagement to take a an expected Tranby Colt of a Spread Eagle[18] & Sumpter Mare.[19] I Saw nothing in training that I thought Superior except an argele filly[20] 2 yrs old

I hope to hear from you at St Louis and in the mean time my greatest anxiety is that you escape the Sickness of the Season, I hope you May See us at home in September yr Brother

J. E DAVIS[21]

ALS (Jefferson Hayes-Davis, Colorado Springs, 1969). Addressed: "Jefferson Davis Esq Warrenton Mississippi."

1 The eighty-three-ton sidewheel steamer *Pavilion* was built in 1836 in Pittsburgh, also her home port, and was abandoned sometime in 1838 (Lytle [comp.], *Merchant Steam Vessels*, 149).

2 Davis' niece Florida wrote to him from Hot Springs, Arkansas, in July (1:524).

3 Bardstown was the site of a girls' boarding school attended by several of Davis' nieces, including Joseph's daughter Caroline (see 1:526, *n.* 7).

4 Probably a member of Zachary Taylor's family, several of whom lived in and near Louisville.

5 Possibly George P. Jouett (1813–62), son of Kentucky portrait artist Matthew H. Jouett. George Jouett was graduated from Transylvania medical school, studied with surgeon Benjamin W. Dudley, and practiced for several years until persuaded by his brother-in-law, Richard Menefee, to practice law. After the death of Menefee in 1841, Jouett turned to commerce to support his family and was the owner of several steamboats. He helped organize the Fifteenth Kentucky (Union) Infantry Regiment in 1861 and died in the Battle of Perryville (*Appleton's*; *Biographical Encyclopaedia of Kentucky*, 260). The reference could also be to William R. Jouett, who married Sally Strother Taylor, Davis' first wife's cousin (see 1:483, *n.* 10). Jouett was born in 1795 in Tennessee and was a captain in the First Infantry, 1829–46; Davis was assigned to the same regiment, 1829–33 (see 1:138, 349). The Jouetts had at least three children, born

in 1838 and after. A lieutenant colonel, Second Infantry, Jouett died May 1, 1852 (Taylor family folder [The Filson Club, Louisville, Kentucky]; Heitman, *Historical Register*, I, 584).

[6] Interlined.

[7] Joseph Davis is evidently speaking of supplies needed for the family and slaves of the Davises' Mississippi plantations. See 1:328, *n.* 2 for a notice of the elder brother's commissary at "Hurricane."

[8] Very likely Jacob Upshur Payne, a prominent New Orleans cotton factor and a friend and business associate of the Davis family for over half a century. Born in Woodford County, Kentucky, Payne moved to Mississippi in the 1830's and established himself in a "mercantile business" at Vicksburg and Warrenton, where he first met Joseph E. and Jefferson Davis. In 1840 he moved to New Orleans and opened a cotton factorage and commission business known first as Payne & Harrison (1840–61); Payne continued to merchandize cotton with various other partners until the late nineteenth century. Owner of a plantation near Washington, Louisiana, Payne lived the last forty years of his life in an "immense brick stuccoed mansion" on First Street, New Orleans. Davis died in the Payne-Fenner home in December 1889 and Payne himself died there March 11, 1900, at the age of ninety-eight. In 1841, Payne married Mrs. Charlotte D. Haynes of Vicksburg; they had three children (New Orleans *Daily States*, March 12, 1900; Seebold, *Old Louisiana Plantation Homes*, I, 352–55; Davis *v.* Bowmar, 155–57 [Mississippi Department of Archives and History, Jackson]). "Mr. Payne" may also refer to George E. Payne, Davis' cotton factor in New Orleans, 1838–44, in the firm of Oakey, Payne & Hawkins. George Payne, living in New York in 1875, stated that he had known the Davis brothers first in the mid–1830's (Davis *v.* Bowmar, 227–28 [Mississippi Department of Archives and History, Jackson]). There is no evidence that Jacob U. and George E. Payne were related.

[9] David McCaleb, Joseph Davis' son-in-law (sketch, 1:439, *n.* 6; 1:Appendix IV, Entry 29).

[10] Obviously a reference to Davis' "Brierfield" plantation in Warren County, Mississippi.

[11] For a note on the "sickly season," when disease was most prevalent in the South, see 1:124, *n.* 3.

[12] Possibly a reference to Nicholas Biddle (sketch, 1:523, *n.* 11).

[13] Joseph Davis' ill health is noted in earlier family letters (1:517, 518, 524).

[14] Tranby was an imported thoroughbred, highly regarded by horse breeders and racers. According to a notice in an 1838 periodical, Tranby was available for stud service at Parker E. Todhunter's farm (*Spirit of the Times*, VII, 415).

[15] Probably Parker E. Todhunter, who appears in note 14 above. His farm, "Oakland," was located some nine miles from Lexington in Jessamine County. Todhunter was a horse breeder of some note, and his family was apparently still living near Lexington as late as 1864 (Simpson to Bull, April 29, 1970 [Jefferson Davis Association, Rice University, Houston]; Hewitt, *Map of the Counties of Bourbon, Fayette Clark, Jessamine and Woodford Kentucky*).

[16] Buzzard was a chestnut stallion, imported from England in 1805 (*American Turf Register*, II, 319). In this period horses were frequently known only by the names of their sires, *i.e.*, Buzzard mare or, as used later in this letter, Sumpter mare and "argele" filly (Buckley to Lasswell, April 11, 1970 [Jefferson Davis Association, Rice University, Houston]).

[17] Possibly James L. Bradley, a prominent racing horse breeder in the Lexington area, 1830–62. He raised many champion horses, and included Henry Clay among his clients (Peter, *History of Fayette County*, 143; *Wilkes' Spirit of the Times*, VII, 371; [Lexington]

Kentucky *Gazette*, March 12, 1830; Crickman [comp.], *Racing Calendars*, I, 36).

[18] Spread Eagle, winner of the Epsom Derby in 1795, was imported from England in 1798 and died in Lexington, Kentucky, in 1805 (*American Turf Register*, II, 322). See also *n.* 16 above.

[19] Sumpter, a chestnut sired by the famous Sir Archie, died in Lexington in 1831 (*American Turf Register*, II, 302). As noted above (*n.* 16), the mare probably was one of Sumpter's foals.

[20] "Argele filly" may refer to a bay filly sired by Argyle that was racing at Lexington in 1838 (*American Turf Register*, IX, 524).

[21] Joseph Emory Davis, Davis' brother (sketch, 1:19, *n.* 1; 1:Appendix IV, Entry 15).

From Ellen Mary Davis

1:526

My Dear Uncle Locust Grove[1] Dec 29th 1838

If I have neglected writing to you it was not becaus I have forgotten your kind promis to take me to school, but my going to school is a subject so undecidable with Grandma[2] that I have not been able to tell you whether she would let me go or not. She sometimes says I may go but she seems so much to dislike for Sis[3] and me both to leave her at once that I told her if I could afford her any pleasure by staying I was willing to do stay. I suppose you <know>[4] that Grandma and Ma[5] are going to move back to Woodville.[6] Grandma says if lives in the same house with Ma perhaps she will be willing for me to go to school in the spring at Bardstown[7] if you like the school and can leave home at that time to go with me. Aunt Ann[8] talks of sending Amanda[9] to school in the spring.

Grandma says all she asks of you is to come to see her and if you cannot do that to write to her, do Dear Uncle come to see us all when we get back to Woodville anyhow. We heard from Aunt Amanda's[10] two or three days since they were all well. Grandma sends her love to you.

Give my love Uncle Joe[11] Cousin Florida[12] and Aunt Eliza[13] and believe me Dear Uncle to be Your ever affectionate Neice

Ellen[14]

P. S. Aunt Ann sends her love to you

ALS (William Burr Howell Papers, Mississippi Department of Archives and History, Jackson). Addressed: "To Mr. Jefferson Davis Brierfield Mis by Jim."

[1] "Locust Grove," plantation home of Anna and Luther L. Smith, Davis' sister and brother-in-law, was located in West Feliciana Parish, some one and one-half miles from St. Francis-

ville. Built in the early nineteenth century, the big house was looted and partially destroyed during the Civil War. Luther Smith was a wealthy physician and planter; his estate, including "Locust Grove," was valued at over $65,000 in 1834 (Luther L. Smith, Inventory of Property, Probate Box 91 [West Feliciana Parish Courthouse, St. Francisville, Louisiana]). The family cemetery at "Locust Grove" contains the grave of Davis' first wife, who died there in 1835.

2 "Grandma" is Jane Cook Davis, Davis' mother (sketch, 1:22, *n.* 4; 1:Appendix IV, Entry 14).

3 Jane Lucinda Davis Farish (sketch, 1:363, *n.* 35; 1:Appendix IV, Entry 90).

4 Interlined.

5 "Ma" is presumably Lucinda Farrar Davis Davis Stamps, Ellen Mary Davis' aunt (sketch, 1:19, *n.* 3; 1:Appendix IV, Entry 20).

6 The Stamps family was living near Fort Adams, Mississippi (1:513); Jane Cook Davis' home was "Rosemont," near Woodville; both she and the Stampses were in Woodville by December 1839 (1:529, *n.* 1).

7 In 1812 the Sisters of Charity were established at St. Thomas' Farm near Bardstown, Kentucky, and in August 1814 they opened a school for girls at Nazareth, about a mile and a half from the farm. A day school named "Bethlehem" was opened near Bardstown in 1818 at the request of Bishop B. J. Flaget, and in 1823 they opened St. Catherine's Academy in Lexington. After the order expanded its activities to Louisville, it established St. Vincent's Orphan Asylum, Presentation Academy, and St. Joseph's Infirmary; during the years prior to the Civil War, several branches of the academy were established in Kentucky, Tennessee, Indiana, and Kansas.

Nazareth Academy held its first public examination in 1825, and four years later it was chartered by the state legislature. Although established under church sanction—the academy received a papal rescript in 1829—eventually most of the students were southern girls from wealthy Protestant families. The 1829 register showed over 200 boarders at Nazareth and by the mid-1850's there were over 300. In addition to the usual reading, writing, arithmetic, music, and art courses, the curriculum included foreign languages, science and social studies. The annual vacation was from the last Thursday in July to the first Monday in September. For a detailed history of the order and the school, see McGill, *Sisters of Charity*.

8 Anna Eliza Davis Smith, Davis' sister (sketch, 1:419, *n.* 30; 1:Appendix IV, Entry 18).

9 Anna Amanda Smith Smith (1:Appendix IV, Entry 53), cousin of Ellen Mary Davis, was one of Anna Eliza Davis and Luther Smith's six children. Born in 1826, she was reared at "Locust Grove" plantation, Bayou Sara, Louisiana. She married Philander Smith in 1850 and was the mother of two children (H. A. Davis, *The Davis Family*, 83). She was living at "Locust Grove" when she died, November 7, 1887 (Boyle to Davis, November 11, 1887 [Museum of the Confederacy, Richmond]).

10 Amanda Davis Bradford, Davis' sister (sketch, 1:363, *n.* 29; 1:Appendix IV, Entry 21).

11 Joseph Emory Davis (sketch, 1:19, *n.* 1; 1:Appendix IV, Entry 15).

12 Florida A. Davis McCaleb Laughlin (sketch, 1:19, *n.* 9; 1:Appendix IV, Entry 28).

13 Eliza Van Benthuysen Davis (sketch, 1:361, *n.* 8; 1:Appendix IV, Entry 25).

14 Ellen Mary Davis Anderson (sketch, 1:363, *n.* 36; 1:Appendix IV, Entry 92).

To George W. Jones 1:527

Near Warrenton[1] Mi[ssissippi]

MY DEAR JONES,[2] 9th Feby 1839

If I were a "whig" I should begin this letter by a phillipic against Amos Kendall,[3] in this, that your much valued favor of 16th Dec. '38[4] did not reach me until the news-papers had brought such intelligence as rendered it probable that my answer would not find you in Washington D. C. the further information recieved by me induces me to send this to your home;[5] a place hallowed in my memory by associations of friendship and kindly feeling.

I will not pretend that I do not regret the decision of the House of Reps. in the Ouisconsin Ty. case. Yet my regrets are mitigated by the assurance that your interests will be advanced by your presence at home and that the happiness you will find in the midst of your aniable family will greatly exceed all you could have hoped for at Washington that hot bed of heartlessness and home of the world's worldly[6]

Although I have seen on former occasions a man's best feelings used as weapons of assault against him, I had not conceived that the disinterested sacrifice you made to support Mr. Cilley[7] and the pain and difficulty you encountered because of your connexion with that affair, could be arrayed against you, and I am glad to perceive that you have not recoiled with disgust from a constituency so little able to appreciate your motives.

Doty[8] is too cunning to last long, and the "little man that writes for the news-papers" will probably find himself too poorly paid to play into his hand again.

The President[9] in refusing your appointment as Govr. of Iowa[10] pursued the same shackled, electioneering policy that caused him to call an Extra session of Congress[11] and covered the financial part of his last message with the spirit of Banking, a policy which may divide <the Democrats>[12] take from them the banner under which the state right's men would have rallied to their aid, but can never propitiate Bank whigs or Federalists; as the head of the democratic party I wish him success, but he has sowed indecision,[13] a plant not suited to the deep furrows ploughed by his predecessor. You perceive that when I write of Politics I am out of my element and naturally slip back to seeding and ploughing about which I hope to talk with you next summer.

It gave me much pleasure to hear that I was not forgotten by Dr. Linn[14] and Mr. Allen[15] I esteem them both, and I *love* the Doctor.

I have written to you I scarcely <know>[12] about what but it all means I am interested in whatever concerns you and wish to hear from you often. My health is better than when we parted, and I hope to visit sinsinawa[5] next summer looking something less pale and yellow than when we met last winter.[16]

Present my remembrances and kindest regards to your Lady[17] and believe me to be most sincerely yr. friend JEFFN. DAVIS

ALS (George W. Jones Collection, Iowa State Department of History and Archives, Des Moines). Addressed: "Genl. Geo. W. Jones Sinsinawa Mound Via Galena Ills. Wisconsin Ty." Endorsed: "*Recd* April. 7. 1839 *Ansd* May 31. 1839." Printed: D. Rowland, *Papers*, I, 2–4.

1 For Warrenton, see 1:482, *n.* 6.

2 George W. Jones (sketch, 1:409, *n.* 2).

3 Amos Kendall (1789–1869), postmaster general under Presidents Andrew Jackson and Martin Van Buren, was born in Massachusetts and graduated from Dartmouth in 1811. After studying law in Groton, Massachusetts, Kendall migrated to Kentucky in 1814. He took over management of the Frankfort *Argus of Western America* in 1816, and by 1826 became a firm supporter of Jackson, helping him, through the newspaper, carry Kentucky in 1828. Kendall was a member of the "Kitchen Cabinet" and one of Jackson's ghost writers. In 1840 he returned to journalism full time but was not successful; he became business agent for Samuel Morse in 1845 and by 1859 was a wealthy man. Kendall remained a Democrat through the Civil War and devoted his later years to religion and philanthropy (*DAB*).

4 The December 18 letter from Jones has not been found.

5 Sinsinawa Mound, situated in the southwestern corner of Grant County, Wisconsin, was a natural mound of an irregular pyramidal shape a few hundred feet high (Taylor, "Mineral Point and Richland County," Wisconsin Historical *Collections*, II, 481; Rodolf, "Pioneering in the Wisconsin Lead Region," *ibid.*, XV, 369). Jones bought the mound in 1827, along with 1,000 surrounding acres which also contained a grove of timber; he established his home there in 1831 and remained until 1842 (Parish, *George Wallace Jones*, 143–47). See also 1:163, *n.* 3.

6 Jones failed to win reelection to Congress as a delegate from Wisconsin in 1838 largely because he had acted as a second in the duel between Congressmen Jonathan Cilley and William J. Graves (February 1838). Jones contested the election in December 1838 on the basis that he had not resigned and no vacancy had occurred. But the House ruled in January 1839 that James D. Doty was entitled to the seat because Jones had been elected as a delegate from the territory of Wisconsin for only two years and not, as Jones believed, for a longer period of time (*Congressional Globe*, 25th Cong., 3rd Sess., 1, 17, 19, 90–91; Parish, *George Wallace Jones*, 172–73).

7 Jonathan Cilley (1802–38) was born in New Hampshire and graduated in 1825 from Bowdoin College. He was admitted to the bar in 1828 and practiced in Thomaston, Maine, where he was editor of the local newspaper, 1829–31. Member, then speaker, of the Maine house, 1831–36, he was elected as a Jacksonian Democrat to

the Twenty-fifth Congress, where he served less than a year. He was killed in a duel near Washington with Kentucky Representative William Graves (*Biographical Directory of the American Congress*, 692). George W. Jones acted as Cilley's second; for Jones's account of the contest, see Parish, *George Wallace Jones*, 157–70.

[8] James D. Doty (1799–1865) was born in New York, studied law, and moved to Michigan, where he was admitted to the bar in 1819. He served as a federal judge, 1823–32, and assisted in bringing about the division of Michigan Territory into Michigan, Wisconsin, and Iowa territories. He won election to the third session of the Twenty-fifth Congress in 1838 and served until 1841 when he was appointed governor of Wisconsin Territory. At the time of his death he was governor of Utah Territory (*Biographical Directory of the American Congress*, 824).

[9] Martin Van Buren was President (sketch, 1:419, *n.* 20).

[10] Jones explained his not receiving the appointment as governor in his autobiography: "President Van Buren was my warm and devoted friend, as was evidenced by . . . his appointment of myself as Surveyor General at Dubuque in December, 1839. He intended to appoint me Governor and would have done so but that several Democrats in the House of Representatives went to him and told him that my appointment would ruin them and him, too, because of the false prejudice which existed against me on account of my connection with the [Jonathan] Cilley duel . . ." (Parish, *George Wallace Jones*, 174).

[11] The third session of the Twenty-fifth Congress, which began December 3, 1838, met to reconsider the Independent Treasury Bill, an administration measure first introduced in September 1837 and finally passed in 1840. John C. Calhoun's support of the bill was balanced by opposition of conservatives allied with Whigs. In the Congress of 1837–39 the Democrats had a majority in the Senate, and the House was evenly divided. For a discussion of the bill and others considered by the Twenty-fifth Congress, see Van Deusen, *Jacksonian Era,* 124–31.

[12] Interlined.

[13] Van Buren's message of December 3, 1838, is printed in Richardson (comp.), *Messages and Papers of the Presidents*, III, 483–505.

[14] Dr. Lewis F. Linn (1795–1843), Henry Dodge's half-brother, was United States senator from Missouri in 1839. Born near Louisville, Kentucky, and orphaned as a boy, he studied medicine in Louisville and served as a surgeon in Dodge's volunteer regiment in the War of 1812. He then completed his studies in Philadelphia and opened practice in Ste. Genevieve, Missouri Territory, in 1816. He served in the state senate in 1827, was appointed to the Senate in 1833, and was continually reelected (*DAB*; *Biographical Directory of the American Congress*, 1222). Linn was the doctor who tended Davis' wounds suffered in an accident early in 1838 (see 1:523, *n.* 5).

[15] William Allen (1803–79), senator from Ohio, was born in North Carolina, reared by his half-sister, and apprenticed to a saddler at an early age. Allen migrated to Ohio in 1819 and began his education, being admitted to the bar in 1827. He was elected as a Democrat to Congress in 1832 and after a term out of office, was elected to the Senate in 1836, serving until 1849. He retired to his farm in Ohio, and held only one more public office, as governor of Ohio, 1874–76 (*DAB*; *Biographical Directory of the American Congress*, 473). It was Allen who accompanied Davis when he (Davis) had a serious accident in Washington in 1838 (see 1:523, *n.* 5).

[16] Davis was in Washington December 26, 1837–April 5, 1838 (1:516, 523).

[17] Josephine Grégoire, of an old French family in Ste. Genevieve, Missouri, married Jones in 1831 when she was seventeen years old (*DAB*; Parish, *George Wallace Jones*, 88, 92–95).

1:528

Will of Jane Cook Davis

[May 20, 1839]

Be it known that I Jane Davis[1] of the county of Wilkinson and State of Mississippi do make and ordain this my last will and Testament in writing; Having made two heretofore and now revoking all others and especially those Two so heretofore made.

First—I give and Bequeath unto my Two Grand daughters Jane L Davis[2] and Ellen M Davis[3] daughters of Robert[4] and Mary E. Davis[5] all the property of which I am now possessed, of whatsoever description, and to be divided between my said Two Gran[d] Daughters as herein after mentioned. V[torn]

Second—I give and bequeath to my abov[e] named Grand Daughter Jane L. Davis: the following Negro slaves Towit—Julyan[6] [torn] Two children Jim[7] and Leo. and any incr[ease] the said Slave Julyan may hereafter h[ave] also a negro Boy Peter, and also a negro woman slave named Sucky and her d[aughter] Charity[8] and her increase. To her and th[e] Heirs of her Body.

Third—I give and bequeath to my above named Grand daughter Ellen M. Davis [the] following negro Slaves Towit Betsy and her Charles,[9] Sarah and her child Henriett[a] Judy the youngest Daughter of Sucky a[re] bequeathed to Jane L. Davis and their in[crease?] To her and the Heirs of her body

Fourth—In the event of the Death of either of my said Grand daughters without issue I will and bequeath the whole of th[e] above named Slaves to the Survivor and th[e] Heirs of the body of Such Survivor.

Fifth—It is further my will and desire that all my stock and Furniture be equal[ly] divided between my said Grand daughter[s] Jane L Davis and Ellen M. Davis and the Heirs of their bodies.

Sixth—Whereas there is a suit now depending in the Circuit Court of Wilkinson County for Several negro Slaves as the property of Sarah Matilda Vaughan[10] between my son-in-law William Stamps[11] and the Heirs of the said Sarah Matilda Vaughan—Now should my son-in-law succeed in recovering those Negroes—It is my will and desire that they be equally divided between my aforesaid Grand daughters Jane L. Davis and Ellen M. Davis and the Heirs of their bodies.

Seventh—It is further my will and desire that my Executors herein after named, place my said Grand daughters with My Daughter Lucinda F. Stamps[12] and that she have the charge of their Education and Government in all [r]espects.

Eighth & Lastly—I do hereby appoint and Constitute my Grand Son Hugh R. Davis[13] and my Son Jefferson F. Davis Executors of this my last Will and Testament.

In Witness whereof I have hereunto set my hand and caused my seal to be affixed Twentieth day of May in the year of our Lord One thousand Eight hundred and Thirty nine.

Attest. JANE DAVIS (Seal)

[torn] STAMPS

L[UCINDA] F[ARRAR] STAMPS

JANE STAMPS[14]

[AES] The within last will and Testament of <Jane Davis>[15] proved by the <oath of the>[15] within named subscribing witness thereto and admitted to probate, and ordered to be Recorded, this 12th Day of February AD 1846. I.FRANCIS GILDART

Judge of Probate

DS, copy (Chancery Clerk's Office, Wilkinson County Courthouse, Woodville, Mississippi). Manuscript worn and frayed. Endorsed: "Recorded in Vol 2 pages 1 & 2 Attest F Conrad Clk Filed 11th. Feby 1846 Conrad Clk."

[1] Jane Cook Davis, Davis' mother (sketch, 1:22, *n.* 4; 1:Appendix IV, Entry 14).

[2] Jane Lucinda Davis Farish (sketch, 1:363, *n.* 35; 1:Appendix IV, Entry 90).

[3] Ellen Mary Davis Anderson (sketch, 1:363, *n.* 36; 1:Appendix IV, Entry 92).

[4] Robert Davis (1:Appendix IV, Entry 89), Jane Cook Davis' deceased son-in-law, was not related to his wife's family, although, like them, he was descended from a line that had emigrated from Wales and settled finally in Mississippi (De Leon, "The Real Jefferson Davis," Southern Historical *Papers*, XXXVI, 76). Born *ca.* 1790–91, he served in the War of 1812, entering with a commission as ensign in 1814 and resigning in 1816 as a second lieutenant (H. A. Davis, *The Davis Family*, 94; Heitman, *Historical Register*, I, 360). In 1820 Robert Davis married the youngest of Samuel and Jane Davis' daughters, Mary Ellen, or "Polly"; they had two daughters, Jane Lucinda and Ellen Mary. Robert died sometime between 1825 and 1830 (H. A. Davis, *The Davis Family*, 94). His brother Hugh married Mary Ellen's sister Lucinda (see 1:Appendix IV, Charts Ten and Thirteen).

[5] Mary Ellen Davis Davis (1:Appendix IV, Entry 23), Jane Cook Davis' youngest daughter, who died in 1824. Being the child nearest Davis' age,

Mary Ellen, or Polly as she was called, and Davis were close childhood companions (Strode, *American Patriot*, 28), and her death, which affected Davis greatly, is mentioned by Davis in a letter to his sister-in-law Susannah Gartley Davis (1:9).

6 Julian, possibly James Pemberton's wife (see 1:395, *n.* 22).

7 Jim was possibly James Pemberton's son (see *n.* 6 above).

8 Charity—see 1:395, *n.* 20.

9 Charles—see 1:496, *n.* 6.

10 Sarah Matilda Vaughan, probably Jane Davis' granddaughter (see 1:363, *n.* 34).

11 William Stamps (sketch, 1:362, *n.* 12; 1:Appendix IV, Entry 63).

12 Lucinda Farrar Davis Davis Stamps (sketch, 1:19, *n.* 3; 1:Appendix IV, Entry 20).

13 Hugh Robert Davis (sketch, 1:362, *n.* 13; 1:Appendix IV, Entry 61).

14 Jane Davis Stamps Alexander (1:Appendix IV, Entry 64), Jane Cook Davis' granddaughter, was born to William and Lucinda Stamps in 1820. In 1845 Jane married William Alexander of Paris, Kentucky (More, Genealogical Data [Jefferson Davis Association, Rice University, Houston]; H. A. Davis, *The Davis Family*, 85); the Alexanders had six children. Jane died in 1884, ten years after her husband (More, Genealogical Data [Jefferson Davis Association, Rice University, Houston]).

15 Interlined.

1:529

From Ellen Mary Davis

My Dear Uncle Poplar Grove[1] Sep 22d 1839

I am afraid I have, by neglecting so long to fulfill my promes to you, given you cause to suppose that I had either forgotten it or intended to break it, but I hope you will change your opinion of me, if indeed you have formed so bad a one, for I can assure you it would give me great pleasure to write to you or to any of my relations who desire me to do so, if I could compose my letters so as to Let them be a source of pleasure instead of fatigue to the receivers; So when you receive no letters from me do not attribute my silence to indifference. Cousin Anna[2] and I have just completed one quarter of our schooling with Miss Calder;[3] I expect you think one quarter almost as good as nothing but the expectation of wet weather in the winter prevents us from commencing another; besides Ma's[4] house is nearly finished and Grandma[5] would be quite lonely as she will not be persuaded to give up housekeeping; I think, as she cannot go about she is happier to have something in which she takes interest than she would otherwise be. If I ever have the happiness to go to school I expect it will be after Sis[6] comes home. Cousin Mary Jane,[7] Nanny[8] and the little boys[9] are still going to school,[10] I believe Nanny thought of writing a postcript in this to you but she has gone to school. Uncle David[11] left here this morning I think he wrote to you yesterday.

Grandma sends her love to you, she wishes you to write to her but would prefer seeing you. Ma, Cousin Jane[12] and Cousin Anna send their love to you. I am dear Uncle Yours affectionately

ELLEN M. DAVIS[13]

Jim sends his love to his Pa.[14]

ALS (Jefferson Hayes-Davis, Colorado Springs, 1969). Addressed: "To Mr. Jefferson Davis Warrenton Miss."

1 "Poplar Grove" was Jane Cook Davis' home near Woodville. See 1:395, *n.* 1.

2 Anna Aurelia Stamps Farish (1:Appendix IV, Entry 66) was Lucinda and William Stamps's second daughter, born in 1823 (More, Genealogical Data [Jefferson Davis Association, Rice University, Houston]). Sometime between 1854 and 1856, Anna married Claiborne Farish, who practiced law in Wilkinson County, Mississippi (*ibid.*; H. A. Davis, *The Davis Family*, 85); the Farishes had four children. Claiborne Farish died in 1889, Anna Aurelia in 1895 (More, Genealogical Data [Jefferson Davis Association, Rice University, Houston]).

3 Miss Calder—see 1:363, *n.* 22.

4 "Ma" is Ellen's aunt, Lucinda Farrar Davis Davis Stamps (sketch, 1:19, *n.* 3; 1:Appendix IV, Entry 20).

5 "Grandma" is Jane Cook Davis, Davis' mother (sketch, 1:22, *n.* 4; 1:Appendix IV, Entry 14). Presumably, Ellen's aunt, Lucinda Stamps, and her grandmother, Jane Cook Davis, were at "Locust Grove," in Louisiana at the time of Ellen's letter to Davis in December 1838 (1:526); the Stampses had had a home near Fort Adams (1:513) but may have moved after Stamps's gin house and 200 cotton bales were destroyed in February 1839 (1:521, *n.* 9).

6 Jane Lucinda Davis Farish (sketch, 1:363, *n.* 35; 1:Appendix IV, Entry 90) was probably attending school in Kentucky (1:534).

7 Mary Jane Bradford Brodhead Sayre (sketch, 1:363, *n.* 20; 1:Appendix IV, Entry 74).

8 Anna Matilda Bradford Miles (sketch, 1:363, *n.* 19; 1:Appendix IV, Entry 77).

9 "The little boys" may be Benjamin Franklin Bradford (sketch, 1:363, *n.* 18), William Stamps, Jr. (sketch, 1:535, *n.* 11), and Isaac Davis Stamps, all of whom were of school age (1:Appendix IV, Entries 73, 68, 69).

10 The school the boys were attending cannot be identified with certainty, for there were several academies for boys in Woodville during these years: Brandon Academy, Wilkinson Academy, Woodville Male Academy, and Woodville Classical School are the best known. Only the latter two are mentioned in the newspaper notices of 1839 and 1840. The Woodville Male Academy, under the supervision of William Halsey, offered a classical education at a new building in Woodville. Tuition was $10 a month, and classes met from nine to four daily (Woodville [Mississippi] *Republican*, August 8, 1840). The Woodville Classical School opened for a third term on October 7, 1839, and met in the basement of the Presbyterian church under the direction of Messrs. Green and Phelps. The school included primary as well as more advanced levels (*ibid.*, September 28, 1839).

11 David Bradford, Davis' brother-in-law (sketch, 1:5, *n.* 10; 1:Appendix IV, Entry 71). His letter, if it were written, has not been found.

[12] Jane Davis Stamps Alexander (sketch, 1:528, *n.* 14; 1:Appendix IV, Entry 64).

[13] Ellen Mary Davis Anderson, Davis' niece (sketch, 1:363, *n.* 36; 1:Appendix IV, Entry 92).

[14] "Jim" is probably the son of Davis' plantation manager, James Pemberton.

1:530 From Lewis Sanders, Jr.

DEAR SIR. Natchez Nov. 30. *1839*[1]

I have Just returned from Kentucky after an absence of five months, on which I recd your Kind letter of the 15. July[2]—this fact will be my apology for not answering sooner. I was detained beyond the time contemplated in the troublesome labour of winding up old business, generally vexatious, and rearely profitable.

I have returned to this place for the purpose of persuing my profession with whatever industry I can master—and expect to remain here for some time; during which I will be truly gratified to see <you>,[3] at all times when you may visit our city—and if opportunity should present itself I will Certain call upon you. or should I have time, make you a special visit.

Your close application to business in the pursuit of planting, is rather anomalous considering your late connexion with the army: as military gentlemen are not much given to employment out of Service. For which however your merit so much the more credit.

I am truly gratified to learn that you have escaped the vortex of Speculation, as also its twin Sister *credit.*[1] I infer this from the tenor of your letter which Speaks of your *slow,*[1] but *safe,*[1] efforts, the only correct one in a country like our. I regret that I have not been so fortunate; whilst I have accumulated some property, I have incured some debts which have been very perplexing to me.

But as I am blest with a sangune temperament, and feel buoyed by hope I think a few years will releive me & give me the possession of a competency, the only, truly, rich estate.

Poor Charles, I do not recollect having seen him since I left school; but when memory, as mine some times does, retrospects the incidents of my last schooling, I fail not to see his self sufficient tho, rather dull, yet good hearted personage, well sustained with flesh and blood, fretting at the geers and gibes and *Mischeivious pranks of your identical self.*[1] Yet after the duel, he seemed to fill a better character, and if memory serves me aright, we all awarded to him a higher place in our esteem. I want to see you to talk about those *gone by days—when our spirits were high*[1] with *future hopes,*[1] days: before care, *or the*[1] mishaps, *or misfortunes, or perplexeties*[1] of life, had eaten Canker like upon our fortunes, days—be our destiny what it may, the like of which we "n,eer shall see again."

Present my respects to your brother,[4] and receive my assurances of friendship & regard Respectfuly L. SANDERS JR[5]

ALS (Hudson Strode, Tuscaloosa, Alabama, 1969). Addressed: "Jefferson Davis Esqr. Near Warrenton Miss."

1 The underlining was apparently added at a later date.
2 Davis' letter of July 15 has not been found.
3 Interlined.
4 Probably Joseph Emory Davis (sketch, 1:19, *n.* 1; 1:Appendix IV, Entry 15).
5 Lewis Sanders, Jr. (1796–1871), a prominent Natchez attorney and businessman. Sanders was born in Franklin County, Kentucky, served in the state legislature, 1825–29, and was Kentucky secretary of state, 1832–34. He had moved to Natchez by January 1838 and entered a partnership with Richard W. Samuels and Robert Rube to operate a livery stable and commission house in Natchez. He owned several tracts of land in and near the town, including the land and stables of the Pharsalia Race Track and a plantation on Pine Ridge, ten miles from Natchez. Sanders married Margaret H. Price in 1821; she and their son Lewis were appointed "attorneys-in-fact" for the elder Sanders when he left Natchez *ca.* December 1851 for California. She sold their various holdings, including their town home, "Holly Hedges," and the Pine Ridge plantation, and had joined him in California by June 1854. Sanders later lived in Woodford County, Kentucky; he is buried at Versailles, Kentucky (Clift, "Biographical Directory of the Kentucky General Assembly, 1792–" [MSS in Kentucky Historical Society, Frankfort]; Records of Deeds, Book Z, 374, 375, 406, 409, Book BB, 86, Book FF, 130, Book GG, 503, Book HH, 12, Book "II," 246, 290, 346, 350, Book KK, 208 [Adams County Courthouse, Natchez, Mississippi]).

ABSTRACT

Census Return

1:531

Warren County, Mississippi, [June 1,] 1840[1]

Lists Jefferson Davis as being between thirty and thirty-nine years of age and the only free person in his household. Forty slaves of varying ages are also listed, only twenty-nine of whom were engaged in agriculture.

Printed document, filled in (NA, RG 29 Records of the Bureau of the Census, Sixth Census, 1840, Warren County, Mississippi, III, 267.

[1] Although it is not possible to ascertain the day on which Davis' household was enumerated, census takers were instructed to record the status of all individuals on June 1, 1840, even though it might be weeks or even months after that date before the head of a household was interviewed (Wright, *United States Census*, 146).

1:532

From Joseph Emory Davis

DEAR BROTHR Lexington July 23rd 1840

Since I left Mississippi I have heard nothing a continual din of Politicks Clerks without employment Speculators with out Capital & Lawyers without business have all engaged in this new trafic and Salleid forth to iluminate the public by lectures upon Government Finane Curency &c not a Steam Boat, Stage, rail Car, or bar room <but rings>[1] with th Cry of Genl. Jackson war upon the Banks Coruption Van Burun, Subtreasury, Speice humbug &c With the Variation of Genl. Harrison hard Cider log Cabbin Old Tip Nationa Bank,[2] until I am ready to exclaim with the poor frenchman "I *very much disgust*"

Arriving at this place I was informed that a discussion would take place at the Court House that evening upon important polical questions, the bell tolled about 8 o'clock and I went with the hope of hearing <Something>[1] better than Hard Cider Log Cabin in a Short time the house was filled with a very orderly and in appearanc with a very respectable and inteligent Audienc after a time Mr. C. Clay[3] rose and in low and Solemn accents <informed>[1] the Company that he had been Accused of producng a division in the whig ranks which he declared to be false and would proceed to prove it,[4] Now it turned out that this important question so big with the fate of Empire was a law of the State passed in 1833[5] prohibiting the introduction of <Slaves>[1] into Kentucky as Merchandize, The enemies of the law Contended (and (I think very fairly) that any interferene with the unqualified property of the Own[er] in a Slave was an abolition principle Mr. Clay proceeded to State he was opposed to abolition & denied that the law contained any abolition principle. Stated that he was opposed to the repeal had voted against <–illegible–> the repeal whil a member of the Legislature of Kentucky But that <he>[1] warned the Citizens of Kentucky of the danger of Connecting themselves with the Cotton planters & Sugar planters of the South that although he pitied their Situation from the *bottom* of his Soul he was opposed to Connecting his destiny with theirs <—illegible—> that the whol Civilized world was opposed to Slavery England France &c and he again Solemny warned them of their danger of Such a connexion <—*should be formed*—>. Having Consumed about two hours in thus repeling the Charge of producing a division in the whig Ranks he Sat down when Mr. T. Marshall[6] rose and after very high wrought Eloquenc upon Mr. Clay's Speech proceeded to State that he was the advocate of <the>[1] Same principles had fought Side by Side with Mr. C in defense of the law in question and though he Could not See that it had any Connexion with the abolition question he was Decidedy opposed to Connecting their destinies with Cotton & Sugar Planters of the South. That the <—white—> population of the non Slaveholding States was about 4 to 1 of <the>[1] whitepopulation of the Slave States, take South Carolina & Kentucky <for example>[1] Kentucky had about 5. Whites to 1 black Carolina 350.000 blacks to 150.000 whites[7] and <asked>[1] if Kentucky was willing to allow 330.000 *half Starved ragged dirty thieving Niggars* to poured in upon <them>[1] drive out the free labor of whites <—to be poured in upon them—> He further Contended with <more>[1] ingenuity <—illegible—> than fairness that the law had produced a wonderful effect<—ing—> in reducing the number of Slaves in Kentucky Since its passage &c

You may readily Suppose the feelin[gs] <—the feelings—> of any Southern man on <hearing>[1] Such principles in Such a place and I determined to reply as Soon as he concluded but a <—illegible—> Call for Wickliff[8] from the Spectators was answered by an apology <—illegible—> That the lateness of the hour &c at the Same time the company began to disperse So that I was prevented. Yet I think it duty to apprise the South of the opinions entertained and advocated by the *whigs* in a State where they expected funds, and when <that>[1] the necessity occurs they may be prepared to act as men. Yours truely

J E Davis[9]

[PS]

My dear Brothr — Gueandotte[10] 25th July 1840

we are thus far and take the Stage in the morning for white Sulphr Springs & So on to New York I Send you a rough Sheet which you may corect and Send to the Press it is not <—as Prefect—> <Such>[1] as I would make it if I had time to Copy it but it is in Substance <—correct—> and in fact Correct but not So full as it Should be

Your Brothr

ALS (Jefferson Hayes-Davis, Colorado Springs, 1969). Addressed: "Jefferson Davis Warrenton Mississippi." Enclosure missing.

[1] Interlined.

[2] Joseph Davis here mentions the issues of the 1840 political campaign in which the Whigs elected their first President, William Henry Harrison. For a discussion of the issues, see Van Deusen, *Jacksonian Era*, especially chapter 7.

[3] Cassius M. Clay (1810–1903), prominent and controversial Kentucky abolitionist, was born on his father's estate in Madison County and attended Transylvania University before his graduation from Yale in 1832. Clay served in the state legislature in 1835 and 1837, and in 1840 was elected to the house from Lexington. Defeated for reelection in 1841, Clay opened a newspaper in Lexington in 1845 and began a campaign against slavery. He opposed the annexation of Texas but served with distinction in the Mexican War, being taken prisoner in 1847. He supported Zachary Taylor in 1848 and joined the Republican party at its formation. In 1861 Lincoln offered Clay a diplomatic post in Russia, but he did not serve there until 1863. He retired to his estate in 1869 and was adjudged a lunatic by a Richmond, Kentucky, court shortly before his death (*DAB*; see also Smiley, *Lion of White Hall*).

[4] Cassius Clay, because he became an active critic of the slave system in his successful 1840 campaign for the state legislature, was accused of splitting the party into Conscience and Cotton Whigs (Smiley, *Lion of White Hall*, 43). Clay's opponent in the election was Robert Wickliffe, Jr., a Cotton Whig (see *n.* 8 below).

[5] The so-called Negro Law of 1833, a law prohibiting further importation of slaves into the state, did not prohibit intrastate trade. The result was that the Bluegrass region around Lexington, well supplied with slaves, was able to sell to other counties at tremendous profits. But the law was also designed to reduce the Negro population gradually; some slaveowners, therefore, were anxious to repeal the law even though it meant undermining their lucrative monopoly (Smiley, *Lion of White Hall*, 44–45).

[6] Thomas Alexander Marshall (1794–1871), nephew of Chief Justice John Marshall, was born in Kentucky and graduated from Yale in 1815. Marshall opened a law office in Frankfort the next year, moved to Paris, Kentucky, in 1819, and was elected to the United States House, 1831–35. Appointed a justice of the state court of appeals in 1835, he retained that office until 1856, and during that time was twice chief justice. He retired to Chicago but returned to Kentucky and served as a Unionist in the legislature, 1863–65. He died at his home in Louisville (*DAB*).

[7] According to official 1840 census returns, the white population of the North was almost ten million and that of the South almost four and a half million (*Historical Statistics of the United States*, 11–12). In 1840 the free white population of Kentucky was 590,253 and the slave and free colored population 189,575; South Carolina's number of free whites was 259,084 and of slave and free colored 335,314 (*Sixth Census of the United States* [Book I], 230, 288).

[8] Robert Wickliffe, Jr. (1815–50), a member of the Kentucky legislature, 1835–37 and 1841, was defeated by Cassius M. Clay in 1840, and a year later Clay challenged Wickliffe to a duel because of insulting remarks made about Clay's political record. The duel ended without bloodshed, but the two remained enemies (Conner and Thomas, "Documents," Kentucky Historical *Register*, LXVI, 305; Smiley, *Lion of White Hall*, 44–49, 51–53; Collins, *History of Kentucky*, II, 170). Wickliffe later was first secretary of the United States legation in Spain and chargé d'affaires to Sardinia (Throck-

morton, *A Genealogical and Historical Account*, 398).

9 Joseph Emory Davis (sketch, 1:19, *n.* 1; 1:Appendix IV, Entry 15).

10 Guyandotte, Virginia (now West Virginia), was founded in 1810 above the mouth of the Guyandot River where it flows into the Ohio near Huntington. "The growth of the town was influenced by the opening of the James River and Kanawha Turnpike in 1830, and Guyandotte became a post for overland travel and an important point of steamboat embarkation on the Ohio River" (Writers of the W.P.A., *West Virginia*, 240).

To William Allen[1]

1:533

Warren County Mi[ssissippi,] 24th July 1840

"I long hae thought my honored friend
A something to hae sent ye,"[2] and though I have nothing now more than my thanks for your kind recollection of me and these in my heart I have often returned to you. I take the occasion of your return from the sphere of your public duties—to break perhaps you will say the only repose which those duties leave you to enjoy—well, I bring my offering of thanks, the sacrifice of a pure spirit would always burn, I am willing that mine should be adjudged by that test.

I received your speech of Feby. eleventh on the assumption of state debts[3] and could but illy express to you the gratification it gave me as your friend and as such I candidly tell you, I consider it the best English sample of the Demosthenean style. I recollect you saw in Mr. Calhoun's speech on the independent Treasy,[4] an especial likeness to the grecian orator I thought he was too sententious, nor indeed could any one opening a question of expediency or dwelling on details of finance speak as Demosthenes did when he addressed men nearly as well informed as himself on the subject of which he spoke and addressed them not to argue but to lay bare before them the true issue and excite them to action—but perhaps like the Vicar of Wakefield said to the lecturer on Cosmogony you may say to me—however with this difference that instead of once you may have heard all this a dozen times before[5] and that instead of the second it is the first time you have heard it from me.

Before I quit the subject of speeches I must tell you of an old democratic friend of mine who lives some distance back in the hills and who notwithstanding the great increase of Post Offices is quite out of striking distance of a mail line—he came to see me in the spring of '38 I handed him your speech on the independent Treasy. Bill[6] after reading it, he asked me to let him take it home and show it to some of his neighbors. I have seen him frequently since but his "neighbors" have not yet gotten through with it—when Lord Byron saw an American edition of his works he said it seemed like to posthumous fame—recurring to my old friend of the hills, he states it as a political maxim that "no honest sensible whig can read Allen's and Benton's[7] speeches without turning their politics"

I am living as retired as a man on the great thoroughfare of the Mississippi can be, and just now the little society which exists hereabout has been driven away by the presence of the summer's heat and the fear of the summer's disease.

Our Staple, Cotton, is distressingly low and I fear likely to remain so until there is a diminished production of it, an event which the embarassed condition of cotton planters in this section will not allow them to consider—if our Yankee friends and their coadjutors should get up a scheme for bounties to particular branches of industry I think the cotton growers may come in with the old plea of the manufacturers "not able at present to progress without it."[8]

With assurances of sincere regard of the pleasure it will always give me to hear from you and to mark your success I am yr. friend

JEFFN. DAVIS

ALS (William Allen Papers, Volume III, Library of Congress). Addressed: "Honble. Wm. Allen U. S. Senator Chilicothe Ohio." Endorsed: "not yet ans 1840." Printed: D. Rowland, *Papers*, I, 4–5.

1 William Allen (sketch, 1:527, *n.* 15).

2 Davis substitutes "honored" for "youthful" in this quotation from Robert Burns's "Epistle to a Young Friend."

3 Allen's February 11 speech is printed in the *Congressional Globe*, 26th Cong., 1st Sess., Appendix, 309–14.

4 John C. Calhoun's speeches in support of the Independent Treasury Bill, made in the second session of the Twenty-fifth Congress, are in the *Congressional Globe* for that session, Appendix, 176–81, 188–95, 243–50, 265–66.

5 The vicar of Wakefield said to the lecturer on cosmogony: "'I ask pardon, sir,' cried I, 'for interrupting so much learning; but I think I have heard all this before'" (Goldsmith, *Vicar of Wakefield*, chapter 25).

6 Allen's remarks in favor of the Independent Treasury Bill, made in the Senate February 20, 1838, are printed in the *Congressional Globe*, 25th Cong., 2nd Sess., Appendix, 250–57.

7 The reference is undoubtedly to Thomas Hart Benton (1782–1858), Democratic senator from Missouri for thirty years. He was born in North Carolina, attended Chapel Hill College, was admitted to the bar, and opened his practice in Tennessee in 1806. Benton was Andrew Jackson's aide and an officer in the War of 1812; he later moved to Missouri where he edited the St. Louis *Enquirer* and resumed his law practice. Elected to the Senate in 1821, he was elected to a single term in the

House in 1853. He died in Washington (*Biographical Directory of the American Congress*, 546).

8 The cotton crop of 1839–40 was the largest on record to that date; over half the bales exported from New Orleans went to Great Britain and a third to the Continent, with a decline in the amount taken by northern mills. Low prices, of course, were the result, the lowest occurring in the months of December, March, and April. The index of world prices, the "Liverpool Circular" (August 7, 1840), indicated a more favorable business trend, and by the end of the season, prices were up 33 percent (Boyle, *Cotton and the New Orleans Cotton Exchange*, 27, 43). For a brief discussion of business relations between southern planters and northern middlemen in marketing cotton in the 1830's–40's, see Cohn, *Life and Times of King Cotton*, 81–89.

From Eliza Van Benthuysen Davis and Caroline Davis 1:534

MY DEAR BROTHER Lexington July 24th 1840

I feel that if I do not write to you just at this Moment that I May not be able to do so untill We reach New York. My hand trembles so Much that I can Scarcely command my pen—they have been at it all day—Doct Mitchell[1]—Caroline,[2] Jane[3] & Catherine[4] are all in the room Mr Davis[5] has left to light his cigar, & perhaps to seek More agreeable Society. We leave in the Morning all except Jane Who remains with Mrs Ficklin[6]—the other Jinny[7] is at Nazareth.[8] Mr Davis did not wish to remain untill after the examination & as Jane is to receive so Many honors, it would not answer for her to leave & she did not appear to desire it. I left poor little Martha with her, I feel lost without the child—would that there were more like her. Julia has grown considerably Doct Mitchell reached New York the day we left home, Mary[9] & the child[10] are at Brother's[11] the Doct hastened on to see his Mother who is dangerously ill; said to be no hopes of her recovery.

Caroline perhaps will remain at the North at school she is very Anxious to do so—<—she is very pretty—>[12] but too mu<—ch of a child—>[12] I think it would be Wrong for her to go home, & as she is not contented at Nazareth it would be wrong to leave her there. Doct Mitchell will remain with his Mother—he had some idea of returning for Mary but was waiting to hear of Mr Davis—thought he had gone up the river. I fear Mary will become impatient at having to remain longer than she desired.

Mr Ficklin[13] has been confined for some weeks, with something the Matter With the bone of one of his legs but he talks as much as ever & I think looks quite as well as ever.

Mrs Ficklin is fearful Jane will be very lonely, as an opperation has to be performed on Mr Ficklin & she will be obliged to remain with him. We are promised a room for her at Mrs. Jeutts[14] Ann will be much company for her. I did not like it much

Dear Uncle

It seems strange to me how much a few days among strangers can change a person—before I left Nazareth I would not have dreamed of writing to you but now you see I write with considerable ease—not ease either for I have a stiff iron pen. Ma[15] has gone down to see some Ladies in the parlour and has a Thousand little things to do so she left me to finish hers for her. O! Uncle you cannot know how much I have wished to get in some little place to my self away from the noise & bustle of the world. I have but one thing to do & find pleasure in nothing else   I wish to give some happiness to Pa[5] but I fear I cannot give much at present therefore I am going to school again to remain two years & when I return perhaps I will not Make my friends ashamed. But I know well that education aloan will not cause the person who possesses it to give <—pleasure—> happiness or to be happy them selves   it is more <the>[16] amiable qualities that are necessary for this. I am sorry Ma said I was dissatisfied with my school as this would lead you to suppose that I <—did not—> had acted wrongly myself or was affraid to stay untill the examination which was not the case. I like Cousin Jane very much   she will remain at your old friend Mrs Ficklin   she does not like it much now but I think she will afterwards. You must forgive this bad & careless letter. Your Niece CAROLINE[2]

Carry perposed to finish My letter to you as I was too Much occupied. I know not what she has written. Mrs Juett—Mrs Woolly[17] & Mrs Ficklin have been here. I was surprised to see Mrs Wooly as I thought she was dead but it was Col Woollys[18] Wife[19] Who died in New Orleans. Mrs Woolly looks old & is Very fleshy—she was very much dressed, Major Woolly or Judge[20] is thin.

Oh! that I could write to you something that would be grattifying but I have not the power. My heart—if ever I had any or something that is in its place gives me much pain. My mind is dull very dull—every thing arround Me appears as a dream, I frequently think can this be real. Am I the same being who twelve years ago was here; I can remember you & Florida[21] as if it was but yesterday.[22]

Carry & Jane are packing every Moment asking Me Something. I [can][23] not write when My feelings are so I will not say excited, but stag[torn]—you will think strange of My going to New York, but I feel [torn] I cannot stay—& as Mr Davis appears perfectly willing for me to g[o][23]—I must do so—if I should die on the way—persons about me Notice the little attacks I have & if Mr Davis leaves me I know they will be More frequent.

Mrs Smith is boarding here, but she did Not recognize Me this Morning & I was not at all desirous for her to do so. I have been to but one meal since we have been here, the effort to dress has prevented Me.

I hope to find a letter here from you on our return which I hope will be soon.

Jane & Cate often speak of you, Carry was conversing the other day with her Pa on the Merrits of the Presidents—& the states that had given birth to them—she said Mississippi never had one & her Pa answered <perhaps>[16] Never would. Cate spoke unexpectedly—Said that Uncle Jeff would be President after while—she is a very good child at least to Me, she seems to feel that she has to take Care of me. Instead that I should take care of her it ammuses me sometimes but not in the same way counsellor Philips is ammused.

Jane & Cate send their love to you also one Who feels that she is your Sister—Good Night—we leave at four in the Morning—Love again from all & that you may be happy is the prayer of your Sister

ELIZA[15]

<Carry[2] Scratched out where I had Written she was rather pretty. She is an enigma to me; I believe she has but little affection for any one unless it is her Pa[5] & Sister Mary.[9] I am sorry she does Not love Me, as she Might feel more happy by doing so—every one that has been about me lately has exhibited kind feelings towards me—& the time may come when she would wish for a friend as sincere—it gives me a pang occasionally—but I must endure it & whilst My husband[5] loves. me I feel I ought not to be miserable; he is very Kind to me—good bye again—remember Me to all & think kindly of your Sister

ELIZA[15]>[24]

ALS (Papers of Jefferson Davis and Family, Library of Congress). Addressed: "Jefferson Davis Warrenton Mississippi."

[1] Charles J. Mitchell, Eliza's stepson-in-law (sketch, 1:521, *n.* 4; 1:Appendix IV, Entry 27).

[2] Caroline Davis Robins Leonard,

Eliza's stepdaughter (sketch, 1:395, *n.* 8; 1:Appendix IV, Entry 31).

[3] "Jane" may be Jane Lucinda Davis Farish, Eliza's niece (sketch, 1:363, *n.* 35; 1:Appendix IV, Entry 90).

[4] Very likely a member of Watson Van Benthuysen's (Eliza's brother) family (Van Benthuysen, "Supplement to the Van Benthuysen, Conklin-Dally and Seaward Genealogies," *passim* [typescript in New York State Library, Albany]).

[5] Joseph Emory Davis, Eliza's husband (sketch, 1:19, *n.* 1; 1:Appendix IV, Entry 15).

[6] Mrs. Joseph Ficklin; see 1:6, *n.* 3.

[7] "Jinny" is probably Jane Davis Stamps Alexander (sketch, 1:528, *n.* 14; 1:Appendix IV, Entry 64).

[8] For Nazareth, see 1:526, *n.* 7.

[9] Mary Lucinda Davis Mitchell, Eliza's stepdaughter (sketch, 1:362, *n.* 11; 1:Appendix IV, Entry 26).

[10] Joseph Davis Mitchell, Eliza Davis' step-grandson and first child of Charles J. and Mary Lucinda Davis Mitchell, was born in France where his father studied medicine (H. A. Davis, *The Davis Family*, 81). After Mary Lucinda's death in 1846, her three children were adopted by their grandfather, Joseph E. Davis (Davis *v.* Bowmar, 76 [Mississippi Department of Archives and History, Jackson]). Joseph Davis Mitchell apparently served for awhile in the Confederate Army (Mitchell to Miles, August 20, 1863, diary entry of May 13, 1865 [Lise Mitchell Papers, Howard-Tilton Memorial Library, Tulane University, New Orleans]). He was unmarried as late as 1870 (H. A. Davis, *The Davis Family*, 81); although his death date is unknown, he was still living in 1911 (tax receipt, December 6, 1911 [Mitchell Family Papers, Howard-Tilton Memorial Library, Tulane University, New Orleans]).

[11] Watson Van Benthuysen (sketch, 1:395, *n.* 7).

[12] This phrase may well be the part Caroline scratched out; see *n.* 24 below.

[13] Joseph Ficklin; see 1:6, *n.* 3.

[14] "Mrs. Jeutt" is possibly the widow of Kentucky portrait artist Matthew H. Jouett. She was the former Margaret Henderson Allen, daughter of William Allen of Fayette County, and was living in Lexington as late as 1849 (Bentley to Laswell, March 17, 1970 [Jefferson Davis Association, Rice University, Houston]; Wilson, "Jouett: A Review," *Filson Club History Quarterly*, XIII, 81*n.*).

[15] Eliza Van Benthuysen Davis, Davis' sister-in-law and Caroline's stepmother (sketch, 1:361, *n.* 8; 1:Appendix IV, Entry 25).

[16] Interlined.

[17] "Mrs. Woolly," the former Sally H. Wickliffe, daughter of Robert Wickliffe of Lexington, married Aaron K. Woolley in 1827 (Clift, *Kentucky Marriages*, 50).

[18] Abram R. Woolley, a native of New Jersey, was appointed a captain in the army in 1812 and served in the Ordnance Corps and Seventh Infantry before his dismissal from the service in 1829, when his rank was lieutenant colonel (Heitman, *Historical Register*, I, 1060). Davis may have met him while both were stationed at Jefferson Barracks in 1829 (1:138, *n.* 3).

[19] Caroline Preston Woolley was born in Virginia in 1806, daughter of Major William Preston. She married Abram R. Woolley in Louisville, Kentucky, in 1827; they had two sons at the time of her death, sometime before May 1840 (Folder 190, Preston Davie Genealogical Collection and Joyes Collection [Preston Family Papers, The Filson Club, Louisville, Kentucky]).

[20] Aaron K. Woolley (or Wooley), born in 1800 in Pennsylvania, entered West Point in 1815 but failed to be graduated. He studied law and opened his practice in Port Gibson, Mississippi, in 1827. He married, the same year, the eldest daughter of Robert Wickliffe, in Lexington, Kentucky (see *n.* 17 above). Woolley was elected to the Kentucky legislature in 1832 and to

the state senate, 1835–39. He was a circuit judge for seven years before his death from cholera in 1849 in Lexington (*Biographical Encyclopaedia of Kentucky*, 418; *Register of Graduates* [1964], 207).

21 Florida A. Davis McCaleb Laughlin, Eliza's stepdaughter (sketch, 1:19, *n.* 9; 1:Appendix IV, Entry 28).

22 See 1:124 for evidence of Davis' presence in Lexington in 1828.

23 Manuscript torn.

24 In the margin of the first page.

From Anna Amanda Smith 1:535

DEAR UNCLE Locust grove[1] agust 27th. 1840

I have intended writing to you but have been so busily employed with my studies, that I may say I have not had time. I Cousin Mary[2] and Anne[3] are going to school at present to Mrs Mylotte[4] who teachs us French English and Music. Ma[5] wanted Cousin Ellen[6] to come down to school but grandmama[7] could not spare her. they were all well when I last heard from them but Cousin Jane[8] who had the fever. sister Lucy[9] has got into her house she is very comfortablely settled. brother Jed[10] goes to school with Cousin William Stamps[11] in Woodville[12] he appears to be learning very fast. if you come down in October with Cousin Jane Davis as we expect Ma says he may return with you.

Cousin Mary[13] writes that her Child is the prettiest Joe[14] that ever was. I think if she could see Sister Cora's[15] she would think it the most beautiful Smith[16] in the world.

all unite in sending our best love to you accept the same from your niece

AMANDA SMITH[17]

ALS (Jefferson Hayes-Davis, Colorado Springs, 1969). Addressed: "Jefferson Davis Esqr Warrenton Miss."

1 See 1:526, *n.* 1 for "Locust Grove."

2 Mary Jane Bradford Brodhead Sayre (sketch, 1:363, *n.* 20; 1:Appendix IV, Entry 74).

3 Probably Anna Matilda Bradford Miles (sketch, 1:363, *n.* 19; 1:Appendix IV, Entry 77).

4 The three girls were doubtless attending the Female Seminary, a school established by Mrs. Mylotte at the former residence of Captain Williams on Upper Jackson Road, three miles from St. Francisville, Louisiana (Woodville [Mississippi] *Republican*, April 4, 1841).

5 Anna Eliza Davis Smith, Davis' sister (sketch, 1:419, *n.* 30; 1:Appendix IV, Entry 18).

6 Ellen Mary Davis Anderson (sketch, 1:363, *n.* 36; 1:Appendix IV, Entry 92).

7 Jane Cook Davis (sketch, 1:22, *n.* 4; 1:Appendix IV, Entry 14).

8 Jane Lucinda Davis Farish (sketch, 1:363, *n.* 35; 1:Appendix IV, Entry 90).

9 Lucinda Jane Smith Boyle (1:Appendix IV, Entry 49), sister of Anna Amanda Smith, was born in 1822

(H. A. Davis, *The Davis Family*, 83). In May 1836 she married William D. Boyle; they had no children (*Be It Known and Remembered: Bible Records*, IV, 18; Ganier, Davis Family Tree [Alfred F. Ganier, Nashville, 1968]; H. A. Davis, *The Davis Family*, 83). Little is known of Lucinda's life except that she inherited "Locust Grove" plantation near St. Francisville, Louisiana, was widowed by 1847, and was living at "Locust Grove" as late as 1887 (Strode, *Private Letters*, 348; H. A. Davis, *The Davis Family*, 83; Boyle to Davis, November 11, 1887 [Museum of the Confederacy]). She died in August 1889 (*Be It Known and Remembered: Bible Records*, IV, 20).

10 Jedediah Davis Smith (1:Appendix IV, Entry 51), brother of Anna Amanda Smith, was born July 31, 1824 (Gravestone ["God's Acre," "Locust Grove" plantation cemetery, near St. Francisville, Louisiana]). His marriage to Susan M. Buck produced no offspring (H. A. Davis, *The Davis Family*, 83; Watts and De Grummond, *Solitude*, 65). He died February 23, 1891 (Gravestone ["God's Acre," "Locust Grove" plantation cemetery, near St. Francisville, Louisiana]).

11 William Stamps, Jr. (1:Appendix IV, Entry 68), Amanda Smith's cousin, attended school in Woodville before going on to Bethany College, Bethany, Virginia. He died there February 9, 1843, at the age of seventeen (More, Genealogical Data [Jefferson Davis Association, Rice University, Houston]; Woodville [Mississippi] *Republican*, March 11, 1843).

12 See 1:529, *n.* 10 for the boys' schools in Woodville.

13 Mary Lucinda Davis Mitchell (sketch, 1:362, *n.* 11; 1:Appendix IV, Entry 26).

14 Joseph Davis Mitchell (sketch, 1:534, *n.* 10).

15 Marie Coralie Guibert Smith (1:Appendix IV, Entry 46), sister-in-law of Anna Amanda Smith, was born in 1822 at "The Valley" plantation on Bayou Sara in West Feliciana Parish, Louisiana. After her father's death, Marie Coralie lived with her mother and brother at "Solitude," a plantation across the bayou from Marie Coralie's birthplace. On April 24, 1839, she married Joseph Davis Smith, a physician, and lived at "Solitude," which Dr. Smith had bought the year before. They had twelve children, four of whom died before reaching maturity. Marie Coralie herself died soon after giving birth to twins on June 30, 1863 (Watts and De Grummond, *Solitude*, 13, Family Record, 24–25).

16 Mary Corlie (or Marie Coralie) Smith Nugent, Amanda Smith's niece and first child of Joseph Davis and Marie Coralie Guibert Smith, was born December 19, 1839, on "Solitude" plantation, West Feliciana Parish, Louisiana. On December 15, 1859, she married Richard J. Nugent. She died September 1, 1867 (Watts and De Grummond, *Solitude*, Family Record).

17 Anna Amanda Smith Smith (sketch, 1:526, *n.* 9; 1:Appendix IV, Entry 53).

APPENDIX I

FRAGMENTARY AND UNDATED LETTERS

FRAGMENT

Sarah Knox Taylor Davis[1] to Margaret Mackall Smith Taylor

Editorial Note: Although this last known letter of Sarah Davis was apparently seen by a number of Davis and Taylor biographers, its present location is unknown. The item has therefore been pieced together from the sources cited, and it is certain that it is not complete. An article in the New Orleans *Daily Picayune*, August 23, 1910, by Trist Wood, indicates that in the missing portions Sarah Davis mentioned she had received two letters from home, and commented that she had received news of the marriage of Mary Street, daughter of the Indian agent at Fort Crawford. The letter was sent to Fort Crawford.

Warrenton,[2] Miss. Aug. 11, 1835

MY DEAREST MOTHER:[3]

I have just received your affectionate letter[4] forwarded to me from Louisville;[5] you may readily imagine the pleasure it afforded me to hear from you. . . . Have you been much annoyed with visitors this year? do tell me who you have been obliged to entertain. How often, my dear Mother, I wish I could look in upon you. I imagine so often I can see you moving about attending to your domestic concerns, down in the cellar skimming the milk or going to feed the chickens. . . . Tell Dick[6] I have a beautiful colt, prettier than his, I expect; when did you hear from dear little Betty?[7] Give my love to her;[8] Mr. Davis sends his best respects to you. did you receive the letter he wrote from St. Louis?[9] My love to Pa[10] and Dick. . . . Remember me most affectionately to Sister[11] and the Doc.[12] Kiss the children.[13] . . .[14] Write to me, my dear mother, as often as you can find time, and tell me all concerning you. Do not[15] make yourself uneasy about me; the country is quite healthy.

MS not found. Partial text from Holman Hamilton, *Zachary Taylor: Soldier of the Republic* (Indianapolis and New York: Bobbs-Merrill, 1941), 107–108; New Orleans *Daily Picayune*, August 28, 1910, p. 9; Hudson Strode, *Jefferson Davis: American Patriot, 1808–1861* (New York: Harcourt, Brace, 1955), 103; Walter L. Fleming, "Jefferson Davis' First Marriage," Mississippi Historical Society, *Publications*, XII (1912), 34. This letter was apparently kept in the Wood family until supposedly given, along with other Taylor material, to the Southern Historical Collection at the University of North Carolina. A search of the Trist Wood Papers at that institution, however, was unsuccessful (Wallace to McIntosh, January 15, 1969, Griffith to Riddle, January 23, 1969 [Jefferson Davis Association, Rice University, Houston]).

[1] Sarah Knox Taylor Davis (sketch, 1:443, *n.* 2; 1:Appendix IV, Entry 94), Davis' first wife.

[2] See 1:482, *n.* 6.

[3] Margaret Mackall Smith Taylor (sketch, 1:483, *n.* 1).

[4] Not found.

[5] Sarah Taylor and Davis were married near Louisville at the home of her aunt, Elizabeth Lee Taylor. See 1:483, *n.* 2.

[6] Richard Taylor (sketch, 1:483, *n.* 11), Sarah Davis' brother.

[7] Probably Mary Elizabeth Taylor, Sarah Davis' younger sister, who was most likely away at school. She was born near Louisville in 1824 or 1826, was educated in Philadelphia, and in 1848 married William W. S. Bliss, her father's aide in the Mexican War. She was mistress of the White House for two years and was an accomplished hostess; her husband was President Taylor's private secretary. In 1853 Bliss died in Mississippi of yellow fever. Mrs. Bliss married Philip P. Dandridge in 1858 and was living in Winchester, Virginia, as late as 1908 (Bixby [ed.], *Letters of Zachary Taylor*, xii–xiii). She died in 1909 (Zachary Taylor, Small File [The Filson Club, Louisville, Kentucky]).

[8] Hamilton's text reads "Give my love to Dr. [Wood]" (*Zachary Taylor*, 108).

[9] The letter from Davis to the Taylors has not been found. It could have been written in May or early June 1835. According to W. L. Fleming ("Davis' First Marriage," Mississippi Historical *Publications*, XII, 29), Davis completed the arrangements for the wedding in St. Louis, and he received part of his army pay through the St. Louis paymaster—although this is not conclusive proof of his presence there—on June 3, 1835 (1:481). In any event, the letter could not have been written before April, since he was in Port Gibson, Mississippi, as late as March 26 (1:473). It is more likely that Davis wrote to his new in-laws on the way from Louisville to Mississippi.

[10] Zachary Taylor (sketch, 1:332, *n.* 3).

[11] Ann Mackall Taylor Wood (sketch, 1:483, *n.* 5).

[12] Dr. Robert Crooke Wood, Sarah Davis' brother-in-law, was born in Rhode Island *ca.* 1800 and started his long army career in 1825 as an assistant surgeon. In 1862 he became assistant surgeon general with the rank of colonel. On March 13, 1865, he was brevetted brigadier general for his Civil War service. He died in 1869 (Bixby [ed.], *Letters of Zachary Taylor*, x; Heitman, *Historical Register*, 1055).

[13] Referring to Sarah Davis' younger sister Betty and brother Dick.

[14] The fragmentary nature of the source texts makes it uncertain whether part of the letter has here been omitted.

[15] Fleming's text reads "Do not you . . ." (W. L. Fleming, "Davis' First Marriage," Mississippi Historical *Publications*, XII, 34).

From Florida A. Davis McCaleb

Diamond Place[1] Oct 15th[2]

If you were not My Uncle Jeff, I should not write to you to-day, for I have a very weak eye, which makes me cross; knowing you to be subject to the like infirmity,[3] and that nothing increases the disease so much as waiting for an answer to a letter. I "do give me credit for my consideration" hasten to thank you for your remembrance of me. I Know you love me very much Uncle Jeff, and have always done so; and you know that I am not forgetful of such kindness. So few bestow such kindness on me, that I cherish it perhaps more fondly, for that reason. You were always too kind to my faults, and too flattering to my few virtues. I remember alway, "the olden time," when we were still friends and school-mates,[4] and then, our golden youth and then, the unwearied affection of after years. Do not believe I shall ever forget, a word kindly spoken a look of encouragement, or the reproval of a fault. I am not changeful, nor ungrateful; then always believe me your truest friend, and most affectionate—

IDA[5]

[PS] Cant you come up to see me? I think you might—when you do so I will return with you. Now do not come only to oblige me for then I shall not <—illegible—> be pleased to go.

ALS (Jefferson Davis Papers, University of Alabama Library, Tuscaloosa). Addressed: "To, Jeff. Davis Esqr Hurricane." Printed: Strode, *Private Letters*, 13–14.

1 See 1:439, *n.* 9.

2 It is unlikely that this letter was written before Davis' return from his trip to Cuba, New York, and Washington, which he began in the fall of 1835 (V. Davis, *Memoir*, I, 165–70). The date of his return is uncertain, but the trip was undoubtedly lengthy, and he had probably not returned long before April 8, 1836, when he received a letter from his mother addressed to him at Warrenton (1:496). The document at hand could not be dated later than the fall of 1838 when Davis built "Brierfield," since it is addressed to him at "Hurricane"; he was definitely in residence at "Brierfield" by December 29, 1838, when he received a letter by messenger at the latter plantation (1:526). Therefore, this letter was most likely written in 1836, 1837, or possibly 1838.

3 Florida also complained of eye trouble in June and July 1833 (see 1:361, 362). Davis had suffered a severe case of malaria in 1835, and after that time had recurrent attacks. "Within at most a few years after 1851, Davis could only discern light with his left eye . . . . By about 1865 it is possible to conclude from available descriptions that Davis suffered from both a corneal ulcer and secondary glaucoma" (K. B. Davis, "Davis and the Mississippi Gubernatorial Contest," 133).

4 Davis went away to school in Kentucky in 1816, when Florida was not yet born, although he did attend an

academy in Wilkinson County part of the time from 1818 until 1823, when he went to Transylvania University. At the latter date, Florida, probably born in 1817 or 1818, could have been no more than six years of age. It is unlikely that they attended the same school for more than a few weeks or months, if ever.

[5] Florida A. Davis McCaleb Laughlin (sketch, 1:19, *n.* 9; 1:Appendix IV, Entry 28).

APPENDIX II

EXTRACTS FROM *JEFFERSON DAVIS . . . A MEMOIR BY HIS WIFE*

Editorial Note: The following extracts, written by Davis, were included by Mrs. Davis in her memoir of him and are printed here rather than in the volume proper because they are undated and undatable. Annotation of events prior to Davis' career will not be attempted.

Concerning Davis and the Nullification Crisis

The nullification by South Carolina, in 1832, of certain acts of Congress,[1] the consequent proclamation of President Jackson,[2] and the "Force Bill,"[3] soon afterward enacted, presented the probability that the troops of the United States would be employed to enforce the execution of the laws in that State, and it was supposed that the regiment to which I belonged[4] would in that event be ordered to South Carolina.

By education, by association, and by preference I was a soldier; then regarding that profession as my vocation for life. Yet, looking the issue squarely in the face, I chose the alternative of abandoning my profession rather than be employed in the subjugation or coercion of a State of the Union, and had fully determined and was prepared to resign my commission immediately on the occurence of such a contingency. The compromise of 1833[5] prevented the threatened calamity, and the sorrowful issue was deferred until a day more drear, which forced upon me the determination of the question of State sovereignty or federal supremacy—of independence or submission to usurpation.[6]

MS not found. Text from Varina Howell Davis, *Jefferson Davis, Ex-President of the Confederate States of America: A Memoir* (2 vols., New York: Belford, 1890), I, 89–90.

[1] South Carolina led Southern discontent over the 1828 "Tariff of Abom-

inations." In response to what many Southerners felt to be unfair policy—the tariff rested heavily upon an agricultural region—John C. Calhoun wrote the South Carolina Exposition, asserting that the protective tariff was an unconstitutional exercise of the taxing power. The remedy, Calhoun suggested, lay in interposition, the supposed right of a state to nullify federal law. The Tariff of 1832 modified that of 1828, but not sufficiently to satisfy South Carolina. With Calhoun again articulating the grievance, South Carolina's state convention declared the tariffs of 1828 and 1832 null and void and prohibited their enforcement in that state after February 1, 1832. Any use of force by the federal government would, according to the ordinance of the convention, destroy the bond between the state and the Union. For further information, see Van Deusen, *Jacksonian Era*, 39–40, 59–60, 71–72.

[2] Part of President Andrew Jackson's reaction to South Carolina's attempt to nullify the Tariff of 1832 was his proclamation of December 10, 1832, which stated the President's belief that "the power to annul a law of the United States . . . [was] *incompatible with the existence of the Union, contradicted expressly by the letter of the Constitution, unauthorized by its spirit, inconsistent with every principle on which it was founded, and destructive of the great object for which it was formed.*" Jackson went on to warn that the laws would be enforced, and asked whether South Carolina was ready to incur the guilt of treason (Richardson [comp.], *Messages and Papers of the Presidents*, II, 640–56). For a sketch of Jackson, see 1:239, *n.* 2.

[3] The Force Bill, signed into law by President Jackson on March 2, 1833, provided that when the usual methods of customs collection were impracticable, the President could move the sites of customhouses, even placing them on board ship if necessary, and further provided that whenever the laws of the United States were obstructed by forces too strong to be overcome by normal procedures, the President was empowered to use the military to ensure their enforcement (*Statutes at Large of the United States*, IV [1846], 632–35).

[4] The First Infantry (Davis was in Company B) was then stationed at Fort Crawford. Davis was on furlough at the time of Jackson's proclamation and the passage of the Force Bill (1:342, 343; *n.* 3 above).

[5] The Tariff of 1833, otherwise known as the Compromise of 1833, was signed into law March 2, 1833. It provided for a gradual reduction in tariff rates over a ten-year period. After July 1, 1842, no rate would be over 20 percent of the value of the goods taxed (*Statutes at Large of the United States*, IV [1846], 629–31). South Carolina accepted the new tariff but attempted to assert the right of interposition once again by nullifying the Force Bill. See Van Deusen, *Jacksonian Era*, 76–79.

[6] During the Senate debates on the Compromise of 1850, Davis recalled his feelings at the time of the nullification controversy. "I well remember, upon another occasion," he said, "when one State stood arrayed against the power of the Federal Government, in the well-known nullification contest, what was the feeling of the army. Though unwilling to refer to myself, yet, as connected with it, I will say that I was then an officer of the United States army, and looked forward to the probability of being ordered to Charleston in the event of actual collision. Then, sir, much as I valued my commission, much as I desired to remain in the army, and disapproving as I did the remedy resorted to, that commission would have been torn to tatters before it would have been used in civil war with the State of South Carolina" (*Congressional Globe*, 31st Cong., 1st Sess., Appendix, 1471 [July 31, 1850]).

Concerning Zachary Taylor and the Construction of Fort Crawford

In 1832, Zachary Taylor[1] became colonel of the First Infantry, with head-quarters at Fort Crawford, Prairie du Chien.[2] The barracks were unfinished, and his practical mind and conscientious attention to every duty were manifest in the progress and completion of the work.

MS not found. Text from Varina Howell Davis, *Jefferson Davis, Ex-President of the Confederate States of America: A Memoir* (2 vols., New York: Belford, 1890), I, 93.

[1] Zachary Taylor (sketch, 1:332, *n.* 3).

[2] Fort Crawford, Prairie du Chien (see 1:231, *n.* 12).

Concerning the Northwestern Indians and the War of 1812

The troubles on the Indian frontier, which had attracted attention in 1808, continued to increase in number and magnitude until, in 1811, General Harrison, afterward President of the United States, marched against the stronghold of the Shawnees, the most warlike of the hostile tribes, and whose chief, Tecumptha (The Walker), was first in sagacity, influence, and ambition, of the Northwestern Indians. While professing peace, he contemplated a general war between the Indians and the whites, and was said to be instigated and abetted by British emissaries. It is known that he sent out, and some suppose bore, the wampum to the Muscagees (Creeks) of Georgia. This supposition is fortified by the circumstances of his blood relationship to the Creeks, and by his absence when his brother, The Prophet, on November 7, 1811, to prevent General Harrison's advance on the principal town, made a night attack on his camp at Teppecanoe. This battle, or rather the fear of its renewal, caused the Indians hastily to abandon their permanent village. General Harrison, with his numerous wounded, returned to Vincennes, and the field of his recent occupations was unoccupied.

On the following June, of 1812, war was declared against England, and this increased the widespread and not unfounded fears of Indian invasion which existed in the valley of the Wabash. To protect Vincennes from a sudden assault, Captain Z. Taylor[1] was ordered to Fort Harrison, a stockade on the river above Vincennes, and with his company of infantry, about fifty strong, made preparation to defend the place. He had not long to wait. A large body of Indians, knowing the small size of the garrison, came, confidently counting on its capture; but, as it is a rule in their warfare to seek by stratagem to avoid equal risk and probable loss, they tried their various strategetic expedients, which were foiled by the sound judgment, vigilance, and courage of the commander; and when the final attack was made, the brave little garrison repulsed it with such loss to the assailants that when, in the following October, General Hopkins came to support Fort Harrison, no Indians were to be found thereabout. For the defence of "Fort Harrison" Captain Taylor received the brevet of major, an honor which had seldom if ever before been conferred for service in Indian war.

In the following November Major Taylor, with a battalion of regulars, formed part of the command of General Hopkins in the expedition against the hostile Indians at the head waters of the Wabash. In 1814, with his separate command, being then a major by commission, he made a campaign against the hostile Indians and their British allies on Rock River, which was so successful as to give subsequent security to that immediate frontier.

MS not found. Text from Varina Howell Davis, *Jefferson Davis, Ex-President of the Confederate States of America: A Memoir* (2 vols., New York: Belford, 1890), I, 111–13.

[1] Zachary Taylor (sketch, 1:332, *n.* 3).

Concerning the Black Hawk War

The second Black Hawk campaign[1] occurred in 1832,[2] and Colonel Taylor,[3] with the greater part of his regiment, joined the army commanded by General Atkinson,[4] and with it moved from Rock Island[5] up the valley of Rock River, following after Black Hawk,[2] who had gone to make a junction with the Pottowatomie band of the Prophet,[6] a nephew of Black Hawk.

This was the violation of a treaty he had made with General Gaines in 1831,[7] by which he was required to remove to the west of the Mississippi, relinquishing all claim to the Rock River villages. It was assumed that his purpose in returning to the east side of the river was hostile, and from the defenceless condition of frontier settlers, and the horror of savage atrocity, a great excitement was created, due rather to his fame as a warrior than to the number of his followers.

If, as he subsequently stated, his design was to go out and live peaceably with his nephew, the Prophet, rather than with the "Foxes," of whom Keokuk[8] was chief, that design may have been frustrated by the lamentable mistake of some mounted volunteers in hastening forward in pursuit of Black Hawk, who, with his band—men, women, and children—was going up on the south side of Rock River.

The vanity of the young Indians was inflated by their success at Stillman's Run,[9] as was shown by some exultant messages, and the sagacious old chief, whatever he may have previously calculated on, now saw that war was inevitable and immediate. With his band recruited by warriors from the Prophet's band, he crossed the north side of Rock River, and passing through the swamp Koshenong,[10] fled over the prairies west of the Four Lakes[11] toward the Wisconsin River. General Dodge[12] with a battalion of mounted miners pursued and overtook the Indians while crossing the Wisconsin and attacked their rear-guard,[13] which, when the main body had crossed, swam the river and joined in the retreat over the Kickapoo hills toward the Mississippi River. General Atkinson with his whole army continued the pursuit, and after a toilsome march overtook the Indians north of Prairie du Chien, on the bank of the Mississippi River, to the west side of which they were preparing to cross in bark canoes made on the spot. That purpose was foiled by the accidental arrival of a steamboat with a gun on board. The Indians took cover in a willow marsh, and there, on August 3d, was fought the battle of the "Bad Axe."[14] The Indians were defeated, dispersed, and the campaign ended.

In the meantime General Scott,[15] with troops from the east, took chief command and established his headquarters at Rock Island. Thither General Atkinson went with the regular troops, except that part of the First Infantry which constituted the garrison of Fort Crawford,[16] with these Colonel Taylor returned to Prairie du Chien.

After a short time it was reported that the Indians were on an island in the river above the prairie, and Colonel Taylor sent a Lieutenant (Lieutenant Davis) with an appropriate command to explore the island. Unmistakable evidence of their very recent presence was found, and contemporaneously Black Hawk, with the remnant of his band and accompanied by some friendly Winnebagoes, appeared under a white flag on the east bank of the river, and the lieutenant returned with them to the fort, where Colonel Taylor treated them as surrendered hostiles. Their trails were followed through the brush to the west side of the island, where signs of canoes having just been pushed off were discovered. The lieutenant* and his party recrossed the island to get their boats, and there saw, on the east side of the river, a large collection of Indians under a white flag. On going to the group it proved to be Black Hawk with a portion of his band, with a few Winnebagoes, who said Black Hawk had surrendered to them, and that they wanted to take him to the fort and to see the Indian agent.[17] The lieutenant went with the Indians to the fort, reported to Colonel Taylor, among other things, his disbelief of the Winnebago story. The grand old soldier merely replied, "They want the credit of being friendly and to get a reward, let them have it."

* Lieutenant Davis.

MS not found. Text from Varina Howell Davis, *Jefferson Davis, Ex-President of the Confederate States of America: A Memoir* (2 vols., New York: Belford, 1890), I, 138–42.

1 For the distinction between the two campaigns of the Black Hawk War, see 1:267, *n.* 8.

2 For a discussion of Black Hawk and the Black Hawk War, see 1:334, *n.* 6, and *nn.* 7, 9, 11, 13, 14 below.

3 Zachary Taylor (sketch, 1:332, *n.* 3).

4 Henry Atkinson (sketch, 1:301, *n.* 7).

5 Rock Island was the site of Fort Armstrong (1:267, *n.* 3).

6 "The Prophet" (sketch, 1:335, *n.* 13).

7 General Edmund P. Gaines attempted to persuade Black Hawk and his "British band" of the Sauk and Fox Indians to move off their tribal lands east of the Mississippi River. These lands had been ceded in 1804, but Black Hawk denounced the cession even though he had once joined in confirming it. With the aid of threats made by Keokuk, the leader of a peaceful faction of the Indians, Gaines succeeded in gaining Black Hawk's agreement to a treaty, June 30, 1831, by which the "British band" was "at all times . . . [thereafter] to reside and hunt . . . upon their own lands west of the Mississippi River, and to be obedient to their laws and treaties." The integrity of Indian lands claimed under the treaties of 1825 and 1830 was to be guaranteed. See Prucha, *Sword of the Republic*, 212–17; Stevens, *Black Hawk War*, 96–98.

8 Keokuk (sketch, 1:335, *n.* 11).

9 Stillman's Run (formerly Sycamore Creek) was located about ten miles south of present-day Rockford, Illinois, along the line of Black Hawk's retreat into Michigan Territory (now Wisconsin). Black Hawk had decided to surrender to General Atkinson, and on May 14, 1832, when a force of pursuing militia under the command of Major Isaiah Stillman encamped on Old Man's Creek five miles to the south of Black Hawk's camp, the Indian leader sent a flag of truce with three bearers in order to make arrangements for a meeting. The surprised and unruly militia, however, fired upon them, killing one. Five Indian scouts sent to observe the proceedings from a distance were also attacked, and when they returned to Black Hawk they

told him that not only had two of their number been killed, but that the three flagbearers had also lost their lives. Thinking his attempt to surrender had been rejected, Black Hawk determined to fight and deployed his braves to await the oncoming militiamen. When they approached, Black Hawk's men attacked, surprising the whites completely and frightening them so thoroughly that they did not stop their pell-mell retreat until they reached Dixon's Ferry, approximately twenty-five miles away. Despite the fact that Stillman's command lost only eleven, perhaps twelve, the men were so demoralized that most of them were discharged. Black Hawk said that he had about forty braves to oppose 300–400 militia; Stillman, on the other hand, asserted that he had only 206 men to face the Indians who formed a line two miles long. Although Black Hawk's estimate of his forces has been generally accepted, one suspects both parties of self-serving statements. If, as Stillman and other witnesses claimed, the battle was fought at the end of the day in poor light, the militiamen might well have been unable to know how many adversaries they faced. Even so, it appears that Black Hawk had considerably fewer men than Stillman, although the extent of the discrepancy is open to conjecture. The similarity in names between the militia commander and the location of the action leads to the conclusion that either Stillman's Run was called by that name prior to the Black Hawk War or, as the editor of Black Hawk's autobiography asserts, it was renamed immediately. In either event, a regular army muster roll for June 30, 1832 (NA, RG 94, First Infantry, Company B), makes no mention of Sycamore Creek, but does mention arriving "on the ground where the Saukies routed Maj Stillmans party the 29. & mustered on the same spot, bank of a creek, called Stillman's Run." See Thwaites, *How George Rogers Clark Won the Northwest*, 117, 140, 147–53; Black Hawk, *An Autobiography*, ed. Jackson, 141–46; Stevens, *Black Hawk War*, 132–38; Prucha, *Sword of the Republic*, 221–23; Armstrong, *Sauks and the Black Hawk War*, 421.

[10] This refers to Lake Koshkonong, Michigan Territory (now Wisconsin), which was then quite swampy. It is located about twenty-five miles southeast of Madison, not far from the southernmost of the "Four Lakes" (see *n.* 11 below). After his victory at Stillman's Run, Black Hawk thought war unavoidable, and withdrew to this area for the protection of his women and children (Prucha, *Sword of the Republic*, 224; Thwaites, *How George Rogers Clark Won the Northwest*, 154).

[11] The "Four Lakes" were described by Davis in February 1831 (see 1:231, especially *n.* 17). Black Hawk moved to this area from Lake Koshkonong, but, because of the pursuit of the army (reinforced by a new levy of militia), and the difficulty in obtaining game, he decided to retreat to the Wisconsin River, then descend and cross to the west bank of the Mississippi (Black Hawk, *An Autobiography*, ed. Jackson, 153–54; Thwaites, *How George Rogers Clark Won the Northwest*, 158–68).

[12] Henry Dodge (sketch, 1:370, *n.* 2).

[13] The attack upon Black Hawk's rear guard, remembered as the Battle of Wisconsin Heights, took place on the Wisconsin River about twenty-five miles northwest of present-day Madison, near the site of Sauk City. Black Hawk reached the river without major incident, but late on July 21, 1832, his rear guard of about twenty men was overtaken just short of the river by a body of militia under the command of Henry Dodge and James D. Henry. Black Hawk joined his guard with about twenty more men in order to cover the retreat of the other warriors and their families across the river. Since darkness was coming on, the militia did not pursue and the Indi-

ans made good their escape. See Armstrong, *Sauks and the Black Hawk War*, 422, 459; Thwaites, *How George Rogers Clark Won the Northwest*, 178–83; and Prucha, *Sword of the Republic*, 227–28. Davis apparently spoke in after years as if he had been present, calling the retreat over the river "the most brilliant exhibition of military tactics that I ever witnessed . . ." (Aldrich, "Davis and Black Hawk," *Midland Monthly*, V, 408–409). In spite of the statement attributed to Davis, it is doubtful that he witnessed the battle; for a full discussion of this and the related question of Davis' participation in the Black Hawk War, see 1:322, *n.* 4.

[14] After bringing his main contingent across the Wisconsin River, Black Hawk fled toward the Mississippi. He was pursued by both the regular troops, who had left the Lake Koshkonong area on July 21, 1832, and by the militia, who apparently broke contact in order to rendezvous with General Atkinson's regulars at Blue Mounds. Although Black Hawk had determined to abandon the conflict and retreat beyond the Mississippi, the army seemed unaware of his intentions, and the pursuit, which may have been motivated by the army's desire to capture Black Hawk, was continued. The Indians reached the Mississippi August 1, but before they could escape, the steamboat *Warrior* arrived, preventing any further attempts at flight. If Black Hawk's account may be believed, he then attempted to surrender, asking the *Warrior*'s captain to send a boat for him. His efforts were unsuccessful because of a misunderstanding between him and the captain who suspected a ruse and demanded that, instead of sending a boat to the Indians, they send one to him. This the Indians refused to do, and after they were given time to remove women and children, the ship "let slip a six-pounder loaded with canister, followed by a severe fire of musketry . . ." (Armstrong, *Sauks and the Black Hawk War*, 468). The ship later withdrew to obtain more fuel, returning the next day when the Indians were already engaged with General Atkinson's regulars and militia. With the army on one side and the *Warrior* on the other, Black Hawk's force had no chance of escaping. Except for a few, including Black Hawk himself, those who remained were either killed, drowned, or captured. The Battle of Bad Axe was fought not on August 3 as Davis wrote, but on August 2, 1832 (*ibid.*, 467–72; Stevens, *Black Hawk War*, 221–25; Black Hawk, *An Autobiography*, ed. Jackson, 157–62; Prucha, *Sword of the Republic*, 229–30).

[15] General Winfield Scott (sketch, 1:124, *n.* 2). When it appeared that a protracted Indian war might ensue, General Scott, with about 1,000 new troops, had been sent west to take command of the operations. Because of the outbreak of cholera, he was unable to move beyond Chicago to the scene of the conflict until after the war was over (Prucha, *Sword of the Republic*, 225–26).

[16] Fort Crawford (sketch, 1:231, *n.* 12).

[17] Joseph M. Street (sketch, 1:386, *n.* 3).

Concerning Davis' First Marriage

In 1835 I resigned from the army,[1] and Miss Taylor[2] being then in Kentucky[3] with her aunt[4]—the oldest sister of General Taylor[5]—I went thither and we were married[6] in the house of her aunt, in the presence of General Taylor's two sisters, of his oldest brother, his son-in-law, and many others of the Taylor family.[7]

MS not found. Text from Varina Howell Davis, *Jefferson Davis, Ex-President of the Confederate States of America: A Memoir* (2 vols., New York: Belford, 1890), I, 162.

[1] Davis' resignation was effective June 30, 1835. See 1:486.

[2] Sarah Knox Taylor Davis (sketch, 1:443, *n.* 2; 1:Appendix IV, Entry 94).

[3] At "Beechland," near Louisville (see 1:483, *n.* 2).

[4] Elizabeth Lee Taylor Taylor (1792–1845), the widowed sister of Zachary Taylor, at whose home Davis and Sarah Taylor were married (Hamilton, *Zachary Taylor*, 107; Taylor family folder [The Filson Club, Louisville, Kentucky]).

[5] Zachary Taylor (sketch, 1:332, *n.* 3).

[6] The marriage took place on June 17, 1835 (1:485).

[7] While sources disagree as to exactly who the guests were, they do agree that several members of the Taylor family were present. If the number of relatives in attendance be an index of family approval, there can be no doubt that there was little objection, among the larger family at least, to the Taylor-Davis marriage. Davis' own listing of the guests is quite imprecise. While he mentions that Zachary Taylor's two sisters attended, the problem of identification is confused by the fact that General Taylor had three sisters. One of these was of course Elizabeth Lee Taylor Taylor (widow of John Gibson Taylor), at whose home the marriage took place, but it is not possible to ascertain whether the other sister present was Sarah Taylor Strother or Emily Taylor Allison. The oldest brother was Hancock Taylor (sketch, 1:484, *n.* 1) and the son-in-law was Dr. Robert C. Wood (sketch, 1:Appendix I, 476). Among the "many others of the Taylor family" were: Joseph P. Taylor (brother of Zachary Taylor and later a general in the Union army) and his family; Ann Mackall Taylor Wood (sketch, 1:483, *n.* 5), Sarah Knox Taylor's sister and the wife of Dr. Wood; Sally Strother Taylor (the maid of honor), Mary Virginia Taylor Randall and Elizabeth Taylor Casey, all cousins of Sarah Knox Taylor and daughters of Elizabeth Lee Taylor Taylor; Nicholas M. L. Taylor, best man and son of Hancock Taylor; Annah Hormsby Taylor, wife of Hancock Taylor; Mary Louise Taylor, the eleven-year-old daughter of Hancock Taylor; and apparently a number of other young children. See Hamilton, *Zachary Taylor*, 107; Taylor family folder (The Filson Club, Louisville, Kentucky); W. L. Fleming, "Davis' First Marriage," Mississippi Historical *Publications*, XII, 33; Wood, "Jefferson Davis' First Marriage," New Orleans *Daily Picayune*, August 28, 1910; statement of Dandridge to "D.B.C.," New York *Times*, October 20, 1906.

APPENDIX III

EXTRACT FROM GENEALOGY OF JEFFERSON DAVIS

by

Kirk Bentley Barb[1]

Editorial Note: Barb completed his genealogy of Davis in 1935. Since the manuscript is in rough draft, some minor stylistic and grammatical changes have been made without notation. Whenever possible, Barb's quotations have been checked, and where variations appear between the source and the manuscript, the latter has been silently changed to conform to the former. Incorrect or incomplete citations have been revised in the same manner to conform to current historical practice. Citations in the text were placed there by Barb and will, even when revised, remain there. Additional citations, when necessary, have been placed in the footnotes.

Jefferson Davis . . . knew little of his ancestry, and apparently cared little. More than a quarter of a century later [after the start of the Civil War] he made the following statement:

> Three brothers came to America from Wales in the early part of the eighteenth century. They settled at Philadelphia.
>
> The youngest of the brothers, Evan Davis, removed to Georgia, then a colony of Great Britain. He was the grandfather of Jefferson Davis. He married a widow, whose family name was Emory. By her he had one son, Samuel Davis, the father of Jefferson Davis.[2]

From the time of the issuance of the above statement to the present writing, practically nothing has been added to the meager knowledge contained therein, though interest and speculation in the matter have been rife. A large number of Davis families have claimed relationship to this great man, resulting in a vast amount of confusion, conflicting claims and traditions. The following will serve as examples:

1. In the Floyd family and some Davis families of Virginia it has been handed down that Jefferson Davis was a descendant of Nathaniel

Davis, a Welshman, who married a child of Niketti, the daughter of Opechananough, brother of Powhatan ([Rev.] Edgar Woods, *Albemarle County in Virginia* . . . [Charlottesville, Virginia, 1901]).

2. The family of Jefferson Davis came from Wales, first to North Carolina and then to Georgia (MSS by Rev. G. C. Smith, Macon, Georgia [Mrs. T. M. Green, Washington, Georgia]).

3. A Davis family of New England with branches in New York claims the Davises of Georgia to whom Jefferson Davis belonged were an offshoot of their family that emigrated south during the eighteenth century.

4. In 1910, Dr. William H. Whitsitt of Richmond, Virginia, made a futile effort to show that Jefferson Davis and Samuel Davies, at one time president of Princeton University, were members of the same family, being descended from two brothers, John and David Davis of the Welsh Tract Settlement in New Castle County, Delaware. His theory had practically nothing to support it and is now disproven.[3]

5. Four brothers, Samuel, William, Micajah, and Evan, sons of John Davis, of Shropshire, on the border of Wales, came to Philadelphia in 1742. Later some or all of them went to Virginia, first to Alexandria, and next to Louisa County, whence the older brothers went to live near the present city of Lynchburg, while Evan, the youngest, went to Oglethorpe's colony in Georgia, settling near Savannah (Davis family of Bedford County, Virginia, T. H. Davis, 1898).

6. The Davis family is of Welsh ancestry, the immigrant being Evan Davis, who came with two brothers, Joseph and Samuel, from Cardiff, Wales . . . to America [in] the early part of the eighteenth century. Joseph was lost at sea; Samuel went to one of the middle states; Evan settled in Pennsylvania *ca.* 1760, later removed to Richmond County, Georgia, and married Mrs. Emory Williams (George N. Mackenzie, *Colonial Families of the United States of America* . . . [New York, 1907]).

7. In 1912 appears "Nathaniel Davis married Hughes, a daughter of Niketti; the oldest child, Robert Davis, married young and moved to Georgia; later some of these Davises moved to Kentucky, whence a weanling was carried to Mississippi who later became the President of the Confederate States" (Nicholas J. Floyd, *Biographical Genealogies of the Virginia-Kentucky Floyd Families* . . . [Baltimore, 1912]).

8. Evan Davis, grandfather of Jefferson Davis, was born in Philadelphia and moved to New Castle County, Delaware, with his parents about June 1716. He was a son of John David and a grandson of Morgan David of Merion Township, Philadelphia County (Harry Alexander Davis, *The Davis Family . . . in Wales and America . . .* [Washington, 1927]).

9. The writer's grandmother, Louisa Davis Barb, and her brother, Colonel T. G. C. Davis . . . made definite claim to being second cousins of Jefferson Davis.

10. Captain Dolan Davis settled in St. Mary's, Maryland. He was the grandfather of Samuel Davis, who was the father of Joseph Emory and Jefferson Davis, President of the Confederacy (Richmond, Virginia, *Times-Dispatch*, March 25, 1917).

11. From another source the following is taken: Evan Davis, Samuel Davis, and Joseph Davis, three brothers, immigrated to America from Cardiff, Wales, about 1730. Evan and Samuel landed at Philadelphia. Joseph was drowned on the voyage over. Samuel went to what is now the Middle West. Evan married a Mrs. Mary Emory Williams in Pennsylvania, and after 1761 moved from Philadelphia to Georgia. He was the grandfather of Jefferson Davis.

It would be most difficult indeed to imagine anything less convincing than all this array of conflicting claims, not a single one of which has an iota of proof of any kind to substantiate it. It is not difficult, however, to understand why they have arisen. In the first place, Davis is one of the most universal of all surnames, thus rendering very easy the confusion of one apparently unrelated branch of the family with another. This, coupled with the fact that the "wish is often father to the thought," has caused these various Davis clans, either consciously or subconsciously, to attempt to connect this illustrious man with their own line. . . .

Nor is it hard to understand why Davis knew little of his ancestry. His grandfather, Evan Davis, had died when his father, Samuel, was almost an infant. Samuel had been reared in a wilderness outpost far removed from the Davis ancestral home in Philadelphia. His mother had seen and known none of the Davises, save her husband Evan, and perhaps his brother, Joseph.

Samuel's knowledge of family history, therefore, must necessarily have been small, but meager as it was, it was greater than that which his son Jefferson possessed. Nor is this fact difficult to understand. Jefferson, the youngest of ten children, was only sixteen years of age at the time of his father's death, and most of these years had been spent away from home in boarding schools. As a result he had been associated with his father very little, particularly at a time when he would have taken much cognizance of any remarks his father may have made relative to his family forebears. Children are simply not interested in such subjects; and a great majority of them, even though of the highest intelligence, cannot tell the maiden names of their grandmothers.

It is now definitely known that Evan Davis, the grandfather of Jefferson, was born in Philadelphia and not in Wales, as Jefferson himself had thought. That Jefferson's father, Samuel, was well aware of this fact is shown by a letter which was first made public in 1910 by Dr. William H. Whitsitt of Richmond, Virginia. . . .

A perusal of the . . . letter [see 1:5] shows conclusively that Samuel was fully cognizant of the fact that his father, Evan, had been born in Philadelphia. . . . If, then, Evan Davis was born in Philadelphia, the records of that city should show some trace of him. And this raises an interesting question. For half a century it has been known, or at least it was stated by Jefferson Davis himself, that his forebears had lived in Philadelphia. One would naturally think that those investigators who were interested in solving the riddle of his descent would have turned their attention to the archives of that city, but apparently none did so.

Having long been interested in the subject, I seized upon the first opportunity that presented itself to look into the public records, with the present writing as the result, and this account, I trust, will set at rest this much confused question.

The first document I wish to call attention to is the following will, which is recorded in Register of Wills, Book H, 256 *ff.* (Philadelphia City Hall, Philadelphia County, Pennsylvania).

THE WILL OF EVAN DAVIS

IN THE NAME of God Amen I Evan Davis of the City of Philadelphia in the province of Pennsylvania Carter being infirm and weak of Body but of Sound and perfect mind and Memory therefore knowing the uncertainty of this Life do make and Ordain this my last Will and Testament in the following manner and form.

IMPRIMIS my Will and Desire is that my just Debts and funeral Expences be fully Satisfyed and paid ITEM I Give and Bequeath unto Mary my beloved wife all my Estate whereof I shall die possessed as well moveable as Immoveable Real & personal by her freely to be possessed for & during her natural life She only paying unto my two Sons hereafter named such Sums of money as I shall bequeath to them at the times prefixed VIZ to my Son Joseph the Sum of ten pounds Current money of Pennsylvania when he Shall Arrive at the full age of Twenty one Years AND to my Son Evan whom I desire may be put Apprentice to a Blacksmith as soon as he shall become fit the Sum of Twenty pounds Current money of Pennsylvania when he Shall arrive at the full age of Twenty one Years likewise But if it so happen that <—my—> Mary my Aforesaid wife should die before my Above mentioned Sons Joseph and Evan or Either of them shall arrive at the full age of Twenty one Years as aforesaid then my Will and Desire is my Estate may be kept Entire until my Above said Son Evan Attain to the full age of Twenty one Years and then to be Equally divided amongst all my Children hereafter named VIZ Benjamin William Samuel Hannah Joseph & Evan Except the two last mentioned Joseph & Evan for my will & Desire is that Joseph Shall have twenty pounds more & Evan Thirty pounds <more>[4] than Either Benjamin William Samuel or Hannah also [it][5] is my Will and Desire that if my Above said wife Mary should live till my two Sons Joseph & Evan Attain to the full age of Twenty one Years as aforesaid and that my two Sons Joseph & Evan receive from her the Sums before mentioned to be paid by her to them Yet Notwithstanding after her Decease that my two Sons Joseph and Evan Each receive ten pounds more than Equal Dividend with the rest of my Children before named And my will and desire is that if Any of my above named Children should die before that my Aforesaid Son Evan shall attain to the full age of Twenty one Years that then *his or hers their or their parts or part Shares or Share Dividends or Dividend be Equally divided amongst the Surviving part of my Children his or hers their or theirs heir or heirs by them to be fully possessed and Enjoyed.*[6] ITEM I Constitute my beloved Wife Aforesaid my whole and Sole Executrix of this my last Will & Testament and I do hereby utterly disallow Revoke and Disannul all and Every other former Testaments Wills Legacies and Bequests & Executors by me in any ways before named Willed and Bequeathed. Ratifying and Confirming this and no other to be my last Will and Testament IN WITNESS whereof I have hereunto

Set my hand & Seal this Seventeenth day of March in the Year of our Lord one Thousand Seven hundred forty & three.

his
Evan ED Davis
mark

SIGN'D SEAL'D PUBLISH'D pronounced & Declared by the Said Evan Davis as his last Will and Testament in the presence of us the Subscribers
JOSEPH HARMER
SAMUEL YOUNG
JNO GREEN

The above will was proved[7] May 14, 1747.

It is my purpose to show that the Evan Davis who placed his mark to the above will was the original Welsh immigrant ancestor of Jefferson Davis in America, that he was Jefferson Davis' great-grandfather, and that Jefferson Davis belonged to the fourth generation of his family in this country, and not to the third as he himself thought....

The fact that he had two ancestors in succession by the name of Evan had apparently confused the issue. The tradition that the Evan Davis who migrated South was the youngest of three or more brothers is borne out by the elder Evan's will. Whether or not the elder Evan had two brothers who, according to the tradition, came to America with him, is a matter of no importance from a genealogical standpoint. Personally, I am much inclined to discredit the theory. If, however, two brothers did accompany him, it is scarcely probable that they settled in or near Philadelphia, as I have diligently searched every record that seemed likely to cast light on the subject, and failed to find any other Davis associated in any way with this particular family.

My lack of faith in the three-brother origin in America of the family of Jefferson Davis is further strengthened by the well-known fact that there is an old traditional story "of having descended from three brothers" who came from England, Ireland, Wales, or some other foreign land, and settled in different localities, that is told and believed by many of the descendants of the first colonists in Pennsylvania and Delaware. In fact, this ancient, stereotyped tradition seems to attach itself to a large number of our old families, and is related with an unction sufficient to make one not acquainted with the uncertainties connected with genealogy accept it as an historical truth.

There is one point which, it appears to me, all historians have overlooked. All of them admit that Samuel Davis was born in 1756 and that he was a son of Evan Davis; and most of them hold, with the tradition, that this Evan was the immigrant ancestor who came to America in the early part of the eighteenth century. Now, if Evan had come as an immigrant early in the century, say about 1705, without his parents, as alleged, he must at that time have been nearly grown, perhaps twenty years of age. If he had been twenty in 1705, he would have been born about 1685. Now, since his first and only son, Samuel, was born in 1756, he would have been seventy-one years of age at the time of this son's birth, a thing which, for rather obvious reasons, most of us are inclined to doubt. This should immediately awaken the suspicion that a whole generation has been left out. It thus becomes much more plausible to accept the younger Evan as Samuel's father.

EVAN DAVIS, THE ELDER

Of Evan Davis, the Elder, the records have but little to disclose. As to his nationality, the tradition says he was a Welshman and what evidence is to be had corroborates this assumption. In the first place, both Evan and Davis are typical Welsh names, the name Evan being practically unknown among people of other nationalities. Secondly, as will be shown later, two of his sons, Joseph and Evan, immigrated to South Carolina, to which colony a large number of Welsh Baptists had gone from the Philadelphia area.

As to his religious creed, Evan was almost certainly a Baptist, as were a large majority of the other numerous Welsh settlers in Pennsylvania. I had hoped to find some mention in the church records of the members of this particular Davis family, but in this I was disappointed, although a very careful search of the records of all the early churches in the vicinity of Philadelphia was made. If they had been Quakers, as were not a few of the Welsh settlers, I would have experienced little difficulty in contacting them, as the Quaker records of that period are very full. So also are the records of the Established Church of England and the Presbyterian Church. But in this respect the early Philadelphia Baptists seem to stand apart. Judging however from the history of their custom in other sections of the colonies, it would appear that they kept ample church records, but for some reason, probably due to their having been destroyed in a fire, the records of the early Philadelphia Baptist Church have failed to come down to our time. This is a fact greatly to be deplored, for, as a result of it, much valuable genealogical and historical information has been irretrievably lost.

As to Evan's occupation, his will and deeds of conveyance show him to have been a carter. In other words, he earned his livelihood by doing hauling of various kinds, using a horse and cart—not what would at the present time be regarded as a very romantic way of making a living, but at least an honest one. Apparently, however, Evan had never been entirely satisfied with his lot as a carter and had looked forward to the time when he might do credit to a more dignified position, for the records disclose that some time between the signing of his will in 1743 and his death in 1747 he became an innkeeper. This is shown in the inventory of his estate, which was signed by his son-in-law, Jacob Dubre, and one John Jones, and which lists him at the time of his death as an innholder by occupation. It would seem also that Evan, like most good Welshmen, was not averse to partaking at least occasionally of the "cup that cheers," for two of the items of the above mentioned inventory were "a quantity of rum" and "a part of a cask of wine." Of course it may be that he kept these two items for the delectation of his guests.

As to his education, his will and his deeds of conveyance were all signed with his mark, showing that he was unable to read and write.

As to the date of his arrival in America, one can only conjecture. The earliest official record of his presence in this country is a deed bearing the date of September 30, 1734, in which one William Hudson of the City of Philadelphia, tanner, and Hannah, his wife, did "grant and confirm unto the said Evan Davis his Heirs and Assigns. A Certain Piece or Lot of Ground situate in the said City of Philadelphia Containing in Breadth on the West Side of Fifth Street Sixty Feet" (Record of Deeds, Book H, XXI, 166 [Philadelphia City Hall, Philadelphia County, Pennsylvania]).[8] But Evan had undoubtedly been in this country many years prior to the above date. If he had been compelled to earn his livelihood as a carter with the large family which he had to support, he could scarcely have accumulated enough surplus cash to have bought improved city real estate during the early years of his sojourn here.

His wife's first name was Mary, her maiden name being unknown. He probably married her in Wales and immigrated to America soon thereafter. Most men at that period, before coming to this country, endeavored to select a helpmate to bring along with them because women were not nearly so plentiful here as men, and wives consequently none too easily secured. By her he had six children who, at the time he made his will in 1743, had all reached their majority except Joseph and Evan. He therefore could not have been married less than twenty-seven years. This would fix the probable date of his marriage and arrival in America at not later than the year 1716. If he had been twenty-one years of age at the time of his marriage, he could not have been born later than 1695. Of course, both these events could, and in all probability did, occur at much earlier periods. I am only attempting to show that they could not have happened at a later time. It is quite likely that Evan Davis arrived in Philadelphia about the year 1701, at which time a number of people "who were members of the Churches of Jesus Christ in the Counties of Pembroke and Carmarthen, South Wales, in Great Britain, professing believers in Baptism, elections, and final perseverance in grace, were moved and encouraged to come to these parts, viz, Pennsylvania."[9] These early Welsh Baptists set up flourishing organizations in Philadelphia and Welsh Tract in New Castle County, Delaware, then a portion of Pennsylvania, which for a number of years continued to obtain fresh accessions from the mother church in Wales.

Evan Davis died in May 1747, as shown by his will, which further discloses that he was survived by a wife, Mary, and six children named as follows: William, Benjamin, Samuel, Hannah, Joseph, and Evan.[10]

That Evan endeavored to give his children better educational advantages than he himself had had is shown by the fact that all of them, save his daughter Hannah, were able to sign their names to their wills and deeds, and therefore [were] presumably able to read and write. That he himself was able to think clearly and know exactly what he wanted is shown by the terse, exact specifications of his will.

Apparently his two youngest sons, Joseph and Evan, still minors in 1743 at the time of the drafting of his will, were his favorites. He makes very clear his desire that they have a larger share of his estate than any of his other children, and of these two, Evan, the youngest and his namesake, appears to have been slightly more favored.

Evan[11] seems to have been devoted to his wife, to whom he bequeathed all his "estate . . . for and during her natural life,"[12] and who, as shown by the following record, died in December 1758, having survived him by eleven years. The estate . . . was administered by her son-in-law, Jacob Dubre, Jr.

> To Jacob Dubree, Jr., next of kin to Mary Davis, deceased, Greeting. . . . Memo. that letters of administration were granted to Jacob Dubree, above named, on the estate of Mary Davis, deceased, etc. . . . Given under the seal of the said office at Philadelphia, the 30th December 1758.
>
> WM PLUMSTED, Reg.
>
> Secured by Jacob Dubree, Sr., of the Northern Liberties of Philadelphia, yeoman, and Jacob Shoemaker, Jr., of Philadelphia, blacksmith (Administration Book G, 138 [Philadelphia City Hall, Philadelphia County, Pennsylvania]).[13]

THE CHILDREN OF EVAN DAVIS

So much for Evan and Mary Davis, the great-grandparents and first American ancestors of Jefferson Davis. Let us now follow briefly the fortunes of their children. Evan Davis left five sons and one daughter, viz, William, Benjamin, Samuel, Hannah, Joseph, and Evan. One would, therefore, expect him to have a large number of descendants, more particularly in that so many different Davis families and Davis clans have claimed relationship to Jefferson Davis. Such, however, as will be presently shown, is not the case. It is largely with a view of ruling out most of these claims that a part of the following documentary records are inserted.

It is admitted by all that Evan Davis migrated south, most authorities say to South Carolina, where he married a Mrs. Williams née Emory. He later removed to Georgia and there had one son, Samuel, the father of Jefferson Davis, and died soon after the birth of this son. Since he removed rather young from Philadelphia, one would not expect to find any records of him in that city, and such is precisely the case.

That Evan's brother, Joseph, went to South Carolina, presumably with him, will presently be shown by irrefutable documentary evidence. There appears no means of knowing whether or not Joseph was ever married and had issue, but I regard the likelihood of it as very improbable. It is certain that he had not married as late as 1762, at which time he signed a deed which will be cited later, and which would have required the signature of his wife, had he had one, to make it legal. Neither is there any means of estimating the date of his death. That he was living at Charleston, South Carolina, as late as 1772 will be shown by a record to be submitted later.

The records of Christ Church, Philadelphia (Marriage Record, Parish Register, 4255), show that Hannah Davis married Jacob Dubre, Jr., January 12, 1758.[14] At that time Hannah must have been at least thirty-five years of age. Marrying at that late period in life, the likelihood of her having many children is rather remote. Doubt as to her leaving issue is still further strengthened by the fact that Jacob Dubre, Sr., made his will in 1769,[15] leaving his plantation and all he possessed[16] to "my loving Son Jacob," for and during his natural lifetime, and, in case his son should die without issue, then the property was to be sold and the proceeds divided, as specified in the will, amongst the children of the elder Jacob's brothers.[17] If Hannah and Jacob had had children at the time the will was drafted, this provision would scarcely have been incorporated (Register of Wills, Book O, 269 *ff*. [Philadelphia City Hall, Philadelphia County, Pennsylvania]).

Samuel Davis died in December 1758, the same year and month in which his mother, Mary Davis, died, leaving a wife, Martha, but no issue, as the following extract of his will discloses.[18]

> I Samuel Davies of the City of Philadelphia Tailor: being possessed of a Sound Mind and Memory, though Weak in Body . . . as to all my Goods and Chattels and in general all that I may be esteemed worth both in real and personal Estate, I leave and bequeathe unto my Dear and well beloved Wife Martha Davis, in consideration of the Love and good Will I have for her. . . . I also appoint the Said Martha my Wife to be my Sole Executr[ix.][19] In Witness whereof I have hereunto affixed my hand and Seal this twenty fourth Day of December, one thousand Seven hundred and fifty eight . . . .

The above will was probated January 1, 1759, and is recorded in Register of Wills, Book L, 202 *ff*. (Philadelphia City Hall, Philadelphia County, Pennsylvania).

That Benjamin Davis died prior to the year 1762, leaving neither wife nor issue, will be conclusively shown by evidence to be submitted later.

William Davis, oldest son of Evan and Mary Davis, died in July 1771, leaving a wife, Christian, but no issue, as shown in the following extract of his will, which was probated July 24, 1771, and recorded in Register of Wills, Book P, 115 *ff*. (Philadelphia City Hall, Philadelphia County, Pennsylvania).[20]

> *I William Davis of the city of Philada. Skiner* considering the Uncertainty of this transitory Life, do make and declare the Presents to contain my last Will and Testament; *That is to say*, I give and bequeath unto *my Dear and loving Wife Christian all my Money Goods Chattells Rights & Credits and all my Houses, Lots, Tenements*. . . . And I do hereby nominate and appoint *her my said Wife & my loving Friend Benjamin Loxley of this City Carpenter* to be *the* Executors of this my last Will and Testament . . . . *In Witness* Whereof; I have hereunto set my Hand and Seal, this *first* Day of *March* in the *fourth* Year of His Majesty's Reign, *Annoque Domini, One Thousand Seven Hundred* and *sixty four*.
>
> *Willm. Davis*
>
> *Signed, Sealed, Published, and Declared in the Presense of us, by the above-named William Davis for & as his Last Will & Testament.*
>
> *Paul Isaac Voto . . .*
> *John Kirke . . . .*

The outstanding characteristic of the Davis family seems to be that its members were as short lived as they were unprolific. Four of the six children of Evan Davis, the Elder, died relatively young. It is not known to what age the other two lived. Unless Joseph had children, which seems very unlikely, the elder Evan had only one grandchild, Samuel Davis, son of the younger Evan. This Samuel lived to a fair age of sixty-eight years, and if two of his children, Joseph and Jefferson, lived to be octogenarians they inherited their longevity not from the Davises, but from Jane Cook, their mother, who lived to the age of eighty-six years.

William Davis' wife, Christian, or Christiana as she termed herself in her will, survived him by four years, dying in March 1775. An abstract of her will, which was probated March 7, 1775, and recorded in Register of Wills, Book Q, 112 *ff*. (Philadelphia City Hall, Philadelphia County, Pennsylvania) follows:

> IN THE NAME OF GOD Amen I Christiana Davis of the City of Philadelphia in the Province of Pennsylvania, Widow, being Sick

and Weak in Body but Through the Goodness of God of Sound and well disposing Mind and Memory thanks be to God for the same, and all other his Mercies, do make my Last Will and Testament as follows . . . And I do give to Hannah Dubree the Wife of Jacob Dubree the Sum of fifty Pounds . . . And I do give unto my Brother in Law Joseph Davis of Charles Town in South Carolina, All the Wearing Apparel now in my Possession that belonged to my deceased Husband . . . . And I do nominate and appoint Benjamin Loxley of the said City of Philadelphia, Carpenter and George Smith of the same Place, Merchant to be the Executors . . . . In Witness whereof I the said Christiana Davis have hereunto set my Hand and Seal the Nineteenth Day of November in the Year of our Lord One thousand Seven hundred and seventy two.

CHRISTIANA DAVIS. . . .

Witnessed by Paul Isaac Voto and Frederick Kuhl.

That Christiana Davis, widow, and Christian Davis, wife of William Davis, were one and the same person is proven by the fact that Benjamin Loxley of the City of Philadelphia, carpenter, was one of the executors of the wills of both William Davis and Christiana Davis, that Paul Isaac Voto was a witness to both of them, and that Christiana Davis, widow, made a bequest to William Davis' sister, Hannah Dubre, and one of his brothers, Joseph Davis.

It will be noted that the above will of Christiana Davis contains an item of the utmost genealogical importance—"And I do give unto my Brother in Law Joseph Davis of Charles Town in South Carolina, All the Wearing Apparel now in my Possession that belonged to my deceased Husband . . . ." This record and another one, which will follow later, show that Evan Davis, Jr., was not the only son of Evan Davis, Sr., who migrated to South Carolina and cast his fortunes with the South. But why should Joseph and Evan Davis have selected South Carolina of all the colonies when there were so many places nearer home where lands were cheap and more fertile? I believe the answer is not difficult to find.

In their colonization of America, the Welsh had two chief ports of entry—Philadelphia and Charleston, South Carolina. It would appear that some of the settlers at Philadelphia had friends from Wales who located at or near Charleston, and that they kept up some form of intercourse with each other. Perhaps some of those who immigrated to the South wrote glowing accounts of the warm, equal, mild climate of the Southern colony which must have sounded good to Pennsylvanians, whose climate was not noted for its sunshine and equanimity. Whether for this or some other unknown but good and sufficient reason, there were frequent migrations, as will be shown later, from the Philadelphia area to South Carolina. . . .

THE DAVIS FAMILY IS TRANSPLANTED TO THE SOUTH

It was unquestionably with some migratory party . . . that Joseph and Evan Davis, the two youngest sons of Evan Davis, the Elder, made their way to the South. Their motives in going were no doubt the same as those which prompted the other Welsh colonists to make the move. But perhaps Evan, the grandfather of Jefferson Davis, had a double incentive. The reader will recall that the elder Evan had stipulated in his will that "my son Evan . . . I desire may be put Apprentice to a Blacksmith as soon as he shall become fit.[21]. . ." It is, therefore, quite likely that the younger Evan was none too much in sympathy with his father's ambitions for him, and that the wide open spaces of South Carolina appealed to him more than did the smoke and din of a Philadelphia smithy. . . .

Joseph and Evan Davis took leave of Philadelphia about the year 1750, because it was at or near this date that Evan, the youngest son, "Attain[ed] to the full age of Twenty one Years"[12] and, no doubt, received the twenty pounds which his father had stipulated in his will should be paid him at that time. This fairly sizable sum for those days probably furnished him with the wherewithal to make the adventure. Evan was now free to launch out on a career of his own, unhampered by parental restrictions. Becoming twenty-one about the year 1750 would place the approximate date of his birth as 1729. These dates are reckoned from the fact that Joseph and Evan were still minors in 1743, the year the elder Evan executed his will, and that at that time Evan was not yet "fit"[21] to "be put Apprentice to a Blacksmith."

President Jefferson Davis was himself of the opinion that his grandfather went directly from Philadelphia to Georgia, but this opinion was based on mere family tradition, and was, therefore, subject to various inaccuracies. Official records show that Evan's brother, Joseph, went to South Carolina. It is therefore logical to conclude that they both first went there, either to Charles Town (Charleston) or to the Welsh Neck Settlement on the Peedee River, where they almost certainly had friends and acquaintances. It is very probable that it was at or near one of these settlements in South Carolina that Evan met and married about 1755 a Mrs. Mary Williams née Emory.

But Evan appears not to have let much grass grow under his feet in South Carolina. He is next heard of in Georgia, where was born to him in 1756 a son, Samuel, the father of Jefferson Davis, and who was named in honor of his brother, Samuel Davis, in Philadelphia. The year of Samuel's birth is reckoned from a statement by President Davis himself. "He [Samuel] died on July 4, 1824, at the age of sixty-eight" (V. Davis, *Memoir*, I, 32).

Evan Davis died, as will presently appear, prior to the year 1762, probably about 1758, and at the time of his death could not have been more than thirty years of age. While frankly admitting that the dates of his birth, his migration south, his marriage, and his death are all calculated, I nevertheless feel confident in asserting that none of them can be more than a year or so from the exact time these events actually occurred.

At this juncture it seems fitting to insert the extract of a deed which is of inestimable genealogical value, and to which reference has already been frequently made in the preceding pages. This deed cites other deeds and is, as a result, rather complicated and much too long to print in full. I have therefore made an abstract of the vital parts of it, being very careful not to change in any way its sense. It discloses a transaction whereby William Davis, one of the sons of Evan Davis, deceased, purchased from the other Davis heirs their interests in certain real estate left by their father, the said Evan Davis.

RELEASE JOSEPH DAVIS AND OTHERS TO WILLIAM DAVIS

THIS INDENTURE Made the first Day of October in the Year of Our Lord One Thousand Seven Hundred and Sixty Two Between Joseph Davis of Broad River in the Colony of South Carolina Carpenter Jacob Dubre Junr. of the Northern Liberties of the City of Philadelphia in the Province of Pennsylvania Yeoman and Hannah his Wife (the said Joseph and Hannah being Two of the Children of Evan Davis late of the said City Carter deceased by Mary his Wife also deceased) and Martha Davis of the said City Widow (she being the Widow and Devisee of the Real and Personal Estate late of Samuel Davis deceased another of the Sons of the said deceased Evan Davis and Mary his Wife) of the one part, and William Davis of the said City of Philadelphia Skinner (the Eldest Son of the said deceased Evan and Mary Davis) of the other part. . . .

Now this Indenture Witnesseth that the said Joseph Davis Jacob Dubre and Hannah his Wife and Martha Davis for and in Consideration of the Sum of One Hundred and forty Pounds One Shilling lawful Money of Pennsylvania unto them well and truly paid by the said William Davis . . . Do Grant bargain sell assign set over remise release and confirm unto the said William Davis . . . his Heirs and Assigns forever . . . the aforesaid several Lots or pieces of Ground . . . and Appurtenances . . . To the only proper Use and Behoof of the said William Davis. . . . And the said Joseph Davis for him and his Heirs The said Jacob Dubre for him and his Heirs and for the said Hannah his Wife and her Heirs And the said Martha Davis for her and her Heirs severally and respectively do hereby covenant to and with the said William Davis his Heirs and Assigns That they . . . the said Joseph Davis Jacob Dubre and Hannah his Wife and Martha Davis and their Heirs respectively And Against all and every other Person and Persons whatsoever lawfully Claiming or to Claim by from or Under them or any of them shall and will Warrant and forever Defend by these Presents. In Witness whereof the said Parties to these presents have Interchangeably set their Hands and Seals hereunto Dated the Day and Year first above written. . . .

JOSEPH DAVIS (S)[eal]
JACOB DUBRE (S)[eal]
her
Hannah H Dubre (S)[eal]
mark
MARTHA DAVIS (S)[eal] . . .

Witness Present at Signing. STEPHEN REEVES, PAUL ISAAC VOTO.

Recorded in Record of Deeds, Book H, XXI, 166–71 (Philadelphia City Hall, Philadelphia County, Pennsylvania).

The reader will recall that in his will the elder Evan bequeathed to his wife, Mary, his entire estate, which at her death was to be *divided equally amongst all his children then living*, except that Joseph and Evan were each to "receive ten pounds more than Equal Dividend with the rest of my Children . . . ."[12] He will also recall that Mary had died in 1758 and that her son-in-law Jacob Dubre, Jr., had been appointed by the court as the administrator of her estate. The final settlement of this estate, although small, dragged on for four years and was finally consummated, as the above deed shows, on the first day of October 1762. This deed shows that Joseph Davis, one of the heirs, was at that time living at Broad River, South Carolina, and that he had made the journey all the way to Philadelphia to be present at the settlement. It also discloses that Samuel Davis, as has already been ascertained from his will, was dead, leaving no children but a widow, Martha, who came in for her husband's share of the estate. It shows that Hannah Davis was married to Jacob Dubre.

But one of the most interesting features about this deed is that no reference is made in it to either Benjamin Davis or Evan Davis. This can mean only one thing, namely that Benjamin and Evan are dead, presumably at least, leaving no issue. This document therefore fixes the approximate date of Evan's death as being sometime between the birth of his son, Samuel, in 1756 and the final settlement of his father's estate in 1762.

Lest someone raise the question as to whether certain statements in the above deed imply the prior deaths of Benjamin and Evan Davis, I wish to quote here a section from another deed which should remove all doubt. This deed shows that five years later William Davis disposed of the land he had acquired from the other Davis heirs in the final settlement of the estate of Evan and Mary Davis.

> This Indenture made the Twenty fifth day of July in the year of our Lord One thousand seven hundred and sixty seven Between William Davis of the City of Philadelphia Skinner and Christian his Wife of the one part and Reuben Haines of the said City Brewer of the other part Whereas in and by a certain Indenture bearing date the fifth day of October One thousand seven hundred and sixty two made between . . . [the] Overseers of the Public School Founded by Charter in the City and County of Philadelphia in the Province of Pennsylvania of the one Part and the said William Davis, Joseph Davis of Broad River in the Colony of South Carolina Carpenter and Jacob Dubre of the Township of the Northern Liberties in the said County of Philadelphia Yeoman and Hannah his Wife (The said William Davis, Joseph Davis and Hannah Dubre being the only issue of Mary Davis late of the City and County of Philadelphia Widow deceased) of the other part. . . . And whereas in and by a certain Indenture bearing date the first day of October One thousand seven hundred and sixty two made between the said Joseph Davis, Jacob Dubree and Hannah his Wife and Martha Davis of the said

City Widow (she being the Widow and devisee of the real and personal Estate of Samuel Davis deceased another of the sons of the said deceased Evan Davis and Mary his Wife) of the one part and the said William Davis of the other part They the said Joseph Davis, Jacob Dubree and Hannah his Wife and Martha Davis did (inter-alia) grant and confirm unto the said William Davis his heirs and assigns All and every the part and parts purpart and purparts Share and Shares and dividend whatsoever of them the said Joseph Davis, Jacob Dubree and Hannah his Wife and Martha Davis of in and to the aforesaid Messuage Lot or piece of ground and premises and all their Estate and Estates property claim and demand of in and to the said Messuage Lot or piece of ground and premises Together with the appurtances To hold to him the said William Davis his heirs and assigns forever as in and by the said recited Indenture recorded at Philadelphia in Book H. vol. 21 page 166 &ca at Large appears Now this Indenture Witnesseth that the said William Davis and Christian his wife for and in consideration of the sum of Two hundred pounds lawful money of Pennsylvania . . . Have granted bargained sold released and confirmed . . . unto the said Reuben Haines his heirs and assigns forever All that the aforesaid Messuage and described Lot or piece of ground . . . In Witness whereof the said parties to these presents have interchangeably set their hands and seals hereunto Dated the day and year first above written, WILLIAM DAVIS (seal) CHRISTIAN DAVIS (seal) . . . .

The deed from which the above extract is taken and which is recorded in Record of Deeds, Book "I," XV, 459–61 (Philadelphia City Hall, Philadelphia County, Pennsylvania), states specifically that the said William Davis, Joseph Davis, and Hannah Dubre are the only issue of Mary Davis, late of the City of Philadelphia, widow, deceased. This leaves absolutely no doubt but that the other three sons, viz: Benjamin, Samuel and Evan had died before the final settlement of the estate had been consummated and that their shares, save that of Samuel, had been divided equally amongst the surviving part of Evan's[10] children. The full text of this deed gives to Reuben Haines a presumably clear title to the land, which William Davis had acquired from the other Davis heirs. I say presumably because there is positively no question but that the title, at least insofar as a fifth part of it was concerned, was actually faulty, for in it William Davis had disposed of land which belonged to Samuel Davis, infant son of his brother, the deceased Evan Davis, Jr.

Whether this ignoring of Evan's family in the final settlement was a deliberate act of fraud, or whether they were unaware of its existence, cannot be ascertained now, but it seems extremely improbable that it could have been the latter. Joseph Davis, who had gone to South Carolina with Evan, would certainly have known of his brother's marriage. It is, furthermore, very unlikely that anyone would have transmitted the news of Evan's death to his family without also letting it be known that he had left a widow. Presuming then that his brother knew of his marriage, the perpetration of a fraud becomes more apparent than actual, for, since Samuel's widow had come in for her husband's share of the estate, one would naturally think that Evan's widow would have been entitled to the same privilege. Such, however, was not the case. It will be recalled that Samuel Davis,[22] in his will, had made his widow his devisee bequeathing to her "all that I may be esteemed worth,"[23] while Evan, so far as known, had died intestate. But, in another sense, this latter fact does not make the fraud less actual, provided it was known that Evan had left issue in the person of a young son, Samuel, who was entitled to his father's full share in the final settlement of the estate of Evan Davis, the Elder, deceased, of which share there was no power on earth that could have justly deprived him.

After reaching South Carolina Evan had married, parted company with his brother Joseph, and moved still further on into Georgia where an untimely death soon overtook him. The news of his death had, of course, been transmitted to his family in Philadelphia and to his brother Joseph in South Carolina; but whether or not this information also carried intelligence of the birth of a son can only be conjectured. At that time settlements were sparse and delivery of mail was very infrequent and uncertain. After the death of her husband, Mrs. Evan Davis, Jr., who had never met any other members of the Davis family, save perhaps Joseph, most likely felt little in common with them and, breaking off all communication for the time being at least, dropped out of the picture as it were. So, when the time for the final settlement of the estate of Evan and Mary Davis came around, all account had been lost of her and her young son, if in fact it had actually been known that a son existed. It may be that the Davis heirs, knowing of the existence of the son, but not knowing his whereabouts, had complied with a certain legal formality and inserted in one of the local Philadelphia papers an advertisement which, as a matter of fact, Evan's widow had no opportunity of seeing.

Whether this or whether the Davis heirs perpetrated a willful and premeditated fraud upon the young Samuel no one can with certainty say now. But of this one point there can be no question, namely that young Samuel was cheated of his inheritance, for he was without question entitled to his father's full share, which would have been one fifth of the entire proceeds of the estate.

SAMUEL DAVIS

That Samuel Davis, though practically an infant when his father died and though brought up in the wilderness reaches of Georgia far removed from the Davis ancestral home in Philadelphia, later made contact with his father's people and learned something of their history is shown by the fact that he possessed more knowledge of the family than he would likely have gained from his mother, whose information along this line must have been extremely meager. That he had definite information concerning the Davis family is shown by the fact that he named his three oldest sons, Joseph, Benjamin and Samuel, for his three uncles, Joseph, Benjamin and Samuel Davis. This contact was almost certainly made with his uncle Joseph, who lived near by in South Carolina, and who had been the only member of the Davis family known to his mother.

Typescript (Mississippi Department of Archives and History, Jackson), 50.

[1] According to John MacDonnell Barb, the son of Kirk Bentley Barb, his father "was born February 23, 1886 in Merion County, Arkansas. He attended North Texas Normal School, Denton, Texas, from 1905–1907, and the University of Texas at Austin from 1907–1908. After teaching for two years he attended the University of Oklahoma and graduated with the degree of Bachelor of Science in 1914. He received his degree of Doctor of Medicine from the University of Oklahoma in 1915. After interning at Allegheny General Hospital, Pittsburgh, Pa., he did post-graduate work at Johns Hopkins University until the outbreak of World War I, when he enlisted as Lieutenant Senior Grade, a surgeon, in the U. S. Navy and served from 1917–1919. In 1920–1922 he was in private practice in Fort Worth, Texas. In August, 1922, he came to Camden, New Jersey, where he was in private practice until he died in August 1954" (Barb to McIntosh, March 11, 1970 [Jefferson Davis Association, Rice University, Houston]).

[2] V. Davis, *Memoir*, I, 3.

[3] William H. Whitsitt, *Genealogy of Jefferson Davis and of Samuel Davies* (New York and Washington: Neale, 1910).

[4] Interlined.

[5] Manuscript torn.

[6] Emphasis Barb's.

[7] Barb undoubtedly meant probated, for docketing on the will reads "Prob. 14. May 1747."

[8] The citation is not to the deed of 1734, but rather to that of October 1, 1762, which describes the earlier transaction.

[9] Elsewhere in the typescript Barb indicates this comes from the minutes

of the Welsh Tract Baptist meeting of Pencader Hundred, New Castle County, Delaware.

[10] The will refers to the wife and children, but, of course, it could make no specific reference as to which of them actually survived the elder Evan Davis. Later endorsements and attachments to the will are likewise uninformative on this point.

[11] Referring to the elder Evan Davis.

[12] Will of Evan Davis (Register of Wills, Book H, *256 ff.* [Philadelphia City Hall, Philadelphia County, Pennsylvania]).

[13] Unlike the other wills and deeds quoted in this manuscript, this one could not be checked, even indirectly, by the editors.

[14] Verified by a recent (1969) certificate of Reverend Ernest A. Harding, Rector, Christ Church, Philadelphia (Jefferson Davis Association, Rice University, Houston).

[15] This is undoubtedly a typographical error in Barb's manuscript, the will having actually been made in 1768.

[16] While the bulk of the estate was willed to Jacob, two slaves were manumitted and some personal items (furniture and silver) were willed to a cousin.

[17] In such a contingency the elder Jacob's nieces and nephews were not to be the only legatees, the others being a daughter-in-law, another woman who was apparently not a relative, "the Overseers of the public School of the Friends," and "the Trustees of the Pennsylvania Hospital."

[18] "Note. In Pennsylvania a will, in order to be legal must mention children, if any exist. When no reference is made to children it is considered prima facie evidence that there were none."

[19] Ink blot in original document.

[20] The original document is a printed form, which was filled in and signed.

[21] Fit, meaning old enough (Barb). See also *n.* 12 above.

[22] The son of the elder Evan Davis.

[23] Register of Wills, Book "L," 202 *ff.* (Philadelphia City Hall, Philadelphia County, Pennsylvania).

APPENDIX IV

GENEALOGY OF THE DAVIS FAMILY

Editorial Note: The chart method has been employed in the following pages for maximum clarity. A summary of the direct paternal line of Jefferson Davis forms the first chart; it is intended to make the charts thereafter more easily comprehended. Dates are given in the charts as a rule only when they are ascertained from primary sources, such as birth or marriage certificates, tombstones, personal testimony, and so forth. Dates from secondary sources are usually treated in numbered footnotes; uncertain or disputed dates are also handled in this manner. The footnote numbers follow their subjects as elsewhere in the volume. The numbers preceding each person's name are arbitrarily assigned to members of the five generations charted here; to illustrate, "1:Appendix IV, Entry 23" refers to Mary Ellen Davis Davis. An alphabetized list with entry numbers concludes this appendix.

The editors do not consider this genealogy complete or final; additional information will undoubtedly make for a number of corrections and these as well as the later generations will appear in subsequent volumes.

CHART ONE
SUMMARY OF DIRECT PATERNAL LINE[1]

1 Evan Davis m. 2 Mary

11 Evan Davis m. 12 Mary Emory Williams

13 Samuel Emory Davis m. 14 Jane Cook

24 Jefferson Finis Davis

[1] 1:Appendix III, 493.

APPENDIX IV

CHART TWO

FIRST AND SECOND GENERATIONS

1 Evan Davis[2] m. *ca.* 1716[3] 2 Mary

Immigrants from Wales

d. (prior to May 14, 1747)[4] | d. December 1758[5]

(six children)

3 Benjamin d. prior to 1762[4]		
4 William d. (prior to July 24, 1771)[4]	m.	5 Christiana d. (prior to March 7, 1775)[4]
6 Samuel d. (prior to January 1, 1759)[4]	m.	7 Martha
8 Hannah[6]	m. January 12, 1758[7]	9 Jacob Dubre, Jr. d. (prior to July 11, 1768)[4]
10 Joseph		
11 Evan[8]	m.	12 Mary Emory Williams

[2] From the ages of Evan's children at the time of his death, Barb reasons that Evan was born not later than 1695 (1:Appendix III, 496).

[3] 1:Appendix III, 496.

[4] Deathdates in parentheses preceded by "prior to" are the probate dates of the wills of Evan, William, Christiana, and Samuel Davis, and of Jacob Dubre, Jr. (Register of Wills [Philadelphia City Hall, Philadelphia County, Pennsylvania]). In the case of Benjamin Davis, the approximate deathdate is derived from the deed of October 5, 1762, in which Benjamin is not listed as being among "the only issue of Mary Davis"; from this Barb concludes that Benjamin was already dead (William Davis & Uxr. to Reuben Haines, Record of Deeds, Book "I," XV, 459–61 [Philadelphia City Hall, Philadelphia County, Pennsylvania]; 1:Appendix III, 505).

[5] 1:Appendix III, 496.

[6] If, as Barb believes, Hannah was at least thirty-five when she married, her birthdate can be approximated as 1723 (1:Appendix III, 498).

[7] Jacob Dubre, Jr., and Hannah Davis, Marriage Record, Parish Register, 4255 (Christ Church, Philadelphia, Pennsylvania).

[8] Since Evan apparently reached his majority in 1750, Barb estimates the year of his birth as 1729, and his death as 1758 (1:Appendix III, 501–502).

GENEALOGY OF DAVIS FAMILY

CHART THREE

SECOND AND THIRD GENERATIONS

11 Evan Davis	m.[9]	12 Mary Emory Williams
	(one child)[10]	
13 Samuel Emory	m.[12]	14 Jane Cook
		b. 1760/61
d. July 4, 1824[11]		d. October 3, 1845[13]

[9] Barb believes the marriage took place *ca.* 1755 (1:Appendix III, 502).

[10] The authorities disagree about the issue of Evan and Mary Davis. Davis himself believed that his father was the only son of Evan Davis (Davis to Hall, July 7, 1884 [Jefferson Davis Association, Rice University, Houston]). Several genealogists state that Samuel had two half brothers, Daniel and Isaac Williams, the children of his mother's first marriage. Barb mentions them by name ("Genealogy of Davis," 25 [typescript in Mississippi Department of Archives and History, Jackson]), as do H. A. Davis (*The Davis Family*, 19) and Whitsitt (*Genealogy*, 50); De Leon also acknowledges the existence of these half brothers (*Belles, Beaux and Brains*, 76), and so does Davis himself (1:2, lxvii). The fact that Samuel named one of his sons Isaac Williams Davis lends credence to the relationship. A daughter, Anna, may also have been born to Evan and Mary Davis (Kerrigan, Genealogical Data [Jefferson Davis Association, Rice University, Houston]; H. A. Davis, *The Davis Family*, 19). H. A. Davis concludes, "No record evidence discovered of her. Said to have married a John Black and had a daughter Jane . . . . Apparently there was a son, as in 1870's a Mr. Black, a civil engineer, introduced himself to Joseph D. Smith . . . as a kinsman; Smith not aware of any relations by name of Black was more or less cold. When he mentioned the occurrence at home and learned of Anna Davis Black he endeavored to locate the man but found no trace of him or where he came from" (*The Davis Family*, 19).

[11] Davis stated that his father died July 4, 1824, at the age of sixty-eight (1:2, lxxviii). Virtually every source states that 1756 was the year of Samuel's birth (1:Appendix III, 502; H. A. Davis, *The Davis Family*, 37; Whitsitt, *Genealogy*, 50; Ganier, Davis Family Tree [Alfred F. Ganier, Nashville, 1968]; Kerrigan, Genealogical Data [Jefferson Davis Association, Rice University, Houston]; More, Genealogical Data [Jefferson Davis Association, Rice University, Houston]; Strode, *American Patriot*, 5). Samuel's tombstone at "Beauvoir," to which his remains were moved in 1942 from Davis Island, also gives his deathdate as July 4, 1824, but adds "Aged 66 years," making 1757 or 1758 the year of his birth ("Beauvoir" cemetery, near Biloxi, Mississippi; "Points of Interest at Beauvoir").

[12] Both Barb ("Genealogy of Davis," 25 [typescript in Mississippi Department of Archives and History, Jackson]) and H. A. Davis (*The Davis Family*, 42) believe the marriage took place in 1783; the latter states that it was July of that year.

[13] Jane Cook Davis' tombstone reads, "Aged 84 years" ("Rosemont" plantation cemetery, near Woodville, Mississippi).

APPENDIX IV

CHART FOUR

THIRD AND FOURTH GENERATIONS

13 Samuel Emory Davis m. 14 Jane Cook

(ten children)

15 Joseph Emory
b. December 10, 1784
d. September 18, 1870[14]

16 Benjamin
b. 1787/88
d. October 22, 1827[15]

17 Samuel[16]

18 Anna Eliza
b. September 1, 1791
d. August 13, 1870[17]

19 Isaac Williams[18]

20 Lucinda Farrar[19]

21 Amanda[20]

22 Matilda
d. March 16, 1834[21]

23 Mary Ellen
d. March 2, 1824[22]

24 Jefferson Finis
b. June 3, 1807/1808
d. December 6, 1889[23]

14 Gravestone ("Hurricane" and "Brierfield" plantations cemetery, Davis Island, near Vicksburg, Mississippi).

15 Benjamin's tombstone states that he was thirty-nine when he died ("God's Acre," "Locust Grove" plantation cemetery, near St. Francisville, Louisiana).

16 H. A. Davis estimates Samuel's birthdate as 1788/89 and his deathdate at about 1835 (*The Davis Family*, 81).

17 Gravestone ("God's Acre," "Locust Grove" plantation cemetery, near St. Francisville, Louisiana).

18 Barb and H. A. Davis state that Isaac Williams Davis was born in October 1792; H. A. Davis believes that he died prior to 1860 ("Genealogy of Davis," 28 [typescript in Mississippi Department of Archives and History, Jackson]; *The Davis Family*, 83–84).

19 H. A. Davis cites June 5, 1797, as Lucinda's birthdate and December 14, 1873, as the date of her death (*The Davis Family*, 84). Douglas McL. More, Lucinda's great-great-grandson, states that she died at the age of seventy-six on December 14, 1873, at "Rosemont," near Woodville, Mississippi (More, Genealogical Data [Jefferson Davis Association, Rice University, Houston]).

20 Amanda's birthdate is considered by Barb and H. A. Davis to be in De-

cember 1799. H. A. Davis states she died in 1881 ("Genealogy of Davis," 28 [typescript in Mississippi Department of Archives and History, Jackson]; *The Davis Family*, 88).

21 Less is known about Matilda than any other of Davis' brothers and sisters. Most sources state that she was born in 1800 or 1801. Virtually every authority has wrongly assumed that she died in infancy or childhood; see 1:419. See also Chart Twelve.

22 Several sources agree that Mary Ellen was born in 1806 (Barb, "Genealogy of Davis," 28 [typescript in Mississippi Department of Archives and History, Jackson]; H. A. Davis, *The Davis Family*, 94; More, Genealogical Data [Jefferson Davis Association, Rice University, Houston]; Strode, *American Patriot*, 28). The Woodville (Mississippi) *Republican*, March 2, 1824, records the death that morning of "Mrs. Mary E. Davis, consort of Mr. Robert Davis."

23 During his youth Davis believed that he had been born in 1807. For a discussion of the confusion over his birthdate, see 1:1, *n.* 1. Davis' deathdate is confirmed by his death certificate (Jefferson Davis Personal Miscellaneous Papers, New York Public Library).

CHART FIVE

JOSEPH EMORY DAVIS FAMILY

15 Joseph Emory Davis m.[25] (unknown)
b. December 10, 1784
d. September 18, 1870[24]
(three children)

26 Mary Lucinda b. May 1, 1816 d. November 22, 1846[26]	m.	February 6, 1838[27]	27 Charles Jouett Mitchell[28]
28 Florida A. b. 1817/18[29]	m.	October 21, 1830[30]	29 David McCaleb[31]
	m.	1848[32]	30 Edmund C. Laughlin b. 1812/13[33]
31 Caroline[34]	m.	*ca.* 1842[34]	32 Thomas E. Robins
	m.	*ca.* 1856[34]	33 Abram F. Leonard
15 Joseph Emory Davis[24]	m.	October 5, 1827[35]	25 Eliza Van Benthuysen b. January 23, 1811 d. October 4, 1863[36]

24 See *n.* 14 above.

25 The three daughters listed were Joseph's children by his first wife, whose identity remains unknown. Elizabeth O'Kelley Kerrigan, Joseph's great-great-granddaughter, stated that "Eliza & Joseph Davis had no children. His three daughters by his first wife were Mary, Caroline & . . . Florida" (Kerrigan to Riddle, April 7, 1969 [Jefferson Davis Association, Rice University, Houston]). DeLeon believes that

Joseph had nine children (*Belles, Beaux and Brains*, 77). The Vicksburg *Daily Sentinel* of November 26, 1838, reports the death of "Mr. W. Davis, son of Joseph E. Davis, Esq."; whether the deceased was Davis' nephew has not been ascertained.

26 Gravestone ("Hurricane" and "Brierfield" plantations cemetery, Davis Island, near Vicksburg, Mississippi).

27 See 1:521. The marriage bond of Charles Mitchell and Mary L. Davis is dated February 5, 1838 (O'Neill, "Warren County Marriages," *Journal of Mississippi History*, XXIX, 46).

28 After Mary Lucinda's death, Charles Mitchell married her cousin Lucinda Bradford (see 1:Appendix IV, Chart Eleven). Charles Mitchell apparently died early in 1886 (V. Davis to Mitchell, February 7, 1886 [Lise Mitchell Papers, Howard-Tilton Memorial Library, Tulane University, New Orleans]).

29 Florida testified on July 2, 1875, that she was then fifty-seven (Davis *v.* Bowmar, 378 [Mississippi Department of Archives and History, Jackson]). H. A. Davis (*The Davis Family*, 80) states that Florida was born in 1817/18; the Woodville (Mississippi) *Republican* of November 13, 1830, in reporting her marriage, describes Florida as Joseph's eldest daughter, which would place her birthdate prior to 1816 (see Entry 26 above).

30 Woodville (Mississippi) *Republican*, November 13, 1830. Florida and David McCaleb's marriage bond is dated October 15, 1830 (O'Neill, "Warren County Marriages," *Journal of Mississippi History*, XXVIII, 326).

31 A newspaper account states that David McCaleb was born October 21, 1803, and died September 7, 1849 (unidentified newspaper clipping, *ca.* 1906, Kerrigan, Genealogical Data [Jefferson Davis Association, Rice University, Houston]).

32 Davis *v.* Bowmar, 244 (Mississippi Department of Archives and History, Jackson). Mrs. Florida McCaleb and Edmund C. Laughlin signed a marriage bond on July 17, 1848 (O'Neill, "Warren County Marriages," *Journal of Mississippi History*, XXIX, 214).

33 Laughlin testified January 12, 1875, that he was sixty-two years old (Davis *v.* Bowmar, 251 [Mississippi Department of Archives and History, Jackson]).

34 H. A. Davis believes that Caroline was born in 1823 (*The Davis Family*, 81). A marriage bond between Thomas E. Robins and Caroline Davis is dated December 17, 1842; another marriage bond, dated December 3, 1856, is recorded for Abram F. Leonard and Caroline Robins (O'Neill, "Warren County Marriages," *Journal of Mississippi History*, XXIX, 146, XXX, 152). An entry dated June 1, 1862, in the Lise Mitchell diary notes that Leonard had had a very bad fall four years previous, which was about a year after his marriage to Caroline (Lise Mitchell Papers, Howard-Tilton Memorial Library, Tulane University, New Orleans). Caroline was still living in 1901 (Leonard to Harper, March 21, 1901 [Lise Mitchell Papers, Howard-Tilton Memorial Library, Tulane University, New Orleans]).

35 Marriage Records (Mississippi Department of Health, Jackson).

36 Eliza's maiden name is sometimes written "van Benthysen"; her tombstone reads only "Eliza V. Davis." The birthdate recorded in the chart is from the tombstone, which gives her deathdate as October 21, 1864 ("Hurricane" and "Brierfield" plantations cemetery, Davis Island, near Vicksburg, Mississippi). Eliza's step-granddaughter, Lise Mitchell, who was with Eliza when she died on October 4, 1863, at Lauderdale Springs, Mississippi, explains that it was the intention of the family to move the body from its temporary resting place to the family graveyard at "Hurricane" (Mitchell, Journal, 51 [Southern Historical Collection, University of North Carolina Library, Chapel Hill]).

CHART SIX
BENJAMIN DAVIS FAMILY

16 Benjamin Davis m. 34 Aurelia Smith[38]
b. 1787/88
d. October 22, 1827[37]

(one child)

35 Mary Ann
b. August 1825
d. April 13, 1828[39]

[37] See *n.* 15 above.
[38] Aurelia was a niece of Luther L. Smith, Benjamin's brother-in-law (H. A. Davis, *The Davis Family*, 40).
[39] "Mary Ann daughter of Dr. Bn. & Aurelia Davis . . . died the 13th of April 1828, aged 2 years & 8 months" (Gravestone ["God's Acre," "Locust Grove" plantation cemetery, near St. Francisville, Louisiana]).

CHART SEVEN
SAMUEL DAVIS FAMILY

17 Samuel Davis[40] m.[41] 36 Lucy Throckmorton[42]

(five children)[43]

37 Benjamin Thomas[44] m.[45] 38 Pauline Taylor

39 Helen[46] m. March 11, 1841[47] 40 Patrick F. Keary[48]

41 Robert H.[49]

42 Samuel A.[50]

43 Joseph[51]

[40] See *n.* 16 above.
[41] H. A. Davis believes the marriage took place about 1818 (*The Davis Family*, 81).
[42] Lucy Throckmorton is thought to have been born about 1800 (H. A. Davis, *The Davis Family*, 81).
[43] Both Barb ("Genealogy of Davis," 29 [typescript in Mississippi Department of Archives and History, Jackson]) and H. A. Davis (*The Davis Family*, 81) exclude Joseph from a list of Samuel's children.
[44] H. A. Davis and Barb give Benjamin's birthdate as July 29, 1820; Barb lists his deathdate as April 29, 1899 (*The Davis Family*, 81; "Genealogy of Davis," 29 [typescript in Mississippi Department of Archives and History, Jackson]).
[45] Barb states that Benjamin was married on August 19, 1855 ("Genealogy of Davis," 29 [typescript in Mississippi Department of Archives and History, Jackson]).
[46] Although Barb excludes Helen in his account of Samuel's offspring ("Genealogy of Davis," 29 [typescript in Mississippi Department of Archives and History, Jackson]), H. A. Davis believes Helen was born in 1822 (*The Davis Family*, 81).

47 Woodville (Mississippi) *Republican*, March 13, 1841.

48 H. A. Davis states that Keary was born in 1817 (*The Davis Family*, 81).

49 Robert H. Davis was born in 1824 and lived to serve in the Confederate Army (H. A. Davis, *The Davis Family*, 81).

50 Ganier and H. A. Davis state that Samuel was born in 1826/27. Although no deathdate can be ascertained, Ganier believes that Samuel died at the age of twenty-one (Davis Family Tree [Alfred F. Ganier, Nashville, 1968]; H. A. Davis, *The Davis Family*, 81).

51 Only Ganier and De Leon list Joseph among Samuel's children; Ganier states that Joseph died at the age of twenty (Davis Family Tree [Alfred F. Ganier, Nashville, 1968]; De Leon, *Belles, Beaux and Brains*, 77).

CHART EIGHT

ANNA ELIZA DAVIS SMITH FAMILY

18 Anna Eliza b. September 1, 1791 d. August 13, 1870[52]	m.[53]	44 Luther L. Smith[54] b. 1769/70 d. December 23, 1833[55]
	(six children)[56]	
45 Joseph Davis b. April 6, 1817 d. January 13, 1876[57]	m.[58]	46 Marie Coralie Guibert b. 1822 d. June 30, 1863[59]
47 Luther L., Jr.[60]		
48 Gordon A.[61]		
49 Lucinda Jane[62]	m.[63]	50 William D. Boyle b. 1805/1806 d. September 21, 1847[64]
51 Jedediah b. July 31, 1824 d. February 23, 1891[65]	m.[66]	52 Susan Madison Buck
53 Anna Amanda d. November 7, 1887[67]	m.[68]	54 Philander C. Smith[69]

52 See *n.* 17 above.

53 Notations from the Smith Bible record Anna Eliza's marriage to Luther L. Smith on March 31, 1816 (*Be It Known and Remembered: Bible Records*, IV, 18).

54 Anna Eliza was Luther's second wife; he was first married to Martha E. Baker, sometimes referred to as Patsy (Luther L. Smith, Inventory of Property, Probate Box 91 [West Feliciana Parish Courthouse, St. Francisville, Louisiana]; Kendall, "Chronicles of a Southern Family," *Louisiana Historical Quarterly*, XXIX, 286). Martha Baker Smith died in 1815 at the age of thirty-seven (DAR [comps.], *Louisiana Tombstone Inscriptions*, VII, 42).

55 Luther's tombstone states that he was sixty-three at the time of his death ("God's Acre," "Locust Grove" plantation cemetery, near St. Francisville, Louisiana).

56 H. A. Davis claims there were

seven children: the seventh, another son, was born in the 1830's and died in the 1840's (*The Davis Family*, 83).

57 Joseph's tombstone states only that he was born in 1817 and died in 1876 ("God's Acre," "Locust Grove" plantation cemetery, near St. Francisville, Louisiana). The exact dates are supplied by family records (*Be It Known and Remembered: Bible Records*, IV, 18–19; Watts and De Grummond, *Solitude*, Family Record).

58 Joseph and Marie Coralie were married April 25, 1839 (Watts and De Grummond, *Solitude*, Family Record; H. A. Davis, *The Davis Family*, 82).

59 Again, the tombstone gives only the years of birth and death ("God's Acre," "Locust Grove" plantation cemetery, near St. Francisville, Louisiana). The more precise deathdate is supplied by family records (*Be It Known and Remembered: Bible Records*, IV, 20; Watts and De Grummond, *Solitude*, Family Record).

60 H. A. Davis and Ganier believe that Luther L., Jr., was born in 1818 (*The Davis Family*, 83; Davis Family Tree [Alfred F. Ganier, Nashville, 1968]). Records made from the Smith Bible note that he died November 1, 1858 (*Be It Known and Remembered: Bible Records*, IV, 19).

61 Notations from the Smith Bible state that Gordon was born March 26, 1820, and died September 19, 1883 (*Be It Known and Remembered: Bible Records*, IV, 18–19).

62 Lucinda's birthdate is recorded as January 20, 1822, and her deathdate as August 24, 1889 (*Be It Known and Remembered: Bible Records*, IV, 18, 20).

63 Lucinda and William Boyle were married May 17, 1836 (*Be It Known and Remembered: Bible Records*, IV, 18).

64 The tombstone states that William D. Boyle died at the age of forty-one (DAR [comps.], *Louisiana Tombstone Inscriptions*, VII, 41).

65 Gravestone ("God's Acre," "Locust Grove" plantation cemetery, near St. Francisville, Louisiana).

66 Susan Buck and Jedediah Smith were married November 18, 1856 (*Be It Known and Remembered: Bible Records*, IV, 18).

67 Records taken from the Smith Bible assert that Anna Amanda was born December 6, 1826 (*Be It Known and Remembered: Bible Records*, IV, 18). Her death is recorded in a letter from her sister Lucinda Jane Davis Boyle to Davis, November 11, 1887 (Museum of the Confederacy, Richmond).

68 Anna and Philander Smith were married November 21, 1850 (*Be It Known and Remembered: Bible Records*, IV, 18).

69 The death of Philander C. Smith is recorded in the Smith Bible as having occurred on October 2, 1853, "in the 32nd year of his age" (*Be It Known and Remembered: Bible Records*, IV, 19).

CHART NINE

ISAAC WILLIAMS DAVIS FAMILY

19 Isaac Williams[70] m.[71] 55 Susannah Gartley[72]

(two children)[73]

56 (son)[74]

57 Joseph Robert[75] m.[76] 58 Fannie Peyton
m.[77] 59 Margaret Cary Green

[70] See *n.* 18 above.

[71] H. A. Davis estimates the wedding date as 1822 (*The Davis Family*, 84).

[72] Many discrepancies exist regarding the spelling of Susannah's maiden name. H. A. Davis says it was Garthy or Guerthy (*The Davis Family*, 84). De Leon states that it was Guertly (*Belles, Beaux and Brains*, 77). Other sources refer to a Susan or Susannah Gartley (Ganier, Davis Family Tree [Alfred F. Ganier, Nashville, 1968]; Kerrigan, Genealogical Data [Jefferson Davis Association, Rice University, Houston]; unidentified newspaper clipping [Walthall Papers, Box 27, Mississippi Department of Archives and History, Jackson]).

[73] The number of children in Isaac and Susannah's family is problematical. Barb ("Genealogy of Davis," 28–29 [typescript in Mississippi Department of Archives and History, Jackson]), H. A. Davis (*The Davis Family*, 84), and Ganier (Davis Family Tree [Alfred F. Ganier, Nashville, 1968]) agree that there were two sons, one of whom was Joseph R.; the other remains unnamed and is believed to have died as a child (see *n.* 74 below). De Leon mentions only one son, Joseph E. Davis (*Belles, Beaux and Brains*, 77); Warner identifies him as Joseph Robert Davis (*Generals in Gray*, 68). Jefferson Hayes-Davis says two of Isaac's children were killed by a tornado which implies, of course, that Isaac had at least three children (Hayes-Davis, Genealogical Data [Jefferson Davis Association, Rice University, Houston]).

[74] Both H. A. Davis (*The Davis Family*, 84) and Ganier (Davis Family Tree [Alfred F. Ganier, Nashville, 1968]) state that Isaac's elder son was born about 1823/24 and was killed by a hurricane about 1830 (see also 1:9, *n.* 11).

[75] Joseph R. was born January 12, 1825, and died September 15, 1896 (Barb, "Genealogy of Davis," 28–29 [typescript in Mississippi Department of Archives and History, Jackson]; H. A. Davis, *The Davis Family*, 84; Warner, *Generals in Gray*, 68–69).

[76] An unidentified newspaper clipping states that Joseph married a Miss Peyton in 1848 (Walthall Papers, Box 27, Mississippi Department of Archives and History, Jackson). The only other identification of Joseph's first wife is an entry dated June 1, 1862, in Lise Mitchell's journal, which refers to "cousin Joe R. Davis . . . and his wife cousin Fannie" (Lise Mitchell Papers, Howard-Tilton Memorial Library, Tulane University, New Orleans).

[77] H. A. Davis notes that Joseph's marriage to Margaret Green took place March 18, 1879 (*The Davis Family*, 84).

CHART TEN

LUCINDA FARRAR DAVIS DAVIS STAMPS FAMILY

20 Lucinda Farrar Davis[78] m.[79] 60 Hugh Davis[80]

(one child)

---

61 Hugh Robert Davis[81] m.[82] 62 Anne Jane Boyle[83]

---

20 Lucinda Farrar Davis Davis m. March 5, 1820[84] 63 William Stamps[85]

(four children)

---

64 Jane Davis[86] m.[87] 65 William Alexander[88]

---

66 Anna Aurelia[89]	m.[90]	67 Claiborne Farish[91]
68 William Stamps, Jr. d. February 9, 1843[92]		
69 Isaac Davis b. April 23, 1823 d. July 3, 1863[93]	m.[94]	70 Mary Elizabeth Douglas Humphreys[95]

78 See *n.* 19 above.

79 According to the chart prepared by Douglas McL. More, Hugh and Lucinda were married December 12, 1816 (Genealogical Data [Jefferson Davis Association, Rice University, Houston]).

80 Lucinda's husband Hugh Davis was a brother of the Robert Davis who married Lucinda's youngest sister Mary Ellen (Kerrigan, Genealogical Data [Jefferson Davis Association, Rice University, Houston]; see also Chart Thirteen). Lucinda Davis Stamps Farrar, in a letter of February 9, 1946, to Floyd R. Farrar, affirms the double kinship and states that her grandmother Lucinda's first husband (Hugh) was drowned in the Homochitto River and their son Hugh Robert born posthumously (Floyd R. Farrar, Shreveport, Louisiana, 1968). H. A. Davis believes Hugh Davis was born about 1792/93 (*The Davis Family*, 84); More gives Hugh's deathdate as July 12, 1817 (Genealogical Data [Jefferson Davis Association, Rice University, Houston]). No blood relationship between Lucinda's and Hugh's respective families has been discovered.

81 According to More's chart, Hugh Robert was born March 3, 1818, and died March 1, 1871 (Genealogical Data [Jefferson Davis Association, Rice University, Houston]); 1818 is the birthdate also assigned by H. A. Davis and Ganier (*The Davis Family*, 84; Davis Family Tree [Alfred F. Ganier, Nashville, 1968]).

82 Anne or Anna Boyle married Hugh Robert Davis on March 26, 1845 (More, Genealogical Data [Jefferson Davis Association, Rice University, Houston]).

83 More lists Anne's deathdate as June 16, 1883 (Genealogical Data [Jefferson Davis Association, Rice University, Houston]).

84 Marriage Records (Wilkinson County Courthouse, Woodville, Mississippi).

85 H. A. Davis states that William Stamps was born about 1799 and died March 4, 1878 (*The Davis Family*, 84). More believes the year of his birth was 1797 or 1798 (Genealogical Data [Jefferson Davis Association, Rice University, Houston]).

86 According to More, Jane Davis Stamps was born December 21, 1820, and died September 14, 1884 (Genealogical Data [Jefferson Davis Association, Rice University, Houston]).

87 Jane was married to William Alexander February 27, 1845 (More, Genealogical Data [Jefferson Davis Association, Rice University, Houston]).

88 William Alexander is thought to have died July 22, 1874 (More, Genealogical Data [Jefferson Davis Association, Rice University, Houston]).

89 Anna Aurelia was born February 2, 1823, and died June 10, 1895, according to the chart prepared by More (Genealogical Data [Jefferson Davis Association, Rice University, Houston]).

90 More states Anna Aurelia and Claiborne Farish were married January 17, 1856 (Genealogical Data [Jefferson Davis Association, Rice University, Houston]); H. A. Davis (*The Davis Family*, 85) gives the marriage date as "about 1854–5."

[91] Claiborne Farish was born about 1819 or 1820 and died November 18, 1889 (More, Genealogical Data [Jefferson Davis Association, Rice University, Houston]).

[92] More gives the birthdate of William, Jr., as December 28, 1825. The Woodville (Mississippi) *Republican* of March 11, 1843, records the death of W. J. Stamps, a student at Bethany College, Bethany, Virginia, on February 9, 1843.

[93] The birthdate on Isaac's tombstone appears to read April 23, 1823 ("Rosemont" plantation cemetery, near Woodville, Mississippi); More's chart lists the date as April 23, 1828. The latter date is more acceptable because Isaac's sister was born on February 2, 1823 (More, Genealogical Data [Jefferson Davis Association, Rice University, Houston]).

[94] The date of Isaac and Mary Elizabeth Douglas Humphreys Stamps's marriage was May 11, 1854 (More, Genealogical Data [Jefferson Davis Association, Rice University, Houston]; H. A. Davis, *The Davis Family*, 174; Mary McLaughlin Stamps Bateson, Application for Membership [The Colonial Dames of America, New Canaan, Connecticut, 1935]).

[95] Isaac's wife, Mary, was born February 13, 1835, and died May 9, 1900 (More, Genealogical Data [Jefferson Davis Association, Rice University, Houston]; H. A. Davis, *The Davis Family*, 174).

CHART ELEVEN
AMANDA DAVIS BRADFORD FAMILY

21 Amanda Davis[96] m.[97] 71 David Bradford b. February 2, 1796[98]

(nine children)

72 David Vincent b. July 25, 1821 d. August 15, 1831[99]		
73 Benjamin Franklin[100]		
74 Mary Jane[101]	m.[102] m.[104]	75 Richard Brodhead[103] 76 Robert Sayre
77 Anna Matilda[105]	m.	78 Edward L. Miles
79 Jefferson Davis[106]	m. m.	80 Helen Sumner 81 Virgie Patterson[107]
82 Lucinda[108]	m.[109]	27 Charles Jouett Mitchell[110]
83 Elizabeth Porter[111]	m.[112]	84 Maunsel White, Jr.[113]
85 Sarah D.[114]		
86 David[115]	m.	87 Ada Pottinger

[96] See *n.* 20 above.

[97] H. A. Davis states that Amanda and David Bradford were married about 1820 (*The Davis Family*, 88).

[98] The birthdate for Bradford is the one found on his tombstone, which also gives the date of his death as March 12, 1844 ("Hurricane" and "Brierfield"

plantations cemetery, Davis Island, near Vicksburg, Mississippi). There is considerable disagreement about the deathdate: in a letter to Varina Howell, dated March 15, 1844, Davis states, "My Brother-in-law David Bradford was assassinated day before yesterday" (Hudson Strode, Tuscaloosa, Alabama, 1969). This would, of course, fix his deathdate as March 13, 1844. The Richmond (Louisiana) *Compiler* of March 15, 1844, also states that Bradford died on March 13, as does the Vicksburg *Weekly Whig* of April 8, 1844, which reports that the fatal shooting took place on Wednesday, March 13, 1844. However, the Vicksburg *Sentinel* (March 18, 1844) and the Vicksburg *Weekly Whig* (March 25, 1844) state that he died March 14, 1844.

99 These are the dates on a tombstone in the "Hurricane" cemetery; the identification on the grave is only "David son of David and Amanda Bradford" ("Hurricane" and "Brierfield" plantations cemetery, Davis Island, near Vicksburg, Mississippi). Since their other son David (Entry 86) lived to marry, the grave is obviously not his (see *n.* 115 below). Moreover, the first David's relatively short life would explain why some genealogists have overlooked him.

100 H. A. Davis believes Benjamin Franklin Bradford was born 1822/23 (*The Davis Family*, 88); Ganier gives his birthdate as 1822 and his deathdate as 1885 (Davis Family Tree [Alfred F. Ganier, Nashville, 1968]).

101 Mary Jane or "Malie" was born in 1825, according to H. A. Davis (*The Davis Family*, 88) and Ganier (Davis Family Tree [Alfred F. Ganier, Nashville, 1968]). Ganier states that she died in 1877.

102 According to H. A. Davis, Mary Jane and Richard Brodhead were married in 1848 (*The Davis Family*, 88); their marriage bond, however, is dated April 3, 1849 (O'Neill, "Warren County Marriages," *Journal of Mississippi History*, XXIX, 215).

103 Richard Brodhead was born January 5, 1811, and died September 16, 1863 (*Biographical Directory of the American Congress*, 601).

104 Mary Jane Bradford Brodhead is believed to have wed Robert Sayre in 1872 (Ganier, Davis Family Tree [Alfred F. Ganier, Nashville, 1968]).

105 Anna Matilda was called Nannie or Nancy according to H. A. Davis, who gives her birthdate as 1826/27 (*The Davis Family*, 88). Ganier's chart lists her birth in 1827 and her death in 1904 (Davis Family Tree [Alfred F. Ganier, Nashville, 1968]). A marriage bond for Edward L. Miles and Anna M. Bradford is dated May 17, 1848 (O'Neill, "Warren County Marriages," *Journal of Mississippi History*, XXIX, 214).

106 Jefferson Davis Bradford was born in 1838, according to Strode (*American Patriot*, 87*n.*) and Ganier (Davis Family Tree [Alfred F. Ganier, Nashville, 1968]). H. A. Davis lists 1828 as the year of his birth (*The Davis Family*, 88). Ganier states that he died in 1910 (Davis Family Tree [Alfred F. Ganier, Nashville, 1968]).

107 Ganier refers to J. D. Bradford's second wife as Virgie Patterson (Davis Family Tree [Alfred F. Ganier, Nashville, 1968]), whereas H. A. Davis gives her name as Virgil (*The Davis Family*, 89).

108 Ganier writes that Lucinda was born November 11, 1831, and died February 7, 1919 (Davis Family Tree [Alfred F. Ganier, Nashville, 1968]).

109 Lucinda married the widowered Charles Mitchell (Entry 27) in 1850 (Ganier, Davis Family Tree [Alfred F. Ganier, Nashville, 1968]). Their marriage bond is dated December 13, 1850 (O'Neill, "Warren County Marriages," *Journal of Mississippi History*, XXIX, 217).

110 See *n.* 28 above.

111 Elizabeth Porter Bradford's birthdate is given as 1829 by Ganier, and as 1831 by H. A. Davis, who lists her middle name as Parker. Both sources cite 1917 as her deathdate (*The Davis

Family, 89; Davis Family Tree [Alfred F. Ganier, Nashville, 1968]).
[112] Elizabeth Bradford married Maunsel White in 1855 (H. A. Davis, *The Davis Family*, 89; Ganier, Davis Family Tree [Alfred F. Ganier, Nashville, 1968]). The marriage bond was signed June 12, 1855 (O'Neill, "Warren County Marriages," *Journal of Mississippi History*, XXX, 58).
[113] H. A. Davis states that White was born *ca.* 1830/31 and died in 1896 (*The Davis Family*, 89).
[114] According to H. A. Davis (*The Davis Family*, 90), Sarah D. Bradford was born in 1833 and died in the 1850's. Ganier notes that a Sara Aurelia was born to David and Amanda Bradford in 1833 and that she died in 1852 (Davis Family Tree [Alfred F. Ganier, Nashville, 1968]). Other sources simply refer to her as Sarah (Hayes-Davis, Genealogical Data [Jefferson Davis Association, Rice University, Houston]; De Leon, *Belles, Beaux and Brains*, 78). A different birthdate—June 1834—is suggested in 1:419. There David Bradford reports that a child is soon to be born, and it seems likely that this would have been Sarah.
[115] Ganier and H. A. Davis agree that the second David was born in 1835; Ganier says that he died in 1903 (Davis Family Tree [Alfred F. Ganier, Nashville, 1968]; *The Davis Family*, 90).

CHART TWELVE

MATILDA DAVIS VAUGHAN

22 Matilda Davis m. 88 Mr. Vaughan
d. March 16, 1834[116]
(no known children)[117]

[116] See *n.* 21 above.
[117] A newspaper notice suggests that a daughter may have been born to this union. As guardian of a Sarah Matilda Vaughan, Jane Cook Davis (Entry 14), mother of Matilda (Entry 22), states she will present an account for final settlement at the county probate court (Woodville [Mississippi] *Republican*, April 12, 1834). See also sketch, 1:363, *n.* 34. *The Republican* (Woodville, Mississippi) of Friday, September 25, 1846, reports the following marriage: "In this place, on Monday morning last, by Hon. Francis Gildart, Mr. John J. Brown to Miss Sarah Vaughan, both of West Feliciana Parish, La." Whether this is the same Sarah Vaughan mentioned above and whether she was Davis' niece have not been ascertained.

CHART THIRTEEN

MARY ELLEN DAVIS DAVIS FAMILY

23 Mary Ellen Davis m.[119] 89 Robert Davis[120]
d. March 2, 1824[118]
(two children)

90 Jane Lucinda m. May 3, 1842[122] 91 Hazlewood Farish
b. 1819/20 b. 1809/10
d. November 23, 1851[121] d. May 5, 1851[123]

92 Ellen Mary[124] m.[125] 93 Thomas Anderson[126]

118 See *n.* 22 above.
119 According to H. A. Davis, Mary Ellen and Robert Davis were married in 1820 (*The Davis Family*, 94).
120 Robert was born about 1790/91 and died between 1825 and 1830 (H. A. Davis, *The Davis Family*, 94). Robert's brother Hugh married Mary Ellen's sister Lucinda; see *n.* 80 above.
121 Jane Lucinda's tombstone states that she was thirty-one at the time of her death ("Rosemont" plantation cemetery, near Woodville, Mississippi).
122 Woodville (Mississippi) *Republican*, May 7, 1842.
123 According to his tombstone, Hazlewood Farish was forty-one when he died ("Rosemont" plantation cemetery, near Woodville, Mississippi).
124 Ellen Mary was born in 1824 and died about 1915 (H. A. Davis, *The Davis Family*, 95; Ganier, Davis Family Tree [Alfred F. Ganier, Nashville, 1968]).
125 Ellen Mary and Thomas Anderson were married *ca.* 1852 according to H. A. Davis (*The Davis Family*, 94) and Ganier (Davis Family Tree [Alfred F. Ganier, Nashville, 1968]).
126 Born in 1820, Thomas Anderson died sometime in the 1860's (H. A. Davis, *The Davis Family*, 95; Ganier, Davis Family Tree [Alfred F. Ganier, Nashville, 1968]).

CHART FOURTEEN

JEFFERSON FINIS DAVIS FAMILY

24 Jefferson Finis Davis m. June 17, 1835[128] 94 Sarah Knox Taylor
b. June 3, 1807/1808
d. December 6, 1889[127]
d. September 15, 1835[129]

24 Jefferson Finis Davis m. February 26, 1845[130] 95 Varina Banks Howell
b. May 7, 1826
d. October 16, 1906[131]

(six children)

96 Samuel Emory
b. July 30, 1852
d. June 13, 1854[132]

97 Margaret Howell m. January 1, 1876[134] 98 Joel Addison Hayes, Jr.
b. February 25, 1855
d. July 18, 1909[133]
b. March 4, 1848
d. January 28, 1919[135]

99 Jefferson, Jr.
b. January 16, 1857
d. October 16, 1878[136]

100 Joseph Evan
b. April 18, 1859
d. April 30, 1864[137]

101 William Howell
d. October 16, 1872[138]

102 Varina Anne
b. June 27, 1864
d. September 18, 1898[139]

[127] See *n.* 23 above.
[128] See 1:485.
[129] The deathdate is confirmed by Sarah's tombstone, which states that she was "Aged 21 Years" when she died ("God's Acre," "Locust Grove" plantation cemetery, near St. Francisville, Louisiana). She would thus have been born in 1813 or 1814. In notes taken from the Taylor Family Tree compiled by Philip Fall, Sarah's birthdate is given as March 6, 1815 (Zachary Taylor, Small File [The Filson Club, Louisville, Kentucky]). Miscellaneous notes about Sarah Knox Taylor in the Trist Wood Papers also give March 6, 1815, as her birthdate (Box 12, Folder 8 [Southern Historical Collection, University of North Carolina Library, Chapel Hill]). See also 1:443, *n.* 2.
[130] Marriage Bond and License, Book F, 691 (County Clerk's Office, Adams County Courthouse, Natchez, Mississippi).
[131] The birthdate is confirmed by Varina in her lifesketch (Jefferson Davis Papers, University of Alabama Library, Tuscaloosa). Her deathdate is recorded in various newspapers, including the New York *Times* (October 18, 1906, p. 9).
[132] Gravestone (Hollywood Cemetery, Richmond, Virginia).
[133] Margaret's birth and death dates are those given by her son, Jefferson Hayes-Davis (Genealogical Data [Jefferson Davis Association, Rice University, Houston]).
[134] According to Jefferson Hayes-Davis, his parents were married January 1, 1876 (Genealogical Data [Jefferson Davis Association, Rice University, Houston]).
[135] Hayes-Davis, Genealogical Data (Jefferson Davis Association, Rice University, Houston).
[136] Gravestone (Hollywood Cemetery, Richmond, Virginia).
[137] Plaque (St. Paul's Episcopal Church, Richmond, Virginia).
[138] Jefferson Hayes-Davis gives December 16, 1861, as the date of his uncle William's birth, and Howell Morgan, in his genealogy of the Howell family, concurs (Hayes-Davis, Genealogical Data [Jefferson Davis Association, Rice University, Houston]; Morgan, Howell Genealogy [Jefferson Hayes-Davis, Colorado Springs, 1970]). The birthdate on the tombstone, however, is October 16, 1861, and in a church memorial inscription is listed as December 6, 1861. The deathdate on the tombstone is October 16, 1871, while the memorial inscription in St. Paul's records October 16, 1872 (Hollywood Cemetery, St. Paul's Episcopal Church, Richmond, Virginia). A letter of condolence from Mary Custis (Mrs. Robert E.) Lee to Varina Davis, November 18, 1872, gives evidence of William's death in that year (Jefferson Davis Papers, University of Alabama Library, Tuscaloosa).
[139] Varina Anne states in her birthday book that she was born on June 27 (Museum of the Confederacy, Richmond, Virginia). Her nephew Jefferson Hayes-Davis confirms her birthdate as June 27, 1864 (Genealogical Data [Jefferson Davis Association, Rice University, Houston]). Both her tombstone and the memorial inscription in St. Paul's record her death on September 18, 1898 (Hollywood Cemetery, St. Paul's Episcopal Church, Richmond, Virginia).

Alphabetical Guide to the Davis Family

Editorial Note: The following list serves for rapid identification of an individual by giving his relationship to a member of his immediate family and his relation to Jefferson Davis; for example, "23 Mary Ellen Davis Davis—daughter of Samuel and Jane Davis; sister—1:548, *n.* 5." The location of the biographical sketch, if one has been included in the volume, follows this description. Female members of the family are listed alphabetically under their last married name.

Entry No.

64 Alexander, Jane Davis Stamps—daughter of William and Lucinda Farrar Davis Davis Stamps; niece—1:528, *n.* 14.

65 Alexander, William—husband of Jane Davis Stamps; nephew by marriage.

92 Anderson, Ellen Mary Davis—daughter of Robert and Mary Ellen Davis Davis; niece—1:363, *n.* 36.

93 Anderson, Thomas—husband of Ellen Mary Davis; nephew by marriage.

49 Boyle, Lucinda Jane Smith—daughter of Luther and Anna Eliza Davis Smith; niece—1:535, *n.* 9.

50 Boyle, William D.—husband of Lucinda Jane Smith; nephew by marriage.

87 Bradford, Ada Pottinger—wife of David Bradford (Entry 86); niece by marriage.

21 Bradford, Amanda Davis—daughter of Samuel and Jane Cook Davis; sister—1:363, *n.* 29.

73 Bradford, Benjamin Franklin—son of David and Amanda Davis Bradford; nephew—1:363, *n.* 18.

71 Bradford, David—husband of Amanda Davis; brother-in law—1:5, *n.* 10.

86 Bradford, David—son of David and Amanda Davis Bradford; nephew.

72 Bradford, David Vincent—son of David and Amanda Davis Bradford; nephew.

80 Bradford, Helen Sumner—first wife of Jefferson Davis Bradford; niece by marriage.

79 Bradford, Jefferson Davis—son of David and Amanda Davis Bradford; nephew.

85 Bradford, Sarah D.—daughter of David and Amanda Davis Bradford; niece.

81 Bradford, Virgie Patterson—second wife of Jefferson Davis Bradford; niece by marriage.

Entry No.

75 Brodhead, Richard–first husband of Mary Jane Bradford; nephew by marriage.

62 Davis, Anne Jane Boyle–wife of Hugh Robert Davis; niece by marriage.

34 Davis, Aurelia Smith–wife of Benjamin Davis; sister-in-law.

3 Davis, Benjamin–son of Evan and Mary Davis; great uncle.

16 Davis, Benjamin–son of Samuel and Jane Cook Davis; brother.

37 Davis, Benjamin Thomas–son of Samuel and Lucy Throckmorton Davis; nephew.

5 Davis, Christiana–wife of William Davis (Entry 4); great aunt by marriage.

25 Davis, Eliza Van Benthuysen–second wife of Joseph Emory Davis; sister-in-law–1:361, *n.* 8.

1 Davis, Evan–great-grandfather.

11 Davis, Evan–son of Evan and Mary Davis; grandfather–1:5, *n.* 6.

58 Davis, Fannie Peyton–first wife of Joseph Robert Davis; niece by marriage.

60 Davis, Hugh–first husband of Lucinda Farrar Davis; brother-in-law.

61 Davis, Hugh Robert–son of Hugh and Lucinda Farrar Davis Davis; nephew–1:362, *n.* 13.

19 Davis, Isaac Williams–son of Samuel and Jane Cook Davis; brother–1:9, *n.* 12.

14 Davis, Jane Cook–wife of Samuel Emory Davis; mother–1:22, *n.* 4.

99 Davis, Jefferson, Jr.–son of Jefferson and Varina Banks Howell Davis.

24 Davis, Jefferson Finis–son of Samuel and Jane Cook Davis.

10 Davis, Joseph–son of Evan and Mary Davis; great uncle.

43 Davis, Joseph–son of Samuel and Lucy Throckmorton Davis; nephew.

15 Davis, Joseph Emory–son of Samuel and Jane Cook Davis; brother–1:19, *n.* 1.

100 Davis, Joseph Evan–son of Jefferson and Varina Banks Howell Davis.

57 Davis, Joseph Robert–son of Isaac Williams and Susannah Gartley Davis; nephew.

36 Davis, Lucy Throckmorton–wife of Samuel Davis; sister-in-law.

Entry No.

59 Davis, Margaret Cary Green–second wife of Joseph Robert Davis; niece by marriage.

7 Davis, Martha–wife of Samuel Davis (Entry 6); great aunt by marriage.

2 Davis, Mary–wife of Evan Davis (Entry 1); great-grandmother.

35 Davis, Mary Ann–daughter of Benjamin and Aurelia Smith Davis; niece.

23 Davis, Mary Ellen Davis–daughter of Samuel and Jane Cook Davis; sister–1:528, *n.* 5.

12 Davis, Mary Emory Williams–wife of Evan Davis (Entry 11); grandmother.

38 Davis, Pauline Taylor–wife of Benjamin Thomas Davis; niece by marriage.

89 Davis, Robert–husband of Mary Ellen Davis; brother-in-law–1:528, *n.* 4.

41 Davis, Robert H.–son of Samuel and Lucy Throckmorton Davis; nephew.

6 Davis, Samuel–son of Evan and Mary Davis; great uncle.

17 Davis, Samuel–son of Samuel and Jane Cook Davis; brother–1:19, *n.* 8.

42 Davis, Samuel A.–son of Samuel and Lucy Throckmorton Davis; nephew.

13 Davis, Samuel Emory–son of Evan and Mary Davis; father of Jefferson Davis–1:5, *n.* 11.

96 Davis, Samuel Emory–son of Jefferson and Varina Howell Davis.

94 Davis, Sarah Knox Taylor–first wife of Jefferson Davis–1:443, *n.* 2.

55 Davis, Susannah Gartley–wife of Isaac Williams Davis; sister-in-law.

102 Davis, Varina Anne–daughter of Jefferson and Varina Banks Howell Davis.

95 Davis, Varina Banks Howell–second wife of Jefferson Davis.

4 Davis, William–son of Evan and Mary Davis; great uncle.

101 Davis, William Howell–son of Jefferson and Varina Banks Howell Davis.

56 Davis, ________–son of Isaac Williams and Susannah Gartley Davis; nephew–1:9, *n.* 11.

8 Dubre, Hannah Davis–daughter of Evan and Mary Davis; great aunt.

Entry No.	
9	Dubre, Jacob, Jr.–husband of Hannah Davis; great uncle by marriage.
66	Farish, Anna Aurelia Stamps–daughter of William and Lucinda Farrar Davis Davis Stamps; niece–1:529, *n.* 2.
67	Farish, Claiborne–husband of Anna Aurelia Stamps; nephew by marriage.
91	Farish, Hazlewood–husband of Jane Lucinda Davis; nephew by marriage.
90	Farish, Jane Lucinda Davis–daughter of Robert and Mary Ellen Davis Davis; niece–1:363, *n.* 35.
98	Hayes, Joel Addison, Jr.–husband of Margaret Howell Davis; son-in-law.
97	Hayes, Margaret Howell Davis–daughter of Jefferson and Varina Banks Howell Davis.
39	Keary, Helen Davis–daughter of Samuel and Lucy Throckmorton Davis; niece.
40	Keary, Patrick F.–husband of Helen Davis; nephew by marriage.
30	Laughlin, Edmund C.–second husband of Florida A. Davis McCaleb; nephew by marriage.
28	Laughlin, Florida A. Davis McCaleb–daughter of Joseph Emory Davis by his first wife; niece–1:19, *n.* 9.
33	Leonard, Abram F.–second husband of Caroline Davis Robins; nephew by marriage.
31	Leonard, Caroline Davis Robins–daughter of Joseph Emory Davis by his first wife; niece–1:395, *n.* 8.
29	McCaleb, David–first husband of Florida Davis; nephew by marriage–1:439, *n.* 6.
77	Miles, Anna Matilda Bradford–daughter of David and Amanda Davis Bradford; niece–1:363, *n.* 19.
78	Miles, Edward L.–husband of Anna Matilda Bradford; nephew by marriage.
27	Mitchell, Charles Jouett–husband of Mary Lucinda Davis and, later, of Lucinda Bradford; nephew by marriage–1:521, *n.* 4.
82	Mitchell, Lucinda Bradford–daughter of David and Amanda Davis Bradford; niece–1:363, *n.* 28.
26	Mitchell, Mary Lucinda Davis–daughter of Joseph Emory Davis by his first wife; niece–1:362, *n.* 11.
32	Robins, Thomas E.–first husband of Caroline Davis; nephew by marriage.

Entry No.	
74	Sayre, Mary Jane Bradford Brodhead—daughter of David and Amanda Davis Bradford; niece—1:363, *n.* 20.
76	Sayre, Robert—second husband of Mary Jane Bradford Brodhead; nephew by marriage.
53	Smith, Anna Amanda Smith—daughter of Luther and Anna Eliza Davis Smith; niece—1:526, *n.* 9.
18	Smith, Anna Eliza Davis—daughter of Samuel and Jane Cook Davis; sister—1:419, *n.* 30.
48	Smith, Gordon A.—son of Luther and Anna Eliza Davis Smith; nephew.
51	Smith, Jedediah Davis—son of Luther and Anna Eliza Davis Smith; nephew—1:535, *n.* 10.
45	Smith, Joseph Davis—son of Luther and Anna Eliza Davis Smith; nephew—1:363, *n.* 24.
44	Smith, Luther L.—husband of Anna Eliza Davis; brother-in-law—1:363, *n.* 26.
47	Smith, Luther L., Jr.—son of Luther and Anna Eliza Davis Smith; nephew—1:363, *n.* 25.
46	Smith, Marie Coralie Guibert—wife of Joseph Davis Smith; niece by marriage—1:535, *n.* 15.
54	Smith, Philander C.—husband of Anna Amanda Smith; nephew by marriage.
52	Smith, Susan M. Buck—wife of Jedediah Davis Smith; niece by marriage.
69	Stamps, Isaac Davis—son of William and Lucinda Farrar Davis Davis Stamps; nephew.
20	Stamps, Lucinda Farrar Davis Davis—daughter of Samuel and Jane Cook Davis; sister—1:19, *n.* 3.
70	Stamps, Mary Elizabeth Douglas Humphreys—wife of Isaac Davis Stamps; niece by marriage.
63	Stamps, William—second husband of Lucinda Farrar Davis Davis; brother-in-law—1:362, *n.* 12.
68	Stamps, William, Jr. son of William and Lucinda Farrar Davis Davis Stamps; nephew—1:535, *n.* 11.
22	Vaughan, Matilda Davis—daughter of Samuel and Jane Cook Davis; sister—1:363, *n.* 34.
88	Vaughan, ________—husband of Matilda Davis; brother-in-law.
83	White, Elizabeth Porter Bradford—daughter of David and Amanda Davis Bradford; niece.
84	White, Maunsel, Jr.—husband of Elizabeth Porter Bradford; nephew by marriage.

APPENDIX V

CALENDARS OF RETURNS AND MUSTER ROLLS

Calendar of Monthly Returns: West Point

Editorial Note: Unlike the later post returns, to which they are similar, monthly returns at West Point do not list Davis on each report. Cadets are named only when their status was unusual, and sometimes not even then. Thus Davis is mentioned when he was sick or in arrest, but is not mentioned when present for duty. Even when he was graduated, in July 1828, he appears only by implication, for the report states simply "*Dropped* 32 Cadets (Graduates)." We may therefore assume that if Davis is not mentioned, he was present for duty.

DATE OF REPORT	ITEM NUMBER	ENTRY	IF NOT PRINTED
September 30, 1824	1:10	Admitted	
October 31	1:13	Present; sick	
November 30			Davis not mentioned
December 31			Davis not mentioned
January 31, 1825			Davis not mentioned
February 28			Report missing
March 31			Davis not mentioned
April 30			Davis not mentioned
May 31			Davis not mentioned
June 30			Davis not mentioned
July 31			Davis not mentioned

DATE OF REPORT	ITEM NUMBER	ENTRY	IF NOT PRINTED
August 31	1:40	Present; in arrest	
September 30		Lists receipt of order concerning Davis' court martial	Davis' status unchanged
October 31			Davis not mentioned
November 30			Davis not mentioned
December 31			Davis not mentioned
January 31, 1826	1:50	Present; sick (most likely Jefferson Davis, but possibly John P. Davis)	
February 28			Davis not mentioned
March 31			Davis not mentioned
April 30			Davis not mentioned
May 31	1:54	Present; sick (most likely Jefferson Davis, but possibly John P. Davis)	
June 30		Present; sick	Repeats previous printed report
July 31			Davis not mentioned
August 31	1:63	Present; sick	
September 30		Present; sick	Repeats previous printed report
October 31		Present; sick	Repeats previous printed report
November 30		Present; sick	Repeats previous printed report

APPENDIX V

DATE OF REPORT	ITEM NUMBER	ENTRY	IF NOT PRINTED
December 31	1:71	Present; in arrest	
January 31, 1827		Present; in arrest	Repeats previous printed report
February 28			Davis not mentioned
March 31			Davis not mentioned
April 30	1:93	Present; sick	
May 31			Davis not mentioned
June 30			Davis not mentioned
July 31			Davis not mentioned
August 31			Davis not mentioned
September 30	1:104	Present; sick	
October 31			Davis not mentioned
November 30			Davis not mentioned
December 31			Davis not mentioned
January 31, 1828			Davis not mentioned
February 29			Davis not mentioned
March 31			Davis not mentioned
April 30			Davis not mentioned
May 31			Davis not mentioned
June 30		Fifty-two cadets on furlough (one of these being Davis)	Davis not mentioned
July 31		Thirty-two cadets graduated and dropped (one of these being Davis)	Davis not mentioned

DATE OF REPORT	ITEM NUMBER	ENTRY	IF NOT PRINTED
September 30	1:128	Lists receipt of order extending Davis' furlough until December 31, 1828	

Calendar of Muster Rolls: West Point

Editorial Note: Army muster rolls in this period were made in two series, bimonthly and semiannual. The abbreviation SA denotes semiannual.

DATE OF REPORT	ITEM NUMBER	ENTRY	IF NOT PRINTED
October 31, 1824	1:14	Admitted September 1, 1824; present; sick	
December 31	1:17	Present	
December 31 SA	1:18	Admitted September 1, 1824; present; age 17 years 6 months	
February 28, 1825		Present	Repeats previous printed report
April 30		Present	Repeats previous printed report
June 30		Present	Repeats previous printed report
June 30 SA	1:31	Present; age 18 years	
August 31	1:41	Present; in arrest	
October 31	1:44	Present	

DATE OF REPORT	ITEM NUMBER	ENTRY	IF NOT PRINTED
December 31		Present	Repeats previous printed report
December 31 SA	1:47	Present; age 18 years 6 months	
February 28, 1826		Present	Repeats previous printed report
April 30		Present	Repeats previous printed report
June 30	1:58	Present; sick; fourth sergeant, first company	
June 30 SA	1:59	Present; sick; fourth sergeant, first company; age 19 years	
August 31	1:64	Present; sick; sergeant of the color guard	
October 31		Present; sick; sergeant of the color guard	Repeats previous printed report
December 31	1:72	Present; in arrest and confinement; sergeant of the color guard	
December 31 SA	1:73	Present; in arrest and confinement; sergeant of the color guard; age 19 years 6 months	
February 28, 1827	1:89	Present; sergeant of the color guard	
April 30	1:94	Present; sick	

DATE OF REPORT	ITEM NUMBER	ENTRY	IF NOT PRINTED
June 30	1:98	Present	
June 30 SA	1:99	Present; age 20 years	
August 31		Present	Repeats previous printed report
October 31		Present	Repeats previous printed report
December 31		Present	Repeats previous printed report
December 31 SA	1:107	Present; age 20 years 6 months	
February 29, 1828		Present	Repeats previous printed report
April 30		Present	Repeats previous printed report
June 30			Report missing
June 30 SA	1:120	Absent on furlough to August 28, 1828; age 21 years	

Calendar of Post Returns: Regular Army

Editorial Note: Regular army post returns are similar to the cadet monthly returns from West Point, except that an officer is always listed, even when he was only present for duty. Davis is not found on any post returns until October 1828, when he was to report to Jefferson Barracks, Missouri.

DATE OF REPORT & POST	ITEM NUMBER	ENTRY	IF NOT PRINTED
October 31, 1828 (Jefferson Bks.)	1:130	Absent without leave; furlough expired October 30, 1828	

DATE OF REPORT & POST	ITEM NUMBER	ENTRY	IF NOT PRINTED
November 30 (Jefferson Bks.)		Absent without leave; furlough expired October 30, 1828	Repeats previous printed report
December 31 (Jefferson Bks.)		Absent without leave; furlough expired October 30, 1828	Repeats previous printed report
January 31, 1829 (Jefferson Bks.)	1:138	Present for duty January 11, 1829	
February 28 (Jefferson Bks.)		Present for duty	Repeats previous printed report
March 31 (Jefferson Bks.)	1:142	Dropped; ordered to regiment March 24, 1829	
April 30			Transferred; not located on any post return
May 31 (Ft. Winnebago)	1:146	Present; not attached to a company	
June 30 (Ft. Winnebago)	1:147	Present; on extra duty; not attached to a company	
July 31 (Ft. Winnebago)	1:149	Present; on extra duty; not attached to a company	
August 31 (Ft. Winnebago)	1:150	Present; attached to Company C August 29, 1829	
September 30 (Ft. Winnebago)	1:154	Present; on extra duty June 21, 1829	
October 31 (Ft. Winnebago)	1:159	Absent on detached service pursuing deserters October 20, 1829	

DATE OF REPORT & POST	ITEM NUMBER	ENTRY	IF NOT PRINTED
November 30 (Ft. Winnebago)	1:162	Present for duty	
December 31 (Ft. Winnebago)	1:163	Absent with leave December 22, 1829	
January 31, 1830 (Ft. Winnebago)	1:169	Present for duty	
February 28 (Ft. Winnebago)	1:170	Present; on extra duty	
March 31 (Ft. Winnebago)		Present; on extra duty	Repeats previous printed report
April 30 (Ft. Winnebago)		Present; on extra duty	Repeats previous printed report
May 31 (Ft. Winnebago)		Present; on extra duty	Repeats previous printed report
June 30 (Ft. Winnebago)		Present; on extra duty	Repeats previous printed report
July 31 (Ft. Winnebago)	1:190	Absent on special duty pursuing deserters July 25, 1830	
August 31 (Ft. Winnebago)	1:201	Present; on extra duty	
September 30 (Ft. Winnebago)		Present; on extra duty	Repeats previous printed report
October 31 (Ft. Winnebago)		Present; on extra duty	Repeats previous printed report
November 30 (Ft. Winnebago)		Present; on extra duty	Repeats previous printed report
December 31 (Ft. Winnebago)		Present; on extra duty	Repeats previous printed report
January 31, 1831 (Ft. Winnebago)		Present; on extra duty	Repeats previous printed report

DATE OF REPORT & POST	ITEM NUMBER	ENTRY	IF NOT PRINTED
February 28 (Ft. Winnebago)	1:236	Present; on extra duty; first return to reflect promotion to second lieutenant	
March 31 (Ft. Winnebago)		Present; on extra duty	Repeats previous printed report
April 30 (Ft. Winnebago)	1:252	Present; acting assistant commissary of subsistence and quartermaster	
May 31 (Ft. Winnebago)		Present; acting assistant commissary of subsistence and quartermaster	Repeats previous printed report
June 30 (Ft. Crawford)	1:267	Absent on special duty at Rock Island	
July 31 (Ft. Crawford)	1:272	Absent on special duty superintending sawmill on the Yellow River	
August 31 (Ft. Crawford)	1:277	Present for duty	
September 30 (Ft. Crawford)	1:282	Absent on furlough	
October 31 (Ft. Crawford)	1:292	Absent on special duty at Dubuques Mines	
November 30 (Ft. Crawford)	1:302	Absent on special duty at Dubuques Mines (order of November 1, 1831)	
December 31 (Ft. Crawford)		Absent on special duty at Dubuques Mines	Repeats previous printed report

DATE OF REPORT & POST	ITEM NUMBER	ENTRY	IF NOT PRINTED
January 31, 1832 (Ft. Crawford)		Absent on special duty at Dubuques Mines	Repeats previous printed report
February 29 (Ft. Crawford)		Absent on special duty at Dubuques Mines	Repeats previous printed report
March 31 (Ft. Crawford)	1:322	Absent on furlough until May 26, 1832	
April 30 (Ft. Crawford)		Absent on furlough	Repeats previous printed report
May 31 (Ft. Crawford)			Davis not listed
June 30 (Ft. Crawford)			Davis not listed
July 31 (Ft. Crawford)			Davis not listed
August 31 (Ft. Crawford)	1:331	Present for duty	
September 30 (Ft. Crawford)	1:339	Absent on special duty at Rock Island (order of September 3, 1832)	
October 31 (Ft. Crawford)		Absent on special duty at Rock Island	Repeats previous printed report
November 30 (Ft. Crawford)	1:342	Absent on furlough	
December 31 (Ft. Crawford)		Absent on furlough	Repeats previous printed report
January 31, 1833 (Ft. Crawford)			Report missing
February 28 (Ft. Crawford)	1:346	Present for duty	

DATE OF REPORT & POST	ITEM NUMBER	ENTRY	IF NOT PRINTED
March 31 (Ft. Crawford)	1:352	Present; sick	
April 30 (Ft. Crawford)	1:353	Transferred; appointed second lieutenant of Dragoons March 4, 1833	
May 31			Transferred; not located on any post return
June 30			Transferred; not located on any post return
July 31 (Jefferson Bks.)	1:367	Present for duty; joined company July 11, 1833	
August 31 (Jefferson Bks.)	1:369	Present for duty; transferred from Company C to staff August 30, 1833	
September 30 (Jefferson Bks.)	1:378	Present for duty	
October 31 (Jefferson Bks.)	1:389	Present; acting staff officer to brigade October 2–21, 1833	
November 30			Transferred; not located on any post return
December 31 (Ft. Gibson)	1:397	Present for duty; left Jefferson Barracks November 20, arrived December 14, 1833	

DATE OF REPORT & POST	ITEM NUMBER	ENTRY	IF NOT PRINTED
January 31, 1834 (Ft. Gibson)		Present for duty	Repeats previous printed report
February 28 (Ft. Gibson)	1:405	Present for duty; company unorganized	
March 31 (Ft. Gibson)	1:408	Present; company unorganized; doing duty with Company A	
April 30 (Ft. Gibson)			Davis not listed
May 31 (Ft. Gibson)			Davis not listed
June 30 (Ft. Gibson)			Davis not listed
July 31 (Ft. Gibson)			Davis not listed
August 31 (Ft. Gibson)			Davis not listed
September 30 (Ft. Gibson)	1:427	Present; acting assistant quartermaster and commissary of subsistence; first return to reflect promotion to first lieutenant	
October 31 (Ft. Gibson)		Present; acting assistant quartermaster and commissary of subsistence	Repeats previous printed report
November 30 (Ft. Gibson)	1:441	Present for duty	
December 31 (Ft. Gibson)	1:444	Present; in arrest	

DATE OF REPORT & POST	ITEM NUMBER	ENTRY	IF NOT PRINTED
January 31, 1835 (Ft. Gibson)	1:450	Present for duty	
February 28 (Ft. Gibson)	1:464	Present; in arrest	
March 31 (Ft. Gibson)	1:474	Absent with leave	
April 30 (Ft. Gibson)			Davis not listed
May 31 (Ft. Gibson)			Davis not listed
June 30 (Ft. Gibson)			Davis not listed

Calendar of Muster Rolls: Regular Army

Editorial Note: Contrary to the practice at West Point, the regular army did not make up bimonthly rolls for the last two months covered by a semiannual muster roll (indicated by the notation SA). Davis is not found on any regular army muster roll until August 1829, when he was first assigned to a company.

DATE OF REPORT & ORGANIZATION	ITEM NUMBER	ENTRY	IF NOT PRINTED
August 31, 1829 (Co. C, 1st Inf.)	1:151	Present; attached August 29, 1829	
October 31 (Co. C, 1st Inf.)	1:160	Absent in pursuit of deserters October 20, 1829	
December 31 SA (Co. C, 1st Inf.)	1:164	Attached August 29, 1829; absent with leave December 22, 1829	
February 28, 1830 (Co. C, 1st Inf.)	1:171	Present; on extra duty	

DATE OF REPORT & ORGANIZATION	ITEM NUMBER	ENTRY	IF NOT PRINTED
April 30 (Co. C, 1st Inf.)		Present; on extra duty	Repeats previous printed report
June 30 SA (Co. C, 1st Inf.)		Present; on extra duty	Repeats previous printed report
August 31 (Co. C, 1st Inf.)		Present; on extra duty	Repeats previous printed report
October 31 (Co. C, 1st Inf.)		Present; on extra duty	Repeats previous printed report
December 31 SA (Co. C, 1st Inf.)		Present; on extra duty	Repeats previous printed report
February 28, 1831 (Co. C, 1st Inf.)	1:237	Present; on extra duty; acting assistant quartermaster	
April 30 (Co. B, 1st Inf.)	1:253	Present; joined and assumed command April 16, 1831; first muster roll to reflect promotion to second lieutenant	
June 30 SA (Co. B, 1st Inf.)	1:268	Present; assumed command April 16, 1831, relinquished command June 27, 1831; company left Fort Winnebago June 24, arrived at Fort Crawford June 26, left Fort Crawford June 27, and arrived at Fort Armstrong June 28, 1831	

DATE OF REPORT & ORGANIZATION	ITEM NUMBER	ENTRY	IF NOT PRINTED
August 31 (Co. B, 1st Inf.)	1:278	Present; company left Fort Armstrong July 2 and arrived at Fort Crawford July 5, 1831	
October 31 (Co. B, 1st Inf.)	1:293	Absent on detached service	
December 31 SA (Co. B, 1st Inf.)	1:308	Absent on detached service	
February 29, 1832 (Co. B, 1st Inf.)		Absent on detached service	Repeats previous printed report
April 30 (Co. B, 1st Inf.)	1:325	Absent on sixty-day furlough; left post March 26, 1832	
June 30 SA (Co. B, 1st Inf.)		Absent on sixty-day furlough; left post March 26, 1832	Repeats previous printed report
August 31 (Co. B, 1st Inf.)	1:332	Present; joined August 18, 1832	
October 31 (Co. B, 1st Inf.)	1:341	Absent on detached service at Jefferson Barracks (order of September 3, 1832)	
December 31 SA (Co. B, 1st Inf.)	1:343	Absent on furlough	
February 28, 1833 (Co. B, 1st Inf.)	1:347	Present for duty	
April 30 (Co. B, 1st Inf.)		Transferred to Dragoons March 3, 1833	

DATE OF REPORT & ORGANIZATION	ITEM NUMBER	ENTRY	IF NOT PRINTED
June 30 SA (Co. B, 1st Inf.)		Lieutenant Miller joined vice Davis transferred	Davis' status unchanged
August 31 (Field & Staff, Dragoons)	1:370	Present; appointed adjutant August 29, 1833	
August 31 (Co. C, Dragoons)	1:371	Present; joined July 11, 1833; appointed adjutant August 30, 1833	
October 31			Report missing
December 31 (Field & Staff, Dragoons)	1:398	Present for duty	
December 31 SA (Co. C, Dragoons)		Transferred; appointed adjutant August 30, 1833	Davis' status unchanged
February 28, 1834			Davis not listed
April 30 (Co. E, Dragoons)	1:410	Present; joined April 25, 1834; first muster roll to reflect promotion to first lieutenant	
June 30 SA (Co. E, Dragoons)	1:420	Present; joined April 25, 1834; commanding Company F; company left post June 18, 1834	

DATE OF REPORT & ORGANIZATION	ITEM NUMBER	ENTRY	IF NOT PRINTED
August 31 (Co. E, Dragoons)	1:424	Present; acting adjutant, assistant quartermaster and commissary of subsistence; company left post for the Pawnee towns June 18 and returned August 16, 1834	
October 31 (Co. E, Dragoons)	1:432	Present for duty	
December 31 SA (Co. E, Dragoons)	1:445	Present; in arrest	
February 28, 1835 (Co. E, Dragoons)		Present; in arrest	Repeats previous printed report
April 30 (Co. E, Dragoons)	1:475	Absent without leave since April 19, 1835	
June 30 SA (Co. E, Dragoons)	1:489	Absent without leave	
August 31 (Co. E, Dragoons)	1:492	Resigned effective June 30, 1835	

LIST OF SOURCES

Editorial Note: The sources used in editing the documents in this volume include printed materials of all sorts, manuscript records of several kinds, and memorial inscriptions on gravestones and plaques. The following list includes sources supplying both Davis documents and materials used in annotation. Although some depositories did not indicate a specific name for certain collections, the editors have attempted to give a complete bibliographical entry for each source.

MANUSCRIPT COLLECTIONS AND LEGAL DOCUMENTS

Adams County Courthouse, Natchez, Mississippi
  Marriage Bonds
  Records of Deeds
American Antiquarian Society, Worcester, Massachusetts
Beauvoir, Jefferson Davis Shrine, Biloxi, Mississippi
Chicago Historical Society
  Abraham Lincoln Collection
Christ Church, Philadelphia, Pennsylvania
  Parish Register
Circuit Court of Wilkinson County, Mississippi
  Marriage Records
Archives, The Dominican Province of St. Joseph, Washington
The Filson Club, Louisville, Kentucky
  Bodley Family Folder
  Challen Family Folder
  Preston Family Papers
  Redd Family File
  Rogers Index

Taylor Family Folder
Henry E. Huntington Library and Art Gallery, San Marino, California
Huntington Miscellaneous Collection
Illinois State Historical Library, Springfield
Black Hawk War Collection
Lewis Cass Collection
Frank E. Stevens Collection
Iowa State Department of History and Archives, Des Moines
Charles Aldrich Collection
Correspondence of Henry Dodge
Henry Dodge Order Book
George W. Jones Collection
Jefferson County Courthouse, Louisville, Kentucky
Marriage Register
Kentucky Historical Society, Frankfort
Biographical Directory of the Kentucky General Assembly, 1792–, compiled by G. Glenn Clift
Library of Congress
William Allen Papers
Papers of Jefferson Davis and Family
Andrew Jackson Papers
Miami University, Oxford, Ohio
Samuel Richey Confederate Collection
Mississippi Department of Archives and History, Jackson
Jefferson Davis *v.* Joseph H. D. Bowmar *et al.*, Warren County, Mississippi, Chancery Court, July 3, 1874–January 8, 1876, *Unreported*
Governors Papers, Series E
William Burr Howell Papers
William T. Walthall Papers
Mississippi Department of Health, Jackson
Marriage Records
Murphy Library, Wisconsin State University–La Crosse
Special Collections
Museum of the Confederacy, Richmond
National Archives

Record Group 29	Records of the Bureau of the Census
Record Group 48	Records of the Office of the Secretary of the Interior
Record Group 49	Records of the Bureau of Land Management
Record Group 77	Records of the Office of the Chief of Engineers
Record Group 94	Records of the Adjutant General's Office
Record Group 99	Records of the Office of the Paymaster General
Record Group 107	Records of the Office of the Secretary of War

Record Group 108	Records of the Headquarters of the Army
Record Group 153	Records of the Office of the Judge Advocate General (Army)
Record Group 156	Records of the Office of the Chief of Ordnance
Record Group 192	Records of the Office of the Commissary General of Subsistence
Record Group 217	Records of the United States General Accounting Office
Record Group 393	Records of United States Army Continental Commands, 1821–1920

New York Public Library
  Jefferson Davis Personal Miscellaneous Papers
  Walter Lynwood Fleming Collection
Philadelphia City Hall, Philadelphia County, Pennsylvania
  Record of Deeds
  Register of Wills
State Historical Society of Wisconsin, Madison
  Diary of Cutting Marsh
  File 1885
Frances Carrick Thomas Library, Transylvania University, Lexington, Kentucky
  Jefferson Davis Papers
  Mrs. Horace Holley's Scrapbook
Howard-Tilton Memorial Library, Tulane University, New Orleans
  Lise Mitchell Papers
United States Military Academy Archives
University of Alabama Library, Tuscaloosa
  Jefferson Davis Papers
University of North Carolina Library, Chapel Hill
  Southern Historical Collection
    C. Seymour Bullock Papers
    Trist Wood Papers
Virginia State Library, Richmond
  Personal Papers
West Feliciana Parish Courthouse, St. Francisville, Louisiana
  Inventory of Property
  Notarial Record
  Probate Boxes
Western Reserve Historical Society, Cleveland
  William P. Palmer Collection
Wilkinson County Courthouse, Woodville, Mississippi
  Land Record

LIST OF SOURCES

TYPESCRIPTS

Beers, Henry Putney. "The Western Military Frontier, 1815–1846." Ph.D. dissertation, University of Pennsylvania, Philadelphia, 1935.

Davis, Kathleen Bailey. "Jefferson Davis and the Mississippi Gubernatorial Contest of 1851 with Selected Letters and Speeches Concerning the Campaign." M.A. thesis, Rice University, Houston, 1971.

Heintzelman, Samuel Peter. "Journal." Typescript, Virginia State Library, Richmond.

Mitchell, Harry E. "History of Jefferson Barracks." Typescript, Missouri Historical Society, St. Louis.

GENEALOGICAL MATERIAL

Barb, Kirk Bentley. "Genealogy of Jefferson Davis." Typescript, Mississippi Department of Archives and History, Jackson.

Bateson, Mary McLaughlin Stamps. Application for Membership. The Colonial Dames of America, New Canaan, Connecticut, 1935.

Ganier, Alfred F., comp. The Davis Family Tree. Chart, 1938 revision, Alfred F. Ganier, Nashville, Tennessee, 1968.

Hayes-Davis, Jefferson, comp. Genealogical Data. Typescript and charts, Jefferson Davis Association, Rice University, Houston.

Kerrigan, Elizabeth O'Kelley, comp. Genealogical Data. Manuscripts, letters, and charts, Jefferson Davis Association, Rice University, Houston.

Mitchell, Mary Elizabeth. Journal and Letters. Typescript, Southern Historical Collection, University of North Carolina, Chapel Hill.

More, Douglas McL., comp. Genealogical Data. Typescript and chart, Jefferson Davis Association, Rice University, Houston.

Morgan, Howell, comp. Howell Genealogy. Typescript, Jefferson Hayes-Davis, Colorado Springs, 1970.

Van Benthuysen, A. S. "Supplement to the Van Benthuysen, Conklin-Dally and Seaward Genealogies." Typescript, New York State Library, Albany.

White, Mary Mitchell. "Interludes." Typescript, Betty White Wills, Tulsa, Oklahoma, 1968.

GOVERNMENT DOCUMENTS

American State Papers. Class V, Military Affairs. 7 vols. Washington: Gales and Seaton, 1832–61.

American State Papers. Class VII, Post Office Department. Washington: Gales and Seaton, 1834.

The Congressional Globe. 23rd–42nd Congresses, 1833–73. 23rd–30th Congresses, Washington: Blair and Rives, 1834–49; 31st Congress–38th Congress, 1st Session, Washington: John C. Rives, 1850–64; 38th Congress, 2nd Session–39th Congress, Washington: F. & J. Rives, 1865–66; 40th–42nd Congresses, Washington: F. & J. Rives & George A. Bailey, 1867–73.

House Reports. 29th Congress, 1st Session.

Journal of the Executive Proceedings of the Senate of the United States of America, 1789–1905. 90 vols. Washington: Duff Green, Government Printing Office, 1828–1948.

The Public Statutes at Large of the United States of America, from the Organization of the Government in 1789, to March 3, 1845. Edited by Richard Peters. 8 vols. Boston: Little, Brown, 1845–48.

Register of Debates in Congress. 18th–25th Congresses, 1825–37. 14 vols. Washington: Gales and Seaton, 1825–37.

NEWSPAPERS AND PERIODICALS

American Turf Register and Sporting Magazine, Vols. I, II, IX (1829, 1830, 1838).

Clinton (Mississippi) *Gazette*, 1835–37.

Dubuque (Iowa) *Daily Telegraph*, December 19, 1882.

Galena (Illinois) *Galenian*, September 5, 1832.

La Crosse (Wisconsin) *Tribune and Leader-Press*, April 26, 1931.

Lexington *Kentucky Gazette*, 1823–24.

Lexington (Kentucky) *Monitor*, June 22, 1824.

Lexington *Kentucky Reporter*, 1821–24.

Milwaukee *Sentinel*, February 3, 1891.

New Orleans *Daily States*, March 12, 1900.

New York *Daily Graphic*, September 7, 1877.

Niles' Weekly Register, 1832–40. (Title varies.)

Richmond (Louisiana) *Compiler*, December 8, 1833, March 15, May 24, 1844.

St. Louis *Globe-Democrat*, January 2, 1883.

St. Louis *Missouri Republican*, September 11, 1832.

Spirit of the Times, Vol. VII (1838).

Vicksburg *Register*, 1831–38. (Title varies.)

Vicksburg *Sentinel*, 1836–40, 1842–47. (Title varies.)

Vicksburg *Whig*, 1839–44, 1846–47. (Title varies.)

Wilkes' Spirit of the Times, Vol. VII (1862).

Woodville (Mississippi) *Republican*, 1823–30, 1833–48. (Title varies).

ARTICLES

Aldrich, Charles. "Jefferson Davis and Black Hawk," *Midland Monthly*, V (1896), 406–11.

LIST OF SOURCES

Anderson, Robert. "Reminiscences of the Black Hawk War," State Historical Society of Wisconsin, *Collections*, X (reprinted edition, 1909), 167–76.

Arndt, John Wallace. "Pioneers and Durham Boats on Fox River," State Historical Society of Wisconsin, *Proceedings, 1912*, LX, 180–220. Madison, 1913.

Aucoin, Sidney Joseph. "The Political Career of Isaac Johnson, Governor of Louisiana, 1846–1850," *Louisiana Historical Quarterly*, XXVIII (1945), 941–89.

Bale, Florence Gratiot. "A Packet of Old Letters," *Wisconsin Magazine of History*, XI (1927–28), 153–68.

Barrickman, W. C., ed. "Marriages and Deaths Published in *The Commentator*," Kentucky Historical Society, *Register*, L (1952), 134–51.

Brunson, Ira B. "Early Times in Old Northwest," State Historical Society of Wisconsin, *Proceedings, 1904*, LII, 156–72. Madison, 1905.

Busby, Orel. "Buffalo Valley: An Osage Hunting Ground," *Chronicles of Oklahoma*, XL (1962), 22–35.

Butler, James D. "Taychoperah, the Four Lake Country," State Historical Society of Wisconsin, *Collections*, X (reprinted edition, 1909), 64–89.

Butler, Louise. "West Feliciana: A Glimpse of Its History," *Louisiana Historical Quarterly*, VII (1924), 90–120.

Calkins, Elias A. "William Hull and Satterlee Clark," State Historical Society of Wisconsin, *Collections*, IX (reprinted edition, 1909), 413–20.

Carpenter, S. H. "Report on the Picture Gallery," State Historical Society of Wisconsin, *Collections*, III (reprinted edition, 1904), 45–65.

Carson, William Glasgow Bruce. "Night Life in St. Louis a Century Ago," Missouri Historical Society, *Bulletin*, I (1944–45), 3–9, II (1945–46), 3–10.

Chapin, John E. "Sketch of Cutting Marsh," State Historical Society of Wisconsin, *Collections*, XV (1900), 25–38.

Clark, Satterlee. "Early Times at Fort Winnebago," State Historical Society of Wisconsin, *Collections*, VIII (reprinted edition, 1908), 309–21.

Clift, G. Glenn, ed. "Kentucky Marriages and Obituaries," Kentucky Historical Society, *Register*, XXXVI (1938), 158–82, 240–62, 306–29, XXXVII (1939), 18–39, 127–50, 238–55, 360–77, XXXVIII (1940), 57–74, 157–75, 202–220, 340–59, XXXIX (1941), 58–80, 116–37, 237–59, 373–91, XL (1942), 47–68, 132–54, 268–89, 376–401, XLI (1943), 63–79, 147–70.

Cole, H. E. "The Old Military Road," *Wisconsin Magazine of History*, IX (1925–26), 47–62.

Coleman, J. Winston, Jr. "Samuel Woodson Price: Kentucky Portrait Painter," *Filson Club History Quarterly*, XXIII (1949), 5–24.

Conner, Eugene H., and Samuel W. Thomas. "Documents," Kentucky Historical Society, *Register*, LXVI (1968), 305–307.

Davis, Jefferson. "Autobiography of Jefferson Davis," *Belford's Magazine*, IV (1889–90), 255–66.

_______. "Life and Character of the Hon. John Caldwell Calhoun," *North American Review*, CXLV (1887), 246–60.

_______. "The Indian Policy of the United States," *North American Review*, CXLIII (1886), 436–46.

De La Ronde, John. "Personal Narrative," State Historical Society of Wisconsin, *Collections*, VII (reprinted edition, 1908), 345–65.

De Leon, T. C. "The Real Jefferson Davis, in Private and Public Life," Southern Historical Society, *Papers*, XXXVI (1908), 74–85.

Dorman, John Frederick, III. "Descendants of General Jonathan Clark: Jefferson County, Kentucky, 1750–1811," *Filson Club History Quarterly*, XXIII (1949), 25–33, 117–39, 278–304.

Draper, Lyman C. "Michel St. Cyr: An Early Dane County Pioneer," State Historical Society of Wisconsin, *Collections*, VI (reprinted edition, 1908), 397–400.

Edwards, Abram. "A Western Reminiscence," State Historical Society of Wisconsin, *Collections*, V (reprinted edition, 1907), 158–60.

Ellis, Albert G. "Upper Wisconsin Country," State Historical Society of Wisconsin, *Collections*, III (reprinted edition, 1904), 435–52.

_______. "Fifty-Four Years' Recollections of Men and Events in Wisconsin," State Historical Society of Wisconsin, *Collections*, VII (reprinted edition, 1908), 207–68.

Evans, William A. "Jefferson Davis, His Diseases and His Doctors," reprint from *The Mississippi Doctor*, XX (June 1942).

Ferris, Ruth, ed. "Captain Thomas Hawkes Griffith," Missouri Historical Society, *Bulletin*, V (1948–49), 289–305.

Fleming, Walter L. "The Early Life of Jefferson Davis," Mississippi Valley Historical Association, *Proceedings, 1915–16*, IX, 151 76. Cedar Rapids, Iowa: Torch Press, 1917.

_______. "Jefferson Davis at West Point," Mississippi Historical Society, *Publications*, X (1909), 247–67.

_______. "Jefferson Davis' First Marriage," Mississippi Historical Society, *Publications*, XII (1912), 21–36.

_______. "Jefferson Davis, the Negroes and the Negro Problem," *Sewanee Review*, XVI (1908), 407–27.

_______. "The Religious Life of Jefferson Davis," *Methodist Quarterly Review*, LIX (1910), 325–42.

Foreman, Carolyn Thomas. "The Bean Family," *Chronicles of Oklahoma*, XXXII (1954), 308–25.

_______. "General Richard Barnes Mason," *Chronicles of Oklahoma*, XIX (1941), 14–36.

Foreman, Grant. "The Three Forks," *Chronicles of Oklahoma*, II (1924), 37–47.

Freeman, C. E. "Two Local Questions," Dunn County (Menomonie, Wisconsin) *News*, October 14, 1909, p. 10.

Gardner, Hamilton. "The March of the First Dragoons from Jefferson Barracks in 1833–1834," *Chronicles of Oklahoma*, XXXI (1953), 22–36.

Grignon, Augustin. "Seventy-two Years' Recollections of Wisconsin," State Historical Society of Wisconsin, *Collections*, III (reprinted edition, 1904), 197–295.

Ham, F. Gerald. "Broadsides and Newspapers in the John M. McCalla Papers, West Virginia University Library," Kentucky Historical Society, *Register*, LVIII (1960), 322–52, LIX (1961), 47–78.

Hempstead, Stephen, Sr. "I at Home: Part IX," edited by Mrs. Dana O. Jensen, Missouri Historical Society, *Bulletin*, XXII (1965–66), 410–45.

Jillson, Willard Rouse. "A Bibliography of Lexington, Kentucky," Kentucky Historical Society, *Register*, XLIV (1946), 151–86, 259–90, XLV (1947), 39–70.

Jordan, Philip D. "The Life and Works of James Gardiner Edwards," *Journal of the Illinois State Historical Society*, XXIII (1930), 459–502.

Kellogg, Louise P. "The Agency House at Fort Winnebago," *Wisconsin Magazine of History*, XIV (1930–31), 437–48.

Kemper, Jackson. "Journal of an Episcopalian Missionary's Tour to Green Bay, 1834," State Historical Society of Wisconsin, *Collections*, XIV (1898), 394–449.

———. "A Trip through Wisconsin in 1838," *Wisconsin Magazine of History*, VIII (1925), 423–45.

Kendall, John S. "Chronicles of a Southern Family," *Louisiana Historical Quarterly*, XXIX (1946), 277–95.

"L. H. L." "Youthful Romance of Jefferson Davis," *Confederate Veteran*, XVII (1909), 387–88.

Leavy, William. "Memoir of Lexington and Its Vicinity," Kentucky Historical Society, *Register*, XL (1942), 107–31, 253–67, 353–75, XLI (1943), 44–62, 107–37, 250–60, 310–46, XLII (1944), 26–53.

LeBron, Jeanne. "Colonel James W. Stephenson: Galena Pioneer," *Journal of the Illinois State Historical Society*, XXXV (1942), 347–67.

Libby, Orin Grant. "Chronicle of the Helena Shot-tower," State Historical Society of Wisconsin, *Collections*, XIII (1895), 335–74.

"List of Hurricanes on the Coast of the South Atlantic States, and on the North Coast of the Gulf of Mexico," *De Bow's Review*, XXIII (1857), 513–17.

Lockwood, James H. "Early Times and Events in Wisconsin," State Historical Society of Wisconsin, *Collections*, II (reprinted edition, 1903), 98–196.

"The Louisiana Ouachita Region," *De Bow's Review*, III (1847), 225–30.

M'Call, Ansel J. "[James] M'Call's Journal of a Visit to Wisconsin in 1830," State Historical Society of Wisconsin, *Collections*, XII (1892), 170–205.

Merrell, Henry. "Pioneer Life in Wisconsin," State Historical Society of Wisconsin, *Collections*, VII (reprinted edition, 1908), 366–404.

Miller, James L., Jr. "Transylvania University as the Nation Saw It, 1818–1828," *Filson Club History Quarterly*, XXIV (1960), 305–18.

"North Louisiana," *De Bow's Review*, XXVI (1859), 601–602.

"North-west Louisiana: Claiborne Parish, Lebanon, Minden," *De Bow's Review*, XI (1851), 89.

"The North-western Region of Louisiana," *De Bow's Review*, IV (1847), 226–29.

O'Neill, J. Cyril, comp. "Warren County Marriages, 1810–1860," *Journal of Mississippi History*, XXVIII (1966), 322–29, XXIX (1967), 43–49, 142–48, 210–17, XXX (1968), 51–59, 151–58.

Padgett, James A., ed. "Official Records of the West Florida Revolution and Republic," *Louisiana Historical Quarterly*, XXI (1938), 685–805.

Parkinson, Daniel M. "Pioneer Life in Wisconsin," State Historical Society of Wisconsin, *Collections*, II (reprinted edition, 1903), 326–64.

Pelzer, Louis, ed. "A Journal of Marches by the First United States Dragoons 1834–1835," *Iowa Journal of History and Politics*, VII (1909), 331–78.

Perrine, Fred S., ed. "The Journal of Hugh Evans, covering the First and Second Campaigns of the United States Dragoon Regiment in 1834 and 1835: Campaign of 1834," *Chronicles of Oklahoma*, III (1925), 175–215.

Pitt, Felix Newton. "Two Early Catholic Colleges in Kentucky: St. Thomas and Gethsemani," *Filson Club History Quarterly*, XXXVIII (1964), 133–48.

"Prairie du Chien in 1827: Letters of Joseph M. Street to Gov. Ninian Edwards, of Illinois," State Historical Society of Wisconsin, *Collections*, XI (1888), 356–69.

Prichard, Walter, ed. "Some Interesting Glimpses of Louisiana a Century Ago," *Louisiana Historical Quarterly*, XXIV (1941), 35–48.

Quaife, M. M. "The Northwestern Career of Jefferson Davis," *Journal of the Illinois State Historical Society*, XVI (1923), 1–19.

"The Question Box," *Wisconsin Magazine of History*, III (1919–20), 227–40.

Rainwater, P. L., ed. "The Autobiography of Benjamin Grubb Humphreys: August 26, 1808–December 20, 1882," *Mississippi Valley Historical Review*, XXI (1934–35), 231–55.

Rodolf, Theodore. "Pioneering in the Wisconsin Lead Region," State Historical Society of Wisconsin, *Collections*, XV (1900), 338–89.

Rowland, Mrs. Dunbar [Eron O.]. "Marking the Natchez Trace: An Historic Highway of the Lower South," Mississippi Historical Society, *Publications*, XI (1910), 345–61.

Salter, William, ed. "Letters of Henry Dodge to Gen. George W. Jones," *Annals of Iowa*, 3rd Ser., III (1897), 220–23.

Scanlan, P. L. "The Military Record of Jefferson Davis in Wisconsin," *Wisconsin Magazine of History*, XXIV (1940–41), 174–82.

Shaw, Arthur Marvin, Jr. "Rampant Individualism in an Ante-Bellum Southern College," *Louisiana Historical Quarterly*, XXXI (1948), 877–96.

Shirk, George H. "Peace on the Plains," *Chronicles of Oklahoma*, XXVIII (1950), 2–41.

Smith, Nannie Davis. "Reminiscences of Jefferson Davis," *Confederate Veteran*, XXXVIII (1930), 178–82.

Smith, William R., and others. "Report," State Historical Society of Wisconsin, *Collections*, I (reprinted edition, 1903), 5–16.

Stambaugh, Samuel. "Report on the Quality and Condition of Wisconsin Territory, 1831," State Historical Society of Wisconsin, *Collections*, XV (1900), 399–438.

Starin, Frederick J. "Diary of a Journey to Wisconsin in 1840," *Wisconsin Magazine of History*, VI (1922–23), 73–94, 207–32, 334–45.

Statement of Mrs. Philip Pendleton Dandridge to "D. B. C.," New York *Times*, October 20, 1906, p. 6.

"Statistical and Historical Collections of Louisiana: Parish of East Feliciana, La.," *De Bow's Review*, XI (1851), 263–68.

Stevens, Frank E. "Hazelwood: Its Master and Its Coterie," *Journal of the Illinois State Historical Society*, XXXII (1939), 313–57.

Street, William B. "General Joseph M. Street," *Annals of Iowa*, 3rd Ser., II (1895), 81–105.

Tanner, Edward. "Wisconsin in 1818," State Historical Society of Wisconsin, *Collections*, VIII (reprinted edition, 1908), 287–92.

Taylor, Stephen. "Mineral Point and Richland County," State Historical Society of Wisconsin, *Collections*, II (reprinted edition, 1903), 480–90.

[Thwaites, Reuben Gold]. "Narrative of Alexis Clermont: In an Interview," State Historical Society of Wisconsin, *Collections*, XV (1900), 452–57.

———. "Narrative of Andrew J. Vieau, Sr.: In an Interview," State Historical Society of Wisconsin, *Collections*, XI (1888), 218–37.

———. "Narrative of Morgan L. Martin: In an Interview," State Historical Society of Wisconsin, *Collections*, XI (1888), 385–415.

———. "Notes on Early Lead Mining in the Fever (or Galena) River Region," State Historical Society of Wisconsin, *Collections*, XIII (1895), 271–92.

———. "The Wisconsin Winnebagoes: An Interview with Moses Paquette," State Historical Society of Wisconsin, *Collections*, XII (1892), 399–433.

———. "The Story of the Black Hawk War," State Historical Society of Wisconsin, *Collections*, XII (1892), 217–65.

———, ed. "Documents Relating to the Catholic Church in Green Bay, and the Mission at Little Chute, 1825–40," State Historical Society of Wisconsin, *Collections*, XIV (1898), 162–205.

———, ed. "The Fur-Trade in Wisconsin, 1815–1817," State Historical Society of Wisconsin, *Collections*, XIX (1910), 375–488.

———, ed. "The Fur-Trade in Wisconsin, 1818–1825," State Historical Society of Wisconsin, *Collections*, XX (1911), 1–395.

Titus, W. A. "Historic Spots in Wisconsin: Portage, the Break in a Historic Waterway," *Wisconsin Magazine of History*, III (1919–20), 184–88.

Turner, Andrew Jackson. "The History of Fort Winnebago," State Historical Society of Wisconsin, *Collections*, XIV (1898), 65–102.

Usher, Ellis B. "Cyrus Woodman: A Character Sketch," *Wisconsin Magazine of History*, II (1918–19), 393–412.

Van der Zee, Jacob. "Early History of Lead Mining in the Iowa Country," *Iowa Journal of History and Politics*, XIII (1915), 3–52.

Van Zandt, Howard F. "The History of Camp Holmes and Chouteau's Trading Post," *Chronicles of Oklahoma*, XIII (1935), 316–37.

Washburne, Elihu B. "Col. Henry Gratiot," State Historical Society of Wisconsin, *Collections*, X (reprinted edition, 1909), 235–60.

Webb, Henry W. "The Story of Jefferson Barracks," *New Mexico Historical Review*, XXI (1946), 185–208.

Wheelock, T. B. "Journal of Colonel Dodge's expedition from Fort Gibson to the Pawnee Pict village," *American State Papers*, Class V, Military Affairs, V, 373–82.

Whittlesey, Charles. "Recollections of a Tour through Wisconsin in 1832," State Historical Society of Wisconsin, *Collections*, I (reprinted edition, 1903), 64–85.

Wight, William Ward, and [Reuben Gold Thwaites]. "Documents Relating to the Stockbridge Mission, 1825–48," State Historical Society of Wisconsin, *Collections*, XV (1900), 39–204.

Wilkinson, Lucille Warfield. "Early Baptists in Washington, D.C.," Columbia Historical Society, *Records*, XXIX–XXX (1928), 211–68.

Wilson, Samuel M. "Matthew Harris Jouett, Kentucky Portrait Painter: A Review," *Filson Club History Quarterly*, XIII (1939), 75–96.

Wood, Trist. "Jefferson Davis' First Marriage: The True Story of His So-called Elopement," New Orleans *Daily Picayune*, August 28, 1910, p. 9.

Young, Otis E. "The United States Mounted Ranger Battalion, 1832–1833," *Mississippi Valley Historical Review*, XLI (1954), 453–70.

BOOKS

Alexander, DeAlva Stanwood. *A Political History of the State of New York*. 3 vols. New York: Henry Holt, 1906–1909.

The American Almanac and Repository of Useful Knowledge, for the Year . . . 1830–1861. 32 vols. Boston: Gray and Bowen, 1829–61.

Appleton's Cyclopaedia of American Biography. Edited by James Grant Wilson and John Fiske. 6 vols. New York: D. Appleton, 1887–89.

Armstrong, Perry A. *The Sauks and the Black Hawk War, with Biographical Sketches, Etc.* Springfield, Ill.: H. W. Rokker, 1887.

Bassett, John S., ed. *Correspondence of Andrew Jackson*. 7 vols. Washington: Carnegie Institution, 1926–35.

Bateman, Newton, and Paul Selby, eds. *Historical Encyclopedia of Illinois*. Chicago: Munsell, 1916.

Be It Known and Remembered: Bible Records. 4 vols. Baton Rouge: Louisiana Genealogical and Historical Society, 1960–67.

Biographical and Historical Memoirs of Mississippi. 2 vols. Chicago: Goodspeed, 1891.

Biographical Directory of the American Congress, 1774–1961. Washington: Government Printing Office, 1961.

The Biographical Encyclopaedia of Kentucky of the Dead and Living Men of the Nineteenth Century. Cincinnati: J. M. Armstrong, 1878.

Bixby, William K., ed. *Letters of Zachary Taylor from the Battle-Fields of the Mexican War*. Rochester, N.Y.: Genesee Press, 1908.

Black Hawk. *An Autobiography*. Edited by Donald Jackson. Urbana: University of Illinois Press, 1955.

________. *Life of Ma-ka-tai-me-she-kia-kiak*. Edited by J. B. Patterson. Boston: Russell, Odiorne, & Metcalf, 1834.

Blake, William J. *The History of Putnam County, N. Y.* New York: Baker & Scribner, 1849.

Blanchard, Elizabeth Amis Cameron, and Manley Wade Wellman. *The Life and Times of Sir Archie: The Story of America's Greatest Thoroughbred, 1805–1833*. Chapel Hill: University of North Carolina Press, 1958.

Boyle, James E. *Cotton and the New Orleans Cotton Exchange: A Century of Commercial Evolution*. Garden City, N.Y.: Country Life Press, 1934.

Boynton, Edward C. *History of West Point, and Its Military Importance during the American Revolution: And the Origin and Progress of the United States Military Academy*. New York: D. Van Nostrand, 1863.

Carhart, Lucy Ann, comp. *Genealogy of the Morris Family: Descendants of Thomas Morris of Connecticut*. Edited by Charles Alexander Nelson. New York: A. S. Barnes, 1911.

A Catalogue of the Officers and Students of Transylvania University. 4 vols. Lexington, Ky.: T. Smith, 1821–24.

Catlin, George. *Letters and Notes on the Manners, Customs, and Condition of the North American Indians*. 2 vols. Reprinted edition. Minneapolis: Ross & Haines, 1965.

Church, Albert E. *Personal Reminiscences of the Military Academy. From 1824 to 1831*. West Point, N.Y.: U.S.M.A. Press, 1879.

Claiborne, J. F. H. *Mississippi, as a Province, Territory and State, with Biographical Notices of Eminent Citizens*. Reprinted edition. Baton Rouge: Louisiana State University Press, 1964.

Clarke, Dwight L. *Stephen Watts Kearny: Soldier of the West*. Norman: University of Oklahoma Press, 1961.

Clement, William Edwards. *Plantation Life on the Mississippi*. New Orleans: Pelican Publishing Co., 1952.

Clift, G. Glenn, comp. *Kentucky Marriages, 1797–1865*. Baltimore: Genealogical Publishing Co., 1966.

———. *Remember the Raisin! Kentucky and Kentuckians in the Battles and Massacre at Frenchtown, Michigan Territory, in the War of 1812*. Frankfort: Kentucky Historical Society, 1961.

Cohn, David L. *The Life and Times of King Cotton*. New York: Oxford University Press, 1956.

Cole, Cyrenus. *I am a Man: The Indian Black Hawk*. Iowa City: State Historical Society of Iowa, 1938.

Collins, Lewis and Richard H. *History of Kentucky*. 2 vols. Reprinted edition. Frankfort: Kentucky Historical Society, 1966.

Cooke, Philip St. George. *Scenes and Adventures in the Army: or, Romance of Military Life*. Philadelphia: Lindsay & Blakiston, 1859.

Cullum, George W. *Biographical Register of the Officers and Graduates of the U. S. Military Academy at West Point, N. Y. from Its Establishment, in 1802, to 1890 with the Early History of the United States Military Academy*. 8 vols. Boston and New York: Houghton, Mifflin, 1891–1930.

Curtis, Nathaniel Cortlandt. *New Orleans: Its Old Houses, Shops and Public Buildings*. Philadelphia and London: J. B. Lippincott, 1933.

Cutting, Elisabeth B. *Jefferson Davis: Political Soldier*. New York: Dodd, Mead, 1930.

Daniel, John W., ed. *Life and Reminiscences of Jefferson Davis*. Baltimore: R. H. Woodward, 1890.

Daughters of the American Revolution, Louisiana, comps. *Louisiana Tombstone Inscriptions*. 11 vols. [Shreveport?, La.]: Louisiana Society NSDAR, 1954–57.

Davidson, A. N. *In Unnamed Wisconsin: Studies in the History of the Region between Lake Michigan and the Mississippi.* Milwaukee: Silas Chapman, 1895.

Davis, Edwin Adams. *Plantation Life in the Florida Parishes of Louisiana, 1836–1846, as Reflected in the Diary of Bennet H. Barrow.* New York: Columbia University Press, 1943.

Davis, Harry Alexander. *The Davis Family (Davies and David) in Wales and America.* Washington: Harry Alexander Davis, 1927.

Davis, Varina Howell. *Jefferson Davis, Ex-President of the Confederate States of America: A Memoir.* 2 vols. New York: Belford, 1890.

De Leon, T. C. *Belles, Beaux and Brains of the 60's.* New York: G. W. Dillingham, 1909.

Dickey, Dallas C. *Seargent S. Prentiss: Whig Orator of the Old South.* Baton Rouge: Louisiana State University Press, 1946.

Dictionary of American Biography. Edited by Allen Johnson, Dumas Malone, and others. 11 vols. New York: Charles Scribner's Sons, 1964.

A Dictionary of American English. Chicago: University of Chicago Press, 1942.

Dictionary of Wisconsin Biography. Madison: State Historical Society of Wisconsin, 1960.

Dimitry, John B. S. *Lessons in the History of Louisiana, from Its Earliest Settlement to the Close of the Civil War, to which are appended Lessons in Its Geography and Products.* New York, Chicago, and New Orleans: A. S. Barnes, 1877.

Dodd, William E. *Jefferson Davis.* Philadelphia: George W. Jacobs, 1907.

Donovan, Frank. *River Boats of America.* New York: Thomas Y. Crowell, 1966.

Doty, William Kavanaugh. *The Confectionery of Monsieur Giron.* Charlottesville, Va.: Michie, 1915.

Duffy, John, ed. *The Rudolph Matas History of Medicine in Louisiana.* 2 vols. Baton Rouge: Louisiana State University Press, 1958–62.

Earle, Alice Morse. *Curious Punishments of Bygone Days.* New York: Macmillan, 1922.

Eckenrode, H. J. *Jefferson Davis: President of the South.* New York: Macmillan, 1930.

Elliott, Charles W. *Winfield Scott: The Soldier and the Man.* New York: Macmillan, 1937.

Flagler, D. W. *A History of the Rock Island Arsenal.* Ordnance Memoranda, No. 20. Washington: Government Printing Office, 1877.

Fleming, Thomas J. *West Point: The Men and Times of the United States Military Academy.* New York: William Morrow, 1969.

Foote, Henry S. *The Bench and Bar of the South and Southwest.* St. Louis: Soule, Thomas & Wentworth, 1876.

———. *Casket of Reminiscences.* Washington: Chronicle, 1874.

Ford, Thomas. *A History of Illinois.* Edited by Milo Milton Quaife. 2 vols. Chicago: R. R. Donnelley, 1945–46.

Foreman, Grant. *Advancing the Frontier, 1830–1860.* Norman: University of Oklahoma Press, 1933.

Frazer, Robert W. *Forts of the West: Military Forts and Presidios and Posts commonly called Forts West of the Mississippi River to 1898.* Norman: University of Oklahoma Press, 1965.

Fry, Henry. *The History of North Atlantic Steam Navigation with Some Account of Early Ships and Shipowners.* Reprinted edition. London: Cornmarket Press, 1969.

General Regulations for the Army; or, Military Institutes. Washington: Davis & Force, 1825.

Gordon, William A., comp. *A Compilation of Registers of the Army of the United States, from 1815 to 1837.* Washington: James C. Dunn, 1837.

Govan, Thomas Payne. *Nicholas Biddle: Nationalist and Public Banker, 1786–1844.* Chicago: University of Chicago Press, 1959.

Hagan, William T. *The Sac and Fox Indians.* Norman: University of Oklahoma Press, 1958.

Hamilton, Holman. *Zachary Taylor: Soldier of the Republic.* Indianapolis and New York: Bobbs-Merrill, 1941.

Heitman, Francis B. *Historical Register and Dictionary of the United States Army, from Its Organization September 29, 1789, to March 2, 1903.* 2 vols. Reprinted edition. Urbana: University of Illinois Press, 1965.

Henry, John Flournoy. *A History of the Henry Family.* Louisville, Ky.: John P. Morton, 1900.

Hewitt, E. A. *Topographical Map of the Counties of Bourbon, Fayette Clark, Jessamine and Woodford Kentucky.* New York: Smith, Gallup, 1861.

[Hildreth, James]. *Dragoon Campaigns to the Rocky Mountains; Being a History of the Enlistment, Organization, and First Campaigns of the Regiment of United States Dragoons; Together with Incidents of a Soldier's Life, and Sketches of Scenery and Indian Character.* New York: Wiley & Long, 1836.

Historical Statistics of the United States, Colonial Times to 1957. Washington: Government Printing Office, 1960.

The History of American Methodism. 3 vols. New York and Nashville: Abingdon, 1964.

The History of Jo Daviess County Illinois. Chicago: H. F. Kett, 1878.

History of Lee County [Illinois]. Chicago: H. H. Hill, 1881.

Howell, George R. and Jonathan Tenney. *Bi-Centennial History of Al-*

bany: History of the County of Albany, N. Y. from 1609 to 1886. New York: Munsell, 1886.

In Memoriam: Cincinnati, 1881, containing Proceedings of the Memorial Association, Eulogies at Music Hall, and Biographical Sketches of Many Distinguished Citizens of Cincinnati. Cincinnati: A. E. Jones, 1881.

[Ingraham, Joseph Holt]. *The South-West. By a Yankee.* 2 vols. New York: Harper & Brothers, 1835.

Irving, Washington. *A Tour on the Prairies.* Edited by John F. McDermott. Norman: University of Oklahoma Press, 1956.

James, Marquis. *The Life of Andrew Jackson.* Indianapolis and New York: Bobbs-Merrill, 1938.

Johnston, William P. *The Life of Gen. Albert Sidney Johnston, Embracing His Services in the Armies of the United States, the Republic of Texas, and the Confederate States.* New York: D. Appleton, 1879.

Jones, J. William. *The Davis Memorial Volume; or our Dead President, Jefferson Davis, and the World's Tribute to His Memory.* Dallas: A. P. Foster, 1890.

Kerr, Charles, ed. *History of Kentucky.* 5 vols. Chicago and New York: American Historical Society, 1922.

Kinzie, Mrs. John H. (Juliette A.) *Wau-Bun: The "Early Day" in the North-West.* Edited by Milo Milton Quaife. Chicago: R. R. Donnelley, 1932.

Knight, Landon. *The Real Jefferson Davis.* Battle Creek, Mich.: Pilgrim Magazine Co., 1904.

Langley, Harold D. *Social Reform in the United States Navy, 1798–1862.* Urbana: University of Illinois Press, 1967.

Latrobe, John H. B. *Reminiscences of West Point from September, 1818, to March, 1822.* East Saginaw, Mich.: Evening News, 1887.

Lloyd, James T. *Lloyd's Steamboat Directory and Disasters on the Western Waters, Containing the History of the First Application of Steam as a Motive Power; the Lives of John Fitch and Robert Fulton, Likenesses & Engravings of Their First Steamboats.* Cincinnati: James T. Lloyd, 1856.

Lynch, James D. *The Bench and Bar of Mississippi.* New York: E. J. Hale, 1881.

Lytle, William M., comp. *Merchant Steam Vessels of the United States, 1807–1868.* Edited by Forrest R. Holdcamper. Mystic, Conn.: Steamship Historical Society of America, 1952.

MacCabe, Julius P. Bolivar. *Directory of the City of Lexington and County of Fayette, for 1838 & 39.* Lexington, Ky.: I. C. Noble, 1838.

McDermott, John Francis, ed. *The Western Journals of Washington Irving.* Norman: University of Oklahoma Press, 1944.

McElroy, Robert. *Jefferson Davis: The Unreal and the Real.* 2 vols. New York and London: Harper & Brothers, 1937.

McGill, Anna B. *The Sisters of Charity of Nazareth Kentucky.* New York: Encyclopedia Press, 1917.

McGrane, Reginald C., ed. *The Correspondence of Nicholas Biddle dealing with National Affairs, 1807–1844.* Boston and New York: Houghton Mifflin, 1919.

McKenney, Thomas L., and James Hall. *The Indian Tribes of North America with Biographical Sketches and Anecdotes of the Principal Chiefs.* Edited by Frederick Webb Hodge. 3 vols. Edinburgh: John Grant, 1933–34.

Mahan, Bruce Ellis. *Old Fort Crawford and the Frontier.* Iowa City: State Historical Society, 1926.

Michaud, J. F. and L. G., and E. E. Desplaces, eds. *Biographie Universelle.* 45 vols. Vol. I, Paris: Desplaces; Vols. II–XLV, Paris: Delagrave, 1843–55.

Moore, John T., and Austin P. Foster. *Tennessee: the Volunteer State, 1769–1923.* 4 vols. Chicago and Nashville: S. J. Clarke, 1923.

The National Cyclopaedia of American Biography Being the History of the United States as Illustrated in the Lives of the Founders, Builders and Defenders of the Republic, and of the Men and Women Who are Doing the Work and Moulding the Thought of the Present Time. 50 vols. and index. New York: James T. White, 1898–1968.

Nevin, Alfred, ed. *Encyclopaedia of the Presbyterian Church in the United States of America.* Philadelphia: Presbyterian Publishing Co., 1884.

A New English Dictionary on Historical Principles. Oxford, England: Oxford University Press, 1919.

Nichols, Roger L. *General Henry Atkinson: A Western Military Career.* Norman: University of Oklahoma Press, 1965.

Nicolay, John G., and John Hay. *Abraham Lincoln: A History.* 10 vols. New York: Century, 1890.

O'Daniel, Victor F. *A Light of the Church in Kentucky, or, the Life, Labors and Character of the Very Rev. Samuel Thomas Wilson, O. P. S. T. M., Pioneer Educator and the First Provincial of a Religious Order in the United States.* Washington: Dominicana, 1932.

Parish, John Carl. *George Wallace Jones.* Iowa City: State Historical Society of Iowa, 1912.

Pease, Theodore Calvin. *The Frontier State, 1818–1848.* Chicago: A. C. McClurg, 1922.

Pelzer, Louis. *Marches of the Dragoons in the Mississippi Valley: An Account of Marches and Activities of the First Regiment United States*

Dragoons in the Mississippi Valley between the Years 1833 and 1850. Iowa City: State Historical Society of Iowa, 1917.

Peter, Robert. *History of Fayette County, Kentucky, with an Outline Sketch of the Blue Grass Region.* Edited by William Henry Perrin. Chicago: O. L. Baskin, 1882.

———. *The History of the Medical Department of Transylvania University.* Filson Club Publication No. 20. Louisville, Ky.: John P. Morton, 1905.

———. *Transylvania University: Its Origin, Rise, Decline, and Fall.* Louisville, Ky.: John P. Morton, 1896.

Phelps, Albert. *Louisiana: A Record of Expansion.* Boston and New York: Houghton, Mifflin, 1905.

"Points of Interest at Beauvoir." Biloxi, Miss.: Jefferson Davis Shrine, n.d.

Polk, William M. *Leonidas Polk: Bishop and General.* 2 vols. New York: Longmans, Green, 1915.

Pollack, Queena. *Peggy Eaton: Democracy's Mistress.* New York: Minton, Balch, 1931.

Portrait and Biographical Album of Jo Daviess and Carroll Counties, Illinois. Chicago: Chapman Brothers, 1889.

Prucha, Francis Paul. *Broadax and Bayonet: The Role of the United States Army in the Development of the Northwest, 1815–1860.* Madison: State Historical Society of Wisconsin, 1953.

———. *A Guide to the Military Posts of the United States, 1789–1846.* Madison: State Historical Society of Wisconsin, 1964.

———. *The Sword of the Republic: The United States Army on the Frontier, 1783–1846.* London: Collier-Macmillan, 1969.

Reavis, Logan U. *The Life and Military Services of Gen. William Selby Harney.* St. Louis: Bryan, Brand, 1878.

Redford, A. H. *The History of Methodism in Kentucky.* 3 vols. Nashville: Southern Methodist Publishing House, 1868–70.

Register of Graduates and Former Cadets of the United States Military Academy. West Point, N.Y.: West Point Alumni Foundation, 1964.

Regulations of the United States Military Academy, at West Point. New York: no publisher, 1823.

Reminiscences of Richard Menefee Redd, Better Known as Colonel "Dick" Redd from Childhood to Old Age. Lexington, Ky.: Clay Printing Co., 1929.

Reynolds, John. *Reynolds' History of Illinois: My Own Times.* Chicago: Chicago Historical Society, 1879.

Richardson, James D., comp. *A Compilation of the Messages and Papers of the Presidents, 1789–1897.* 10 vols. Washington: Government Printing Office, 1896–99.

Risch, Erna. *Quartermaster Support of the Army: A History of the Corps, 1775–1939.* Washington: Government Printing Office, 1962.

Robinson, Elrie. *Early Feliciana Politics.* St. Francisville, La.: St. Francisville Democrat, 1936.

Robinson, Fayette. *An Account of the Organization of the Army of the United States; with Biographies of Distinguished Officers of All Grades.* 2 vols. Philadelphia: E. H. Butler, 1848.

Rowland, Dunbar. *Courts, Judges, and Lawyers of Mississippi, 1798–1835.* Jackson, Miss.: State Department of Archives and History and the Mississippi Historical Society, 1935.

———. *History of Mississippi: The Heart of the South.* 2 vols. Chicago and Jackson, Miss.: S. J. Clarke, 1925.

———. *The Official and Statistical Register of the State of Mississippi, 1908.* Nashville: Brandon, 1908.

———, ed. *Encyclopedia of Mississippi History.* 2 vols. Madison, Wis.: Selwyn A. Brant, 1907.

———, ed. *Official Letter Books of W. C. C. Claiborne, 1801–1816.* 6 vols. Jackson, Miss.: State Department of Archives and History, 1917.

———, ed. *Jefferson Davis, Constitutionalist: His Letters, Papers and Speeches.* 10 vols. Jackson, Miss.: State Department of Archives and History, 1923.

Rowland, Eron (Mrs. Dunbar). *Varina Howell: Wife of Jefferson Davis.* 2 vols. New York: Macmillan, 1927–31.

Rugg, Mary Louise Dement. *Dement Dodge Patterson Williams.* n.p.: no publisher, 1954.

Salter, William. *The Life of Henry Dodge from 1782 to 1833.* Burlington, Iowa: no publisher, 1890.

Scanlan, Peter Lawrence. *Prairie du Chien: French, British, American.* Menasha, Wis.: George Banta, 1937.

Schaff, Morris. *Jefferson Davis: His Life and Personality.* Boston: John W. Luce, 1922.

Seaman, Ezra C. *Essays on the Progress of Nations.* Reprinted edition. New York: Johnson Reprint, 1967.

Seebold, Herman de Bachellé. *Old Louisiana Plantation Homes and Family Trees.* 2 vols. New Orleans: Pelican Press, 1941.

Shields, Joseph Dunbar. *Natchez: Its Early History.* Louisville: John P. Morton, 1930.

Silver, James W. *Edmund Pendleton Gaines: Frontier General.* Baton Rouge: Louisiana State University Press, 1949.

Sixth Census or Enumeration of the Inhabitants of the United States, as Corrected at the Department of State, in 1840. Book I. Washington: Blair and Rives, 1841.

Smiley, David L. *Lion of White Hall: The Life of Cassius M. Clay*. Madison: University of Wisconsin Press, 1962.

Smith, Justin H. *The War with Mexico*. 2 vols. New York: Macmillan, 1919.

Sonne, Niels Henry. *Liberal Kentucky, 1780–1828*. New York: Columbia University Press, 1939.

Spooner, W. W., ed. *Historic Families of America*. 3 vols. New York: Historic Families, 1907.

Stevens, Frank E. *The Black Hawk War including a Review of Black Hawk's Life*. Chicago: Frank E. Stevens, 1903.

Strode, Hudson. *Jefferson Davis: American Patriot, 1808–1861*. New York: Harcourt, Brace, 1955.

———. *Jefferson Davis, Tragic Hero: The Last Twenty-five Years, 1864–1889*. New York: Harcourt, Brace & World, 1964.

———, ed. *Jefferson Davis: Private Letters, 1823–1889*. New York: Harcourt, Brace & World, 1966.

Tate, Allen. *Jefferson Davis: His Rise and Fall*. New York: Minton, Balch, 1929.

Throckmorton, Charles Wickliffe. *A Genealogical and Historical Account of the Throckmorton Family in England and the United States*. Richmond, Va.: Old Dominion Press, 1930.

Thwaites, Reuben Gold. *How George Rogers Clark Won the Northwest and Other Essays in Western History*. Chicago: A. C. McClurg, 1903.

———. *The Story of Wisconsin*. Boston: D. Lothrop, 1890.

Van Benthuysen, Alvin S. and Edith McIntosh Hall. *The Van Benthuysen Genealogy*. Clay Center, Kans.: Wilson, 1953.

Van Deusen, Glyndon G. *The Jacksonian Era, 1828–1848*. New York: Harper & Brothers, 1959.

Van Zandt, Franklin K. *Boundaries of the United States and the Several States*. Geological Survey Bulletin 1212. Washington: Government Printing Office, 1966.

Wagers, Margaret Newnan. *The Education of a Gentleman: Jefferson Davis at Transylvania, 1821–1824*. Lexington, Ky.: Buckley & Reading, 1943.

Warner, Ezra J. *Generals in Blue: Lives of the Union Commanders*. Baton Rouge: Louisiana State University Press, 1964.

———. *Generals in Gray: Lives of the Confederate Commanders*. Baton Rouge: Louisiana State University Press, 1959.

Watts, Beulah de Verieré Smith, and Nancy Jane Lucas De Grummond. *Solitude: Life on a Louisiana Plantation, 1788–1968*. Baton Rouge: Claitor's Publishing Division, 1970.

Webster's Geographical Dictionary. Springfield, Mass.: G. & C. Merriam, 1957.

Webster's Seventh New Collegiate Dictionary. Springfield, Mass.: G. & C. Merriam, 1967.

Weigley, Russell F. *History of the United States Army*. New York: Macmillan, 1967.

Wentworth, John. *Early Chicago: Fort Dearborn*. Chicago: Fergus, 1881.

Whitehill, Walter M. *Dumbarton Oaks: The History of a Georgetown House and Garden, 1800–1966*. Cambridge, Mass.: Belknap Press of Harvard University Press, 1967.

Whitsitt, William H. *Genealogy of Jefferson Davis and of Samuel Davies*. New York and Washington: Neale, 1910.

Who Was Who in America: Historical Volume, 1607–1896. Chicago: A. N. Marquis, 1963.

Wild, J. C. *The Valley of the Mississippi*. Edited by Lewis F. Thomas. St. Louis: Chambers and Knapp, 1841.

Wiltse, Charles M. *John C. Calhoun: Nullifier, 1829–1839*. Indianapolis: Bobbs-Merrill, 1949.

Winston, Robert W. *High Stakes and Hair Trigger: The Life of Jefferson Davis*. New York: Henry Holt, 1930.

Workers of the Writers' Program of the Work Projects Administration in the State of Louisiana, comps. *Louisiana: A Guide to the State*. New York: Hastings House, 1941.

Workers of the Writers' Program of the Work Projects Administration in the State of Maryland, comps. *Maryland: A Guide to the Old Line State*. New York: Oxford University Press, 1940.

Workers of the Federal Writers' Project of the Works Progress Administration, comps. *Mississippi: A Guide to the Magnolia State*. New York: Hastings House, 1949.

Workers of the Writers' Program of the Work Projects Administration in the State of West Virginia, comps. *West Virginia: A Guide to the Mountain State*. New York: Oxford University Press, 1941.

Wright, Carroll D. *The History and Growth of the United States Census, Prepared for the Senate Committee on the Census*. Washington: Government Printing Office, 1900.

Young, Otis E. *The West of Philip St. George Cooke, 1809–1895*. Glendale, Calif.: Arthur H. Clark, 1955.

INDEX

References are to item numbers save where otherwise indicated.

INDEX

INDEX